VIRGINIA/
GENEALOGICAL DATA FROM
REVOLUTIONARY WAR
PENSION AND
BOUNTY LAND WARRANT
RECORDS

Volume 1 -- Aaron through Cyrus

Compiled By

Patrick G. Wardell
Lt. Col., U. S. Army Retired

HERITAGE BOOKS, INC.

Published 1988 By

HERITAGE BOOKS INC.
1540E Pointer Ridge Place, Bowie, Maryland 20716
(301)-390-7709

ISBN 1-55613-170-4

A Complete Catalog Listing Hundreds Of Titles On
Genealogy, History, And Americana
Available Free Upon Request

FOREWORD

This book is the first of several volumes of genealogical data pertaining to Virginia people and their
families that has been extracted from some 2,670 reels
of microfilm at the US National Archives. Family history researchers can view the complete records at the
the National Archives or may obtain copies of the mic-
films by mail, or may purchase reels for home viewing.
For the convenience of users of this book, the perti-
nent reel for each serviceman's record is indicated.

Most of the bounty land warrant records for Revolutionary War servicemen were destroyed by a fire in Washington, DC, in 1800. However, the pension records
are fairly complete, and they are replete with excel-
lent source data. Records include affidavits of the
applicants and their witnesses, local court actions,
Congressional actions, extracts from family bibles,
discharge papers, service certificates, marriage certificates, as well as letters from descendants request-
ing data on Revolutionary War ancestors. Those letters
often contained additional genealogical data which is
also provided herein.

This book includes not only data on the men who entered the Army or the Sea Service from Virginia but also those who entered from other states or countries but
were born, married, or lived at one time in Virginia or
had members of their families reside in Virginia before
or after the Revolutionary War.

Not all of the Revolutionary War veterans or their
widows or family members applied for pensions or bounty land warrants. Those who did apply were not always
successful for various reasons, such as insufficient
proof of service or marriage, or failure to submit the
required documents or forms to the National Pension Office, or to the Government Land Office. In some cases,
the veteran or his spouse died before the pension or

warrant could be approved. The mails at the time being slow and government bureaucracy being even slower, considerable time passed between application and approval. Many frustrated applicants solicited the help of their Congressmen to speed up the process. Proof of marriage was often difficult to obtain because of the loss of public records, particularly in Virginia where fire destroyed courthouses in a number of counties. Affidavits from witnesses to service or marriage were often difficult or impossible to obtain when the applicants were of advanced age or had moved out of state.

There were, of course, fraudulent claims. Some were discovered when the claims were made, while others were found out later. Some people who had been awarded pensions were dropped from the rolls as a result.

Laws for receiving pensions and bounty land were not consistent, since Congress made a number of changes after the first awards were allowed. Consequently, some claimants who were initially rejected were able to submit a successful claim later. However, some who waited too long missed out because of a rules change.

The reader's attention is invited to the many variations in the spelling of names, which was prevalent in those early days. When looking for a particular surname, the reader should also look for similar sounding names; e.g. ALLEN vs. ALLAN, STEWART vs STUART, BRIAN vs BRYAN, NEAL vs NEILL, or CAREY vs CARY.

Variations in ages of the claimants from one court appearance or affadavit to another were prevalent. Not having public records of births in those times, as well as the failing memory of elderly and aged claimants and witnesses, were the main causes of discrepancies.

Some of the microfilmed documents were very difficult to read, especially when the handwriting of the preparers of court documents or family bible entries was poor, or the ink was badly faded or blotched. The compiler of this book often had to make an educated guess as to the names and dates recorded.

An index which lists all people who are not the subject of an entry is provided. Women are listed by both maiden and married names, when known.

This work is a companion piece to the book, WAR OF 1812: VIRGINIA BOUNTY LAND & PENSION APPLICANTS, by the same compiler, published by HERITAGE BOOKS, INC, in 1987.

General Abbreviations

adm	administrator	LWT	last will and testament
ae	age		
aec	age about	m	mother
afb	applied for bounty land warrant	MB	marriage bond
		mbnn	mentioned but not named
AFF	affidavit		
afp	applied for pension	md	married
b	born	mns	mentions
bc	born about	mvd	moved
BLAR	bounty land applica-ton rejected	o	of (used with /)
		PAR	pension application rejected
BLW	bounty land warrant		
bro	brother	PN	pension, pensioned
c	about	POW	prisoner of war
ch	child, children	QLF	query letter in pension or bounty land warrant record
co	county		
d	daughter		
dd	died	R	microfilm reel number for record
decd	deceased		
desc	descendant	recd	received
esf	entered service from	res	resident, residence
f	father	RW	Revolutionary War
gdc	grandchild(ren)	s	son
gdd	granddaughter	sis	sister
gdf	grandfather	sol	soldier
gdm	grandmother	sub	substitute
gds	grandson	surv	surviving
gtd	granted	svc	military service
h	husband	w	wife
KIA	killed in action	wid	widow
liv	living		

AARON, William, esf Amherst Co, VA; bc 1753; dd Oct 1841 nr
    Carnesville, Franklin Co, GA; md 11/3/29 Rebecca Rudd,
    Franklin Co, GA; wid PN there & dd after 1857. R1
AARONS, Abraham, esf Pittsylvania Co, VA; b 3/17/1759, Lan-
    caster Co, PA; to Pittsylvania Co with parents ae 12; PN
    Adair Co, KY. R1
ABBEY, Edward, VA & PA militia; PN 1829 Simpson Co, TN, ae 79,
    w Rebecca aec 60. R1
ABBOTT, Elijah, esf Stafford Co, VA; PN 1824 Bourbon Co, KY,
    ae 61, w aec 60, d ae 20, 2 small gdc. R1
  Reuben, BLW issued 8/20/1791. R2
  William, esf Halifax Co, VA; bc1756 King & Queen Co, VA; dd
    1/4/1848, Halifax Co, VA; md 12/2/1784 Mary Parker, bc
    1765; wid PN 1848; ch births: Rebekah M 1/23/1788, Eliza-
    beth 10/26/89, Carter Sebury 10/2/91, Lusanna Sharp
    1/5/94, Polley 8/14/96, Wesley Mansfield & Keturah (twins)
    9/27/1798, Delphia 1/1/1801, Onisha 5/9/03, Standfield
    11/4/05, Isaac 5/20/09; births of ch of George A Irion &
    Rebecca Hunt, md 12/3/05: William H 3/28/07, Robert K
    10/21/08, Polly Ann 12/25/10; sol sis Elizabeth liv 1832.
    R4
ABEL, Thomas, esf Shenandoah Co, VA; bc 1759; dd 8/30/1822,
    Haywood Co, NC; md 9/1/82-85 Elizabeth, b 3/9/1763; wid
    PN 1839 NC; sol will 1822 listed s Samuel, 7 d's, step-
    son John Woodfin; 2nd ch Delia (Abel) Hughes b 1/3/1788,
    res Buncombe Co, NC, 1845. R4
ABELS, see ABEL, Thomas. R4
ABERNATHY, David A, esf 1776 NC; b 7/29/1759, Dinwiddie Co,
    VA; dd 1838 Giles Co, TN; PN there 1832; md Christiana
    Forney in NC. R5
  Robert, esf Brunswick Co, VA; bc 1752; PN 1832 Lincoln Co,
    NC. R5
ABLE, Thomas, see ABEL, Thomas. R5
ABNER, Paul, see ABNEY, Paul. R5
ABNEY, George, esf 1775 SC; b 2/10/1752, Halifax Co, VA; afp
    1822 Switzerland Co, IN, when w Sarah/Salley ae 66; sol PN
    1832 Hamilton Co, IN. R5
  Paul, esf Albemarle Co, VA, s/o Dannett & Mary; dd 6/15/1815
    Gallatin Co, IL; md 3/1785 Rhody/Rhoda/Rodah, b 12/1768
    d/o Eli & Sary Ann Norman, Greenville, SC; wid PN 1847
    Gallatin Co, IL; ch births: Thomas 12/3/1785, John 1/2/88,
    William 2/3/90, Elias 2/23/92, Abner 11/14/95, Michael
    11/15/97, Joshua 12/99, Nancy 2/1801, Delilah 5/18/06,
    Henry 8/09, & Mathy 8/11; births of s Abner's ch: Willi-
    am 10/1/1814, Patsy 5/1/14/17, Rhody 2/27/19, Sarah
    5/28/21, Willis 2/2/25, Charity 5/14/27, & Jonathan
    10/18/29. R5
  William, esf Albemarle Co, VA; bc1757; dd 6/31/1845, Rock-
    castle Co, KY; PN there 1818; md (2) 8/1811 Judith Clark,
    Estill Co, KY; surviving ch by 1st w 1820: Dicy/Decy 31,
    Betsey 29, Charles 26, William 24, Jane 22, Polly 20, Da-
    vid 17, Milly 15, Sally 13, Elisha 11, Joshua 9; by 2nd w

1

ABNEY (continued)
   in 1820: Amanda 8, America 6, Andrew Jackson 4, Elizah 2;
   wid PN ae 79, Rockcastle Co, KY, 1853. R5
ABSALOM, Edward; heirs-at-law William Pace, Margaret Gaskins,
   Mary Cavender, William Absolom, & Henry Absolam of Prin-
   cess Anne Co, VA, gtd BLW 1/6/1845. R5
ABSHIRE, Abraham, esf 1779 Bedford Co, VA; bc 1761; PN Frank-
   lin Co, VA, 1832; dd 7/28/42 leaving wid. R5
ABSOLAM, Edward, see ABSALOM, Edward. R5
ABSTON, John, esf 1780 Pittsylvania Co, VA, s/o Joshua (capt-
   ain in VA militia); afp ae 97 Collin Co, TX, 1856; PAR for
   lack of witnesses to service; QLF 1911 from great gds
   George W. Fitzhugh, McKinney, TX. R5
ACKELBARNER, Joseph, see EICHELBERGER, Joseph. R6
ACRE, Philip, esf Frederick Co, VA; b 8/20/1754; PN 1838 Wash-
   ington Township, Harrison Co, IN; dd 8/8/43, Harrison Co,
   IN; md 3/18/1788 Catharine Zimmerman, PN 1848 & gtd BLW
   ae 88, Harrison Co, IN, 1855; d Anna aec 56 in 1845. R7
   James, esf Caroline Co, VA; bc1754; dd 6/17/1845, Roane Co,
   TN; md 1/1/1823 Esther Jones, Meigs Co, TN; wid bc 1793,
   PN 1853 Roane Co, TN, dd 9/5/84, Cave Creek, Roane Co, TN;
   youngest d ae 8 in 1824. R7
ACREE, John, esf Caroline Co, VA; b there 3/21/1760, s/o Abra-
   ham & Anne; dd 3/6/1837 or 3/2/1838; PN 1832 Sullivan Co,
   TN; md 11/21/1793-4 Lucy Schools, Caroline or King & Queen
   Co, VA, b 6/30/1774, d/o John & Salley; wid res 1846 Sul-
   livan Co, TN; ch births: Elizabeth 2/21/1795, Matthew T
   6 or 7/21/96, Salley 7/21/98, Uriah 12/2/1800, Susanna
   4/19/03, Fanney 2/8/06, Polley 8/4/08, John 12/13/10, Lucy
   12/5/12, William 6/7/15; s Matthew T res 1853 Sullivan Co,
   TN. R7
ACRON, Gabriel, see EAKINS, Gabriel. R9
ADAMS, Benjamin, esf 1776 Norfolk or Orange Co, VA; bc1759; PN
   1830 Jessamine Co, KY; in 1820 w aec 60, ch: Polly aec 17,
   Fanney 14. R8
   Benjamin, ddc 6/20/1846; heirs-at-law George W. Adams & Pol-
   ley Adams gtd BLW Jessamine Co, KY, 1855. R8
   Bryant, esf 1777 Wilmington, NC; b 1756 Three Creeks, VA; to
   Franklin Co, VA, with parents ae 5; md ? 1821 Johnston Co,
   NC; PN there 1836; to Montgomery Co, AL; back to Johnston
   Co, NC, after w dd. R8
   Elisha, esf Bedford Co, VA; bc 1763 Charlotte Co, VA, s/o
   Peter, & bro/o Philemon, Zerniah, Abijah, Benoni, Ephraim,
   & Simeon; PN 1833 Franklin Co, VA. R9
   Ellison E, esf 1776 King William Co, VA; bc 1755; PN there
   1821 when w Jenny aec 40 & ch: Betsy aec 6, Grant aec 2,
   John aec 11 months, & Sally ae 12. R9
   Francis, svc with French troops, to VA with Count Rochambeau
   1780; bc 1751; res Fauquier Co, VA, till 1791; dd 1/1/1837
   Mercer Co, KY; md 1781 Nancy ---, Frederick Co, VA, who bc
   1754; wid PN 1838 Mercer Co, KY; 5th ch Susannah (Adams)
   Cummins aec 48 in 1838. R10

2

ADAMS (continued)
  Gavin, esf Culpeper Co, VA; b 6/7/1763 Fauquier Co, VA; res
    1837 Bartholomew Co, IN; dd 1842 Jackson Co, IN; ch: Wil-
    liam (res 1854 Oldham Co, KY), Mrs. Elizabeth Seely (res
    1855 Bartholomew Co, IN), Martha/Patsy Anderson (res 1856
    Washington Co, IN), Delphia Adams (b KY). R10
  George, dd during RW; md 4/1769 Nancy Parker, Fauquier Co,
    VA, who later md Hugh Bramblett (dd 7/25/1818); wid PN ae
    84 Scott Co, KY, 1838; Martin, s/o Hugh & Nancy Bramblett,
    ae 50 testified in 1838 that m had 3 ch by George. R10
  Henry, esf Bedford Co, VA; b there 2/3/1761; dd 11/29/1834,
    Russell Parish, that co; md 12/22/1791 Rebecca Chaffin who
    PN ae 67 that co 1841. R10
  Jacob, BLW issued 1/7/1793. R11
  James, esf Halifax Co, NC; b 6/2/1758, Sussex Co, VA; to NC
    ae 12 with parents; to Davidson Co, TN, c1812; PN Wake Co,
    NC, 1832. R11
  James, BLW issued 1/7/1793. R11
  James; afp 1829 Warren Co, KY; PAR. R11
  James, esf VA; b 10/18/1753, Albemarle Co, VA; res during RW
    Fluvanna & Charlotte Co, VA; hired bro Thomas as sub for
    part of enlistment; dd 1835; md 1772 Jane Cunningham, who
    PN 1832 Elbert Co, GA, where Thomas res; QLF states w/o
    sol was --- Lynch, d/o Col. John Lynch of Lynchburg, VA, &
    ward of Robert Adams; QLF also mentioned Dozier Thornton,
    b 4/14/1755 Lunenburg Co, VA, & dd 9/1843 Franklin Co, GA,
    & md 1783 Lucy Hill, & was s/o Mark (b 1725) & Susannah
    (Dozier) Thornton. R11
  Jeremiah, esf Rowan Co, NC; b 1759 Bedford Co, VA; to Rowan
    Co aec 2 with parents; res 1832 Mecklenburg Co, NC; dd
    5/14/1835; 11 ch by 1st w; md (2) 1810 Elizabeth (wid/o
    William Hart by whom she had 4 ch including Lentite, who
    aec 50 in 1854; wid, ae 55 in 1827, had 3 ch by sol, eld-
    est Lewis bc 1811; wid PN 1854 Mecklenburg Co, NC; sol sis
    Martha Burnett ae 71 Iredell Co, NC, 1829. R11
  John, esf 1776 Fairfax Co, VA, MD sea service; PN 1832 Fair-
    fax Co, VA, ae 83; in 1852 s James stated sol decd. R12
  John, esf VA, PN ae 60 Montgomery Co, KY, 1818; dd c1/1/1819
    R12
  John, esf 1777, Mecklenburg Co, VA; b 2/13/1759; md bef 1794
    Calarine ---, Mecklenburg Co, VA; sol res 1833 Montgomery
    Co, TN, & dd 4/21/1835; wid PN 1840; eldest s David aec
    54 res IL 1839. R12
  John, esf Louisa Co, VA; b 10/10/1754; dd 12/10/1832 Garrard
    Co, KY; md 1778 Suckey --- who b 1/4/1758; wid dd Garrard
    Co, KY, 3/20/1846; John & Suckey had 11 ch, eldest Lucy b
    6/4/1778: heirs-at-law 1843 were John, Nancy, Robinson, &
    Thomas Adams who gtd BLW; age of sol ch 1850: Lucy Riggs-
    by 72, Margaret DeHouse 70, Overton 65, John 63, James 61,
    Mary DeHouse (twin to James), Astin 57, William 55, Patsy
    & Sucky (twins) 51; s Astin md d/o Edward & Polly DeHouse
    (ae 96 in 1850) who were md 1782 Louisa Co, VA. R12

ADAMS, Jonathan, esf 1778 NJ; bc1763; md (2) Fall 1791 Margar-
et ---, NJ; res 1824 Harrison Co, VA; dd 4/21/1835; wid PN
ae 72 Barbour Co, VA, 1843; ch births: Mary 1/12/1782 (md
--- Reed), Washington 3/12/1775, Sarah/Sary 4/30/1796, Da-
vid 3/12/1798, Anne 8/23/1801, Margaret 5/22/03, William
9/1/05, Tebbytha/Tabitha 8/15/07, Edy/Edie 2/2/09, Ireny/
Irena 1/22/11; other births given: Isaac Tyson 1/12/1814,
Hyram Tribbel 7/4/1823. R13
   Littleton, esf 1775 Fauquier Co, VA; bc 1753 MD; to Fauquier
Co c1771; dd there 2/9/1834; md 3/4/1793 Harriet Smith who
PN ae 75 there 1839. R13
   Peter, esf Boones Station, KY, in VA regiment; b 3/11/1759
Rowan Co, NC; bro/o John, nephew/o Jacob Hunter; PN 1833
Washington Co, KY; gdf/o James H. Adams, Guston, KY. R14
   Robert, esf Charlottesville, Albemarle Co, VA; PN ae 64 Law-
rence Co, OH, when w & gdd ae 11 res with him; QLF states
sol md Martha Fletcher & had ch John, James, Robert, Hugh,
Mary, Eliza, & others. R15
   Sylvester, esf Loudoun Co, VA; bc 1763 there, s/o Daniel &
bro/o Nathaniel (bc 1767); PN 1857 Rockcastle Co, KY. R16
   Thomas, esf 1779 Albemarle Co, VA; bc 1758, s/o James who dd
3/15/1789 & Cicely who dd 2/10/1845; md 10/4/1786 Salley
---, bc 1766; res 1836 Elbert Co, GA; wid PN there 1839;
ch births: Elizabeth 7/15/1787, Thomas F 6/5/91, Mourning
McL 2/8/93, James B 3/25/95, Culvrain 3/9/97, Richard C
6/24/98, Abner 3/10/1800, John 5/30/01, & Nicholas M
7/29/04; d Elizabeth md 1/19/09 Anthony Perryman & their
ch births: Eliza E 2/15/10, Albert Galiton 2/24/12; s
James B md Polly & their ch births: Elizabeth B 6/9/1818
(dd 12/6/1821), Fayett Henry 2/10/20, Ann Hailey 6/2/21;
s Nicholas M res Elbert Co, GA, 1832; s Abner res there
1839. R16
   Walter, esf 1779 Rowan Co, NC; b 1/19/1753, Fauquier Co, VA;
to Rowan Co with parents 1776; bro/o George; PN Graves Co,
KY, 1833. R17
   William, dd 7/8/1835, Lawrence Co, IL; 3 ch liv 1853: Claiborn H res of Palestine, Crawford Co, IL, William D, Jane
Adams Clark; Claiborn H afp of sol 1857; PAR. R17
   William, esf 177d King William Co, VA; dd 12/10/1837 New Ma-
drid, MO; md 12/10/1832 Sarah Lee, Bedford Co, TN, at her
f's house; wid gtd BLW 1855. R17
ADCOCK, John A, esf 1781 Buckingham Co, VA; bc 1758 there; PN
1834 Robertson Co, TN. R18
   John, esf 1776 VA; bc 1754; PN 1819 Smith Co, TN; res David-
son Co, TN, 1821 with w ae 31 & 5 ch (eldest 13, youngest
1 1/2). R18
   William, esf 1776 Albemarle Co, VA; PN aec 75 Franklin Co,
VA, 1818; family 1822 w aec 70 & d Jane McGee ae 40. R18
ADDAMS, Benjamin, see ADAMS, Benjamin. R18
ADDISON, Richard, esf 1776 Berkeley Co, VA; PN ae 65 Hampshire
Co, VA, 1818, w Priscilla then ae 62. R18
ADKINS, Charles, see ATKINS, Charles. R19

4

ADKINS, Hezekiah, esf 1775-80 Montgomery Co, VA; b 9/20/1759,
    Goochland Co, VA; afp Cabell Co, VA, 1835; PAR; wid Mary
    afp Cabell Co, VA, 1854; PAR. R19
  James, esf 1778 Orange Co, VA; b there 11/14/1745; to Clark
    Co, KY, c1806; PN there 1833; d Fanny McDaniel res there
    then ae 60; QLF mentions Thomas Otho Adkins (gdf/o Mrs.
    Charles B Nelcomp who res Brooklyn, NY, 1914) md 2/23/1834
    Martha/Patsy Ward, KY. R19
  James, esf 1775 Culpeper Co, VA; dd 8/9/1828; md 12/19/1770
    Elizabeth --- who afp aec 80, Scott Co, KY, 1836; PAR; ch
    births: John 1/8/1772, James 5/8/79, Pheby 4/9/83, Judy
    7/27/85, Levi 1/20/87; Nancy 4/16/90. R19
ADKINSON, David, esf 1777 VA, PN aec 69 Lawrence Co, KY, 1823,
    when fam w Sylvenious aec 35 & ch: Enoch aec 15, Fanna aec
    11, Goolsberry aec 9, Martin aec 6, Nickallbery aec 3, El-
    liott aec 1. R19
  James, see ATKINSON, James. R19
  William, records lost in fire 1800 in Washington, DC, but PN
    from 9/4/1789. R19
ADKISSON, Ellis, esf 1781 Bedford Co, VA; bc 1762 Amelia Co,
    to Madison Co, KY, c1808 where PN 1832; QLF 1920 from ggdd
    Olive Adkisson, Guston, KY; QLF 1940 from desc J D Adkis-
    son, Roseville, IL. R19
AGEE, Jacob, esf 1778 Buckingham Co, VA; bc there c1757; dd
    there 5/1838; only surv ch Mary A Snoddy ae 71 res there
    1866; QLF states a Jacob Agee, b 1745, Buckingham Co, VA,
    md --- Ford & dd 1832, & had neighbor Walter A. Ford. R20
  Joshua, esf 1776 Buckingham Co, VA; b there 1/4/1757; dd
    12/1837 Wilkes Co, GA; afp 1832 Lincoln Co, GA; PAR; wid
    dd 1835; surv ch Mary Crum & Nancy Wynn res 1855 Lincoln
    Co, GA. R20
AGNEW, John, esf 1776 Botetourt Co, VA; PN aec 77 Bath Co, VA,
    1818; res 1820 Rockbridge Co, VA, liv alone. R20
AHART, Jacob, esf Orange Co, VA; b 7/15/1744, PA; to VA when
    infant; md c1782, VA; to Caswell Co, NC, c1782; PN there
    1782. R20
AIKEN, James, see AIKINS, James. R21
AIKENS, James, see AIKINS, James. R21
AIKINS, James, esf 1780 Granville Co, NC; esf 1781 Mecklenburg
    Co, VA; s/o James; PN ae 72 Roane Co, TN, 1832; dd 3/26/44
    there; md 1808/9 Dyce Henson, Lancaster Co, SC; wid PN aec
    66 Cass Co, MO, 1856; wid res 1859 Lykins Co, KS Territory
    R21
AILESWORTH, George, see AILSWORTH, George. R21
AILSTOCK, Absalom, esf VA; b Louisa Co, VA, free born mulatto;
    PN ae 70 Rockbridge Co, VA, 1832. R21
AILSWORTH, George, esf 1776 New Kent Co, VA; afp ae 70 White
    Co, TN, 1828; dd there 12/21/1841; md 8/8/1792 Susannah
    Harlow, Henrico Co, VA; wid PN ae 66 White Co, TN, 1843;
    eldest ch b 8/12/1793. R21
AITCHLEY, Abraham, see ATCHLEY, Abraham. R21
AKERD, esf 1779 Frederick Co, VA; b 9/15/1757 nr Philadelphia,

AKERD (continued)
    PA; to Frederick Co, VA, ae 8 with parents; to Mason Co,
    VA, 1807 where PN 1834. R22
AKERS, John, esf 1780 Buckingham Co, VA; b there c1758; PN
    1833 Franklin Co, VA; QLF states a William Akers, b1730 &
    dd 1810, md Elizabeth Martye, bought land Nelson Co, VA,
    1751, later res Campbell Co, VA, ch: s William, Peter, Si-
    mon, John, & 7 d, further s William, Peter, & John all RW
    sol's, John sol at Battle of Bunker Hill. R22
AKIN, James, esf Chesterfield Co, VA; b 1759 Cumberland Co,
    VA; PN 1833 Fayette Co, GA; res Greenville Co, NC, before
    res GA. R22
ALBAN, George, esf 1776 Winchester, VA; b 2/14/1758 Frede-
    rick Co, VA; PN 1832 Island Creek Township, Jefferson Co,
    OH; dd 1/27/1840 Steubenville, OH; ch mbnn; QLF 1897 from
    ggds Charles W Alban, St Louis, MO; QLF 1923 from desc A T
    Secrest, Pleasant City, OH. R23
ALBERT, William, esf 1776 PA; PN ae 67 Winchester, VA, 1821;
    bro Abraham esf Northampton Town, (now Allentown), PA, la-
    ter res VA; gdd Elmina Roome res 1854 Vicksburg, MS; in
    1857 sol youngest d Catherine Clark afp Vicksburg, MS, El-
    mina Roome then decd; Catherine PAR. R23
ALBRITTON, John, see ALLBRITTON, John. R23
ALCOCK, Thomas, esf 1777 Caroline Co, VA; b there 11/1744; PN
    1833 Stafford Co, VA. R24
ALDAY, Seth P, esf 1779 Charlotte Co, VA; bc 1762 there, s/o
    Perren; PN 1840 ae 78, res Fannon Creek, Union District,
    SC; dd 11/24/1847, leaving aged wid Sarah, who moved Meade
    Co, KY, where PAR. R24
ALDER, George, esf 1776 MD; PN 1818 Loudoun Co, VA; dd
    8/28/1824; md 11/17/1778 Lucy Ann , d/o John & Sarah Wynn,
    Prince Georges or Charles Co, MD; Lucy Ann b 9/26/1762;
    her f dd 10/13/1782 & m dd 5/22/1777; ch births: James
    8/14/1779, John 9/20/81, James Latimore 5/16/83, Sary Roby
    1/23/1785 (dd 8/23/1802), George Hawkins 6/22/1789, Eli-
    zabeth Latimore 2/2/1793, Mary Hawkins 11/9/95, Nancy
    Hawkins & twin Sary Roby 10/28/1800, Marcus 11/1807; wid
    PN 1840 Loudoun Co, VA, last name then spelled Allder;
    wid sis Priscilla Ann b 4/16/1764 & her sis Eleanor Ann
    b 11/13/67. R25
ALDERSON, Thomas, esf Rockingham, VA; b 8/22/1744, Bucks Co,
    to VA as ch; PN 1832 Monroe Co, VA. R26
ALDMAN, Thomas, BLW assigned to Robert Means. R26
ALDRED, Henry, esf 1776 Winchester, VA; b 4/24/1755; PN 1818
    Adams Co, OH, w aec 65 & s aec 17 (dumb & insane). R26
ALDRIDGE, John Simpson, esf 1776 VA; b 2/9/1761; res Clermont
    Co, OH, 1819; dd 11/17/1842, Rush Co, IN; md 11/18/1783
    Mary Lakin, MD, b 6/20/1760, dd 11/27/1843; wid PN Rush
    Co, IN, & after her death, PN paid to ch Nathan, Erasmus,
    Delilah Layton, & Elizabeth Stiers; ch births: Joseph La-
    kin 9/27/1784, Rachel Plummer 3/21/86, Ranzy 9/20/89,
    Eliza 3/10/91, Mary 2/5/93, Sarah 5/10/95, John 2/27/98,

ALDRIDGE (continued)
Delilah 12/23/99, Nathan 9/3/1803; Elizabeth md Rafe Stiers; Joseph Lakin dd 7/24/1816; gdc births: Leroy Swamp-
stead (s/o Sarah) 7/28/23; John Simpson Aldridge 6/25/15,
Delilah Ann Aldridge 2/11/19, Lucinda Aldridge 5/31/19,
Samuel Stiers Aldridge 8/10/24, Reuhame Aldridge (d/o Jos-
eph & Rachael) 7/14/05, John Aldridge 1/1/08, Mehale Al-
dridge 8/13/18, Henry Aldridge 5/5/13, William (s/o Ranzy
& Sarah Aldridge) 12/23/09, Mary Aldridge 12/23/15, Nackly
Aldridge 12/24/11 (dd 7/13/18), Joseph Aldridge 12/20/13
(dd 7/30/15); gdc 1844: ch/o John Aldridge (decd) were
Elizabeth w/o Rice Boswell, Eliza, Ruhamar, Darlington D,
Jason, Joseph Franklin, Philander, John S, & Barr E; ch/o
Joseph Aldridge (decd) was Henry; ch/o Polly (Aldridge)
Smith (decd) were Anna & Mahala; ch/o Rachel (Aldridge)
Stiers (decd) were John, Alfonso, & Cyrus. R27
William, esf Frederick Co, MD, for VA svc; b 5/1757; PN 1832
Boone Co, KY. R27
ALESHIDT, Henry, see ALESHITE, Henry. R27
ALESHITE, Henry Sr, esf 1778 Millerstown (later Woodstock),
Shenandoah Co, VA; b2/19/1754 nr Powell's Fort, that co;
bro/o John C; PN; res Page Co, VA, 1833. R27
John C, esf 1777 Page Co (then Shenandoah Co), VA; b on
Smith's Creek, Shenandoah Co, VA, 12/23/1755; PN Page Co,
VA, 1832. R27
ALEXANDER, James, esf King William Co, VA; PN aec 56 there
1818. R28
James, esf VA; dd 4/10//1817; md 4/10 1776 Orange Co, VA, to
Jerusha ---, b 4/17/1755; wid PN 1838 Boone Co, KY; ch
births: John T 5/2/1777, James 11/9/78 (md 4/25/1802-3),
Benjamin 12/6/83, William 10/17/85, Polly 8/29/87, Washington 2/18/89, Nelson 3/1/91, Willis 8/28/97; ch/o s John
& w Lydia births: Betsey 11/10/98, Polly 11/6/1800, & Sally 1/8/03, Harris 1/27/05, Jerusha 12/18/07, & James
2/27/10; ch/o son James births: John 1/10/1804, George
2/26/05; & William 12/26/189--. R28
Jeremiah, esf 1780 Washington Co, VA; b 7/4/1763 MD; dd AL
1/26/1847; PN 1832 Morgan Co, AL; res 1840 Walker Co, AL;
s-in-law Martin Orear, adm of sol's estate 1854 stated sol
left no w but ch: Luticia Orear, Easter Stephenson, John,
Martha Inman, & Abigail Randolph. R29
John, afb in TN; BLAR; dd there c1825; s John afb ae 77 Lea-
venworth, KS, 1864; BLAR, since no claims for BLW for RW
svc allowed after 1860. R29
Joseph, esf 1776 Ohio Co, VA, for svc in PA & VA; b Co Ty-
rone, Ireland; to America 1771; dd 10/1/1834 West Alexander, PA; md 11/25/1813 Sarah Woodburn, Washington Co, PA;
wid PN ae 83 West Alexander, PA, 1855. R29
Peter, esf 1777 Augusta Co, VA; b there 4/1758; afp Woodford
Co, KY, 1834; dd 2/14/1842; md 3/27/1787 Jannett Steele;
wid PN ae 81 Woodford Co, KY, 1843, when res with s-in-law
Warren Hearne; s David dd 8/1783; QLF 1908 from Dr Frede-

ALEXANDER (continued)

 rick D Keppel, Cazenovia, NY, states sol b Scotland; QLF
 1928 from ggdd Janet Alexander Lannert, Racine, WI. R29

 Solomon, esf 1780 nr Winchester, VA; PN ae 95 Lancaster, PA,
 1832. R29

 William, esf Ohio Co, VA (now Washington Co, PA); svc with
 VA & PA units; b 2/17/1757 Chester Co, PA; dd 9/4/1835; md
 4/24/1787 Elizabeth McClelland, Washington Co, PA, who b
 there 11/5/1765; wid PN 1838 Coolspring Township, Mercer
 Co, PA; sol bro/o John & Joseph; ch births: Margaret
 1/14/1788, Mary 1/4/90, Elizabeth 1/9/92, John 2/25/94,
 William 12/26/95, James 9/25/98, Elias 12/25/99, Esther
 5/20/1803, Joseph 1/29/08, Ebenezer 7/23/10. R30

 William, esf 1776 Pittsylvania Co, VA; b 4/15/1752 Cumberland Co, VA; raised by gdf; to Pittsylvania Co ae 23; to
 Rockingham Co, NC, 1818; to Wilkes Co, NC, 1822, where PN
 1832. R30

 William, esf Augusta Co, VA; PN ae 81 Knox Co, TN; dd
 6/15/1838; QLF 1914 from desc Mrs H C Moore, Atlanta, GA.
 R30

 William, esf 1780 Northumberland Co, VA; PN ae 67 Mercer Co,
 KY, 1820, when w ae 62 & 2 s, youngest b 12/14/1802, one
 s George; QLF 1923 from ggdd Mrs. Mary Huckelbridge, Bun-
 ker Hill, IL, states sol wife Margaret Bailey. R30

ALFORD, Jacob, esf 1777 Goochland Co, VA; to KY c1785; dd Garrard Co, KY, 6/3-23/1803; md Nancy Hunter, Louisa Co, VA,
 who PN ae 77 Garrard Co, KY, 1839, still res there 1844;
 ch births; Charles 12/10/1779, John 2/5/82, Lucy 9/21/83,
 Mary 3/17/89, William 8/31/91, Jesse 5/23/93 (res Garrard
 Co, KY, 1839), Stephen 3/28/95; QLF 1917 from desc Miss
 Martha Chinn, Vandalia, MO. R31

 John, BLW issued 5/29/1792. R31

 John, esf Amherst Co, VA; b 5/8/1760, Frederick Co, VA; to
 TN 1806; PN 1832 Davidson Co, TN; dd 4/24/1837. R31

ALFRED, Thomas, sea svc from VA; wid Susan PAR; wid also PAR
 as wid/o Jesse Kennedy/Kenady, VA. R31

ALGOOD, John, see ALLGOOD, John. R32

 William, esf 1776 VA in GA regiment; PN ae 67 Surry Co, NC,
 1828, when family w Sarah & 4 d; dd 10/2/1847; QLF 1936
 from desc A R Yates, Bogalusa, AL. R32

ALLAN, John, esf 1777 Lancaster, PA, for VA regiment; PN ae 64
 Schoharie, NY, 1818, w Eve then ae 66. R32

ALLAN, Moses, esf 1776 Fauquier Co, VA; PN ae 75 Wilson Co,
 TN, 1829 w then ae 72; dd 22 Aug 1843 there, surv by ch:
 Archibald, Elizabeth (Allan) Wood, & Mary (Allan) Atwood;
 s Archibald adm of sol estate; attorney for adm was Moses
 Allen, Jr (possibly gds) since Archibald had many ch. R32

ALLAY, Samuel, esf 1777 Henrico Co, VA; b there 1747; to Wake
 Co, NC, for 20 years, then to TN; PN Sumner Co, TN, 1832
 R32

ALLBRITTON, John, esf 1774 Goochland Co, VA; esf 1779 Union
 District, SC; b 12/6/1747, Newcastle, Hanover Co, VA; dd

8

ALLBRITTON (continued)
12/19/1836; PN 1832 Franklin Co, GA, later res Elbert Co,
GA; QLF 1930 from gggdd Sarah F (Mrs A J) King & s Dean,
both of Kalispell, MT, states sol s John Manly Albritton
to KY where md Mary Todd. R32
ALLDER, George, see ALDER, George. R32
ALLEE, David, esf Henry Co, VA; b 4/25/1762, Pittsylania Co,
VA; PN 1833 Cooper Co, MO; QLF 1939 from desc J A Birdsong
of Clarksburg, MO. R32
ALLEMBAUGH, Peter, esf 1775 Greenbrier Co, VA; PN ae 82 Madi-
son Co, KY, 1832, when wife decd & sol res with one of his
ch. R32
ALLEN, Archibald, esf 1781 Fauquier Co, VA; b 2/7/1751 West-
moreland Co, VA; to Nelson Co, KY, c 1786; to NC c1805; to
IL 1828; afp Putnam Co, IL, 1840; PAR, since svc less than
6 months. R33
  Benjamin, esf 1780 Staunton, Augusta Co, VA; afp ae 81 Mc-
  Minn Co, TN; PAR, proof of svc. R34
  Charles, esf 1770 Warren Co, NC, in company of f Capt Char-
  les; b 3/8/1758 Culpeper Co, VA; PN 1832 Williamson Co,
  TN. R34
  Charles, esf 1781 Craven Co, SC; b 1764 Charlottesville, VA;
  PN 1832 Laurens District, SC; gtd BLW there 1855. R34
  Charles, esf 1779 Cumberland Co, VA; b there 1764; PN 1832
  Halifax Co, VA; QLF states sol w --- Wilbourne; other QLF
  1909 from ggdd Mrs H E Hall, Farmville, VA. R34
  Charles, esf 1776 Albemarle Co, VA; PN aec 67 Warren Co, KY,
  1818; w Ursula liv 1831. R34
  Daniel, esf 1781 VA; BLW issued 5/29/1792; PN ae 60 Rock-
  bridge Co, VA, 1820, when w ae 80; no ch mentioned. R34
  David, esf 1777 VA; res 1799 Pittsylvania Co, VA; Apphia Al-
  len, adm of estate 1801, gtd BLW; QLF states sol w Apphia
  Fauntleroy Lewis. R35
  David, esf 1776 Hanover Co, VA; PN ae 63 Fayette Co, KY,
  1818; liv alone 1820, 8 ch having grown & left abode. R35
  Ethen, esf VT, commander of Green Mountain Boys; taken POW &
  brought to England; surv by wid; only s Ethan A apb 1829
  Norfolk, VA, for all heirs of sol; sol d Lucy Hetchuck res
  Plattsburgh, NY, 1832; QLF 1910 from desc Mrs John T Mac-
  Crea, New York City, states sol wid Phebe Green; other QLF
  states sol b 1/10/1737 Litchfield, CT; other QLF states he
  dd 2/12/1789, Burlington, VT, & w Frances Buchanan. R36
  George, esf Wake Co, NC; b 1744 Hanover Co, VA; PN 1832 Ire-
  dell Co, NC; QLF states sol w Susanah Reeves; other QLF
  states sol dd 1836. R36
  Henry, esf Culpeper Co, VA; dd there 8/11/1831; md 12/1781
  Catharine McConchie/McKonkey, Fauquier Co, VA; wid PN 1837
  ae 79 Culpeper Co, VA, & dd 7/26/1840; QLF 1905 from desc
  Mrs Benjamin Staunton, Lake Mills, WI, states Catharine b
  1761. R36
  Isham, esf 1779 Richmond, VA; PN ae 59 Hanover Co, VA, 1823;
  dd 10/24/1834; md 3/22/1792 Elizabeth ---; ch births: Rob-

ALLEN (continued)
    ert 7/6/1793, George Mosby 8/10/95 (dd 2/1827), John F
    8/6/97, Charles 9/22/99; wid PN ae 62 Boone Co, KY, 1838,
    & dd 7/9/53; heirs 1854 there Bill Allen, John F Allen,
    Lucy M Grant, Adaline Allen, Agnes F Johnson.
    R37
John, esf 177 VA; PN ae 57 Brunswick Co, VA, 1818; dd ae 57
    Brunswick Co, VA, 5/11/1822; md 12/1783 Nancy Morgan,
    Mecklenburg Co, VA; wid PN ae 70 Washington Co, KY, 1838.
    R38
John, esf Warren Co, NC; b 11/1752 Culpeper Co, VA; PN 1832
    Chester District, SC; res there since 1799. R39
John, esf 1779 Culpeper Co, VA; PN ae over 70 Richland Town-
    ship, Clinton Co, OH, 1832. R39
John, esf 1775 Fauquier Co, VA; PN ae 63 Woodford Co, KY,
    1818. R39
John Sr, esf 1775 VA; PN ae 64 Madison Co, AL, 1818; fam in
    1818 w ae 62, s ae 20, d ae 18, gdc ae 2; to Davidson Co,
    TN, 1825. R39
John, esf VA; LWT 3/21/1785, probated 12/4/1797 Henrico Co,
    VA, lists bequests to: Allen s/o Nathaniel Hunt of Hali-
    fax Co, VA, to Achilles s/o Charles Allen of Mecklenburg
    Co, VA, to Lewis Buckner s/o David Allen of Halifax Co,
    to Martha d/o Julius Allen of Henrico Co, VA, to Susanna
    d/o John Watlington of Pittsylvania Co, VA; file contains
    data on another John Allen of VA who moved to VA & dd
    1803, adm for his estate Joseph B Allen of NJ; (There were
    so many John Allen's in the VA RW forces that oftentimes
    the National Pension Office found it difficult, if not im-
    possible to file data properly). R39
John, esf VA; dd James City Co, VA, before 3/1792; ch by 1st
    w: Julius, Archer, William, Elizabeth, & Mary; ch by 2nd
    w: Isham & John; d Elizabeth md Edmund Bacon & they had s
    William S, who, as legal representative of sol heirs, afp
    1847; PAR for insufficient proof of svc.
    R39
John, esf VA; LWT 12/13/1815, probated Prince George Co, VA,
    4/8/1817 listing ch: Polly, Thomas, William, Allen, & Lil-
    ly Fenner; legal representative of sol heirs Thomas G Fen-
    ner afp 1849 Prince George Co, VA; PAR for insufficient
    proof of svc. R39
John, esf 1777 VA; b 7/1/1757; dd 11/1/1816; md 11/14/1782
    Ann Sims, Louisa Co, VA; wid b 9/13/1760 & PN 1838 Char-
    lotte Co, VA, res there 1843; ch births: James 2/14/1784,
    Sarah 11/10/85, Sims 7/3/87, Lucy Sims 11/27/89, & Nancy
    10/6/90; births of d Mrs Rowlett ch: Lucy Sims 2/21/1805,
    William Philip 11/29/06, John James 6/17/10, & Mary Ann
    18--. R39
John, esf before 1779 James City Co, VA; md 8/15/1781 Jane,
    d/o William Tandy, Albemarle Co, VA; to KY 1785; dd there
    8/18/1816; wid PN ae 75 Bourbon Co, KY, 1840, when d Mrs
    Jane Grosjean ae 44; QLF from Jane Allen Wilson states sol

ALLEN (continued)

 b Albemarle Co, VA, dd Bourbon Co, KY, will probated there 9/1815, further LWT/o William Tandy probated 10/1812; other QLF 1930 from desc Archie E Allen, Greencastle, IN. R39

John, see ALLAN, John. R39

Moses, esf 1779, VA; PN ae 64 Washington Co, VA, 1822. R40

Moses, see ALLAN, Moses. R40

Philip, see ALLIN, Philip. R41

Reuben, BLW issued 7/6/1793. R42

Richard, esf c1776 Cumberland Co, VA; dd c1833 there; d Drucilla Parker afp ae 68 Rockcastle Co, KY, 1850 as only surv heir; s David afp ae 85 Halifax Co, VA, 1852 as only surv heir, stating f left no wid but ch: David, Anderson, Simeon, Charles, Patsey Rainey/Ramsey, & Priscilla Parker; both PAR for insufficient proof of svc; QLF states sol b 1740-45, further sol d Martha (Patsey a nickname for Martha in those days) b 5/20/1768 & md Francis A Ramsey b 12/17/1764, further Francis Ramsey also RW sol who PN & dd 1842 Rockcastle Co, KY. R42

Richard, esf 1776 Goochland Co, VA; PN ae 77 Roane Co, TN, 1832; f res Goochland Co, VA, when sol enlisted. R42

Robert, esf 1775 Amelia Co, VA; PN ae 75 Madison Co, AL, fam then s William; QLF 1920 from desc Miss Sallie Lee Lightfoot, Paris, TX, states sol res with d Sarah, w/o Thomas Lightfoot, Lawrence Co, AL, & dd there c1840. R42

Samuel came to VA 1773; esf 1780 Augusta Co, VA; PN ae 86 Monroe Co,VA, 1832; d md 1820 Esther --- who dd 1/24/1822; sol had 2 s; one s to OH; other s George ae 43 Monroe Co, VA, 1826 when had w & 8 ch. R42

Vincent, esf 1775 Culpeper Co, VA; b 5/11/1756 Essex Co, VA; to Culpeper Co with fam c1767; PN 1832 Lincoln Co, NC; dd 5/30/1834; md 1/27/1776 Elizabeth ---, Culpeper Co, VA; wid PN ae 84 Lincoln Co, NC, 1838, & dd 10/19/48; ch surv 1843: John, Stanley, Margaret, & Vincent Hale; AFF by V Hale Allen & Barbary Allen 1853 Gaston Co, NC; QLF 1921 from ggds J W Allen, Nashville, TN. R43

William, esf 1779 MD; s Jeremiah afb 1828 Chambliss Store, Bedford Co,VA, on behalf of sol ch: Charles, Rachel White, William, Jeremiah B, Sally Beasley, Milly Lumpkin, James, Robert, Frances Ashwell, Polly Ashwell, Matthew, & John; BLW gtd; QLF 1840 from gds Eliel Allen, Baltimore, MD. R44

William, esf Henrico Co, VA; b there 12/26/1760; PN 1832 Granville Co, NC; md d/o Archer Johnson Sr who res near Good's Bridge on Appomattox River, Amelia Co, VA; wid liv 1833; QLF 1932 from desc Bernice M (Mrs A D) Kirk, Owensboro, KY, states sol w had twin sis: Mrs Kissey White & Mrs Fanny Norris. R44

William , esf 1777-8 Caroline Co, VA; PN there aec 62; dd VA 1828; d Mrs Reynolds res nr Richmond, VA, 1834, with 5 or 6 ch in poor straits. R44

William, esf 1775 Fauquier Co, VA; PN ae 76 Mason Co, KY, 1834; to KY winter 1793; dd there 5/20/1839; md 8/8/1781

11

ALLEN (continued)
  or 1784 Frances Pepper, Fauquier Co, VA; wid PN ae 81 Ma-
  son Co, KY, 1843, having then 5 or 6 ch; QLF 1931 from
  descendant Andrew H Allen, East Orange, NJ, states sol b
  6/20/1756 Lunenburg Co, VA, further sol's half-bro George
  Shackelford ae 78 Mason Co, KY, 1843. R44
ALLER, Conrad, esf 1777 Shepherdstown, VA; bc 1750; of German
  ancestry & spoke English poorly; PN 1833 West Bethlehem
  Township, Washington Co, PA. R44
ALLEY, Abraham, see ALLEY, Abram. R45
  Abram, esf 1779 VA; PN ae 70 Prince George Co, VA, 1833; bro
  Hamlin also res there then. R45
  Isaiah, esf 1781 Hanover Co, VA; b 1750 Henrico Co, VA; PN
  1832 Warren Co, KY; mvd to Nashville, TN, 1835 where son
  res. R45
  James, esf 1777 Guilford Co, NC; b 1753 Henrico Co, VA, on
  Clinch River in what now Lee Co; PN 1833 Roane Co, TN, &
  dd there 8/2/1834; md 4 or 5/1781 Massey Saunders at Hel-
  lico Block House; wid PN aec 80 Morgan Co, TN, 1839, & dd
  4/1849; ch 1839: William decd, Betsy aec 55, James ae 49,
  Fanny aec 48, Sally aec 46, David ae 45, Doshea ae 43; Leah aec 41, & Joseph ae 37; David res 1839 Morgan Co, TN;
  sol d --- md Jeremiah Hatfield c 1806; Elizabeth Hatfield
  ae 61 res Morgan Co, TN, 1844, her guardians since infancy
  being James & Massey Alley. R45
  John, esf Russell Co (then part of Washington Co), VA;
  b 7/8/1764, s/o James; afp 1841 Franklin Co, VA; PAR for
  insufficient proof of svc; bro-in-law Samuel Porter. R45
  Samuel, esf 1777 Washington Co, VA; b 6/25/1761 Henrico Co,
  VA; to Brookville Township, Franklin Co, IN, 1810, & PN
  there 1833; dd 8/12/1847 Shelby Co, IN; md 1786 Mary Os-
  borne/Osburn nr Abingdon,VA; wid PN aec 85 Decatur Co, IN;
  ch births: Jonathan 4/17/1787 (md Catharine), Doddridge
  11/1/88 (md Jane), Cyrus 4/17/91 (md Charity), Thursey
  3/17/93 (md Miss McCarty), Joyday 5/2/95 (md Mr Gant),
  Sampson 8/20/97 (md Creecy), Lanzel 7/26/1800 (md William
  Fowler), Elihu 2/28/03 (md Catharine), Azby C 2/20/06 (md
  --- Hobbs), Samuel 5/1/08 (md Nancy), & Solomon 10/25/10
  (md Catharine); all ch liv 1844 when sol & w had 68 gdc
  liv & 15 decd & 48 ggdc liv; QLF 1931 from ggdd Maud Bliss
  Allen (Mrs W J) Allen, Salt Lake City, UT, states Cyrus md
  Charity Nelson, further Joyday/Joyce md (1) Allen Ramsey
  Jr, (2) James C. Gant). R45
  Shadrick, esf Brunswick Co, VA; b there 1751; also esf NC;
  PN 1822 Iredell Co, NC; NC svc as sub for uncle Miles Al-
  ley of Northampton Co, NC. R45
ALLGOOD, John, esf Mecklenburg Co, VA; to Washington Co, TN,
  after RW, thence to KY; PN aec 75 Breckenridge Co, KY,
  1833. R45
  John, esf 1778 Mecklenburg Co, VA; b 5/12/1751 Richmond Co,
  VA; to Elbert Co, GA, 1788; to Walton Co, GA, 1826 where
  afp 1832; PAR for insufficient proof of svc. R45

ALLGOOD, John, esf 1778 Mecklenburg Co, VA, as sub for f Ish-
mael; b 1760 nr Mecklenburg Court House, VA; to Elbert Co,
GA, 1786; to Monroe Co, TN, 1826 where PN 1832 & d there
11/17/53; md 3/12/1835 Seleta Lankford, Madisonville, Mon-
roe Co, TN; wid PN there 1854 ae 67; wid res 1866 McMinn
Co, TN, & res 1870 Polk Co, TN, ae 80, she kin to Jesse
White. R45
ALLIN, Isaac, esf 1776 Lunenburg Court House, Lunenburg Co,
VA; afp ae 68 Scott Co, VA; PAR because owner of too much
property; fam then w aec 46, 2 s ae 13 & ae 3, 2 d ae 11 &
ae 6. R45
  Philip, esf 1776 Mecklenburg Co, VA; b VA & reared in King &
  Queen Co, VA; PN aec 72 Clarke Co, VA. R45
  Samuel, esf Bedford Court House, Bedford Co, VA; later esf
  Orange Co,NC; b VA 12/30/1756; PN 1832 Pulaski Co, KY; QLF
  states sol dd 1840 Pulaski Co, VA, w was Nancy Easter. R45
  Thomas, esf 1776 Granville Co, NC; b 1757 Hanover Co, VA; to
  Granville Co,NC, as ch with f; PN 1832 Mercer Co, KY, & dd
  there 6/26/33; wid Mary dd 6/28/33 surv by s: John J, Tho-
  mas, Charles W, Grant, Philip, & Ben C; sol bro Grant res
  1832 Smith Co, TN. R45
ALLISON, Burch, esf 1789 Montgomery Co, MD; b there 2/24/1764;
  to Loudoun Co, VA, for 5 years, thence to Burke Co, NC, in
  1799 where PN 1834; bro Posey ae 63 res there then; sis
  Mrs Jarrett Smith. R46
  Gauyn, ESF 1776 Washington Co,PA (area where VA claimed ju-
  risdiction); b 1/28/1789 Lancaster Co, PA; afp 1834 Saint
  Clair Township, Allegheny Co, PA; PAR for insufficient svc
  (less than 6 months); bro Archibald res 1834 Washington
  Co, PA. R46
  John; VA svc but not in RW; svc in Chesapeake War c1805; gtd
  BLW ae 83 Petersburg, VA. R46
  John, esf VA; dd 4/16/1803 Washington, Wilkes Co, GA; md
  4/24/1788 Rebecca McRea, Alexandria, VA; wid gtd BLW ae 76
  Wilkes Co, GA, 1839 (6,000 acres on Licking Creek, Fleming
  Co, KY); wid PN 1839; sol LWT 4/14/1803 listed w Rebecca,
  ch: Robert McRea (dd 1821), James (dd 1805), John Jr (dd
  1805), & William Candour (dd 1832); a Nancy A McCrea tes-
  tified in Wilkes Co, GA, court. R46
ALLPHIN, Ransom, esf 1776 VA; PN ae 81 Campbell Co, KY, 1831,
  w then decd c30 years; ch mbnn. R47
  Zebulon, esf 1781 Orange Co, VA; b there 5/5/1766; afp 1851
  Kenton Co, KY; PAR for insufficient proof of svc; s Ran-
  som & bro Ransom. R47
ALLVIS, John, see ALVIS, John. R47
ALLUMBAUGH, Peter, see ALLEMBAUGH, Peter. R47
ALMOND, John, esf 1775 King & Queen Co, VA; PN ae 77 Spotsyl-
  vania Co, VA, 1832; d 10/2/1845 Orange Co, VA; md 1789
  Lizza, d/o Francis Hume, (MB dated 8/4/1789), Culpeper Co,
  VA; wid PN ae 79 Orange Co, VA 1846. R47
  William, esf 1775 VA; PN ae 63 Campbell Co, VA, 1818; fam in
  1820: w Susanna, William ae 12, Catharine ae 10, Clemen-

ALMOND (continued)
   ine, Katy, & Kelley ae 1; res Highland Co, OH, 1836; sol
   dd 12/4/1839. R47
ALMY, John, esf 1776 Norfolk, VA, while there as mariner; la-
   ter esf RI; b 3/3/1758 Tiverton, RI, s/o Gideon & Sarah;
   dd 3/20/1844; md 4/3/1796 Abigail Bailey, Little Compton,
   RI, d/o Isaac & Sarah; wid PN there 1849 ae 74; dd 1/1853.
   R48
ALSOP, Benjamin, esf 1775 Spotsylvania Co, VA; b there
   3/17/1758; dd 12/1/1832; f dd 1776-8; sol ch: Elizabeth C
   w/o William Spindle, Sarah Ann w/o Stapleton Crutchfield.
   R48
 James, esf 1780 VA; b VA; PN ae 69 Mercer Co, KY, 1832. R48
ALTIZER, Emery, esf VA; dd 9/1819; md 7/1773 Mary --- of Berk-
   eley Co, VA, at Hagerstown, MD; w PN aec 81 Montgomery Co,
   VA, 1840 where res c50 years; ch mbnn. R48
ALTOP, Thomas; BLW issued 7/6/1793. R48
ALVERSON, Elijah, esf 1780 Colchester, Fairfax Co, VA; b there
   after RW to Caswell Co, NC, thence to Union District, SC,
   thence to Spartansburg, SC, thence to White Co, TN, where
   PN 1834 & dd 5/23/1857; md 5/27/1827 Wina/Winney/Nina
   Couch, Spartansburg District, SC; wid PN ae 46 White Co,
   TN, 1868; ch mbnn; 3 s in US Army; QLF 1928 from desc Ed-
   ward R Alverson, Oakland, CA. R48
 James, esf 1777 Fairfax Co, VA; PN 1818 Union District, SC;
   res ae 60 Chester District, SC, 1821; dd 5/21 or 27/1834;
   md 1780-1 Sabitha ---, Fairfax Co, VA; wid dd 9/17/1842;
   ch liv 1838: William, Moses, John, Elender, Nancy, Mary/
   Polly who md James Roach. R48
 John, esf Culpeper Co, VA; b there 1757; PN 1832 Botetourt
   Co, VA, where had res since 1783. R48
 John, esf VA; PN 1818 Columbia, SC; ae 63 in 1822 when w ae
   53; ch at home then: Zachariah ae 18 & Frances ae 14; dd
   2/25/1829. R48
 John S, esf 1778 nr New London, Bedford Co, VA; b 1755; PN
   1832 Madison Co, KY; res 1833 Lincoln Co, KY. R48
ALVEY, John, esf 1776, VA; dd 6/12/1815 Union Co, KY; MB with
   Fanny Lloyd, Prince William Co, VA, 12/3/1778; md 2/1779;
   wid Fanny/Frances PN ae 81, Union Co, KY, 1841. R49
 Robert, esf Prince William Co, VA; dd 10/3/1820 Union Co,
   KY; MB with Susan Kitchen 10/21/1782 Prince William Co,
   VA; md there 10/22/1782; wid b 2/17/1765 & PN 1842 Union
   Co, KY; QLF states sol w dd 1843, further one of her ch a
   widow res Cincinnati, OH, with 6 ch 1847. R49
ALVIS, Elijah, esf VA; PN ae 66 Louisa Co, VA, 1818; PN ae 66
   Louisa Co, VA, 1818; MB 10/15/1784 Goochland Co, VA, with
   with Elizabeth Clarke (surety for bond Shadrach Alvis);
   in 1820 wid ae 50-60, ch: Polly aec 30, Nancy aec 30, Jane
   aec 23, Betsy aec 15; wid PN ae 77 Goochland Co, VA, & res
   there 1843. R49
 Henry H, esf 1779 Richmond, VA; b Goochland Co, VA; afp ae
   78 Patrick Co, VA, 1836; afp ae 78 Tompkinsville, Monroe

ALVIS (continued)
Co, KY; PAR for insufficient proof of service. R49
Jesse, esf 1778 VA; b 8/1757; PN 1819 Shelby Co, KY; in 1820
had w plus s's ae 15 & 11, d's ae 21, 13, & 8; to Washing-
ton Co, IN, 1827 to res with s David. R49
John, esf c1778 Hanover Co, VA; PN ae 78 Fayette Co, KY,
1835; dd 3/29/1847; md 8/29/1795 Nancy Bingham, Hanover Co
VA; wid b 7/1776 & PN 1848 Athens, Fayette Co, KY & recd
BLW there 1855. R49
Zachariah, esf 1779 VA; PN ae 72 Goochland Co, VA, 1832. R49
AMBURN, Joseph, esf 1776 Worcester Township, PA, as substitute
for f Jacob; b there 1761; to Grayson Co, VA, 1797, where
PN 1832; to IN 1853 to visit 5 of ch; res 1854 Marion, IN;
res 1856 Randolph Co, IN; QLF 1924 from gggds Clifford L
Amburn, Muncie, IN. R50
AMENT, Anthony, esf 1776 Lancaster, PA; b 1757 York Co, PA; to
Shenandoah Co, VA, 1782; to Hardin Co, KY, 1804, where PN
1833. R50
Philip, esf 1775 York, York Co, PA; b 1/1/1755; to Albemarle
Co, VA, c1788; to Bourbon Co, KY, 1800 where PN 1834. R50
AMICKS, Matthew, see AMYX, Matthew. R51
AMMENET, John, esf 1776 Buckingham Co, VA; PN ae 79 Madison,
Co, AL, 1832; QLF spells name AMMONETTE, states sol dd Ma-
dison Co, AL, 3/1833. R52
AMMON, Christopher, esf 1778 Culpeper Co, VA; b there 1759; to
Rockingham Co, VA, 1779 where PN 1832; dd 4/24/1842. R53
AMMONDS, Peter, BLW issued 12/27/1794. R53
AMMONETTE, Charles, esf Powhatan Co, VA, where b 10/13/1738 &
PN 1832; dd 2/14/1833, Chesterfield Co, VA; md 2/1/1797 or
2/2/1798 Phoebe Hall; wid PN ae 76, Chesterfield Co, VA, &
recd BLW 1855; res with s Thomas 1866, Bellair, VA; wid ae
91 Chesterfield Co, VA, 1867. R53
AMMONS, Joshua, esf 1775 Craven Co, SC; b 1/22/1756, Brunswick
Co, VA; PN 1832 Marlborough District, SC; dd 4/11/1833;
QLF 1917 from descendant Mrs J C Mobley, Social Circle, GA
R53
AMONETT, Charles, see AMMONETTE, Charles. R53
AMOS, Martin, see AMOSS, Martin. R53
AMOSS, Martin, esf 1776 Albemarle Co, VA; b there (now in Flu-
vanna Co); PN aec 71 Ohio Township, Gallia Co, OH, 1832;
QLF from descendant Mrs O E Nichols, Hebron, IN, states
sol from England to Greenbrier Co, VA, before RW & was a
blacksmith during RW. R53
AMYX, Mathew, esf VA; PN 1789 for disability from wounds; res
1827 Cumberland Co, KY, with s Mathew Jr; dd 3/12/1832;
QLF states sol & bro Andrew were sons of Mathew who infirm
from old age 1771 & esf Botetourt Co, VA.   R53
ANDERSON, Alexander, esf 1777 Frederick Co, MD; esf 1779 Rock-
bridge Co, VA; b 10/1761, York Co, PA; PN 1832 Stewart Co,
TN; m moved with him to VA. R54
Armistead, esf 1776 Pittsylvania Co, VA; b 9/2/1756, Amelia
PN 1832 Union Co, KY; QLF states sol dd 1832. R54

ANDERSON, Bailey, esf 1776 Ninety-Six District, SC; esf "Long
    Island" on Holston River in VA (area later TN); esf GA;
    b11/13/1754; res TX 1833 when afp Parish of Natchitoches,
    LA; member of state legislature of KY; only s liv in 1856;
    QLF 1932 from desc Mrs Grayce Gossom Bell, Horse Cove, KY;
    QLF states sol s/o John who b Scotland & sol dd 8/1840,
    Harrison Co, KY; QLF states sol's s b 1796 & dd 1850 nr
    Memphis, TN. R54
  Charles, esf ae 16 Caroline Co, VA; b eastern VA; after RW
    to Rockbridge Co, VA; dd 3/6/1841 on visit to Augusta Co,
    ch liv 3/31/1845 James ae 47, Charles ae 32, Richard ae 30
    (all res Rockbridge Co, VA), Clarissa ae 43 w/o Daniel Ro-
    binson of Augusta Co, VA, Catherine ae 34 w/o Washington
    Crouse who mvd Albemarle Co, VA, to MO 1844; sol bro of
    William of Caroline Co, VA, also RW sol; PAR for insuffi-
    cient proof of svc. R54
  Daniel, esf 1775 Shenandoah Co, VA; b 4/1753; PN 1819 She-
    nandoah Co, VA; dd 11/6/1840; family in 1840 w ae 57, d's
    ae 23 & 14, s ae 27; surv ch Jeruth & Catherine w/o Moses
    Wood. R54
  David, esf 1776 Chesterfield Co, VA; b 7/16/1756 Cumberland
    Co, VA; PN 1832 St Patrick's Parish, Prince Edward Co, VA,
    where sol res 50 years; dd 8/5/1835 there; md 9/21/1785
    Lucy Horsley who PN ae 70 there 1838, res 1843 Mecklenburg
    Co, VA; sol had younger bro Thomas, who mvd to GA. R54
  David, esf 1778 Craven Co, NC; b 1763 Halifax Co, VA, s/o
    George; PN 1832 Laurens District, SC; dd there 4/1836 lea-
    ving several ch; QLF 1901 from desc W C Adamson states sol
    b 4/9/1764 & dd 4/26/1836 & f George was also RW sol. R54
  George, esf Person Co, NC; b 1754 nr Potomac River, VA; aec
    5 when parents mvd to NC; PN aec 78 Henderson Co, TN; half
    bro John Cash. R55
  George, BLW issued 10/21/1792. R55
  George, esf 1781 Augusta Co, VA; dd there 6/29/1814; md Mary
    Breden there 2/12/1789; wid PN there 1846, ae 79; QLF 1912
    from desc Lemuel L Bolles, US Army, North Yakima, WA. R55
  Henry, esf 1776, Romney, VA, PN ae 70 Lawrence Co, OH, 1819,
    w then ae 70; QLF 1925 from desc Mrs Charles N (Blanche N)
    Dyer states sol res Boone Co, KY, 1818 & mvd that year to
    Campbell Co, KY. R55
  Jacob, esf 1777 Shepherdstown, Berkeley Co (later Jefferson
    Co), VA; PN ae 62 Frederick Co, VA, 1819; LIF 1919 from
    desc Mrs W D (Grace F) Powers, Indianapolis, IN, states
    sol came from old Rappahannock Co, VA, & was her great gdf
    through his d. R55
  Jacob, esf Caroline Co, VA; b there 1760; to Cumberland Co,
    1784, thence to Pittsylvania Co, VA, where PN 1832; dd
    there 4/1841 or 4/18/1844; md 1/1806 Frances Green, Hali-
    Co, VA; w PN ae 74 Pittsylvania Co, VA, 1853, where still
    res 1855; Charlotte Anderson AFF 1853 in support of wid
    claim for PN & Jacob Anderson AFF 1855; QLF states sol ae
    90 as res with s Jacob Jr, Pittsylvania Co, VA, 1840. R55

16

ANDERSON, Jacob, esf 1777 Frederick Co, VA; b 7/5/1758; PN
1832 Montgomery Co, VA; dd 2/21/1842, Pulaski Co, VA; md
3/24/1779 Christina/Christiana Wyser/Wiser/Weyser at home
of her parents Adam & Eliza Wyser nr Winchester, VA; wid
afp ae 83 Pulaski Co, VA, 1843; PAR for insufficient proof
of marriage, & dd there 7/28/1846; when ch: George decd,
Nancy Shepherd decd, Susan decd, Elizabeth Woolwine, Peggy
Gray, Eve Sanger/Songer, Polly S Barger, Jacob, & William;
wid 3rd ch of parents & had bro George & Henry & sis Margaret & Catherine; in 1845 Mary S Barger of Pulaski Co, VA
stated she sis of Christiana & was 8th ch of parents; Mary
Shufflebarger, ae 85, stated 1857 she sis of Christiana, &
in 1843 Capt Henry Wyser, bro of Christiana, age 83 & dd
1844; in 1843 Henry Wyser Jr was Justice of the Peace in
Pulaski Co, VA, & was nephew of Christiana, he being ae 79
in 1857. R55

James, esf Hampshire Co, VA; b DE 10/22/1743; to MD, thence
to Frederick Co, VA, with parents as ch; also esf Ky 1780;
PN 1833 Knox Co, IN, & mvd to IN 1816; md but w & ch mbnn;
QLF 1936 from desc Mrs O L Drum, Vincennes, IN. R56

James, esf 1779 Harrodsburg, KY; b 4/1760 Prince William Co,
VA; PN 1832 Montgomery Co, KY; dd 2/15/1835 leaving 1 ch,
whose guardian was John A Moore; QLF states sol w was Mary
& sol PN Clarke Co, KY. R56

James, alias Asher CROCKETT, esf 1778 Hampshire Co, VA; b
there 9/1760; PN 1832 Cabell Co, VA; medical certificate
from Montgomery Co, VA, shows sol used name of Asher Crockett when md there to Sarah Blankenship 9/11/1800 & enlisted under name of James ANDERSON; sol dd 1/16/1845 Millers
Fork, Wayne Co, VA; wid PN ae 69, Wayne Co, VA, & d there
9/9/1862 leaving ch Andrew CROCKETT, Elizabeth (w/o Joseph
Kelly), & Charlotte (w/o Edward Miller); s Andrew J Crockett res 1877 Wayne Co, WV; QLF 1900 from desc Gertrude
Crockett, Kansas City, MO. R56

John, esf Wilkes Co, NC; b 1758 Bedford Co, VA; PN 1832
Whitley Co, KY, where dd 2/22/1838; md 12/1796 Sarah Pierceful in VA; wid "Sally" PN ae 78 Clay Co, MO 1857; in one
afp stated md in Knox Co, KY; AFF by sol s John 1857 Johnson Co, MO, stated he b 11/4/1795 & sol md Sarah Pierceful
as 2nd w 1798 Knox Co, KY, & that sol & Sarah had 8 ch who
lived to maturity. R57

John, esf 1777 Frederick Co, VA; b there 7/30/1758; esf 1779
SC; mvd to SC after RW, thence KY, thence Davidson Co, TN,
where PN 1832; dd there 3/12/1836; md 8/3/1784 Ann Clark;
wid PN ae 72 Davidson Co, TN, 1838; ch births: Benjamin
10/13/1785, John 3/10/87, Robert B 1/26/89, George 2/14/91
Oliver 3/27/92, William F 3/16/94, Isaac 11/7/96, Summer-
field 12/1/98 (md 7/10/1816), Berimien D 11/29/1801, Bayles E 11/7/02, Merium 1/21/08. R57

John, esf 1778 Hanover Co, VA; b 12/25/1757; PN 1832 Spencer
Co, KY; QLF 1919 from desc Miss Mary Harte Walter, Perry,
MO. R57

ANDERSON, John, BLW; QLF states sol md Mary, sis/o his cousin
Col Richard Clough Anderson & that Mary d/o Robert Anderson (1712-1792) & Elizabeth Clough (1722-1779) of Goldmine
VA, further Mary's gdd/o Robert Anderson & Cecelia Massey
of St Peter's Parish; QLF mns another John Anderson, (dd
10/13/1817), who moved to Scott Co, VA, 1773, md Rebecca
Maxwell (dd 2/21/1824) & they had 8 ch: William, John (md
Elizabeth McNier), Audley, Isaac (md Margaret Rhea), Mary
(md John Skellem), Elizabeth (md William Christian), Sarah
(md Rev. Andrew Galbraith), & Jane (md Rev. John Heniger).
R57

John, esf 1776 Hampshire Co, VA; PN ae 70 Bourbon Co, KY, in
1820 when w ae 64; ch mbnn. R57

Jordan, esf 1777 Chesterfield Co, VA; b 12/1759, PN Chesterfield Co, VA, 1832; QLF 1924 from desc Mrs J R Rich, Princeton, Mercer Co,WV, states sol b 12/28/1759, dd 3/28/1850
R57

Joseph, esf Fauquier Co, VA; afp there 1821 ae 65, when w ae
57, ch: Thomas ae 23, Milly ae 18, William ae 14, all not
md, plus md ch: Daniel 28, Joseph 25, Henry ae 20; w had
d's by previous marriage & a gdc Polly Freeman, plus a son
John ae 31; PAR for insufficient proof of svc. R57

Joseph, esf 1776 Botetourt Co, VA; PN aec 69, Giles Co, VA,
1819; w aec 60 in 1821; ch mbnn; sol dd c1827, w dd c1830;
ch afp 1853; QLF mns a Joseph Anderson of Augusta Co, VA,
whose d's: Rachael (md 3/10/1786 James Shields), Geny/Jeny
(md 11/8/1790 Samuel Torbet), all of Augusta Co, VA. R57

Leonard, esf 1776/77 Rockingham Co, VA; esf 1781 NC; b 1755
Augusta Co,VA; PN 1832 Logan Co, KY; dd 4/16/1838; md 1791
Rosanna Hadden,SC; wid PN 1844 ae 74, when AFF made by 2nd
s Alexander ae 50 & by wid bro Robert of Todd Co, KY; wid
still living 1849; eldest ch William b 1792. R57

Nathan, esf 1781 Manchester,VA; b1/23/1764; PN 1832 Chester-
field Co, VA; dd 10/31/1834; md 1785 Mariana/Mary Mayo (MB
dated 4/10/1785), Chesterfield Co,VA; wid PN ae 77 Henrico
Co, VA, 1845; QLF 1909 from desc Edward D Anderson, USA,
Atlanta,GA; QLF 1903 from desc Mrs J E Perkinson, Danville
VA. R57

Nathaniel, esf 1776 VA; dd 2/1799 Caroline Co, VA; md Sally
Jones 12/2/1787, Hanover Co, VA; wid md (2) c1800 William
Anderson of Caroline Co, VA, who dd there 6/14/1836; Sally
PN 1836 & dd there 8/28/1840 at home of s Herbert (s/o of
William) who ae 45 in 1850; wid other ch: Armistead, Mary
B (w/o John Richardson/Richerson),Catharine T (w/o William
E Green in 1850); in 1785 sol bro John res nr Hanover, Ha-
nover Co, VA, also res there wid bro's Merriwether, Jekyl,
& Skelton Jones; Sarah d/o sol & Sally Jones, b7/19/1790 &
dd 7/21/1839. R57

Peter, esf 1777 VA, afp ae 73 Wood Co, VA, 1832; PAR for insufficient proof of svc. R57

Peter, esf 1777 Bedford Co, VA; b there 1756; PN 1832 Jonesborough, Hawkins Co, TN. R57

ANDERSON, Richard, esf Caroline Co, VA; d 4/1813 Buckingham Co
VA; md 12/2/1784 Martha Meadows/Meador, Cumberland Co, VA;
wid PN ae 74 there 1839; ch births: James 10/11/1785, Salley 12/7/87, Billy 11/20/89, John 11/91, Elizabeth 11/94,
? 3/15/96, Rebekah, Lawrence May; Cumberland Co clerk AFF
that Martha last name on marriage record was Meador. R58

Richard Clough, esf 1776 Hanover Co, VA; b there; to Jefferson Co, KY, after RW; dd 10/16/1826; md 9/17/1797 Sally
Marshall (MB dated 9/14/1797), Jefferson Co, KY; wid PN ae
68, Chillicothe, Ross Co, OH, 1848, & dd 8/26/1854; s William M liv 1849; QLF states sol b 1/2/1750; QLF states a
William Marshall b 8/27/1720, King & Queen Co, VA, dd 1810
Henry Co, KY, also RW sol. R58

Robert, esf Rockbridge Co, VA; b 3/25/1763 York Co, PA; PN
1833 Pulaski Co, KY & dd there 8/24/1844; md there 1814/5
Nancy Ping (wid/o of John Brown, md 1789, who also RW sol)
wid PN ae 93 there 1853; Nancy had many ch by 1st h including dau liv 1853; Robert Ping ae 47 res there 1853. R58

Robert, esf 1777 Hanover Co, VA; b 1/29/1761; PN 1833 Jackson Co, TN; dd 4/18/1836; md 11/24/1789 Mary/Molly Martin,
Hanover Co, VA; wid PN ae 75, Jackson Co, TN, 1839; ch
births: Mathew 5/20/1790, Sarah 3/11/92, William 2/18/95,
Elizabeth 7/18/98, Robert 3/25/1801, John 1/17/04. R58

Robert, esf Louisa Co; dd 5/15/1826 Davidson Co, TN; md Bedford Co, VA, 3/29/1784 Mary Read (MB surety William Read);
wid dd 1/1/1846 Giles Co, TN, leaving ch Samuel R, Mrs Mary Cole, & Mrs Joannah Cole; s Samuel R ae 49 Davidson Co,
TN, 1851; ch of Joanna Cole (dd 1851) were Robert, David,
Richard, Rebecca Blow, & Martha Simpson, all of TN; surv
ch of wid PN 1851; QLF states sol wid d/o William Reade, &
sol ch were Robert, Johanna J, Mary, & Samuel Reade. R58

Spencer, esf 1776 Prince William Co, VA; afp 1818 there; PN
ae 70 Fauquier Co, VA, 1820, when w Susan ae 76, & both of
them liv with s. R58

Thomas, esf 1779/80 Chesterfield Co, VA; b there 4/1/1762;
PN 1832 Abbeville District, SC; QLF states sol dd there c
1840. R58

ANDREW, John, esf Chester, PA; PN ae 69 Brooke Co, VA, 1819; w
decd in 1820; sol res then with d & son-in-law; mvd Harrison Co, VA, 1821. R59

ANDREWS, Adam, esf 1777 VA; PN ae 68 Botetourt Co, VA, 1818;
dd 7/11/1825; QLF 1935 from desc Mrs. F J Farnsworth, Minneapolis, MN. R59

Benjamin, esf VA; dd 7/11/1803 Chesterfield Co, VA; md Elizabeth Dodd 11 or 12/1776; wid PN ae 92 Chesterfield Co,
VA, 1843; ch births: Simon 10/2/1777, Nanny 12/2/78, Masey
11/10/81, Andrew 2/24/85, Daniel 5/12/87, Benjamin 1/24/91
other births in family bible: Tamey Ellison (s/o William &
Betsy Wilson) 4/13/1802, Lawson Wilson 12/22/03. R59

Elkanah, sea svc, esf 1777 Accomac Co, VA; PN ae 57 there
1824 when family w ae 40, & ch: Robert aec 20, Richard aec
11, Samuel aec 8; sol still res there 1832. R61

ANDREWS, Ephraim, esf 1781 VA; BLW 1807 Hawkins Co, TN. R61
  Isham, esf 1780 Chesterfield Co,VA; b there 1747; dd there
    10/3/1845; md there 2/3/1786 Mary Perkinson, who PN there
    1847 ae 81; eldest ch Fanny b 5/28/1787. R61
  John, esf 1781 Lunenburg Co, VA; b4/4/1764 Dinwiddie Co, VA,
    s/o Mark; to Adair Co, KY, 1802, thence to Williamson Co,
    TN, where PN 1832; QLF 1939 from desc Mrs. Oscar Barthold,
    Weatherford, TX. R62
  Robert, PN half pay for life; military chaplain; dd 1/1/1804
    leaving ch: Ann w/o William Randolph, Elizabeth, Catherine
    w/o J B Wilkinson, Robert who dd without issue, & John; in
    1833 heirs were ch: Catherine, Elizabeth, John, & gdc: Ro-
    bert Randolph & Catherine Taylor, orphans of Ann Andrews
    Randolph; heirs PAR. R63
  Thomas, esf 1780 Cumberland Co, VA; b there 12/12/1761; PN
    1833 Bedford Co, VA; QLF from desc Hazel E Lee, La Junta,
    CO, states sol md Tabitha Lee, further Capt. John Lee of
    Bedford Co, VA, b 1730, dd 5/19/1818, further William Lee,
    RW sol of Bedford Co, VA, dd 9/23/1803 & md Avie Noell of
    Bristol, England, & Westmoreland Co, VA. R64
  Thomas, esf 1775 Lunenburg Co, VA; b 4/4/1758 Dinwiddie Co,
    VA; to Fayette Co, KY, 1815 & PN there 1832; dd 1/22/1833;
    md 3/31/1791, Margaret ---, Mecklenburg Co, VA; wid PN ae
    77, Fayette Co,KY, 1838; ch births: Nancy 2/28/1792, Abra-
    ham 6/2/93, Nely 6/9/96, Perley 9/8/98, Rebecca 3/29/1802;
    other family bible births (all surname Andrews): Daniel
    7 or 9/1815, Abraham 5/28/18, Salley 5/17/1797, George W
    3/15/1819, Eliza J 10/5/20, William W 5/10/22, Hannah E
    1/22/24, Margrit 2/8/26, Thomas D 2/27/27. R64
  Varney, esf 1776/7 Halifax Co, VA; b 1754 Mecklenburg Co, VA
    PN there 1833. R64
  William, esf 1776 Harford Co, MD; PN ae 66 Amherst Co, VA,
    at which time w decd & ch Polly ae 26, Ann ae 24, Betsy ae
    22 res with him; QLF 1930 from Miss Helen Louise Andrews,
    Wellington, KS, states sol w was Martha Lane, further Jo-
    seph Andrews, b 4/15/1780, dd 1844, War of 1812 sol who md
    Susanna Ellis; QLF 1923 from desc Mrs George Oliver, Eus-
    tis, FL, requests RW PN data on William Ellis of VA. R64
  William, sea svc, esf 1777 Accomac Co, VA; afp 1824 ae 66,
    Accomac Co, VA?; res with sis Rachel Pew; AFF by Elkanah
    Andrews that he served on same ship with William. R64
  William, esf VA & GA; records lost in fire at US War Office;
    PN increased GA 1816; dd 5/3/1821; QLF 1937 from great-
    great gdd Corola L White, Decatur, IL, states William esf
    Dinwiddie Co, VA, possibly, & was granted BLW for land in
    Brunswick Co, VA. R64
ANGELL, James, BLW issued 10/31/1792. R66
ANGLETON, Sarah, PN as former wid/o sol John Robertson. R66
ANGLIN, Philip, esf 177- VA; b 12/30/1742 Albemarle Co, VA;
  afp ae 91 Henry Co, VA, 1834; PAR for insufficient proof
  of svc. R66
ANGLIN, John, see ANGLING, John. R66

ANGLING, John, esf 1781 Caswell Co, NC; b 1757 Louisa Co, VA;
PN 1832 Dickson Co, TN; dd 12/10/1836; md 8/5/1810 Eliza-
beth Carver, Wilson Co, TN; wid PN ae 72 Dickson Co, TN,
1853; wid gtd BLW there 1855. R66
ANNIS, Levi, sea svc, dd 1816; md 1787 Peggy --- who PN 1837
Accomac Co, VA, & gtd BLW ae over 80 there 1851; ch gtd PN
1853; s Custis, War of 1812 sol, liv 1851. R67
Micajah, esf 1777 VA; b Accomac Co, VA; PN 1819 Worcester Co
MD when had w & d. R67
ANTILL, Jacob, esf Berkeley Co, VA; dd 8/11/1800; md 2/20/1781
Dorcas, d/o John Dawkins, Berkeley Co,VA; wid b 9/30/1763,
PN 1839 Henry Co, KY; s John, who res 1853 there, stated m
dd many years since; QLF 1929 from desc Miss Mary Rankley,
Turners Station, KY; QLF states sol esf 1776, further that
a John Dawkins RW sol from NC. R68
ANTLE, Jacob, see ANTILL, Jacob. R68
APPERSON, John, name also spelled EPPERSON, esf 1780 Spotsylvania Co, VA; b there 12/4/1763; PN Boles Township, Franklin Co, VA; dd there 9/30/1834; md 1/4/1785 Alcey/Alice, d
of William & Ann Favour/Favor, Culpeper Co, VA; wid PN ae
83 Clay Co,IL; eldest ch William ae 20/21 in 1808; s Francis b 2/14/1800; births ch of s Francis & Jane Duff: Elbert Sevier 7/29/1826, Mary Elizabeth 7/18/28, John Alexander 4/17/31, Stephen Randolph 3/19/34, Alsey Ellen
3/27/37, Charles Wesley 4/12/1841; a Francis Epperson was
clerk of court Clay Co, IL, 1852; sol's bro Reuben, who b
3/7/1779, res Russell Co, VA, 1853; QLF 1834 from William
Epperson, Kaysville, UT, gives data on Apperson family of
of VA: William Epperson b 2/22/1770 Bedford Co, VA, Hyrum
Percy Epperson b 11/1/1830 IN, William P Epperon b 9/23/59
IL; QLF 1910 from sol great gdd, Lucy Apperson Weaver, Sa-
lida, CO, states sol w dd 1857 Clay Co,IL, further Richard
Apperson b 8/22/1796, Culpeper Co, VA, md Sarah/Margaret
Aiken, mvd later to Clay Co,IL; QLF 1902 from desc John A
Gardner, St Louis, MO, states sol b Culpeper Co, VA; QLF
1913 from great gdd Mrs Edward Compton, Chicago,IL, states
f William Favor also RW sol from Culpeper Co, VA; QLF 1929
from desc Mrs. Pickens Gates, Huntsville, AL. R69
Peter, esf 1776 VA; PN 1818 Spotsylvania Co, VA. R69
Richard,esf VA; BLW issued 1808;res 1807 Franklin Co,KY. R69
APPLEGATE, Garrett, esf 1778, VA; esf 1781 PA; b 11/2/1758,
PN 1833 Heth Township, Harrison Co, IN; QLF 1907 from
great gdd, Mrs Elsie Applegate Drapier, Indianapolis, IN;
QLF 1905 from desc Hardin Heth Littell, Buffalo, NY. R70
James, svc Northwest Indian War not RW; wounded Battle of St
Clair's Defeat when res Berkeley Co,VA & md there; PN 1826
Flemingsburg, Fleming Co, KY, when res Greenup Co,KY. R70
Robert, esf 1778 Yogohania Co, PA, for VA svc; b 3/13/1759
Princeton, NJ; PN 1832 Allegheny Co, PN; s Irwin res with
sol 1845 Harrison Co, IN, where mvd c1842. R70
APPLEWHAITE, John, sea svc; esf 1776 VA; dd 1800 Hampton, VA;
in 1834 d Judith Cary Applewhaite, sole heir, adm of sol's

APPLEWHAITE (continued)
    estate, she still liv 1853 Norfolk, VA; sol's d Sarah Gil-
    bert res 1833 Norfolk, VA. R71
ARBUCKLE, James, esf Prince Edward Co, VA; b there 5/1761/62;
    to NC; PN 1834 Braden Co, KY; bro David also RW sol. R71
  Matthew, no PN; see claim of William RICHMOND of VA. R71
  Thomas, esf Botetourt Co, VA; est Whitley Station, KY, 1780;
    PN ae 86 Washington Co, IN, 1833; court appearance in 1838
    Jefferson Co, IN; QLF 1909 from desc, Mrs. Wayne Robison,
    Columbus, IN, states sol s/o James, who res 1749 Augusta
    Co,VA, further sol had bro's John (dd 1845 Madison Co,OH),
    William (dd 1836 Mason Co, VA), Capt Mathew (dd 1781 Bath
    Co or Greenbrier Co, VA). R71
  William, esf Augusta Co, VA, afp 1833 Mason Co, VA; PAR for
    insufficient proof of svc; QLF 1919 from desc Nelson W.
    McMullin, Louisville, KY. R71
  William, drafted 1779 Prince Edward Co, VA; afp ae 75 Laurel
    Co, KY; PAR, no svc, having hired John Mead as sub. R71
ARCHER, Edmund, esf 1777 Culpeper Co, VA; b there 4/27/1759;
    to KY 1795;PN 1832 Oldham Co,KY, when s Jesse W res French
    Lick, Orange Co, IN, & d res KY; QLF states sol recd last
    PN payment 1840 & his LWT listed 5 s & 2 d. R72
  Evans, esf 1780 Portsmouth,VA; PN aec 69, Hartford,KY, 1823.
    R72
  Isaac, esf 1778 VA; PN ae over 65 Sullivan Co, TN, 1818,
    res there 1820 ae 71 & w aec 72. R72
  John, sea svc, esf VA; dd 10/18/1793; LWT 10/15/1793, proba-
    ed 7/28/1794, Norfolk,VA, listed w Elizabeth, bro Edward &
    w, niece Anna Maria Archer, sis Frances, nephew John Arch-
    er; sol md 3/12/1792 Elizabeth Calvert res/o her m Mary,
    Norfolk,VA; wid md (2) Alexander Martin, dd c1812; wid afp
    1832 ae 74, PN 1842 ae 86,liv 1851; QLF 1906 from desc Mrs
    Emma Stevens Ganson, Kansas City,MO, states sol s/o Robert
    & ancestor m's side, & sol d Frances md Dougald Ferguson &
    they parents/o her gdm who md William Stevens Jr. R72
  Joseph, esf VA, fatally wounded at Battle of Brandywine; s/o
    William of Amelia Co, VA; bro Joseph dd leaving 4 ch: Wil-
    liam S (member of US Congress in 1834), Elizabeth, Martha,
    & Ann; these ch gtd BLW as heirs of uncle Joseph. R72
  Peter Field, BLW issued 1806; res Richmond, VA. R72
  Richard, BLW issued 9/9/1789. R72
  Stephen, esf 1775/6 Philadelphia, PA, sea svc; esf later for
    army svc Staunton, Augusta Co, VA; esf 1781 for army svc
    in PA; PN 1818 Green Co,PA; md (1) Elizabeth ---; res 1820
    Monongalia Co, VA, ae 75, with w Elizabeth ae 55, d Eliza-
    beth aec 35 (invalid), d Mary ae 26; dd 5/12/1824; md (2)
    6/12/1823 Martha, b 8/21/1800 York Co, PA, d/o William &
    Margaret Sign; wid md (2) 4/3-4/1835 John Rice who dd 9/47
    or 9/48; wid PN 1855 Monongalia Co, VA, as sol's former
    wid; QLF states Martha "Mattie", after sol dd, ran off
    with her bro-in-law, who was md at time, to OH, & she had
    ch by him, & ending up in poorhouse in OH, where she md to

ARCHER (continued)
   an Irishman, John Rice, having 5 d's & 1 s by him. R72
ARGABRIGHT, George, esf before 1778 Rockingham Co, VA; b 1759
   Lancaster, PA; to Rockingham Co, VA, aec 9; PN there 1832;
   md there 3/27/1832 Christina Eaton; dd 2/22/1840; wid PN
   ae 69 Cass Co, IN, 1854. R72
ARGUBRIGHT, Jacob, esf 1778 Rockingham Co, VA; b 10/20/1760,
   Lancaster Co, PA; to Rockingham Co, VA, as ch; to Albemarle Co, VA, after RW, thence to Monroe Co, VA, where PN
   1832; w mbnn; sol bro's John & Abram RW svc with him. R72
ARGUBRITE, Jacob, see ARGUBRIGHT, Jacob. R72
ARINGTON, John, see ARRINGTON, John. R72
ARMAN, Thomas, esf 1777 Botetourt Co, VA; afp ae 69/70 Pulaski
   Co, KY, 1822 when w ae 60, & ch: Nancy aec 30, Mary ae 28
   (md), Harry, Thomas ae 22, Elizabeth ae 20; sol PN 1824 &
   dd 8/1831 St Francis Co, MO; md 1787/88 Charity ---, Rutherford Co, NC, who b 12/13/1759; wid back to KY after sol
   dd & PN 1839 Pulaski Co, KY; wid dd there 2/14/1845, surv
   by ch: Nancy, Mary, & Henry, adm of estate being Charles
   Ashley; d Elizabeth md George Crump; d Mary b 9/13/1793 &
   md Charles Ashley who b 1/23/1789; birth of Charles & Mary
   Ashley's ch: Callaway 4/12/1811, Moses 7/17/1815, Thomas
   5/24/18, Cinsy 6/6/20, Andy 4/8/23, Susanna 1/1/28, Elizabeth 4/2/29. R73
ARMANTROUT, Charles, see ARMONTROUT, Charles. R73
ARMENTROUT, Charles, see ARMONTROUT, Charles. R73
ARMISTEAD, Richard, esf 1776 Kingston Parish, Gloucester Co,
   VA, where b; dd 1824; md 1770 Elizabeth Jarvis,Mathews Co,
   who PN ae 84 there 1836; wid dd 12/23/1836 leaving d Elizabeth Tumberlin/Tumblin, d Susan, & s Isaac; AFF 1858 by
   Elizabeth Tumblin that she b 8/22/1773. R73
   Thaddeus, esf c1777 Cumberland Co, VA; b there 11/3/1753; to
   Smith Co, TN, 1803 where afp 1832, & PAR for insufficient
   svc; dd Smith Co, TN, 12/12/1848; w dd c1813; ch liv there
   1853 John ae 55, Thaddeus aec 50 who afp for f svc, & PAR
   for same reason. R73
   Thomas, esf 1776 VA; retired 1782 disabled from 3 wounds at
   1/2 pay; dd 9/1/1809 King William Co, VA; wid Jane --- dd
   before 1833; ch: Abiah (md --- Albert), Ann (md --- Mitchell), Catherine T (md William B Pierce, 2nd Everard Hall),
   Martha B (md John Towler), Jane/Juli Ann; gdc Louisa & Octavo Berthea; d Martha AFF 1847 Baltimore, MD, that her h
   John Towler was War of 1812 sol & her uncle Gregory Smith
   was colonel in RW; sol ch afp 1833 but PAR because sol wid
   already decd. R73
   William, esf VA; dd 11/23/1822; 1/2 pay gtd 1850 to adm of
   his estate. R73
   William, esf 1777 Elizabeth City Co, VA, where b; PN ae 76
   Clark Co, AL; dd 3/1/1842; s John K res Pine Hill, Wilcox
   Co, AL, 1838; also s Westbrook; QLF 1925 from great gdd
   May M Forwood states sol b 1762; QLF states s John middle
   name Kimbell. R73

ARMON, Thomas, see ARMAN, Thomas R73
ARMONTROUT, Charles,esf 1781 Rockingham Co,VA; b there 5/1763;
    PN 1833 Preble Co, OH, where dd 5/6/1836; md 6/23/1807
    Christiana/Christena Gray, Harding Township, Montgomery Co
    OH; wid PN ae 71 Monroe Township, Preble Co, OH, 1853; fam
    mvd there c1811. R73
ARMSTEAD, William, esf 1776 Kingston Parish, Gloucester Co, VA
    where b 1758; PN 1834 Mathews Co, VA; dd 2/4/1836. R73
ARMSTRONG, Abel, est 1777 Staunton, Augusta Co, VA; b 6/3/1758
    or 6/4/1758; PN 1832 Monroe Township, Logan Co, OH; dd
    8/26/1837, surv ch mbnn; QLF 1909 from great gdd Mrs Ida
    Beavers, Seattle, WA, states sol b 1755 Augusta Co, VA, &
    dd Logan Co, OH, 1835; QLF 1929 from desc Mrs A Lee Pray,
    Leroy, IL. R74
  Adam, BLW issued 4/12/1792. R74
  Alexander, esf 1776 Bedford Co, VA; to KY 1780 & again esf
    1781; b 1752 Bedford Co, VA; PN 1834 Monroe Co, IN. R74
  Ambrose, esf c1778 Essex Co, VA; PN ae 72 Fayette Co, KY,
    1832; QLF states sol dd 1881 ae 82 & buried Johnson Co, IN
    R74
  Henry, esf 1778 Rockingham Co, VA; later esf Botetourt Co,
    VA; b 2/28/1754 VA; to KY 1807; PN 1833 Adair Co, KY. R74
  Isaac, esf 1777/78 Augusta Co, VA; b 7/1762 MD; to Loudon Co
    VA ae 8; to Augusta Co, VA, ae 15; to Greenbrier Co, VA,
    after RW; to TN c1817; PN 1832 Anderson Co, IN; res 1837
    Putnam Co, IN. R74
  James, esf 1778 Henry Co, VA; b 3/17/1758; dd 3/15/1819; md
    1/7/1782 Nancy Lanier/Linear, Henry Co,VA, who b 9/2/1766;
    wid afp 1838 Overton Co, TN, & PAR; her res 1853 Overton
    Co, TN; ch births: William 12/18/178-, Elizabeth 3/12/85,
    John 3/3/87, George 4/4/89, Landon 12/18/91, James Jr
    5/9/94, Hugh 7/27/96,Catharine 1/1797, Nancy 5/25/99, Pol-
    ly 9/13/1801, Mi;cajah 8/13/05, Robert 10/2/07; family bi-
    ble marriages: Hugh F 11/17/1815, George 7/7/11, Landon
    11/13/09, James Jr 9/3/12, Polly 1/2/17, Nancy 12/20/15,
    George to Sally South 11/7/1824, Robert 1/19/26, Hugh F to
    Elizabeth Poindexter 8/10/28, Micajah L to R B Overstreet
    4/3/28, Pyle to Mahaly Gamewell 4/4/33; other family bible
    births: P H Armstrong 12/2/1817, Elizabeth Cross 1/8/23,
    William who s/o George 1812, Anaren 4/14/14, Armistead
    1/13/16, Amanda M who d/o Hugh 10/4/16, Frank 11/25/09,
    Maclin who s/o Elizabeth Cross 3/31/03, William who s/o
    Elizabeth Cross 4/16/07, Mary A, d/o M L & R B Armstrong,
    8/22/30, Nancy M who d/o R G Armstrong 8/26/26, Polley who
    d/o R L Armstrong 8/20/30, Mahala 12/5/10, Mary Jane who
    d/o Pyle 7/10/34, George 3/21/36, Andrew 11/9/37, Thomas
    Jefferson 3/19/39; family bible deaths: William Armstrong
    7/16/1784, James 3/15/1819 in 61st year, Kitty Armstrong
    in 23rd year, James M 9/1/21, Patsy 11/6/21, Hugh Sr
    4/29/24, William Sr 12/28/24, George 10/7/27, Rebecca B
    3/30/32 in 22nd year, Polly who d/o Robert & Susanna Arm-
    strong 7/29/32, Nancy who w/o H C Armstrong 1833 in 34th

ARMSTRONG (continued)
    year; AFF by Landon Armstrong 1857 states John B Cross md
    his sis 1800; AFF 1853 by Will Armstrong, nephew of James,
    Grundy Co, TN; AFF 1853 by Colonel Landon Armstrong, s/o
    sol & wNancy, Overton Co, TN. R75
James, esf 1776 Bucks Co, PA, where b 7/1761; to Loud Co, VA
    1783, thence to Franklin Township, Franklin Co, OH, where
    PN 1832; f at one time res in Pendleton Co, VA. R75
Jesse, BLW issued 11/2/1792. R75
Jesse, esf 1776 VA; s George gtd BLW 1833 King George Co, VA
    at which time f was decd. R75
John, est 1778/79 Essex Co, VA; PN 1832 South Farnham Parish
    Essex Co, VA; dd 3/30/1847 ae 70 years & 7 months, Rich-
    mond Co, VA, leaving ch: Purkins, John P, Lucy W Hanks,
    Joseph H; QLF 1921 from desc Mrs. Arthur Mortimer, Virden,
    IL. R75
Joshua, esf 1777 Cumberland Co, VA; b 8/1/1756 Lancaster, PA
    PN 1833 Greene Co, IL; dd 9/25/1845; md 7/7/1785 Sarah
    d/o Morris Morris, Rockingham Co, VA; wid PN ae 82 Jersey
    Co, IL, 1846; sol's bro John POW in RW & bro Joseph KIA in
    RW; QLF 1930 from desc J A Stice, Shelbyville, IL, states
    sol b Carlisle,PA; QLF 1918 from great gds Byron Armstrong
    of Jacksonville, IL, states he s/o C C Armstrong (b Jersey
    Co, IL) who now res Girard, Macoupin Co, IL; QLF 1914
    great gds A L Armstrong, Clinton, MO, states sol md Sarah
    L Mars or Ross; QLF 1909 from great gds William E Bridges,
    Kansas City, MO, states he gds/o sol d Margaret & William
    Bridges of O'Fallon, IL. R75
William, esf 1778 Augusta Co, VA; b 12/12/1759 Little Calf
    Pasture, Augusta Co, VA; PN there 1832; dd 10/29/1853; QLF
    states sol possibly h/o Ann (b 5/15/1755, dd 12/25/1842) &
    family mvd to Northampton Co, VA, shortly after marriage &
    had d b there, then mvd back to Augusta Co, VA; QLF 1924
    from desc Mrs J A Holtzclaw, Chattanooga, TN. R76
ARNETT, David, esf Louisa Co, VA, where b 6/18/1752; PN 1831
    Barren Co, KY. R76
ARNOLD, Benjamin, esf c1779 Laurens Co, SC, while res with gdf
    & later mvd back to VA with gdf, where esf Henry Co, VA, &
    later esf as sub for uncle Hendrick Arnold of Amherst Co;
    b 1/28/1762 Buckingham Co, VA; f dd before RW; PN 1833
    Warren Co, TN; QLF 1935 from desc William H Arnold, Texar-
    kana, AR; QLF states gdf of sol was Benjamin b 1719. R77
Elisha, esf 1776 Lunenburg Co, VA; b 1758 Mecklenburg Co, VA
    PN 1832 Henry Co, VA; QLF states Elisha Henry Arnold, b
    8/3/1758, Mecklenburg Co, VA, s/o James Arnold & his 3rd w
    Martha Atkins, further sol md 1/1/1779 Sally (b 7/10/1764,
    d/o Samuel Marshall & Cassandra Allfriend) who dd c1837 in
    Henry Co, VA, further sol & w Sally had 6 s & 4 d, further
    sol dd Fall of 1849 Henry Co, VA. R77
Francis, esf 1777 New Market, Spotsylvania Co, VA; b 1/1758
    that Co, VA; PN 1818 White Co, TN, where dd 2/5/1830-1831;
    md 8/5/1790 Elizabeth Parker, Greenville District, SC; wid

ARNOLD (continued)

    b 12/23/1775 & mvd to Coffee Co, TN, after h dd; she PN 1840 White Co, TN, & res 1851 Coffee Co, TN, with s Peter; wid dd before 3/1853; births of 14 ch: William (eldest) 6/20/1791, then 6 more s, then d, then s Peter 9/28/1803, s Calberd 4/28/07, then s, then s 1/21/1811, then 1 more s; s Hayes res 1853 White Co, TN, & adm of his m's estate. R77

Hezekiah, esf Spotsylvania, VA; b 1764 King George Co, VA; PN 1834 Stokes Co, NC. R77

James, esf 1777 Culpeper Co, VA; PN 1832 aec 77 Woodford Co, KY; bro Lewis never returned from RW svc; QLF states sol md to Lucy. R78

John, esf 1778 Spotsylvania Co, VA, as sub for f Anthony; b 6/24/1758 Caroline Co,VA; to Clark Co, KY, Fall 1803 where PN 1834; dd 7/15/1840; sis Mrs Sally Benning ae 69 there 1834; QLF 1936 from great great gds Harvey D Arnold, Goree, TX, states sol md --- Owen & dd Nicholasville,KY; QLF 1895 from s James who res Sanger, Clark Co, KY. R78

Josiah, esf 1776 VA; PN 1819 Muhlenberg Co, KY; in 1821 sol ae 67, w aec 63; mvd to Pike Co, IN, 1829 to live near ch. R78

Lindsey/Lindsay, esf 1781 NC in VA regiment; PN ae 63 Rutherford Co, NC; dd NC 3/1832; md 11/18/1785 Elizabeth Davis (Louisa Co, VA, MB dated 11/14/1785 with Jonathan Davis as surety); wid PN ae 74 Louisa Co, VA, 1843; d Susan who b 2/7/1790 res Louisa Co, VA, 1843; AFF Coffee Co, TN, 1850 by Nancy Arnold ae 75, who afp stating sol who PN Morgantown, NC, had dd by drowning 12/1/1830, further she md sol 8/10/1781, Spartansburg District, SC; AFF 1843 Louisa Co, states sol dd 1832 Rutherford Co, NC, further he left w & several children in 1787 & never returned. R78

Lindsey, BLW issued 1/7/1793. R78

Solomon, esf 1780 Warren Co, NC; b 1758 Lunenburg Co, VA; PN 1833 Moore Co, NC; dd 10/23/1844 there; MB 1/29/1784 with Mary Ourley (surety John Arnold), Warren Co, NC; wid PN ae 77 Moore Co, NC, 1845. R79

Thomas, esf 1777 Ninety-Six District, SC; b 10/5/1763-66 Buckingham Co, VA; PN 1833 Autauga Co, AL; dd 3/23/1844; md 10/26/1786 Mary --- who b 5/3/1766; wid PN 1854 Selma, Dallas Co, AL; ch births: Temperance 11/26/1789 (md Peter Ross 8/15/1804), William b 7/1/1791, John 4/4/93, Thomas H 3/7/97, Sally P 4/27/99, Ann H 6/22/1802 (md Hance H Dunklin 3/11/24); births of ch/o Peter & Temperance Ross: Thomas A 7/4/05, Mary 9/6/07, Susan 4/20/10, Lucinda 8/14/12, Andrew J 11/25/14; QLF 1924 from great great gds W S Regan of Kansas City, MO; QLF 1927 from great great gdd G B Ellis, Texarkana, TX; QLF 1930 from great gdd Mrs. Sallie T Harris, Dallas, TX; QLF 1930 from great gdd Dot Arnold Pavey (Mrs G M), Dallas, TX. R79

William, esf 1776 Henry Co, VA; b 8/31/1749 Cumberland Co, Co, VA; apf 1832 Rutherford Co, TN; PAR for insufficient

ARNOLD (continued)
　　svc. R79
ARRANCE, James, BLW issued 1/15/1793. R80
ARRASMITH, Massey (alias SMITH, Massa Arra); esf VA, PN 1829
　　Campbell Co, KY. R80
　Nancy, former wid/o Casper Potterf who recd PN & BLW for MD/
　　VA svc. R80
ARRINGTON, Adler, esf Buckingham Co, VA, where b 3/1761; PN
　　1832 Campbell Co, VA. R80
　John, esf 1781 VA; b 1757 Lunenburg Co, VA, PN 1832 Halifax
　　Co,VA; dd 11/20/1837; md 4/30/1790 Susannah Vaughan, Gran-
　　ville Co, NC; wid PN ae 61 Halifax Co, VA, 1838; wid apf
　　increase ae 90 there 1867; AFF by wid bro John Vaughan ae
　　79 & by wid sis Mary Wosham ae 83 Mecklenburg Co, VA, 1850
　　R80
　Samuel, esf 1779 Amherst Co (that section now Nelson Co),VA,
　　PN ae 81 Nelson Co, VA, 1843. R80
　Thomas, esf 1777 Fairfax Co, VA; afp ae 65 Prince William
　　Co, VA, 1818; PAR for insufficient proof of svc; bro Wil-
　　liam ae 75 (also RW svc) & sol both res Prince William Co
　　VA, 1832; sol afp again 1836 & PAR; QLF 1907 from desc
　　Anne L Rollins states sol dd ae 104 New York, NY. R80
　William, BLW issued 1/7/1793. R80
ARROWSMITH, James, see SMITH, James Arrow. R80
ARTHER, James, esf 1776 Bedford Co, VA; b 10/24/1750 King Wil-
　　liam Co, VA; PN 1833 Pittsylvania Co, VA. R80
ARTHUR, Catherine, former wid/o MACKAY, Walter. R80
　James, see ARTHER, James, above. R80
　James, esf 1781 Hardy Co, VA; b 5/1784 Burlington, NJ; PN
　　1832 Butler Co,OH, having res OH 33 years; in 1828 had W &
　　4 ch; sis Elizabeth Arthur & Lydia Hall res then Clermont
　　Co, OH; QLF 1898 from great gdd Mrs. J L Hartwell, Dixon,
　　IL, states sol w was Rachel Brown, buried Clermont Co, OH,
　　further sol res Batavia, IL; QLF 1909 from great gdd Mrs.
　　Cora Arthur Glenn, Altawa, IL. R80
　James, esf MD; d 12/12/1810 Dinwiddie Co, VA; md 5/25/1782
　　Elizabeth Gilliam, Prince George Co, VA; wid PN ae 75 Ame-
　　lia Co, VA, 1840; wid f dd 4/1801; wid res ae 80 Amelia,
　　Co, VA, 1844; d Elizabeth md 3/29/1801 Andrew Torborne;
　　wid sis Mary md 5/25/1782 Capt. William Poythress, Prince
　　George Co, VA. R80
　Joel, esf 1780 Bedford Co, VA, where b 1781; to Greenbrier
　　Co, VA, c1802, thence Jackson Co, OH, c1812, where PN 1832
　　Jefferson Township. R80
　John, esf 1776 Prince Edward Co, VA; later esf Bedford Co,
　　PA, where PN 1819 Greenfield Township ae 63; QLF 1933 from
　　desc Grace Annette Wills, Washington, NJ. R80
　John, esf 1780 Bedford Co, VA, where PN 1843 ae 85; dd there
　　8/24/1850; md there 10/1784 Elizabeth, b 9/28/1769, d/o
　　John & Sarah Adams; ch births: Thomas A 1/3/1787, Dosia
　　11/23/89, Willis 2/27/91,Larkin 2/5/93, Lilly Ann 3/12/95,
　　John 9/15/97, Sally 4/27/1800, Caleb 7/27/02, Winnifred

ARTHUR (continued)
    1/8/18--, name illegible 3/21/07, Melindah 1/17/14, Emley
    Jane 1/3/16, Elizabeth 9/16; bro Thomas also RW sol who md
    Sally Dixon; QLF 1933 from desc T D Killian, Atlanta, GA.
    R80
  Stephen, esf 1780 Bedford Co, VA; b 3/8/1760; afp Powell Co,
    KY, 1833; PAR for insufficient proof of svc. R80
  Thomas, esf 1778 Bedford Co, VA; dd 11/1805; md 11/29/1782
    Sarah "Sally" Dixon, Bedford Co, VA; wid PN aec 76 there
    1843 & still res there 1849; ch in 1843: John aec 59, Hen-
    ry aec 57, Thomas aec 55; wid still res there 11849; sol
    bro John aec 85 there 1843, also RW sol; QLF 1938 from Am-
    brose Arthur, Williamsburg, KY, states sol buried Knox Co,
    KY, further sol s Ambrose War of 1812 sol, buried Knox Co,
    KY. R80
  William, esf 1780 Bedford Co, VA, where b 11/14/1762 & where
    PN 1833; dd 7/9/1847 leaving 1 ch Susan H Arthur; QLF 1940
    from desc George L Saunders, Denver, CO. R80
ARTIS, Isaac, esf 1777 Cornfield, Berkeley Co, VA; PN Fayette
    Co, PA, 1818; ae 63 in 1820 when w Chloe ae 64 & no ch liv
    with them. R80
ARUNDALL, John, esf 1776 PA; PN ae 61 Fairfax Co, VA, 1818; dd
    2/16/22; md (1) Ann Davis who dd; md (2) 9/10/1793 Jemima,
    sis of Ann, Fairfax Co, VA; wid PN 1838 & dd 10/22/47 lea-
    ving ch: Nancy, Mary Ann Gosporn, Elizabeth Keene, Polly
    Mayhugh, Charles A, & Peter C; Charles A afp 1856 on be-
    half of sol surv ch; Pension Office doubted that sol mar-
    riage occurred before 1794, & had court try Charles A for
    fraud. R80
ARUNDELL, John, see ARUNDALL, John. R80
ASBERRY, William, esf Fauquier Co, VA; BLW issued 7/7/1792; dd
    3/12/1814 Fleming Co, KY; md 8/1782-3 Susan Glascock, Fau-
    quier Co, VA, her res near Goosonik, that Co; family to KY
    after 20 years Fauquier Co; wid md (2) 1815 Thomas Bateman
    in Fleming Co, KY, & he dd 11/1820; wid PN as Susan Bate-
    man ae 87 Mason Co, KY, 1844; AFF 1845 by Hannah ae 75 w/o
    Burtis Ringo (RW sol now ae 83, md 1790 Fauquier Co, VA)
    that surv ch of sol 1845: Caleb, Benjamin, Elizabeth w/o
    Thomas Glascock, & Mrs. Plumer. R81
ASBURY, George, esf 1776 Bedford Co, VA; PN ae 68 Franklin Co,
    VA, 1824, where dd 11/12/1834; md 5/27/1785 Mary Hatcher
    at home of her f Benjamin, Bedford Co, VA; MB 5/24/1785 &
    md by Rev. Jeremiah Hatcher; wid PN ae 84 near Trenton,
    Dade Co, GA, 1844; s Coleman res Madison Co, OH, attorney
    for m. R81
ASH, Francis, esf 1779 VA, as sub for f George; dd 4/27/1828;
    md 2/12/1789 Elizabeth "Betsy" Gerrard, Frederick Co, VA;
    wid PN ae 78 in 1850; AFF 1850 by James Blackmore ae 78,
    Fauquier Co, VA, who md sis of sol, that sol dd 1827. R8
ASHBROOK, George, esf 1781 Montgomery Co, which section now
    Wythe Co, VA; b 11/1763 Hampshire Co, VA; afp 1838 Wash-
    ington Co, MO; PAR for insufficient svc. R81

ASHBROOK, Thomas, esf 1781 Hampshire Co, VA, where b 1758 on
Potomac River; PN 1834 Washington Township, Owen Co, IN.
R81
ASHBURN, Luke, sea svc, esf Lancaster Co, VA, where PN 1833 ae
84; dd 12/24/37; md c1792 Susan "Suckey" Roberts, Lancast-
er Co, VA; wid PN ae 70 there 1846. R81
ASHBURY, Benjamin, BLW issued 7/28/1790. R81
ASHBY, Daniel, esf 1780 Hampshire Co, VA; b 8/30/1759 Frede-
rick Co, VA; PN 1832 Hopkins Co, KY; dd 9/13/1836. R81
   Fielding, esf 1779 Frederick Co, VA, where b 1762; PN 1833
   Oldham Co, KY. R81
   John, afp of 1/2 pay; PAR. R81
   Joseph, esf Halifax Co, VA, where b; PN ae 85 there 1844.
   R81
   Peter, esf Hampshire Co,VA; b 1751 Frederick Co,VA; to Hamp-
   shire Co, VA, c1777; PN 1832 Hopkins Co,KY; dd 1/28-29/33;
   md 1776 Winnifred Timmons, Frederick Co, VA, who dd ae 75
   1839 Hopkins Co, KY; wid bro ae 83 there 1844; ch in 1845:
   Jesse, Henry, Peter, Ann w/o Lewis Robertson (all of Hop-
   kins Co, KY), Frances w/o Isaac Harman of Henderson Co, KY
   & Hannah w/o James Howell of Livingston Co, MO; in 1852 ch
   Frances ae 63, Anna ae 61, Jesse ae 55, & Peter ae 51 all
   afp & PAR; sol erroneously carried on PN rolls as Peter
   ASHLEY for some time. R81
   Stephen, esf 1776 VA; dd before 1846 when ch John, Absolom,
   Enos, Daniel, Rosy Timmons, & Ann Prather all decd; BLW
   issued to sol heirs 1847; ch & heirs of s John: (E Robert-
   son, Matilda Robertson, William J Ashby, Enos G Ashby,
   John Crabtree, Lucinda Crabtree, Enos J Ashby, Vincent Ho-
   well, Nancy Howell, Emily Ashby, Stephen J Ashby, Daniel S
   Ashby, Sarah Ashby, John Stodghill, Elizabeth Stodghill);
   ch & heirs/o s Absolom: (James Ashby, Alfred W Barr, Ann
   Barr, Lewis Ashby, Wilson W Ashby, Robert Pritchett, Jami-
   ma Pritchett, Philip Prather, Polly Prather); ch & heirs/o
   s Enos: (John Threlkell, Huldah Ashby, Rice Ashby, Hester
   Ashby, Martha C. Threlkell, Presley Ashby, Daniel S Ash-
   by); ch & heirs/o s Daniel: (John Ashby, Stephen Ashby,
   Cindrella Ashby, Rebecca Ashby, Ann Ashby, Sarah Turley,
   Daniel Turley, Nancy Ashby, James P Ashby, Mary Ashby, Sa-
   rah Ashby, William C Coffman, Sarah Ashby Jr, Daniel Ashby
   Jr, Martha E Coffman, Absolom S Ashby); ch & heirs/o s
   Stephen: (Lewis Fugota, Nancy Fugota, Lewis Ashby, Rosy
   Ashby, William J Ashby, Mary C Ashby, Austin Smith, Cath-
   arine Smith, Elizabeth Ashby wid, Enos G Ashby, Prather
   Ashby, Enos J Ashby, Tabitha Ashby, Stephen D Ashby, Vin-
   cent Ashby, Thomas Prather, Priscilla Prather); ch & heirs
   /o George & Rosy Timmons: (Liner Bronson, Sarah Bronson,
   Mason Timmons, Hannah Timmons,A B Pedcock, Martha Pedcock,
   James A Timmons, James Prather, Margaret Timmons, Bayless
   Bronson, Richard Timmons, Stephen Sisk, Elizabeth Sisk);
   ch & heirs/o Thomas & Ann Prather: (Charles Murphey, Leleticia Murphey, Rebecca Ashby, Joseph Crabtreee, Elenor

ASHBY (continued)
   Crabtree, James Prather, William Crabtree, Rosy Crabtree,
   Philip Prather, Washington Prather, Stephen Prather). R81
ASHCRAFT, Amos, esf 1775 PA; b 1757 VA; PN 1833 Howard Co, MO,
   as Amos Sr aec 76; QLF 1921 from desc Mrs. John W Pearce,
   Colorado, TX. R81
  Daniel, see ASHCROFT, Daniel. R81
  John, esf 1781 PA; PN ae 95 Harrison Co, VA, 1832, when s
   Uriah res there; QLF 1934 from desc Mrs L H Houston, Hart-
   selle, AL, states sol b Scotland. R81
  Uriah, esf 1778 Fayette Co, PA; b 1762 or 4/6/1765 Lancaster
   Co, PA; PAR since svc was local against Indians, & not in
   regular RW forces. R81
ASHCROFT, Daniel, esf 1781 VA; b 3/13/1768 PA; to VA 1780; f,
   who settled KY, killed by indians along with 3 uncles & 1
   aunt; PN 1833 Grayson Co, KY; mvd Lawrence Co, IL, 1840 to
   be near sons; dd there 6/6/1842; md 10/18-27/179- Sarah
   "Sally" Dye (b 3/22/1775), Hardin Co, KY; wid PN Richland
   Co, IL, 1844; ch births: Jadiah/Jediah 12/12/1795, Hannah
   11/12/97, James 7/14/1800,Isaac 11/22/02, Eleanor 10/22/06
   Melia/Emelia 9/25/08, Luizean/Lewiza Ann 3/10/11, & John
   1/24/14; marriage of ch: Jediah & Anna (aec 23) 2/10/1820,
   Lewiza Ann & Thomas Williams 4/30/40, Emelia & Thomas J
   Roy (b 1/8/12) 10/20/33; gdc births: ch/o Jediah (Sarah
   Ann 10/3/20, Elizabeth 2/6/22), ch/o Lewiza Ann Williams
   (Emelia R 3/14/41), ch/o Isaac (Sally Elin 4/4/321, Rebec-
   ca Petty 2/12/1836, Mandy Jane 7/1/38). R81
ASHER, Bartlett, esf 1779 Culpeper Co,VA; PN ae 65-68 Owen Co,
   IN 1832; dd 6/1841, Owen Co, IN; md 3/21/1791 Margaret d/o
   William Curry (MB 3/12/1791), Jefferson Co, KY; wid dd in-
   testate 2/9/1845 Vermillion Co,IL, leaving ch: John res
   Van Buren Co, Iowa Territory, Daniel of Owen Co, IN, Levi
   of Vermillion Co, IL, Thomas of Adams Co, IL, Bartlett of
   Adams Co, IL, Edmund of Putnam Co, IN, Catharine (w/o Wil-
   liam Walters) of Owen Co, IN, Nancy (w/o Peter Hayse) of
   Owen Co, IN, Levia (w/o George Thompson) of Edgar Co, IL,
   Alley (w/o John Johnson) of Adams Co, IL, Jane (w/o Frede-
   rick Staggerwalt) of Owen Co, IN, & William who decd 1845.
   R82
  Charles, esf 1779 Culpeper Co, VA; PN ae 68 Mercer Co, KY,
   1832. R82
ASHERST, William, esf 1780 Accomac Co, VA; b c1762 Halifax Co,
   VA; PN 1832 Caldwell Co, KY; dd 2/16/1851 Crittenden Co,
   KY, while visiting s William; md 11/29/1831 Mary "Polly"
   Nash, a wid, Livingston Co, KY, & she PN ae 64 Caldwell Co
   KY, 1854; QLF 1925 from great great gds Linn Asher. R82
ASHLEY, John, BLW issued 5/29/1792. R82
  Peter, see ASHBY, John. R82
  Thomas, esf 1776 Botetourt Co, VA; PN 1818 Bath Co, KY; in
   1820 sol ae 66, w ae 55, d ae 22, s Peter ae 19, d Milly
   ae 18. R82
ASHLOCK, James, esf 1776 Halifax Co, VA; PN ae 61 Sumner Co,

ASHLOCK (continued)
   TN, 1819; dd 1822; md 1784 Charlotte ---; wid dd 2/28/1841
   Sumner Co, TN, leaving s Philip (b 1789) who PN 1846; in
   file were following births, not associated with sol & all
   surname Anderson: Baly 11/4/1799, Nancy 1/24/1800, Polly
   Ann 7/4/1827, Sary Maxfield 1/2/1818, Drucilla Elizabeth
   11/6/1830, Charlotte Temple 2/15/1831, Robert Pearson
   10/20/1832, Eliza Jane 4/11/1834, & Ailse Carline Francis
   6/7/1825. R83
   Jesse, esf 1781 NC; b Halifax Co, VA, ran away from home to
   Tazewell Co, VA; PN ae 78 Overton Co, TN, 1832, where dd
   12/21/1846; md there 3/15/1842 Sarah "Sallie" Scott who md
   (2) 5/17/1849 Wesley Killman; wid res 1886 Cumberland Co,
   KY, without 2nd h; ch by sol: Margaret S who b 1/13/1843 &
   George Washington who b 3/24/1846, both b Overton Co, TN;
   s George 1869 of Monroe Co, KY, & sol d Margaret w/o Milton Pennington gtd BLW as only surv ch & both res Cumberland Co, KY, 1870; QLF 1937 from L E Cramb, Fairbury, NE,
   states probably the Jesse who md Sarah Scott was s/o Jesse
   RW sol & made fraudulent claim for PN, further records of
   Pittsylvania Co, VA, show marriage 9/6/1785 of Jesse Ashlock & Anne Scott as well as marriage 11/7/1785 of William
   Ashlock & Sarah Sullivan, further a William Ashlock was RW
   sol, further probably Jesse Richardson Ashlock b11/15/1800
   who son of Josiah (res 1790 Rutherfordton, NC) was great
   gdf/o w/o L E Cramb, further w/o L E Cramb was d/o William
   Jesse Ashlock, further w/o Josiah Ashlock was Elizabeth
   Sutton whose f dd 1814. R83
   William, esf 1781 Halifax Co, VA, where b 10/9/1762; to KY
   c1805; PN 1832 Nelson Co, KY. R83
ASHTON, John, esf 1776/7 VA; PN ae 69 King George Co,VA, 1827;
   dd 9/1831; QLF 1918 from desc Katherine S Glenn, Chicago,
   IL. R83
ASHURST, William, see ASHERST, William. R84
ASHWORTH, Harrison, esf 1781 VA; b 3/7/1763 Charlotte Co, VA,
   where PN 1837, where dd 5/9/1837; md there 3/13/1781 Eli-
   zabeth Ford who PN ae 68 there 1838; ch mbnn. R84
   Joel, esf Charlotte Co, VA, where b 1757; PN Grayson Co, VA,
   1833; dd 10/21/47; md 8/3/1796 Milly Brizendine, Charlotte
   Co, VA; wid PN 1851 Carroll Co, VA, & dd 1/29/54. R84
ASKEW, James, disability PN 1789; all papers destroyed in War
   Office fire 1814; QLF from desc Miss Martha Lou Houston,
   Columbus, GA. R84
ASLIN, Thomas, esf 1777 Dinwiddie Co, VA; PN aec 70 Lincoln Co
   TN, 1827; no family but himself then. R84
ASPENWALL, John, BLW issued 12/13/1791. R84
ASRE, Jonathan, esf Wythe Co, VA; later esf Chatham Co, NC; b
   3/8/1746 Chester Co, PA; afp ae 86 Troup Co, GA, 1832; PAR
   for insufficient proof of svc; s Joseph res MS or LA. R84
ASSELIN, Thomas, see ASLIN, Thomas. R84
ASTON, Alexander, esf 1780/81 Goochland Co, VA; b 2/17/1765
   Bucks Co, PA; mvd with family to Hanover Co, VA, thence

ASTON (continued)
    Goochland Co, VA; PN 1841 Wilson Co, TN. R84
ATCHLEY, Abraham, esf Botetourt Co, VA; b 1759 near Princeton,
    Middlesex Co, NJ; to Montgomery Co, VA with parents ae 7;
    res 1778 Loudoun Co, VA; afp 1820 Sevier Co, TN, when fam-
    ily w Nanna Alsey ae 47 & ch: John ae 16, Thomas ae 13,
    Easther ae 11, James ae 9, William ae 7, George ae 4; afp
    1834 Jackson Co, AL, & again there 1839; all PAR; bro Tho-
    mas; s William afp 1854 Jackson Co, AL, & PAR. R85
ATCHLEY, Thomas, esf 1775 Middlesex Co, NJ; esf 1777 Loudon Co
    VA; esf 1781 Botetourt Co, VA; svc in Indian Wars 1794; b
    5/3/1755 Middlesex Co, NJ; PN 1832 Sevier Co, TN, where dd
    10/11/1836 or 11/5/1836; md 1780 Lydia Richards, Loudoun
    Co, VA; wid b 8/18/1762; wid PN 1839 Sevier Co, TN, & res
    there 1849; ch births: Hannah 2/23/1782, Mary 11/13/83,
    Sarah 11/28/85, Isaac 12/9/87, Benjamin 1/24/90, Joshua
    2/26/92, Liddy 4/22/94, Thomas 4/19/96, Jean 8/1/98, Eli-
    zabeth 10/14/1800, Roda 2/25/02, & Noah 1/19/07; in 1844 s
    Isaac res Sevier Co, TN; QLF 1926 from great great gdd Mrs
    Maud Horn, Houston,TX, states sol & bro's mvd to Sevier Co
    TN, including bro William; QLF 1931 from great great gdd
    Mrs Dixie M Miller, Johnson City, TN, states sol buried
    Alder Branch, Sevier Co, TN; QLF states w Lydia dd 1850 &
    s Isaac dd 8/19/1854; QLF 1937 from desc Miss Johnnie Ro-
    berts, Dalton, GA, states w Lydia dd 1851. R85
ATHELL, Benjamin, see ETHELL, Benjamin. R85
ATHEY, James, res near Parkersburg, Wood Co, VA, when afp 1834
    & PAR; later admitted in court to no RW svc; file mns Jo-
    nathan James Athey who esf 1178 VA. R85
  William, esf 1777 Loudoun Co, VA; PN ae 57 Allegany Co, MD,
    1818; dd 10/30/1818. R85
ATHY, Thomas, esf 1777 Fairfax Co, VA; PN ae 72 Hampshire Co,
    1818; QLF states wid named Martha. R85
ATKINS, Alexander, esf 1777, VA; PN ae 65 Scott Co, KY, 1818.
    R86
  Ambrose, esf 1777 Orange Co, VA, where b; PN ae 78 Culpeper
    Co, VA, 1832, where mvd 1777. R86
  Charles, esf Granville Co, NC; b 5/5/1760 Lancaster Co, VA;
    PN 1832 Upson Co, GA. R86
  Edward, esf VA; PN ae 62 Franklin Co, KY, 1818; res Mercer
    Co, KY, 1820; family mbnn. R86
  John, esf 1780 Lunenburg Co, VA; PN ae 72 Abbeville District
    SC, 1832. R86
  John, esf 1776 VA; PN aec 67 Orange Co, VA, 1820, when w aec
    67, plus Betty Groom ae 49 & her ch Solomon & Betty Groom
    res with him; sol dd 3/18/1837; QLF states sol s Joseph RW
    sol from Orange Co, VA. R86
  John, esf 1779 Henry Co,VA, where b 1755; afp ae 78 Cool Ri-
    ver, Fayette Co, VA; PAR, insufficient proof of svc. R86
  Lewis, BLW issued 11/17/1794. R86
ATKINSON, David, esf c1778 VA, b 1751 Essex Co, VA; PN 1837
    Caroline Co, VA. R88

32

ATKINSON, Elisha, esf Cape Fear, New Hanover Co, NC; later esf
    Craven Co, NC; b 1745 Isle of Wight Co, VA; PN 1833 Muh-
    lenburg Co, KY, where mvd 1805. R87
  Isaac, esf 1777 VA; PN ae 66 Woolwich Township, Gloucester
    Co, NJ, 1818; dd 9/23/38 Port Elizabeth, NJ; md 1819 Anna
    Alloways, Crane's Mill, NJ; wid PN ae 65 East Creek, Cape
    May Co, NJ, 1853; QLF states sol also in NJ militia War of
    1812 Cape May Co, NJ, further Anna Alloways was sol 2nd w
    & she dd c1872 West Creek, Cape May Co, NJ. R87
  James, esf 1778 Pittsylvania Co, VA, where b 4/3/1747; PN
    1833 Pike Co, KY; dd c4/1837, leaving no wid but several
    ch mbnn. R87
  John, esf 1777 Alexandria, VA; PN ae 62 Richmond, VA, 1818;
    dd 12/31/1832 leaving wid Sally who aec 55 in 1820. R87
  John, esf 1780 Pittsylvania Co, VA; b9/18/1755 Cumberland Co
    VA; to Maury Co, TN, 1811, thence Williamson Co, TN, 1813,
    where PN 1834; dd 4/2/37; md 11/6/1777 Mary Armstead, Cum-
    berland Co, VA; wid b 2/17/1758 & PN; wid bro Thaddeus b
    11/3/1755; QLF 1918 from great great gdd A B Radford, Saw-
    tell, CA, states sol Baptist preacher & uncle/o inventor
    Eli Whitney; QLF states eldest s Samuel md Nancy Binns;
    QLF 1937 from desc Beatrice (Mrs Burton Wands), Los Ange-
    les, CA. R87
  Joshua, esf 1781 Essex Co, VA; PN ae 78 Adair Co, KY, 1833.
    R87
  Reuben, esf 1777 Essex Co, VA, where PN 1832. R87
  Richard, esf under name of THOMAS, Richard 1776, Martinsburg
    VA, using alias because before RW was sol in British Army;
    PN aec 75 Monongalia Co, VA, 1820, when w ae 77 & d Marga-
    ret aec 30 res with him. R87
  Thomas, esf 1776 Essex Co, VA; PN ae 78 Cumberland Co, VA,
    1833; in 1828 sol stated he ae 78, s John ae 28, d Nancy
    ae 23, Cumberland Co, VA. R87
  William, BLW issued 3/26/1792. R87
  William, esf Cumberland Co, VA; afp ae 66 Grainger Co, TN,
    but dd before claim recd at Pension Office so PAR; w older
    than sol. R87
ATKISON, Henry, esf 1776 Sussex Co, VA; b 9/16/1760 VA; mvd
    Hancock Co, GA, 1800; PN ae 73 Wilkinson Co, GA, 1832 when
    aged w & s Littleton res with him. R87
ATTWELL, Charles B, esf 1781 Prince William Co, VA; b Dumfries
    that Co, 1765; PN ae 68 Loudoun Co, VA, 1838; res Prince
    William Co, VA, 1832, ae 67. R88
ATWELL, Charles B, see ATTWELL, Charles B. R88
AUBONY, Thomas, BLW issued 12/13/1791. R90
AUSTEN, James, see AUSTIN, James. R93
AUSTIN, James, esf 1777 Prince Georges Co,MD where b 4/18/1756
    & mvd Bedford Co, VA, 1788; PN 1832 Russel Parish, Bedford
    Co, VA; QLF states maiden name of sol m was CHASE. R93
AUSTIN, Joel, dd intestate 4/10/1792 Charlotte Co, VA, per AFF
    of s Stephen there 1846; md Fall of 1782 Anne --- there;
    wid PN ae 80 Campbell Co, VA, 1838. R92

AUSTIN, John, esf 1776 Hanover Co, VA; PN ae 67 Sumner Co, TN;
QLF 1916 from great great gdd Miss Amanda M Stone. R92

John, esf 1775 Fauquier Co, VA; PN ae 96 LaGrange, Oldham Co
KY, 1832; dd 10/14-19/1845; md 11/3/1784 Elizabeth Lindsay, Fauquier Co, VA; wid apf KY 1846 but PAR because of
current laws on age of widows after h decease; youngest s
Daniel, b 5/24/1798, res Oldham Co, KY, 1850; elder ch of
sol: William (eldest), Lucy, James, & John; in 1846 Henry
Browning of Henry Co, KY, made AFF that he half bro/o Elizabeth Lindsay & they had same m; QLF states sol b England
R92

John, eldest of 5 bro who esf Pittsylvania Co, VA, where dd
10/4/1827; md 9/11/1788 Polly Bennett; wid afp ae 78 Union
District,SC, 1840; PAR for insufficient proof of svc; wid
decd by 1852; d Nancy afp 1853 Union District, SC, 1853, &
PAR. R92

Stephen, esf Surry Co, NC; b 11/1755 Pittsylvania Co, VA;
but res Grayson Co, VA, when esf, & res there 20 years after RW; mvd to TN, thence AL, thence Wayne Co, TN, where
PN 1832; res Hardin Co, TN, 1841. R93

Walter, esf 1777 Hanover Co, VA, where PN 1818 aec 60. R93

AUXER, Samuel, esf 1777 VA; dd 1800-1804 at Blockhouse on Big
Sandy River, Floyd Co,KY; md 7/15/1779 Sarah d/o Nathaniel
& Ann Brown; wid b 1/6/1765; wid md (2) Jesse Kelly who dd
in svc War of 1812; wid md (3) John Phillips who dd c1835;
PN 1843 Johns Creek, Johnson Co, KY, under name of Sarah
Phillips; ch/o sol & Sarah Brown births: Nathaniel 6/1780
(md d/o John Back), Nancy 7/20/1782, Mary Barbary 2/7/1784
John 11/178-, Daniel, Samuel 8/7/91, Enoch 2/22/1795 (md
Mary ---), Frances Emelia 3/1800; John Back, f-in-law/o
Nathaniel Auxer, b 1760 Culpeper Co, VA, esf Washington Co
VA, & served with Samuel Auxer under General George Rogers
Clark; births of ch/o Enoch & Mary Auxer: Sarah Jane 1834,
Lyda Jemima 3/23/36, Samuel W 1/8/38, Nancy B 5/4/40; QLF
1912 from great great gds Andrew Auxer, Pikeville, KY. R93

AUXIER, Samuel, see AUXER, Samuel. R93

AUXTIER, Samuel, see AUXER, Samuel. R93

AVIS, Robert, esf 1776 VA in Capt. William Darke's Company; PN
ae 74 Jefferson Co, VA, 1829, when had 4 d's; dd 6/15/34,
leaving w & ch mbnn; QLF 1923 from desc Miss Virginia Merrills, Bellesville, IL, states sol md 7/31/1777 Martha
Dark & d Martha b 1778. R97

AWBERY, Samuel, see AWBRY, Samuel. R97

AWBRY, Samuel, esf 1777 Loudoun Co, VA; PN ae 73 Hardin Co, KY
1832 nr Breckinridge Co line; res there 20 years; QLF 1931
from desc Mrs N B Davidson, Louisville, KY, states sol ae
82 Hardin Co, KY, 1840, his w Margaret Craven, further s
Craven had d Margaret Craven Awbry, who md David Donand
South, who f/o Eliza, who m/o Mrs Davidson. R97

AYERS, Elihu, see AYRES, Elihu. R98

Francis, esf 1776 VA; dd c1845; md Mary ---, who dd c1838;
youngest & only liv ch Sarah Soward afp ae 77, Nebo, Pike

AYERS (continued)
    Co, IL, 1905; PAR because, by law, PN had not been claimed
    by sol or his wid & therefore ch had no title to claim af-
    ter 1852. R98
AYLOR, Jacob, esf 1775 Culpeper Co, VA, where b 2/1749; PN
    1833 Madison Co, VA. R98
AYRES, Elihu, esf 1778 Wilkes Co, NC; b 1/26/1761 Pittsylvania
    Co, VA; PN 1832 Patrick Co, VA; dd 3/19/1844; md Spring of
    1786 Lydia ---, Halifax Co, VA; wid PN ae 81 Patrick Co,
    VA, 1844, & dd there 8/13/45; ch who apf 1846 Carroll Co,
    VA: Elkanah ae 50, Nancy w/o Hiram H Dean, Kitty w/o Hen-
    ry H Dean, Affey w/o John Scott, Cassamara, Martha w/o Sa-
    muel Richardson, Lucy w/o William Allen, & Lydia w/o Arch-
    ibald Burnett; ch PAR. R98
  Francis, see AYERS, Francis. R98
  Henry, esf 1775 Bedford Co, VA; PN ae 79 Robertson Co, TN,
    1833; md 1/1781 Susan ---, Surry Co, NC; wid b 8/7/1762,
    Dinwiddie Co, VA; wid PN 1843 Robertson Co, TN; several
    ch including Lemuel; QLF 1920 from Miss Nellie Ayres, Se-
    dalia, MO, states sol b 1753. R98
  James, esf aec 14 as Minuteman in SC; mvd to Henry Co, VA,
    1778 where enlisted; b 1/6/1761 Cumberland Co, VA, s/o Da-
    niel; family mvd to Kershaw Co, SC, c1765; afp 1834 Pick-
    ens District, SC, & PAR. R98
  John, esf Buckingham Co, VA; bc 1760; dd 11/1828 Buckingham
    Co, VA, where md 12/4/1777 Jane d/o William Sally; wid PN
    there 1842 ae 81; ch births: Magdalene 8/16/1778, Ann
    2/20/81, Edmond 2/4/83, Salee 5/25/91, Elizabeth 2/9/94,
    Susannah 3/26/96, Patsey 8/11/98, John H 5/3/1801, Jane
    6/9/03, & Olive S 2/3/06; AFF by d Olive S 1842, Bucking-
    ham Co, VA; QLF 1919 from Miss Nellie Ayres, Sedalia, MO,
    states sol w was Jane Salle/Sallee; QLF 1939 from desc Mrs
    Mildred Shirley, Anderson, SC. R98
  Nancy, PN as former wid/o James RUSSEY. R98 ·
BABB, Seth, esf 1781 Winchester, Frederick Co, VA; b 2/1/1760;
    PN 1832 Greene Co, TN, where res 40 years; dd 8/26/36; md
    1/22/1791 Mary McClelen/McClelland, Greene Co, TN; wid PN
    ae 82 there 1844; ch births: Ezz/Err 10/2/1791 who md
    3/19/1812, Hiram 3/10/1793 who md 9/3/1816, Ruth 8/25/1895
    who md 3/23/1830, Mary 6/22/1797 who md 8/22/1820, Huldah
    4/28/1799, Seth Jr 4/4/1802 who md 6/1/20, Rachel 3/11/03,
    Rhody 7/4/05 who md 9/1829, Nancy 3/30/07. R99
BABER, James, esf 1779 Bedford Co, VA, where b 6/2/1762; mvd
    Rutherford Co, NC, for 32 years, thence Gwinnett Co, GA,
    where PN 1832; dd 7/17/36; md 1785 Milley/Melley ---, Bed-
    ford Co or Campbell Co, VA; wid b 6/13/1762 & PN 1843 Cobb
    Co, GA; ch births: Anna 9/25/1785, William 3/14/87, Sally
    11/30/88, Robert 4/13/91, Jane 3/10/93, John 9/9/97, Barn-
    abas Arthur 12/25/99, & George 3/31/02; QLF states sol w
    Mildred Arthur, & sol res nr Monticello, VA; QLF 1937 from
    desc Clara Melton (Mrs W S) Sims Jr, Jackson, MS. R102
  Obadiah, esf VA; dd 1/28/1822; md c1780 Hannah Martin, Flu-

BABER (continued)
    vanna Co, VA; to Clark Co, KY, then part of Fayette Co,
    with 3 ch 1786; wid b Goochland Co, VA, her family moving
    to Fluvanna Co, VA, 2 or 3 years after she b; wid afp 1844
    Montgomery Co, KY, while res home/o s-in-law Randall Gor-
    don (b 7/13/1784) who md d Rachel 2/10//1803; wid PAR for
    insufficient svc; wid bro Elisha dd in RW svc, & her bro
    William also RW sol; sol surname at times spelled BEAVER;
    wid sis Rachel (md --- Bush), who b 8/20/1768 Goochland
    Co, VA, made AFF 1844 that she & bro's William, Orson, Va-
    lentine, John, & sis Elizabeth mvd to Clark Co, KY, 1786;
    sol 1st ch Hiram b 12/251/1782. R102
  William, see BARBER, William. R102
BACK, John, esf 17788 Washington Co, VA; b 6/17/1760 Culpeper
    Co, VA; to "Clench", Washington Co, with parents aec 12;
    to KY aec 34; PN 1835 Wayne Co, KY; bro Jacob ae 70 then;
    sol ch res Monroe Co, IN, 1838. R102
BACON, Richard, esf 1779 Lunenburg Co, VA, as sub for bro-in-
    law Robert Dixon, where b & raised; PN ae 71 Madison Co,
    AL; s Washington afp 1854 Bowlingsville, DeKalb Co, AL, &
    PAR. R105
  Robert, BLW issued 11/5/1789. R105
BADGET, Thomas, esf 1779 Louisa Co, VA, where b; PN there 1833
    ae 72; QLF 1918 from desc Mrs. E L Mason, Charlotte, NC.
    R106
BAGBY, John, esf 1775 Halifax Co, NC; b 1757 Hanover Co, VA;
    PN 1832 Gwinnett Co, GA; dd 3/1/1837. R106
  John, esf 1778 Louisa Co, VA; b 5/25/1761; PN 1832 Barren Co
    KY where mvd 1817; dd there 11/17/1834; md 12/20/1792 Ma-
    tilda Davis, Amherst Co, VA; wid b 11/19/1772 & PN Barren
    Co, KY, 1839, where still res 1848; ch births: Elvira
    11/4/1793, Landon 12/30/95, Roderick 8/10/98, name illegi-
    ble 4/3/1801, Richard 12/23/02, Nancy 6/05, William 6/3/08
    Theodocia Morris 7/9/10, Charles Davis 11/18/13; QLF 1925
    from desc R E Bagby, Stillwater, OK, states sol s Landon
    svc in War of 1812 from Louisa Co or Rockbridge Co, VA, &
    recd PN & dd St Joseph, Buchanan Co, MO, further sol bro
    James (bc1751 VA & dd VA c1818) also RW sol; QLF 1916 from
    desc Mrs G G Tucker, Wichita, KS. R106
BAGENT, John, see BEGEANT, John. R106
BAGGS, James, PA svc, esf Chester Co, PA; PN ae 66 Brooke Co,
    VA; res 1822 Richland Co, OH; dd 2/1/1827; md 11/30/1780
    Susannah ---; in 1820 family w plus s's ae 20 & 34, d's ae
    24 & 27; wid b 10/4/1758 & res 1837 Richland Co, OH. R107
BAGWELL, Isaiah, VA sea svc; esf 1778 Accomac Co, VA, where b
    9/13/1760, where PN 1832; dd 10/8/1839 leaving 1 ch. R107
BAHR, John, see BARR, John. R107
BAILES, Eldridge, esf SC & NC; b 1760 VA & to Santee River, SC
    as ch; to Madison Co, AL 1818; PN AL 1831; dd 8/27/1835;
    md 1791 Sarah Burnett, Rutherford Co, NC; MB 11/14/1791,
    surety Clayton Burnett; wid PN ae 80 Lowville, Madison Co,
    AL, 1854; last surv ch ae 75 res Des Arc, AR, whose BLAR

36

BAILES (continued)
    since ae over 21 in 1855. R107
BAILEY, Abraham, see BALEY, Abraham. R108.
    Anselm, esf 1776 New Kent Co, VA, where PN ae 62 in 1820 fa-
        mily then w Susannah ae 28, Rebecca ae 6, Martha ae 4, An-
        selm ae 1, & a boy ae 16; 7 small ch in 1827. R108
    Elisha, esf 1781 Albemarle Co, VA; b 11/20/1763 s/o John &
        Mary; PN 1833 Adair Co, KY, where dd 11/30/1841; md Hannah
        d/o Thomas & Peggy Gay 12/19/1782; wid b 3/11/1764 & PN
        1843 Adair Co, KY; ch births: Thomas T 4/3/1784 (md Polly
        Atkinson 7/12/1809), Polley L 4/1/86, John 7/22/88, Betsey
        12/31/9-,Samuel B 1/19/96,Hiram 8/18/98, Terry 12/27/1800,
        Blane 1/13/03, Benjamin 8/25/09, Hetty 1/24/92. R108
    Henry, esf 1778 Sussex Co, VA, where PN ae 78 in 1832; dd
        1/3/1843 leaving 1 ch & some gdc. R109
    Isham, esf 1777 Albemarle Co, VA; PN ae 78 Pocotalio, Kana-
        wha Co, VA, 1833; decd by 1836, when ch Isham, Winny, Mar-
        tha (w/o Uriah Parish) apf & PAR. R109
    Ishmael, esf 1777 VA; PN aec 70 Buckingham Co, VA, 1819; dd
        6/1/33; md Summer of 1784 Julina/Juliana ---, who PN ae 78
        Buckingham Co, VA, 1840; 3 ch mbnn. R109
    James, BLW issued 7/6/1793. R109
    James, esf 1776 Dumfries, Prince William Co, VA; b 10/1751
        near there; PN 1832 Roxbury Township, Washington Co, OH;
        res there c18 years. R109
    James, esf 1779 VA, PN aec 70 Surry Co, VA, 1833. R109
    John, PN 1/2 pay, member of Clark's IL Regiment of VA; file
        lost by PN Office. R110
    John, esf 1776 Brunswick Co, VA; s/o William; afp ae 62 Bath
        Co, KY, 1824, when fam 2 small ch by 2nd w Jane; AFF 1825
        by sis Mary Yarbrough ae 67 Bath Co, KY; PAR. R110
    Manoah "Noah", esf 1777 Cumberland Co, VA; afp ae 66 Halifax
        Co, NC, 1824, his s then aec 13; PAR R111
    Martin, esf VA; dd ae 75 Monroe Co, KY, 6/22/1826; md Susan-
        na Robinson (ae 18) 7/7/1784, Surry Co, NC; wid b & raised
        Caroline Co, VA; wid afp ae 85 Monroe Co, KY, 1851 & PAR;
        ch births: Francis 5/6/1785,William 2/28/87, Edmon 5/6/85,
        Patsey 4/9/91, Susannah Staton 9/2/93, Anna Mary 1796,
        Winston 9/9/98, Lehigh 3/1/1801, John F 1/14/04; other fa-
        mily bible births: Edward K McMillion 5/24/1794, John P
        Bailey 4/7/1822, A A Bailey 3/10/1819; following surv ch
        afp 1851 & PAR: Patsey ae 60, Nancy Lester ae 55, Lehigh
        ae 50, & John F ae 47. R111
    Moses, esf ae 16-18 VA; b Henrico Co, VA; to Amherst Co, VA,
        after RW, thence GA, thence Madison Co, AL, where PN 1832
        ae 77; QLF 1932 from desc Virginia B (Mrs Wirt) Franklin,
        Oklahoma City, OK. R111
    Noah, esf c1777 VA; b 1749 Cumberland Co, VA; PN 1832 Stokes
        Co, NC. R111
    Peter, esf 1778/9 NC; b 10/7/1762 Henrico Co, VA; family mvd
        to Charlotte Co, VA, 1773/4, thence Mecklenburg Co, VA,
        f went off to RW leaving sol & stepm, whom f md Henrico Co

BAILEY (continued)
   VA, after sol m dd; sol mvd to Montgomery Co, TN, where PN
   1834; in 1836 d res nr Madisonville, Hopkins Co, TN, s nr
   Lafayette, Christian Co, KY; s Peter A liv in 1839 whose d
   Elizabeth M A then res Nebo, Hopkins Co, KY, w/o Anderson
   B Harralson; later investigation by PN Office whether sol
   old enough to have served in RW. R111
Philip, esf c1779 Amherst Co, VA; b 1749 Goochland Co, VA;
   PN 1833 Bedford Co, VA, as Peter Bailey Sr in Russell Par-
   ish; s moved to MO before 1833. R111
Richard, esf 1780 as sub for William Harrison, Sussex Co, VA
   where b 1764; PN 1832 Barren Co, KY. R111
Richard, esf 1779 Fauquier Co, VA, where b 2/22/1762; afp
   1836 Lauderdale Co, AL; afp again 1843 Laurence Co, AL;
   PAR. R111
Southy, BLW issued 6/10/1808; another BLW 7/2/27. R112
Thomas, esf 1778 Loudoun Co, VA; b 4/8/1761 Halifax Co, VA,
   where PN 1832. R112
Thomas, esf 1776 VA; b Surry Co, VA; PN 1817 for disability
   from battle wound; res ae 59 Surry Co, VA, 1818; w & large
   family of ch mbnn; sol dd 10/31/32. R112
Thomas, esf 1778 Louisa Co, VA; d 7 Jul 1825 Hardin Co, KY,
   aec 66; md 1780 (MB 5/6/1780) Nancy, d/o Nicholas Gentry,
   Louisa Co, VA; family mvd Hardin Co, KY, 1810; ch: John
   Hubbard, Charles Carter, Betsy, Joseph, Marina, Lewis,
   Willis, Edwin, Walter, Nancy, & Katy; ch ages 1848: John
   H c65, Charles Carter c61, Lewis c46, all res Hardin Co,
   KY, where sol wid then PN ae 86; wid sis/o John & niece/o
   Edmond Stringer; s Lewis had d Margaret June b 9/16/1824.
   R112
William, BLW issued 4/16/1794. R112
William, esf 1778 Amherst Co, VA; b 12/24/1756 Albemarle Co,
   VA; to Smith Co, TN, 1817 where PN 1836 & dd 1/4/1847 lea-
   ving no wid but ch: Jonathan, Wyuatt, Susan Shepherd, Lu-
   cinda Horseley, Saluda Walker, Sarah Wilkerson, & gds Jo-
   nathan B Stovall; AFF 1837 Sumner Co, TN, by Bartholomew
   Stovall. R112
William, esf 1776 VA; PN ae 67 Albemarle Co, VA, when family
   w ae 47 & ch ages: Samuel 15, James 14, William 12, John
   10, Reuben 3, Nancy 22, Betsy 18, Lucinda 9, & Martha 7.
   R112
William, esf 1776 VA; PN 1827 Fauquier Co, VA; dd 6/28/1832
   Culpeper Co, VA; md Nancy Newby (license 2/11/1782), Fauquier Co, VA; wid ae 78 Culpeper Co, VA, 1838, & PN there
   1843; s ae 40 liv 1827. R112
William, esf 1776 Albemarle Co, VA, where PN 1820; dd Kanawha Co, VA, 3/1/1837; md Sarah "Sally" Sprouse, who PN ae
   80 Putnam Co, VA, 1851 where dd 7/17/1851; ch births: Nancy 5/6/1798, Betty A 9/10/1802, Salley 11/28/03, Samuel
   4/19/05; James 9/24/08, William 4/16/10, John 1/22/11, Lucinda 8/11/12, Martha 8/18/14, & Reuben P 4/2/17; d Nancy
   md Matthew Philips & dd c1844, leaving 7 ch including her

BAILEY (continued)
    eldest Nancy; d Betsey md David Graham, res Buckingham Co,
    VA; d Salley dd aec 2; s Samuel res Putnam Co, VA; s John
    dd c1851 Kanawha Co, VA, leaving ch Mary, Eliza, & Martha
    Jane, s James res Kanawha Co, VA; d Martha w/o Joseph Lan-
    ham, res Putnam Co, VA; d Lucinda decd 1853 when sol surv
    ch afp, application signed by William & Reuben P. R112
William, esf 1782 Fauquier Co, VA; dd 9/1848; md 8/1782 Emi-
    ly --- who afp ae 86, Polk Co,TN, 1851, & PAR. R112
William, esf 1776 Albemarle Co, VA; PN ae 72 Union District,
    SC, 1832; dd 7/23/41; md 7/1836 Margaret ---, Union Dis-
    trict, SC, who md (2) 1843 David Porter, who absconded in
    1850, never returned; wid afp ae 51 Whitfield Co, GA, 1851
    & PAR. R112
BAILIS, Eldridge, see BAILES, Eldridge.
BAILY, Callam, esf 1775 Goochland Co, VA; b 1/1/1749 Louisa Co
    VA; mvd to Barren Co, KY 1807 where PN 1833; QLF 1933 from
    desc Mrs Raymond Jones, Washington, DC; QLF states sol
    name Callum H Bailey who md Judy --- & dd 1842. R113
    David, esf 1779 Botetourt Co, VA; b 9/8/1755 Chester Co, PA;
    to MO 1822; PN 1835 Washington Co, MO. R113
    John, esf VA; recd 1/2 pay PN; dd 10/22/1822 without issue,
    adm of estate James Rogers of KY; wid referred to in 1849,
    Fayette Co, PA, when heirs afp there & PAR. R113
    Thomas, esf 1775 Sussex Co, VA, where b; PN ae 77 York Dist-
    rict, SC, 1833, where dd; gds William Bailey made Aff 1852
    Mecklenburg Co, NC. R113
    William C, esf 1777 Alexandria, VA, esf MD 1792 for Indian
    Wars; b VA; PN ae 66 Miami Co, OH, 1820, while res with s-
    in-law; dd 9/2/1837; w Ann ae 59 in 1820; in 1836 d Mrs
    Gates a wid with large family of ch; QLF 1902 from great
    gdd Cora Gates Davison, Denver, CO, states her f Albert
    Goddard Gates & her m Elizabeth, d/o sol. R113
BAIRD, Thomas, esf 1776 Cumberland Co, VA; esf 1780 Jefferson
    Co,VA, where mvd 1780; to Knox Co, IN, c1800, where PN ae
    83; dd 10/24/34; md 9/20 1791 Jane --- (b 6/18/1764), Jes-
    samine Co,KY, who PN 1839 Sullivan Co,IN; ch births: Char-
    les 5/28/77, Mary 1/28/79, Jane 11/28/81, Thomas 12/83,
    illegible name 1/87; Elizabeth 6/8/89, Ann 10/8/92, Rich-
    ard 1/9/97, illegible name & date, Amelia 1803, & Joseph
    1805; s Joseph AFF 1839, states these birth dates for sol
    ch: Anna 10/8/1792, Archibald 1/9/1797; Martha 11/19/1799,
    all b KY, plus Amelia 9/19/1802, Joseph 9/11/05, Amanda
    7/27/09, all b Knox Co, IN. R113
BAITH, George, esf Frederick Co, VA, where m res; b 1762 Lan-
    caster Co, PA; PN Crawford Co, IL, where dd 10/4/1844; md
    9/15/1789 Susanna Willson, Clark Co, KY; wid b 4/9/1770, &
    afp 1845, & PAR (spelled her last name BATHE then). R114
BAKER, Anthony, esf 1780 Hampshire Co, VA; b 1761/2 Shenandoah
    Co, VA; PN 1833 Hardy Co, VA. R114
    Charles, esf 1780 Burke Co, NC; b 1762 Culpeper Co, VA; PN
    1837 Cass Co, GA; QLF 1929 from great gdd Caroline (Mrs

BAKER (continued)

James H) Elgin, Tulsa, OK, states sol buried Bartow Co, GA R115

David, esf 1776 Culpeper Co, VA; b 6/3/1749; after svc join- ed m in Burke Co, NC, f having dd while sol in svc; PN there 1832; dd 9/15/1838; md 8/9/1793-95 there Dorothy Wi- seman who b 2/5/1765; wid PN 1849 Yancey Co, NC, & gtd BLW there 1855; wid dd 8/23/55; ch mbnn. R115

Elijah, esf 1779 Albemarle Co, VA; PN 1832 while res of both Washington Co & Jefferson Co, MO, ae 74; res 1828 Hopkins Co, KY, with w, all ch being md by then. R115

Glover, esf 1777 VA; PN 1816 for disabilility from wound; res ae 67 Bedford Co, VA, 1822; QLF 1922 from great great gds Frank Baker McKee, Albert Lea, MN, states sol w was Mary Ferrall of Bedford Co,VA; QLF states sol dd 1/7/1828. R116

John, esf 1777 Loudoun Co, VA, for GA svc; 1780 for VA svc; PN ae 71 Davidson Co, TN, 1820, occupation tailor & no fa- mily res with him; QLF states sol md Ann Norfleet. R117

John, esf 1777 Chesterfield Co, VA; b 12/24/1750 Hanover Co, VA; PN 1832 Cumberland Co, KY, dd 9/4/1838, leaving 3 ch mbnn; QLF 1927 from great great gds W W Jones, Columbia, KY; QLF 1930 from great gdd Miss Menifee R Cheek, Nash- ville, TN, states her gdm Elizabeth Cheek was d/o sol & b 10/6/1806 Cumberland Co, VA. R117

John, esf Stafford Co, VA, where b 1/1747; afp 1843 Wilson Co, KY; PAR for insufficient proof of svc. R117

Joseph, esf 1780 NC; PN ae 77 Garrard Co, KY; dd 3/1/1838; md 1778 Susanna ---, Wythe Co, VA; in 1820 family was w & 10 ch, with those still at home s aec 15 & ae 13, d aec 8; wid PN ae 76 Garrard Co, KY, 1838; Abraham Baker ae 52 AFF 1838 that he 2nd s/o sol. R118

Michael, esf 1779 PA; b 3/27/1753 Southwark Borough, London, England; to America as indentured servant; escaped to join RW forces; to Franklin Co, OH, 1812, where PN 1818; dd 9/13/1831 Greene Co, IL; md 2/14/1791 Point Pleasant, VA, Mary Craig/Carig, wid/o Andrew McGahee/McGahey; wid dd 10/18/1837 Greene Co, IL; in 1818 sol family was w Mary, s William ae 23, s John ae 18, s Michael ae 14, d Nancy ae 25, gds ae 6 & gdd ae 11; surv ch 1855: John of Greene Co IL, James, Michael, Nancy Brown; wid 1st h Andrew also RW sol & md Mary in Cumberland Co, VA; sol ch births: Sarah 12/8/1791, Anna 9/30/93, William 4/28/9-, James 2/17/9-, & John 3/24/1802; other items in family bible: Michael Mor- ris Baker (s/o John & Mary Baker) b 8/18/1828, Nancy Baker md 11/2/1826 John Phillips; in 1855 sol s-in-law John Rose ae 65, h/o Sarah who dd 5/4/48 Greene Co, IL, they being md 1813 Franklin Co, OH. R118

Nicholas, esf Culpeper Co,VA; PN ae 74 Woodford Co,KY, 1818; dd 11/2/1832; in 1821 family was w ae 60 & ch: Phillip ae 16, Robert ae 12, Betsy ae 19, Anna ae 17, & Susan ae 14; wid PN ae 79 Lawrence Co, IN, 1843; wid was decd 1848 when

BAKER (continued)

following ch afp: Daniel, Susan Seatch, Anna Speer, William, Armsted, Robert, Philip, Elizabeth Peyton, & Eliza Stephens. R118

Philip Peter, esf 1779 Shenandoah Co, VA; b 21/26/1759; PN 1836 Shenandoah Co, VA; dd 5/2/1837; md 12/28/1784 Elizabeth Dorothy Volkner who b 5/6/1765; wid PN Shenandoah Co, VA, 1839; ch births: Rebecca 9/24/1785, Isaac 12/25/87, Catarina 12/14/89, Philip 6/29/92, Henrich 10/5/94, Willhelm 3/9/97, Jacob 10/26/99, Joseph 2/4/1802, Christina 6/29/04, Samuel 8/4/06, & Luthwig 12/17/08; sol sis Christina & Rosa; s William res Shenandoah Co, VA, 1839; QLF 1937 from great great gds Ned D Baker, Oakland, CA. R119

Richard, esf 1778 New Kent Co, VA; also War of 1812 sol; PN ae 58 Henrico Co, VA, 1818; dd 12/3/1827 there, leaving s Richard by 1st w; md 7/1810 or 7/1811 Frances --- & had 3 ch by her including Elizabeth b 11/8/1815 (other 2 ch dd young); wid afp ae 67 Richmond, VA, 1837; PAR since marriage to sol occurred after date allowed by PN Law. R119

Robert, esf 1776 Fincastle Co (now Washington Co), VA; b Augusta Co, VA, 1/17/1754; PN 1833 Montgomery Co, MO. R119

Samuel, esf Fauquier Co, VA; PN ae 92 Tuscaloosa, AL, 1832; family 1776 was w & 4 ch res Fauquier Co, VA; QLF states a Samuel Baker, b 1756-60 & dd 1840, md Sarah Schriver in Loudoun or Culpeper Co, VA; QLF mns a Philip Baker (1724-1786) who md Juliana Schumaker of Loudoun or Culpeper Co, VA. R119

Sarah, PN & gtd BLW as former wid/o William Foster. R119

Solomon, esf 1781, Martinsburg, TN Territory; indian spy; b 1763 Berkeley Co, VA; afp ae 70 Lewis Co, VA, 1833; PAR for insufficient proof of svc. R120

Thomas, esf Cumberland Co, VA, for GA sea svc, res Goochland co, VA; b 3/1762; PN 1826 Henderson Co, KY; dd 2/12/1829; in 1826 family at home w aec 55-60; ch mbrn & recd PN due sol at time of his death. R120

William, esf 1779 Chesterfield Co, VA, where b 12/17/1764; to Cumberland Co, KY, 1805 where PN 1832; QLF from desc Miss Pauline Baker, Salisbury, MO, states sol md --- Kimborough; QLF 1925 from Judge H C Baker, Columbia Co, KY. R121

BALDOCK, Richard, esf 1780/81 Amherst Co, VA; afp ae 78 Monroe Co, KY, 1841; PAR. R121

BALDWIN, Benjamin, esf VA; in 1854 W H Baldwin of Blanchester, Clinton Co, OH, afp for himself & other heirs of sol; PAR; QLF from Hazel Hayes (Mrs Harry A) Metzger, great great gdd of a Benjamin Baldwin, an RW sol buried Edwardsville Cemetery, Warren Co, OH. R122

John, esf 1780 Amelia Co, VA, where b 1762; PN 1834 Mason Co Co. R123

John, esf 1777 Prince Edward Co, VA, where b 6/25/1758; dd 4/24/1837; md 9/27/1797 Agness ---, Powhatan Co, VA, who PN ae 80 Prince Edward Co, VA, 1848. R123

BALDWIN, William, esf 1776 Prince Edward Co, VA, where b
12/27/1750; to Union Co,SC, 1786; to Daviess Co, IN, 1817;
PN Reeve Township, Daviess Co, IN, 1833. R125
BALES, Jesse, see BAYLES, Jesse. R125
BALEY, Abraham, esf Chesterfield Co, VA; PN ae 80 Franklin Co,
KY, 1833. R125
  Ishmael, see BAILEY, Ishmael. R125
  Martin, see BAILEY, Martin. R125
  Stephen, esf Fauquier Co, VA; afp ae 68 Monroe Co, GA, 1833;
  PAR since svc less than 6 months. R126
BALL, Aaron, esf 1777 VA; PN ae 59 Essex Co, VA, 1818, family
then w & 6 ch mbnn. R126
  Burgess, BLW issued 5/28/1789; colonel. R126
  Daniel, BLW issued 1/24/1794. R126
  David, esf 1778, VA; PN ae 66 Fauquier Co, VA, 1819; ch "all
  grown up" 1820. R127
  Edmund/Edmond, esf 1779 King & Queen Co, VA, where b 1755;
  PN 1832 Woodford Co, KY; dd 7/30/1833; md 1787 Sarah Tho-
  mas, Northumberland Co, VA; wid PN ae 74 Woodford Co, KY,
  1842. R127
  James, esf 1778 VA; AFF by s William, Bedford Co, VA, 1828,
  that f had not yet recd BLW issued 1/19/1829; afb was in
  behalf of heirs of sol mbnn; QLF 1933 from desc Mrs Junie
  F Grayson, Charlottesville, VA. R127
  James, esf 1776 Hampshire Co, VA; PN ae 69 Fayette Co, KY;
  dd 3/27/1830 Owen Co, KY; md 5/1771-2 Margaret Bray, Hampshire Co, VA, who PN ae 83 Owen Co, KY, 1836; wid dd
  8/29/42; ch births: Henry 12/24/1775 (res 1836 Nicholasville, Jessamine Co, KY, where lived for 24 years), James
  10/30/77 (res 1836 Nelson Co, KY), John 10/19/79, Abraham
  10/19/81, Isaac 10/21/83, Catrine 9/7/85, Jacob 8/22/87
  (res 1843 Owenton, Owen Co, KY), Mary 8/23/92, Margaret
  12/1/95, Susannah 12/15/97, Milley 10/28/1800; in 1836 wid
  sis Jane (wid/o Peter DeWitt who md 7/1774 Hampshire Co,
  VA) res Clark Co, KY, ae 81. R127
  Stephen, esf VA; PN ae 85 Essex Co, VA, 1834. R128
  Valentine, esf Chesterfield Co, VA, early in RW; PN ae 78
  Campbell Co, KY, 1833. R128
  William, esf Leesburg, Loudoun Co, VA; PN 1828 Winchester,
  Frederick Co, VA; dd 7/7/1829; md 3/27/1785 Elizabeth Ri-
  ley, Frederick Co, VA, who PN ae 70 there, & d 5/5/1855
  there, leaving only ch Samuel H; AFF 1854 by d Mrs Eliza-
  Massie & sol wid, then ae 98, Frederick Co, VA; a Joseph
  Massie testified for sol wid 1838 Frederick Co, VA. R128
BALLANGER, William, esf 1777 VA; PN ae 61 Nicholas Co,KY, 1818
R128
BALLARD, Bland W, esf 1779 Spotsylvania Co,VA, PN ae 75 Shelby
Co, KY, for RW svc 1834; esf KY for War of 1812, 5 wounds;
dd 9/5/53, Shelby Co, KY, where res c 61 years; md Eliza-
beth Weaver there 10/28/41; wid b 3/1768, she former wid/o
--- Garrett/Garnett; wid PN 1854 Louisville, Jefferson Co,
KY, & gtd BLW there 1855; in 1854 sol nephews Bland & A J

42

BALLARD (continued)
    Ballard res there. R129
  Devereux, esf Halifax Co, NC; b 1756 on Nottoway River, VA;
    afp 1832 Sumter District, SC, & PAR. R129
  Francis, esf 1777 Nash Co, NC, as sub for bro William; b
    1/1761 c7 miles from Petersburg, VA; to Edgecombe Co (lat-
    er Nash Co), NC, as ch; to Pensacola, FL, c1787; PN Copiah
    Co, MS, 1833; dd 10/30/1833. R129
  James, esf 1779 Spotsylvania Co, VA, where PN ae 69 in 1832;
    a Belinda Ballard testified in his behalf but no relation-
    ship given; QLF states a Thomas Ballard, w, & 3 small ch
    massacred KY by indians 1783, further this Thomas f/o Col.
    James Ballard (1812 sol) & Bland Ballard, the famous indi-
    an fighter & spy who res Shelbyville, KY; QLF 1928 from
    desc Frank Morris, LaGrange, KY. R129
  James, esf 1780 Orange Co, VA, where b 1752; to KY c1794; PN
    Montgomery Co, KY, 1834. R129
  James, ae 76 in 1832; to KY with f Bland 1780, where James
    was spy, ranger, scout, & hunter for RW troops; afp 1838
    Shelby Co, KY, but PAR since PN Law did not permit PN for
    type of svc (not true military nor member of military or-
    ganization); bro/o Bland W who aec 70 Shelby Co, KY, 1832.
    R129
  John, esf 1779 Loudoun Co, VA; PN ae 60 Staunton, Augusta Co
    VA; dd 11/9/1821; w ae 46 in 1820; QLF 1927 from Burnett H
    Ballard, Falls Church, VA, states his great gdf John Bal-
    lard of Lunenburg Co, VA, was RW sol 1775-78 & mvd 1785 to
    TN, further that writer's f, gdf, & great gdf all named
    John Ballard; PN Office reply to query was that writer's
    John Ballard made no claim for PN or BLW, thus no record
    on him. R129
  Micajah, esf 1780 Bedford Co, VA; PN ae 83 Lawrence Co, OH,
    1819; dd 6/6/1821; in 1820 family w ae 83, d ae 50, s Har-
    ris ae 51. R129
  Philip, esf Orange Co, VA; PN ae 75 Logan Co, VA, 1832; dd
    4/13/1833; wid Mary gtd BLW 1833. R130
  Thomas, esf 1780 Kershaw District, SC; b 3/1751 Albemarle Co
    VA; PN 1839 Gwinnett Co, GA; AFF 1847 by s Colonel Thomas
    Ballard, ae 47 of Lancaster District, SC, stated that sol
    dd 12/28/1843 at res of d Susanna Caston, there; other ch
    Mrs Mary Russell liv 1847; QLF states sol s/o Thomas who
    dd 1781 Albemarle Co, VA. R130
  William, esf 1779 Albemarle Co, VA; b 3/18/1760; PN ae 72
    Scioto Township, Pickaway Co, OH, 1832; dd 3/13/1842-1843
    Franklin Co, OH; md 1/7/1830 Catharine Toxell, there; wid
    1853 Madison Co, OH; wid ae 72 res South Charleston, Clark
    Co, OH, 1855. R130
BALLENGER, John, esf 1777 Culpeper Co, VA, where b 1759; PN St
    Clair Co, AL, 1832. R130
BALLEW, Joseph, esf 1780 Burke Co, NC; b 1757-8 Buckingham Co,
    VA; PN Shelby Co, TN 1832; res 1845 White Co, AR, near res
    of some of his ch. R130

BALLEW, Richard, esf 1779 Burke Co, NC; b 1763 Buckingham Co,
VA; res with f & bro Peter when esf; PN 1833 Poplar Creek,
Knox Co, KY, where res 30 years; bro Peter also res there
1833. R130

  Robert, see BALLOW, Robert. R130

  Stephen, esf 1779 Rowan Co, NC; later esf Burke Co, NC; s/o
  Robert; b Amherst Co, VA; PN aec 70 Burke Co, NC (name at
  times spelled BALLOU). R130

BALLOW, Charles, esf 1776 Williamsburg, VA; PN ae 67 Shelby Co
KY, 1818; dd 9/13/1818; md 9/25/1787 Elizabeth Marshall,
Lincoln Co, KY; wid PN ae 76, Trimble Co, KY; wid ae 78 in
1848; d America Hawkins res Trimble Co, KY; other ch mbnn.
R131

  Robert, esf 1779 Burke Co, NC, as sub for uncle Robert Bal-
  lew; esf 1781 Amherst Co, VA; b Buckingham Co, VA; to Knox
  Co, KY, 1800; to Morgan Co, AL, 1819, where PN 1832 ae 74.
  R131

BALMAIN, Alexander, esf VA, military chaplain; dd 6/16/1821;
md 10/31/1786 Lucy Taylor, who PN ae 81 Frederick Co, VA,
1838; AFF 1838 by wid bro Robert Taylor of Winchester, VA.
R131

BALMER, John, esf 1779 Northampton Co,VA; esf 1780 Middlebrook
PA; afp ae 73 Montgomery Co, NC, ae 73, & PAR; no family
"under his control" at time of application. R131

  John, see BARMER, John. R131

BALMORE, John, see BARMER, John. R131

BALSEY, Christian, esf 1776 Reading, Berks Co, PA; b 5/1/1756
Berks Co, PA; PN 1832 Augusta Co, VA, where moved soon after marriage; dd 6/1837; md c1779 Anna Elizabeth ---, Cumberland Co, PA, who PN ae 83 Augusta Co, VA, 1842; births
of ch: Anna Cattrina 5/27/1780, George Adam 10/31/81, Johannes 12/29/83, Christian 1/9/86, & Elizabeth 3/28/90; s
Jonathan/Johanne liv 1842. R131

BALTHROP, Augustine, esf 1778 Bute Co (now Warren Co), NC; b
1761 Westmoreland Co, VA & mved with older bro to Bute Co,
NC, 1777; PN 1832 Warren Co, NC, where md 4/8/1814 Holly
Burrow/Burrows; wid PN ae 70 while res with d Mecklenburg
Co, VA, 1853; wid res 1855 Franklin Co, NC; QLF 1926 from
desc Mrs. L A Pennebaker, Clarksville, TN. R131

BANDY, Thomas, esf 1781 Bedford Co (now Franklin Co), VA; b
6/22/1748 Cumberland Co, VA; mvd Botetourt Co, VA, thence
Sumner Co, TN, where PN 1833; dd 10/18/35; md (1) Polley/
Polly --- & 5 ch by her; md (2) 10/12/1777-8 Nancy Burns;
wid b 3/1757 & PN 1837 Sumner Co, TN, & dd 8/12/1852; ch
births: Cary/Carey 10/30/1769, Richard 7/10/71, Elizabeth
2/7/73, Martha 8/8/75, Thomas 8/8/75, James 12/27/86, Elihu 6/9/88, Elizabeth 4/4/90,Robert Dobson 2/15/92, Horasha
8/13/94; s Cary & Thomas res Smith Co, TN, 1837; other family bible births: Nancy Bandy 2/12/1811, Samuel Vanover
2/8/1811, Juicey Vanover 2/18--; QLF 1926 from Mrs Truman
H Connor, Ft Worth, TX, great gdd/o a Richard Bandy, a War
of 1812 sol from TN. R132

BANE, Ellis, esf 1777 Washington Co, PA; b 10/1/1743 Chester
    Co, PA; to Cape Capon on Potomac River, VA, ae 11; PN 1833
    Rich Hill Township, Greene Co,PA; dd 8/29/38; ch mbnn; QLF
    states sol md --- Patton?, & ch were Jesse, Mordecai, El-
    lis, Henry, Bythinia, Elizabeth, & Anne, further Bythinia
    md John Gray (b 2/18/1761 & dd 8/19/1834) who esf Washing-
    ton Co, PA, & later res Greene Co, PA. R132
  John, see BANES, John. R132
BANES, John, esf 1779-80 Mecklenburg Co, VA, for NC svc; PN ae
    72 Sumner Co, TN, 1832; dd 9/2/1840 Perry Co, IL; md c1782
    Susannah ---, Mecklenburg Co, VA; wid dd 4/23/1842; s Els-
    worth b 9/17/1783 & dd c1814; d Sarah b 2/7/1786 who md
    Isaac Carmack, & she afp 1844 Perry Co, IL, & PAR. R132
BANGHAM, Richard, esf 1776 King & Queen Co, VA; PN 1819 Char-
    lottesville, VA. R132
BANISTER, John, esf 1779 Prince William Co, VA, where b c1763;
    PN 1833 Anderson District, SC. R133
BANKS, Edward, see BRUS, Edward. R134
  Jacob, esf Goochland Co, VA, where b 8/1754; PN there 1832;
    svc in Albemarle Co, VA, as wagonmaster; dd 1/5/1835, with
    remainder of PN to 3 of his 4 ch who mbnn. R134
  James, sea svc, esf VA; dd 1795 Hampton, VA; md (1) ?, & md
    (2) 3/30/1787 Mary Smith, Warwick Co,VA, who PN ae 75 Eli-
    zabeth City Co, VA, 1845; wid dd 5/19/1848 leaving d Mary
    A w/o John M Willis, gdd Caroline Godwin, & s-in-law Tho-
    mas Lateman. R134
  John, esf 1779 VA; PN ae 73 Goochland Co,VA; dd 11/24/1842;
    md Spring 1772 Salley Jenkins, Cumberland Co, VA; wid PN
    ae 89 Goochland Co, VA, 1845, her res 1854 there; ch mbnn;
    QLF 1919 from descendant Mrs. Socrates Drew, Minneapolis,
    MN. R134
  John, esf 1776 Gloucester Co, NJ; b 11/25/1757, s/o Richard;
    PN 1832 Floyd Co, VA; dd 8/30/1850; md c9/10/1830 Mary Ad-
    ams, Patrick Co, VA; wid PN ae 85 there 1854; ch: d Ruth
    w/o George Shelor, Polly, William, & Thomas; QLF states
    George Shelor, s/o Daniel Shelor & May Wickham, also RW
    sol. R134
  William, 1781 esf Amherst Co, VA; b 6/3/1761, or 6/23/1762,
    Culpeper Co, VA; to KY after RW; PN 1832 Putnam Co, IN, &
    dd there 9/5/1839; md 12/10/1801 Elizabeth Brown, Garrard
    Co, KY; wid b 7/27/1781; wid PN 1855 Putnam Co, IN, & res
    there 1863; ch births: Nancy 8/4/1802 (dd 1/22/27), Fran-
    ces 6/16/05 (dd 10/06), Mary 2/15/07 (dd 2/12/46), Eliza-
    beth 2/8/09, Daniel P 9/30/10, William S 2/2/14, Emily A
    12/19/15, Almirium 2/5/18 (dd 9/4/47), John Smith 3/7/20,
    Joseph R 7/15/23 (dd 12/4/46), Wesley J 7/28/25; other fa-
    mily bible data: John Banks & Louisa md 11/21/1843, Emily
    A Banks Jr b 5/10/1845; in 1855 sol s Daniel P & Wesley J
    res Putnam Co, IN; QLF 1909 from sol gdd Mrs Martin Wright
    of Muncie, IN. R135
BAPTISTE, John, BLW issued 1/20/1796. R136
BARBEE, Daniel, esf 1775 Culpeper Co, VA; PN ae 75 Danville,

BARBEE (continued)
    Mercer Co, KY, 1832; dd 6/28/1834; in 1832 Elizabeth Rooney ae 68 testified sol md her sis; sol bro/o Capt Thomas & Joshua (ae 72 Mercer Co, KY, 1834). R136
  Elias, esf 1781 Culpeper Co, VA, where b 6/14/1763; to KY 12/1782; PN 1832 Green Co, KY; 5 bros all RW sol: Thomas, John, Daniel, William, & Joshua; in 1832 Joshua ae 72, Daniel ae 75, Mercer Co, KY; QLF 1912 from desc W C Rogers, Lebanon, KY, states sol dd 1843. R136
  John, esf VA; dd 9/23/1835; md 6/27/1782 (MB 6/24/82) Mary Dyson; wid PN ae 75 Fauquier Co, VA, 1838, & dd 11/9/1845 there, leaving ch: William H, John T, Joseph A, James M, Samuel B, Mary Hitch, Martha Grant, & Ann Singleton; QLF mns a John Barbee who f/o six s in RW: Thomas, John, William, Elias, Ezekiel, & Daniel. R136
  Joshua, esf 1777 Culpeper Co, VA; PN 1832 Mercer Co, KY ae 71; bro Daniel ae 75 then res same Co. R136
  Thomas, BLW issued 7/15/1789; QLF 1920 from kin Mrs Carlos Michler, Akron, OH, states sol esf Culpeper Co, VA, further either Thomas or Daniel Barbee had d Rose who md William Bradford, Culpeper Co,VA, & they had d Lucy who md Fred Yiser, latter being parents/o Rose (grandm/o querier) who md Capt A S McGroarty of Danville, KY. R136
BARBER, James, esf 1779 nr Romney, Hampshire Co,VA; b Winchester, VA, 10/16/1761; esf 1791 for Indian Wars nr Steubenville, OH; PN 1840 Bath, Medina Co, OH; md Mary Rowland, Hampshire Co, VA; QLF 1927 from desc Mrs Lola Grabill of Ashland, OH, states sol d 1842; QLR 1939 from desc Mrs Arthur Mallory, LaGrange, GA. R137
  John, BLW issued 4/3/1794. R137
  William, esf 1781 Halifax Co, VA; b 5/17/1745 Dinwiddie Co, VA; PN 1833 Surry Co, NC. R138
  William, esf VA; PN 1786 for disability; res 1822 Mecklenburg Co, VA; QLF 1933 from desc Mrs W O Hughes, West Point MS, states sol esf Mecklenburg Co, VA, PN for loss of eyesight; QLF 1913 from desc William Henry Crutcher, Louisville, KY, states b 1724. R138
BARBEY, Elijah, esf Stafford Co, VA; PN aec 53 Bourbon Co, KY, 1818; afp increase 1820 when w Nancy ae 37, ch: Joseph aec 7, Sally aec 4, Benjamin aec 3, William ae 5-6 weeks. R139
BARBOUR, Mordecai, esf Culpeper Co, VA, where b 10/21/63; PN 1831; res 1834 Petersburg, VA; dd 1/21/1846 Greene Co, AL; w dd before him; 4 ch including J S & Maria (wid in 1846); 1 ch of sol liv 1847. R139
BAREITH, John, see BARETH, John. R140
BARETH, John, 1781 esf Winchester,VA; PN ae 67 Wayne Township, Champaign Co, OH; dd 3/21/1837; md 1/8/1783 Elizabeth, d/o Peter Moore, Yorktown, PA; wid PN ae 74 Champaign Co, OH, 1838; she res 1844 Wayne Township, that Co. R140
BARHAM, Benjamin, esf 1776 VA; PN ae 64 Southampton Co, VA, 1818; dd 1822 leaving wid & 7 ch. R140
  Hartwell, esf 1776 VA; PN ae 66 Stokes Co, NC, 1825, having

BARHAM (continued)
   w & step d aec 18; QLF states sol res Sussex Co, VA, 1784.
   R140
   James, esf 1781 Southampton Co, VA, where b 5/18/1764; to NC
      after RW; to KY 1813 where PN 1833 Trigg Co; to TN 1846 to
      be near ch; dd 1/8/1865 nr Springfield, Greene Co, MO; QLF
      1932 from great great gdd Mrs Faye Parker, Stamps, AR,
      states sol b 1755 England. R140
BARKER, Charles, esf 1777 VA; PN ae 71 Pike Col OH, 1822; QLF
      1940 from desc Ethel (Mrs Walter) Moser, Fort Thomas, KY,
      states sol from Washington Co, VA, & md Frances Chiles.
      R141
   David, esf 1779 Caswell Co, NC; b 3/23/1761 Louisa Co, VA;
      PN 1832 Caswell Co, NC; dd 11/14/39; ch mbnn. R141
   Edward, esf King William Co,VA; PN ae 78 Smyth Co, VA, 1833;
      dd 3/30/1845, leaving wid Elizabeth, whom he md 1774-78;
      wid dd 6/15/1849; heirs at law of sol apf 1852, Washington
      Co, VA, & PAR because unable to prove marriage of sol and
      Elizabeth; ch then: Sally w/o Micajah McCormick Jr, Eliza-
      beth w/o William Calliham, Edward, Polly w/o Ezekiel Call-
      ham, John (dumb), Vesta w/o Obadiah Calliham; other heir
      William Barker s/o sol decd d Lucy; Sally McCormick stated
      in court 1853 ae 72-75 & eldest liv ch/o sol. R141
   George, esf 1776 Washington Co, VA; esf 1778 NC; b 1758
      Rockbridge Co, VA; PN 1834 Morgan Co, KY; res 1836 Parke
      Co, IN, to be near only s. R141
   John, esf 1777 Sussex Co, VA; PN ae 70 Somerset, Pulaski Co,
      Co, KY, 1832; dd 4/23/1835; md 10/1783 Lucy Irby, Prince
      George Co, VA; wid PN ae 80 Pulaski Co, KY, 1839, when ch:
      Sally Floyd (eldest) ae 54, Betsey ae 52, & Irby ae 44; ch
      decd then: Lucy b c1789, Thomas b c1791, & Edmund b c1793;
      QLF 1914 from Dr B L Barker, Monticello,IL, states sol had
      1 more ch John F (youngest), & descendants of John anxious
      to join Daughters of the American Revolution. R142
   Nathaniel, esf 1781 Loudoun Co, VA; b Charles Co, MD; PN ae
      81 Fairfax Co, VA, 1832; dd there 7/13/1833; md 11/1/1771
      Letitia "Letty" Elsey/Ellzey, Loudon Co, VA; wid PN ae 82
      Fairfax Co, VA,1838; ch births: Anna 8/1775, Joel 11/20/76
      then 2 s dd infancy, Susanna 12/2/1781, John 10/27/83, En-
      och 11/11/85, Mary 10/5/87,William 7/10/89, Jemima 2/15/91
      Penny 1/1/93, & Leady 9/3/1794; QLF 1930 from great gdd
      Medda Barker (Mrs J C) Nelson, Sharpsburg, KY. R142
   William, esf 1781 Monongalia Co, VA; b 1765 Loudoun Co, VA;
      afp 1834 Henry Co, KY, PAR for insufficient proof of svc;
      QLF states sol dd Fayette Co, KY. R143
BARKSDALE, Henry Hickerson, esf 1781 Pittsylvania Co, VA; dd
      11/27/1810; md 8/8/1782 (MB 8/2/1782) Molly, d/o Richard
      Bayne, Pittsylvania Co, VA; wid PN ae 77 Halifax Co, VA,
      1840, & dd 7/28/46, adm/o her estate Elisha Barksdale; re-
      mainder of wid PN to only surv ch 1850: William H, Richard
      H, Anna, Unity Spencer, Judith Pollard, Patty Grant, Cyn-
      thia H Crouch, & Claiborne B; court action shows sol mid-

BARKSDALE (continued)
   dle name as Higgerson. R144
   Samuel, esf 1776 Albemarle Co, VA, where b 10/25/1759, & PN
   there 1832; dd 6/20/42; md 3/31/1793 Jemima Wingfield, Albemarle Co, VA; wid PN there 1842 ae 69. R144
BARLOW, Christopher, esf 1776 Culpeper Co, VA, where b on Robinson River 1/1/67; mvd to Rockingham Co, VA, after RW
   for 8 years, thence Washington Co, KY, where PN 1834; md
   1768-9 Barbara Moyers, Culpeper Co, VA; wid PN ae 94 Washington Co, KY, 1838 when d Jerusha Adams AFF there aec 68;
   sol bro Lewis, also RW sol, mvd to IN. R144
   Joseph, esf 1779 VA; to Boone Co, KY, c1818; PN there ae 60
   1820 at which time no family but res with bro; QLF states
   sol res there at time/o 1840 Census with w Catherine. R145
   Lewis, esf 1776 Staunton, Augusta Co, VA; b 1755 Culpeper Co
   VA; mvd to KY, thence c1820 to IN where PN 1832 Shelby Co;
   family in 1830 w Judah ae 75, Elizabeth ae 28, George aec
   12, Bluford aec 10; a William Barlow AFF in support of sol
   claim; QLF 1908 from great gdd Mrs A B Sims, Des Moines,
   IA; QLF 1905 from great gds H G Williams, Whiteland, IN,
   states sol drew 1 PN payment at Edinburgh, IN, & his wid
   drew 1 payment there too. R145
BARMER, John, esf aec 30 Southampton Co, VA, where b; mvd after RW to Montgomery Co, NC, where PN 1833 ae 80-85; md
   there; res there over 50 years in 1853. R145
BARNARD, Benjamin, esf Powhatan Co, VA, where b 2/20/1757; PN
   1832 Chesterfield Co, VA. R145
   Peter, esf 1777 Gloucester Co (area later Mathews Co), VA;
   dd 4-5 years after RW; heirs afp, but no record of names,
   & PAR; QLF states sol bro/o John & Abner of Fluvanna Co or
   Gloucester Co, VA. R146
BARNES, Andrew, BLW issued 3/20/1797. R147
   Armistead, esf 1776 Norfolk, VA; PN ae 63 Madison Co, VA,
   1819; w ae 50 in 1821. R147
   Bingamond/Benjamin, esf 1781 Culpeper Co, VA; b 2/1/1766; PN
   1832 Gallatin Co, KY; AFF Trimble Co, KY, 1832 by William
   Barnes, adm/o decd sol's estate & 1 of his heirs; QLF 1928
   from desc Mrs Faye M Scherieble, Minneapolis, MN. R147
   Charles, BLW issued 5/31/1794 for svc in SC; in file data on
   a Charles Barnes, who came to America while sol under Lord
   Dunsmore, in expedition against indians on Scioto River in
   1774, presumably came to VA; family records states sol mvd
   to Newark, OH, 1811 from Frederick Co, VA, at advanced ae
   with s Charles Jr & dd 1818 Mary Ann Township, OH; s Charles b 4/1797 Frederick Co, VA, dd 12/21/1873, f/o Stewart
   who b OH 1834; Stewart's s Oren J (b OH 5/22/1877) sent in
   family records to PN Office 1928. R147
   Chesley/Chessley, esf 1780 Guilford Co, NC; b 1760 on Slate
   River, VA; PN 1832 Rockingham Co, NC; dd 9/8/1840; md Mary
   Means (MB 2/10/1783), Guilford Co, NC; wid PN ae 81 there
   1844; ch births: Robert 4/26/1784, John 1/12/86, Nathaniel
   2/1/88, Pleasant 2/19/91, Ann 9/12/93, Martha 3/31/96,

BARNES (continued)

Nancey 8/6/98; Mary 3/4/1800, & Susannah 12/20/06; in 1852 wid decd, & d Martha Gann, Rockingham Co, NC, agent for PN heirs, her signature witnessed by W & Nathaniel Gann. R147

George, esf 1780 Hillsborough, VA; on way to KY, attacked by indians, who carried off 2 s; PN ae 75 Christian Co, KY, dd before 7/31/1854, leaving ch but only William mentioned. R148

James, esf 1776 VA; PN ae 66 Smith Co,TN, 1823 when w ae 50, dd 4/11/1825. R148

John, esf Spotsylvania Co, VA; PN aec 60 Harrison Co, KY, 1818; dd there 8/5/40; md 1782, 1783, or 11/27/1784 Milly, Culpeper Co, VA; wid PN aec 73 Harrison Co, Ky, 1841; 4 ch at home 1820: Sally ae 16, Armistead ae 15, Samuel ae 14, & Betsey aec 12; eldest ch James, b 1785-6, liv 1845; QLF states sol b England 1740. R148

John, BLW issued 11/12/91. R148

Richard, esf 1781 Henry Co, VA; b 1763 Baltimore, MD; to IN from KY 1832; afp Hendricks Co, IN, 1845; PAR since svc not in truly military unit. R149

Shadrach, see BARNS, Shadrach. R149

BARNET, Joseph, esf 1779 Franklin Co, VA, where b 5/1760-1; PN 1832 Harrison Co, VA. R150

BARNETT, Ambrose, esf 1777 Orange Co, VA; PN ae 58 Nicholas Co KY, 1818; dd 12/17-18/1832; md 10/31/1781 Sally ---, about 12 miles from Orange Court House, Orange Co, VA; wid PN ae 75 Nicholas Co, KY, 1839, & res there 1849; wid dd 2/6/52; ch births: John 4/12-13/1785, Susanah 6/13/87, Maryan 10/28/89, William 4/11/93, Mariah 9/30/9-, Robert 2/18/99, James 6/29/1801, & Sary/Sally 8/20/1803-4; QLF 1932 from Mrs O W Elmore, Versailles,KY, desc/o another Ambrose Barnett from Fauquier Co, VA, who md Judith Neville & their d md 1798 Henry Steel (b 1770) nr Winchester, VA. R150

Charles, esf 1780 Albemarle Co, VA, where b 1764-5; mvd to TN 1800, thence NC c1808; PN 1833 Granville Co, NC; to Albemarle Co, VA, c840; sol "a man of color" dd Granville Co TN, leaving " wid & parcel of children in very distressed situation." R150

David, esf 1779 Caswell Co, NC; b 1754 Lunenburg Co, VA; PN 1832 Greenville District, SC. R150

Isaac, afp Lewis Co, VA, 18--; PAR. R150

James, esf VA; reared Amherst Co, VA; PN 1828 Madison Co, KY & dd 8/27/35 there ae 86; md 3/4/1790 there Marcey/Massy d/o Nathan Hawkins; wid PN aec 71 there 1839, res there 1843; name of Nicholas Hawkins on MB; QLF 19-- from great great gds Louis P Barnett, Columbia,MO; QLF 1935 from desc Lenora Higginbotham (Mrs William M) Sweeny, Astoria, Long Island, NY, states sol b 1/16/1750; QLF states sol dd at Richmond, KY. R150

James P, esf as sub for f John in Guilford Co, NC, where mvd as ch; b 1762 Amherst Co, VA; PN 1832 Lincoln Co, KY. R150

BARNETT, John, BLW issued 4/21/1796. R151
   John, esf 1779, VA; PN ae 55, Nicholas Co,KY; res 1826 John-
   son Co, IN, to be near ch; dd there 9/8/1828; md Elizabeth
   Self 2/1783, who PN aec 57 Nicholas Co, KY, 1820; wid dd
   9/26/40; ch births: James 6/23/1784, William 9/27/86,
   Spencer 3/28/89,George 8/17/91,Lucy 5/4/96,Thomas 3/23/98,
   John 6/25/1800, Elizabeth Ann 8/15/06, & Ambrose 7/24/09;
   ch 1848: James (Nicholas Co,KY), William, Spencer, Thomas,
   & Ambrose (all Johnson Co, IN), George in MO, Elizabeth
   Ann Record (Shelby Co, IN); QLF 1901 from gdd Mrs George
   W Barnett, Trefalgar, IN, states sol b 7/23/1764 Orange Co
   VA, youngest of 17 bro's who were RW sol's, & PN Coryden,
   IN, further sol name John P Barnett; QLF 1918 from desc
   Idela (Mrs Theodore F) Craven, Indianapolis,IN, states sol
   middle name Perry & enlisted ae 16 as fifer; QLF 1910 from
   desc Mrs J T Fleming, Logan,UT; QLF 1925 from desc Mrs Mae
   Ralston Guthrie, Vincennes,IN, states sol res near what is
   now Edinburgh, IN, & rode to Corydon to collect PN; QLF
   1930 states 6 of 17 bro's who drew PN were Artax, James,
   Jonathan, Ambrose, Daniel, & John Perry, further one bro f
   of James Horatio Barnett (b 1798) who md Louisa Harlow in
   1804, ancestors/o querier. R151
   Leona, former wid/o Lewis HOWEL/HOWELL. R151
   Michael, esf 1779 Augusta Co, VA; PN ae 71 Jefferson Co, TN,
   1833; dd 3/24/52; md 4/1817 (MB 4/15/17) Esther Daniel, in
   Jefferson Co, TN; wid PN aec 67 there 1853. R151
   Peter, see BARNARD, Peter. R151
   Robert, esf VA; to KY 1788; res Lincoln Co, KY, till death
   3/31/1831; in 1834 surv ch (Ann, Hannah, William P, & Ro-
   bert, all of Lincoln Co, KY, & Betsey Mae w/o Benjamin May
   of IN) afp; PAR since sol svc less than 6 months. R151
BARNS, James, esf 1796-7 Mecklenburg Co, VA; b 12/14/1748 on
   Potomac River in Northumberland Co, VA; PN 1832 nr Terre
   Haute, Vigo Co, IN; to Blount Co, TN, 1837 to res with ch;
   AFF 1838 there by James Barns Jr. R153
   Shadrack, esf 1778 Amherst Co, VA; b 2/6/1764 Culpeper Co,
   VA; PN 1833 Gallatin Co, KY; dd 12/31/44; QLF 1933 from
   great great gdd Zola C (Mrs Howard M) Smith, St Paul, MN;
   QLF 1928 from great great gdd Mrs L B Medley, Minneapolis,
   MN. R154
BARNWELL, James, PN aec 70 Fauquier Co, VA, 1823, then no fa-
   mily res with him. R155
BARR, Hugh, esf 1780 Halifax Co,VA, when res with f Michael in
   Caswell Co, NC; PN ae 73 Barr Township, Daviess Co, IN; md
   (1) ? Fredericktown,MD, who dd 1822; md (1) ? who dd 1832;
   dd 4/24/42 at res/o s Michael, Edgar Co, IL, where mvd in
   1835; survivors were ch: Michael (ae 51 in 1852 h/o sis/o
   James Johnson), James, Polly w/o John Aikman, & Hugh; also
   surv ch/o s Byram who dd 1842: George T, John H of Daviess
   Co, IN; Polly & John Aikman dd 1852, leaving ch: Barton,
   Scisely w/o William Robeson, James, Hugh, Samuel, Elizabeth w/o --- Hawkins, Mary w/o Isaac McCormick, Maria w/o

BARR (continued)
William Helvestine, Robert, William, Martha & John B; sol
had 2 older bro's who also RW sol's: Daniel (decd in 1833)
& Robert (res TN 1827); QLF 1931 from great great gds H H
Purkhiser, Mitchell, IN. R155
Isaac, esf 1776 Fauquier Co,VA; PN ae 69 Stokes Co, NC, 1820
when family d Patsy aec 20, d Elizabeth aec 15, & s Joshua
aec 13; dd 12/1832; QLF 1895 from desc David Barr, Wash-
ington, DC, s/o George Ray Barr, who eldest s/o Dr William
Barr of Abingdon, VA, who s/o sol; QLF 1938 from desc Mrs
R L Chuning, Los Angeles, CA, states sol b 1751 Fauquier
Co, VA, & dd Stokes Co, NC, h/o Ann Foster. R155
James, esf 1776 Sussex Co, NJ; b 9/24/1753 Philadelphia, PA;
PN 1832 Berkeley Co, VA; QLF states sol w Rachel. R155
James, esf 1778 Guilford Co, NC, when f res Pittsylvania Co,
VA; b2/7/1762 Guilford Co,NC; PN 1832 Jackson Co, GA. R155
John, esf 1781 VA; BLW 1804 Frederick Co, VA, when signed as
Johannes Bahr. R156
Philip, esf 1776 VA; PN ae 68 Shenandoah Co, VA, 1818; fami-
ly in 1820: d Elizabeth ae 27 & son Stapleton ae 17; QLF
1904 from gds W F Barr, Brice, OH, states sol came with
bro's from Northern Ireland, md Mary Bond, res near Wood-
stock, Shenandoah Co, VA, had 7 s including William (f/o
querier) who was War of 1812 sol who dd Centervillage, De-
laware Co, OH, 1873. R156
William, esf 1776 for svc with PA & VA troops; PN ae 68 St
Clair Township, Allegheny Co, PA, 1818; dd there 12/1842;
md 2/10/1785 Mary ---, Allegheny Co, PA; wid PN aec 81 Lower St Clair Township, that Co, 1842. R156
William, BLW issued 1/7/1793. R156
BARRAM, Fielding, esf 1776 Williamsburg, VA; to SC after RW, &
to LA 1806; PN ae 64 Parish of East Feliciana, LA, 1824; 1
liv heir at death Rowena w/o George W Christine afp & afb
1853 Parish of East Baton Rouge, LA. R156
BARRET, Francis, esf 1779 Hanover Co, VA, where b 2/20/1763;
PN 1832 Cumberland Co, KY; res 1833 Green Co, KY; in 1832
a John Barret clerk of court of that Co. R156
Richard, see FRANKS, Richard. R156
William, BLW issued 5/28/1789. R156
BARRETT, Henry, esf Prince William Co, VA, where b near Dum-
fries; PN aec 80 Wythe Co, VA, 1833. R157
John, see BARETH, John. R157
John, esf 1781 Henry Co, VA; afp ae 84 Buncombe Co, NC, 1836
& PAR. R157
Jonathan, dd in svc while POW in NY (proven in Prince Willi-
am Co, VA, as early as 1784), leaving wid Amy, an aged m &
2 ch; wid afp & PAR. R157
Lewis, esf 1776 Hanover Co, VA, where b 1/7/1752; PN 1832
Wilkes Co, GA. R157
Miles, esf VA; dd c1832 Green Co, TN; md c1783 Judith ---,
Patrick Co, VA, who dd c1825; 1st ch d Mary Lawson aec 72
afb 1855 & gtd BLW. R157

BARRETT, Samuel, esf 1776 Shenandoah Co, VA; b 2/21/1758; PN 1832 Wood Co, VA. R158

Sarah, former wid/o William HARPER. R158

BARRON, Fielding, BLW issued 5/29/92. R159

James, VA sea svc & US Navy; aide to f Commodore James Barron who commander in chief/o VA navy; afp ae 65 Philadelphia, PA, 1834; PN 1834 Washington, DC; afp increase 1850 Norfolk,VA; dd 4/21/51; wid Mary A PN 1853 Portsmouth, VA. R159

John, esf 1776 Montgomery Co, VA; b 10/3/1749 Talbot Co, MD; PN 1834 Pulaski Co, KY, where dd 3/14/41; md 4/12/1781 Susannah ---, Washington Co, NC; wid b 9/17/1762, & PN 1842 Pulaski Co, KY, when eldest ch ae 61; s James ae 52 in 1843; QLF states sol md Susannah McBee, Washington Co, NC, 4/12/1781. R159

Richard, VA sea svc; former wid Ann Hubbard gtd 1/2 pay settlement 1850. R159

Samuel, VA sea svc, esf 1779 aec 17; sailor dd 11/1810, leaving s Samuel, & d (md 1818 & dd 1821, who left d md 1836 "not yet of age"); s Samuel of age 11/1829, & in US Navy & adm/o f's estate 1850, gtd PN Norfolk, VA, for svc/o f who bro/o Commodore James Barron. R159

William, esf on New River, Montgomery Co, VA; b 1755 Talbot Co, MD; PN 1833 Washington Co, TN, where res 50 years; QLF states sol dd Pulaski Co, KY. R159

BARROTT, Peter, esf VA; PN ae 62 Person Co, NC, 1818; family 1820 w Sarah aec 57, s Jabez ae 20, s John ae 16, d ae 13; QLF 1899 from great gdd Mrs Mary Barrett Whitmire, Waverly IA, states sol dd Rexborough, NC; QLF 1904 from desc Mrs Elsie Layman, Jacksonville, IL. R160

BARROW, Daniel, esf 1776 Brunswick Co, VA, where bc 1757; esf 1779 NC; PN 1834 Jackson Co, IL; surname at times spelled BANOW; QLF 1936 from great great gdd Mrs Albert S Johnson, Indianapolis, IN (mns family bible), her descent through sol s David who b 8/1807 Wayne Co,KY, h/o Elizabeth Young; QLF 1916 from desc Estella A (Mrs Thomas J) Felton, Chicago, IL; QLF 1927 from great great gdd Mrs J B Longerot of Yuma,AZ; QLF 1922 from desc Mrs Margaret M Bain, Ohio, CO; QLF 1932 from great gds R W Barrow, Macon, MO, states his gdf Daniel Barrow & Daniel's bro Nathan came as young men to Monticello, Wayne Co, KY, md d's/o Bright Gilstrap, & mvd with them to MO. R160

John, see BARRON, John. R160

William, esf 1789 Guilford Co, NC; b 1/8/1762 Brunswick Co, VA; PN 1833 Pulaski Co, KY; dd 9/3/39; md 3/29/96 Susanna Miskell; wid PN ae 73 Pulaski Co, KY, & dd 8/7/1850; birth of ch: Rebecca Lee 2/26/1797, Charles Miskell 11/25/98, Nancy 2/3/1800, David 10/2/01, Thomas 4/30/03, Samuel 12/17/04, Susanna 3/11/06, Hanna 5/1/08, Mary 2/16/10, William Jr 6/18/11, Moses 4/26/13, John 1/10/1815, Isaac 8/2/16; & Salley 3/27/19; other family bible births: Thomas Wilson 3/18/1847; Polly Wilson 6/2/48; Archie B Cherry

BARROW (continued)
      4/13/49; sol d Rebecca L Sadler res 1850 Pulaski Co, KY, &
      also a Samuel Sadler res there; Aaron (bro/o sol) ae 61 &
      w Martha ae 64 res 1833 Pulaski Co, KY. R160
BARTEE, David; esf 1781 ae 16 Charlotte Co, VA, sub for f John
      & PN ae 66 there. R161
BARTHE, George, see BAITH, George. R162
BARTLET, John, BLW issued 7/12/1810 Bridgeport, VA (now WV).
      R163
BARTLETT, Edmund, esf 1776 Spotsylvania Co, VA; b 12/23/1759;
      to MO 1830 from KY; PN 1833 Huntsville, Randolph Co, MO.
      R164
    John, esf 1780, Winchester, Frederick Co, VA; PN ae 57 Jeff-
      erson Co, KY, 1821 when w ae 54, & ch: John (eldest), La-
      vender ae 19, Jefferson ae 12, & all living w sol s John;
      QLF 1919 from desc Lorena Luckett (Mrs James S) Bush, of
      Brooklyn, NY, states sol b 1764 & dd New Castle, KY; QLF
      1915 from Mrs J E Law, Clarksburg, WV, desc/o another John
      Bartlett who PN ae 73 Allen Co, KY, 1823; see below. R164
    John, sea svc, esf 1776 near Suffolk, VA; PN ae 73 Allen Co,
      KY, 1823; res 1825 Williamson Co, TN. R164
    Philip, surgeon; dd 7/1/1809; adm of estate John Jones afp
      for heirs 1846 Elizabeth City Co, VA; PAR. R165
    William, see BERKLEY, William. R166
BARTLEY, John, BLW issued 7/6/1793. R166
    John, esf 1776 near Winchester, Frederick Co, VA; PN ae 73
      Greene Co, PN, 1819; w dd during RW; ch mbnn. R166
    Thomas, esf PA; later esf VA; PN aec 78 Monroe Co, KY, 1838;
      md KY; wid Margaret res Monroe Co, KY, 1854. R166
BARTON, Elisha, esf 1781 Fauquier Co,VA, where b 1757; PN 1834
      Bedford Co, VA. R167
    John, esf NC; dd 1/3/1839 at res Grayson Co, VA; md 9/4/1793
      Elizabeth Pennington, Wilkes Co (later Ashe Co), NC; wid b
      8/10/1774 "in the Hollows of the Yadkin River on the east
      side of Blue Ridge", d/o Micajah Pennington (b 4/28/1743)
      & Rachel Jones (b 6/12/1744), who md 1/28/1761; wid afp
      1857 Grayson Co, VA; PAR, insufficient proof of h svc; ch
      births: Eady 8/30/1799 (1st liv ch, 3 dd as infants),
      Isaac 5/27/1804, Rachel 6/8/06, Charety 2/27/09, Absalam
      4/28/11, John 7/25/12, Feby 5/1/14, & John 3/20/17; QLF
      1931 from desc Kat (Mrs John S) Welborn, High Point, NC.
      R167
BASHAM, Obediah, see BASSHAM, Obadiah. R168
BASHAW, John, esf 1776-7 VA; PN ae 60 Fluvanna Co, VA, 1818;
      family 1820 w ae 60, s ae 19, d ae 17, d ae 14. R168
    Peter, esf 1780 Fauquier Co, VA, where b 3/31/1763; PN 1832
      Davidson Co, TN, where res 1864 ae 101; QLF 1900 from Sons
      of the American Revolution states sol dd ae 101 near Nash-
      ville, TN; QLF states sol md Frances Bashaw. R168
BASKERVILLE, John, esf VA; dd 6/3/1832 Buckingham Co, VA; md
      12/25/1792 Mildred "Millie" Pendleton there; wid PN ae 79
      there 1842, & res ae 85 Appomattox Co, VA, 1848; female ch

BASKERVILLE (continued)
    mbnn. R168
    Samuel, esf 1776 Cumberland Co, VA; BLW issued 4/9/1800; PN
      ae 63 Madison Co, OH, 1818; family in 1820 res with him w
      Statina ae 56, ch: William B ae 23, Samuel B ae 22, James
      M ae 17, Richard A 15, Judith ae 26, & Ann M ae 12; res
      there 1828. R168
BASKET, Martin, see Baskett, Martin. R168
    Martin, esf 1780 Fluvanna Co, VA; esf 1782 NC; b 12/6/1761
      Goochland Co, VA; PN 1833 Shelby Co, KY, dd there 5/26/33;
      md 11/7/1783 Frances Shepherd, Fluvanna Co, VA; wid sis/o
      John & b 12/2/1766; wid PN 1838 Shelby Co, KY; ch births:
      John 1/9/1785 (dd 5/1785), Thomas 3/27/86 (dd 3/19/1822),
      Nancy 3/25/89, Elizabeth 5/7/91, Henry M 10/11/93, Mary
      7/24/96, Jesse 6/15/99, Sarah 2/1/1802 (dd 2/18/10), Mild-
      red 6/28/04, & Frances 6/8/10; other family bible dates:
      Joab Michell b 8/1829-39, Thomas Henry (s/o Jesse Baskett)
      b 9/27/36, Nancy Baskett md 10/30/06 William Webber, Tho-
      mas Baskett md 9/27/08 Peggy Doudle, Elizabeth Baskett md
      9/29/08 William E King, Henry M Baskett md 10/20/13 Sarah
      Ford, Mary Baskett md 12/24/18 Daniel Connelly, Mildred
      Baskett md 12/19/22 Gideon Michell, Elizabeth King dd
      2/24/22,Thomas Michell dd 18--,Mildred Michell dd 3/14/30,
      Mary Connelly dd 8/21/34, & John Moore dd 6/8/38; QLF 1907
      from great gds Walter S Baskett, McFall,MO, who also great
      gds of RW sol Elisha Ford. R168
BASS, Edward Sr, esf 1754 Chesterfield Co,VA,where b 8/15/1754
      & PN there 1832; QLF states sol w Judith, further d Martha
      md Jordan Martin. R169
    James, esf Norfolk Co, VA, where b 8/1760, PN 1832 Bedford
      Co, TN, where mvd c1819; QLF 1923 from desc Mrs Frances M
      Ransom, Washington, DC. R169
    John, esf 1777 Chesterfield Co, VA, where b 6/22/1761; PN
      there 1832; QLF 1939 states sol John Sr ae 79 Chesterfield
      Co census 1840. R169
    Joseph, esf 1780 Chesterfield Co, VA, where b 11/30/1758; to
      Dinwiddie Co, VA, 1807, where PN 1832; dd there 3/30/1840;
      md 12/5/1790 Jane "Jenney" Manlove, Chesterfield Co, VA;
      wid PN ae 71 Dinwiddie Co, VA, 1844, & dd 1/17/52; in 1844
      her bro Joel Manlove res Dinwiddie Co. R169
    Philip, esf NC; res Union Co, SC, 1791; dd 1/12/1815 Barren
      Co, KY; md 1/22/1782 Martha "Patsy" Mullins, Pittsylvania
      Co, VA; wid PN 1845, Monteau Co, MO, & dd there 9/11/50 ae
      86; ch: Dread, Sarah, Nancy, Isaac, Bird, Elizabeth, Pol-
      ly, & Katy; ch res 1851: Elizabeth (Cedar Co, MO), Polly
      (w/o John Goodman, Morgan Co,MO), Tolbert (Cooper Co, MO),
      Sally (wid/o Plesent Wood, Barren Co, KY), Catherine (w/o
      John Sartore, Monteau Co, MO). R169
    William Sr, esf Chesterfield Co, VA, where b 5/10/1763; mvd
      to Powhatan Co, VA, c1814, where PN 1832; dd 5/10/39 Ches-
      terfield Co, VA; md 10/1789 Sarah Shackleford, there; wid
      PN ae 69 there 1843; wid sis Nancy Sublet ae 67 then; sol

BASS (continued)
    bro John aec 70 Chesterfield Co, VA, 1832. R169
BASSETT, Nathaniel, esf 1778 Prince Edward Co,VA; b 10/12/1758
    Cumberland Co, VA; to Hawkins Co, TN, 1800 where PN 1832;
    dd there 12/18/1833, leaving ch mbnn. R170
  William, esf 1776 Botetourt Co, VA; b 4/18/1755 Surrey Co,
    England; mvd to KY, thence Ripley Co, IN, where PN 1833;
    dd 2/6/1840; md 11/27/1786 Peggy ---, who PN ae 70 Ripley
    Co, IN, 1840; ch births: Nancy 8/27/1787; Thomas 4/14/91,
    James 11/18/93, Sally 1/13/96, Elizabeth 2/2/1798, Polly
    8/14/1801,Rebecah 9/13/03, Melinda 2/8/05, William 10/8/08
    & Harriet 7/14/1811; s William md 6/18/29 Nancy ---; QLF
    states sol dd near Cross Plains, IN, & buried there on the
    old family homestead; QLF 1924 from desc Mrs F E Battin,
    Pierre, SD, states sol wid dd 9/26/1844. R171
BASSHAM, Obadiah, esf 1777-8 Cumberland Co, VA; PN Breckin-
    ridge Co, KY, 1818; ae 63 there 1823 when family w ae 60,
    s Francis ae 15; sol dd 5/28/1840. R171
BASYE, Richard, esf 1777 Fauquier Co, VA; dd 11/4/1822; md
    11/4/1781 Nancy Stallard; wid md (2) 8/25/25 Walter Stal-
    lard, who dd 8/18/27; wid PN ae 82 Spencer Co, KY, 1843.
    R171
BATCHELOR, Peter, esf 1777 VA; PN 1818 Botetourt Co, VA; ae 65
    in 1820 when w ae 79, d Nancy ae 30, gds Reuben Shropshire
    ae 14. R172
BATEMAN, John, BLW issued 8/8/1795. R172
  Susan, former wid/o William ASBERY. R172
  Thomas, esf 1776 Edgecombe Co, NC; b 1/29/1755 Bedford Co,
    VA; afp ae 78 Green Co, MS, 1833; PAR, insufficient proof
    of svc; res 1838 P. O. Leakesville, Green Co, MS. R172
BATES, Ephraim, esf 1777 near Catfish Camp, VA (later Washing-
    ton Co); b 5/24/1743 Morristown, Morris Co, NJ; PN Union
    Township, OH, 1833; dd 1/3/1834; s Isaac 63 in 1833; QLF
    1930 from desc Mrs Homer E Apperson, Cambridge, OH; QLF
    states sol d 6/17/1829, Howard Co, MO, per family bible, &
    w was Rebecca Wiley. R174
  James, esf 1776 New London, Bedford Co, VA; b 1760 Essex Co,
    VA; later esf NC; PN Grant Co, KY, 1833. R174
  James, esf 1777-8 Halifax Co, VA, where PN 1832 ae 72; dd
    there 9/2/1847; md 1/28/1793 Levina Frances Nance there;
    wid PN ae 76 there 1847; QLF states sol md (1) Elizabeth
    Vaughan (b VA 1758-60), (2) Levina Nance, further sol ch
    were: James, William, Samuel h/o Polly Rice, Matthew,
    Molly, Mildred w/o Thomas Gwin, Winifred w/o John Gwin who
    nephew/o Thomas Gwin, Micky w/o John Hamilton of VA, Su-
    sanna w/o David Tyler, Elizabeth, & Polly. R174
  Thomas, esf 1777 Fauquier Co,VA; PN ae 64 Scott Co,KY, 1818.
    R176
  William, esf 1779 Prince Edward Co, VA; b 7/14/1765; PN Bath
    Co, KY, 1818. R176
  William, esf ae 14 Louisa Co,VA; b 1764 Stafford Co, VA; afp
    Amherst Co, VA, 1845; PAR insufficient proof of sv. R176

BATHE, George, see BAITH, George. R177
BATSON, Mardica, esf 1776 VA; PN ae 63 Bourbon Co, KY, 1818;
    dd 1/6/1829; family in 1821 was Rachel Batson ae 61 & Wes-
    ley Batson (no relationship stated); QLF states sol's wid
    Rachel dd Dayton, OH. R177
BATTERSHELL, Freeman, esf VA; md 3/1786 Nancy ---, & their res
    Clark Co & Bourbon Co, KY; sol dd 4/16/1818; wid PN ae 75
    Bourbon Co, KY, 1842, & res 1848 Clark Co, KY; ch births:
    Mary 1/22/1787, Elizabeth 11/7/89, Susannah 1/20/92. Sarah
    2/8/94, Rachel 12/18/95, Nancy 2/2/1798, Peggy 1/22/1800,
    & John 7/14/05; births of ch/o Jacob Hanah Johnson: Cyn-
    thia 11/11/1826, Elizabeth 10/16/28, Margret 10/17/30,
    Nancy 10/7/32, Armilda 7/16/35, Matilda 8/28/37; & Squire
    5/4/39; William Battershell md Elizabeth 10/13/1831, their
    ch births: James 2/2/33, John E 1/14/35, Saryan 3/17/37;
    QLF 1933 from desc Mrs A M McArthur, Santa Barbara, CA,
    states sol her m's great gdf; QLF states family bible does
    not list two ch/o sol & w: William b 1805-6 & Cyntha 1809,
    further that ch Cyntha & Susanna md bro's Osburn & Kelly
    Tucker respectively; response QLF by PN Office was Osburn
    & Cyntha stated 1842 they knew sol well, no relationship
    given. R177
BATTERTON, Samuel, esf 1777 Loudoun Co, VA; PN ae 60 Bourbon
    Co, KY, 1818; in 1820 family w ae 65-67, d who b 9/1798, &
    s; sol dd 6/12/11833; QLF states sol b 1758, w named Lydia
    & sol bro/o Moses. R177
BATTES, Noel, esf 1776 Albemarle Co, VA; to GA few years after
    RW; PN ae 78 "Chandlers Beat", St Clair Co, AL; w mbnn; md
    VA. R178
BATTLES, Shadrach/Shaderick,"a man of color", esf 1778 Amherst
    Co, VA; PN ae 74 Albemarle Co,VA, 1820, w then ae 60. R178
BATTON, Henry, esf 1777 near Uniontown, Fayette Co, PA; b 1750
    Chester Co,PA; after RW res in PA, VA, & IN; PN 1833 Foun-
    tain Co,IN; QLF states sol res Porter Co, IN, 1840, ae 91.
    R178
BATTSON, Mordecai, see BATSON, Mardica. R178
BAUGH, Henry, esf Wythe Co (then Montgomery Co),VA; b 4/4/1760
    Lancaster Co, PA; to Pulaski Co, KY, 1808, where PN 1832;
    dd 10/9/1836; md 1786 (license 3/28/86) Margaret Philippi,
    Montgomery Co, VA; wid PN ae 72 Pulaski Co, KY, 1841; 3rd
    ch Adam ae 50 there 1841. R178
  Jacob; esf 1774 & 1777 Wythe Co,VA; b 10/19/1852-4 Lancaster
    Co, PA; afp 1833 Pulaski Co, KY, aec 80; PAR. R178
  Joseph, esf 1777 Cumberland Co, VA; b 1758 Powhatan Co (then
    Cumberland Co), VA; afp 1843 Calloway Township, St Charles
    Co, MO; PAR, insufficient proof of svc; QLF 1924 from desc
    Kate Baugh (Mrs C M) Anderson, McPherson, KS; QLF states
    sol dd 1846, further sol md Nancy Gentry & their ch: Wil-
    liam, Benjamin, Judith, Alsey, Nancy, Mary, Patsey, & Lu-
    cinda. R178
BAUGHAN, Richard, see BANGHAM, Richard. R178
BAULDWIN, Edward, esf 1782 Caswell Co, NC; b 10/26/1766 Pitt-

BAULDWIN (continued)
   sylvania Co,VA; PN 1832 Hopkins Co,KY, where dd 9/17/1841;
   md 8/27/1786 Drusilla Trigg at home/o her m Mary, Caswell
   NC; wid dd 1/27/1846, leaving 4 ch: Mary Hill, Hiram, Herbert, & Nancy; sol bro Henry res Henderson Co, KY, 1843;
   wid bro Joshua Trigg res 1843 there; sol heirs afp 1851,
   Hopkins Co, KY, when s Hiram ae 57; PAR; surname at times
   spelled BALDWIN. R178
BAUMGARTEL, Leonard, see BAUMGARTNER, Leonard. R179
BAUMGARTEN, Henry, see BAUMGARTENER, Henry. R179
BAUMGARTENER, Henry, esf 1780-82 Strasburg,VA; PN ae 61 Franklin Co, OH, 1818; in 1820 ae 65 & had w ae 54, s ae 18, d
   ae 16, & d ae 9. R179
BAUMGARTNER, Leonard, esf 1782 Winchester, VA; gtd BLW 1828 ae
   73, York Co, PA. R179
BAWCUTT, William, esf 1777; PN ae 68 Winchester, VA, 1828; dd
   8/10/1839, Augusta Co, VA; md there 4/29/1803 Sarah Dixon,
   who PN ae 74 there 1853; wid LWT, dated 10/18/1862, lists
   following: s Archibald D, d Letitia & her ch (Elizabeth,
   Samuel, James, & Robert Byers), Nancy (NRG) w/o Thornton
   Berry, Betsy Lesley (NRG), Rachel Margaret (NRG) w/o John
   S Byers, slave Ben, gds John S Byers; LWT probated Augusta
   Co, VA (NRG means no relationship shown); wid dd 8/29/63;
   s Archibald ae 55-60 then; births of ch/o John Byers: Mat-
   tie 5/28/1844, James T 9/3/48, David Marshall 4/9/50, Mary
   A 1/23/52, & John H 3/26/54; sol d Letitia w/o James Byers
   dd 4/22/69 leaving 7 ch; s Archibald D dd 10/1863. R179
BAWLING, Charles, see BOWLING, Charles. R179
   William, see BOWLING, William. R179
BAXTER, William, esf 1776 VA; b 4/18/1758 Baltimore Co, MD; PN
   1832 Brooke Co,VA; QLF 1926 from desc Mrs E B Miller, West
   Point, MS, states sol liv ae 91 Brooke Co, VA. R180
BAY, David, esf 1776 Westmoreland Co, PA (area then claimed by
   VA); PN ae 63 Champaign Co,OH; w dd 1820, when family s ae
   17 & s ae 19. R181
BAYLES, David, esf 1781 PA; b 7/9/1762 Frederick Co, VA; afp
   1833 Champaign Co, OH; PAR, insufficient proof of 6 months
   svc; AFF 1837 by bro Haydon & sis Betsey Straight, Monon-
   galia Co, VA; QLF 1902 from gds Mason Bayles, Mt Pleasant,
   IA, states sol esf Uniontown, PA, res many years near Mor-
   gantown,VA, & sol War of 1812; Mason Bayles Civil War svc.
   R181
   Elijah, esf Prince William Co, VA; also svc in Indian Wars;
   b 1760, Stafford Co, VA; parents to Prince William Co, VA,
   soon after birth; PN 1832 Sumner Co, TN; dd 3/3/43. R181
   Hezekiah, esf 1776 Loudoun Co, VA; b 4/16/1757 NJ; PN 1832
   Madison Co, AL; md 1778 Loudoun Co, VA. R181
   Jesse, esf 1776 ae 16 Winchester,VA; PN 1818 Bracken Co, KY;
   to Brown Co,OH, 1821; dd 4/27/30; md 4/1787 Jane d/o Moses
   & Rachel Lunsford, Stafford Co, VA; wid PN ae 84 Mason Co,
   KY, 1838, then res with her s Moses Lunsford by former h.
   R181

BAYLEY, Noah, see BAILEY, Noah. R182
   Robert, VA sea svc; dd 9/4/1829 ae 70; md 1/14/1778 Nancy
    d/o William Christopher; wid dd 8/14/1846 ae 84; ch liv
    when f dd: Elijah, Molly, John, & Elizabeth/Betsy w/o ---
    Wessels; in 1855 Elizabeth Wessels, only surv ch/o sol ae
    50 & afp alleging f sailor in navy on board ship ACCOMAC;
    PAR, insufficient proof of svc. R182
   William, see BAILEY, William. R182
   Zadock, PN ae 57 Accomac Co, VA, 1818, when had d Ritter ae
    11 & res with s; sol dd 11/29/1839; surname spelled BAILEY
    at times. R182
BAYLIS, Henry; afb Frederick Co, VA, 1809; BLAR; QLF 1913 from
    desc B W Petty, Grove Hill, Page Co, VA. R182
   William, esf 1777 Frederick Co, VA, where PN 1818 ae 59; fa-
    mily 1821 w ae 57, d Susan ae 18, d Maria ae 15, & d Eliza
    ae 12; md 1780; sol res 1837 Rives Co, MO; sol dd 6/18/43
    or 6/17/44, leaving ch: Mrs Lucy Buck of MS, Mrs Mary/Ma-
    ria L Tutt of MO; gdc mbnn 1850.
BAYLISS, John, esf 1780 VA; PN ae 68 Knox Co, TN, 1818; w ae
    60-65 in 1820 & no ch at home; sol dd 8/6/1824; QLF 1921
    from desc Mrs J L McGarity, Monroe, GA, states sol w most
    likely named Anne, or Elizabeth Anne; QLF 1937 from desc
    Millard Caldwell, US Congressman from FL. R182
BAYLOR, George, esf Caroline Co, VA; died of wounds on Island
    of Bermuda 11/19/1784 where he had gone to recuperate; md
    5/30/1778 Lucy d/o Mann Page the Elder of Mannsfield, near
    Fredericksburg, VA; wid md (2) 1/24/1792 Colonel Nathaniel
    Burwell of James City Co,VA, who dd 3/3/1814; wid PN ae 77
    Clarke Co,VA for svc of George Baylor; in 1802 John W Bay-
    lor only s & heir of sol. R183
   Walker, PN 1789 for disability incurred in svc; to KY 1821;
    dd 1823; in 1934 Miss J C Watkins, Houston, TX, great gdd
    of General Walker Baylor of War of 1812 afp; PAR. R183
BAYLY, Laban, VA sea svc; perished at sea 1794; 1/2 pay PN gtd
    1839 to John J Bayly, adm/o estate of sailor; surname at
    times spelled BAILEY. R183
BAYNE, John, esf 1781 Lunenburg Co, VA; b 1764 Westmoreland Co
    VA; PN 1834 Halifax Co,VA, where dd 5/21/57; md 10/25/1822
    Sally Canada there; wid PN 1857 there ae 66. R183
BAYSE, Richard, see BASYE, Richard. R183
BAYTOP, James, esf 1776; PN ae 66 Gloucester Co, VA, 1820 when
    had 2 d's. R18
   John, esf 1779 VA; dd 1/1799 King & Queen Co, VA; 1/2 pay PN
    gtd 1837 to Philip Taliaferro, adm/o sol estate. R183
BAZWELL, David, esf Mecklenburg Co, VA, where b 1759; to Per-
    son Co, NC, with f & esf NC; to Williamson Co, TN, c1820,
    where PN 1833, when bro John ae 62; dd 12/29/36; md Susan
    --- 6/29/1793; wid afp ae 66 Maury Co, TN, 1840; PAR. R183
BAZZELL, David, see BAZWELL, David. R183
BAZZILL, John, esf 1781 Winchester, VA; PN ae 56 Fauquier Co,
    VA, 1818, when family w ae 59-60, d ae over 20, d aec 12,
    & s aec 20. R183

BEACH, Lodowick B; esf 1779 Chesterfield Co, VA, where b 2/28/1758; to Williamson Co, TN, 1821 where afp 1832; PAR. R184

Richard Bayse, see BEECH, Richard Bayse. R185
BEARCROFT, Lott, BLW issued 1793. R185
BEADLES, Edmund,esf 1779 King William Co,VA,where b 8/31/1764; PN there 1834; AFF there 1834 by Joel Beadles, b 1/12/1761 (no relationship shown); QLF 1936 from Catherine Beadles, Hayfield, KY, states a John Beadles mvd with w Martha Vaughn & 9 ch from Pittsylvania Co,VA, to Graves Co, KY. R185

Joel, esf 1778 King William Co, VA, where b 1/12/1761; PN there 1834. R185
BEAHAM, James, BLW issued 1790. R185
BEAL, John, esf Southampton Co, VA, where b; PN 1832 ae 74 there; md 5/16/1815 Julia ---; wid PN ae 68 Nottoway Co, VA, 1853, & gtd BLW 1855 ae 75 Southampton Co, VA; in 1882 Mary A Lankford of Carrollton, Isle of Wight Co, VA, a wid stated she d/o sol. R186

Nathaniel, see BEALL, Nathaniel. R186

Shadrach of Benjamin Cooper (so-called for distinction), esf 1779 Southampton Co, VA, where b 1763; PN there 1832. R186

Shadrach, esf 1778 Southampton Co, VA; PN ae 60 there 1832. R186

William, BLW issued 1794. R186
BEALE, John, see BEAL, John. R186

Richard E, esf 1776 Stafford Co, VA; PN ae 72 Fauquier Co, VA; dd 1/8/1835; md 1/1808 Mary Elizabeth, wid/o William Grayson, Prince William Co, VA; wid PN ae 74 Washington, DC, 1853

Robert, BLW issued 1794. R186

Robert, dd 1789 Fayette Co, PA; md 1781 wid Elizabeth (---) Stephenson, who gtd BLW 1808 Shelbyville, KY; ch in 1800: Betsy Brooke Beale aec 18 who later md Adam Steele, & Robert aec 13. R186

William, esf 1776 Winchester, VA; PN ae 67 Effingham Co, GA, 1819; family in 1821 w Jane ae 68, Grace Beale ae 28 & her 7-months-old ch (relationship not shown), & gds William Beale ae 8; QLF states sol parents John (b 1730) & Mary (Ross) Beale, John also RW sol. R186
BEALL, Archibald, esf 1776 Bedford Co, VA; b 10/3/1756; to KY 1783; PN 1833 Bourbon Co, KY; dd 7/31/1840; md 3/1785 Milly ---, who PN ae 79 Bourbon Co, KY, 1846; in 1845 eldest ch aec 60. R187

Nathaniel, esf 1779 VA; BLW gtd 1809 Ohio Co, KY. R187
Robert, see BEALE, Robert. R187
BEALLE, Robert, see BEALE, Robert. R187
BEALOR, George, esf Shepherdstown, VA; b 1762 Anspack, Russia; to America (Staten Island, NY) 1777; to Philadelphia, PA, thence Shepherdstown,VA; after RW to Bedford Co,PA, thence Somerset Co, PA; PN 1833 Turkeyfoot Township, Somerset Co, PA; QLF 1931 from desc R S Bane, Henry Co, IL; QLF 1932 from desc Mrs Julia Drake McCracken, Cameron, WV, states

BEALOR (continued)
    sol ch Elizabeth, Nancy, George H, Thomas, Charles, Frede-
    rick, Joseph, & Mary, further d Nancy md Jesse Bane & they
    great great grandparents/o querier; QLF 1932 from desc Mrs
    Walter L Horn, Chicago, IL. R187
BEAM, Michael, esf 1777 Loudoun Co, VA; b 1758 PA; PN 1832
    Jersey Township, Licking Co, OH; QLF 1927 from desc Mrs
    George H Bonnell, Worthington, OH; QLF states sol res with
    Michael Beam Jr 1833 in OH; QLF 1904 from great gds E C
    Beem, Columbus, OH; QLF states sol dd 1855. R188
BEAN, James, esf 1779 Brock's Gap, Rockingham Co, VA, when res
    with family of Thomas Beggs, f/o James Beggs; b 9/22/1762,
    Shenandoah Co, VA; PN 1833 Harrison Co, KY. R189
  John, BLW issued 1790. R189
  Richard, esf 1776 Bedford Co, VA; b 8/1752 Northern Neck,
    Northumberland Co, VA; PN 1833 Lewis Co, KY. R189
BEARD, Francis, esf 1777 York Co, PA, where b 4/15/1753, esf
    1781 where mvd 1779; PN 1833 Preble Co, OH. R190
  Jacob, esf 1781 Shenandoah Co,VA, where b 8/29/1762; PN 1833
    Vernon Township, Clinton Co, OH, where mvd 1831; dd there
    3/27/39; md 9/3/1820 Rosana/Rosena Wendel, Shenandoah Co,
    VA; wid PN ae 66 Clinton Co, OH, 1855. R190
  James, esf 1781 Rockingham Co, VA; b 1761 Augusta Co, VA;
    afp 1845 Rockingham Co, VA; PAR. R190
  Robert, esf 1777 Cumberland Co, VA; esf 1780 Augusta Co, VA;
    PN ae 76 Henry Co, GA, 1833; dd 11/27/1836; md 8/16/1790
    Sarah Hatfield, Augusta Co, VA; wid PN ae 72 Henry Co, GA,
    1841; wid ae 78 Cobb Co, GA, 1849; sol bro John res Madi-
    son Co, GA, 1842. R190
  Robert, esf 1780 Augusta Co, VA; b 3/1/1764; PN Washington
    Co, TN, 1832. R190
  Samuel, esf 1779 Botetourt Co, VA, where b 6/1755; PN 1832
    Henderson Co, TN. R190
  Samuel, esf 1776 Bedford Co, VA, where dd 10/1814, & where
    md 9/8/1778 Mary Mitchell; wid PN ae 83 there 1840; wid dd
    7/28/43; ch births: Harvey 9/7/1780, Betsy 6/22/82, Robert
    7/8-, & Nancy -/24/1786; in 1840 2nd s James H res Bedford
    Co, VA. R190
BEARDEN, John, esf 1777 Spartansburg District, SC; b 3/11/1764
    Spotsylvania Co, VA; to Bedford Co, TN, 1824, where PN
    1833, as John Sr; QLF 1921 from great great gds W H Bear-
    den, Auburn, IL; QLF 1929 from desc Grace Philpott (Mrs
    Bert E) Young, Bloomington, IN. R191
  Richard, see BEARDON, Richard. R191
BEARDON, Richard, esf 1781 Spartansburg District, SC, 7/6/1760
    Granville Co, VA (sic); afp 1826 Wayne Co,TN, when w Sarah
    56 & s John ae 19; PAR, insufficient proof of svc. R191
BEASELEY, Cornelius, see BEAZLEY, Cornelius. R192
BEASLEY, Benjamin, esf 1779 King & Queen Co,VA; b 2/1760 Caro-
    line Co, VA; to NC, thence Grayson Co, VA, where PN 1832;
    dd 4/24/41 Patrick Co, VA; md 9/30/1791 Rachel Prather,
    Stokes Co,NC; wid PN 1847 ae 78; ch births: John 9/5/1792,

60

BEASLEY (continued)
    Susanna 2/24/1794,   Enoch 3/28/96, Nancy 3/21/98, & Ammon
    3/27/1800; sol bro Thomas res Patrick Co, VA, 1833. R192
  John, esf 1776 Accomac Co, VA; PN ae 82 Williamsburg, VA,
    1818; dd 8/21/1819 Accomac Co, VA. R192
  Smith, esf Accomac Co, VA; PN aec 58 Williamsburg, VA, 1818;
    family in 1820: w Fanny aec 60, s Edward ae 8, Accomac Co,
    VA. R192
BEASLY, Leonard, esf 1781 Amelia Co, VA, where b 8/11/1764; to
    Laurens District, SC, 1800, where PN 1832; QLF 1932 from
    desc Elmer W Beasley, Hartford, CT, states sol dd 1844.
    R192
BEATTY, George, esf Loudoun Co, VA; dd 11/1798-99 Montgomery
    Co, KY; md 2/5/1786 Sarah ---, Loudoun Co, VA; wid md (2)
    John Beatty, bro/o sol, & also RW sol himself (see below);
    wid PN ae 74 Montgomery Co, KY; ch/o sol & Sarah births:
    Thomas 11/24/1786-7, James 2/5/88, Melly 4/12/91, Roberta
    9/6/92, Andrew 2/12/96, & ch unnamed; QLF 1915 from desc
    Grace Wyckoff, Los Angeles, CA. R193
  Henry, esf 1776 Frederick Co, MD, where b 1760; to Frederick
    Co,VA, 1780 where esf 1781, & PN 1833; ae 74 in 1836. R193
  James, esf 1775-6 PA in VA regiment; PN ae 80 Cumberland Co,
    PA, 1832. R193
  James, BLW issued 3/4/1796. R193
  John, esf 1778 Loudoun Co, VA; PN ae 63 Montgomery Co, KY;
    dd 6/9/1839; md 7/16/1801 Sarah, wid/o bro George (above),
    Montgomery Co,KY; ch/o sol & Sarah births: Daniel 7/11/02,
    George 12/1/03, Elizabeth 5/26/06, & Cyrene 12/23/08; QLF
    states Sarah & John md Mt Sterling, KY. R193
BEATY, Andrew, esf 1777 Washington Co, VA; b PA; to Cumberland
    Co, KY, 1799, where PN 1834 ae 74 near TN border, when bro
    Alexander ae 66 in same area; sol dd 7/19/1836; QLF states
    a different Andrew Beaty b Ireland, came to America before
    RW, locating at Cow Pasture Springs, VA, thence to Monroe
    Co, IN, by 1800 & dd 1819 ae 72, buried near Bedford, IN,
    leaving s John, s James, & 2 or more d's, further this sol
    great gdf of querier Frank C Wade who res Terre Haute, IN,
    1936. R193
  Walter, not VA connected, but wid May's bro, Robert Miller,
    who bc 9/6/1757, made AFF 1838 when res Wythe Co, VA. R193
  William, esf 1779-80 Loudoun Co, VA; b 10/20/1762 Sussex Co,
    NJ; PN 1832 Scott Co, KY. R193
BEAVER, Jeremiah, esf 1780 Granville Co,NC; b 5/19/1757 Amelia
    Co, VA; PN 1833 Caswell Co, NC; son-in-law John Walker res
    there then. R194
  John, esf PA; afp 1829 Bedford Co, VA; PAR; surname at times
    spelled BEVER. R194
  Obadiah, see BABER, Obadiah. R194
BEAVERS, John, esf 1780 Mecklenburg Co, VA; PN ae 70 Barren Co
    KY, 1832. R194
  Samuel, esf 1780 Loudoun Co, VA, where b 1/18/1762; to Fair-
    fax Co, VA, 1794, thence Washington Township, Muskingum Co,

BEAVERS (continued)
OH, 1815, where PN 1832; dd there 6/23/1844; md 5/8/1789
(MB 5/6/1789) Jane Flood of Cameron Parish, Loudoun Co, VA
who PN ae 79 Muskingum Co, OH, 1847 & res 1855 Zanesville,
OH; QLF 1920 from gdd Mary W (Mrs C P) Simpson, Sullivan
Harbor, ME. R194
BEAZELEY, James, esf 1776 Orange Co,VA; b 8/10/1760; dd Orange
Co, VA 5/18/1821; md 1/14/1779 Mary Sanford (b 9/11/1760);
wid PN 1842 Greene Co, VA; ch births: John 8/6/1780 (md
12/23/1802 Lucy Porter (b 9/22/1780), Sanford 3/24/83,
Nancy 5/11/86, Elizabeth 2/4/89, Robert 5/9/91, James
2/18/94, Polley 4/10/97, Lucy 9/217/99 & dd 3/17/1801, &
Durrett 2/9-11/1802. R194
BEAZELY, James, see BEAZELEY, James. R194
BEAZLE, Len, see BEASLY, Leonard BEASLY. R194
BEAZLEY, Cornelius, esf 1777 Caroline Co, VA; PN ae 66, Frede-
rick Co,VA, 1824; in 1820 w decd & no ch liv with him; res
1835 Berryville, Frederick Co, VA; res 1837 P. O. Bowling
Green, Pike Co, MO, with d; PN increased when ae 82 there
1840. R194
  Cornelius, b Charlottte Co, VA; afp aec 90 Marengo Co, AL,
  1844; PAR. R194
  Ephraim, esf 1779 Caroline Co,VA; b 2/11/1762; PN 1832 South
  Farnham Parish, Essex Co, VA; dd 7/1/1833. R194
  James, see BEAZELEY, James. R194
BECHER, John, esf 1778 Lebanon Co, CT; PN ae 56, Berne Town-
ship, Berks Co,PA; dd 3/22/1819; wid Mary Ann dd 11/11/37;
ch & only heirs 1854: John (Berks Co, PA), William, Barba-
ra Nyswender (both of Franklin Co, OH), Margaret Mullner
(Philadelphia, PA), Benjamin, Jacob, Catharine Paxon (Che-
ster Co,PA), Samuel (Lancaster Co, PA), Lydia Cook (Clarke
Co, VA); QLF 1928 from great gdd Ednah Wilson (Mrs H K Mc-
Adams, Lexington, KY, states sol's f Emanuel BUCHER emi-
grant from Germany & md Mary Albert of Reading, Coaleco
Township, Lancaster Co, PA, further sol had a md d Betty
Sagner. R194
BECK, Jeffrey/Geoffrey, esf 1778 Randolph Co,NC; b Augusta Co,
VA; PN aec 81 Pickens District, SC, 1833. R195
  Jesse, esf 1781 Albemarle Co, VA, where b 9/1758; PN 1832
  Amherst Co, VA; dd 5/4-8/41 there; md there 12/5/1785 Ann
  Hughes; wid PN ae 77 there 1843; ch births: Susannah
  9/1/1788, Fanney 3/16/90, Elihu 8/22/91, William 7/23/93
  (dd 7/4/94), Jesse 4/1/95, John 4/5/97, & Reuben 3/18/99.
  R195
  John, BLW issued 6/3/1791; esf MD?, dd 8/29/1816 Ohio Co,VA,
  where mvd 1791, res near West Liberty; md 6/13/1784 Rebecka d/o Nathaniel Miller, Chestertown, Kent Co, MD; wid PN
  ae 76 near Wheeling, Ohio Co, VA, 1840; wid stated 1843 ae
  81; wid dd 8/22/53; ch births: Elizabeth 3/9/1785 (dd
  9/1796), Mary 10/8/86, Rebekah 12/14/88, John Wesley
  7/4/91, Alexander Miller 3/16/93 (dd 4/8/96), William Fletcher 10/20/95, Francis Asbury 9/3/97 (res 1840 Ohio Co,

BECK (continued)
VA), George Washington 8/3/99 (dd 6/11/1806), James Amenious 5/11/1801 (dd 8/4/02), Susanna Miller 6/9/03, & Rachel 8/7/06 (dd 12/26/06); ch surv sol: Mary Lauck, Rebekah Burns, John Wesley, William Fletcher, Francis Asbury, Susannah; d Rebekah Burns dd, leaving ch: George, Alexander, Elizabeth, & Susannah Burns; in 1840 Reverend Simion Lauck made AFF Ohio Co, VA; wid sis Elizabeth Walker res Kent Co MD 1839; in 1840 Samuel Beck ae 71 & Samuel Miller ae 85, both natives of Kent Co, MD, res Brooke Co, VA; QLF 1912 from great gdd Mrs Victor F Cooper, Harrisville, WV. R195

John Sr, esf VA; b 2/4/1762; dd 7/11/1824 Elbert Co, GA; md 6/5/1784 Sarah Wanslow, Albemarle Co, VA, who b 3/6/1765; wid afp 1856 Murray Co, GA, & PAR, insufficient proof of sol svc; family bible data: Sarah L Beck b 4/3/1803, John Henderson md 1/29/1805 Matilda Beck, Charles N B Carter md 5/3/1838 Eugenia M Beck;James Beck Henderson b 10/24/1806; James Beck dd 6/14/1787, John Beck Jr dd 2/28/1789; QLF states sol md Sara Wansley, & their s William Andrew; QLF 1931 from Mrs A L Dabney, Monroe,LA, states different John Beck (b VA 1754,dd 1818) md Ann Huguenin (b 1773, dd 1836) & they res Scott Co, GA, & querier's ancestors. R195

BECKET, Humphrey, see BECKETT, Humphrey. R196

BECKETT, Humphrey, esf 1777 Frederick Co, VA; PN ae 61 Albemarle Co,VA, 1818; in 1828 family w Susannah ae 69, d Patsey ae 30, d Jemima ae 25; w dd 10/29/1829; sol to Pendleton Co, KY, 1831, to Pickaway Co, OH, 1832, & dd 9/16/39. R196

BECKHAM, James; esf 1776-7 VA; PN ae 56 Frederick Co,VA, 1818; dd 4/22/28; ch recd PN 1840. R196

William, esf 1776 VA; PN ae 63 Amherst Co, VA, 1821 when family w Salley ae 58, d Susanne ae 14; res 1829 Buckingham Co, VA. R196

BECKNEL, Thomas, esf 1780 Wilkes Co,NC; b 3/1763 Albemarle Co, VA; PN 1832 Madison Co, KY, where gtd BLW 1857; QLF 1911 from gds (maternal side) W K Azbill, Cleveland, OH, states sol d aec 104. R196

BECKTEL, George, esf Millerstown, Shenandoah Co, VA; PN aec 56 New Holland, Lancaster Co, PA, 1818; in 1820 w Susan ae 35. R196

BEDINGER, Christopher, esf 1776 PA; PN ae 59 Frederick Co, VA, 1818; in 1820 w Mary aec 60, plus 4 d's, eldest aec 25 & youngest aec 11; sol dd 7/23/1824; md 8/10/1786-7 Mary Sanders, Morris Co, NJ; wid PN ae 73 Hardy Co, VA, 1838; AFF 1839 by Joseph Parker ae 67 that he md Phebe Sanders, sis/o sol w Mary, & that sol & w in 1792 had 4 ch. R198

Daniel, esf 1776 VA; BLW issued 8/25/1789; dd 3/17/1817-8 Jefferson Co, VA; md 4/1791 Sarah Rutherford, Berkeley Co, VA; wid PN ae 67 Jefferson Co, VA, 1838; wid dd 7/14/44; surv ch 1852: Susan B w/o N E Cornwall, Henrietta w/o E I Lee, & Henry; sol gdc 1852: ch/o decd d Elizabeth Bedinger Washington (Benjamin F, Daniel B, Lawrence B, Sally,

BEDINGER (continued)
George, John T, Mary E, Mildred B, Susan, Georgiana w/o
John W Smith), ch/o decd d Margaret Bedinger Foster (Mar-
garet w/o James H Morrison), ch/o decd d Mary Bedinger
Bryan (John L Jr, Sarah B w/o William S/L Long), ch/o decd
d Virginia Bedinger Lucas (William Jr, Sally E w/o Everett
W Bedinger, Daniel B, Virginia); QLF 1936 from desc Eliza-
beth (Mrs W R) Swan, Columbus, OH. R198

George Michael, esf 1775 Shepherdstown, Berkeley Co, VA; svc
in Indian Wars also; b12/10/1756 York Co, PA; PN 1836 Nicholas Co, KY, where dd 12/8/1843; md 2/11/1793 Henrietta
Clay, at home/o her sis Matty Bedford, Bourbon Co, KY; wid
PN ae 68 there 1844, when res with s Daniel P; sis Matty
Bedford res 1844 there stated sol wid 5 years older than
she; AFF 1834 by sol bro Henry ae 81 Berkeley Co, VA; wid
requested PN increase 1865; QLF 1930 from Mrs A K Lewis of
Big Timber, MT, states she & bro gdc/o sol s Daniel P, &
ch/o Daniel's d Olivia w/o Richard H Lindsay. R198

Henry, esf 1777 VA; BLW issued 8/25/1795; PN 1828 Berkeley
Co, VA; dd 5/14/1843 Jefferson Co, VA, surv ch: Mrs Nancy
Swearingen, & Elizabeth w/o Braxton D Davenport of Jeffer-
son Co, VA. R198

BEDLE, Francis, esf 1777 Washington Co, PA, where f & family
mvd Fall 1775; b 11/13/1758 NJ; PN 1832 Warren Co, OH; d
Rhoda Mills, a wid res Cincinnati,OH, afp 1858 stating sol
dd c1837. R198

BEDSELL, John, see BETSILL, John. R198

BEECH, Lodowick B, see BEACH, Lodowick B. R200

BEECH, Richard Bayse, esf Lunenburg Co, VA; dd 4/7/1810; md
there 8/14/1774 Mary Akin; wid afp ae 90 there 1839 & PAR;
ch births: James B 10/11/1775, William B 2/8/79, Pheby B
9/14/82, & Lodowick B 9/10/86; other family bible data:
Lodowick B Beech md 8/28/1811 Elizabeth Beech, Mary Ann
Cheatom (d/o William Ellis Jr & w/Nancy) b 12/12/1809; Be-
thiah (d/o Phebe Bailey) b7/10/1815; AFF 1839 Lunenburg Co
VA, by wid sis Elizabeth Akin Ellis. R200

BEECHER, John, see BECHER, John. R200

BEEKMAN, William, esf 1775 Rowan Co, NC; esf 178- Princeton,
Somerset Co, NJ; b 8/27/1755 near Germantown, NJ; after RW
res Loudoun Co, VA, then Hampshire Co, then Mason Co, KY,
then Ross Co (later Pike Co), OH; dd 6/13/1834 Mifflin
Township, Pike Co, OH; md 7/1781 Sarah Furman, NJ; wid b
7/10/1761 & PN 1843 Mifflin Township, Pike Co, OH; wid dd
6/24/47; ch births: Gabriel 5/10/1782, Christopher 9/6/84,
William 1/1/1788, Abraham 10/13/90, Aaron 3/31/93, Mary
11/26/95 (md Josiah Pillars), John 5/22/99 (dd 7/1851), &
Elizabeth 12/12/02 (md Thomas Johnson); other family bible
births, all BEEKMAN: William 6/11/1803, Mary 12/13/1806,
Furman 2/18/1809, Delilah 11/2/1810. R201

BEELER, George, see BEALOR, George. R201

BEELER, Jacob, esf 1775 NC; mvd to NC 4/1770 from Frederick Co
VA; PN ae 70 Sullivan Co, TN, 1832; QLF states Jacob bro/o

BEELER (continued)
    Joseph; QLF 1914 from Newton Hacker, Jonesboro, TN, states
    his great grandm Martha d/o sol. R201
BEESLY, Isaac, esf 1778 Monongalia Co, VA; b 1753 Loudoun Co,
    VA; afp 1833 Lewis Co, VA; PAR, no proof of svc. R203
BEETEM, Adam, esf 1776 Berks Co, PA, where b 1759; esf 1780
    VA; PN 1833 Henry Co, KY; QLF 1914 from desc Charles Gil-
    lett Beetem, Montgomery Co, PA. R203
BEGEANT, John; esf 1777 Winchester, VA; b 8/10/1761; PN 1824
    Frederick Co, VA, w then ae 62. R203
  William, esf 1781 VA; PN ae 78 Loudoun Co, VA, 1833; f sol
    in French & Indian War under General Braddock. R203
BEGLEY, Henry, esf 1782 Montgomery Co (now Wythe Co), VA; b
    3/4/1756 Hampshire Co, VA; afp 1844 Morgan Co, TN, & PAR;
    md at res/o Richard Davis; bro William AFF 1844 Montgomery
    Co, TN. R203
BEGLY, Henry, see BEGLEY, Henry. R203
BELCHER, Bartlet; esf 1780 Patrick Co, VA; b 6/8/1764 Chester-
    field Co, VA; PN 1832 Hawkins Co, TN; dd 4/8/48; md Alice
    ---- 7/20/1799, Patrick Co, VA; wid PN ae 81 Hancock Co,
    1849; ch births: Sarah 2/17/1801, George 6/11/03, John
    2/16/05, Lana 3/31/07, Joseph 1/5/10, & Elizabeth 10/5/13.
    R203
  Robert, esf 1776 VA; PN aec 60 Spartanburg District, SC,
    1820; w dd 5/1837; res with s Jacob 4/38 Monroe Co, TN;
    returned 10/38 to Spartanburg, SC, to res with other ch;
    dd 4/26/45. R203
BELEW, Solomon; esf 1778 Orange Co, VA; PN aec 63 Pendleton Co
    KY, 1818, where dd 9/18/18; md 6/9/1778 Elinia, Orange Co,
    VA, at home/o Colonel Robert Johnson where they res; wid
    b 6/9/1756 & PN 1840 Pendleton Co, KY; 1st s Elijah, who b
    6/9/1779, liv 1840. R204
BELFIELD, John, BLW issued 12/11/1797; QLF states Major John
    Belfield an original member of Society of the Cincinnati.
    R204
BELKNAP, Thomas, esf 1776 Kingston, Ulster Co,NY; dd Hampshire
    Co, VA, 12/18/1835; md 10/17 1791 Naomi Dare, Philadelphia
    PA; wid PN aec 68 Hampshire Co, VA, 1839, & gtd BLW 1855
    Braxton Co, VA; d Nancy ae 18 Pendleton Co, VA, 1810; QLF
    1933 from gdd Eliza Belknap Albert, Ogden, UT; (following
    data in file on a War of 1812 sol Thomas Belknap: b Frede-
    rick Co or Pendleton Co, VA, 1779-1797, s/o John; esf 1814
    Hampshire Co, VA; PN 1871 Braxton Co, WV; dd 11/30/1883 on
    Cedar Creek, Otter District, that Co ; md (1) Mary "Polly"
    Friend who dd that Co 3/4/1850; md (2) 7/26/50 Emsey Fish-
    er, that Co; wid PN ae 60-65 that Co 1885, & dd 3/2/1907;
    in 1885 d Lucerne ae 22 & s John ae 25). R205
BELL, Benjamin; esf 1780 Washington Co,PA; b 1762 Berkeley Co,
    VA; to PA with father, as small ch; afp 1843 Clay Co, IN,
    when bro Nathaniel ae 86 res Johnson Co, IN; PAR, svc not
    in regularly organized military unit; QLF 1933 from desc
    Elouise (Mrs Scott C) Hanna, Minneapolis, MN. R205

BELL, Daniel, esf 1779 Stafford Co, VA, where b 4/14/1765; PN
1835 Mason Co, KY; dd c1840; surv d liv 1875. R205
  Henry, BLW issued 1/7/1814; afp 1811 Campbell Co, VA, & PAR.
  R205
  John, esf 1776 Paxton Township, Lancaster Co,PA, for VA svc;
  after RW returned to home/o f Dauphin Co,PA; PN ae 81 Pike
  Township, Clearfield Co, PA, 1833. R206
  John, esf 1782 Prince William Co, VA; b 5/15/1762; PN Prince
  William Co, VA, 1833; requested PN increase 1834 Washing-
  ton, DC. R206
  John, esf 1780 Augusta Co, VA, where b 9/1755 Long Glade in
  that Co; PN 1834 Long Glade. R206
  John, esf 1775 Stafford Co, VA, where b 1750; PN 1842 Marion
  Co, KY, when w Sarah already decd, & sol res with s John
  for past 20 years; s John dd 1842. R206
  John, esf Augusta Co, VA; bc 1757; PN 1795, disability from
  wounds; dd c1831; md Margaret Patterson. R206
  Joseph, esf 1776 VA; b 2/1755 Augusta Co, VA, where PN 1832.
  R207
  Nathaniel, esf 1778 Washington Co,PA; b 1757 Berkeley C, VA;
  afp 1843 Johnson Co, IN; PAR, insufficient svc; bro Benja-
  min res ae 81 Clay Co,IN, 1843; QLF states sol w Mary ---.
  R207
  Richard, esf VA as indian spy for VA troops; PN 1833 Harrison Co, VA; dropped from PN rolls 1835 by PN Office, who
  stated PN improperly gtd, (svc not in regularly organized
  unit). R207
  Robert Sr, esf c1777 Montgomery Co, VA, where PN 1833; b
  12/25/1758. R207
  Samuel, esf 1782 Sampson Co, NC; b 5/1749 Surry Co, VA; PN
  1832 Robeson Co, NC; QLF 1902 from great gds F W Maxwell,
  Springfield, IL. R207
  Samuel, esf 1777 Augusta Co,VA, where b 1759; PN there 1834;
  dd there 5/15/1838; md 12/7/1815 Rebekah Hays; wid PN ae
  75 Augusta Co, VA, 1854. R207
  Samuel, esf 1781 MD; PN ae 55 Harrison Co, VA, 1818; res Washington, DC, 1833 when family: s Benjamin ae 17, s Aza ae
  12, d Sarah ae 14, & s Samuel ae 9; gds George S Beall res
  1856 Parkersburg, Wood Co, VA; QLF 1931 from great gdd Mrs
  Marjorie McCaddon Wirt, Peoria, IL; surname spelled BEALL
  at times. R207
  Thomas, esf 1781 Berkeley Co, VA; b 7/25/1756 on Rock Creek
  in MD which area now in Washington, DC; PN 1833 Washington
  DC; PN 1833 Washington Co, TN; dd 3/30/1837; md 2/22/1783
  Mary Edwards, Berkeley Co, VA; wid dd 8/6/1839; surv ch in
  1854: Brooks H ae 60 (res Washington Co, TN), Joseph ae 67
  (res Greene Co, TN); Andrew ae 57 (res Greene Co, TN), Rebecca ae 54 (res Washington Co, TN); QLF 1919 from great
  great great gdd Mrs R C Howard, Greeneville, TN, states s
  b Iredell Co, NC, & had other ch John & Jake, & s Brooks
  was War of 1812 sol. R207
  Thomas, esf 1777 Albemarle Co, VA, where b 1760; esf 1780 KY

BELL (continued)
    where later esf for War of 1812; PN 1833 Henry Co, KY; dd
    5/11/1841 leaving wid. R207
  Thomas, esf 1777 Frederick Co, VA; b Frederick Co, MD; afp
    1835 Bullitt Co, KY, while res Nelson Co, KY; PAR, insuf-
    ficient svc. R207
  Thomas, BLW issued 3/1/1796. R207
  William, esf 1777 Franklin Co, VA; b 5/1754 Orange Co, VA;
    PN 1833 Barren Co, KY, where had res for c38 years. R207
  William, esf 1777 VA; PN ae 85 Muskingum Co, OH, 1818. R207
  William, esf 1781 VA; afb ae 91 Spotsylvania Co, VA, 1855;
    PAR, insufficient svc. R207
BELOTE, Jonas, esf 1777 Accomac Co, VA, where b 12/8/1760; PN
    1834 Fayette Co, TN; BLW 1855 Hardeman Co, TN; dd 4/7/57;
    QLF 1897 from desc Katharine M Cannon, Forest Glen, MD;
    QLF 1925 from desc Miss Thuria Belote, St Louis, MO; QLF
    1917 from Byrd Belote, Valdosta, GA, states sol of French
    parentage; QLF states sol buried La Grange, TN; QLF 1917
    from great gdd Mrs F B Clarke, Quitman, GA; QLF 1928 from
    great great gdd Alice Emily Topy, Louisville, KY. R209
BELOTTE, Jonas, see BELOTE, Jonas. R209
BELVIN, Aaron, esf 1776 VA; PN ae 64 Gloucester Co, VA, 1818.
    R209
BENEGER, George, see BENIGER, George. R213
BENGE, David, esf 1779 Wilkes Co, NC; b 8/1760 Albemarle Co,
    VA; to KY 1790; PN 1834 Clay Co, KY; dd 3/3/1854; QLF 1940
    from desc Stella Risner, Pineville, KY. R213
  Obadiah M, esf Surry Co, NC; b 1763 Surry Co, VA; afp 1843
    DeKalb Co, AL, & PAR; dd there 3/23/1846; md after 1800
    Sarah ---, who afp 1852 DeKalb Co, AL, & PAR; wid res 1853
    Hollingsville, AL; ch births: Patsey 9/22/1786, Elizebeth
    6/30/88, W B 3/22/90, GC 2/21/1802, & Robert 6/1/03. R213
BENIGER, George, esf 1781 Frederick Co,VA; b 8/28/1763 Lancas-
    ter Co, PA; to Berkeley Co, VA, 1806, thence 1807 Belmont
    Co, OH; afp 1833 Green Township, Fayette Co, OH, & PAR; dd
    3/27/1837, surv ch: Sarah Gregory, Mary Stinson, George, &
    Samuel; George & Samuel res 1854 Fayette Co, OH; AFF 1854
    by John Stinson there; QLF states sol s/o Jonathan Bingar
    & Elizabeth Mercer (originally from MD) who md 6/17/1768,
    further sol md 2/8/1793 Mary Bennett; another QLF states
    sol md Mary Mattock. R213
BENJAMIN, Joseph, esf 1775 Amelia Co, VA; PN 1818 ae 70 Cecil
    Co, MD; in 1820 family w ae 59 & d ae 14; dd 10/7/1825;
    QLF 1902 from gds Dr D Benjamin, Camden, NJ; QLF 1924 from
    desc Mrs J N Deyo, Roselle Park, NJ, states sol b 1748 &
    dd 1830. R214
BENNATT, Richard, esf 1776 VA; PN ae 74 Lunenburg Co,VA, 1832;
    dd 9/17/1832. R214
BENNETT, George, esf 1781 SC; b 12/29/1759 Frederick Co, VA;
    afp 1833 Spartanburg District, SC; PAR. R218
  John, sol in Lee's Legion; BLW issued 2/17/1792. R219
  Jordon, esf VA, losing leg Battle of Guilford; dd 10/4/1822

BENNETT (continued)
    10/4/1822 Mecklenburg Co, VA; md there 12/1795 Ann "Nancy"
    Murphy; wid PN ae 76 there 1852; wid gtd BLW ae 79 there
    1855. R219
  Joseph, esf 1776 Mecklenburg Co, VA, where b; PN ae 76 there
    1833; to Rutherford Co, TN, 1838 to be near ch. R219
  Peter, esf 1780 Granville Co,NC; dd 4/9/1922; md c1773 Eli-
    zabeth ---, King William Co, VA; wid dd 7/8/1845; afp ar-
    rears 1851 Knox Co, TN, by her heirs Dorias Bennett & R M
    Bennett; PAR, insufficient proof; heirs res Morgan Co, TN,
    1857 referred to sol as Peter G Bennett; QLF states sol md
    Elizabeth Pomfret, further adm/o sol estate was s Haywood,
    further wid s-in-law Samuel White adm/o her estate, he ae
    61 in 1851; QLF states sol d Nancy Ann w/o Richard Beard-
    en, & sol d Polly w/o Samuel White, further sol other ch:
    Sally, Jane, James D, & Haywood G. R219
  Richard, see BENNATT, Richard. R220
  Richard, esf 1777 VA; PN ae 56 Scott Co, KY, 1818; res ae
    Owen Co, KY, 1820, when family w & ch who ae 3 & 9 months;
    dd 1829. R220
  Richard, esf 1781 Richmond, VA; 1st w dd 1813; afp ae 63
    Warren Co, OH, 1825 when had 7 ch; PN ae 69 there 1832; dd
    1/14/1835; md (2) 1826 Margaret Turvey, had s Abram by her
    (he aec 3 in 1836); wid PN ae 70 Lawrence Co, OH, 1857;
    sol older bro William RW sol; other bro Daniel; s Abram
    liv 1857. R220
  William, esf 1777 Saratoga Co, NY; b 1/18/1746; PN 1832 Ty-
    ler Co, VA; dd 2/20/1843. R220
  William, esf 1780 VA; dd 7/17/1826; md 11/17/1782 Mary Ed-
    wards, Brunswick Co, VA; wid afp ae 82 Coffee Co, TN, 1846
    & PAR. R220
  William; s Henry afp Pittsylvania Co, VA, 1854, & PAR. R220
  William, sea svc; esf VA; dd 1846; adm/o sol estate Coving-
    ton Bennett applied for 1/2 pay PN 1846, Pungoteague, VA,
    & PAR. R220
BENNEVILLE, Daniel, see DeBENNEVILLE, Daniel. R221
BENNINGTON, Job; esf 1777 PA; PN ae 67 Rockbridge Co,VA. R221
BENSON, Enoch, esf 1780 Culpeper Co, VA, where b 12/1756; mvd
    to Greenville District, SC, 1785; PN 1832 Gwinnett Co, GA;
    bro Zachariah his sub for part of svc; QLF states sol eld-
    est s Reuben. R221
  Henry "Harry", dd 11/1/1828 Lawrence Co, MS; md c1792 in VA
    Nancy ---, who dd Lawrence Co, MS, 6/28/1834; ch: Cynthia,
    Hiram J, Herod, Alfred, Jana, Lina, Minna, Pharaoh, Parth-
    ena, & Job; Herod, Alfred, & Job all decd in 1857; sol ch
    who afp 1857 Lawrence Co,MS: Cynthia w/o Prue Benson, Par-
    thena w/o W H McMurtrey, Lina w/o John Newsom, Jana w/o
    John Martin, Minna w/o Benjamin B Barnes, Hiram J, & Pha-
    raoh. R221
  Levin, esf 1774 Augusta Co, VA; PN ae 77 Greenbrier Co, VA,
    1832; dd 11/14/1835; md 8/17/1779 Jane ---; wid afp ae 81
    Knox Co, IL, 1844, & PAR; QLF 1889 from desc James B Mc-

BENSON (continued)
    Crellis, Washington, DC; QLF 1903 from great gdd Mrs Sarah
    Benson Ranne, Hanover, IN; QLF 1889 from great gds L C
    Jones, Madison, IN. R222
  William, esf 1777 Culpeper Co or Prince William Co,VA, while
    res with Uncle Porter; b 9/17/1759; f dd 1765, & m mvd to
    home/o sol's f's sis, Molly Miller; m dd c1768; sol dd
    4/14/1834, Wilkes Co, GA; md 9/19/1786 Sarah Seale, Prince
    William Co, VA, she sis/o John; wid PN ae 82 there 1853, &
    dd 6/30/1854; large family of ch. R222
BENTLEY, Efford, esf 1776 Amelia Co, VA, where b; PN ae 73 Ma-
    dison Co, AL, 1833, where mvd 1823; dd 7/1837; QLF states
    full name of sol Peter Efford Bentley, he enlisting ae 16.
    R223
  Jeremiah, esf 1777 Amelia Co, VA; b 5/1/1759; PN 1818 Giles
    Co, TN, when w aec 57; res 1821 Lawrence Co, TN, where dd
    5/1841 leaving s John who res 1854 Lauderdale Co, AL. R223
  William, esf VA; BLW issued 12/12/1794; PN 1818 Powhatan Co,
    VA; d Jane Ligon afp 1851 Petersburg, VA; QLF from desc
    Mrs W L Peel, Atlanta, GA. R223
BENTLY, Thomas, esf 1781 Pitt Co, NC, where PN 1833; b 1759
    VA. R223
BERGERHOFF, Nicholas, esf 1777 Philadelphia, PA; PN ae 62 Pen-
    dleton Co, VA, 1819; in 1820 family w Elizabeth & 5 d's:
    Catharine ae 24, Susanna ae 22, Mary ae 18, Sally ae 16, &
    Lydia ae 17; sol res 1832 Crawford Co, OH; QLF 1901 from
    gdd Sarah C Daughmer, Little Sandusky, OH, states sol na-
    tive/o WV. R225
BERKELY, George, see BERKLEY, George. R225
BERKLEY, George, esf 1779 VA; dd 1819 Charlotte Co, VA; md Sa-
    rah "Sally", d/o John Wheeler, 11/2/1784; wid PN ae 70
    Charlotte Co, VA, 1839; wid res 1845 Campbell Co, VA, ae
    79. R225
  John, esf 1779 King George Co, VA, where b 11/20/53; PN 1832
    Scott Co, KY; QLF 1920 from great gdd Molly Berkley (Mrs
    John Adams) Herring states sol ch: Robert (gdf/o querier &
    md 1806 Mary Cooper), William, & John. R225
  William, esf 1777 Loudoun Co, VA; b 1/7 or 1/17/1755 Frede-
    rick Co, VA, s/o William who dd Loudoun Co, VA; PN 1832
    Winchester, Clark Co, KY; some bro's spelled name BARTLETT
    while others BARCLAY or BERKLEY; QLF states sol b PA & res
    Rockbridge Co, VA. R225
BERKSHIRE, Maria, former wid/o Joshua PREWITT. R225
BERLIN, Jacob; esf 1776 Easton, PA; b 1750 Berks Co, PA; mvd
    1792 to Frederick Co, VA, where PN 1832; res there 1841.
    R225
BERNARD, Benjamin, see BARNARD, Benjamin. R225
  Thomas, esf 1776 VA; b Cumberland Co,VA; to OH 1807 where PN
    1818 ae 61; dd 6/12/33 or 6/11/34, buried in Pleasant Hill
    Cemetery, Highland Co,OH; md 12/29/1792 Virginia/Mary, d/o
    Meshack Hicks, Goochland Co, VA; wid dd 5/6/1847 at home/o
    s-in-law Francis H Smithson, Clinton Co, OH; ch in 1850:

BERNARD (continued)
   Elizabeth aec 58 w/o Francis H Smithson, John aec 54, Sarah w/o William Morris, George W (b 9/1799 Goochland Co,
   VA), Thomas aec 49, Mary/Polly aec 45 w/o John Underwood,
   Susan/Susana (already decd, w/o Samuel Ross/Reese), Nancy
   aec 38 w/o Thomas Riley; ch/o decd d Susan: Mary Ellen,
   Thomas, Harriett, John, William, & Samuel; sol bro Richard
   minister in Highland Co,OH, 1820, who md 1798 Mary Walker,
   Rockbridge Co, VA, mvd family 1805 to Highland Co, OH, &
   dd there 1835; Meshack Hicks, bro/o sol w, res 1847 Gooch-
   land Co, VA, h/o Ann Elizabeth; in 1847 sol wid bro John,
   sis Nancy Carroll, & sis Salley liv; all/o sol ch liv 1850
   Highland Co, OH, except John; surname spelled BARNARD at
   times; QLF 1936 from desc Frederick F Bernard, Glendale,
   OH; QLF 1909 from desc F F Bernard, Cincinnati, OH. R225
   Walter, esf 1776-7 Loudoun Co, VA;f b Frederick Co, MD, bap-
   Rock Creek Church; PN 1832 ae 74 Franklin Co (then Henry
   Co), VA. R225
BERRY, Benjamin, esf 1775 NJ, where b near Monmouth Court
   House; mvd to VA fall/o 1778, where esf 1780 Rockingham Co
   & PN there 1832; dd 12/14/34 leaving ch mbnn; bro John liv
   1832. R226
   Benjamin, esf 1776 King George Co, VA, where b; mvd to Mason
   Co, KY, c 1813 where PN 1833 aec 77; dd before 1/5/37 lea-
   ving 1 ch William; sol bro Reuben, 10 years younger, res
   Bracken Co, KY, 1831; QLF states sol s/o Joseph & b 1756
   King George Co, VA, further sol md Sarah, & their ch: Da-
   niel, Franklin, William, Nancy, Jane, Rebecca, Elizabeth,
   Martin, Susan, & Benjamin. R226
   Francis, esf Washington Co, VA; b 1762 Augusta Co, VA, but
   principally raised Washington Co, VA; to TX 1822 where afp
   1852 Caldwell Co; PAR. R226
   George, esf 1776 VA; PN 1818 Logan Co,KY; res 1822 Henderson
   Co, KY, ae 71; dd 10/29/23; QLF 1932 from great great gdd
   Mrs J H Carlile, Paducah, TX, states sol b 6/26/1756. R226
   James, esf 1777 Bucks Co, PA; PN 1818 Russell Co, VA; res
   1833 Montgomery Co, VA, ae 83; dd 12/4/36 leaving wid Mar-
   garet; QLF from desc Sue H Berry, Washington, DC; QLF 1895
   from desc Henry Berry, Washington, DC; QLF 1906 from desc
   Miss A M Honeywell, Hoopeston, IL; QLF 1931 from desc Ce-
   cile B McIntosh, Flushing, Long Island,NY, states sol mid-
   dle name Washington & md Margaret Plot. R226
   James, esf VA; PN 1809, disability from wounds; dd 2/12/1822
   Madison Co, KY; md 3/28/1785 Sarah Grubbs, Lincoln Co, KY;
   wid afp aec 78 Madison Co, KY, 1839, when s ae 55 there;
   PAR, sol svc less than 6 months. R226
   Joel, esf 1775 King George Co, VA, where b 1754; PN 1833
   Pendleton Co, KY; to IN 1838; dd 2/28/43 leaving d; QLF
   states sol s/o William & dd Rushville, IN; QLF 1917 from
   desc Martha B Kimble, Brookville, IN. R227
   John, esf 1778 Augusta Co, VA, where b 12/27/1760; PN 1832
   Harrison Co, KY, where dd 8/12/38; md 6/4/1802 Elizabeth

BERRY (continued)

Claypole, Bourbon Co, KY; wid PN ae 71 Harrison Co, KY, 1853, & res there 1855; QLF 1911 from desc Henrietta M Berry, University Park, CO, states sol wid dd 1863. R227

John, PN Shenandoah Co, VA; PN papers lost 1814 when British burned Washington, DC; PN increase 1818 automatic, not requiring sol request; QLF 1926 from desc Edith (Mrs Elwood) Stevenson, Faribault, MN; QLF states sol originally PN in 1804. R227

Peter, esf 1779; s Thomas gtd BLW 1828 Bedford Co, VA. R227

Robert, MD sea svc, esf Annapolis, MD; res Gloucester Co, VA when dd 1813; md 11/4/1773 Lucy Rhodes, after which mvd to Annapolis, MD; wid PN ae 84 Gloucester Co, VA, 1835; wid dd there 9/6/1842 leaving s James res there & d Ann (wid/o Richard Pitt); Ann's ch Richard & Doulouss over age 21 in 1854. R227

Thomas, esf 1778 Berkeley Co, VA; b 8/25/1761 Carlisle, PA; to OH 1793, where PN ae 70 Butler Co 1832. R228

Thomas, esf King George Co, VA; PN ae 59 Washington, DC, in 1818; PN increase ae 62 Fairfax Co, VA, 1820, when w ae 50 & 5 ch: Nancy ae 26 (a cripple since infancy), Ann ae 18, Ankret? ae 16, Elizabeth ae 14 & Eliza ae 10; dd 1/7/1829; md 3/4/1781 Catherine E, d/o John Stephens, King George Co VA; wid b 2/19/1769, & PN ae 69 Fairfax Co, VA, 1838; wid res there 1843 ae 74; wid final PN payment 3/4/46. R228

William, sea svc (Marines), esf Baltimore,MD; dd OH 1822; md 2/26/1793 Hannah Oldacres, Fauquier Co, VA; wid dd 5/27/45 Scott Co, IN, leaving ch John, Seymour, Isaac, Andrew, Catherine Hougland, Sarah Babbitt, & Abraham; all ch except Abraham res there 1850, & recd arrears of m's PN. R228

William, esf 1781 Rockbridge Co, VA; b 3/18/1763 Augusta Co, VA; to Fayette Co, KY, 1794, thence Scott Co, KY, 1797; to Mercer Co, OH, c 1808, where PN 1832 St Mary's. R228

William, esf 1774 near Staunton, Augusta Co,VA; b 10/10/1755 that Co; PN 1833 St Louis Co, MO; QLF 1914 from desc Miss Mattie R Davis, Lexington, KY, states sol b 10/10/1754, dd 12/19/38, md (1) 1776 Rebecca McCleary, Augusta Co, VA, & md (2) Margaret Collins. R228

William, esf 1776 Hampton, VA; PN ae 71 Greenville District, SC, 1818, when w Sarah ae 65-70; sol mvd to Benton Co, AL, after 12/1829 to res with d Ellender/Elener, w/o Salathiel Clements, & dd her house 6/27 or 6/28/38; in 1825 sol had ch (none liv at home): Robert C, James, Ellender, of whom Robert C & Ellender survived him. R228

William, esf Loudoun Co, VA; PN ae 90 Hampshire Co, VA, 1834 & dd there 5/22/36; md 5/1793 (MB 5/22/93) Elizabeth Watkins, Cameron Parish, Loudoun Co, VA; wid PN aec 81 Hampshire Co, VA, & res ae 97 Butler Co, OH, 1855. R228

BERTRUG, Peter, esf 1777 Augusta Co, VA; b 2/15/1750 Fairfax Co, VA; to Tyler Co, VA, 1822 where PN 1833 res Fish Creek Settlement; dd 4/5/39; QLF states sol d Elizabeth md Samuel Glover. R229

BEST, James, esf 1778 Nansemond Co, VA; ae 57 Clark Co, KY; dd 5/10 or 5/11/1836 Estill Co, KY; md 12/24/1783 Susan, Nansemond Co, VA; wid b 9/14/1757, & afp 1840 Jackson Co, MO, & PAR for proof of marriage; large family of ch including Elizabeth, who wid/o Matthew Conner & who had 6 ch in 1821 eldest being ae 10 or 11; QLF 1932 from great gdd Cecelia (Mrs C E) Hardesty, Pueblo, CO. R229

BETHEA, Elisha, esf Gates Co, NC; PN ae 72 Nansemond Co, VA, 1833, where dd 4/4/1833 leaving wid Rachel & 3 ch. R230

BETHEL, John, see BETHELL, John. R230

BETHEL, John, esf 1780 Henrico Co, VA, where b 12/15/1755; PN 1833 Jefferson Co, TN; dd 12/17/48 Granger Co, TN; md 8/10/1798 Margaret d/o William Brabson & stepd/o Mary May, Wythe Co, VA; wid f dd 2/9/1801; wid b 4/28/1777 & PN 1849 Granger Co, TN. R230

BETSELL, John, see BETSILL, John. R230

BETSILL, John, esf 1779 VA; PN ae 59 Charleston, SC, 1820 when f w Sarah, d Charity, d Sarah, & s John Madison. R230

BETTERSWORTH, Richard, see BETTISWORTH, Richard. R230

BETTESWORTH, Richard, see BETTISWORTH, Richard. R230

BETTISWORTH, Charles, esf 1778 King George Co, VA; b 11/23/1761 Washington Parish, that Co; PN 1832 Adair Co, KY; res 1834 near Carthage, Hancock Co, IL, with s Evin, when other ch res IL; QLF states sol dd 6/1842. R230

  Mary, former wid/o Robert/Robertson McKinney. R230

  Richard, esf 1776 Hanover Co, VA; PN 1818 Warren Co, KY; res there 1821 ae 70 when w Elizabeth aec 55, d Sally aec 20, & d Betsy ae 13; sol dd 11/9/1825; QLF 1905 from desc Mrs Ruth Bettersworth Norcross, Los Angeles, CA; QLF 1939 from desc great great gds Kenneth Stansfield, Nashville,TN. R230

BETTSWORTH, Charles, see BETTISWORTH, Charles. R232

BEVERS, James, esf 1776 VA; b 3/4/1763; PN 1823 Limestone Co, AL, when had d's ae 20, 22, & 24; dd 12/1826; QLF 1930 from desc Mrs Lucile G Pleasants, Los Angeles, CA, states sol f was Captain James Beavers of Loudoun Co, VA, militia. R232

BEVILL, Edward, esf 1778 Mecklenburg Co, VA, where b 9/16/1762; PN 1832 near Sulphur Springs, Madison Co, AL, 1832, where mvd 1825. R232

BEVILLE, Edward, see BEVILL, Edward. R232

BIBB, Benjamin, esf 1780 Loudoun Co, VA, where b 1746, & where PN 1832; dd 1/14/35; md 8/5/1790 Agness Tate, who PN ae 71 Louisa Co, VA, 1842 & dd there 3/27/67, leaving s Richard G then ae 65, who adm/o m's estate; sol MB signed by Uriah Tate; QLF 1912 from gds Dr R H L Bibb (ae 64), Austin, TX, s/o Richard G Bibb. R233

  Henry, esf Louisa Co, VA, where b; during RW res in same home as Benjamin Bibb above; PN ae 75 Louisa Co, VA, 1832; dd 1/14/42. R233

  James, esf 1777 Goochland Co, VA; b Louisa Co, VA; to Barren Co, KY, c1807; PN ae 78 Green Co, KY, 1832; QLF 1913 from great great gdd Stella Pickett Hardy, Batesville,AR, states family bible/o sol s Fleming shows sol dd 11/23/1846 ae 93;

72

BIBB (continued)
   QLF states sol s/o Captain William Bibb & bro/o William,
   1st governor of AL. R233
   Thomas, esf 1780 Louisa Co, VA, where b 1754-5, & where PN
   1833, bro/o Henry who res there then ae 76; QLF 1929 from
   desc Caroline H Frazier, Huntington, WV. R233
BIBEE, Thomas, esf 1776 Amherst Co, VA; b Goochland Co, VA; PN
   1834 Cocke Co, TN, when res with steps. R233
BIBLE, Adam, esf 1778 Augusta Co, VA; dd 2/2/1826; md 9/1783
   or 9/1785 Magdalene d/o George Shoemaker, Rockingham Co,
   VA; wid PN ae 75 there 1839; s John ae 51 in 1840. R233
BICKEL, George, esf 1780 Monongalia Co, VA; also svc in Indian
   Wars 1793-4; b 1764 Berkeley Co, VA; afp 1833 Lewis Co, VA
   & PAR; wid Mary afp aec 70 Braxton Co, VA, 1858, & PAR but
   gtd BLW for sol svc in Randolph Co, VA, Indian Wars. R233
BICKERS, Nicholas, esf Orange Co, VA, where b 8/16/1744; PN
   there 1833; QLF 1919 from desc Frank Marshall (Mrs C P)
   Fox, Greeneville, TN, states sol LWT probated 8/27/1833
   Orange Co, VA, listing ch: Joanna Bickers Marshall, Benja-
   min C, Moses, Polly Bickers Hawkins, & Joel; QLF states w
   named Janey. R233
BICKLE, George, see BICKEL, George. R234
BICKLEY, Charles, esf 1775 Russell Co, VA, & PN aec 83 there
   1836; dd there 6/1/39 leaving 5 ch of 7 surv; QLF states
   sol had s Sebastian H. R234
   William, esf 1777 Buckingham Co, VA; PN ae 77 Mason Co, KY,
   1833. R234
BICKLY, Charles, see BICKLEY, Charles. R234
BIDDIE, John, esf Union District,SC; b 7/17/1762 Lunenburg Co,
   VA; PN 1832 Union Distict,SC; dd 10/14/41 Marshall Co, AL;
   md c1810 Sarah, Union District, SC; wid PN 1842 Marshall
   Co, AL. R235
BIDGOOD, Philip, BLW issued 2/18/1793. R235
BIGBIE, William, esf 1777; PN & BLW ae 72 Floods, Buckingham
   Co, VA, 1828. R235
BIGBY, William, see BIGBIE, William. R235
BIGGS, Benjamin, esf 1777 Ohio Co, VA; also War of 1812 svc;
   BLW issued 6/3/1791; dd at home 12/2/1823 near West Liber-
   ty, Ohio Co, VA; md 8/26/1795 Priscilla d/o Allen Metcalf,
   Ohio Co, VA; family of 10 ch, 7 still liv 1848; wid PN ae
   70 near West Liberty, Ohio Co, VA, 1849; QLF 1926 from gds
   Daniel E Biggs (b 7/23/1841) of Parkersburg,WV, states sol
   b 1/31/1753 Philadelphia, PA, s/o Benjamin, an Englishman
   who md 1747 Henrietta P D Munday in or near London, England & family came at once to Philadelphia, further cites
   sol ch births: Henrietta M 7/11/1796 w/o William Irvin,
   Juliann 4/13/98 w/o William Anderson, Benjamin F 7/6/1800
   h/o Lydia A Carney, Allen M 6/11/02 md (1) Mary Trimble &
   (2) Mrs Nancy Bell, George 4/3/04 h/o Margaret Anderson,
   Margaret M 8/26/06 & dd ae 18, Zaccheus 6/7/09 h/o Viney
   Gorsuck, Washington L ?/22/11 h/o Mary A Roland, Priscilla
   I 1813 w/o John Beatty, John H 12/1815 h/o Sarah A Cramp,

BIGGS (continued)
all data from family bible; querier Daniel E s/o Benjamin
Biggs & Lydia, youngest d/o Daniel Carney; QLF 1919 from
desc Miss Nell Moore, Salem, IL; QLF 1898 from gdd Mrs J L
Webb, Denver, CO. R237

John, esf 1778 VA; PN ae 70 Giles Co, VA, when w aec 60 & no
ch liv at home. R237

John, esf 1779 Williamsburg, VA; PN ae 79 Adair Co, KY, 1830
& dd 4/7/1840; md 1/25/1784 Sarah Roe, Caroline Co, VA, &
res Carswell Co, NC, 1790 with 3 ch; later had 7 more ch;
wid PN ae 85 Adair Co, KY, 1843; AFF there 1845 by her bro
Anthony. R237

John, esf 1779 PA; b Scotland or Ireland; PN ae 80 Greene Co
TN, 1832; dd 12/1/33 Blount Co, TN; md in VA 1782-3 Isa-
bella, who dd 7/17/32, McMinn Co, TN; ch births: Margaret
11/7/1783, Ginny 5/5/85, Alexander 5/15/87, Mary 11/19/89,
Isabella 3/30/92, & John 8/31/94; surv ch 1845: Margaret
Carson, Jane Anderson, Alexander, Isabella, John, William,
& James (ae 45). R237

John, BLW issued 2/19/1828 to sol heir-at-law Thomas Biggs,
Giles Co, VA. R237

Joseph, esf VA; PN 1796 Brooke Co, VA; res 1825 Belmont Co,
OH, 1825; dd 2/1/1833; md 1/14/1794 Mary Daily; wid afp ae
70 Marshall Co, VA, 1840, & PAR, not md before 1794. R237

Randolph/Randall, sea svc, esf Alexandria, VA; dd 5/27/1815
Pendleton Co, VA; md 1780 Mary ---, Westmoreland Co, VA;
wid afp ae 77 Campbell Co, KY, 1838, & PAR; s Thomas made
AFF then (b 1/19/1782); wid again afp ae 85 under name of
Polly Biggs, Kenton Co, KY, 1845, & PAR; wid dd 6/21/49
Covington, KY; d Mrs Nancy Payne afp 1850 Hamilton Co, OH,
stating parents md 1778 Westmoreland Co, VA, & res Loudoun
Co,VA, after RW, further f 1st name Randal; Nancy PAR; QLF
1898 from gds John M Biggs, Louisville, KY, states sol bu-
ried near what is now Williamstown, KY. R237

Stephen, esf 1775-6 Spotsylvania Co, VA; to Greenup Co, KY,
1794; afp ae 80 there 1835; PAR, insufficient proof of sv.
R237

William, esf VA; dd 3/1827 Madison Co, IL; heirs-at-law 1833
St Clair Co, IL, who afp: wid Nancy, Samuel Scott & w Nan-
cy, William Scott h/o Mississippi Biggs (decd), Sampson
Biggs, Catey Ann Biggs, William S Galbreath & w Jemima,
Matthew J Cox & w Henrietta; PAR. R237

BILLINGS, Abraham; esf 1780 Pittsylvania Co, VA, where b 1754;
afp ae 83 Ralls Co, MO, 1835 & PAR; dd there 9/15/39; ch &
only heirs who afp there 1840: John, George, Abraham Jr,
Mary Nunns, Jane Hampton, Margaret Carson; s George res in
1855 Newburg, Macon Co, MO; ch PAR. R239

Jasper, esf 1778 Surry Co (now Wilkes Co), NC; b 4/3/1759
Pittsylvania Co, VA; to NC aec 15 with f; PN 1832 Wilkes
Co, NC; dd 11/12/35; md 6/14/1795 Elizabeth Richardson,
Wilkes Co, NC; wid PN ae 76 there 1850; ch mbnn; wid res
with ch after h dd. R239

BILLS, John E, esf 1779 Hampshire Co, VA, where b 1763; PN
    1833 Hardy Co, VA; dd 7/9/52 Wood Co, VA; md 7/2/1818 Mary
    Reel, Hardy Co, VA; wid PN ae 65-70 Wood Co, VA, 1853, &
    gtd BLW 1856 Parkersburg, VA. R240
  William, esf 1778 Radnor, PA; PN 1818 Philadelphia Co, PA, &
    dd 11/15/19; QLF 1924 from desc F H Stevenson, Philadelph-
    ia, PA, states sol w Polly; QLF 1904 from desc Mary Hough-
    ton, Philadelphia, PA, states sol b 1758. R240
BINER, George, esf 1780 Loudoun Co, VA; b 3/15/1765 Philadel-
    phia, PA; to Loudoun Co, VA, as small ch; PN 1833 Harrison
    Co, OH. R240
BINEGER, George, see BENEGER, George. R240
BINGHAM, Benjamin, esf 1777 Culpeper Co, VA; PN ae 76 Blount
    Co, TN, 1832. R241
  Robert, esf VA or MD; dd 3/26/1811 Wilkes Co, NC; md there
    12/7/1785 Elizabeth McNeil; wid afp ae 90 Watauga Co, NC,
    1857, & PAR; also afb & BLAR; s G M made AFF 1858 Soda/Lo-
    da, NC. R241
BINGLEY, Lewis, esf 1777 VA; dd 10/13/1799, James City Co, VA,
    where md 2/28/1788 Elizabeth Morris; wd ae 74 Howard Co,
    IL, & res Petersburg, that Co, 1848; wid md (2) 12/13/1802
    Zachariah Vance who also RW sol (see his name for data on
    his 1st w & on ch by Elizabeth Morris, who also PN for his
    svc); births of ch/o Lewis & Elizabeth: John M 12/18/1789
    (dd 12/2/1836), Nathaniel 10/8/1792, Mary 10/19/95, & Eli-
    zabeth 12/9/97; QLF states sol wid dd 1850 Petersburg, IL;
    QLF 1912 from following desc: Mrs Sarah Garner Bryant of
    Eureka KS, Mrs Fannie Garner Hughes of Bement IL, & Mrs
    Amanda Garner Jewell, Tuscola, IL. R242
BINNS, William, BLW issued 7/14/1792. R242
BIRCH, John, esf 1779 Reading, Berks Co, PA; b 11/7/1752; PN
    1818 Bath Co, KY, w then ae 53; dd 8/30/37 Montgomery Co,
    KY; md 1/19/1786 Jane Epperson/Apperson, Albemarle Co, VA;
    family 1821 Bath Co,KY: w Jane, d ae 20, s ae 16, s ae 13,
    & d ae 10; sol sis Polly Mayberry res there then; in 1820
    sol bro George ae 65 Montgomery Co, KY; wid PN ae 69 there
    1839, res 1849 Scott Co,KY, & res 1855 Powell Co, KY. R242
  William, see BURCH, William. R242
BIRD, Henry, see BYRD, Henry. R242
  Joshua, esf 1776 King George Co, VA; PN ae 75 Nelson Co, KY,
    1819; QLF 1916 from desc Ninette Layton, Jacksonville, FL.
    R243
  Levin, sea svc, esf VA; in 1849, 6 heirs, including John D
    Tyler of Onancock, VA, queried on entitlement to compensa-
    tion, stating earlier claim gtd to Thomas M Bayly who f/o
    VA Congressman Thomas H Bayly; QLF 1938 from desc H K Bow-
    ers, Kansas City, MO, states sol from Accomac Co, VA, & at
    times spelled surname BYRD. R243
  Reuben, esf 1780 Hillsborough,NC, 1820; a mulatto; PN aec 56
    Powhatan Co, VA, when family w aec 37 & d aec 7. R243
BISCOE, James, VA sea svc, esf 1778; b 7/3/1760; PN Franklin
    Co, VA, 1832, & dd there 7/11/53; md 12/16/1832 Polly Ken-

BISCOE, (continued)
    dall there; wid PN ae 48 there 1854;   QLF 1928 from desc
    Annette Jane Hedges, Indianapolis, IN. R244
BISH, Frederick, esf Shenandoah Co, VA; b 7/1758 Strasburg,
    Germany; to America c1764; PN 1833 Greene Co, PA; res 1839
    Highland Co, OH, where s Jacob res. R244
BISHOP, Elisha, esf 1779 Berkeley Co, VA; b 1760 Anne Arundel
    Co, MD, s/o Thomas; PN 1833 Henry Co, KY; QLF states sol
    res Henry Co, KY, 1840; QLF 1931 from desc Lela W (Mrs L
    D) Prewitt, Forest City, IA. R245
  Henry, esf Botetourt Co, VA; b 4/1757; PN 1832 Floyd Co, VA;
    dd 6/2/39; md 5/1785 or 6/1/1785 Fanny d/o Daniel Simpkins
    (MB 5/23/85) Montgomery Co, VA; wid PN ae 76 Floyd Co, VA,
    1841; in 1843 wid ae 81; in 1856 John Bishop one of heirs
    of sol. R245
  James, esf 1777 Dinwiddie Co, VA, where b, & where PN 1832
    ae 72; bro/o Jeremiah. R245
  Jeremiah, esf 1776 Dinwiddie Co,VA, where b; & where PN 1832
    ae 77; bro/o James; dd 4/1/36; QLF 1936 from desc Ruth L
    (Mrs Dudley D) Fouche, Jackson Heights, Long Island, NY.
    R246
  Richard, esf 1779 VA; PN ae 70 Harrison Co, KY, 1818; res ae
    66 Nicholas Co, KY, 1820 with w ae 63; res 1828 Lexington,
    KY. R247
  Solomon, esf 1775 Frederick Co, VA; PN ae 77 Nelson Co, KY.
    R247
  Stephen, esf 1776 VA; PN ae 65 Buckingham, VA, 1820, when w
    Charlotte ae 68. R247
  William, esf 1781; PN ae 71 Surry Co, VA, 1832; dd 4/27/39
    Prince George Co, VA; md 9/10/1796 Winifred "Winny" Willi-
    ams, Surry Co or Prince George Co, VA; wid PN ae 80 Surry
    Co, VA; wid res 1856 Prince George Co, VA, with Uriah Wil-
    liamson who md her d Mary 1825; d Parmelia Bailey res 1855
    Prince George Co, VA. R247
  William, esf VA; afp 1818 Stafford Co, VA, & PAR. R247
  Wyatt, esf 1779 Surry Co, VA, where b 1759; PN 1833 Franklin
    Co, AL. R247
BISWELL, John, esf 1776-7 Pittsylvania Co, VA; PN aec 60 Fay-
    ette Co, KY, 1818; res 1820 ae 60 Jessamine Co, KY, when
    no one but himself in family. R249.
  John, BLW issued 5/2/1794. R249
BLACK, Alexander, esf c1780 near Staunton, Augusta Co, VA; b
    2/22/1760 Bennett's Forge, Berkeley Co, VA; to Augusta Co,
    VA, with f; afp 1835 Crawford Co, IN, when bro Robert res
    IL, & PAR, insufficient svc; md Bennings Gap, Pendleton Co
    VA. R251
  George, esf 1776 Shepherdstown, VA; b 1/1760 Bucks Co, PA;
    PN 1786 Frederick Co, VA, for disability. R251
  James, esf 1781 Rockbridge Co, VA; b 1761 Augusta Co, VA;
    afp 1845 Abbeville District, SC, & PAR. R251
  John, esf 1778 Williamsport, Washington Co, MD; esf Martins-
    burg, Berkeley Co, VA, 1781; b 3/13/1763; to Williamsport

BLACK (continued)
  aec 15 with f; afp 1834 Highland Co, OH; PAR, insufficient
    svc in regularly organized unit; res 1839 Clermont Co, OH;
    res 1852 Union Township, Brown Co, OH; dd before 1856; s
    William H res Brown Co, OH, 1856; sol bro/o William & Sa-
    muel. R252
  John, esf 177-, Augusta Co, VA; b 10/4/1750; dd 11/20/1830,
    Bourbon Co, KY; md there 7/15 or 7/17/1792 Milly Norton;
    wid b 3/7/1774, & afp 1843 Clark Co, KY; PAR, insufficient
    proof of svc; ch births: Mary 12/14/1808 & Christopher
    12/3/1810; other family bible data: James Walker Black md
    9/6/1832 Mary Aldridge, William Black md Elizabeth Cowen,
    Mary Jean Thomas dd 2/18/18--; wid bro James ae 80 Greenup
    Co, KY, 1843 AFF he RW sol from Rockingham Co, VA, & his
    bro John served in same company with John Black; James
    Norton res Clark Co, 1852. R252
  Robert, esf Montgomery Co, VA; b Augusta Co, VA; PN ae 82
    Woodford Co, Ky, 1832; QLF 1926 from desc Mrs Jerre B No-
    land; QLF states sol b 1751, further Isabella Rice w/o ei-
    ther sol or of Rudolph Black who res Bracken Co, KY, 1835.
    R252
  Samuel, MD/VA sea svc; esf 1779 in boat company on Potomac
    River; afp ae 64 Adams Co, OH, when w ae 58 & ch all grown
    up; PAR. R252
BLACKARD, Willoughby, esf Caswell Co, NC; b 8/12/1758; PN 1832
    Wythe Co, VA; QLF 1928 from great great gdd Mrs R B Moore,
    Charlottesville, VA. R253
  Willyoube, see BLACKARD, Willoughby. R253
BLACKBOURN, Clemont, esf 1776 Mecklenburg Co, VA; b 2/11/1760
    Lisbon, Portugal; PN 1840 Madison Co, AL, where mvd 1818;
    QLF 1929 from desc Mrs J D Simmons, Gunnison, MS, states
    sol b of English parents. R253
BLACKBURN, Benjamin, PN 1821 Tuscaloosa Co, AL, 1821; formerly
    res VA & TN; QLF states sol res Augusta Co, VA, & near
    Jonesboro, TN; QLF 1925 from desc Mrs Hal Burrage Arm-
    strong, Austin, TX, states sol wounded at Battle of Point
    Pleasant. R253
  James, esf 1776 MD; esf VA 1783; PN ae 68 Warren Co, OH,
    1820 when w ae 55, s James ae 19, d Rebecca ae 16, & s
    decd. R253
  William, esf 1776 Fairfax Co, VA, where b 2/12/1757; mvd to
    Wilkes Co, NC, thence TN; PN 1832 Caldwell Co, KY, where
    res with w & ch for 4 years; dd 3/13/41, leaving ch mbnn;
    QLF 1940 from great great gds Edward F Blackburn, Prince-
    ton, KY; QLF states sol res ae 82 with Harrison Blackburn
    1840. R253
BLACKEMORE, George, see BLACKMORE, George. R253
BLACKMORE, George, esf 1778 Blackamore Station near Clinch
    River; b 5/14/1763 Fauquier Co, VA; PN 1833 Lincoln Co, TN
    where dd 8/24/37; md 1787 (MB 9/10/87 security George Daw-
    son Blackmore) Sarah/Sally Thompson, Sumner Co, NC; wid PN
    ae 72 Lincoln Co, TN; QLF 1909 from great gdd Jessie Rives

BLACKMORE (continued)
    Blakemore, Kansas City, MO, states sol & w dd at Fayette-
    ville, TN. R255
  John, see BLAKEMORE, John. R255
  Thomas, see BLAKEMORE, Thomas. R255
BLACKNALL, Thomas, esf 1776 Gloucester Co,VA, where b 2/18/60;
    to Granville Co, NC, c1800 where PN 1832; QLF 1905 from
    desc O W Blacknall, Kittrell, NC. R255
BLACKSHIRE, Ebenezer, esf DE; gtd BLW 1805 Greene Township,
    Greene Co, PA; PN 1828 Monongalia Co, VA; large family of
    ch in 1807; QLF states sol esf Kent Co, DE, where b c1762.
    R255
BLACKWALL, Thomas, see BLACKNALL, Thomas. R255
BLACKWELDER, Isaac, esf 1776 Mecklenburg Co, NC; b 11/17/1757
    Mecklenburg Co, VA; to Mecklenburg Co, NC, with parents as
    infant; PN 1834 Cabarrus Co, NC; QLF 1890 from gds J S
    Blackwelder, Chicago, IL, states surname/o sol originally
    SCHWARTZWALDER before RW, further sol bro Isaac, Daniel, &
    John all RW svc. R255
BLACKWELL, Ann, former wid/o Edwin HULL. R256
  David, esf 1775 Albemarle Co, VA; esf 1778 Surry Co, NC; PN
    ae 73 Roane Co, TN, 1832. R256
  David, esf 1779 Hanover Co, VA, where b 8/24/1764 near New-
    castle; PN 1832 Hanover Co, VA. R256
  David, esf 1775 Fauquier Co, VA; b 11/1750-53 Northumberland
    Co, VA; PN 1833 Prince William Co, VA; dd 6/25/41 Fauquier
    Co, VA; md 5/29/1776 Ann d/o Zacharias & Mary Lewis; wid
    mvd 1842 to Washington Co, MD, to res with s Arthur, & PN
    there 1844 ae 85; wid dd 4/23/47 Hancock, that Co; births
    of ch: Lewis 3/15/1777, Elizabeth Steptoe 8/17/78, Alexan-
    der 3/80, George William Brent 2/7/82, Walter 8/7/84, Ar-
    thur 4/30/87, Ann 4/13/89, Samuel 4/12/91, Caty/Kitty
    3/3/93, John 1/5/95, Lucy 3/1/97, Harriet 11/6/98, Mary
    5/12/1801, & William 8/03; ch surv wid: Elizabeth Jordan,
    Ann Newman, Harriet Sniveley, Mary Ohr, Samuel, & Arthur;
    in 1855 Mary Brent, Prince William Co, VA, stated she d/o
    sol; s Arthur adm/o wid estate, Hancock, MD, 1855. R256
  John, esf 1780 Burke Co,NC; bc 1755 Culpeper Co, VA; PN 1836
    Hickman Co, TN; dd 2/12/39; QLF 1937 from great gdd Mrs N
    R Henderson, LaGrange, GA. R256
  John, esf 1780 Culpeper Co, VA; b 7/25/1758; PN 1833 Shelby
    Co, KY; QLF states 9 persons in sol family. R256
  John, BLW issued 2/26/1793; QLF 1912 from great great gdd
    Mrs B B Mahone, Richmond, VA. R256
  Joseph, esf 1775 VA; b 8/1757; PN 1818 Fauquier Co, VA; fa-
    mily w Mary W & ch: Sarah aec 15, Mary aec 9, Christopher
    aec 7, Joseph aec 5, & m-in-law Mrs Brent; QLF 1937 from
    Mrs Janie H (Mrs J Hughes) Wilson, Alexandria, VA, states
    sol s/o William (4/25/1731-9/10/1772) & Elizabeth Crump
    (of Northumberland Co, VA), further sol md (1) 8/14/1787
    Anne Gibson, Fauquier Co, VA, & (2) Mary Waddy Brent; QLF
    1914 from great gdd Mrs W F Harwood, Lynchburg, VA, states

BLACKWELL (continued)
     sol 1st w full name Anne Grayson Gibson; QLF 1912 from
     desc Mrs Emma S Marsteller, Clarendon, VA. R256
   Joseph, esf 1778 VA; b Fauquier Co, VA; dd 10/1836; md Ann
     Eustace, d/o Agatha Eustace, 12/1784; wid Ann b 1/12/1761,
     who md (1) 1779 RW sol Edwin Hull (d 9/1780) & she gtd wid
     PN for his RW svc; wid PN for 2nd h svc 1838 Fauquier Co,
     VA, & dd there 12/40; ch: Ann w/o John H Gaskins, Agatha
     w/o Enoch Jeffries, Lucy w/o William R Smith, John, Willi-
     am, James, & Joseph; sol gdc: ch/o s Joseph (Jane, James
     D, Betsey Edmonds, & Octavia w/o John Chilton); QLF 1915
     from Harriet Conway, Herndon, VA, states she gdd/o Susan
     Harrison who d/o Joseph & Ann G Blackwell. R256
   Robert, esf 1777 Culpeper Co, VA; b 12/28/1760; PN 1820 Gar-
     rard Co, KY, when had w & 2 ch; res 1830 St Louis, MO; dd
     2/27/37; QLF 1903 from great great gdd Mrs Morris Bartlett
     of Maitland, FL, states sol b Fauquier Co or Hanover Co,
     VA. R256
   Robert, esf VA aec 16 as sub for f John; esf 1791 for Indian
     Wars; gtd BLW aec 90 KY 1855 where had w & married ch mbnn
     & res alternately Anderson & Franklin Co's, KY. R256
   Thomas, esf 1775 VA; PN ae 69 Union Co, KY, when family w ae
     61 & ch: Sophia ae 35, Grant ae 33, Judy ae 29, Thomas ae
     23, & Betsy ae 21. R256
   William, esf VA; b VA; dd Iredell Co, NC; BLW issued to Eli-
     zabeth Scott only surv ch, & heir-at-law to sol 7/17/1832;
     QLF 1940 from desc Velner (Mrs Edward J) Carpenter of
     Greensboro, NC. R256
BLACKWILL, Robert, see BLACKWELL, Robert b 12/28/1760. R256
BLAIKLEY, William, esf 1775 VA; PN 1818 Edgefield District,SC;
     later stricken from PN rolls as not having "Continental
     Service" as claimed. R256
BLAIN, James; esf 1776 VA; PN ae 66 Owen Co, IN, 1820; never
     md; QLF states sol & bro James BLAINE esf MD or VA & came
     to IN 1818. R256
BLAIR, Allen, esf 1781 Amherst Co, VA, where b 7/8/1754 near
     Rockfish River; PN that Co 1832; dd 4/23/33; md 12/22/1778
     Mary Ann Staples, Amherst Co, VA; wid PN aec 76 there 1838
     when s John S/L liv; QLF 1925 from desc Violet Blair (Mrs
     Sterling C) Robertson, Phoenix, AZ. R257
   James, esf 1778 Burke Co, NC; b 3/6/1761 Augusta Co, VA; PN
     1832 Habersham Co, GA; QLF from desc N P Parkman; QLF 1928
     states sol dd 1839 & had d Anne who md Allen Elston. R257
   James, see BLAIN, James who PN 1820 IN. R257
   John, BLW issued 9/19/1789 to heir & legal representative
     Archibald Blair; QLF states sol in VA artillery. R257
   John Neal; esf 1775 Augusta Co, VA; PN ae 76 Greenbrier Co,
     VA, 1818. R257
   Samuel, esf 1779 Burke Co, NC; b 6/14/1758 Amelia Co, VA; PN
     1833 McMinn Co,TN; QLF 1931 from desc Harry T Burn, Sweet-
     water, TN, states sol dd 1836 Monroe Co, TN. R257
BLAKE, George, esf 1776 Augusta Co, VA; b 1751 Chester Co, PA;

BLAKE (continued)
   to Augusta Co, VA, as ch; to IN 1816 where afp Jefferson
   Co 1834; PAR. R258
   James, esf 1780 Southampton Co, VA; in 1789 sol mvd to Wake
   Co, NC, where dd soon thereafter; md 8/11/1777 Sarah Clif-
   ton (b 4/6/1756), sis/o Josiah (b 7/1762), d/o Lydia; wid
   dd 7/26/1839, only surv ch John & Mary who gtd PN arrears
   Orange Co, NC, 1843, when sol bro Thomas ae 98 AFF Montgomery Co, NC, that he & bros James, Samuel, John, Ethelred,
   & Benjamin RW sol's; family bible pages sent with claim
   partially unreadable, but give following data on sol ch
   births: Richard 9/10/1783,Nancey 3/4/1786, Lydia 11/21/78,
   Dorothy Clifton 4/18/17--, & Polly 7/10/81. R259
   Thomas, esf 1777 as sub for John Blake, Augusta Co, VA; PN
   ae 72 Greenbrier Co, VA, 1832. R260
   Thomas, esf Southampton Co, VA; PN aec 86 Montgomery Co, NC,
   1832, when nephew Isham Blake res Fayetteville, NC; sol md
   before RW & had 1-2 ch; QLF states sol s William also RW
   sol; QLF 1936 from desc Mrs A G DeLoach, Atlanta, GA. R260
BLAKELY, Aquilla, esf 1776 Patrick Co, VA; b 10/10/1740 Fauquier Co, VA; PN 1832 Blount Co, AL, where res 15 years,
   previously res Grayson Co, VA, & Jefferson Co, TN. R261
BLAKEMORE, George, esf VA; PN 1832 Frederick Co, VA, where dd
   7/25/33 leaving no wid but ch: John M (res 1851 Front Royal,VA), George N, Thomas, Lucy N, Buck, & Eliza N Elliott;
   QLF states sol b 6/17/175- & res Prince William Co, VA,
   further s Caleb b 1781 & md 1803 Washington Co, MD, further s George md there 1808, further sol w Easther or Hesther ---; QLF states sol middle name Neville & gtd BLW 1795.
   R261
   George, see BLACKMORE, George, PN 1833 Lincoln Co, TN. R261
   John, esf 1781 Frederick Co, VA; PN aec 70 Henry Co, KY,
   1832; QLF states sol res there 1840 ae 78; QLF from desc
   Mrs Philip A Spence, Wytheville, VA, states sol f/o Joseph
   who res Scott Co, VA; QLF states sol dd 1840, & was bro/o
   George & Thomas; QLF states sol b1762 & dd 1856. R261
   Thomas, esf 1777 Frederick Co, VA; KIA Battle of Germantown;
   only heir George Blakemore, also RW sol, gtd BLW 6/9/1812
   for Thomas' svc. R261
BLAKENEY, William, esf 1776 Carlisle, PA, as privateer; esf
   1778 in VA regiment in PA; PN ae 73 Pittsburgh,PA, 1820;
   dd 7/14/21; QLF 1916 from desc Winona Bleakney Peterson,
   University Place, NE. R261
BLAKEY, George, esf 1776 Buckingham Co, VA; PN ae 81 Logan Co,
   KY, 1832, where dd 9/8/42 ae almost 93; md 1/10/1787 Mar-
   garet Whitsitt, Henry Co, VA; wid PN ae 75 Logan Co, KY
   1843; ch births: Pamela 12/27/1787, Reuben 12/21/1789,
   William W 2/5/92, Thomas 6/17/94, Elizabeth W 9/13/96,
   Churchill H 8/7/99, James W 9/13/1801, & Sarah P 4/1/04;
   ch marriages: William W md 1/9/21 Susan C H Breathitt,
   Thomas md 1/28/23 Ann H Whitsitt, James W md 1/28/23 Nancy
   I Haden, Churchill H md 1826 Sally I Haden, George D md

BLAKEY (continued)
2/23/30 Lucy L Thomas, & Pamela md 12/13/08 William Haden;
ch deaths: Reuben 9/20/1790, William W 10/10/1824, & Chur-
chill H 9/23/26; sol bro William also RW sol whose records
of svc spell surname BLACKEY. R261
BLAKLEY, Aquila, see BLAKELY, Aquilla. R261
BLALACK, David, see BLALOCK, David. R262
BLALOCK, David, esf near Petsboro, Chatham Co, NC; b Brunswick
Co, VA, 1752; f KIA in skirmish with British troops in NC;
PN 1833 Fayette Co, TN, where dd 2/28/42; AFF 1857 Shelby
Co, TN, by surv d Margaret Robinson that only other ch/o
liv was Mary Webb, whom she had not heard from in over 15
years. R262
David, esf Granville Co, NC; b Hanover Co, VA; to Rutherford
Co, NC, c1827, where afp 1834 ae 78; PAR, svc less than 6
months; s William afp Cass Co, GA, & PAR. R262
Jeremiah, esf 1776 NC; bc 1754 Hanover Co, VA, where family
mvd before RW; PN 1832 York District, SC; dd 10/28/33; md
12/20/1782 Lucy, who PN ae 79 York District, SC, 1841; ch
births: Mary Wiseman 2/29/1786, William 9/1/89 (res 1841
York District, SC), John 9/8/92 & Elizabeth 1/2/1809. R262
John, esf 1778 VA; b 9/4/1762 Brunswick Co, VA; to Burke Co,
NC, 1831; PN 1832 Carter Co, TN, 1832; to Burke Co, NC, to
be near ch 1838; dd 3/10/46; md 1/8/1797 (MB 1/6/97 secu-
rity John Dormant) Polly Dormant/Dorman, Orange Co, NC;
wid PN ae 67 Yancey Co, NC, 1849, & gtd BLW Grassy Creek,
that Co, 1855; wid dd 10/7/56; QLF 1940 from desc Maj. Forest Blalock, Los Angeles, CA. R262
BLAN, Jesse, esf 1776 VA; b 1756 Prince William Co, VA; PN Kanawha Co, VA, 1832; dd c4/16/1835. R262
BLANCIT, Joel; esf 1776 Henry Co,VA; b 4/7/1761 Amelia Co, VA;
PN 1832 Patrick Co, VA. R265
BLAND, James, BLW issued 3/26/1792. R265
James, esf 1777 VA; dd 1/8/1803 Essex Co, VA; md 1782-3 Amy
Samuel, King & Queen Co, VA, & res near village of Newton
there; wid PN ae 83 Chesterfield Co, VA, 1843 while res
with d Mrs James Taylor; in 1795 d Elizabeth aec 13; in
1843 Henry Samuel ae 75 & John Samuel ae 64, Caroline Co,
VA, stated sol wid their aunt; in 1843 Barbara Taylor aec
72, Essex Co, VA, stated that James Taylor who s-in-law/o
sol was her h's nephew. R265
BLANE, George, esf Amherst Co, VA; dd 5/1817 there; md 1790
(MB 3/3/1790) Rachel Demasters/Masters, at which time sol
was widower; wid afp ae78 res Nelson Farm, Amherst Co,
VA, 1851; PAR, insufficient proof of svc; surname sometimes spelled BLAINE. R265
BLANKENBAKER, Nicholas, esf 1781 Culpeper Co, VA; PN ae 73
Shelbyville, Shelby Co, KY, 1832. R265
BLANKENSHIP, Abel; esf Campbell Co, VA; dd 6/1820; md fall of
1782 Fanny, who afp ae 79 Russell Co, KY, 1839, & PAR;
wid dd 1844; sol s/o Hudson; AFF 1853 Russell Co, KY, by
sol cousin Jesse Blankenship ae 86 that sol & Jesse's bro

BLANKENSHIP (continued)
>Daniel entered svc together Campbell Co, VA, that Abel res res Bedford Co, VA, after RW, & that Jesse md sis of wid/o Abel; Nancy Pierce stated 1853 Jamestown, Russell Co, KY, she legal heir to sol; sol md Fanny ---, Halifax Co, VA. R266

>Abraham/Abram, esf 177- Chesterfield Co, VA, where b 1759; mvd to Bedford Co,VA, 1784, where PN 1833 & dd 3/8/45; md 1781 Susan Wiatt, Chesterfield Co, VA; in 1830 had d ae 35 who had ch ae 11 & ae 14; wid PN ae 87 Franklin Co, VA; d Polly 1845 ae 45; sol sis Melly md 10/31/1789 Peter Kinnett. R266

>Benjamin, esf 1777 Hampton,VA; PN ae 59 Shelby Co, OH, 1819; res 1836 McLean Co, IL, where mvd to be near ch; dd 1844; s J C res Bloomfield, IA, 1850; QLF 1908 from gdd (on her m's side) Mrs Alice Defrees Denton, Atchison, KS, states her paternal gdf Joseph Defrees RW sol from Philadelphia, PA, & dd fall/o 1826 near Piqua, OH. R266

>Daniel, see BLANKINSHIP, Daniel. R266

>Henry, esf 1779-80 Bedford Co, VA; b Chesterfield Co, VA; PN ae 76 Campbell Co, VA, 1832. R266

>John, esf 1781 Lunenburg Co, VA, where b 1760; PN 1832 Pittsylvania Co, VA. R266

>Josiah, esf 1780 Chesterfield Co, VA, where b & raised, & PN there 1832 ae 73-4; to Petersburg, VA, 1831; bro Bland aec 65 Chesterfield Co, VA, 1832. R266

>Reuben, esf 1779 Bedford Co, VA; b 1765 Chesterfield Co, VA; to GA after RW; PN 1832 Shelby Co, AL, where res 2 years; res 1837 Talladega Co, Al; res 1838 Coosa Co, AL; dd leaving wid 10/27/50. R266

>William, esf Henry Co, VA; afp ae 74 Pike Co, KY, 1835; PAR, svc less than 6 months. R266

>Wommock/Womack, esf 1775 Richmond, VA; res 1781 Amelia Co, VA; PN ae 68 Greene Co, MS, 1821, when res with w ae 70 & s ae 21; dd 2/4/31. R266

BLANKINSHIP, Daniel, esf 1777 New London, VA; bro Reuben & bro Henry both RW svc; PN ae 80 years, 5 months, & 21 days on 7/26/1841; dd 6/29/49 Coosa Co, AL, & w dd before him; ch surv: Mary Ann ae 54 w/o James Blankenship, Solomon ae 50, Henry ae 48, Edmund ae 46, & Frances ae 44 w/o Mark Blankenship; surv ch PN 1849, Coosa Co, AL. R266

>Reuben, see BLANKENSHIP, Reuben. R266

>William, see BLANKENSHIP, William. R266

>Wommock/Womack, see BLANKENSHIP, Wommock/Womack. R266

BLANTON, Thomas, esf 1779 VA; PN ae 63 Rutherford Co, TN, 1823 when w Drucilla ae 57, d Susanna ae 20, & s William ae 18; dd there 5/27/46; md 10/28/1783 Scilly Anglea, Littleton Parish, Cumberland Co, VA; wid PN ae 81 Rutherford Co, TN, 1847; wid ae 85 there 1848. R266

>William, esf VA; dd c1817; wid Hannah dd 1833, leaving ch: John, Elizabeth, Vincent, Rutha, Joel, Mary, Hannah, Claiborn (all decd in 1855), & Aggy; d Aggy Johnston, 6th ch/o

BLANTON (continued)
    sol, afp ae 71 Washington Co, VA, 1855, claiming sol also
    svc with George Washington at Braddock's Defeat in French
    & Indian War; Aggy PAR. R266
BLEAKLEY, Robert, esf 1773 on Blackwater River, Henry Co, VA,
    against indians; esf for RW 1776; b 1/12/1756 Caroline Co,
    VA; after parents dd, mvd to Bedford Co, VA, ae 13, thence
    shortly to Henry Co, VA; PN 1832 Wayne Co, KY, where dd
    3/18/33; md (1) ?; md (2) 10/1820-1 widow Margaret (King-
    kade) Maloney, Anderson Co, TN; wid md (1) John Maloney,
    Jefferson Co, East TN, who esf in regular army 1806 Hiwas-
    see Garrison & dd 7/24/1812, Sparta, TN; wid afp 1806 for
    svc of 1st h & PAR; wid PN ae 73 Wayne Co, KY, 1853 & res
    later 1853 with d Eleanor/Elly ae 53 who w/o George Bran-
    ham ae 63 Clinton Co, KY; ch/o John & Margaret Maloney liv
    1853: Edmond, Hanna Collins, Jane Love, Eleanor/Elly Bran-
    ham; in 1852 David, bro/o John Maloney, ae 74 res Rhea Co
    TN, a War of 1812 veteran; John, only ch/o Robert Bleakley
    & Margaret Kingkade, liv 1853; sol name sometimes spelled
    BLAKELY. R268
  William, esf 1782 Bedford Co, VA; b 8/6/1763; afp 1843 Bed-
    ford, KY. R268
BLECHYNDEN, Charles; esf 1778 Rockingham Co, VA; PN ae 75 Pen-
    dleton Co, VA, 1833. R268
BLEDSOE, James, esf Culpeper Co, VA; dd 3/19/1799 Franklin Co,
    KY; md 8/1785 Judith, Culpeper Co,VA; d Sally b 5/30/1786;
    wid md (2) 3/18/1807 William Forsee, Franklin Co, KY, who
    dd there 9/11/38; wid afp ae 78 Carroll Co,KY, 1844 & PAR;
    AFF then by d Sally/Sarah w/o John Tandy of that Co, when
    also AFF there by Ann Wayland, sis/o wid Judith. R268
  Miller, esf 1777 Orange Co, VA; PN ae 70 Oglethorpe Co, GA,
    1832; QLF states sol dd ae 78 when res with s-in-law Whit-
    field Landrum, further sol LWT dated 12/1/1838; QLF states
    sol b 4/13/1761 & md Patience Owsley; QLF states LWT, with
    codicil dated 7/45 lists d's Polly, Sidney, Jane, & Unice,
    & s's Moses, Peachy, & Miller, further s Peachy who b 1793
    md Nancy Ison or Atkinson; QLF 1928 from desc Mrs Eleanor
    Butter, Quitman, GA; QLF 1928 from desc Iona Bledsoe (Mrs
    V) Ragsdale, Illmo, MO, states sol name William Miller
    Bledsoe & he s/o Joseph & Betty Bledsoe. R268
BLEUFORD, William, see BLUFORD, William. R268
BLEVENS, Daniel, esf 1777 VA; b & raised Botetourt Co, VA; PN
    63 Roane Co,TN, 1816; ch in 1823: Daniel ae 15, William ae
    11, John ae 8, Polly Eliza ae 2, & Thomas ae 13 days; res
    Morgan Co,TN, 1834; dd 9/5/39; family surv 1853 Rockcastle
    Co, KY: Nancy & Polly Maden. R269
  James, esf 1780 Montgomery Co, VA; esf 1781 NC; b 12/25/1762
    New England, & brought to Henry Co, VA, as infant; mvd to
    Montgomery Co,VA, aec 10; PN 1832 Shawswick Township, Law-
    rence Co, IN; surname at times spelled BLIVINS. R269
  James, see BLEVIN, James. R269
  John, see BLEVINS, John. R269

BLEVENS, Nathan, see BLEVINS, Nathan. R269
BLEVIN, James, esf 1776 Henry Co, VA; PN ae 80 Morgan Co, KY,
     1834; dd 11/28/43 Lawrence Co, KY; md 1/4/1793 Hannah O,
     VA; wid PN ae 93 Lawrence Co, KY, 1857. R269
BLEVINS, Daniel, see BLEVENS, Daniel. R269
   James, see BLEVENS, James
   John, esf Grayson Co,VA; dd c12/17/1832 Lee Co, VA; md Sally
     Stevens, Claiborne Co, TN, c8/1/1832, who md (1) there
     c8/31/1805 Joel Stinson, who dd c4/11/1828; wid afp ae 69
     Hancock Co, TN, 1856, & PAR. R269
   Nathan, esf Montgomery Co, VA; b on Haw River, NC; PN ae 69
     Ashe Co, NC, 1832; dd 4/8/1834; md 9/1802 Lydia, who PN ae
     73 Monroe Township, Troy, Miami Co, OH, 1854. R269
   William, esf ae 16 Montgomery Co, or Wythe Co, VA, 1776; b
     1769 Pittsylvania Co, VA; afp 1836 Vermillion Co, IL; PAR,
     svc not in regularly organized military unit. R269
BLICK, James, esf 1776 Dinwiddie Co, VA; b 4/5/1760 Dinwiddie
     Co, VA, & mvd to Brunswick Co, VA, as ch; PN there 1832;
     dd 10/29/37. R269
   John, esf 1780 Dinwiddie Co, VA; b 3/17/1762; res Dinwiddie
     Co, VA, till 1830; PN 1833 Caldwell Co, KY; dd c9/8/41.
     R269
BLIZZARD, Burton, esf 1777 Rockingham Co, VA; PN ae 76 Pendle-
     ton Co, VA, 1833; dd 3/17/1837; md 12/1780 Sarah Keister,
     who PN ae 77 Pendleton Co, VA, 1839. R271
BLODGETT, Abisha, esf 1781 Stafford, Tolland Co, CT, where b
     11/24/1763; to NY, thence PA, thence Ohio Co, VA, where PN
     1833; res 1837 Marshall Co, VA; QLF states sol dd 4/15/40
     Marshall Co, VA, leaving wid Hannah & s Benjamin. R272
BLOSS, Valentine, esf 1776 Augusta Co, VA, where b 1757; PN
     1833 Cabell Co, VA; AFF 1850 Wayne Co, VA, by s E Bloss
     that sol dd 9/4/1850. R274
BLOUNT, Nathaniel, see BLUNT, Nathaniel. R274
BLOXSON, Scarborough, VA sea svc, esf 1777 on ship ACCOMAC; PN
     ae 79 Norfolk Co, VA, 1832; dd 10/36; md c1790 Leah, who
     PN ae 86 Accomac Co, VA, 1842, & res there 1852. R274
BLUE, David; no RW svc, but sol in Northwest Indian Wars 1791;
     PN 1800 Berkeley Co, VA; res 1822 Fleming Co, KY; mvd 1829
     to Parke Co, IN, to be with ch; dd there 1/1855, leaving a
     wid. R275
   David, esf 1779 Berkeley Co, VA, as sub for Jacob Blue; b
     6/9/1760 s/o Jacob, Bucks Co, PA; to KY 1808; afp 1838 Un-
     ion Co, KY; PAR, service less than 6 months. R275
   Peter, esf 1781 Hampshire Co, VA; dd 7/25/1844 Fayette Co,
     OH; md 1/1878 Susannah Keltch, Hampshire Co, VA; wid afp &
     afb ae 89 Fayette Co, OH, 1856; PAR & BLAR; s John P then
     ae 67; QLF states sol full name Peter Keyser Blue. R275
BLUFFORD, William, see BLUFORD, William. R275
BLUFORD, William, esf VA; d 1800 Baltimore Co,MD; md 8/14/1780
     Sarah Gardner (elopement); wid PN ae 79 there 1837 & res
     there 1848; ch births: Rachel 7/25/1781, Elizabeth 3/9/83
     (dd 6/30/86), Ann Hutchon 1/26/85, Priscilla 1/7/86 (dd

BLUFORD (continued)
1/1789), Heir 1/7/89 (dd 4/30/93), George Washington
10/6/90, Hancock Lee 6/2/92 (dd 9/--), Hariot & twin Henry
10/26/94, Jonathan 11/17/96, & Mary 3/99; other family bible data: William Bluford, s/o John Zimmerman & Ann Bleuford, b 1/29/1791; Heir Bleuford, d/o Ann Blueford, b
2/--; William Bleuford dd in 36th year; Maria Bleuford b
10/24/180-. R275
BLUNDOM, Elijah, see BLUNDON, Elijah. R275
BLUNDON, Elijah, esf 1776 VA; PN 1819 Northumberland Co, VA,
   where ae 67 in 1822 & res with s. R275
BLUNT, Natt, esf 1775 VA; PN ae 73 Botetourt Co, VA, 1821; w
   then decd & no ch res with him. R276
 William, esf 1775 VA; PN ae 62 Muskingum Co, OH, 1818. R276
BLY, Jacob, esf 1780 Woodstock, VA; dd c 1803 Shenandoah Co,
   VA, 1803; md 1780 Catharine Humble; wid PN ae 75 Frederick
   Co,VA, 1837; ch births: Elizabeth 2/8/1780, Rachel 5/3/82,
   Sarah 6/17/85, Rebeka 4/9/90; Phebe 11/11/92, & Mary
   3/27/88; wid sis/o Michael Humble, who decd in 1837. R276
 John, esf 1776 VA; PN ae 64 Shenandoah Co, VA, when family
   w Barbara ae 46 & ch: Jonathan ae 18, s ae 14, Samuel ae
   6, Mary ae 12, & Dorothy ae 10. R276
BOARD, John, esf Washington Co, MD; b 1751; afp 1835 Fauquier
   Co, VA, & PAR, insufficient svc; dd 3/8/1836; md 1788 (li-
   cense date 3/7/88) Ann/Nancy Doughty, Loudoun Co, VA; wid
   afp ae 88 Barbour Co, VA, 1850 & PAR; QLF 1938 from great
   great gds Forrest F Blalock, Los Angeles, CA, states sol
   res Warrenton, Fauquier Co, VA, further querier also great
   great gds/o Elijah Walker who RW sol. R277
 Patrick, esf Berkeley Co, VA; b 6/12/1750 Pigeon Hills, PA;
   PN 1832 Wood Co, VA; dd 11/6/39; md 5 or 6/1789 or 1790 to
   Mary Keezer, Washington Co, MD; wid PN & BLW ae 75 Ripley,
   Jackson Co,VA, & res there 1855; several ch including Tho-
   mas; eldest ch b 10/1791; QLF 1932 from desc Mrs J R Run-
   nels, Sioux City, IA, states sol's w Polly Kicer of York,
   Green Co, PA. R277
BOATMAN, William; esf 1777-8 near Redstone Fort, PA; b 12/1757
   Fauquier Co, VA; PN ae 77 Highland Co, OH, 1834. R278
BOATWRIGHT, John, esf 1781 Cumberland Co, VA; b 1764 Amherst
   Co, VA; to Prince Edward Co, VA, 1797 where PN 1833. R278
BOAZ, James, esf 1777 Bedford Co, VA; b 5/30/1749 Buckingham
   Co, VA; PN 1833 Patrick Co,VA; sol dd 11/12/1850; ch 1851:
   Milly, Tabitha Taylor, Robert (res 1852 Patrick Co, VA),
   Agnes w/o Daniel Pedigo, Mary Elliott, & Phebe Chandler;
   QLF 1909 from desc John D E Boaz, Nashville, TN, states
   sol had bro Shadrach who 5 years older. R278
 Meshach, esf 1776 Prince Edward Co, VA; PN ae 68 Buckingham
   Co, VA, 1821 when d Molly Meglasson ae 34 & gdd Mary Fran-
   ces Meglasson ae 10; dd 5/13/1828; QLF 1927 from desc Mrs
   Maude H Beckham, Farmville, VA, states sol had bro's James
   & Michael. R278
BOBBITT, William, esf 1779 VA; b 10/25/1754 bro/o John; afp

BOBBITT (continued)
     1826 Monroe Co, VA; in 1826 family was w aec 57 & d ae 23.
     R278
BOBO, Absalom; esf 1781 Spartanburg District, SC; b 1764, Al-
     bemarle Co, VA; afp 1845 Union District, SC, while res of
     Spartanburg District, SC; PAR, insufficient svc. R278
   Joseph, esf 1780 Prince William Co, VA, where b 1760; afp
     there 1846; PAR, insufficient proof of svc. R278
BOCK, Michael, esf VA; b 1757 near Fredericktown, MD; to VA
     1769, where res on Monongalia River; PN 1833 Harrison Co,
     VA; dd 3/23/1838, leaving no wid but ch: John, Michael,
     Nicholas, David, Solomon, Abigail Shaver, Margaret Enomon-
     ger, Sarah, Hanna w/o John Baker, & Catharine Shaver (decd
     in 1860, who left ch: Michael, Sarah, & Margaret Shaver);
     sol's d Elizabeth md Jacob Wolf & dd before f, leaving ch:
     Margaret, Aron, Susanna, & Sarah Wolf; upon reexamination
     of PN claim by US Attorney 1835, it was shown sol did not
     render alleged svc, & his name dropped from PN rolls. R278
BODINE, John, esf 1775 near Martinsburg, Berkeley Co, VA; PN
     ae 75 Ross Co, OH, 1819; dd 9/2/1822; QLF 1912 from desc
     Mrs Mary E Sinnott, Rosemont, PA; QLF 1930 from desc Mrs
     H H Glascock, Veedersburg, IN; QLF states sol dd Ross Co,
     OH, ae 78. R279
BOGGS, Francis, esf 1776 Greenbrier Co, VA; b 1754 Chester Co,
     PA; mvd after RW to Kanawaha Co, VA; afp 1833 on Big Elk
     River, Nicholas Co,VA; PAR, insufficient proof of svc with
     regularly organized troops. R280
   Jeremiah, esf 1781 Fauquier Co, VA; b 3/22/1753 Prince Wil-
     liam Co, VA; afp 1839 Newton Co,GA, & PAR; s Jeremiah BOG-
     GUS Jr afp aec 62 Jasper Co, GA, 1853 & PAR. R280
BOGGUS, Jeremiah, see BOGGS, Jeremiah. R280
BOGLE, Andrew, esf 1777 Cumberland Co, PA; b 4/26/1753 s/o Jo-
     seph who dd 1790; sol dd 11/29/1813 Blount Co, TN, where
     mvd 1786; md 5/24/1774 Elizabeth, d/o Hugh Campbell, York
     Co, PA; wid b 1748; wid apf 1844 Blount Co, TN; PAR, less
     than 6 months svc; ch births: Ann 4/7/1775, Joseph 2/6/78,
     Hugh 1/31/80; Andrew 11/6/81 (dd 12/13/1842 Blount Co,TN),
     & Polly 5/5/85; f Joseph md 6/8/1752 Jane McAntires, Lan-
     cashire,England, & their ch births; Andrew, James 6/22/55,
     Margret 1/25/57 (dd 8/30/175-), Joseph 7/5/59, Rebecca
     12/22/61 (dd 6/23/62), 0. 8/2/63 (dd 8/18/63), Samuel
     5/24/65, Jane 12/27/66 (dd 4/18/67), Agnes 3/20//69, Jeane
     10/3/71; f Joseph Sr dd 9/6/1790; Jean dd 6/14/1797; QLF
     1935 from desc Louise Bogle (Mrs Reuben) Hayes, Knoxville,
     TN; QLF 1931 from desc Mrs T C Young, Birmingham, AL. R280
   Joseph, esf 1777 Cumberland Co, PA; esf 1779 Rockbridge Co,
     VA; dd 5/1/1814; md 1/20/1786 Margaret Houston, Greene Co,
     TN; wid PN ae 81 Monroe Co, TN, 1845. R280
BOHANNON, Ambrose, BLW issued 5/29/1792. R280
   John, esf 1779, dd 7/10/1832 Shelby Co, KY, ae 77; md Helen
     1/7/1774 Pittsylvania Co, VA; wid afp ae 77 Shelby Co, KY,
     & PAR, sol svc not in regularly organized troops. R280

BOHON, Benjamin, esf 1775 VA; dd 10/8/1825; md 7/15/1780 Sarah
    Threlkeld; 1st ch b 4/1781; wid PN ae 72 Mercer Co, KY,
    1836; her bro George present at her marriage, & res ae 77
    Mercer Co, KY, 1837; sol's bro John (4 years older) res ae
    81 Mercer Co, KY, 1836. R280
  John, esf 1775 Orange Co, VA, where b 12/25/1756; PN 1832
    Mercer Co, KY 1832; QLF 1915 from desc Cora (Beck) High-
    leyman, Sedalia, MO, states she d/o William Beck & Rebecca
    Bohon, d/o Walter Raleigh Bohon (b 2/20/1788 VA, or Har-
    rodsburg, KY, & dd 6/21/1884) & Martha Catherine Jones (b
    3/2/1808 & dd 1/12/1859), further Walter Raleigh Bohon s/o
    sol & w Sallie Johnson. R280
BOICE, Abraham, see BOYCE, Abraham. R281
BOIN, Reuben, see BOWEN, Reuben. R281
BOISSEAU, John, esf 1780 Dinwiddie Co, VA, where b 3/14/1764;
    mvd to Logan Co, KY, with family 1806; PN 1834 Simpson Co,
    KY; QLF 1918 from great gds O G Boisseau, Holden, MO,
    states sol dd c1831-2. R281
BOLDEN, John, see BOLDER, John. R281
BOLDER, John, esf VA; PN ae 73 Wiscassett, Lincoln Co, ME,
    1819; res 1819 with s John, Litchfield, that Co; dd Fall
    1826; s Sargant afp still due f, Bath, ME, 1850. R281
BOLEN, John, esf c1780 Henry Co, VA, where b (then Pittsylva-
    nia Co); PN ae 72 Sullivan Co, IN, 1832. R281
BOLENER, Adam, esf 1781 near Winchester, VA; b 10/1765 near
    Reading, Bucks Co, PA; PN 1832 Hardy Co, VA. R281
BOLES, Zachariah, esf 1777 Chesterfield Co, VA; afp ae 80 Sul-
    livan Co, IN, when w ae 76 & they res village of Carlisle
    with s ae 42 who had 9 ch; sol had other s in VA & TN & d
    (wid with 10 ch) who res Green Co, KY; no action indicated
    on PN application; surname at times spelled BOWLES. R281
BOLEY, Prestley, esf VA; PN aec 55 Bedford Co, VA, 1818; in
    1821 family w Polly ae 37, & ch: Harriet ae 16, Martha ae
    14, John ae 12, & William ae 10; dd 5/20/38; QLF 1908 from
    desc Anna Bryan Boley (Mrs R F) Garner, San Bernardino, CA
    states sol full name Pressley M Boley. R281
BOLING, Edmon/Edmond; esf 1776 Stafford Co,VA; PN ae 69 Greene
    Co, TN, 1829 where had res c30 years, when had w & 5 small
    ch & bro Joshua ae 57 also res there. R282
  Jarret, esf 1778 Stafford Co, VA, where b 1/18/1762; PN 1834
    Tazewell Co, VA; QLF states sol full name Jarret Wesley
    BOWLEN; QLF 1928 from desc Mrs R B Bodell, Princeton, Mer-
    cer Co, WV; QLF 1920 from desc Minnie Boone, Richmond, VA.
    R282
BOLLING, Joseph, see BOWLING, Joseph. A282
  Robert, esf 1778 Petersburg, VA; b near there 1759; PN there
    1832; wid liv 1845. R282
  Robert, VA sea svc, esf 1776; md 12/1780 Clara Yates, Amelia
    Co, VA; sol dd c1790 Dinwiddie Co,VA, when ch infants; his
    LWT dated 9/7/1789 & probated there 2/21/91; wid gtd BLW
    1817 & dd 8/1832; ch who afp 1850 Brunswick Co, VA: Susan,
    w/o Samuel Gilliam, & Robert Jr; ch PAR. R282

BOLLZ, Joseph, see BOWLING, Joseph. R282
BOLT, Abraham, esf 1789 Spartanburg District, SC; esf 1781 VA;
    b 824/1764 Fauquier Co, VA; to Laurens District, SC, 1784
    where PN 1832 as Abraham Sr; QLF 1935 from desc Mrs P H
    Perkins Jr, Atlanta, GA, states sol spelled first name Ab-
    ram. R282
BOLTENHOUSE, John, see BOULTENHOUSE, John. R282
BOMAN, John, esf 1781 Henry Co, VA; b 1/6/1759 Halifax Co, VA;
    PN 1834 Patrick Co, VA, when bro ae 64 there. R283
BOMAR, John, esf 1779 Halifax Co, VA; to Hardin Co, KY, 1808;
    PN 1833 Hart Co, KY, when had bro res Halifax Co, VA; QLF
    states sol md Miss Burk of Halifax Co, VA, their 9 s's:
    John, Fielding, Edward, Bibby, William, Booker, Armistead,
    Spencer, & Reuben, plus a d; QLF states sol had 4 bro's,
    William, Alexander, Peter, & Thomas all of Halifax Co, VA,
    further William dd 1802 & Alexander dd Essex Co, VA, 1786.
    R283
BOMGARDNER, David, see BUMGARNER, David. R283
BOND, John, esf 1779 King William Co, VA; PN ae 66 Owen Co, KY
    where dd 3/12/42; md 7/11/1813 Joannah Holliday, Gallatin
    Co, KY; wid PN ae 59 Grant Co, KY, 1853; wid res Owenton,
    Owen Co, KY, 1873. R284
  Richard, esf 1777 VA; esf 1781 as sub for f Nathan; b 7/1763
    Amherst Co, VA; PN 1832 Franklin Co, GA, where dd 1/1837;
    md c1783 Susannah, Amherst Co, VA; wid dd 11/6/1843, leav-
    in ch: Sarah b 2/28/1784 & md John Crider, Sophia b 1792 &
    md --- Hendricks, Frances b1794 & md --- Lanten, Lindsey b
    2/28/1801, & Richard b 12/6/1788 who md 4/9/1811 Franklin
    Co, GA; births of ch who dd before m: Permele 5/22/1786,
    Elizabeth 2/12/91, William 1/27/98, & Peniser 1801; John
    Crider, h/o Sarah/Sally, decd in 1853; s Richard afp for
    sol surv ch 1851 Cobb Co, VA, & PN gtd. R284
  William, esf 1781 Wilkes Co, NC; b 9/24/1766 Charlotte Co,
    VA, s/o Jesse; PN 1832 Warren Co, TN. R284
  William, esf 1776 VA; dd 7/22/1830; md 12/11/1777 Virginia
    Ann, Cumberland Co, VA, who PN ae 79 Williamson Co, TN,
    1839; ch births: John 11/4/1778, Page 11/23/79, William
    7/19/83, Lucy 9/8/90, ? 10/23/95, & Maurice 10/23/1806.
    R284
  William, esf 1777 Cumberland Co, VA; PN ae 86 Franklin Co,
    KY, 1826; dd 3/20/27; md (2) 12/2/1790 Sarah/Sally Cran-
    son, Woodford Co, KY; wid PN ae 75 Anderson Co, KY, 1838;
    QLF 1917 from desc Mrs Edwin Moss, Williamsburg, Whitely
    Co,KY; QLF 1920 from desc Mrs J C Van Arsdell, Lawrence-
    burg, KY. R284
  Wright, esf Halifax Co, VA; bc 1755 Charlotte Co, VA; PN
    1833 Hawkins Co, TN, having no ch at time. R284
  Wright, esf 1775 Cumberland Co, VA, where b 4/13/1759; mvd
    to Bedford Co, VA, c1800, where dd 2/10/1843; md 11/1781
    Martha/Patsey Brown, Cumberland Co, VA; wid PN ae 83 Bed-
    ford Co,VA, 1843; ch births: Salley 1/23/1783 & dd 7/5/98,
    Allen 7/21/85, Mehala 12/4/87,William 7/8/90 & dd 7/20/90,

BOND (continued)
    Anney 10/7/1791, Pleasant 7/2/94, Mary Spearman 9/15/97,
    Rhoda 2/6/180-. R284
BONDS, John, see Bond, John. R284
BONNER, John, esf Sussex Co, VA, where b 8/20/1764; PN Wilson
    Co, TN, 1832; bro Thomas res 1832 Madison Co, TN; wid mbnn
    & she PN 1843 from Nashville, TN, Pension Office. R286
  Joseph, esf PA; PN aec 66 Monongalia Co, VA, 1818; in 1820 w
    aec 60, d's Peggy & Ruth, plus gdc Nancy & John, both ch/o
    Peggy; QLF 1927 from desc James Edgar Brown, Chicago, IL;
    QLF 1940 from Mrs Tracy Zierman, Mobile, AL, states her
    great great gdf Joseph Bonner dd GA 1822, further he b VA
    & md Susannah in GA. R286
  William, esf 1776 York Co, VA, where b 12/29/1759; PN 1833
    Bath Co, VA, where dd 2/9/1847; md 4/13/1790 Hannah, who b
    2/23/1768; sol referred to as William Sr in LWT, his exe-
    cutor being Scipio A Bonner; wid PN 1849 Bath Co, VA; QLF
    1930 from desc Col. Harrison J Price, Richmond, VA. R286
BONNETT, Jacob, esf 1780 from what now Harrison Co, VA; served
    with twin bro Lewis, bro Peter, & bro John; bc 1761 on Ce-
    dar Creek, now in Frederick Co, VA; PN ae 72 Lewis Co, VA,
    1833, when bro's Lewis & Peter made AFF, & when bro Samuel
    ae 65; dd 12/1847 Lewis Co, VA, leaving no wid, but ch:
    Martha w/o Samuel Horne, Delilah w/o Abraham Hess, Eliza
    w/o Fleming Sprouse, & Lucinda w/o Jesse Butcher, all res
    Lewis Co, VA in 1860; other ch decd: Samuel, Gracie West &
    Elizabeth Allhue who had surv ch; sol PN later suspended,
    since service as indian spy not considered as regular type
    (see next paragraph); QLF states sol had s William liv du-
    ring RW. R286
  Lewis, esf 1779 in what now Harrison Co, VA; b 1762 in what
    now Hardy Co, VA; bro John killed 4/1783 while they fight-
    ing indians in Lewis Co, VA; bro/o Lewis, Jacob, & Peter;
    Jacob & Lewis twins & 4 years older than sol; bro Peter 18
    months older than sol; stated in AFF that bro's Lewis, Ja-
    cob, & Peter did not serve in RW, but only fought against
    indians; QLF 1921 from desc Mrs A A Glenn, Chicago, IL.
    R286
  Peter, esf VA; PN ae 69 Lewis Co, VA, but name later dropped
    from PN roll s as not having regular svc in RW, according
    to bro Samuel's statement; QLF 1921 from desc Mrs Gladys
    Somerfield, Arkansas City, KS. R286
BONNEWELL, Thomas, VA sea svc, esf VA; s/o John; bro's James &
    John served on ship that Thomas commanded; also bro's Ar-
    thur, Charles, & Smith; to KY & dd there c1824; following
    heirs recd PN 1832: Rosanna P Young of New Richmond, Nancy
    A Matthews res near Leesburgh, OH, Margaret Colburn & Ame-
    lia Craymor of St Thomas, MO, & Henrietta Stokeley; sur-
    name at times spelled BONEWELL. R286
BONNEY, Thomas; esf ae 15 Princess Anne Co, VA, where b c1760;
    PN there 1832 ae 72. R286
BONNIFIELD, Samuel, esf 1778 Culpeper Co, VA; b 1750 Prince

BONNIFIELD (continued)
Georges Co, MD; afp ae 83 Randolph Co, VA; PAR, insuffici-
ent proof of svc; afp again there 1846, & PAR; QLF 1904
from desc C J Maxwell, Dallas, TX; QLF 1911 from desc
Franklin Maxwell, Dallas, TX. R286
BONWELL, James, esf 1776 Accomac Co, VA; PN aec 68 Brown Co,
OH, 1818. R287
BOOCHER, Abraham, see BOOKER, Abraham. R287
BOOKER, Abraham, esf 1776 Pittsburgh, PA; svc in VA regiment;
PN ae 72 Alleghany Co, PA, 1832; dd 2/2/1833; md 11/1793
or 12/1793 Frances McElroy, Alleghany Co, PA; wid PN ae 70
Peebles Township, that Co, 1849; in 1820 sol had 4 s's ae
20, 15, 12, & aec 9 plus 2 d's; QLF 1908 great gds J Boyd
Duff, Pittsburgh, PA; QLF 1916 from desc W H Reader, New
Amsterdam,IN; QLF 1921 from desc Miss Abbie E Urban, Rich-
mond, IN, states sol surname BOUGHER; QLF 1919 from great
great gdd Mrs C C Friend, Lawrence, KS. R287
George, esf 1781 Winchester, Frederick Co, VA ; b near there
1769; PN 1843 Union Township, Madison Co, OH, ae given as
80. R287
Lewis, esf 1777 Essex Co, VA, 1777; BLW issued 5/12/1803.
R287
Samuel, esf 1777 Amelia Co, VA, where b 8/9/1758; to Washington Co, KY, 1818 where PN 1835, where dd 12/22/47, & md
there 3/2/1829 Nancy A Nantz; wid PN there 1853, when William B Booker & Dr P R Booker made AFF they attended wedding of sol & Nancy Nantz; sol s W B res Springfield, Washington Co, KY, 1835; Thomas Nantz witness for sol wid PN
application; QLF 1934 from great great gds Joseph Linton
Sawyer, Houston, TX, states sol s Paul Jones Booker b near
Staunton, VA, & mvd to KY 1808. R287
Samuel, BLW issued 1807 to s's George & Samuel of Cumberland
Co, VA, sol then being decd; Richard Booker witness for
claim 1806. R287
BOON, John, esf 1774 Rowan Co, NC; b VA 7/16/1755; to Rowan Co
NC, with parents as ch; after RW mvd to Guilford Co, NC,
where PN 1833, & where dd 1/27/37; md there (3) 7/7-8/1822
Anne Montgomery of that Co; wid PN ae 59 Alamance Co, NC,
1856; sol & Anne had 1 ch that dd ae 2; wid gtd BLW 1856;
QLF states a John/Jonathan Boone, an RW sol of Rowan Co,
NC, had w Rebecca. R288
John, esf 1777 York Co, PA; b near York, that Co, nephew/o
Daniel Boone of KY; PN ae 78 Monroe Co, VA, 1833; dd
7/17/1833; md 1787-8 Elizabeth Alford/Alfred, Augusta Co,
VA, who dd 2/15/1841; surv ch who afp 1841: John ae 57,
Nancy Burdett ae 53, Henry b 3/10/1802, Frances Myres ae
37, & Sally Humphreys; PAR, no proof of sol marriage, per
deposition of Augusta Co, VA, Co clerk; QLF 1914 from desc
Mrs J L Goss, Clinton, MO; QLF 1925 from great gds James D
Boone, Fayetteville, WV, states he gds/o sol s Henry, further sol s/o Israel Boone who f/o Daniel Boone of KY; QLF
1928 from desc Helen E (Mrs A H) Dickinson, Huntington,

BOON (continued)
   WV; QLF states sol d Nancy Burdett res/o Roane Co, VA, &
   sol s John res/o Braxton Co, VA. R288
BOORD, Patrick, see BOARD, Patrick. R288
BOOTEN, Travis, see BOOTON, Travis. R288
BOOTH, Beverly; esf 1776 Southampton Co, VA; PN ae 80 Surry Co
   VA, 1832 when titled "Reverend"; dd there 11/22/33, & md
   there 2/4/1819 Mary Cornwall/Presson of that Co; wid PN ae
   73 there, & res there 1855 when gtd BLW; wid dd 7/2/55,
   leaving d Mary E w/o John C Rogers, latter res/o Surry Co,
   VA, 1859. R289
   George, esf 1778 Northumberland Co, VA; PN aec 74 Rutherford
   Co, KY, 1832. R289
   James, esf 1773 Richmond Co, VA; PN aec 76 Woodford Co, KY,
   1832; dd 5/16/34; QLF 1907 from great great gdd Mrs F A
   Carothers, Bardstown, KY. R289
   James, esf 1778 Richmond Co, VA; dd 12/12/1817; md aec 26 to
   Caty Draper ae 18 Richmond Co, VA, 1787 (MB 5/15/87); wid
   afp ae 74 Pike Co, MO, ae 74; PAR, sol svc based upon svc
   of James Booth, above. R289
   John, esf ae 14 Harrison Co,VA, 1782; afp 1834 ae 66 Jeffer-
   son Co, IN; PAR when a witness swore claimant b 3/15/1775.
   R289
   Thomas, esf VA; PN 1786 for disability; res 1825 Franklin Co
   VA. R289
   William, VA sea svc; esf 1777 VA; dd 9/1789 leaving no heirs
   at time; bro Thomas res Somerset Co, MD; heirs afp 1841
   Northumberland Co, VA; PAR. R289
BOOTHE, James, see BOOTH, James who dd 1817. R289
BOOTON, Travis, esf with bro William 1780 Culpeper Co, VA, res
   of that Co; dd 4/1814 Madison Co, KY; md 7/1787 Rutha Es-
   till, Greenbrier Co, VA; wid d/o Captain James Estill, who
   KIA Indian Wars; wid md (2) William Kavanaugh, who dd w/o
   issue 10/1829; wid PN ae 84 Madison Co, KY, 1852 when only
   ch Mary Ann (by 1st h) aec 64 & w/o Joel Embey then ae 87.
   R290
   William, esf 1779 VA with bro Travis; dd c1815 Mason Co, VA;
   md 1777-8 Amelia/Emmelia Sturgeon, Monroe Co, VA; wid dd
   8/1841 Mason Co, VA; AFF 1854 Greenbrier Co, VA, by Hiram
   Sturgeon Booton ae 50 that liv heirs of sol & wid then:
   himself, Elizabeth Bott, Eleanor Newman, Rhoda Everman,
   Mary Fisher , & William Harvey Booton; Eleanor/Ellen w/o
   Waller Newman who ae 74 in 1854; heirs gtd PN. R290
BOOTWRIGHT, Samuel, esf 1779 VA; b 1764 Hanover Co, VA about
   10 miles from Richmond; to Mecklinburg Co, NC, 1787, where
   PN 1832; dd 5/4/1834; QLF 1935 from desc Mrs S E Payne,
   Hawkinsville, GA. R290
BOOZ, John, esf 1777 VA; PN ae 78 Woodford Co, KY, 1820 when
   "no family with him"; QLF states sol res there ae 92. R290
   Richard, esf 1778 with f John, Lunenburg Co, VA; b 7/25/1764
   Amelia Co, VA; f mvd family to Lunenburg Co, VA, before RW
   & later to KY; sol afp ae 69 Rockingham Co, VA, as Richard

BOOZ (continued)
    Sr, when s Henry made AFF there; afp ae 77 Preble Co, KY, 1841; both PAR, insufficient proof of svc. R290
BOOZE, John, BLW issued 5/5/1790. R290
BORDERS, Christopher, esf 1779 VA; b 8/15/1763 near Schuykill River,PA; to MD as ch with f, thence NC, thence to VA; res VA 22 years, thence to OH where PN 1834 Butler Township, Darke Co; QLF 1917 from great gds Foster Stewart. R291
  Peter, esf 1781 Loudoun Co, VA; b 1767 Lancaster Co, PA; to Loudoun Co, VA, aec 4; afp 1835 Sangamon Co, IL; PAR, insufficient proof of svc; res 1850 Logan Co, IL; QLF 1935 from great great gdd Miss Margaret Hamil, Kansas City, MO, states her f's m Mary Ann Borders was d/o or gdd/o sol, & that sol dd 1859 ae 95 Menard Co, IL, & buried there. R291
BORER, Charles, esf 1777 Hampshire Co, VA; PN ae 72 Pendleton Co, VA; QLF states sol dd ae 83 there. R291
BOSS, Adam, esf Baltimore, MD; b 3/17/1762 Bucks Co, PA; mvd with f to Baltimore Co, MD, when ae 13; elder bro Jacob RW sol; to Fauquier Co, VA, thence to KY 1822, thence Cincinnati, Hamilton Co, OH, where PN 1832; dd 6/17/1833 there; md 1/24/1822 Harriet Ransdell, Prince William Co, VA; wid PN ae 60 Cincinnati, OH, 1833, gtd BLW there 1858, & gtd PN increase there ae 69. R292
BOSTEYON, Adam, see BOSTON, Adam. R292
BOSTICK, Absalom, esf 1780; b 12/15/1760; afp 1837 Halifax Co, VA; PAR; Absalom Bostick, executor of sol LWT, made AFF 1855 that sol dd 11/25/1840. R292
BOSTON, Adam, esf VA; b 1/18/1764; dd 3/5/1832 Frederick Co, VA; md 1785 Juliet/Juliania How, Berkeley Co, VA; wid PN 1841 Clarke Co, VA; ch births: Margaret 5/18/1786, Mary 10/14/87; Phebe 9/30/89,Elizabeth 11/27/91, Nancy 2/27/94, Sarah 11/26/95, Fanny 8/17/97, & Kitty 4/9/99 who dd 10/1/1801. R292
  Reuben, esf 1779 Orange Co, VA, where b; PN ae 80 Anderson Co, KY, 1832. R292
BOSWELL, Machen/Machin, esf VA; dd 12/10/1793; gds Thomas M B Roy afp 1845 Urbanna, Middlesex Co, VA, stating his uncle Dr Thomas Boswell adm/o sol's estate; PAR. R293
  Reuben, see BOZZELL, Reuben. R293
BOTHMAN, Barnhart; esf Philadelphia, PA, for VA svc; b 1754 in Germany; PN 1832 Unity Township, Columbiana Co, OH, where mvd from Bucks Co, PA; dd 1/12/43; md 3/2/1785 Catharine, Haycock Township, Bucks Co, PA; wid PN aec 74 Unity Township, Columbiana Co, OH, 1845. R295
BOTKIN, Thomas, esf 1780 Staunton, Augusta Co, VA; md Margaret Devericks, Augusta Co, VA, 4/24/1786; sol dd 2/14/1822; wid PN ae 72 Pendleton Co, VA, & res ae 79 Highland Co, VA 1849. R295
BOTT, Frederick, esf 1779 Dinwiddie Co, VA; PN ae 75 Montgomery Co,VA, 1832; dd 5/14/42; md 3/12/1791 Martha Wall, Bedford Co, VA; wid b 3/2/1764, & PN 1844 Montgomery Co, VA. R295

BOTTOM, Miles, esf 1778 Amelia Co, VA, where b 1751; PN 1834
  Warren Co, TN; dd 9/12/41. R295
BOTTS, Moses, esf 1780 Loudoun Co, VA, where b 2/25/1750; PN
  1832 Bath Co, KY, where res c30 years; QLF 1932 from great
  gds R D Brown, Huntington Beach, CA, states sol dd c1840
  KY; QLF 1939 from desc Mrs Luther C Brown, Salem, IN. R295
 Seth, esf 1775 Battletown, Frederick Co, VA; PN ae 63 Clark
  Co, KY, 1818; QLF states sol dd 1827. R295
BOUCHER, Richard, esf 1775 Berkeley Co, VA; PN ae 69 Mason Co,
  VA, 1821 when w decd & sol res with s & unmarried d. R295
BOUGH, Jacob, see BAUGH, Jacob. R296
BOUGHER, Abram, see BOOKER, Abraham. R296
BOULDIN, Wood, esf 1776 Charlotte Co, VA, where dd 3/13/1800;
  md there 4/3/1777 Joanna Tyler of that Co; wid PN there ae
  86 in 1838, when liv ch: Louis, James (then in US House of
  Representatives), Robert, Thomas, & d; wid surv by 1 s & 1
  d; QLF 1896 from great gds P Bouldin Jr, Stuart, VA. R296
BOULTENHOUSE, John, esf 1777 Morris Co, NJ, company part/o VA
  regiment; PN ae 59 Miami Co, OH, 1820 when family w ae 47,
  s Henry ae 17, & s Abraham ae 12; name sometimes spelled
  BOLTINGHOUSE. R296
BOUNEY, Joseph, esf 1776 VA; PN ae 65 Floyd Co, KY, 1819; family 1820 w Sarah aec 33 (pregnant) & ch Nancy b 4/7/1799,
  Martha b 3/13/1810, Hiram b 4/23/12, Carlisle 5/28/14, Rebecca b 8/27/16, & Margaret 11/1/17; wid survived sol.
  R296
BOURN, Ebenezer, esf 1778 with VA troops while exploring coun-
  try & hunting on Ohio River; b 1753 Lebanon, Windham Co,
  CT; PN 1828 Harrisonville, Monroe Co, IL; dd 8/29/39. R297
 James, esf 1780 Culpeper Co, VA; b 1759-60 Orange Co, VA; PN
  1833 Montgomery Co, KY; s Walker res there 1837; sol sis-
  in-law Catherine md sol bro & res sol home during his RW
  svc, she being ae 70 Jessamine Co, KY. 1833. R297
 John, esf 1776 VA; PN aec 66 Orange Co, VA 1818. R297
BOURNE, John, esf 1777 VA; md Aug 1775 Mary who PN ae 78 King
  William Co, VA, 1837; sol dd 3/1792; s Daniel b 9/9/1776.
  R297
 Judith, former wid/o sol Frederick Zimmerman. R297
BOUSH, Charles S, VA sea svc; esf 1777 VA; dd 2/1809; adm/o
  estate William B Lamb of Norfolk Co afp & PAR. R297
 Goodrich, esf VA; dd intestate during svc, leaving wid, who
  dd intestate leaving 4 ch all of whom decd in 1854, but 1
  gdc living then afp & PAR. R297
 Robert, esf VA; dd 10/15/1809; adm of estate Dr James Corn-
  ish afp & PAR. R297
BOWDEN, Elias, esf 1779 VA as sub for William Bowden; esf Isle
  of Wight Co 1780; PN aec 70 Henry Co, TN, 1832; md Isle of
  Wight Co, VA, 12/22/1785 Celia Lawrence; sol dd 2/25/1843;
  wid dd 12/5/52 Henry Co, TN, leaving ch: Dempsey Thomas,
  Francis, Gay, Mary Olive, Margaret Givin, Jackey Howard, &
  Benjamin T; Benjamin T afp for all heirs 1855 ae 51 & PN
  gtd. R298

BOWEN, Andrew, see BOWER, Andrew. R299
  Bracy, esf Mecklenburg Co, VA, where b 1762; to Rutherford
    Co, NC, 1822 where PN 1832. R299
  Charles, esf Crab Orchard, Washington Co, VA; b 9/1749 on
    farm on James River, VA; also Indian Wars svc after RW; PN
    1832 Blount Co, TN, when res with wid/o decd s William;
    res Putnam Co, IN, 1834 with s Charles; a gdc res Bain-
    bridge, IN; bro Reese KIA in Battle of Kings Mountain; QLF
    states bro William also RW sol. R299
  John, esf 1780 Mecklenburg Co, VA, where b 1763; PN 1833
    Gwinnett Co, GA; dd 1/24/50 leaving ch mbnn; QLF 1926 from
    desc Helen Dowling (Mrs R T) Hulsey. R300
  John, BLW issued 1/17/1811. R300
  John, esf VA; dd 1817; md 1786 Elizabeth d/o James Mayo near
    Charlottesville, VA; wid b 2/25/1762 & PN 1840 Albemarle
    Co, VA, & dd there 1848 leaving ch Nancy (b2/13/1782, eld-
    est), Frances, James, Ephraim, John, Avis, Mary, Eliza-
    beth, Susan, Catharine, Lydia, & Martha; sol bro Micajah
    ae 85 made AFF North Garden, Albemarle Co, VA, 1840 he al-
    so RW sol; AFF 1840 by John Harris who md 1792 Nancy, sis
    of sol wid, Nancy having dd many years before. R300
  John P, esf 1775-6 King George Co, VA, where b; PN there aec
    78 in 1832. R300
  Micajah, esf 1781 Albemarle Co, VA; b 8/8/1753 Lunenburg Co,
    VA; mvd to Albemarle Co, VA, as small ch with parents; PN
    there 1833. R300
  Reuben, esf 1775 Albemarle Co, VA; b Lunenburg Co, VA; PN ae
    76 Hawkins Co, TN, 1832; dd 5/17/39; md 6/10/1787 Sarah R
    Hicks, Albemarle Co, VA; wid PN ae 81 Lee Co, VA, 1844; at
    times surname spelled BOING. R300
  William, esf 1779 Culpeper Co, VA; PN there ae 70 as William
    Bowen Sr 1832; dd 10/1/32 Rappahannock Co, VA, & wid dd 2
    months later; ch: Anne w/o John Beam, William, Thomas, &
    Silas, latter 2 decd before f dd; gdc: ch/o Thomas (John,
    Polly, & Thompson) + Anne d/o Silas; heirs afp 1833 Rappa-
    hannock Co, VA, & PN gtd. R301
  William, esf Charlottesville, Albemarle Co, VA; b 8/1758;
    afp 1837 Nicholas Co, KY; PAR, insufficient proof of svc;
    s William. R301
BOWER, Andrew, esf 1777 Berkeley Co, VA; b 2/16/1753 York Co,
    PA; PN 1833 Montgomery Co, IN. R301
BOWERS, Balaam, esf 1777 Brunswick Co, VA; b 10/1764; PN 1832
    Greensville Co, VA, where res 1836; dd 1/8/41; s Balaam Jr
    & d Betsey Hodges liv 1841. R302
  John Brittain, esf 1780 Southampton Co, VA, where b 1763;
    afp Orange Co, NC, 1824 when family w & 5 ch, including s
    (eldest) ae 10 & youngest b 12/15/1823; PAR, but PN there
    1834. R302
  Morris, BLW issued 7/14/1792. R303
BOWLES, George, esf 1780 Bedford Co, VA; dd 6/7/1824; md Betsy
    Arthur there 1774-5; wid PN ae 88 Franklin Co, VA, 1843 at
    which time s Reuben ae 60-70 & d older than Reuben. R304

BOWLES, Matthew, esf 1777 James City Co, VA; b Ireland & came
to America with f when aec 5; also svc in War of 1812; PN
ae 78 Grayson Co, KY, 1833; dd 3/24/37 Perry Co, IN; also
known as Matthew C Bowles; md 4/4/1826 Nancy Chism, Grayson Co, KY, who PN aec 66 there 1854. R304
   Thomas, esf 1777 Hanover Co, VA, & PN ae 72 there 1832; dd
   12/7/39. R304
   Zachariah, esf 1777 Hanover Co, VA, & PN ae 65 there 1819;
   in 1820 family w ae 50, s ae 24, s ae 22, & s ae 17; R304
BOWLEY, Presley, BLW issued 7/14/1792. R304
BOWLING, Charles, esf Stafford Co, VA; b 4/13/1763 Westmoreland Co, VA; mvd c1830 to Fairfield Co, OH, where PN 1833
res Amanda Township; QLF 1909 from great gds O L Watkins,
Indianapolis, IN. R304
   Edward, esf Amherst Co, VA; b 8/25/1744 St Marys Co, MD, &
   mvd c1769 to Amherst Co, VA; mvd after RW to Clarke Co, GA
   where PN 1832. R304
   James, esf 1775 Amherst Co, VA; b 1752 St Mary's Co, MD; PN
   1832 Amherst Co, VA; dd 11/12-13/1836; md 4/7/1777 Letitia
   "Letty" More Gillaspie at her f's house on Piney River,
   Nelson Co, VA; wid PN ae 76 Amherst Co, VA, 1838; had many
   children. R304
   Jarret, see BOLING, Jarret. R304
   Joseph, esf VA; res 1820 Crawford Co, IN; PN aec 73 Orange
   Co, IN, 1826 where dd 1/30/36; md (2) Spring/o 1818 Martha
   Williams, Madison Co, KY; wid PN ae 71-75 Greene Co, IN,
   1859 when res with d Sally w/o Enoch Stone, & when s Will-
   iam BOLLING ae 40 res Jackson Township, Orange Co, IN; in
   1836 James Belcher, s-in-law of sol by 1st marriage, res
   Orange Co, IN; Nettie Briscoe ae 48, sis of sol wid, res
   Greene Co, IN, 1836. R304
   Thomas, esf 1776 VA; dd 1/1810 Spotsylvania Co, VA; md Sarah
   Ford, Stafford Co, VA, 11/25/1793; wid mvd to IN 1829, afb
   ae 84 Harrison Co, IN, 1849, & BLAR; afb ae 93 Harrison Co
   IN, 1856 & gtd BLW. R304
   William, esf 1775 Westmoreland Co, VA, where b 7/13/1758; to
   Stafford Co, VA, after RW, & res there till c1828 when mvd
   to Fairfield Co, OH, where PN 1833; bro Charles AFF 1833
   that he served with sol in RW. R304
BOWMAN, Abraham; esf 1775-6 VA; b 10/16/1749; PN 1829 Fayette
Co, KY; dd 11/9/37; md Summer/o 1782 Mrs Sarah Bryan, Lin-
coln Co (now Mercer Co), KY; wid b 9/8/1757, & PN Fayette
Co, KY, 1839, & dd 12/8/45; ch births: Mary (also called
Polly) 3/11/1783 who md John Keen who decd 1863, Abraham
Jr 2/27/85 (res Fayette Co, KY, 1863), John 1/31/87, William 11/18/89 (dd bef 3/1863 leaving ch Robert T & John),
George H 9/21/92, Sarah 7/8/96 w/o S Woolfolk, Elizabeth
8/16/98 who md Joseph Bowman & dd 11/9/37 leaving ch (Sarah, Isaac, & Abram who decd in 3/1863), Mary Ann, Catharine w/o Richard Dabney, & Nancy w/o William Stanhope;
document brought to court by John B Bowman listed births:
David Bryan 4/30/1779, & Nancy Keen 9/3/03; document also

BOWMAN (continued)
  lists following "colored" births: Aaron 12/21/1793, Bobb
  4/7/96, Jery 10/26/98, Antoney 2/23/1800, Lize 11/13/01,
  Nathan 11/05, Kaster 8/29/11, Dafney 11/17/12, Reuben
  12/16/12, Levi 8/15/13, Absolum 1/9/15, Nelson 5/23/15,
  Sam 6/30/18, Charles 3/27/19, & Fanny's ch James 9/22/20;
  QLF states sol f George bc 1720 England, settled Strasburg, Shenandoah Valley, VA, & had s Abraham, s John, & s
  Cornelius (b 1740 VA, a preacher who settled Madison Co,
  VA), all RW sol's; QLF 1939 from desc C S Johnson, St Louis, MO, states sol b Strasburg, VA; QLF states sol md Sa-
  rah Henry Bryan & dd South Elkhorn, KY; QLF states sol s/o
  George Bowman & Mary Hite, d/o Joist Hite, the great colo-
  nizer; QLF 1922 by great great gdd Emily Bowman (Mrs Charles L) Provost, New Iberia, LA, states her f Ernest Bowman
  s/o Dr Isaac Bowman of Lexington, KY, who s/o Joseph Bowman who md 1st cousin Elizabeth Bowman. R305
Daniel, esf 1780 VA; b 3/15/1759 Frederick Co, MD; PN 1832
  Rutherford Co, TN; dd 12/6/43 leaving wid. R305
Isaac, esf 1777 Shenandoah Co, VA, where dd 9/9/1826; heirs
  afp 1834, & PAR, insufficient proof/o svc; bro/o Abraham,
  who also RW sol; surv execs/o estate Isaac P Bowman (s/o
  sol) & George Brinker afp 1853, & PAR since no law yet co-
  vered heirs of RW sol's. R305
John, esf 1777 VA; b & Amherst Co, VA; to TN c1791; PN ae
  70 Roane Co,TN, 1822 where dd 3/25/41; md VA 1785 Barbara
  Hooper; wid b 1762-73, & PN 1843 Roane Co, TN; dd 1866;
  eldest s ae 20 in 1808; in 1822 d Sally ae 24 & s Lewis ae
  19; QLF 1919 from desc Mrs V B Hinsch, Rolla, MO. R305
Mackness, esf 1777 VA; PN ae 74 Chesterfield Co, VA, 1832.
  R305
Margaret, former wid/o Benjamin Garvin. R305
Marshall, esf 1778-9 Burke Co, NC; b 10/13/60 Amherst Co,
  VA; to Burke Co, NC, aec 16 with parents; back to Amherst
  Co after RW, thence to Kanawha Co, VA, where PN 1833 res
  on Coal River; to Benton Co, MO, 1840 to be near ch. R305
Nathaniel, esf NJ; LWT dated 7/7/1789, probated Halifax Co,
  VA, 2/22/1790 leaving all property to bro John of Peters-
  burg, VA; BLW issued to bro John 5/18/03. R305
Shearwood, esf 1779 Burke Co, NC; b 1758 Amherst Co, VA; PN
  1833 Burke Co, NC. R305
William, esf 1781 Henry Co, VA; b 5/4/1759 Halifax Co, VA;
  to NC with f 1780; PN 1833 Marion Co, TN. R305
William, esf 1777 Amherst Co, VA; PN ae 71 Washington Co, IN
  1832; bro John & sis h Joseph Lane res TN 1833; dd 4/2/43.
  R305
William, esf 1778 Goochland Co, VA; dds 1/12/1808 Rutherford
  Co, NC; md 12/1779 Mary Cosby, Goochland Co,VA; ch births:
  Elizabeth 12/9/1780, Nancy 7/20/82, Asa 10/2/83, Patsy
  6/26/86, Cosby 3/23/88, Eli 9/28/90, Eadeth 4/21/92, Wil-
  liam 3/31/94, Polly 1/9/97, & Catherine 3/22/1800; wid dd
  1852 Lumpkin Co, GA, leaving ch Polly McKan, Edy McKan,

BOWMAN (continued)
    Patsy Richardson, Catharine Richardson, Betsy Young, Cosby
    & Eli; s Eli afp for all survivors 1853 Rutherford Co, TN,
    & PAR. R305
BOWNE, Thomas, BLW issued 10/28/1789. R306
BOWSER, James, esf 1782 VA; heirs Nathaniel Bowser, Betsy Bow-
    ser, Thomas Bowser, Moses Ash, Caroline Ash, Lydia Ash,
    Thomas Ash, & Curtis Ash afb 1833 Nansemond Co, VA, & gtd
    BLW. R306
BOWYER, Henry, esf 1777 Botetourt Co, VA, where mvd from Augu-
    sta Co, VA, c1763; PN 1828 Botetourt Co, VA, & dd there
    6/13/1832; md 8/9/1792 Agatha Madison there; wid PN there
    1838 & res there 1843 ae 69 & dd 10/6/47; s Henry W res
    1850 Botetourt Co, VA. R306
  Michael, BLW issued 6/24/1796. R306
  Philip, esf 1777 Shenandoah Co, VA; PPN ae 78 Augusta Co, VA
    1823 when no family; had w in 1777. R306
  Thomas, esf VA; dd 8/21/1840; md 5/26/1814 Nancy who afp ae
    68 Montgomery Co, VA, 1858, when she had ch liv; PAR. R306
  Thomas, BLW issued 12/31/1795 to exec Henry Bowyer. R306
BOWZER, Thomas, see BOWYER, Thomas. R306
BOXWELL, Joseph, esf 1781 Winchester, Frederick Co, VA; PN aec
    65 Hampshire Co, VA, 1818; res 1822 with w Leona ae 42, &
    ch: Moses ae 19, Sally ae 17, Elizabeth ae 13, Martha ae
    12, Mary ae 11, Joseph ae 7, Letty ae 6, John ae 4, & Nan-
    cy ae 1; res 1830 Allegany Co, MD, to be near s; QLF 1895
    from desc John W Boxwell, St Paul, MN. R306
  Robert, esf 1781 Frederick Co, MD; PN ae 61 Allegany Co, MD
    1818; in 1820 had w ae 59, & ch: Robert ae 20, William ae
    19, Mary ae 16, Elizabeth ae 13, Deborah ae 11, & John ae
    9; sol d 1825; QLF states sol younger bro/o Joseph who al-
    so RW sol, further that sol enlisted ae 16. R306
BOY, Jacob, esf 1779 Loudoun Co, VA; b 1751 York Co, PA; PN
    1832 Sullivan Co, TN, where dd 5/20/33; name originally
    spelled BUCH in German; md Mary Drummond, Sullivan Co, TN,
    (MB 10/18/1796); wid PN ae 73 there 1848, d there 7/26/56;
    s Andrew res Blountville, TN, 1849. R306
BOYCE, Abraham, esf VA; b 9/27/1760 s/o Nicholas; md 8/7/1786
    Hannah, d/o Thomas Wells, Reading, PA; wid b 10/30/1770 &
    dd 8/21/1845 leaving ch: Abraham, Jacob, John, Robert, Ma-
    ry w/o Jonathan Wamsher, Sarah w/o William Davis; birth of
    ch: Nicholas 7/20/1787, Abram 11/5/89, Jacob 5/14/92, John
    7/31/94, Hannah 12/10/96, Mary 11/19/97, William 9/1801,
    Robert 9/29/02, Anny 6/19/05, Margaret 4/16/07, Ezekiel
    1/19/09, Jeremiah 3/13/11, David 3/1/12, & Sarah 10/17/15;
    other data from family bible: d Hannah w/o Jesse Griffith
    dd 4/9/1824, s Ezekiel dd 8/9/26, Asa Petre, s/o d Hannah,
    b 3/10/1815. R306
  William, BLW issued 2/3/1800. R306
BOYD, Alexander; esf 1778 PA; PN for svc disability; dd before
    9/4/1807; BLW issued 2/3/1829 to d Nancy Boyd, only heir,
    Bedford Co, VA. R307

BOYD, Daniel, esf 1779 Loudoun Co, VA; PN ae 84 Fauquier Co,
VA, 1821 when family w ae 51, ch ae 7 & 9. R307

David, esf Culpeper Co, VA; sol & w Sarah Dabney both dd in
1823-4 Tatnall Co, GA; in 1856 surv ch who afp: s Adin ae
52 & d Blancett/Blanchy Jones ae 68, res Lowndes Co, GA;
PAR per current law on PN to RW sol ch; sol w referred to
also as Sarah Cauthorn. R307

Francis, esf 1776 Halifax Co, VA; PN ae 60 Fayette Co, OH,
1818; dd 12/17/1824; in 1821 had w Anne, & d Anne ae 16;
QLF 1932 from desc Scott L Boyd, Santa Barbara, CA; QLF
states sol w Nancy Ann who survived him & dd OH. R307

Henry, esf 1775 Loudoun Co, VA; BLW issued 8/31/1786; PN ae
76 Washington Co, TN, 1832. R307

Henry, esf 1779 Halifax Co, VA; PN ae 74 Todd Co, KY, 1833.
R307

James, esf 1776 Cecil Co, MD; b 10/3/1759 Chester Co, PA,
area now in Cecil Co, MD; to VA 1784 where PN 1829 Monroe
Co; dd 4/23/1846 leaving wid Flora who res there 1847; QLF
1939 from desc Grace Boyd Thornhill, Buckhannon, WV, stating sol md Florence Bicket/Beckett & their ch: Thomas b
1788, Nathan h/o Miss Dunn, John h/o Sallie Kyle, Jennie
w/o James McDowell, further her ancestor sol s Thomas, who
md Margaret Young & dd ae 88 Buckhannon, WV, 1876. R307

James, esf 1777 Surry Co, NC, sub for f; b 5/8/1763 Bucks Co
PA; PN 1832 Patrick Co, VA, 1832. R307

John, esf 1779 Winchester, VA, where b 3/25/1763; res Rock-
ingham Co, VA, 1791-1808; dd c10/8/1844 at home/o s-in-law
D T Hays, Hopkinsville, Christian Co, KY, leaving wid Mar-
garet (md Augusta Co, VA) & ch: George W who dd AR leaving
ch (Alonzo, Amanda, Oscar, Newton, Emma, Harriet, John,
Lucretia, & Charles), Sarah Summers who dd without issue,
John who dd leaving ch unnamed, Peggy & her d Mary Boyd,
Wilton who dd leaving ch unnamed, Jane w/o D T Hays, James
& Benjamin; adm/o sol estate John W Hays, res Christian Co
KY, gave family data to court & afp for sol heirs; PAR for
insufficient proof of svc. R307

Patrick, esf 1777 Augusta Co, VA, where b; PN ae 73 Monroe
Co, VA, 1832 where dd 3/1/1835; md 4/26/1787 Ann/Anna Mc-
Dowell, Greenbrier Co, VA ; wid PN ae 74 Monroe Co, VA,
1841; QLF 1933 from desc Mrs Lucy Boyd Brown, Charlotte,
NC; QLF states sol b 1759; QLF states a Patrick Boyd, RW
sol who dd 1827, md Margaret Query c1774, & their s Colonel Thomas res NC. R308

Robert, esf 1776 SC; dd 1812; wid Sarah (md VA) dd 3/4/1844;
s Robert afp 1856 Russell Co, VA, & PAR for insufficient
proof of svc. R308

Samuel, esf 1780 Ninety-Six District, SC; b 1764 Bedford Co,
VA; to KY 1787; to Wayne Co, IN, 1811 where PN 1832; dd
11/27/35; md 12/12/1785 Isabella, Chester Co, SC; wid PN
ae 76 Wayne Co, IN, 1840 when s James (b 12/5/1786) res
there; QLF states sol f James & bro's John & Abraham all b
VA & RW sol's in SC, further sol b 5/20/1763 & md Isabella

BOYD (continued)
    Higgins; QLF states sol f James md Martha Burns, further
    sol bro Abram bc 1765 & enlisted ae 16 for RW svc; QLF
    1912 from desc Mrs D M Vesey, Fort Wayne, IN, stating sol
    f James KIA, further sol w Isabella Higgins b SC 2/13/1764
    & that sol & w res near Jacksonburg, IN, 1811 till dd; QLF
    1906 from desc William H Bradbury, Richmond, IN, who had
    d Anna; QLF 1895 from gds J B Martindale, Chicago, IL; QLF
    states sol full name Samuel C Boyd. R308
  William, esf VA; PN ae 64 Fleming Co, KY, 1818; s Thomas res
    Flemingsburg, KY, 1821; sol dd 12/30/1828. R308
  William, esf 1777 Louisa C, VA; b 1756-7 Hanover Co, VA; PN
    1833 Ablemarle Co, VA. R308
  William, no RW svc but svc in Indian Wars 1790; res Nottoway
    Co, VA, later KY; PN 1841 Bath Co, KY, where dd 7/20/47;
    md 7/27/1791 Nancy Bailey (MB 7/25/91 signed by John Bai-
    ley), Madison Co, KY; wid PN aec 80 Bath Co, KY, 1842, res
    there 1856 ae 87; sol bro Spencer AFF Bath Co, KY, 1849.
    R308
BOYDSTUN, William, esf 1776 Montgomery Co, VA; b 3/24/1753
    Frederick Co, MD; to Washington Co, NC, 1780 & esf there;
    PN 1833 Cocke Co, TN; QLF states sol f David b MA 1731, dd
    1811, esf MA; QLF 1935 from desc Mrs E M Olson, New York.
    R309
BOYER, John, esf Ninety-Six District, SC; b 11/18/1759 Nor-
    thumberland Co, VA; mvd to Baltimore, MD, after RW; mvd
    c1812 to Hamilton Co, OH, where PN 1832; res 1837 Rush Co,
    IN; dd 7/5/39 leaving no wid or liv ch but 8 gdc; only d
    Nancy dd before him. R309
  Jonathan, esf VA; afp ae 84 Somerset Co, PA, 1828; PAR, in-
    sufficient proof of svc; bro Joseph AFF 1828. R309
  Lewis, BLW issued 3/7/05 when res Rockingham Co, VA; PN 1828
    Miami Co, OH; QLF 1920 from great gdd Miss J E Davidson,
    Los Angeles, CA; QLF states sol dd 9/19/43. R309
BOYERS, Jacob, esf 1776 PA; esf 1781 VA; b 8/12/1756; PN 1818
    Niagara Co,NY; dd 7/10/26 Newstead, Erie Co, NY; md 4/1786
    Margaret Gearhart, Chester Co, PA; wid b 3/13/1769; wid PN
    3/28/1839 Newstead, NY; ch births: Frederick 9/10/1786,
    John 9/28/88, Elizabeth 3/12/91, Anna Martha 4/22/93, Mary
    9/10/97, & Margaret 7/16/1800. R310
  Lewis, see BOYER, Lewis. R310
  Michael, esf 1777 Lancaster Co, PA, where b 1755; esf Wash-
    ington Co, VA; PN 1834 Claiborne Co, TN. R310
BOYLE, Andrew, see BOGLE, Andrew. R310
  Michel, see BOYLS, Michel. R310
  Robert, esf 1777 Bedford VA, where PN 1833 ae 87, then in-
    sane; s John appointed his caretaker by court. R310
BOYLES, Charles, see BOYLL, Charles. R311
  David, see BOYLLS, David. R311
BOYLL, Charles, esf 1775 Halifax Co, VA; PN ae 68 Floyd Co, IN
    1819; res 1820 Jackson Co, IN, ae 79 when family w mbnn,
    her s Charles ae 14, d Lydia ae 12, gds Enoch ae 11; BLW

BOYLL (continued)
   issued to sol ae 84 Jackson Co, IN, 1828. R311
BOYLLS, David, esf c1779 Loudoun Co, VA; PN ae 67 Clark Co, IN
   1818; dd 6/17/45 Lawrence Co, IN, where md 12/1/1825 Polly
   Sappington; wid PN ae 65 there 1856; ch: Columbus Pery dd
   infancy, David, George, & Melissa; QLF 1923 from desc Minta Phipps MacDonald, Chicago, IL, states her half sis Hazel Mundy Lewis also desc/o sol, also aunt Ara Belle Guthridge, Princeton, IN, desc/o sol, further sol buried Proctor Graveyard, Ft Ritner, IN; QLF 1913 from gdd Mrs Ara
   Belle Boyles Guthridge, Princeton, IN, states her m America Boyles d/o sol, & still liv, further sol dd 6/17/47
   Leesville, IN. R311
BOYLS, Charles, see BOYLL, Charles. R311
   Michel, esf NJ; bc1763 near Morristown, NJ; later esf 1780
   VA; res with f Allegany Co, MD, during RW; shortly after
   RW, f sold property in NJ & mvd to Hampshire Co, VA; afp
   ae 70 Randolph Co, VA, 1833; PAR. R311
BOYT, William, esf 1778 Nansemond Co, VA, where b; PN there in
   1833 ae 75; dd 10/8/43; md 8/1792 (MB 8/4/92) Sally Jones,
   Nansemond Co, VA; wid PN ae 72 there 1843. R312
BOZORTH, Jonathan, esf 1776 PA; b 12/13/1754; PN 1823 Grayson
   Co, KY; dd 9/14/1830; md Mary Hargis (b 11/22/1761) in VA;
   ch: Elizabeth & Sally, both b before 1783, John, Jeremiah,
   William, Mary, & Eli (bc 1800); wid dd 1/11/1839 leaving
   ch Sally Shaw, Polly Brown, John, Jeremiah, & Eli. R312
BOZZELL, Reuben, esf 1777 Augusta Co, VA; esf 1781 Henry Co,
   VA; b 12/1755 Spotsylvania Co, VA; to Mecklinburg Co, NC,
   1782 where PN 1833; QLF 1938 from great gdd Mrs M B Big-
   gerstaff, Ponca City, OK, states sol buried Sandy Ridge
   Township, Union Co, GA. R312
BRABSTON, William, esf VA; dd 2/9/1801 Granger Co, TN; md
   8/4/1788 Mary Runnion (marriage license signed by Adren
   Runnion), Montgomery Co, VA; wid afp states md Wythe Co
   (formed from Montgomery Co 1790); wid b 5/4/1769 & md (2)
   3/3/04 Peter May, Yorktown, VA, & he dd 3/14/43; wid PN ae
   77 Granger Co, TN, 1847; births/o ch/o sol & Mary: Rachel
   Scot Brabston 5/7/1789, & William Buckhannon 1/28/94; ch/o
   Peter May & Mary: Vinston 4/11/09 & John 4/6/11; other fa-
   mily bible births: John May 1/5/1836, James May 3/31/1840.
   R313
BRACEY, Thomas, see BRESSIE, Thomas. R313
BRACKENRIDGE, Alexander, BLW issued 4/14/1790. R313
BRADBERRY, John, esf 1776-7 PA; esf 1781 Mecklenburg Co, VA; b
   1750 Amelia Co, VA; to Wilson Co, TN, 1800; to Giles Co,
   TN, 1828 where afp ae 88 in 1838; PAR. R314
BRADEN, James, esf 1780 Augusta Co, VA, where b 2/10/1763; afp
   Anderson Co, TN, 1837, 1839, & 1843, all PAR; dd 7/15/48
   leaving wid Elizabeth, who dd 11/1/1851 leaving ch: And-
   rew, Brummett, Elsey Huff, & William; these ch all liv
   1852 when William afp Anderson Co, TN, for sol ch; PAR for
   insufficient proof of svc. R314

BRADEN, John, esf as sub for f Edward 1777 Augusta Co, VA, & b
there 1760; to TN 1792 where PN 1832 Claiborne Co; dd
8/3/1840 leaving w Sarah; wid afp 1841, & PAR. R314
BRADFORD, Charles, esf 1777 Culpeper Co, VA; after RW mvd to
Washington Co, PA, where md d/o Colonel Heath; dd c1794
leaving wid & 4 ch, all of whom decd in 1834; d Julia md
John Finley & dd leaving ch Henry Heath & Julia Ann both
res Washington Co, PA, 1834; s Charles who was War of 1812
sol & dd 9/26/1813; s Fielden 3rd ch/o sol; BLW issued to
sol gdc 1834; Charles Allen s/o sol sis res Washington, DC
1834. R314
Enoch, 1778 Fauquier Co, VA; dd 7/6/1823 Scott Co, KY; md
4/1/1785 Mary Chinn at res/o her bro-in-law John Randall,
Fayette Co, KY; wid afp 1849 & 1852 Scott Co, KY, & PAR;
sol bro Fielding AFF there 1849 ae 82; sol bro John, decd,
of Lexington Co, KY, 1st editor of a newspaper in KY; AFF
1849 by sol s Daniel; AFF 1949 by T Metcalfe, half bro of
sol widow; AFF 1849 by William Wigginton s-in-law/o RW sol
Lewis Corbin who served with Enoch Bradford in RW. R314
Henry, see JEANNEREL, Claude Francois. R315
Samuel Kellette, esf 1777 VA; dd 1793 Spotsylvania Co, VA;
md (eloped to MD) 5 or 6/1781 Jane, d/o Edward Carter of
Spotsylvania Co, VA; wid md (2) John Vermonnet/Vermonet,
who dd 1815; wid PN ae 78 Culpeper Co, VA, 1843; in 1827
ch/o sol: Samuel res Culpeper Co, Sally Carter Gray res
Charlottesville, & Harriet wid/o Charles B Hunter/Hunton
of Culpeper, all VA; gds S S Bradford liv 1843. R315
William, esf VA 1777; PN ae 68 Sumner Co, TN, 1828; in 1845
s D M res Huntsville, AL, stated sol dd c1832 & wid res in
TN; QLF states sol b 1760 Fauquier Co, VA, md (1) Miss
Steel, (2) Catherine Morgan, (3) Nancy Baylis & had many
ch by them; QLF 1919 from desc Mrs C C Clark, Brownwood,
TX; QLF 1933 from great great gds Chester C Burdick, Jef-
ferson City, MO. R315
BRADLEY, Augustine, see BRADLEY, Austin. R316
Austin, esf Culpeper Co, VA where b (now Madison Co); PN ae
85 Culpeper Co, VA, 1832; dd 12/15/32; md 11/13/1788 Frankey Hurt, Culpeper Co, VA; wid PN ae 72 Rappannnock Co, VA
1838. R316
Burrel, esf Edgecombe Co, NC; b Sussex Co, VA; mvd with f to
Edgecombe Co, NC, aec 9, where PN 1832 ae 78. R316
Daniel, esf 1780 Cumberland Co, VA; PN ae 75 Pittsylvania Co
VA, 1832. R316
David, esf 1777 Cumberland Co, VA, ae 18; b Roanoke, VA; POW
& taken to Jamaica for 3 years, thence Halifax, Nova Sco-
ta, where res 1842 ae 83 near Manchester, Musquodoboit Co;
dd 1843-4 ae 84; md Susan in Nova Scotia & left no ch; wid
afp 1852 ae 90, & PAR. R316
James, esf 1780 Caroline Co, VA, where b 1761, & where PN
1832. R317
John, esf 1777 Culpeper Co, VA; PN aec 76 Rutherford Co, TN,
1832; QLF states sol dd 1848-58, md Mary d/o Joseph Vance,

BRADLEY (continued)
　　& res near Murfreesboro, Rutherford Co, TN. R317
　　John, esf 1781 Cumberland Co, VA, where b 8/10/1751; to TN
　　　1805; PN 1832 Wilson Co, TN. R317
　　William, esf VA; disability PN 1786 Rockbridge Co, VA; dd
　　　2/5/1819; records lost when British burned Washington, DC,
　　　in War of 1812; QLF states sol md (1) Elizabeth Susan ---,
　　　md (2) 3/12/1791 Mary Elizabeth Carlock, Rockbridge Co,
　　　VA, who survived him. R318
　　William, esf 1777 Powhatan Co, VA; b 1759 Cumberland Co, VA;
　　　PN 1833 Pittsylvania Co, VA, where res at end/o RW. R318
　　William, esf 1777 VA; dd c4/6/1821 Been Creek on James River
　　　VA; md 2/10/1804 Elizabeth Lynch, Buckingham Co, VA; wid
　　　to TN 1823; wid afp & afb ae 91 McMinn Co, TN, 1856; PAR &
　　　BLAR. R318
BRADLY, James, see BRADLEY, James. R319
BRADSHAW, Benjamin, esf 1777 Fluvanna Co, VA; b 5/28/1758 Al-
　　bemarle Co, VA; PN 1834 Jefferson Co, TN; md 1/22/1787
　　Fanny Melton, Fluvanna Co, VA, where she b; wid PN ae 74
　　Jefferson Co, TN, 1843; ch births: Nancy 1/28/1788, Mary
　　5/1/91, Betsy 12/9/93, Patsy 1/8/95, Larner 3/22/99, &
　　Pierce W 7/22/1803; other family bible data: Daniel C Mar-
　　tin b 9/28/1818, Alfred B Sparkes b 10/2/1817, George Cle-
　　venger dd 10/14/1837, Polly Denniston dd 8/23/1820. R319
　　Claiborne/Claybourn, esf 1776 Goochland Co, VA; PN 1832 Mer-
　　　cer Co, KY, ae 73; dd 5/3/42; md 1781 Elizabeth Clamintz;
　　　wid PN aec 81 Mercer Co, KY, 1843 when res with s William
　　　& his w Barsheba; d Sally b 10/24/1782; s John AFF 1843;
　　　AFF 1843 by Edward Houchins ae 76, h/o of Nancy who sis/o
　　　sol wid; William Bowman & Mary Cosby md same day & place
　　　as sol & w. R319
　　John, esf 1776 Monroe Co, VA; b 2/2/1759; PN 1833 Pocahontas
　　　Co,VA; dd 12/1834; QLF 1935 from great great gds H C Brad-
　　　shaw, Bluefield, WV, states federal monument to sol loca-
　　　ted Huttonsville, Pocahontas Co, WV. R319
　　John, esf 1778 Goochland Co, VA, where b 4/18/1763; PN there
　　　1832. R319
　　Jonas, esf 1778 Charlotte, Mecklenburg Co, NC; b 1759 Cum-
　　　berland Co, VA; dd 2/6/1840; md 1782 Elizabeth, who PN ae
　　　87 Lincoln Co, NC, 1845; ch births: Pride 12/9/1783, John
　　　9/5/85, Susannah 2/10/87, Jonah 9/8/89, Field 6/10/91,
　　　Charles 2/23/94, & Larkin 7/12/1801. R319
　　Larner, esf 1776 Goochland Co, VA; PN ae 65 Mercer Co, KY,
　　　1821 when family w ae 63 & 3 d's (2 minors). R319
　　Robert, esf 1777 Goochland Co, VA; BLW issued 2/3/1784; dd
　　　2/1832 Rowan Co, NC; md (1) ? & had only ch Betsey who md
　　　Timothy Merrill, & Betsey res TN 1847; sol md (2) ? in Ro-
　　　wan Co, NC, & they had ch Polly, Unity, Orston, William, &
　　　Robert; only surv ch Orston AFF ae 59 Rowan Co, NC, 1856
　　　when afp & gtd; AFF by sol bro John aec 85 Goochland Co,
　　　VA, 1847 who also RW sol; QLF states one/o sol w's Eliza-
　　　beth Haden. R319

BRADSHAW, William, esf VA; wid Selaw afp aec 84 Southampton Co VA, 1838 & PAR for insufficient proof of svc; d Matilda res 1853 Vicksville, Southampton Co, VA. R319

BRADY, Benjamin, esf 1781 Newgate, Loudoun Co, VA; b 4/14/1761 York Co, PA; to Loudoun Co, VA, 1765; PN 1832 Allegany Co, MD; QLF 1938 from great gdd Miss Susie A Brady, Cumberland MD; QLF states sol w probably Barbara Miller. R320

James, see BRADEN, James. R320

John, esf VA, PN 1820 Garrard Co,KY; dd 9/18/1828; md 3/1786 Keziah, Orange Co, VA; wid PN ae 83 Lincoln Co, KY, 1838; wid res ae 87 Pulaski Co, KY, 1843; AFF 1838 by George 5th ch ae 38 stated eldest bro John now ae 51; other ch James, William, Nancy, & Richard. R320

John, esf 1780 Culpeper Co, VA; dd 8/1/1824; md Roseman Butt 10/1798 there; wid md (2) 10/1832 John Porter, Warren Co, KY, & he dd 9/24/33 Butler Co, KY; wid afp ae 83 there in 1849 & PAR insufficient proof of svc; sol only ch by Roseman was Elizabeth Gothens, who ae 36 Butler Co, KY, 1849; wid bro John Butt made AFF ae 80 Warren Co, KY, 1849 that he md 3/20/1800. R320

Thomas, esf 1781 Halifax Co, VA, where b 10/17/1762; mvd to Highland Co, OH, 1810 where PN 1832. R320

William, esf 1776 PA; esf 1777 Washington Co, PA; b 5/4/1760 Sussex Co, NJ; family to Washington Co, PA, when he ae 14; to Scioto Co, OH, 1799 where PN 1833. R320

BRAGG, Benjamin, BLW issued 11/14/1794. R321

William, esf 1781 Loudoun Co, VA; esf 1782 Montgomery Co, MD aec 17; b 5/18/1765 near Alexandria, Fairfax Co, VA; to TN 1790 where PN 1832 Cocke Co. R321

William, esf 1780 Lunenburg Co, VA, where b 1760; PN there 1834; dd 4/22/1834; md 1/7/1794 (MB same date) Cicely Wilson, Mecklenburg Co, VA (also called Cecelia); wid PN ae 77 Lunenburg Co, VA, 1834. R321

William, esf 1775 Fauquier Co, VA; PN ae 64 Oglethorpe Co, GA, while res Madison Co, GA, 1819; dd 1834; md 3/1778 Ruthy, who PN ae 84 Madison Co, GA, 1842; ch births: George 4/19/1779 & dd 1787, William 4/12/81, Selah 11/4/83, Joseph 7/3/86 & dd 1797, Nancy 1/18/89, Susannah 5/24/91, George 3/10/93, Ruthey 9/24/95, & Humphrey A 12/12/1802; wid dd 11/30/1844 surv by ch Joseph, Nancy Ballenger, Susannah Berryman, George, & Humphrey A, per court record, Madison Co, GA, 5/5/1845. R321

BRAITHWAITE, William, esf 1778 Fredericktown, MD; PN ae 74 Frederick Co, VA, 1826; dd 7/13/31; md 5/1786 Catharine Brookover, Frederick Co, VA (license issued 5/18/86); wid PN ae 68 there 1838; ch in 1826: Elizabeth ae 33, Violett ae 24, Mary ae 20, Emelene ae 17, & gds William H Clark ae 12. R322

BRAKE, Abraham, esf Moorefield, Hardy Co, VA, when f res of Buckhannon Fort; b 8/1763; afp 1834 Harrison Co, VA, & PAR insufficient proof of svc; QLF states sol bro/o John & Jacob. R322

103

BRAKE, John, esf as indian spy near Moorefield, Hardy Co, VA; b 1754; PN 1834 Harrison Co, VA, but dropped from PN rolls 1835 because had not rendered alleged svc. R322
BRAMBLET, Nancy, former wid/o George Adams. R322
  Reuben, esf 1777 Fauquier Co, VA; b 3/15/1757; PN 1832 Gallatin Co, KY. R322
  Reuben, esf 1781 Fauquier Co, VA; b 3/1758; to SC 1794; afp 1832 Laurens District, SC, & PAR; afp 1855 by Lewis Bramblett, Laurens District, SC, for any PN due sol; PAR. R322
BRAMBLETT, James, esf 1780 Bedford Co, VA; PN ae 69 Breckenridge Co, KY, 1833; QLF states sol b VA 1762, dd 1849 Albany, KY, md 1789 Milly Shrewsbury, & their s Ambrose S b 1790, dd 1849, md 1816 Sarah Elliott, further sol d Lydia md Nathaniel Chrisman; QLF states sol gdf/o Governor Thomas Bramlette of KY. R322
BRANCH, Olive, esf Bedford Co, VA; b 1760; PN 1832 Buckingham Co, VA. R323
  Thomas, esf Powhatan Co, VA, where b 7/20/1757 near Mannakin Town; afp 1845 Prince Edward Co, VA, but dd 9/22/50 there before gtd PN; md 12/31/1789 Nancy Clements, Amelia Co, VA (MB 12/26/1789 signed by William Clements); wid afp ae 87 Prince Edward Co, VA, 1856, & PAR, but gtd BLW. R323
BRANDENBURGH, Anthony, esf 1779 Harrodsburg, KY, for svc in VA regiment; b Germantown, PA; to Somerset Co, PA, 1781; to Warren Co, OH, 1807 where PN 1833 aec 71. R323
BRANDOM, Thomas, esf 1780 Mecklenburg Co, VA; b 1746 Hanover Co, VA; PN 1833 Mecklenburg Co, VA, where dd 12/17/1834; md 9/17/1770 Margaret who PN ae 87 Mecklenburg Co, VA; ch births: Nancy 9/2/1771, Agnes 6/2/1773, Waldon 7/5/75, Suckey 9/12/1777, Edward 11/10/79, Elizabeth 2/3/1782, Peter 6/30/84, Thomas 8/30/86, Margaret Walden 1/22/91, John 9/30/92, & Jesse 5/7/96. R323
BRANDON, Francis, esf 1781 Halifax Co, VA, where b 5/16/1756; afp there 1833, & PAR, insufficient proof of svc. R323
  Peter, esf 1775-6 Winchester, VA; PN ae 69 Bullitt Co, KY, 1819; family in 1820 w ae 53 & ch: Robert ae 20, William aec 14, Mary ae 17, Agnes ae 15, & Jennett ae 13; sol dd 7/9/1834. R323
  Thomas, see BRANDOM, Thomas. R323
BRANHAM, James, BLW issued 7/6/1793. R324
  William, BLW issued 10/11/1796. R324
  William B, esf 1780 Orange Co, VA; PN ae 69 Bourbon Co, KY, 1832 where dd 1/8/1845; md 6/21/1840 Mrs Mary Burroughs/ Burris, Nicholas Co, KY; wid PN & gtd BLW there 1855 ae 81; in 1853 Alex Burroughs, s/o sol wid by her 1st h, res there; QLF 1922 from desc Mrs A E Holch, Peru, NE; QLF 1896 from gdd Mrs James Chism, Mt Sterling, KY. R324
BRANN, Andrew; esf VA; res KY 1798; gtd BLW. R324
  Jeremiah, esf 1778 Westmoreland Co,VA, where b; to OH c1790 where PN aec 70 Butler Co 1832; dd c7/27/34; md c3/20/1789 Sarah Reeder, Hampshire Co, VA; wid PN ae 77 Ross Township Butler Co, OH, 1840; wid gtd PN increase ae 85 there 1849

BRANN (continued)
    & dd c1850; f/o wid mvd his family c 1790 to Columbia, OH;
sol bro Nicholas & Mathias also RW sol; Rebecca, wid/o Nicholas Brann (dd 1797) md Westmoreland Co,VA, d c1846 Butler Co, OH, & heirs/o Nicholas afp 1855 Darke Co, OH. R324
    Joseph, esf VA, BLW issued 1798 Fayette Co, KY. R324
    William Sr, esf 1777 Westmoreland Co, VA, where b 5/16/48;
PN 1834 there when family w ae 82; had 13 ch (10 s & 3 d,
5 of s having War of 1812 svc); when esf had w & "several
helpless ch." R324
BRANNON, John, BLW issued 10/5/1791; QLF 1935 from desc Maude
K Hicks, Brazil, IN. R324
    Thomas, BLW issued 5/29/1792. R324
BRANSFORD, William, BLW issued 5/21/1794; QLF states sol b
1761 Chesterfield Co, VA, further sol great great gdd Mrs
B L Bishop, Patchogue, NY, DAR member, further sol desc/o
John Bransford, English immigrant, who came to VA with w
Mary 1729, both of English nobility. R324
BRASHEARS, Richard, esf VA & left svc Dec 1781; heirs rec one-
half pay PN 1846; QLF 1926 from desc Walter Brashear, Lou-
isville, KY, who also desc/o Marshom Brashear. R325
BRASHER, Richard, esf VA; md 11/14/1773 Susan Pitman, who dd
9/10/1842; sol only surv ch Mrs Mary Drake afp ae 78 Sou-
thampton Co, VA, 1853 when AFF made there by Mark Drake ae
82; PAR. R325
BRATCHER, Charles, esf 1779 Bedford Co, VA, where b 1762; PN
1833 Campbell Co, TN. R326
BRAXTON, James, esf 1776-7; also svc Wayne's Indian War 1794;
PN ae 81 for disability from wounds 1839 Caroline Co, VA;
dd 3/13/42; md 1804 Mary Coleburt, Caroline Co, VA; wid
afp ae 73 King George Co, VA, 1855, & PAR. R326
BRAY, David, esf Rowan Co, NC; b 1743 Brunswick Co, VA; to
Northampton Co, NC, as ch; PN 1832 Surry Co, NC; dd 7/8/36
leaving ch: William, Hanon, Nathan, David, Amy, Martha
Alberty, & Reuben; gds Lewis W, s/o David Jr, liv 1852.
R326
    Elisha C, "no pension file found for this veteran." R326
    John, esf 1776 Middlesex Co, VA; b 2/13/1751 NJ; PN 1833
North Brunswick Township, Middlesex Co, VA; dd 4/28/34; md
2/2/1832 Ellen/Eleanor; wid b NJ; wid md (2) 9/8/1835 Daniel Kincheloe & he dd 10/24/1855 Clarksburg, VA, he being
War of 1812 sol who esf 1814; wid PN ae 60 Bridgewater
Township, Somerset Co, NJ, 1858 as John Bray's wid. R326
    John, esf 1777 Romney, Hampshire Co, VA; PN ae 56 Switzer-
land Co, IN, 1818 where dd 6/10/32; md 4/15/1820 Mrs Elizabeth "Betsey." Coonies, Gallatin Co, KY; in 1821 sol had
d Carolina ae 2, d Amelia ae 3 months, & s Daniel who AFF
1824 Switzerland Co, IN, that he in 1816 visited land office in Cincinnati, OH, with f & that a Samuel Bray recd
some/o the land; wid md (3) 10/4/1834 Robert Bakes, Switzerland, IN, who dd 3/119/47; wid PN ae 55 there 1853 as
Elizabeth Bray; QLF 1935 from desc Anna H (Mrs E J) And-

BRAY (continued)
    res, Madison, IN. R326
BRAYHILL, James, esf Halifax Co, VA; b c4/29/1760-1 Caroline
    Co, VA; after RW res Pittsylvania Co, VA, Wilkes Co, NC,
    McMinn Co, TN, Sangamon Co, IL, thence c1833 Tazewell Co,
    IL, where PN 1837 aec 76; dd 1/7/1842; md Rebecca Bailey;
    s James afp for m there 1845. R327
BRECHEN, William Sr, esf 1779 Person Co, NC; b 4/25/1754 Hano-
    ver Co, VA; to TN 1805 where PN 1833 Bedford Co; dd there
    3/10/34; md Margaret before 1794; wid afp aec 90 Marshall
    Co, TN, 1843, when res with s Josiah who still res there
    1853; PAR, no proof of marriage; surname also spelled BRE-
    CHEEN & BRECKEN. R327
BRECKINRIDGE, Robert, esf 1778 VA; BLW issued 4/14/1790; PN
    1828 Louisville, Jefferson Co, KY; also BRACKENRIDGE. R327
BREDON, James, see BRADEN, James. R327
BREEDEN, Enoch, esf 1776 King William Co, VA; b 1/1759 MD; to
    Charles City Co, VA, with parents ae 7; f esf VA & never
    returned from RW; to Spotsylvania Co, VA, after RW where
    PN 1832; to Winchester, Franklin Co, TN, 1835; dd 8/28/41;
    had 5 ch, 4 moving wih him to TN, & 1 already there; QLF
    1910 from great gds A B Lipscomb, Louisville, KY, who also
    great gds/o RW sol William Lipscomb of VA; QLF 1900 from
    Granville Lipscomb, Flat Rock, TN. R328
BREEDING, John, esf New Kent Co, VA; b 1757; PN 1834 New Kent
    VA. R328
BREEDLOVE, John, esf 1780 Culpeper Co, VA; b 4/5/1752; PN 1832
    Madison Co, VA; res 1832 with ch Adams Co, OH; QLF 1917
    from desc Frances L Breedlove (Mrs William Robert) Smith,
    Washington, DC. R328
  William, esf 1781 Albemarle Co, VA; PN ae 71 Simpson Co, KY,
    1833; dd 2/28/38; QLF 1910 from desc Mrs Henry Wood, Rolla
    MO; QLF states sol md 10/1/1785 Mary d/o David Watts, fur-
    ther a Richard Breedlove md Milly d/o David Watts. R328
BRENT, John, BLW issued 5/29/1792. R329
  John, esf 1775 VA; PN 1818 near Carthage, Smith Co, TN, when
    had w Jane & 6 ch; in 1820 w ae 43 & ch: Nancy ae 9, Fran-
    ky ae 6, Elizabeth ae 2; sol dd 7/21/33; md 1/9/1779 Jane,
    who afp ae 74 Smith Co, TN, 1837, & PAR insufficient proof
    of marriage; in 1842 s Samuel ae 50 AFF that sol dd Smith
    Co, TN, & wid Jane since decd leaving ch: Samuel, Susannah
    Hall, Polly Johnson, & Elizabeth Hall & that parents md c
    1783; AFF 1849 Smith Co, TN, by Thomas Hall h/o sol d Eli-
    zabeth that sol wid dd 7/19/1838, Lawrence Co, AL. R329
  William, esf VA; afp 1828 Jefferson Co, MS; PAR insufficient
    proof of svc. R329
BRENTON, Adam, esf 1778 Fayette Co, PA; esf 1781 VA (now KY);
    b 5/8/1763 Hampshire Co, VA; Indian Wars svc 1794; afp Ow-
    en Co, IN, 1834; PAR insufficient proof of svc. R329
  James, esf 1780 VA; PN ae 68 Petersburg, Pike Co, IN, 1832,
    where dd 6/16/36; md 9/21/1830 Mary Ainsley, Pike Co, IN;
    wid b 10/3/1783, & PN Washington Township, Pike Co, IN,

BRENTON (continued)
    1843, still & res there 1855; no ch. R329
  John, esf 1778 Monongahela Co, PA, for svc in VA regiment;
    res KY after RW; to Clark Co,IN, 1819 where PN 1832 ae 70;
    dd there 3/21/47, w dying before him; AFF 1853 by Ursula
    West & Mary McCleary that they only surv heirs/o sol. R329
  Robert, esf 1778 Monongahela Co, PA, sub for f Henry; bro/o
    John above who svc in same regiment; to Clark Co, IN, 1805
    where PN 1832 ae 74. R329
  William, esf 1777 Monongahela Co, PA, in VA regiment sub for
    Davis Brenton; served under Capt. James Brenton; mvd from
    KY 1799 to Clark Co, IN, where PN 1832 ae 72; dd 11/21/38,
    leaving wid; QLF 1933 from great great gds Horace F Bren-
    ton, Red Oak, IA; QLF 1927 from desc Mrs W C Diers. R329
BRESSIE, Thomas, esf 1776; sol had s Francis (dd minor wo iss-
    ue) & s Thomas M of KY & NC who md Elizabeth Jamieson &
    whose LWT dated 7/15/1824 probated 5/26/28 Norfolk Co, VA;
    in 1845 Elizabeth now md to James D Fisher who had dd lea-
    ving wid & d Sarah Frances Fisher; Elizabeth dd 1845 lea-
    ving d Sarah Frances Fisher (res Norfolk Co, VA), who dd
    leaving paternal gdf Israel Fisher; in 1845 also liv Fre-
    derick Cason, Lewis Cason, & Maria Cason (uncles & aunt by
    half-blood/o Elizabeth Bressie Fisher), & Elizabeth's cou-
    sin Frances d/o Rheuben Cason; Elizabeth's sis Sarah Vau-
    ghan m/o Elizabeth F Vaughan; sol also had other surv ch
    liv: Joceming, William, Patsy of Richmond, & Mary w/o Tay-
    lor Simes; heirs afp 1845, & PAR. R329
BREST, John, esf 1780 Berkeley Co, VA; b 3/25/1760; PN Bourbon
    Co, KY, 1832. R329
BRESTON, Edward, esf Loudoun Co, VA; afp aec 80 Iredell Co, NC
    when res with d, aec 40, w/o Uriah Patterson; PAR. R329
BREWER, Barrett, esf 1781 Charlotte Co, VA; b 8/1763 Louisa Co
    VA; f mvd family to Charlotte Co when sol ch & dd Henry Co
    VA, 1794; sol to GA 1783; PN 1833 Montgomery Co, AL; res
    Abbeford, Mason Co, AL, 1838; dd 7/6/1844 leaving ch, in-
    cluding John P who res Pike Co, AL, 1853. R330
  Henry, esf 1779 Martinsburg, Berkeley Co, VA; b 3/1765; PN
    1818 Adams Co, OH, where dd 2/20/1829; wid dd 1829; surv
    ch 1830: Mrs Polly Davis, Romney, VA, Mrs Peggy Hansberry,
    Fairfield Co, OH, Mrs Sally Williams, Anna w/o James Bold-
    man, Elijah, Susan & Charles, last 4/o Adams Co, OH. R330
  John, esf 1777 nr Winchester, VA, as sub for f Richard; b
    3/25/1762; PN Fayette Co,PA, where dd 1/7/48; md Mary Mar-
    tin 11/22/1790 Winchester, VA; wid PN ae 77 Fayette Co, PA
    when surv ch Martha w/o Abner Lacy, Elizabeth w/o Abram
    Geary, Sarah w/o Isaac Geary, Richard, John, & Mary; QLF
    1876 from desc Mrs M Ansbaugh, Newark, Licking Co, OH, d/o
    sol d states sol middle name Andrew & he res/o Huntington,
    PA. R331
  William, esf 1777 Prince William Co,VA; b 3/22/1744 St Marys
    Co, MD; to KY 1793, where PN 1834 Henry Co; d Elizabeth
    Brewer Wallace AFF 1853 that f dd leaving no wid. R331

BREWSTER, Sheriff, esf 1781 Mecklenburg Co, NC; b 3/1763 on
    Potomac River, VA; PN 1832 Walton Co, GA; surname at times
    spelled BRUSTER; QLF states sol md Eleanor Dunlap. R332
BRIAN, Thomas, see BRYAN, Thomas. R333
BRIANT, Benjamin, see BRYANT, Benjamin. R333
  William, see BRYANT, William. R333
  Zachariah, esf 1779 Amherst Co, VA; PN ae 67 Daviess Co, KY,
    1832; to Spencer Co,IN, 1837 where most/o family res. R333
BRICKEY, Peter, esf 1780 Botetourt Co, VA; b 4/10/1761; afp
    1832 Botetourt Co, VA, & PAR, svc less than 6 months; dd
    there 1834; md there c1820 Elizabeth Dunn, who gtd BLW aec
    56 Carter Co, TN, 1855; QLF 1936 from Irving Dilliard, St
    Louis, MO, who states he desc/o a Peter Brickey (dd 1786
    Botetourt Co, VA) through s Jarrett/Jared, res Washington
    Co, MO, 1840. R333
  William, esf 1776 Westmoreland Co, VA, where b 1/9/1756; PN
    there 1832; QLF 1921 from desc Mrs T M Johnson, Princeton,
    Mercer Co, WV. R333
BRIDGEMAN, Joseph, BLW issued 7/6/1793. R333
  Thomas, esf c1779 VA; b Dinwiddie Co, VA; dd c1819 & family
    mvd to Iredell Co, NC, thence to Hardin Co, IL, 1852; md
    Mary on border between NC & SC; wid afp aec 90 Hardin Co,
    IL, 1859, & PAR. R333
BRIDGES, Benjamin, esf 1777 James City Co, VA, where b 1759;
    to KY 1795 where afp Jefferson Co 1834; PAR, insufficient
    proof of svc; s Benjamin res there 1853. R333
  John, esf 1776 VA; PN ae 66 Boone Co, KY, 1822; dd 3/20/38;
    dd 3/20/38; md 3/12/1785 Jane, Stafford Co, VA; wid PN ae
    73 Boone Co, Ky; ch included Levina, b 10/25/1785, who md
    12/24/1801 Henry Riley, their ch births: Seton S 6/4/1803,
    Isom A 2/27/06, Sarah I/J 1/8/08, Jesse I/J 1/16/12, Fiel-
    ding H 10/3/13, Conny C 10/23/15, Agnes W 10/31/17, & Hen-
    ry W 10/25/19; QLF states sol wid Jenny dd Covington, KY;
    QLF 1882 from gds William Bridges, Covington, KY. R333
  John, esf 1776 Charlotte Co, VA; b Gloucester Co, VA; mvd to
    Charlotte Co 1769; PN ae 90 Mercer Co, KY, 1832, & dd
    8/14/36. R333
  Joseph, esf 1775 Caroline Co, VA, where b 2/1/1750-1; esf
    later Granville Co,NC; PN 1832 Chatham Co, NC; dd 3/22/37;
    md 12/24/1778 Frances Davis, Granville Co, NC; wid b
    1/30/1755; PN, & dd 5/3/1841, leaving ch William H, Horace
    D, & Nicholas; ch births: Horace D 7/20/1790, William H
    7/1/93, George Rodney 1/18/95 & Nicholas Richard 12/15/96;
    s Lt. George Rodney dd 2/21/1816 shot dead by military de-
    serter near Ft Montgomery, MS Territory; s William H md
    10/1/1816 Sally Justice, their ch births: Cornelia Adaline
    11/25/18, Joseph Morgan 10/21/20, Delhi Cochren 12/10/22,
    Martha Emila 9/30/25, & Seniorah Susannah 10/25/27; s Ho-
    race D md (1) 10/22/12 Martha Gee (dd 9/28/23) & (2) Loui-
    sa G Johnson 5/26/25; s Nicholas Richard md 12/20/27 Emma
    P Johnson, their ch births: Frances Ann 1/13/29, Horace
    Hampton 10/15/30 (dd 10/3/31), Eving Livingston 3/24/32,

BRIDGES (continued)
  Preston Johnston 1/3/34 (dd 9/30/35), Pauline Agness
    11/30/35, & Mary Sibbels 9/29/37; other birth in family
    records Elizabeth Wilson 7/29/40; QLF 1932 from desc Glen-
    norra (Mrs C H) Krieger, Fort Thomas, KY. R334
  Ransom, BLW issued 10/22/1791. R334
  Ransone, esf 1776 VA; PN ae 64 Mathews Co, VA, 1820 when fa-
    mily w Nancy ae 45, s John ae 15, d Polly ae 18, & d Bet-
    sey ae 7. R334
BRIDGET, James, esf 1777 Augusta Co, VA; PN ae 69 Rockbridge
    Co, VA, 1820. R334
BRIDGEWATER, Levi, see BRIDGWATER, Levi. R334
  Samuel, see BRIDGWATER, Samuel. R334
  Samuel, esf 1776 VA; b 4/18/1749; dd 5/11/1827 Scott Co, IN;
    md 6/2/1771 Mary Ann, Mecklenburg Co, VA; wid b 10/23/1755
    & PN 1844 Scott Co, IN; ch births: Margaret 6/6/1772, Mary
    1/11/73, Anna 8/22/75, John E 7/77, Casiah 3/12/79, Rebec-
    ca 11/30/80, Levi 1/31/82, Rachel 2/5/84, Sarah 12/17/86,
    Samuel 8/7/88, Christian 7/11/90, Elias 1/14/92, Eliza-
    beth 4/5/94, Patience 7/9/96, & Ellenor 5/26/98; AFF 1853
    by s Christian that sol wid dd 3/21/47 Scott Co, IN. R334
  William, see BRIDGWATER, William. R334
BRIDGWATER, Levi, esf 1776 VA; PN Washington Co, IN, 1822 ae
    61; dd 9/30/31; md 1783 or 1785 Patience Stilwell, Fayette
    Co, PA; wid b 8/21/1769 & PN 1839 Washington Co, IN, & res
    1849 Orange Co, IN; ch births: Elias 9/26/1785, Elinor
    8/20/87, Jack 3/11/89, Isaac 3/11/90, Daniel 9/1/92, Polly
    12/11/94, Rebecca 4/28/97, Joseph 6/9/1800, Solomon
    12/24/03, Elijah & Elisha 9/22/05, & John 11/11/07. R334
  Samuel, esf Henrico Co, VA; b 10/29/1750; dd 7/13/1810 Nel-
    son Co, VA; md 4/25/1789 Hanna Jopling (MB 4/24/89 for sol
    & wid Hannah Wood signed by Josiah Jopling), Amherst Co,
    VA; wid b 10/1/1767 & afp 1846 & 1848 Nelson Co, VA, both
    PAR, insufficient proof of svc; sol bro William AFF ae 89
    there 1846; sol s/o Jonathan; births of negro slaves:
    Sary Ann 6/8/1774, Frank 6/18/91, Alexander 9/25/93, Rach-
    el 9/26/95, Aggness 1/8/98, James 4/1/00, Samuel 2/28/02,
    & Nathan 1807. R334
  William, esf 1781 Henrico Co, VA; b 6/29/1757; PN 1832 Nel-
    son Co, VA; bro Nathaniel AFF ae 89 there 1832. R334
BRIDWELL, Simon, esf 1776 Stafford Co, VA, where b 1756; to KY
    1807 where PN Spencer Co 1832. R334
BRIGGS, Benjamin, esf 1777 VA; b 4/3/1765 Augusta Co, VA; PN
    1833 Lincoln Co, KY. R335
  David, esf 1780 Louisville, KY; b 10/23/1760 Westmoreland Co
    VA; PN 1832 Logan Co,KY, where dd 9/22/1835; md 11/13/1786
    Margaret Crawly/Crawley, Fauquier Co, VA; wid b 1/19/1759,
    & PN 1842 Logan Co, KY; she gtd BLW 1855 Warren Co, KY;
    ch births: Jeney 4/25/1788, Judah 1/23/90, Elizabeth S
    4/20/92, William 1/29/94,Charloty 12/2/95, Thomas 1/15/98,
    George 7/14/1800, Hesakiah 3/10/02, Charles 1/22/04, David
    1/22/06, John 1/22/08, Marian 1/12/10, Margaret L 1/22/12;

BRIGGS (continued)
   s George res Logan Co, KY, 1842. R335
BRIGHT, Francis, VA sea svc; esf 1776 VA as captain of armed
     cruiser BRIGANTINE; dd 12/18/1811, surv ch: Elizabeth, Su-
     san Hannah, & Margaret Mary; d Elizabeth, decd in 1832,
     surv ch Susan H Moore, Elizabeth w/o Henry Edlee, Virginia
     F, Catherine M, & Julia S Travis; d Susan Hannah w/o Samu-
     el F Bright decd in 1832; d Margaret Mary dd as minor;
     Henry Edlee, adm/o sailor's estate 1832 York Co, VA, afp
     for heirs, & PAR, sailor having resigned commission before
     end of War (1878). R340
   Windle/Wyndle, esf 1778 Augusta Co,VA; esf 1779 Middlebrook
     NJ; b 10/8/1755 near Baltimore,MD; f mvd family to Augusta
     Co, VA, 1756; sol bro/o George; mvd to Bath Co, VA, 1795,
     thence Greenbrier Co, VA, thence 1811 to KY where PN 1823
     Green Co; dd 4/6/32 Marion Co, KY; md 5/13/1786 Barbara
     Kisner, Augusta Co, VA; wid PN ae 72 Marion Co, KY, 1832;
     ch births: Mary 12/25/1786, George A 9/21/88, Elizabeth
     6/24/90, Sarah 4/19/93, Susanna 4/20/96, Margaret 3/18/99,
     & Nancy 4/1/1801; s George res Marion Co, KY 1838. R340
BRIGHTWELL, Anderson, esf 1778 King William Co, VA; PN ae c58
     Charlotte Co, VA, 1821; dd 4/3/37; md 1786 Nancy d/o Run-
     nald Brightwell, who signed MB 12/14/86, also signed by
     Charles & Barnard Brightwell, Prince Edward Co, VA; wid PN
     ae 76 Pittsylvania Co, VA, 1839. R340
   Charles, esf 1779 Prince Edward Co, VA; b 1756-7 King Willi-
     am Co, VA; PN 1832 Prince Edward Co, VA. R340
BRILL, Michael, esf 1781 Frederick Co, VA; b 1762 PA; afp 1837
     Muskingum Co, OH, when w aec 60; PAR for svc less than 6
     months. R340
BRILLIFONT, James, esf 1776 Charles City Co, VA; PN there 1818
     ae 64; w ae 57 in 1820. R340
BRIMMER, Isaac, esf 1776 VA; b 1/11/1759; PN 1832 Culpeper Co,
     VA. R341
BRINKER, Henry, esf Winchester,VA; PN ae 71 Springfield, Hamp-
     shire Co, VA, 1832. R342
BRINKLEY, Aaron, esf 1777 VA; s/o Henry/o Nansemond Co, VA; to
     Edgecombe Co, NC, after RW; dd 1804; md 5/11/1773 Sarah,
     d/o Henry Griffin, Nansemond Co, VA; wid afp aec 90 Edge-
     combe Co, NC, 1836 when eldest s ae 66; PAR, insufficient
     proof/o svc. R342
   William, esf 1780 Shenandoah Co, VA, where afp 1822 ae 67, &
     PAR; no family 1822. R342
BRISCOE, Reuben, BLW issued 5/26/1789. R342
BRISTER, Aaron (colored), esf 1776 Dumfries, Prince William Co
     VA; PN ae 56 Palmyra, NY, 1818; mvd to Bath Co, NY, c1795,
     thence Palmyra, NY, 1805; sometimes called Alexander BRIS-
     TER; dd 8/1821; md 1777-8 Betsey Tolibee; wid PN aec 81
     Wayne Co, NY, 1843; 10 ch with 4 liv 1843: Mrs Lucy Jarvis
     ae 55, Robert ae 38, Mina ae 33, & Betsey aec 31; sol & w
     slaves at time of marriage; sol fam 1820 w Betsey ae 46, s
     James ae 10, d Mina ae 8, & d Betsey ae 6. R342

BRITAIN, John, see BRITTAIN, John.   R343
BRITT, John, BLW issued 11/2/1792.   R343
  Obed, esf 1777 Goochland Co, VA, b 2/12/1759; PN 1832 Perry
    Co, TN; s W S res Perryville 1833; QLF 1929 from desc Ger-
    trude Britt Oustott, Nashville, TN.   R343
BRITTAIN, John, VA sea svc; sailing master on PATRIOT & LIBER-
    TY; decd in 1850; d Mrs Susan Dixon afp 1849 as only heir,
    she being m-in-law/o Joseph F Battley; PAR.   R344
BRITTEN, John, esf 1779 NJ for svc in VA regiment; b 7/1758;
    PN 1818 Jersey, Steuben Co, NY; in 1820 family w Hannah ae
    52; s John ae 18, s Richard ae 16, d Matilda ae 14, & Emi-
    ly ae 12; QLF 1930 from desc Nellie M (Mrs D P) Yerkes,
    Northville,MI, states sol w Hannah Lott who PN c1840. R344
BRITTON, John, see BRITTAIN, John.   R344
  John, esf 1777 nr Baltimore, MD, for svc in VA regiment; b
    Hertfordshire, England; to America c1770; BLW issued 1821
    Kennebec Co, ME; PN aec 80 Litchfield, Lincoln Co, ME,
    1832.   R344
  Joseph, esf 1779 Winchester, VA; PN ae 70 Harrison Co, VA,
    1832.   R345
  Samuel, BLW issued 3/16/1792 to Mary Britton, adm/o his es-
    tate.   R345
BRIZENDINE, Bartlett, esf 1780 VA; PN ae 59 Essex Co,VA, 1821;
    family res with sol 1823 w Nancy, & 3 ch, eldest ae 11; dd
    11/19/36; md 3/1798 Nancy, who afp ae 75 Essex Co, VA, &
    PAR since md after 1793; heirs Susan & Mary Ann Brizendine
    afp 1852, & PAR.   R345
  Leroy, esf 1780 Lunenburg Co, VA, where res with f; b VA
    5/25/1761; PN 1832 Sumner Co, TN; dd 3/23/39; wid Lucy
    signed for sol final PN receipt 4/18/39 through attorney
    Young P Brizendine, Nashville, TN.   R345
  Reuben, esf 1781 Essex Co, VA; PN aec 71 Charlotte Co, VA,
    1832.   R345
  William, esf 1781 Charlotte Co, VA; b 1743 Essex Co, VA; PN
    1832 Franklin Co, VA.   R345
BROACH, Benoni, esf VA; dd 3/3/1814, King & Queen Co, VA; md
    there 10/1785 Ann, who PN there 1838 ae 74.   R346
  Charles, esf 1777 Essex Co, VA; PN ae 56 King William Co, VA
    1819; family in 1820 w Martha ae 55 & ch: Ann ae 28, Peggy
    ae 22, Charles ae 20, & William ae 17; dd 9/1829; md Mar-
    tha in Spring 1784; wid PN ae 75 King William Co, VA, 1838
    & decd in 1839.   R346
BROADDUS, John, esf 1780 Caroline Co,VA, where b 5/7/1764; afp
    there 1832, & PAR, svc not in regular military unit.   R346
  Pryor, esf 1789 Caroline Co, VA; PN ae 69 King & Queen Co,
    VA, 1832; dd 12/21/43; PN due to sol pd to one/o his 2 ch
    mbnn 1844.   R346
  Reuben, esf 1779 Caroline Co, VA, where b 1760; afp there
    1832, & PAR, svc less than 6 months.   R346
BROADUS, William, esf 1776 VA; PN 1830 Harpers Ferry, Jeffer-
    son Co, VA, where dd 10/7/30; md (2) 11/5/05 Martha R Ri-
    chardson, Hanover Co, VA; wid PN 1853 Charlestown, Jeffer-

BROADUS (continued)
son Co, VA, & dd 2/21/63 Jefferson Co, VA; sol ch by 1st
w: William, Harriet w/o John Brood, Juliet w/o Henry Ward
(s William Henry & s Philip Woodville), Kitty w/o William
Thompson (ch Richard, Martha, Mary & William), & Patsey
w/o Merriwether Thompson; sol ch by 2nd w: John, Robert
(dd before 1832), Maria E, Lavinia D, & Sarah Ann (ae 78
in 1865); QLF states sol gdf/o Richard A Thompson, Secre-
tary of the Navy; QLF 1891 from great gds W S Thompson,
Washington,DC; QLF 1921 from desc Mrs J V Boswell, Springfield, MO, states sol md 1790 a Mrs Jones & their d Catherine Wigginton Broadus b 2/9/1790 md William Mills Thompson; QLF states sol bro/o Thomas & John. R346
BROADWATER, Charles Lewis, VA sea svc, esf 1776 Fairfax Co,
VA; PN there 1830 ae 78; w dd earlier; gdc in 1882: Ann M
Elgin, St Louis, MO, Arthur Broadwater, Fairfax Co, VA,
John C H Broadwater, Montgomery Co, MO, Thomas J Broadwater, Memphis, MO, Guy L Broadwater, Chico, CA, Sydney
Broadwater, Moberly, MO, Julia Duncan, TX, Ann Broadwater
wid/o Charles H Broadwater, Quincy, IL, & Elizabeth Farr
(decd); great gdc 1883 Elizabeth, Guy, Samuel Albert, &
William, all ch/o Elizabeth Farr & res Chenoa,IL; QLF 1908
from desc Julia A Sebastian, Edwardsville, IL; QLF 1909
from great gdd Fannie Elgin (Mrs Everett) Brooks, St Louis
MO; QLF states sol b 1752 Fairfax Co, VA, dd there 1841, &
had s Charles. R346
BROADWAY, Samuel, esf 1778 Prince Edward Co,VA; b 5/1763 Anson
Co, NC; PN 1833 Macon Co, NC. R346
BROCK, George, esf 1779 Shenandoah Co, VA, where b Aug 1762;
afp 1834 Washington Co, IN, 1834; PAR, insufficient proof
of svc. R347
   Henry, esf 1775, PN aec 74 Jefferson Co, KY, 1821 when fami-
ly w & 6 ch res with him, all 3 d's over age 21, & 3 s's
ae 18-21. R347
   Jesse, esf Guilford Co, NC; b 12/8/1751 Cumberland Co, VA;
PN 1833 Harlan Co,KY, having res there c34 years; QLF 1931
from desc Mrs Rose Brock Jones, Frankfort, KY. R347
   Uriah, esf 1776 Portsmouth, VA; PN ae 56 Missouri Territory
1819; BLW issued 1831 Randal Township, Cape Girardeau Co,
MO. R347
BROCKMAN, Joseph, esf VA; PN ae 78 Albemarle Co, VA, 1821 when
no w or ch res with him; QLF 1920 from desc Nola Sparks
(Mrs Edward H) Eichelzer, Detroit, MI. R347
   Sarah, former wid/o James DANIELS. R347
   Thomas, esf 1776 VA; afp ae 75 East Fork Settlement, Montgomery Co, IL, 1834; PAR for insufficient proof of svc; QLF
states s John res Knob Noster, MO. R347
BROCKUS, John, esf 1775 VA; PN ae 72 Grainger Co, TN, when had
w & "small family"; in 1821 family w Mary ae 43 & ch: Betsey ae 7, John ae 6, & David ae 4; QLF 1934 from desc Martha Ellis (Mrs Arthur H) Hopkins, Rensselaer, IN. R347
BROMAGEN, Jarvis, esf 1779 Morgantown, Monongalia Co, VA; b

BROMAGEN (continued)
   1762; PN 1833 Bath Co, KY, where res 35 years, & res still
   1841. R349
BROMIGIN, Jarvis, see BROMAGEN, Jarvis. R349
BROMLEY, Margaret, former wid/o Ralph FALKNER. R349
BROOCKE, William, see BROOKS, William. R350
BROOCKS, William, see BROOKS, William. R350
BROOK, George, esf 1775-6 VA; PN ae 69 Henrico Co,VA; QLF 1909
   from desc H Y Brooke, Montgomery Co, AL. R350
   John, BLW issued 6/21/1796. R350
BROOKE, Dudley, esf 1781 Buckingham Co,VA; b 7/22/1761-2 Ches-
   terfield Co, VA; PN 1833 Robertson Co, TN, where res c18
   years; QLF states sol had s Dudley B Jr, & had gds aec 100
   liv TN 1938. R350
   Edmund, esf 1781 Essex Co, VA; PN 1828 Georgetown, DC; QLF
   states sol had s Robert who War of 1812 sol, & Robert f/o
   Michael, Robert, & Francis. R350
   Francis T, esf 1780 VA; PN ae 65 Spotsylvania Co, VA, 1832;
   gtd PN increase 1832 Richmond, VA; in 1848 judge/o Supreme
   Court of Appeals in VA; gtd PN increase 1850; AFF 1848 by
   "near" relative John Taliaferro, member of Congress from
   VA. R350
   Humphrey, esf 1777 King William Co,VA, where b 9/18/1760; PN
   1832 Frederick Co,VA; QLF 1909 from desc H Y Brooke, Mont-
   gomery, AL. R350
   Walter, VA sea svc; Commodore in VA Navy; heirs gtd BLW for
   his svc: d Mrs Graeff, d Mary C Rooker, W T Brooke, B E
   Brooke, Lucy A Brooke, Virginia Brooke, Jabez Rooker, Mary
   C Rooker, John Graeff, & Ann Graeff; heirs afp, & PAR; QLF
   1917 from great great great gdd Ethel L Smither, Richmond,
   VA. R350
   William, see BROOKS, William. R350
BROOKES, Jonathan, esf 1778 Caswell Co,NC; b 6/7/1762 Glouces-
   ter Co, VA; to Brunswick Co, VA, with f as·ch, thence to
   Caswell Co, NC; PN 1832 Guilford Co,NC; nephew Robert Hol-
   derness res Caswell Co, NC, then; QLF states sol md Ann
   d/o John Lewis (a lawyer) & Sarah Iverson, Spotsylvania
   Co, VA, & they had 5 ch, eldest Rev. Iverson Brooks who b
   1793 Rockingham Co, NC. R350
BROOKOVER, John, esf c 1780 MD aec 18; esf 1781 VA; b near
   Bladensburg, MD at "The Woodyard"; after RW md & settled
   near Winchester, VA; PN aec 72 Wood Co, VA, 1832 where res
   for 20 years; res Parkersburg, VA, 1837. R350
BROOKS, Benjamin, BLW issued 10/24/1789. R351
   Charles, esf 1776 Leesburg, VA; PN ae 60 Knox Township, Jef-
   ferson Co, OH, 1819; in 1820 family w ae 59, d Christina
   ae 19 & gdc ae 10 & 2; .md (2) 8/1836 Malinda Richey, Ohio
   Township, Allegheny Co, PA, where dd 5/25/1845; wid afp
   1857 Sewickleyville, Allegheny Co,PA, & PAR since md after
   1794. R351
   David, esf 1777 Prince Edward Co, VA; PN ae 73 Claiborne Co,
   TN, 1832. R351

BROOKS, Elias, esf Chesterfield Co, VA; b Essex Co, VA; PN ae
    73 Chesterfield Co, VA, 1832; QLF states sol s/o Elias Sr.
    R352
  George, esf 1779 Ninety-Six District, SC; esf 1781 Mecklen-
    burg Co, VA, where b 4/4/1762; PN DeKalb Co, GA, 1837; res
    1855 Cobb Co, GA; dd 4/27/56. R352
  George, esf 1776 Kingston Parish, Gloucester Co, VA, where b
    & where dd 1791; md 1779 Barsheba Diggs; wid PN ae 74 Ma-
    thews Co, VA, 1837, when bro Bailey Diggs AFF; eldest ch
    Mary Hudgins b 5/5/1781 & AFF 1838 Mathews Co, VA. R352
  Henry, esf 1775 Bedford Co, VA; PN ae 78 Orange Co, IN, 1832
    & mvd 1834 to MO to be near s's who res Lafayette Co, MO.
    R352
  James, esf 1780 Bedford Co,VA, where b 6/1760; PN 1832 Camp-
    bell Co, VA, where bro Nelson made AFF 1833. R352
  James, esf 1777 VA; PN ae 76 Bardstown, KY, 1819; w dd Fall
    of 1824 Nelson Co, KY, & her property to her ch. R352
  James, esf 1781 Prince Edward Co, VA; b 3/30/1765 Amelia Co,
    VA; PN 1832 Wilkes Co, NC; dropped from PN rolls 1835, be-
    cause name not on roll/o company in which he allegedly had
    svc; dd 4/20/1838; md c1790 Nancy Wood; wid ae 67 in 1820
    & dd 12/25/46, with 4 of her 7 ch surv: Zachariah, Sarah
    Byrd (Wilkes Co, NC), Nancy Childers, & Lucy Rice, who afp
    & PAR. R352
  John, esf 1777 Baltimore, MD; later esf Augusta Co, VA; mvd
    after RW to KY, thence TN where PN ae 81 Fayette Co, 1833;
    ch mbnn then; QLF states sol s Jonathan RW sol from Augus-
    ta Co, VA, & sol John Sr. R353
  John, BLW issued 6/23/1793-5. R353
  John, esf 1780 Bedford Co, VA; PN ae 77 Allen Co, KY, 1833;
    QLF states sol still res there 1840. R353
  Littleton, esf 1776 Sullivan Co, NC (later TN); b 1758 Brun-
    swick Co, VA; PN 1833 Hawkins Co, TN; dd 8/19/40 leaving
    ch mbnn. R353
  Middleton, esf 1780 Halifax Co, VA; b Caroline Co, VA; to GA
    1786, where PN ae 73 Jackson Co; QLF 1914 from great gdd
    Miss Giralda Brooks, Fairburn, GA, states sol md Sallie
    Smith & they had s Thomas, who md Margaret Storey, who pa-
    rents/o John Madison Brooks, f/o querier. R354
  Nelson, esf 1779 Bedford Co,VA, where b 7/1760 (now Campbell
    Co); PN there 1832; dd there 10/10/33; md there c1782
    Frances Trent; wid PN there 1838, & AFF there 1844 ae 82;
    wid sis Mina md 1772 Barnet Finch Sr, who AFF there 1838;
    Mina Trent Finch AFF 1839 there that she c10 years older
    than sis Frances. R354
  Robert, esf 1781 Mecklenburg Co, VA, where b 6/3/1762; to NC
    1800, thence GA 1818 where PN Marion Co 1833. R354
  Robert, esf VA; d 1804 Caroline Co, VA; md there c1784 Rhoda
    Jones; wid PN aec 80 there 1845; ch William & John (decd
    in 1845); AFF 1845 there by Nancy Eubank, wid/o Royal Eu-
    bank, that she md at least 10-15 years after sol & Rhoda,
    & Nancy's ch Elizabeth & Mrs Sally Taylor who ae 43. R354

114

BROOKS, Thomas, esf 1779 area now Sullivan Co, TN; b 5/1760;
PN 1832 Hawkins Co, TN; QLF quotes General Accounting Office report that sol dd 9/5/1840 having res Hawkins Co, TN,
50 years, & left wid Catherine who recd arrears of PN upon
death/o sol. R355
Thomas, esf Spotsylvania Co, VA; PN ae 85 Goochland Co, VA,
1829 when crippled w res with him; sol sold slave Henry to
s James 1827, & sold slaves Albert & Sewy 1825 to Fielding
Brooks as part of transaction for Fielding to provide food
& clothing to sol & w for rest/o their lives. R355
William, esf Walker Co, GA; b7/6/1757 Charles City Co, VA;
afp 1833 Troup Co, GA; PAR, insufficient proof/o svc; bro
Isham also RW sol. R355
William, esf 1776 Culpeper Co, VA, naval svc as marine; b
5/1747; afp 1830 Shelby Co, IL, when res with married d, &
other ch liv in other states; 7 ch (4 s & 3 d) liv then; w
dd c1821. R355
William, esf 1778 Hartford Co, NC; b 8/14/1734 Middlesex Co,
VA; PN 1832 Gates Co, NC. R355
William, esf 1781 Essex Co, VA, where b 1759; PN 1832 Char-
lotte Co, VA; dd 10/14/36; md 5/1788 Ann/Nancy, Essex Co,
VA; wid PN ae 77 Charlotte Co, VA, leaving ch John, Fran-
ces, Elizabeth, William C, & Catharine Roberts; ch births:
John 1/28/1790, Frances 11/18/92, Elizabeth 6/29/96, William C 7/28/1800, James 1/21/02, & Catharine 12/6/06; surname also spelled BROOCKE, BROOCKS & BROOKE. R355
William, esf 1777 Culpeper Co, VA; b 2/3/1752 Fauquier Co,
VA; PN 1832 Tazewell Co, VA, where dd 1/24/41; md 9/5/1769
Nancy who afp ae 94 Tazewell Co, VA, 1843, & PAR for proof
of marriage; QLF 1928 from desc Charles F Brooks, Bluefield, WV. R355
William, esf Culpeper Co, VA; to Rutherford Co, NC, after RW
where w dd; sol dd 10/15/1836 while on visit to s Middleton who res Rocky Mount, Fairfield District, SC; sol other
ch: James, Thomas, Philip, & Susanah; d Susanah afp ae 87
Greene Co, TN, 1857 when her eldest liv ch James B Chedester ae 46; PAR, insufficient proof/o svc. R355
BROOME, John, esf 1777 Romney, Hampshire Co, VA; PN ae 69 Washington Co, OH, 1818; family 1820 w Chary ae 51 & d Ruth
ae 15 res Fearing Township, that Co. R356
Thomas, BLW issued 10/20/1789. R356
BROSIUS, Abraham, esf 1776 Berks Co, PA; PN ae 64 Augusta Co,
VA, 1818 when family w & 3 d's; in 1820 family w ae 65 &
2 d's all res with s, Staunton, VA; sol dd 1/6/1833; QLF
1916 from desc Mrs J C Rexford, Owosso,MI; QLF 1892 states
data needed for settlement of estate in Holland; QLF 1884
from great gds W G Brosius,Knightstown, IN, states data on
sol needed for settlement of estate in Germany; surname at
times spelled BROSUS. R356
BROUGH, William, esf 1775 VA; res aec 76 Hampton, VA, 1826, &
dd there 9/1832; s Joseph W (1 of sol 2 ch) afp ae 40 Norfolk, VA, 1849; sol gdc Helen & Robert, ch/o decd d Eliza

BROUGH (continued)
    D Repilow, afp 1850; both PAR, insufficient proof of svc.
    R356
BROUGHTON, Job; esf 1775 Surry Co, NC; esf 1777 GA; b Bruns-
    wick Co, VA, 10/30/1755; PN 1833 Goose Creek, Knox Co, KY;
    dd 3/27/37; md 6/26/1774 Mary who b 3/10/1757; wid PN 1838
    Knox Co, KY, when res with s William ae 52; sis/o sol Win-
    ny Davis. R357
BROWDER, Isham, esf 1776 VA; dd 1830 Hickman Co, KY; s John by
    1st w res Hopkins Co,KY, 1853 ae 63; sol md (2) 12/10/1810
    Elizabeth Scearce/Scarce, Woodford Co, KY; wid PN ae 77
    Hopkins Co,KY, 1853; sol also had s Herbert Claiborne; sol
    dd 1830 Hickman Co, KY; QLF 1936 from desc Ella M Crow,
    Santa Cruz, CA; QLF 1926 from desc Mrs Addie Browder Pas-
    chall, Fulton, KY, states sol 3 s's in War of 1812, & 2 of
    them KIA Battle of Tippecanoe; QLF states 1st w/o sol Ra-
    chel Slayton. R357
  Jesse, esf 1776 VA; dd 2/7/1783; md 12/15/1780 Mary "Polly"
    Browder; wid md (2) 9/25/1784 Thomas Penticost, who dd
    2/7/1830; wid afp ae 81 Dinwiddie Co, VA, 1844 as former
    wid/o sol, & PAR. R357
BROWN, Aaron, esf 1776 Bedford Co, VA; b 1756 Cumberland Co,
    PN 1833 Monroe Co, TN; dd 4/29/36 leaving wid Nancy & ch:
    Elizabeth Hunly, Dicey Heisel, Mary Christian, Joseph,
    Phebe Staples, George, Lewcinda, Nancy, Wilson, James, Sa-
    rah Purvines, & John; wid dd 12/7/42; her sis Dicey Brown,
    widow ae 78, AFF McMinn Co, TN, 1845 when sol s Joseph ae
    53 & other heirs afp Monroe Co, TN, & PAR. R358
  Amos, esf 1780 Lincoln Co,NC; b 1766 VA; to NC as ch; PN Ma-
    con Co, NC, 1832; dd 8/28/42 Notley, Cherokee Co, NC; md
    3/18/1785 Elizabeth Brown, who b 5/1770; wid PN 1844 Macon
    Co, NC, & gtd BLW Cherokee Co, NC, 1855; ch births per s
    Thomas 1850, who stated part/o family bible birth records
    lost when bible got wet: Margaret 11/5/1786, Abby 3/15/88,
    Thomas 2/1/90; Alfred 12/16/91, Elizabeth 10/26/92, Sarah
    11/15/94, Zekiel 3/19/06, & Alma 5/21/09; ch liv 1857:
    Thomas, John Wesly, Alfred, Jane, Elizabeth, & Sophia; sol
    heirs 1860: J W Brown, Rollin, Fannin Co,GA, Thomas Brown,
    Notley, Cherokee Co, NC, Jane Brown, Notley, NC, Sophia
    Shepherd, Franklin, Macon Co, NC, Elizabeth Young, Cleave-
    land, Bradley Co,TN, Alford Brown, Elm Springs, Benton Co,
    AR, Sarah Belk's (decd) heir Darling Belk, Tunnell Hill,
    GA, Margaret Foster's (decd) heir A B Foster, Altoona, GA.
    R358
  Arabia, esf 1777 Bedford Co, VA; b 121/27/1755; PN 1832 Gar-
    rard Co, KY, where dd 3/13/44; md 5/1778 Elizabeth "Betsy"
    Dooley; wid PN ae 87 Garrard Co, KY, 1844; family bible
    partially damaged but remaining ch birth data: Stephen
    6/25/1779, ch 1/1/1782, --chel 9/18/83, Arabia J 3/16/85,
    Peggy 8/28/86, Doshy 9/10/88, Stephen U 8/17/17--, Henry
    5/16/92, Elizabeth 2/17/17--, ch 11/1795 (dd 11/1806), ch
    5/6/97, & ch 4/99; other family bible data: John Branham b

116

BROWN (continued)
    4/13/1798, Barthena Branham b ?; s Arabia J liv 1863; QLF
    1923 from desc Mrs Martha Tinsley Kennen, Laddonia,MO; QLF
    1934 from great great great gdd Miss Mary Branham, Orlan-
    do, FL; QLF 1929 states sol w b 3/1757 & dd 9/23/1850 Gar-
    rard Co, KY, further s Stephen md 3/12/1801 Martha Pearl,
    Lincoln Co, KY, further sol s Harvey b 1/1/1782 & md Pati-
    ence Owsley 12/31/1804 Garrard Co, KY, further sol d Ra-
    chel b 9/18/1783 md (1) 11/12/1796 John Branham, Lincoln
    Co, KY, & (2) Tyree Harris, further sol s Arabia Jackson b
    Bedford Co, VA, & md 3/15/1804 Nancy McKinzey, Garrard Co,
    KY, further sol d Sophia W b 8/17/1790 & md 7/18/1811 John
    Spratt, Garrard Co,KY, further sol d Nancy b 5/6/1797 & md
    2/26/1817 Thomas Spratt, further sol d Deshy b 9/10/1788,
    sol d Louvina b 4/12/1799 & md 12/22/1817 Baylor Jennings,
    Garrard Co, KY, & dd 7/18/81; QLF 1932 from desc Miss Bes-
    sie G Brown, Gallatin, TN. R359
Aris, esf Mecklenburg Co, VA; md Fall/o 1779 Joanna Crocksin
    (ae 17) there; to Spartansburg District, SC, after 2nd ch
    born; dd 8/1822; wid PN aec 85 Pickens District, SC, 1846;
    10 ch; 4th ch md 3/27/1812 ae 22-3; AFF 1847 Spartansburg
    District, SC, by d Agness Thompson that ch/o of sol: John,
    William, Nancy, Agness (md 1798), Betsy, Katy, Polly, Jo-
    anna. R359
Basil/Bazel, esf Fayette Co, VA (later PA); PN for disabili-
    ty 1786; res there 1828; QLF 1930 from desc Mrs R P Car-
    der, Ontario, CA, states sol mvd to Shelby Co, KY. R359
Benjamin, esf 1777 Rowan Co, NC; b 1757 Halifax Co, VA; PN
    1832 White Co, TN. R360
Benjamin, esf 1780 Wilkes Co, NC; b 2/17/1763 Orange Co, VA;
    PN 1833 Elbert Co, GA; dd 2/27/46. R360
Bernis, esf Albemarle Co, VA; dd 10/30/1814; md 11/14/1779
    Henrietta Rhodes, Albemarle Co, VA; wid afp there 1842 ae
    81; PAR, not in regularly constituted military unit. R360
Brightberry, esf 1780 Brown's Cove, Albemarle Co, VA; b that
    Co 2/13/62 s/o Sarah Brown; md 1/10/1788 Suca, b 6/21/66;
    ch births: Milley 11/7/1788 (md 10/1/07 Thomas H Brown who
    b 4/16/1785), William 10/1/90, Edmund 4/7/92, Brightberry
    11/17/94, Nimrod 4/5/97, Clifton 8/6/99, Suca T 9/17/1803
    (dd 10/14/05), Horace 4/14/07 (md 11/12/33 Lucey E who b
    5/6/14) & Amanda 1/16/09 (md George Brown); sol dd 1/26/46
    leaving ch Horace, Clifton, William, Edmund, Brightberry,
    & Amanda, who afp 1846 & PAR. R360
Charles, esf 1776 VA; PN ae 76 Hopkins Co, KY 1829; w & ch
    mbnn; QLF 1921 from great gdd Mrs Mattie Brown Holing, Le-
    xington, KY; QLF 1908 from gds John D Brown, Kansas City,
    MO, s/o sol s Dr Coleman D Brown, states sol from Essex Co
    VA, & PN 1830 Mercer Co, KY. R361
Charles, esf 1776 Caroline Co, VA; PN ae 68 Mercer Co, KY;
    PN increase ae 77 there 1829 when family w & at least 2 s,
    latter not res with sol & w; sold slave to Coleman D Brown
    1829. R361

BROWN, Claiborn, esf Bedford Co, VA; md there Sarah Harmon who
    dd 11/1828 at home/o s Harmon, per his AFF 1842 Clinton Co
    KY, when he apf; PAR, since both parents decd. R361
  Daniel, esf 1776 Augusta Co, VA; b 10/1757 Bucks Co, PA; PN
    1832 Gosham Township, Madison Co, IL. R362
  Daniel, esf 1778 Culpeper Co, VA, where b 12/1/1748; PN 1832
    there & where dd 7/14/33; md there 12/25/1779 Elizabeth
    Hill (ae 15); wid PN 1837 & dd 1/2/52 leaving 5 ch & heirs
    of decd ch; AFF there 1837 by William Lewis h/o sol sis md
    1782; QLF 1925 from great great gds John Strother Coving-
    ton, Culpeper, VA, who also great great gds/o RW sol Fran-
    cis Covington bro/o William Covington, further Francis Co-
    vington md Lucy Strother, & William Covington md her sis
    Margaret, both d/o Capt John Strother, veteran of French &
    Indian War & member of Committee of Safety during RW. R362
  David, VA sea svc naval surgeon; dd 1798 unmarried, leaving
    only heir William Brown, who dd & left s John & s Richard;
    John dd leaving s William L (aec 48, Petersburg, VA, 1849)
    & d Mrs Mary Burcher, aec 44, Elizabeth City Co, VA, 1849;
    Richard Brown dd leaving ch: Jane K (ae 44 w/o James Mas-
    senburg, Elizabeth City Co 1849), Susan M ae 34, Elizabeth
    M (ae 36 w/o John Young, Elizabeth Co 1849), Sarah Ann (ae
    32 w/o Thomas Whitfield, Norfolk, VA, 1849), & John W aec
    26 in 1849; AFF 1835 by Noah Brown, Essex Co, NJ, that he
    s/o David Brown killed by indians c1780 in western part of
    NY & that David went to VA to serve in VA navy as surgeon,
    further that f dd intestate leaving 18 ch; heirs afp & all
    PAR. R363
  Edward, esf 1781 VA; bc 1760; afp aec 71 Lewis Co, VA, 1834;
    PAR, svc less than 6 months; s John L. R363
  Frederick, esf 1781 Augusta, Richmond Co, GA, while SC res;
    b VA; PN ae 70 Columbia Co, GA, 1836. R365
  George, esf 1780 Charlotte Co, VA; b 1752 Chesterfield Co,
    VA; after RW res 5 years in NC, 30 years in KY, & 18 years
    in IL; PN 1835 Washington Co, IL; dd 3/24/42. R365
  Henry, esf VA; b 8/10/1760 Bedford Co, VA; PN there as Henry
    Brown Sr 1832; QLF 1928 from great gds Moncure C Carpenter
    of New Brunswick, NJ, states sol dd 1841; QLF 1911 from
    great gdd Mary C Baker, Huntington, IN. R365
  Henry, esf 1781 Spotsylvania Co, VA; PN ae 70 Scott Co, KY,
    1818; family in 1820 w Mary ae 55, s William ae 16, d Nan-
    cy ae 27, & d Betsey ae 19. R365
  Henry, esf 1779 Bedford Co, VA; b 10/25/1759 Prince George
    Co, VA; PN ae 72 Campbell Co, VA, bro/o Edward of same Co;
    dd there 12/26/1849; md 8/29/1827 Elizabeth L Jones, Buck-
    ingham Co, VA; wid PN & gtd BLW ae 76 Campbell Co, VA,
    1855. R365
  Henry, esf 1776 Essex Co, VA; dd 1798 Mercer Co, KY; md 1780
    or 1781 Frances, who PN aec 80 Mercer Co, KY, 1838; AFF by
    sol bro Charles (md 1784) 1838 there; AFF there by sol d
    Esther Morgan 1839 ae 46; AFF there 1839 by sol sis Sally
    Graves that sol f also RW sol, further sol eldest ch Polly

BROWN (continued)
    now aec 58 if liv, 2nd ch Betsy aec 56 if liv, John aec 54
    if liv, & 3 other ch. R365
  Hubbard, esf 1781 Bedford Co, VA; b 1760 Brunswick Co, VA;
    PN 1834 Gibson Co, TN. R365
  Isaac, esf 1780 Charles City Co, VA; PN ae 69 there 1829 fa-
    mily then w, s ae 20, d ae 21 & gdc ae 4 mbnn. R366
  Isaac, esf 1775 Loudoun Co, VA; PN aec 60 Columbiana Co, OH,
    1818; in 1820 family w Esther ae 66, & d Rachel ae 30; dd
    10/26/1825 while on visit to sis in Belmont Co, OH; md
    3/22/1779 Esther/Hester Williams at her m's home, Harford
    Co, MD; wid PN ae 86 Augusta Township, Carroll Co, OH,
    1840; eldest d b 8/26-7/1780; s b 12/1781; other ch; wid
    bro David made AFF 1839 Fayette Co, PA. R366
  Isham, esf 1776 Prince Edward Co, VA; PN ae 70 Giles Co, TN,
    1819; ch in 1824: William, Nancy, George, Abraham, James,
    Polly Watson, Sally Webb, Lucy Finch, Patsy Crecy, & Bet-
    sey; sol res 1830 Arrow Rock Township, Saline Co,MO. R366
  Issachar, esf 1780 Upper Dublin Township, Montgomery Co, PA;
    PN ae 71 Loudoun Co, VA, 1832; dd c1840. R366
  Jacob Roberts, esf Amherst Co, VA, where b; BLW issued for
    disability from wounds 5/23/1783; dd 5/18/1805; youngest d
    Caroline Matilda w/o Dr Anthony F Golding afb 1846 Laurens
    District, SC; other sol ch surv then: Willis & Sarah Mor-
    gan Hall; other heirs then: Rebecca Anne Brown, Sarah C
    Goodwyn, Robert C Brown, & Thomas T Brown; QLF states sol
    sol RW surgeon & his great great gdd Mrs E B Chase, Colum-
    biana, SC, DAR member #55460; QLF 1889 from gdd Mrs Carrie
    Colton, Spartanburg, SC. R366
  James, esf 1780 Dinwiddie Co, VA, where b 5/24/1759; PN Da-
    vidson Co, TN, 1832. R367
  James, esf 1782 Hampshire Co, VA; b 1756 Cumberland Co, PA;
    PN 1832 Lewis Co, VA; name dropped from PN roll 1834 after
    examination of claim showed svc not rendered as claimed;
    bro/o John; QLF 1916 from desc James W Davis, Chicago, IL;
    QLF 1915 from possible desc Mrs J D Springston, Portland,
    OR, states sol dd 9/13/1835 Harrison Co, VA, & his w Sarah
    Sheppard dd 3/1/1835. R367
  James, esf 1774 Montgomery Co, VA; b 3/1755 Botetourt Co,VA;
    PN 1834 Wayne Co, KY, & dd there. R367
  James, esf 1776 VA; b 1760 Prince William Co, VA; res Fair-
    fax, Kennebec Co, ME, 1819. R367
  James, esf 1780 Leesburg, Loudoun Co, VA; PN ae 62 Richland
    District, SC, 1818; in 1820 family w Esther ae 49, & ch: d
    Polly ae 19, d Labey ae 16, d Nancy ae 14, s James ae 11 &
    d Martha ae 9. R367
  James, esf 1776 Charlotte Co, VA, where dd 12/16/1829, will
    probated there 3/1/30; md 12/13/1787 Martha "Patty" Vena-
    ble, Prince William Co, VA; wid PN aec 76 near Charlotte
    Court House, Charlotte Co, VA, 1838, & res there 1848; QLF
    desc Mrs F M Ward, Victoria, TX; QLF 1906 from desc Mrs W
    G Moon, St Louis, MO; QLF 1906 from great gds J T William-

BROWN (continued)
son, Columbia, TN. R367

James, esf 1776 Orange Co, VA; PN aec 65 Smith Co, TN, 1819;
dd 6/22/32; md 8/20/1790 Mary Ramsay, Burke Co, NC; wid PN
ae 69 Smith Co, TN, 1838, & res 1849 Macon Co, TN; eldest
s Spicer b 1791-2, made AFF 1841 Smith Co, TN; 5 other ch
mbnn; sol sis Ailse w/o James Sutton res there 1819. R367

Jeremiah, esf 1775 Fauquier Co, VA, where b 10/1757; PN 1832
Amherst Co, VA, when bro Jesse ae 67 there; QLF states sol
dd 1846. R368

Jesse, esf 1776 Surry Co, VA, where PN 1832 ae 76. R368

John, esf 1777 VA; afb 1828 by heir Jennings Brown, Bedford
Co, VA, who gtd BLW. R369

John, esf 1777 Shepherdstown, VA; b 1751; res 1777 York Co,
PA; PN 1818 York, that Co & dd there 11/18/25; md 6/6/1778
Barbara, German Lutheran Church there; wid b 8/1750, & PN
ae 86 York Co, PA, 1836; ch births: John 1/13/1780, Christiana 11/5/82, & William 9/13/84. R369

John, esf VA, dd 1811 Pulaski Co, KY; 1st h/o Nancey, who md
(2) Robert Anderson, also RW sol, for whose svc she also
gtd PN. R370

John, see BROWN, John G. R370

John, BLW issued 7/7/1792. R370

John, esf 1780 Lunenburg Co, VA, where b 1/25/1761, PN there
1833; to Rutherford Co, TN, 1835 where some/o ch res; QLF
1938 from desc Mrs Alyce Brown Wood, Woodbury, TN. R370

John, esf 1781 Hampshire Co, VA; PN ae 67 Lewis Co,VA, 1832;
name dropped from PN rolls 1835, as not rendering alleged
svc. R370

John, esf 1781 Culpeper Co, VA, sub for Daniel Brown, where
b 10/15/1759; PN there 1832; QLF states sol dd 12/1834 & w
Lucy Doggett, they res near Stephensburg, Culpeper Co, VA;
QLF 1931 from desc Miss Oreon Bruce, Alexandria,VA, states
sol dd 12/31/1834, md Lucy Daggett of Caroline Co, VA, &
they had 12 ch, including querier's gdf John D who War of
1812 sol. R370

John, esf 1775 Princess Anne Co, VA, where b 7/5/1759, & PN
there 1832. R370

John, esf 1775 Bedford Co, VA; never md; dd Wayne Co,KY; bro
Thomas & sis Jane (wid/o John Craig, & m-in-law of James
Coyle) afp 1842 Wayne Co, KY, for arrears/o sol PN; James
Coyle, adm/o sol estate, stated sol dd 12/22/1832, leaving
siblings: David, Betsy Jones, Mary Campbell, James, Tho-
mas, Peggy Woody, Anna Reece, & Jane Craig. R370

John, esf 1778 Petersburg, VA; PN ae 72 Baltimore, MD, 1820;
large family then, including d Margaret ae 15 & d Mary Ann
ae 13; QLF 1913 from desc Mrs Charles O Norton, Kearney,
NE. R370

John, esf 1778 James City Co, VA; PN ae 55 New Kent Co, VA,
1818. R370

John, esf 1777 Pittsylvania Co, VA; PN ae 61 Campbell Co,
VA, 1820 when no family. R370

BROWN (continued)

John, esf 1779 Westmoreland Co, VA; b 8/25/1763; PN 1818 Hampshire Co, VA, as John Brown IV; dd 2/10/43 Pickaway Co OH; md 11/1792 Anne Murphy, Westmoreland Co, VA; wid b 9/10/1765; afp 1843 Harrison Township, Pickaway Co, OH, & PAR for no proof/o marriage; ch births: Corbin 9/13/1793, Frances E 1/10/1795, Eliza M 9/14/1800, William & Margaret 3/1/03, & Richard 5/16/08; other family bible births: Peggy Hustin 3/1/1803, Fanny McCullough 1/10/1795, F Brown 3/10/1784, & Eliza M Hansbrough 9/14/--. R370

John, esf 177- Amherst Co, VA; PN 1811 for disability from wounds Woodford Co, KY, where dd 8/20/22; md (1) ? 1/1778, who dd 1805; md (2) 3/23/06 Nancy Clock, wid/o Tyre Glenn, Woodford Co, KY; wid afp 1853, & PAR for proof of svc; wid gtd BLW ae 83 Shelby Co, KY, 1855; sol s Jacob dd c1847-8; sol s Anderson ae 63 Marion Co, MO, 1854; sol ch by 2nd w: George, Lucinda, Nancy, Maurice, Joshua, & Sydney Scott; sol sis b Amherst Co,VA, md George Waugh, & res ae 93 Gallia Co, OH, 1864. R370

John G, esf 1777 VA where b; PN ae 74 Muskingum Co, OH, 1821 when w Alie ae 76 & blind & they res with d & her ch; sol dd 2/6/32 Monroe Township, Perry Co, OH, where 1st w dd before him; md (2) 4/3/1825 Mary "Polly" Spillman, Muskingum Co, OH; wid res 1853 ae 56 Athens Co, OH, & PN ae 58 Perry Co, OH, 1855; sol s George Washington made AFF 1827 Athens Co, OH, that sol had d Betsy w/o Isaac Shreve & d Sally w/o John Gale by 1st w. R370

Joseph, esf 1776 Jonesborough, TN; b 1756 Bedford Co, VA; PN 1833 Lincoln Co, MO, when res with nephew Levi Brown. R372

Joseph, esf 1776 Loudoun Co VA; esf 1781 Fayette Co, PA; b 1/18/1757 Bucks Co, PA; afp 1833 Bullitt Co, KY, & PAR for proof/o svc; s Joseph ae 50 Meade Co, KY, 1852 stated that sol dd there 9/20/49, leaving ch: Isaac, Hannah Kennedy, William W, Martha, Frances Armstrong, Joseph, & Abigail Wilson, who afp 1852, & PAR; twin bro William also RW sol who res Arkansas Territory. R372

Josiah, esf 1778 NY sub for f; esf 1779 MA; esf 1781 NC; esf 1781 VA; b Salem, Westchester Co,NY; PN ae 69 Hinckly, Medina Co, OH, 1833; 6 ch mbnn; dd c1843. R373.

Lewis, esf c1777 Henrico Co,VA, with f Joseph; dd 2/14/1815; md 5/1787 Clarissa Smith, Buckingham Co, VA; wid PN ae 71 Overton Co, TN, 1842, & res there 1855 ae 87 when gtd BLW; Clerk/o Buckingham Co, VA, record indicates marriage/o sol & Clarissa on 7/14/1784. R373

Low, esf 1774 Montgomery Co, VA, for svc in Indian Wars; esf there later for RW; PN ae 76 Tazewell Co, VA, 1832. R373

Moses, esf 1780 Dinwiddie Co, VA, where b 5/26/1752; PN 1830 Davidson Co, TN, 1830. R373

Neal, esf Petersburg, VA; dd aec 67 Raleigh, NC, 1823; md 1786 (MB dated 1/4/86) Rebecca Matthias, Norfolk Co, VA; wid dd aec 84 Raleigh,NC, 1839, leaving ch: Mary ae 54 wid of Josiah Davis, & Neal ae 44 of Wake Co, NC, who afp 1843

BROWN (continued)
    & gtd PN due to their m. R374
  Oliver, esf 1775 Lexington, MA, where b 6/1753; PN Brooke Co
    VA, 1818; in 1820 w Abigail ae 65 & d Elizabeth ae 20; sol
    res 1845 Brooke Co, VA, & gds William res there then; QLF
    1940 from great great gdd Mrs Winona Whittington Pfander,
    Peoria, IL, who also gdd/o Asa/Azariah Whittington, War of
    1812 sol; QLF 1908 from desc William L Beatty, Chicago,
    IL. R375
  Paten, esf VA; PN 1818 Butler Co, KY; in 1824 sol aec 60, w
    ae 40, & 9 ch (2 over ae 21, next 2 d, then 5 small s's &
    d's); sol dd 9/19/33 Butler Co, KY; md (2) 10/12/1806 Sal-
    ly Buckner, Logan Co, KY, & had 5 ch by her; wid PN ae 69
    Butler Co, KY, 1853. R375
  Patrick, esf 1778 Hanover Co, VA, where b 1760; PN 1832 Jef-
    ferson Co, IN; dd 12/29/35. R375
  Peter, esf nr Esopus, NY, 1775; esf later PA; b 4/1748 Ger-
    many; PN 1832 Rockingham Co, VA; dd 5/23/35; md 7/10/1778
    Elizabeth who PN ae 78 Rockingham Co, VA, 1836; ch Eliza-
    beth b 7/6/1779 (md --- Dietrick), Magdalen b 9/20/81 (md
    --- Duma), & Peter. R375
  Peyton, see BROWN, Peyton. R375
  Pollard, esf 1781 Culpeper Co,VA, ae c 18; PN Abbeville Dis-
    trict, SC, 1832 ae 69; bro Robert res 1832 Habersham Co,
    GA. R375
  Robert, esf Wilkes Co, NC; b 6/1762 Amelia Co, VA; PN 1835
    Humphreys Co, TN; dd 3/20/1840; md 3/1790 Milley Preston,
    Wilkes Co, NC; wid PN ae 73 there 1849; 1st ch b 2/1791;
    2nd ch Eli b 1/12/93 who md 3/31/1818 Martha Alison, their
    ch births: Teresa Caroline 1/7/1819, Malinda Anna 2/4/21,
    Madison Alison 4/15/23, Robert Dickson 7/25/25, Franklin
    Jackson 12/23/27, Calvin Lindsey 8/2/30, Sarah Francina
    3/19/33, Martha Elizabeth 8/18/35, & twins Frances Marrion
    & Eli Francis Marrion 4/20/38; Martha (Alison) Brown res
    Henry Co, TN, 1849. R376
  Robert, esf 1776 Culpeper Co, VA; PN aec 73 Habersham Co, GA
    1832; dd 1/20/40; md 1790 Jane who dd 1/3/46; s Hugh ae 45
    Habersham Co, GA, 1852; sol bro Pollard res Abbeville Dis-
    trict, SC, 1832, also VA RW sol; QLF 1924 from desc Mrs
    Charles Gork, Macon, GA, states sol had d Mary. R376
  Robert, esf VA; dd 1814; Thomas J Evans, adm of sol estate,
    afp, & PAR. R376
  Samuel, esf 1780 Pittsylvania Co, VA, where b 4/1762 or /64;
    PN 1835 Carlinville, Macoupin Co, IL; res 1847 Morgan Co,
    IL. R377
  Samuel, esf 1775 MA; b Lexington, MA; to VA 1789; PN ae 68
    Belmont Co, OH, 1818; w dd before 6/16/23 leaving him with
    9 ch: Peter Davis, Levi, Mariah, Samuel Washington, Isaac
    Hubbard, Hannah, Henry Cordis & twins Elizabeth & Jane (ae
    2), with eldest ch then 16; sol dd Spring 1828, St Clairs-
    ville, Belmont Co, OH; QLF 1918 from great gds Francis Ma-
    rion Richardson, Freeport, IL, states sol md twice & had

BROWN (continued)

> total of 19 or 20 ch, eldest being Elisha, others: Isaac Hubbard, Montgomery, Peter, Charles, Samuel, Henry, & Van Buren, further Van Buren f/o Swingren Brown, who f/o Eliza who m/o querier; QLF states sol Samuel C Brown; QLF 1897 from gds James H Brown, Denver, CO, cousin to John Brown Lennon of Bloomington, IL, also gds/o sol; QLF states sol b Leicester, MA, & w name Lydia. R377

Stark, esf 1776 Amherst Co, VA; b 7/6/1756; PN 1832 Walton Co, GA, where dd 2/5/40 leaving no wid but 3 ch, including d Dosha who md James Wood at ae 19; Dosha AFF ae 66 Henry Co, TN, 1846 that she only surv ch/o sol, her h James Wood then decd; sol d Maredith dd c1828; sol d Matilda md John Stokes. R378

Stephen, esf Buckingham Co, VA; b 1756 Cumberland Co, VA; to Bledsoe Co, TN, 1818 where PN 1833; dd 8/31/37; unnamed ch gtd arrears of sol PN 1841. R378

Thomas, esf 1781 Prince William Co, VA; b 3/7/1763; PN 1832 Grainger Co, TN. R379

Thomas, esf Tryon Co (now Rutherford Co), NC; b 2/28/1753 Augusta Co, VA, s/o William; family to Rowan Co, NC, when sol ch; bro/o William, Alexander, & Robert, all RW sol; to Warren Co, TN, c1808 where PN 1833. R379

Thomas, esf 1778 Surry Co, NC; esf 1780 Wythe Co, VA; b Orange Co, VA; PN aec 90 Estill Co, KY, 1832; dd 12/14/35 there; md 1777-8 Phebe, Halifax Co, NC; wid PN aec 76 Estill Co, KY, 1838, & dd there 3/1/40; ch births: Polly 1/4/1780, Thomas 7/24/83, James 1/15/86-7, Nancy 2/2/88, Patsy, Elizabeth, Midy, Lydia, John; s James md 6/11/1806 Philadelphia Sherrow, Garrard Co, KY (MB same date signed by her guardian Reuben Sherrow) R379

Thomas, esf 1779 Bedford Co, VA; b 2/5/1749 PA; to Amherst Co, VA, with parents ae 3; PN 1832 Russell, Bedford Co, VA R379

Thomas, esf 1780 Prince William Co, VA, where b 9/7/1760; PN 1832 Preston Co, VA; QLF states sol dd 1840 & h/o Anna Ash who survived him; QLF 1904 from desc James E Brown, Chicago, IL; QLF states sol dd 1844 Preston Co, VA. R379

Thomas, esf 1780 Culpeper Co, VA; PN ae 87 Scott Co, KY; dd 2/17/33 leaving ch mbnn; QLF 1926 from desc Sara R (Mrs Harry Marshall) Dixon, Richland, GA. R379

Thomas, esf 1777 VA; b 6/4/1754; PN 1821 Monroe Co, KY, when family w Martha ae 87, d Betsey aec 21, d Polly aec 18, & gds James Brown ae 11; sol dd 12/31/42; s Thomas res Tompkinsville, Monroe Co, KY, 1834 & res there 1835. R379

Thomas C, esf 1778 Hampshire Co, VA, where b 8/1761; mvd to Floyd Co, KY, c1827 where PN 1832 & gtd BLW 1855; sol dd there 4/17-19/57; md there 12/15/1831 Mary Brown; wid PN ae 50 there 1857, & res 1877 P. O. Prestonburg, KY; QLF states sol middle name Cowan. R379

Waller, esf 1780 Caswell Co NC; b 1749 Spotsylvania Co, VA; PN 1832 Pike Co, GA; dd 9/30/33; s John; QLF 1925 from

BROWN (continued)
    great great gdd Mrs L P Stuart, Camden, AL. R379
  William, esf Guilford Co, NC; b 8/27/1760 Pittsylvania Co,
    VA; PN 1833 Monroe Co, MS; res 1850 Choctaw Co, MS, where
    s's & s-in-law res; bro Samuel also RW sol; QLF 1939 from
    desc Hugh Brown, Nashville, TN. R380
  William, esf 1776 Jonesborough, NC (now in TN); b 1756 Bed-
    ford Co, VA; to SC with parents ae 6, thence East TN ae 21
    or 22; to Lincoln Co, MO, c1814 where PN 1832; s Levi res
    there 1834; sol twin bro Joseph also RW sol & PN 1833; f
    John also RW sol who dd c1809; sol res Thompson Township,
    Pike Co, AR, 1838; sol svc in same units with f John & bro
    Joseph. R381
  William, esf 1775 Cumberland Co, PA; esf 1777 Frederick Co,
    VA; b 1737 Lancaster Co,PA; PN 1832 Fayette Co, PA; s John
    res there 1851; other ch mbnn; QLF states sol. dd 3/1/35 ae
    96. R381
  William, esf 1778 Loudoun Co, VA; PN ae 86 Lawrence Co, KY,
    1833. R381
  William, esf 1776 Henrico Co,VA, where b 1760; PN 1832 Shel-
    by Co,KY; appointed William Brown Jr his Power of Attorney
    1832 Spencer Co, KY. R381
  William, esf 1776 Wythe Co (now Tazewell Co), VA; PN ae 77
    Giles Co, VA, 1832. R81
  William, esf 1777 Bedford Co, VA; b 1760 Fairfax Co, VA; to
    St Genevieve Co, MO, 1818 where PN 1832; res Ralls Co, MO,
    1835. R381
  William, esf c1776 Culpeper Co, VA; b VA; PN aec 68 Warren
    Co, KY, 1822 when had w aec 43 & d Nancy ae 6. R381
  William, esf 1778 Caroline Co,VA, where PN 1818 aec 60. R381
  William, esf 1776 Culpeper Co,VA; bc 5/20/1758 Essex Co, VA;
    PN 1832 Culpeper Co, VA; dd 12/12/43; md 2/9/1786 Lucy
    Campbell; wid PN ae 78 Rappahannock Co, VA, 1844, when AFF
    there by sol sis Elizabeth Popham ae 79; AFF then by sol
    sis Phebe Brown ae 89 Culpeper Co, VA; s mbnn 1845. R381
  William, esf 1780 VA; afp ae 78 Floyd Co,KY, 1825, where res
    with d, wid/o George Pack, & her family; PAR, svc not in
    regularly constituted unit. R381
  William Ambrose, esf Culpeper Co, VA; dd 8/23/1832 Overwhar-
    ton Parish, Stafford Co, VA; md 12/16/1787 Mary Grigsby
    Traverse/Travis that Co; wid afp 1839 Mercer Co, KY, & PAR
    insufficient proof/o svc; wid dd c11/15/41; s Ambrose AFF
    there 1853 ae 58, he b 1/29/1795, eldest s & 4th ch; other
    sol ch then liv: Margaret James aec 65 (eldest ch), Ellen-
    der Barnet ae 59, Lucinda Luke aec 53, & John T aec 46;
    sol bro/o Pheby Brown ae 85 Culpeper Co, VA, 1840, & Eli-
    zabeth Popham ae 71 there then. R381
  Windsor, esf Alexandria,VA, where dd 1785; b Ireland; grand-
    niece & only heir Mary Elizabeth w/o William King gtd BLW
    Washington, DC, 1832, she only surv ch/o Robert Dougherty
    (sol nephew) & w Margaret (now Mrs Miller), who AFF Wash-
    ington, DC, 1832. R381

BROWNING, Enos, esf Culpeper Co,VA; dd 1815 Washington Co, VA; md 1777-8 Jane Teim, NC, who dd 9/15/42 Island Creek, Logan Co, VA; ch: Edmund (eldest, ae 75 in 1853), Francis, James, John (ae 59 Wyoming Co, VA, 1853), Jacob, Caleb (bc 1798, decd in 1854), Betsey (dd intestate c1830 leaving ch Josiah, James, Lucinda, Harley, & Guy), Henry (decd in 1854), & Charles (decd in 1854). R382

Francis, esf 1778 Hillsborough, NC; PN ae 79 Russell Co, VA, 1832; dd before 10/55; w dd first; ch mbnn; QLF states sol s/o John (b 1728 Culpeper Co, VA) & Elizabeth Wimercast md 1744, further sol b 11/24/1753 Culpeper Co, & dd 7/18/1855 & md Miss Vermillion & res Lebanon, Russell Co, VA. R382

Isaac, esf VA; dd 11/1/1808 Hopkins Co, KY, where s Joel D afp 1844, & PAR; QLF states sol bro/o William, Francis, & James who all RW svc. R382

Levi, esf 1780 Halifax Co, NC; b 4/16/1758 Southampton Co, VA; PN 1832 Halifax Co, NC; ch mbnn; QLF 1938 from great great gdd Viola V Smith, Halifax Co, NC. R382

Robert, esf 1781 Caswell Co,NC; b 3/15/1764 Culpeper Co, VA; f dd 1807; PN 1833 Caswell Co, NC; dd 4/11/43; md there 12/13/1791 Frances Kinsborough/Kimborough/Kinborough; wid afp there 1844 ae 70, & PAR as not being wid at date/o applicable PN law; wid dd 9/22/46; QLF 1934 from great great gdd Mrs Dale F McGee, Malvern, AR. R382

BROWNLEE, Alexander, esf 1777 VA; KIA Battle of Guilford; afp & afb by s & only heir James Brownlee, Botetourt Co, VA, 1845; PN & BLW gtd. R383

James, esf 1777 Fluvanna Co, VA; PN 1818 Waynesborough, Augusta Co, VA; in 1820 sol aec 70 & w aec 50; dd 3/13/36 Augusta Co,VA, where md 1/28/1825 wid Mary Eve; wid PN aec 68 there 1855; sol surname at times spelled BURLEY. R383

John, esf 1777 Augusta Co, VA; PN ae 60 Green Co, KY, 1818; in 1820 sol had w & ch: Sally ae 25, Polly ae 22, Jane ae 16, Caroline ae 12, & 2 s's aec 21 (1 named William) & gdd ae 4; QLF 1916 from desc Anna Brownlee (Mrs Albert S) Gaus of Pittsburgh, PA. R383

William, esf 1777 VA; BLW issued 3/6/1795; QLF from desc Mrs Walter Benson, Austin, TX, states sol esf Augusta Co, or Rockbridge Co, VA, & recd grant/o ld in Green Co, KY. R383

BROYHILL, James, see BRAYHILL, James. R383

BROYLES, Daniel, esf 1780 Culpeper Co,VA, where b 5/1/1762; PN 1832 McMinn Co, TN; res 1836 Bledsoe Co, TN; dd 12/12/47, leaving ch including James M who County Clerk/o Monroe Co, TN, 1839. R383

Michael, esf 1776 Culpeper Co, VA, where b 6/1740; esf 1778 Western NC (now TN); PN 1833 Washington Co, TN; QLF states sol dd 1833 & was s/o Jacob BROYLES/BROIL, who dd Culpeper Co, VA, 5/19/1763. R383

BRUCE, Benjamin, esf Albemarle Co, VA; dd 12/31/1809 Clark Co, KY, leaving w & ch: Sarah/Sallie Gordon (b 6/27/1776), Agnes Wills, Austron/Austin, Derret, Ely, Elizabeth Haggard, & Nancy Wills; md 3/26/1773 Milly, Albemarle Co, VA; 8 ch;

BRUCE (continued)

    sol will dated 12/1809 & probated 1/22/10; wid b 3/29/1753
& afp 1842 Clark Co, KY; PAR insufficient proof/o svc; one
d md Thornton Wills; QLF states sol w Mildred, d Nancy md
Thornton Wills, d Agnes md Isaac Wills, d Sally md William
Gordon, d Elizabeth md Nathaniel Haggard, s Barnett md Lucy, & s Durritt md Sally, & sol ch signed 1817 deed Winchester, KY; QLF 1926 from desc Ruth Beall of that Co. R384

  George, esf 1776 VA; PN ae 60 Nelson Co, KY, 1820; to Greene
Co, OH, 1829 to res with 2 sons, all of family in KY being
decd. R384

  William, esf Warren Co, NC; b Richmond Co, VA; PN ae 73 Lincoln Co, KY, 1832, where mvd c1802; dd 3/5/42; QLF states
sol b 6/10/1759 VA, md (1) Hannah Morgan of VA, & (2) Kitty Gaines; QLF states sol bro's James & Isaac RW svc. R384

  William, esf 1779 Culpeper Co, VA, where b 1762; to Sumner
Co, TN, 1795, where PN 1832; QLF states sol dd 1846; QLF
1914 from desc Mrs James Johnson Quinn, Houston, TX. R384

BRUEN, Peter Bryan, see BRUIN, Peter Bryan. R385

BRUIN, Peter Bryan, esf 1775 VA; PN ae 64 Claiborne Co, MS,
1820; dd 2/1827 Bruenburgh,MS; ch: Eliza w/o William Briscoe, Matilda Cummins, Mariah, Sophia; Eliza only surv ch
1845 res Natchez, MS; sol gdc 1845: Richard Cummins of IN,
Caroline (d/o Mariah) w/o P W Briscoe, O P Watson (s/o Sophia), Louisa (d/o Sophia) w/o --- Tebbetts, Mary w/o David Roydon, Mariah w/o --- Dix, & Minerva w/o Samuel Walker of AR. R385

BRUMBACK, Peter, esf 1777 GA; esf 1779 NC; res Fairfax Co, VA,
after RW to 1806 when mvd to KY, where PN ae 70 Shelby Co
1818; res 1834 Boone Co, KY, ae 80, where dd 4/6/1846; BLW
issued 4/13/1791; md 1788 (MB 1/10/1788) Elizabeth Simpson
in Loudoun Co, VA; wid b Fairfax Co, VA, & PN aec 80 Boone
Co, KY, 1848; 12 ch; in 1820 ch: d ae 14, d ae 12, s ae 9,
& s ae 7; wid bro George ae 73 Boone Co, KY, 1849; QLF
1933 from great gdd Ora Brumback (Mrs E W) Simpson, Owenton, KY, states sol b Germany; QLF 1927 from great great
gdd Celia T Pettijohn, Akron, OH, states sol Hessian sol &
left British army to join rebel forces; QLF states sol ae
17 when came to America & lived to be 100; QLF 1918 from
Mrs W P Hooper, Walla Walla, WA. R385

BRUMFIELD, Humphrey, esf 1776 Montgomery Co, VA; b 6/22/1752
Amelia Co, VA; PN 1833 Gallia Co, OH. R385

  Robert, esf 1776-7 King William Co, VA; b 6/24/1754 Cumberland Co, VA; to King William Co ae 6, where afp 1835; PAR,
no proof/o svc; bro William also RW svc. R385

BRUMMAL, Benjamin, esf 1779 Chesterfield Co, VA; to Cumberland
Co, KY, 1806 where PN 1832 ae 74. R385

BRUMMET, Thomas, esf 1777 VA; PN ae 61 Anderson Co, TN, 1818;
dd 11/20/42; md c5/17/1793 Mary Burris, Knox Co, TN; ch
births: Hannah 5/14/1794, Delila 1/15/96, Belinda 12/14/98
William 12/8/1800, Elijah 1/25/02, Sarah 5/15/04, Anna
5/15/06, Rhoda 9/14/08, Sintha/Sinthia 6/22/10, James A

BRUMMET (continued)
7/31/12, & Thomas 11/13/14; wid afp ae 77 Anderson Co, TN,
1843, & PAR for proof/o marriage; wid dd there 11/6/1847;
surv ch 1852, all in Anderson Co, TN: William (still there
1854), Elijah, James A, Thomas, Sarah Braden, Anna White,
& Sinthia Bradshaw; AFF 1843 there by Elijah Burris, who b
3/15/1761, & had s Elijah b 2/15/1792; surv ch afp, & PAR
since m not wid in 1838; QLF 1936 from Mrs Arthur S Crump,
Transylvania, LA, states great gdf Banner Brummett b Bris-
tol, VA, 1789. R385
BRUNER, George, esf 1778 Frederick Co,VA; b 1762 Frederick Co,
MD; PN 1837 Frederick Co, VA. R386
BRUS, Edward, esf Halifax Co, VA; PN ae 67 Washington Co, TN,
1818; in 1820 sol res Carter Co, TN, with w & 2 ch. R386
BRUSTER, James, esf 1781 Rockingham Co, VA, where b 1763; to
Jessamine Co, KY, 1792, thence IN 1814, thence Mercer Co,
KY, 1833 where PN 1834; sol sis Polly w/o Nathaniel Dunn
res Jessamine Co, KY, 1833; sol nephew William Alexander
res IN 1834; QLF 1929 from Mrs Alan B Philputt, Indianapolis, IN, states she great great gdd of a James Brewster,
who b 1720 Co Derry, Ireland, came to America ae 18, & dd
Jessamine Co, KY. R387
BRYAN, Barrick, esf 1776 Prince William Co, VA; PN ae 72 Henry Co,KY, 1823, where dd 10/4/1840; md 8/28/1788 Ann Hancock, who PN aec 73 Trimble Co, KY, 1843, & res 1853 Carroll Co, KY; ch births: Elizabeth 8/26/1789, Mary 2/1/92,
Jane 10/16/93,Sarah 2/18/96, Ann 3/11/99, John H 6/8/1801,
Samuel 11/17/03, William 1/27/07, Melinda 2/17/11, & Foster 5/24/13; a Mary Ann Van Winkle b 7/31/1815; QLF 1927
from desc Mrs Betty M Brown, Springfield, IL. R388
James, see BRYANS, James. R388
John, esf 1777 VA; dd 9/1825 Campbell Co, VA; md 9/2/1788
there Catharine d/o Reese Evans (MB 9/1/88 f consenting, &
witnesses Daniel & Jane Evans); MB lists sol as John Jr;
ch mbnn; wid PN ae 77 there 1842; sol bro Anthony RW sol;
QLF 1915 from William Alanson Bryan, Honolulu, HI, desc/o
sol bro Andrew. R388
Reuben, esf 1776 Fauquier Co,VA; PN ae 68 Surry Co, NC, 1824
when w aged & infirm, s's grown, & 2 d's nearly grown, & 1
small gdc aec 6 (its m decd); in 1826 w Margaret ae 32 & a
gds res with sol. R389
Samuel, esf 1777 while res Rowan Co,NC, for svc with NC & VA
troops; PN ae 76 Marion Co, IN, 1832, & dd 3/4/37; md Mary
d/o Col Jonathan Hunt & w Isabella 10/5/1775 Rowan Co, NC;
ch: Ann, Phebe, William, Abner, Luke (b 11/22/1784, & md
1807 Mary d/o Capt John Sanders & w Sarah), Thomas, Sarah,
Mary, Daniel, Hampton, & Samuel; wid PN ae 87 Marion Co,
1839 when res with s's Luke & Thomas; sol great gdf was a
Dane, who res Denmark until s Morgan b, then mvd family to
Ireland, & s Morgan later came to PA in America where md
Martha Strode, a Hollander whose parents went to France to
escape religious persecution; Martha Strode's parents dd

BRYAN (continued)
   at sea enroute to America, leaving ch Jeremiah, Samuel, &
   Martha; ch/o Morgan & Martha: Joseph, Eleanor, Mary, Samu-
   el, Morgan, John, William, James, & Thomas; William, s/o
   Morgan & Martha, md Mary who d/o Squire Boone & Sarah Mor-
   gan & sis/o Col Daniel Boone; William & Mary's ch: Samuel,
   Daniel, William, Phebe, Hannah, John, Sarah, Abner, Eliza-
   beth, & Mary; William & Mary mvd 1779 to KY, settling at
   Bryan's Station on Elkhorn Creek in Fayette Co, where in-
   dians killed William & his s William; this sol s/o William
   & Mary Boone Bryan; QLF 1923 from desc Mrs Joseph E Bird,
   Nampa, ID; QLF 1912 from great gdd Millie Downing, Farina,
   IL, states sol dd Southport, IN, & w dd there ae 84, fur-
   ther Capt John Sanders also RW sol. R389
Seth, see BRYAN, Zephaniah. R389
Thomas, esf Chesterfield Co,VA; b 4/19/1764; PN 1833 Laurens
   Co, GA, where dd 5/13/44; md 10/1792 Margaret d/o William
   Simpson, Richmond Co, GA; wid PN ae 87/88 Laurens Co, GA,
   1854; ch births: Bennet 2/2/1795, James 10/2/96, Mary Ann
   7/6/98, & Elizabeth 1/2/1800; ch living 1855: Thomas, Eli-
   zabeth, Sarah, & Martha. R389
William, esf 1781 Rockingham Co, VA, where b 3/15-16/1762;
   PN there 1832; QLF 1917 from great gdd Miss Lucy Barbour
   Ewing, Harrisonburg, VA; QLF 1922 from desc William Bryan,
   Rockingham Co, VA. R389
Zephaniah, esf 1776 Connelstown, Westmoreland Co,PA, for svc
   in 8th VA Regiment; PN ae 82 Plumb Township, Allegheny Co,
   PA, 1853; dd 5/9/38; md (2) 8/16-17/1799 Jane who PN ae 85
   Allegheny Co,PA, 1853; eldest ch by Jane b 6/21/1790; oth-
   er ch mbnn; QLF states sol dd 4/20/1838 ae 88, Allegheny
   Co, PA. Rec 389
BRYANS, James, esf 1776 VA; PN 1818 Botetourt Co, VA; in 1820
   sol ae 70, w ae 65, d ae 26, twin d's Betsy & Else ae 23,
   d Peggy ae 19, & s Augustine ae 16. R389
BRYANT, Benjamin, esf 1780 Amherst Co, VA; PN ae 82 Warren Co,
   KY, 1832; dd 3/6/1835; md Fall of 1771 Nancy Gragg, Augus-
   ta Co, VA; wid PN ae 83, Warren Co,KY, 1838 when 4 ch, who
   b before 1775, over ae 64. R389
Charles, esf 1779 VA; afp ae 57-8 Laurens District, SC, when
   w ae 41 & ch: Elizabeth ae 22, George ae 21, Maria ae 10,
   Nancy ae 7, Rodger ae 4 & Joseph ae 2; afp 1821 Greenville
   District,SC; PN ae 65 there 1823 when res with w ae 44 & 5
   ch: Elizabeth ae 24, Maria ae 13, Nancy ae 10, Roger ae 7,
   & Joseph ae 5; BLW issued 6/29/1811. R390
James, esf 1789 Bedford Co, VA; PN ae 83 Grainger Co, TN,
   1832; dd 7/2/39, leaving wid mbnn. R390
James, esf 1780-1 Henry Co, VA; b 1753 Amherst Co, VA; PN
   1832 Monroe Co, IN; dd 11/3/53 Owen Co, IN; md 1/20/1836
   Ruth Dyer there; wid PN, gtd BLW there 1855; QLF 1901 from
   Judson W Jones, Liberty, Clay Co, MO, states he desc of
   James Bryant Jr (w Jane) of VA, who s/o James Sr of Mana-
   kintown, VA, & bro/o John. R390

BRYANT, Jesse, BLW issued 7/6/1793. R390
  Jesse, esf 1775 VA; b 11/1757 Surry Co, VA; PN 1832 Wake Co,
    VA. R390
  Jesse, esf 1777 VA; PN 1818 near Newport , Cooke Co,IN, for-
    merly res of Prince Edward Co, VA; John H Bryant ae 56 who
    as legal heir to sol (res Greene Co, TN, c38 years, & now
    decd) afb 1855 Rhea Co, TN, in behalf of Thomas Bryant, f
    of John H. R390
  John, esf 1777 VA; PN ae 61 Fredericksburg, VA, 1818 (crip-
    le on crutches). R391
  John, esf Buckingham Co,VA; b 1754 Albemarle Co, VA; PN 1838
    Jackson Co, AL. R391
  John, esf Amherst Co, VA; PN 1818 Lincoln Co, KY; in 1820 ae
    69, a tailor with failing eyesight, Mason Co, KY. R391
  John, esf 1780 Powhatan Co, VA; b 1/1/1760 Powhatan Co, then
    part/o Cumberland Co, VA; to KY 1786, where high sheriff/o
    Garrard Co, & where PN 1832; dd there 7/4/33; md 5/18/1786
    or 5/25/86 Mary Owsley, Lincoln Co, KY; wid PN ae 71 Gar-
    rard Co, KY, 1840, when s William liv; W J Graves/Groves,
    b there, made AFF 1840 that sol w was d/o his great gdf &
    sis/o his gdm; QLF states sol w d/o Governor Owsley of KY,
    & that sol f James, bro William, uncles Isaac & uncle Tho-
    mas all RW svc, coming from Manakintown, VA, further sol
    res Bryantville, Garrard Co,KY, near Lancaster; QLF states
    James Bryant Jr f/o sol; QLF 1916 from desc W T Foster of
    Washington,DC; QLF 1897 from gds G W H Kemper, Muncie, IN;
    QLF states sol f James Jr, b1720 VA & dd there, s/o James
    Sr & Elizabeth Lafever, & md (1) Jane Guerrant & had 4 ch
    by her (John, William G, Jane, & Sarah), md (2) Jane For-
    see & had 4 ch by her (James, Stephen, Silas & Mary). R391
  John, esf 1782 Powhatan Co, VA; PN ae 61 Garrard Co, KY,
    1832; dd there 2/3/38; md 2/18/1788 Sarah Brown, Cumber-
    land Co, VA; wid PN ae 72 Garrard Co, KY, 1843, & dd there
    3/9/46; ch liv 1848 Greenbury & Mary, who afp then as adm
    of estate/o m. R391
  Jonathan, esf 1775 MA, esf later PA; esf 1776 VA; PN ae 65
    Trenton, NJ, 1820, then sexton/o St Michael's Church, w ae
    65 & gdd Jane Ann Davenport ae 12. R391
  Parmenas, esf Fluvanna Co, VA; dd 3/1842; md 11/18/1788 Mar-
    garet, who afp ae 84 Nelson Co, VA, 1853, when AFF by Syl-
    vanus Bryant that sol his eldest bro, & m with rest of fa-
    mily mvd to Nelson Co, VA, after RW; MB 11/15/1788 Amherst
    Co, VA, between sol & Peggy Bibb, signed by John Bibb; wid
    PAR, insufficient proof/o svc. R391
  Peter, esf 1776 Richmond Co, VA, where b 3/4/1760; PN 1833
    Shelby Co, KY; res with sol there 1820 s aec 13, d aec 20,
    & d aec 18. R391
  Robert, esf 1776 Prince Edward Co, VA, where b 4/11/1755; PN
    1833 Wilkes Co, NC; to Blount Co, TN, with s Thompson; dd
    there 1/17/42, leaving ch Thompson & John; w dd many years
    before. R391
  Thomas, esf 1776 Halifax Co, VA, where b 8/20/1758; PN 1832

BRYANT (continued)
    Surry Co, NC, where dd 2/18/39; md 3/18/15 Ruth Dunagan/
    Dunigan/Donnegan there, she formerly/o Grayson Co, VA; wid
    PN ae 73 Surry Co, NC, 1853, gtd BLW there 1855, dd there
    6/2/1861; ch there 1868: Thomas ae 51, Sarah ae 50 w/o
    William Daniely ae 53, John ae 48, & Mary ae 45 w/o Joel
    Harrison ae 59; sol bro John RW sol who never returned
    from Battle of Camden; sol sis Sarah Lawson, res/o Surry
    Co, NC, 1833. R392
  Thomas, esf 1776 Culpeper Co, VA; b 3/3/1759 Northumberland
    Co, VA; PN 1832 Greene Co,TN; to Daviess Co, MO, 1842; QLF
    states sol dd c11/27/47 & buried near Trenton, Grundy Co,
    MO. R392
  Thomas, esf 1780 Spotsylvania Co, VA, where b 1761; PN 1832
    Henry Co, KY, when bro Jesse made AFF ae 66 Lexington Co,
    KY. R392
  William, esf 1776 Prince Edward Co, VA; PN ae 65 Davidson Co
    TN 1820 when family w Elizabeth ae 52 & s Hartwick Meekins
    ae 12; dd 7/2/39; gtd BLW 1808 Charlotte or Prince Edward
    Co, VA; s Harwick Meekins afp 1845 Bellefont, AL. R392
  William, esf 1777 VA; PN 1820 Morgan Co,GA; res 1825 Gwinett
    Co, GA, when had 3 small ch; res 1831 ae 74 Campbell Co,
    GA, when mns s's; md 8/22/1833 Mary Ann Barnett at home of
    Zadock Barnett, Oglethorpe Co, GA; wid PN ae 87 Campbell
    Co, GA, 1852, & ae 95 there 1856. R392
  William G, esf 1781 Powhatan Co, VA; b 1765 Cumberland Co,
    (now Powhatan Co) VA; PN 1834 Versailles, Ripley Co, IN;
    to Smith Co, TN, to visit sis & remained TN; dd 11/17/40;
    s mbnn 1839. R392
BUCHANAN, Henry, esf 178- VA; PN 1819 York Co, VA; in 1822 ae
    61 when had 3 ch ae 12, 9, & 4; dd 4/20/41; QLF 1933 from
    Mrs Jessie M Buchanan Wright, Los Angeles, CA, states she
    great gdd/o William Buchanan s/o Joshua Sr, further Joshua
    Sr b Scotland c1720-40 s/o George bc 1690, further Joshua
    Sr to VA thence to Allen Co, KY, c1795, & had ch: Andrew,
    James, Henry bc 1765, John bc 1771, Joshua Jr bc 1778,
    William, Thomas, & Hannah. R393
  Robert, esf 1777 Orange Co, NY, for svc in NJ Regiment; PN
    ae 67 Greenbrier Co,VA, 1819; family 1820 w ae 69-70. R393
  William Willis, esf 1775 Portsmouth, NC; esf 1776 VA; afp ae
    96 Baltimore,MD, 1844, while res Clark Co, GA, but former-
    ly res Mecklenburg Co, VA; PAR, insufficient proof of svc.
    R393
BUCHANNAN, John, esf VA; KIA 1777 at Germantown, leaving bro
    James who gtd BLW 3/29/1787 & dd before 4/16/1833; BLW gtd
    1833 to heir John Buckannon, Franklin Co, KY; QLF 1927
    from desc Mrs Hampton Fleming, Richmond,VA; QLF states sol
    sol from Augusta, Fincastle Co, now Smyth Co, VA. R393
BUCHANON, John, esf Fannett Township, Cumberland Co (later
    Franklin Co),PA for svc in PA & VA Regiments; PN 1818 Fan-
    nett Township; dd 2/4/1826. R393
BUCHER, Abraham, see BOOKER, Abraham. R393

BUCHER, Philip Peter, esf Frederick Co, VA, where b 6/5/1751
     on Opequon River; PN there 1832. R393
BUCK, Charles, esf 1777 Botetourt Co, VA; b 2/3/1758 Frederick
     Co, VA; to Gallia Co, OH, c1802 where afp 1834; PAR, svc
     less than 4 months; QLF states a Charles Buck b 1750 VA,
     s of Charles & bro of Thomas & John, md Mary Richardson,
     further John md Miriam Richardson, & Thomas md 12/14/1774
     Ann Richardson, he RW sol & dd 6/4/1842. R394
   Thomas, esf 1777 Dunmore Co (later Shenandoah Co) VA; b 1756
     Frederick Co, VA, where PN 1833; family mbnn. R395
   William, esf 1776 for svc in PA & VA Regiments; PN ae 73
     Athens Co, OH, 1818; dd 3/10/37 St Mary's, Mercer Co, OH;
     md 8/1798 or 9/1798 Phebe Smith, near Chillicothe,Pickaway
     Co, OH; wid md (2) Fall of 1844 Nicholas Christian, White
     Hall, Greene Co,IL, & they mvd to Pokagen, Cass Co, MI, to
     res with her s Enoch Buck; Nicholas Christian dd 11/13/53
     there; wid PN there 1854 ae 76 as former wid/o William
     Buck, & gtd BLW later in 1854, Grundy Co, IL, were s Enoch
     mvd; ch/o sol & Phebe in 1820: Hannach ae 19 & md, John ae
     17, Jesse aec 14, Enoch b 1810 in OH, Samuel ae 8, Char-
     lotte ae 6, & James ae 3. R395
BUCKALOE, John R; esf Edgefield District, SC; later esf Meck-
     lenburg Co, NC; b Loudoun Co, VA; f dd in RW; afp aec 78
     Marengo Co, AL, 1834; PAR, insufficient proof/o svc; sur-
     name at times spelled BUCKALEW. R396
BUCKANAN, Henry, see BUCHANAN, Henry. R396
BUCKER, Philip Peter, see BUCHER, Philip Peter. R396
BUCKHANNON, John, see BUCKHANNAN, John. R396
BUCKHOUT, John, BLW issued 8/26/1789. R396
BUCKLEY, Abraham, esf VA; dd 10/17/1807 Frederick Co, VA; md c
     8/1774 Catharine, who afp 1840 Clark Co, OH, & PAR, since
     "a soldier of the same name received a certificate of full
     pay"; wid dd aec 85 Donalsville, Clark Co,OH, 1/20/41 lea-
     ving ch: Elizabeth, Hannah Kingore/o Donalsville, & Catha-
     rine Turner & Mary Brown both/o Cambridge, Guernsey Co,OH;
     d Elizabeth afp 1848 Clark Co, OH, on behalf of decd m Ca-
     tharine, & PAR. R396
   James, esf 1780 Pittsylvania Co, VA, to serve in Capt John
     Buckley's company; b 2/1763 Loudoun Co, VA; PN 1832 Weak-
     ley Co, TN; dd 11/20/1835; md VA 9/4/1788 Mary Ridgeway;
     wid PN ae 77 Weakley Co, TN, 1850, when her bro James AFF
     ae 74, a neighbor; ch births: Betty Ann 8/17/1789, James W
     12/31/91, Mary 3/11/94, & Nancy Williams 7/22/96; wid dd c
     10/2/50 there, leaving ch: J W, W W, Colman, Susan Webb,
     Ann Howard, & Louisa Killebrew; wid dd intestate, & Thomas
     Killebrew appointed adm/o her estate. R396
   Job, esf 1778 Winchester,VA; dd 1795; md (1) Catharine & had
     ch mbnn by her; Catharine dd & sol md (2) 5/13/1793 Susan-
     nah Newcomb near Winchester, Frederick Co VA; wid md (2)
     William Hinson, Frederick Co,VA, who dd 5//3/1850; wid afp
     ae 95 Richmond Co, VA, 1855 as former wid/o sol Job, & PAR
     for insufficient proof of svc. R396

BUCKLEY, Joshua, esf 1779 Winchester, VA; PN ae 59 Fairfield
Township, Butler Co, OH, 1819; family in 1820 Ephraim ae
19, Emily ae 12, & Lucinda ae 10. R396
Michael, BLW issued 11/16/1802 to adm/o his estate Charles
Barber, Kershaw District, SC. R396
BUCKNER, Dorothea B, former wid/o William McWILLIAMS. R397
Thomas, BLW issued 2/27/1796; QLF states sol from Gloucester
Co, VA, md 1780 Elizabeth Cooke or Throckmorton, & their
res Clay Bank, near Gloucester Point, Abingdon Parish; QLF
states sol w Elizabeth Taliaferro; QLF states sol b 5/1728
s/o Baldwin M & Dorothy Buckner of Gloucester Co, VA. R397
William, esf 1780 Pittsylvania Co, VA; b 7/4/1760; PN 1829
Washington Co, VA, where mvd from Carter Co, TN; w dd be-
fore 3/18/1816. R397
William, VA sea svc; esf Kingston Parish, Gloucester Co, VA;
POW England 1781; dd 2/14/1804 Mathews Co, VA; ch in 1834:
Mary w/o Thomas Norman, Elizabeth w/o Francis Armistead,
Dorothy 1st w/o Dr Bartlett Gayle, & Susan w/o Ephraim
Beazeley; sol gds in 1834: ch/o Bartlett & Dorothy Gayle
(Alexander, William Mathew, & Joshua), ch/o d Susan who md
(1) Robert Hudgins of Mathews Co, VA, & (2) Ephraim Beaze-
ley, & had several ch by each h; heirs afp 1834, & PAR for
length/o svc unknown; QLF 1931 from great great great gdd
Mrs William E Callender, Norfolk, VA. R397
BUFFINGTON, David; esf 1781 near Romney, Hampshire Co, VA,
where b; PN ae 70 Walnut Township, Fairfield Co, OH, 1832,
where mvd to 1822; dd there 10/6/36; md 3/2/1784 Margaret,
Hampshire Co, VA; wid PN ae 82 Walnut Township 1845; ch
births: Mary 5/11/1786, Rebeckah 9/6/88 w/o John Frizzle,
John 11/18/90, Catharine 4/16/93, Susannah 8/14/94, Peter
2/22/97, Richard 11/21/1802, Mary Ann 6/20/06, & William
8/1/08. R399
BUFORD, Abraham; esf before 1779 VA; PN 1828 Georgetown, Scott
Co,KY; BLW issued 5/3/1793; dd 6/29/33 leaving wid Martha;
QLF 1938 from desc Mrs Byron Williams, Neosho, MO. R400
Jane, former wid/o Thomas QUIRK. R400
John, BLW issued 7/14/1792. R400
John, esf 1780 Bedford Co, VA, where b 2/12/1764; PN 1833
Garrard Co, KY, when res there c40 years. R400
John, esf 1776 Bedford Co,VA; b 10/13/1757 Orange Co or Cul-
peper Co, VA; PN 1834 Bedford Co, VA; dd 2/11/1852; md by
Rev Nathaniel Shrewsbury 12/28/1786 Rhoda Shrewsbury there
& she PN there 1852 ae 88; surv ch then: Elizabeth Fields,
Rhoda Caswell, Milley Foutz, Frances Cleaveland, Doldy
Foutz, John, & Samuel. R400
Simeon/Simon, esf 1775 Culpeper Co,VA, where b 9/19/1757 bro
of Abraham, above; to Barren Co, KY, 1789 where PN 1833;
QLF states sol w Margaret Kirtley; QLF 1926 from desc Wil-
liam T Van Culin, Philadelphia, PA, states sol Simeon Sr &
dd 1840 Barren Co, KY, further querier's sis Lillie DuPuy
Van Culin Harper wrote book, COLONIAL MEN AND TIMES, 1916
about sol, further surname sometimes spelled BEAUFORD or

BUFORD (continued)
   BEAUFORT; QLF from desc Mrs Gertrude McK Gwinner, Lexing-
   ton, MO, states sol w Margaret Kirby, further querier gdd
   of James Philip McKean & w Harriet Shields who mvd Alexan-
   dria, VA, to Washington,DC, c1844; QLF 1916 from great gds
   H D Helm, Newark, NJ. R400
BUHER, Jacob, BLW issued 11/5/1789; QLF states a Jacob BUHER b
   Germany, & esf Winchester, VA, & his wid Ann Mary Whetzel
   Bucher or Booker. R400
BUKER, Jacob, BLW issued 11/5/1789. R401
BULL, Curtis, esf ae 14 as drummer boy early in RW; b Accomac
   Co, VA, 1762, bro/o Rachel Gray who b 1760; PN 1832 Saint
   George Parish, Accomac Co, VA. R401
  Daniel, esf aec 16 Accomac Co, VA, 1775, where b 1759, kin/o
   Curtis, above; PN 1833 St George Parish, that Co; dd there
   4/35 leaving one ch Eliza Taylor. R401
  Thomas, esf 1776 VA, near PA border; lost all records 1781
   at burning of Squire Boone's Fort, KY; PN ae 79 Byrd Town-
   ship, Cape Girardeau Co, MO, 1832; res 1838 Washington Co,
   IL, where moved 6 months before from MO to be near rela-
   tives. R401
BULLARD, John, esf ae 19 Prince William Co, VA; b 5/1757 PA;
   mvd with parents to Prince William Co, VA, as ch; PN ae 75
   Rutherford Co, TN, 1832. R402
  Thomas, esf 1778 Duplin Co (now Sampson Co),NC; b 12/13/1759
   VA; PN 1833 Bladen Co, NC; QLF 1938 from desc Juanita Bullard (Mrs J W Jr) Oglesby, Quitman,GA; QLF 1905 from great
   gds B F Bullard, Savannah, GA. R402
BULLEFANT, James, see BRILLIFONT, James. R403
BULLIN, Isaac; esf 1779 Albemarle Co, VA; PN ae 62 Stokes Co,
   NC, 1825; dd 5/6/1828; md 9/1784 Susannah Jackson, Henry
   Co, VA; wid PN ae 74, Stokes Co, NC, 1839 when ch: Henry
   b 3/25/1785, Edward b 5/88, unnamed twins decd, William b
   5/93, Jackson b 7/95, Juston b 5/97, Isaac b 6/99, & Mar-
   tin b 7/3/1802; AFF 1839 Stokes Co, NC, by William Pafford
   that he md sis/o sol 1779-80; sol wid dd 1852, when s Ed-
   ward, legal representative of heirs, Stokes Co, NC. R403
BULLOCK, David, esf 1776 Louisa Co, VA, sub for Rice Bullock;
   b there 12/17/1759; PN there 1832; dd 12/16/33; md 1806
   Catharine W Roy (MB 3/2/06 signed by Walker Roy), Caroline
   Co, VA; wid PN 1844 Fredericksburg, VA, & res Caroline Co,
   VA, 1853 ae 75. R403
  David, esf 1779 Albemarle Co, VA; b Hanover Co, VA; PN ae 71
   Louisa Co, VA, 1832; dd 7/30/38; md 2/12/1782 Jane Terry,
   Louisa Co, VA; wid afp there 1840 ae 84; PAR since not wid
   at date of PN Act. R403
  James, esf 1780 Spotsylvania Co, VA, where b 12/18/1760; PN
   there 1833; dd 3/10/36; wid mbnn 1837; sol sis Sarah White
   ae 67 Stafford Co, VA, 1833; QLF states sol s/o James Sr,
   & md (1) Miss Wingfield, (2) Annie d/o John Waller & w Ag-
   nes Carr, res/o Berkeley Parish, Spotsylvania Co, VA, &
   John Waller d there 1777, further sol dd central KY. R403

BULLOCK, Joseph, esf VA in early part/o RW; dd 9/22/1822 Spot-
    sylvania Co, VA; md 12/25/1783, (MB 12/24/83 lists bride's
    1st name as Patsy, nickname for Martha) Martha Fletcher,
    Spotsylvania Co, VA; wid afp ae 77 there 1843, & PAR, in-
    sufficient proof of svc; ch births: Charlotte 2/14/1784,
    John 1/1/86, Thomas 10/2/88, James 9/7/90, Nancy 8/11/92,
    Polly 9/22/94, & Betty 8/2/96; other family bible births:
    Jane 4/23/1813, Thomas 6/21/16, & William Edmund 2/2/23,
    all surname Bullock; s John AFF there 1843. R403
  Rice, esf VA; apf 1784 & PAR; adm/o estate Joseph C Boxley,
    Louisa Co, VA, 1834. R403
BUMGARNER, David, esf 1777 Shenandoah Co, VA, where b 5/1758;
    PN 1832 Waggoners Bottom, Mason Co, VA; dd there 10/9/35;
    md 4/18/1786 Catharine Burner, Shenandoah Co, VA; wid PN
    1851 Mason Co, VA, when had 9 ch mbnn, eldest aec 64, & 5
    ch res there. R404
BUMLEE, James, see BROWNLEE, James. R404
BUMPASS, William, esf Hanover Co, VA, where b 1/20/1755; PN
    1832 there; dd 6/7/37; md (1) ? & had s Thomas & s William
    by her; md (2) there 3/1796 Elizabeth Harris (MB 3/9/96
    with spinster "Betsy" Harris) & had s Edmond E & s Overton
    by her; wid dd 10/22/48; s Edmond E afp there 1851 for all
    heirs, & gtd PN arrears. R404
BUNCH, Richard, esf 1780 Bedford Co, VA, where b; to Mercer
    Co, KY 1789; PN ae 73 Washington Co, KY, 1832. R405
BUNDRON, Francis, esf 1781 Rockingham Co, NC; b 1764 Bucking-
    ham Co, VA; PN 1833 Claiborne Co, TN, when bro res Warren
    Co, TN. R405
BUNDY, Francis, BLW issued 3/26/1792. R405
  Francis, esf 1780 Caroline Co, VA; PN aec 60 Culpeper Co, VA
    1818; in 1820 sol ae 67 or 68 with one small boy aec 12.
    R405
BUNNELL, John, esf 1782 NY; PN ae 57 Harrison Co, VA, 1818; in
    1820 family w ae 48, s Charles ae 12 & d Margaret ae 3; dd
    4/1/23 there; md there 5/8/1792 Hannah Smith; wid md (2)
    --- Byers who dd c1834; wid PN ae 67 Marion Co, OH, 1840
    as former wid/o sol; d liv 1847. R406
BUNTIN, William, esf Amelia Co,VA, where b 1764; PN 1832 Hali-
    fax Co, VA; dd 3/16/41 Henry Co, TN; md (1) Elizabeth, who
    dd 11/1/34; md (2) 11/12/37 or 12/12/37 Nancy, wid/o Samu-
    el D Smoot, Henry Co,TN; wid PN there 1885 ae 81; sol d by
    1st w was w/o John Wilson, res there 1837; surname some-
    times spelled BUNTON. R406
BUNTING, Solomon, esf 1776 Northampton Co, VA; b 9/20/1742; PN
    1818 Accomac Co, VA; in 1820 family w Leah aec 50, d Peggy
    ae 16, & d Sally aec 11. R406
  William, esf 1781 Accomac Co, VA, & PN there 1818 aec 55.
    R406
BUOY, Robert, esf 1771 VA for Indian Wars; esf 1777 Berkeley
    Co, VA; b 1756; afp 1836 Vermilion Co, IL; PAR, svc less
    than 6 months. R406
BURBRIDGE, George, esf 1780 Spotsylvania Co, VA, when res with

BURBRIDGE (continued)
     f; b there 1762; bro Lincefield; PN 1832 Scott Co, KY; QLF
     states sol had 4 s's in War of 1812 including Capt Robert;
     QLF 1932 from desc Elizabeth A (Mrs C A) Pierce, Tallulah,
     LA, states sol dd 1830 & res Georgetown, KY. R408
   Lincefield, 1776 Spotsylvania Co, VA, where b 1/3/1760; PN
     1832 Clark Co, KY; dd 6/20/42, surv by ch mbnn; bro George
     also RW sol; QLF 1932 from desc Mrs W C Glenn, Chicago, IL
     states sol res Clark Co, KY, 1840; QLF 1939 from desc Mae
     M Luttrell, Hale Center, TX, states sol bro/o John & Wil-
     liam. R408
BURCH, Francis, esf 1777 Charles Co, MD; PN aec 58 Lynchburg,
     Campbell Co, VA, 1818. R408
   George, VA sea svc, esf 1777 King & Queen Co, VA, where b
     1759; f owner/o sloop WILLIAM & MARY pressed into VA naval
     svc; to Caswell Co, NC, 1783, thence Williamson Co, TN;
     PAR, svc not on regular naval ship; f b same day as George
     Washington. R408
   John, esf Charles Co, MD; b 1/18/1759 Prince Georges Co, MD;
     mvd with f to Prince William Co, VA, during RW where esf;
     after RW to Fauquier Co, VA, for 17 years, thence Amherst
     Co, VA, for 16 years, thence Barren Co, KY, where PN 1832;
     dd 3/1/84; md c1796 Elizabeth, Loudoun Co, VA, who PN ae
     71 Barren Co,KY, 1850; ch births: Robert B 7/11/1797, Mar-
     garet F 6/21/99, Landon I 8/9/1801, Anne 9/20/03, Fanney P
     12/19/06, William D 10/9/09, & John 1/12/16; s Robert B
     AFF 1850 he md 5/31/21, had 12 ch mbnn; QLF 1936 from desc
     Una (Mrs L T) Ward, Lebanon, OR, states sol md Elizabeth
     Benham who dd 1853 near Knoxville, IA. R408
   John, see BIRCH, John. R408
   Joseph, esf 1779 Albemarle Co,VA; b 6/28/1763; PN 1832 Scott
     Co, KY, where dd 12/1842; md 7/26/38 Ann J Hawkins; wid PN
     ae 68 Gallatin Co, KY, 1856. R408
   William, esf 1776 Albemarle Co, VA; PN ae 70 Rockford, Surry
     Co (later Yadkin Co), NC, 1828, where dd 6/10/1835; md (1)
     ? & all ch by her decd in 1828; md (2) Summer of 1829 Re-
     becca Kays, Rockford Co, NC, & ch by her: William (decd in
     1865) & Elizabeth, ae 47 Halstead, KS, 1881 w/o Edgar S
     Brown; sol wid PN ae 69 Randolph Co, IN, 1865 where res
     since 1852; her nephew Daniel H Keyes res Winchester, IN
     1881. R408
BURCHEL, Daniel; esf 1776 VA; PN 1818. R409
BURCHETT, John, see BURCHITT, John. R409
   Robert; PN 1823 Halifax Co, VA. R409
   William, esf 1776 Lunenburg Co, VA, where b 10/7/1754; PN
     1832 Cumberland Co, KY. R409
BURCHITT, John, esf 1779 Lunenburg Co, VA, where b 1761; PN
     1833 Cumberland Co, KY. R409
BURCHNELL, James; res Lewis Co, VA, 1834, when confessed to
     fraudulent application for PN. R409
BURDETT, Jarvis, esf 1777 Bedford Co, VA, as sub for bro Wil-
     liam; b Caroline Co, VA, & mvd to Bedford Co before RW; PN

BURDETT (continued)
    ae 75-80 Franklin Co, VA, 1833. R409
BURGER, Nicholas, esf 1778 Albemarle Co, VA; PN ae 71 Union Co
    KY, 1832. R411
BURGESS, Edward, esf 1780 VA; PN aec 74 Floyd Co,KY, 1818 when
    res c12 years; res 1822 Lawrence Co, KY, with w Nancy who
    aec 75; QLF states sol esf Goochland Co, VA, dd c1834, &
    md Nancy Ann Francis. R412
  John, esf 1775 Fluvanna Co, VA, where b; PN there 1833 ae 89
    & dd 2/16/35 leaving s Daniel M. R412
  Ruth, former wid/o James GUNNER. R412
  William, esf 1778 Rockingham Co, VA; PN ae 77 Goochland Co,
    VA, 1818; dd 12/22/23. R412
BURK, George, esf 1779 Shenandoah Co, VA; PN ae 69 Jefferson
    Co, IN, when w ae 78 & d ae 43. R413
  James, VA sea svc, esf 1777 for svc on PATRIOT; gtd 666 2/3
    acres from VA state for svc; PN ae 73 Elizabeth City Co,
    VA, 1832. R413
  John, esf 1779 Hagerstown, MD; PN aec 60 Washington Co, VA,
    1821 when family w Mary ae 55 & grown up ch (2 d's & 1 s);
    dd 3/29/39; md 5/2/1786 (MB 5/1/86) Mary "Polly" Stevens,
    Bedford Co,VA; wid PN ae 77 Lee Co,VA 1844; ch births: Ly-
    dia 1/11/1788, John 1/15/90, Caty 3/15/92, Thomas 9/29/93,
    Robert 9/28/97, Lucy 8/9/1800, & David 4/11/04; other fa-
    mily bible birth James Stevens 1/30/1782. R413
  John, esf 1776 Wilkes Co, NC, with f James when they res on
    Yadkin River; f dd in svc 8/1776; sol b 7/23/1760 in area
    now Rockbridge Co, VA; to KY 1795, thence 1811 to Wayne Co
    IN, where PN 1832; dd 2/1/1836 with one/o heirs being Lew-
    is Burk; QLF states w Alcy Robinson who md (1) --- Sebas-
    tian. R413
  Michael, esf Culpeper Co,VA, where b; mvd to Madison Co, KY,
    c1807 where PN 1833 ae 95. R414
  Samuel, esf 1775 Culpeper Co, VA; PN ae 73 Jessamine Co, KY,
    1832; dd 3/16/41 Shelby Co,KY; md 9/2/1786 Mary d/o Thomas
    Hurley of Culpeper Co, VA, at Rectortown, Fauquier Co, VA;
    wid PN ae 74 Shelby Co, KY, 1844, & liv 1848; ch births:
    Sally 7/7/1788,Susie 9/11/90,James 10/22/92, Polly 2/4/94,
    Devarol 11/9/96, Jerome B or Jeer 5/22/99 (md 10/10/1842
    Mary Elizabeth Campbell Elliston), Willies or Willis
    11/19/1802 (md 4/4/33 Priscilla Ann Solomons who b 2/2/15)
    & Joanah 11/10/04; QLF 1922 from great gdd Mrs F W Milles-
    paugh, Nashville, TN, written by her h F W Millespaugh, a
    member of the Sons of the American Revolution. R414
  William, esf 1778 King George Co, VA soon after marriage; dd
    3/1803; md 2/1/1778 Susanna Sweney, St Paul's Parish, that
    Co; wid PN ae 88 Fauquier Co, VA, 1838. R414
BURKE, Isham, esf 1778 Wilkes Co, GA; b 10/24/1761 Amherst Co,
    VA, s/o John; to Spartanburg District, SC, thence GA as
    ch; PN 1833 McNairy Co, TN. R415
  John, BLW issued 7/6/1793. R415
  John, esf 1781 res New River, Montgomery Co, VA; b 7/15/1761

BURKE (continued)

 Shenandoah Co, VA; afp 1834 Monroe Township, IN, & again afp 1841 Clark Co, KY, when w aec 74; PAR, less than six months svc. R415

 Robert, esf 1777 Culpeper Co, VA, where b 1761; to KY 1798 where PN 1833 Owen Co; dd there 8/28/45; md 1/13/1788-90 Hannah Jones, Shenandoah Co, VA; wid PN aec 75 Owen Co, KY 1848; marriage recorded Shenandoah Co, VA, 1/10/1793; ch mbnn. R415

 Tobias, BLW issued 4/6/1793. R415

 William, esf 1776 VA; PN 1808 for disability from svc; gave up that PN, but PN again ae 60, Winchester, Frederick Co, Co, VA, 1820, when w ae 63; dd there 1/23/26; d Margaret, w/o Peter Kremer, res there 1854 ae 70; surname at times spelled BURK; QLF 1930 from desc Mrs W H Mathew, Gary, IN. R415

 William, esf 1776 Culpeper Co, VA, where PN 1818 ae 67; QLF 1921 from great great great gdd Mrs F H Millespaugh, Nashville, TN. R415

BURKES, Samuel, esf 1779 Surry Co, NC; b 7/24/1764 Prince Edward Co, VA; PN 1832 Rutherford Co, TN; res 1840 Madison Co, MO; surname at times spelled BURKS; QLF states sol res 1840 with William Burks, Twelve Mile Township. R415

BURKET, Frederick, esf 1777 Augusta Co, VA; PN ae 81 Greene Co TN, 1833; res 1836 Hawkins Co, TN; w aec 70 in 1829. R415

BURKHART, Henry, esf 1781 Shenandoah Co, VA; PN ae 71 Smyth Co VA, 1832; dd 12/11/38 leaving ch mbnn. R415

BURKS, Isham, esf 1779-80 VA; b 1759 s/o John & Sarah; PN 1829 Boone Co, MO; dd 8/22/39; md Spring of 1778 Elizabeth Rowland; wid b 1/14/1764, & PN 1841 Boone Co, MO; ch births: Charles 10/11/1780, Sally 7/15/82, Betsey 2/27/86, Robert Rowland 5/6/89 (dd 12/20/91), Nancy 7/23/91, Isham 11/8/94 John 7/21/97, William 9/28/1800, Mahala 12/3/02, Wesley 5/27/06, & James Pane 5/29/08; gdc births: Isham Burks Fletcher 6/3/1809, William See Fletcher 7/18/11, Sally See Fletcher 10/11/13, Jane (d/o James & Elizabeth Gilliland) 4/12/1817, & Sally Gilliland 8/27/22; family bible deaths: John Burks murdered 7/23/1829, Sarah Simpson (m/o John Rowland & Elizabeth Burks) 1/28/1829 ae 80-90, Nancy Mahe formerly Nancy Sexton 11/18/1830 ae 22, youngest s/o Rowland & Mahala Frost 11/20/1830, Elizabeth Gilliland 10/10/1829; QLF states sol wid PN while res with s-in-law George Sexton, Boone Co, MO. R415

BURNER, Abraham, esf 1777 Woodstock, Shenandoah Co, VA; b that Co; to Pendleton Co, VA, 1778; PN ae 62 Randolph Co, VA, 1819, where dd 6/18/27; md 6/5/1780 Mary Magdalen Hull, Pendleton Co, VA; wid PN ae 76 Pocahontas Co, VA, & dd 1/18/40; ch: 7 s's & 2 d's including eldest Daniel, b during RW, & Jacob H who res 1839 Burnersville, Lewis Co, VA; 5 ch survived m; sol bro Henry b 6/28/1762 Shenandoah Co, VA, & to Licking Co, OH, 1817, & res there 1839. R418

 Daniel, esf 1770-75 Millers Town, Shenandoah Co, VA; afp aec

BURNER (continued)
72 Overton Co,TN, 1825 when w aec 76 & ch: Barbary Living-
ston, Abram/Abraham, Elizabeth Bell, Isaac, Susan, Sally
Jones, Polly Coons, John, & Nancy Harmon; PAR, less than
6 months svc. R418
BURNETT, John, esf 1779 Mecklenburg Co, VA; dd 5/22/1809; md
1780 Sarah who afp ae 83 Spartanburg District, SC, 1846, &
PAR, insufficient proof/o svc; ch mbnn; eldest ch md Henry
Bishop, & res there 1846; QLF 1925 from desc Mrs Laura E
Bridges, Independence, MO; QLF 1906 from great great gdd
Minnie M Brashear, Kirksville,MO, states sol w Sarah John-
son. R419
  Joseph, esf Bedford Co, VA, where dd 1787; md c1775 Mabel,
  d/o Absalom Stetton, there; wid dd 10/18/45; ch Absalom,
  Lucy who b 8/24/1780, Anna, & another mbnn; only surv ch
  1850 Lucy, who then Mrs Archibald Wilkes, afp & gtd PN arrears. R419
  Richard, esf 1780 Hanover Co, VA; esf there 1781 sub for bro
  John; bc 1757; afp ae 74 there 1832 & dd 7/24/33 before PN
  application approved; sol will of 8/4/29 listed w & nephew
  Richard Burnett Jr, witnessed by Isaac Burnett, & probated
  8/27/33; md Margaret Hughes who dd childless c7/1834; her
  will of 7/10/34, probated there 7/22/34 listed niece Ann
  wid/o her nephew John Hughes, niece Margaret Talley & her
  ch (James, Mary , Francis, Louisa, & Martha), bro John, &
  nephew David Hughes, plus Tazewell, Sally, Elizabeth, Emily, & Ira Barker; sol bro George aec 69 in 1832.
  William, esf 1769 Prince William Co, VA, a bondservant who
  ran away from master to join troops; b 7/24/1764 on banks
  of Appomattox River; afp 1841 Rhea Co, TN; PAR, svc not
  truly military. R419
  Williamson, esf VA; b Buckingham Co, VA; dd 6/3/1833 Bedford
  Co, VA; md 3/15/1792 Priscilla Carter, Buckingham Co, VA;
  wid PN ae 66 Bedford Co, VA, 1840; ch James H & Nancy both
  b Buckingham Co, VA; wid res Bedford Co, VA, 1843; s James
  AFF ae 48 there 1840. R419
BURNETTE, Williamson, see BURNETT, Williamson. R419
BURNHAM, Gurdin, CT sea svc; esf 1775 CT; b 2/13/1756 East
Hartford, CT; mvd to SC after RW, thence Powhatan Co, VA,
thence Buckingham Co, VA, where md; to IL 1832, thence to
Vigo Co, IN, 1833 where PN then when w, 3 s's, & d. R420
BURNITT, William, esf Mecklenburg Co, VA; b King & Queen Co,
VA; to Rutherford Co, TN, c1802 where PN 1832 ae 73; QLF
states sol dd 1845. R422
BURNLEY, Garland, esf Orange Co,VA; dd there c1790 leaving wid
Frances & ch Sarah G S, Judith, & Lucy B; wid dd 1825 Hen-
rico Co,VA, testate; d Sarah md William D Taylor & dd 1815
leaving ch Garland B, Frances A, Jane M who md Thomas Garland, Hardenia M, Edmund S, & William J; d Judith md Tho-
as Adams & dd 1816 leaving ch Sarah F w/o Peachy Taliaferro, Charles P, & Thomas B; d Lucy B dd c1819 unmarried.
R422

BURNLEY, Henry, esf 1776 VA; f res Bedford Co, VA; PN ae 78
Columbia Co, GA, 1834, when bro Stephen (b 5/8/1770) AFF
Warren Co, GA; QLF states sol nickname Harry, & b cc 1752
s/o Israel & Hannah Terrell, esf Charlotte Co, VA, md Lucy
(Barksdale) Davenport a wid & they had s Richmond who sur-
vived them, further sol dd Warren Co,GA; QLF 1895 from gdd
Miss Mary J Burnley, Grovetown, Columbia Co, GA, states
sol esf Norfolk, VA, & was youngest s/o f; QLF 1923 from
desc Miss Emma Dicken, Meridian, MS. R422
   James, see BROWNLEE, James. R422
BURNS, Andrew, esf Henry Co, VA, where res; PN ae 75 Perry Co,
KY, 1833, where AFF then by bro William. R423
   Bryan, BLW issued 7/14/1792. R423
   George, esf 1777 Rockingham Co, VA; b 3/12/1757 Loudoun Co,
VA; to Randolph Co,VA, 1800 where afp 1833, res Lower Fork
on the Dry Fork of Cheat River; PAR, insufficient proof of
svc; two witnesses stated applicant b during RW & not old
enough to serve in War; left there by 1834. R423
   Jeremiah, esf 1776 Bedford Co, VA; b 10/1752; PN 1818 Greenup Co, KY; dd 10/13-24/1824 there or Lawrence Co, KY; md
3/20/1794 Elizabeth/Riza Rowland, Franklin Co, VA; in 1820
sol family w & ch: s's ae 27, 11, 9, & d's ae 16/ 14/ & 5
liv with him; wid PN ae 79 Louisa, Lawrence Co, KY, 1850;
QLF 1893 from gds Thomas B Hatcher, South Omaha, NE; QLF
1913 from great gds M S Burns, Louisa Co, KY. R423
   John, esf Wilkes Co, NC, where res; b 1763 Amelia Co, VA; PN
1832 Laurens District, SC; decd by 7/52 leaving s Christopher. R423
   John, see BYRNE, John. R423
   John, esf 1777 King & Queen Co, VA; b 7/12/1763; PN Switzerland Co, IN, 1820 when family w Lucretia ae 31 & ch: David
ae 9, Robert ae 7-8, Jane ae 5-6, Elizabeth 4-5, George B
ae 2-3, & John M ae 4 months; dd there 7/7/27; md Lucretia
Vinasdol 6/13/1810 Waynesville, Warren Co,OH; wid PN & BLW
Carrollton, Carroll Co, KY, 1857 ae 72; QLF 1889 from d &
only surv ch, Mrs Elizabeth Harris, Crawfordsville, IN,
states m d 9/1/1860, further sol b Scotland, was surgeon
in RW, was large man weighing c400 pounds. R423
   John, esf 1777 Henry Co, VA; dd 1/29/1805; md 9/10/1773 Ann,
Henry Co, VA; ch births: Allee 6/30/1774, Charles 2/3/75,
John 1/17/77, William 3/12/79,Sarah 2/7/81, Miles 5/24/84,
Mary 11/22/86, Samuel 4/1/88, & twins Uriah & Ezekeah
9/15/90; d Sarah md 11/25/1802 John Leatherwood b 1/2/1779
& their ch births: Mary 12/31/04, Edward 3/18/07, John
3/17/09, & Samuel 5/14/11; wid md (2) Daniel McKizeck, who
dd Spring/o 1821; wid afp ae 91 Haywood Co, NC, 1845 when
d Sarah Leatherwood made AFF; PAR, insufficient proof of
svc; Sarah Leatherwood AFF there 1854 that m decd. R423
   Michael, see BURRUSS, Michael. R423
   William, esf Pittsylvania Co, VA; b VA; PN ae 76 Clay Co, KY
1832; QLF 1901 from desc Mrs Clara E Stewart, Washington,
DC; QLF states s dd Booneville, Owlsley Co,KY, after 1840;

BURNS (continued)
    QLF states sol ae 87 res with Sarah Bishop 1840; QLF 1931
    from desc C E Burns, Frankfort, KY. R423
BURNSIDE, John, BLW issued 5/28/1791. R424
    Jonathan, esf 1779 Loudoun Co, VA; PN ae 54 Fairfield Co, OH
    1818; res 1820 Licking Co, OH, ae 59, & family w ae 57, s
    John ae 13, & d Charlotte ae 11; dd 1/19/35 Hebron, Lick-
    ing Co, OH; surv ch Andrew & Ellen Smith gtd BLW, Greene
    Co, OH, 1852. R424
BURNSIDES, Andrew, esf 1781 Craven Co, NC; b Charlotte Co, VA;
    PN ae 69 Laurens District, SC, 1832; large family mbnn.
    R424
BURRAGE, Charles, esf VA; PN ae 71 Spotsylvania Co, VA, 1819,
    a tavern keeper; dd there 7/28/20; md 11/1780 Catharine
    Cammack there (MB dated 11/20/80); eld ch Mary (Burrage)
    Gray b 8/6/1781; wid PN ae 78, totally blind, Mercer Co,
    KY, 1837 when AFF by James Cammack ae 68-70, gds/o Frances
    Cammack. R425
BURRELL, Francis, esf 1778 Monongalia Co, VA; b 9/1760 near
    Washington, DC; mvd to Galliapolis, thence IN, where afp
    1846 Jackson Co, & PAR; liv ch then: Mary Miller, Rebecca,
    Hannah, Jane, Bartholomew, & Jesse; ch liv 1852: Jesse,
    Bartholomew, Rebecca, Mary/Polly w/o Brison Miller & Jane.
    R426
BURRIS, Jacob, see BURRUSS, Jacob. R426
    Martin, esf Albemarle Co, VA, where b 2/11/1754; to Surry Co
    NC c1788; PN 1832 Morgan Co, IL; dd 1/16/39 leaving ch un-
    named. R426
    Nathaniel, esf 1779 Orange Co, VA; PN ae 71 Mercer Co, KY,
    1832, where res 1837; QLF states sol b 1759 VA & dd 1855
    Salvisa, KY, & buried Mercer Co, KY. R426
BURROUGH, Dobson, see BURROW, Dobson. R427
BURROUGHS, George, esf 1776 Halifax Co,VA, where dd 4/15/1818;
    md there 9/15/1784 Jean Scates (sol surname spelled BURUS
    on MB); wid & ch to Rockingham Co, NC, 1818; wid dd 4/2/47
    leaving ch William, Ann Duncan, & Mary Curry; only surv ch
    Mary Curry afp ae 43 there 1854, & PAR; LWT of William
    Scates, Halifax Co, VA, 1805 listed d Jean Burras. R427
BURROW, Dobson, esf 1776 Dinwiddie Co, VA; PN ae 81 Randolph
    Co, NC, 1839; m Lucy, bro Barney, bro-in-law Thomas Year-
    gin all referred to in 1837; dd 3/18/40; QLF 1919 from de-
    scendant Mrs W Y Smith, Springfield, MO, through d/o sol
    who md Zebidee Wood of Randolph Co, NC. R427
BURROWS, Michael, esf 1781 Culpeper Co, VA; b 1751 Richmond Co
    VA; afp Howard Co, MO, 1834, & PAR. R428
BURRUSS, Jacob, esf 1778 Orange Co, VA; PN ae 77 Smith Co, TN,
    1832, where dd 10/1/32; md 3/1781 Susannah d/o Gen Joseph
    Martin, Henry Co, VA; wid PN ae 75 Smith Co, TN, 1838; wid
    sis/o William Martin who ae 66 there 1832. R429
BURRUSS, Michael, esf Culpeper Co, VA; PN ae 81 Henry Co, VA,
    1832. R429
BURT, Edward, esf 1780 VA; afp ae 70 Sussex Co, VA, 1833; PAR,

BURT (continued)
less than 6 months svc; QLF states bro & sis of sol were:
Harwood, Matthew, Phillip, John, Francis, William, Robert,
Garland, Moody, Susan, Martha, Mary, & Anne. R429
Moody, esf 1779 Charlotte Co, VA; b 12/25/1757 Halfway House
between Williamsburg & Yorktown,VA; bro Robert RW sol; afp
1838 Anderson District, SC, & PAR, less than 6 months svc;
in 1834 had d's Sarah Pope & Martha H w/o Lewelling Goode,
latter two persons already decd in 1841, leaving ch Sarah,
Martha, Thomas, & John Goode; in 1858 sol gdc Mackerness
Goode & Martha H Hammond; sol sis Nancy Hall res 1840 An-
derson District, SC. R429
BURTON, Henry, esf 1777 VA; esf 1778 NC; PN ae 63 Humphreys Co
TN, 1822 when family w Kesiah aec 59, d Patsey aec 18 who
md, & d Charlotte aec 15; QLF states sol b VA, dd McNary
Co, TN, & md Kesine Farley. R430
Hutchens, esf 1780; afp ae 68 Mecklenburg Co, VA, 1832; PAR,
less than 6 months svc. R430
May, esf 1777 Orange Co,VA, where dd 5/13/1829; md 9/29/1776
Sarah Head; surv ch 1839: Lucy Collins, Fanny Buckner,
Benjamin, Hannah Bradford, Judith Webb, Sarah Payne, Margaret Douglass, Martha Craig, & Mary M Eddins; wid dd
9/14-28/1842, Greene Co, VA; ch births: Lucy 4/28/1778,
Fanny 2/6/80, Elizabeth 6/17/81, Benjamin 6/22/84, Hannah
6/20/86, Judith 9/9/88, Sarah 5/9/90, Peggy 2/13/92, Martha 5/31/94, Harriet 2/27/97, & Mary Mariah 10/8/98; oth-
er birth data: Lucy Ann 3/27/1816, d/o James & Sarah Head;
s Benjamin afp 1846 Madison Co, VA, for sol surv ch: Benjamin, Fanny Buckner, Hannah Bradford, Judith Webb, Martha
Craig, & Mary Mariah Eddins, & PN gtd; QLF 1936 from desc
Stella V Bradford, Philippi, WV, states sol Capt May, Jr;
QLF 1929 from Mrs Philip Spence, Wytheville, VA, desc of
RW sol Benjamin Head f/o Sarah who w/o May Burton Jr, further parents of May Jr were May Burton Sr & Hannah Medley.
R430
James, esf Orange Co, VA, where dd 8/21/29; wid Elizabeth PN
there 1833; ch 1828: James, William, John, Bezaleel, Frances Goodridge, Anne Elizabeth, Nancy Brown, Ursula, Eliza-
beth Stone, & Polly A Brent; in 1833 Bezaleel/Bezabel ae
20, only surv s/o sol; QLF 1928 from desc Helen M (Mrs H
E) Warren, Oceanlake, OR. R430
Jarret/Garrett, esf 1775-6 Stafford Co,VA, where res; afp ae
74 Mason Co, KY, 1833; PAR, svc not in regularly organized
unit. R430
John, esf 1780 Mecklenburg Co, VA, where b 1761; to Rutherford Co, TN, 1807, thence Sangamon Co, IL, 1827 where PN
1833; dd 1/30/39 leaving ch mbnn. R430
John, esf 1776 Henrico Co, VA; PN for disability from wounds
1803; dd there 12/27/28; md there c1771 & w dd 1827; surv
ch William & Mrs Sarah A Foose who res 1855 Baltimore, MD,
& she still res there 1856 as sol only surv ch; Sarah b
1/11/1817 had 3 small ch in 1856; QLF 1909 from desc Mrs

BURTON (continued)
    J V Sheehan, Ann Arbor, MI, she also desc/o RW sol Thomas
    Elmon. R430
    John, esf 1781 Berkeley Co,VA; afp ae 75 Cambridge Township,
    Guernsey Co, OH, 1838, & PAR, insufficient proof/o svc; dd
    11/10/45 there; md 11/12/1785 in VA; family to PA c1791, &
    to OH c1803; w dd 4/24/24; surv ch who afp Guernsey Co, OH
    1850: Bazil ae 56, John ae 63, Mrs Christian Clark who b
    11/1792, & Mrs Margaret Speers who b 1/12/1806, she res
    Belmont Co, OH, 1852; ch PAR. R430
    Joshua, esf 1775 Fredericktown,MD; esf 1776 VA; esf 1779 PA;
    PN ae 69 Pickaway Co, OH, 1818; w ae 70 in 1821. R430
    Marshall, esf 1777 Shenandoah Co, VA; PN ae 60 Giles Co, VA,
    1819; in 1820, w but no ch res with sol then. R431
    Richard, esf 1775 Chesterfield Co, VA, where b 5/28/1752; PN
    there 1832. R431
    Robert, esf 1781 Campbell Co, VA; b 10/18/1764 Amelia Co, VA
    & family mvd to Campbell Co c1773; sol to Rockingham Co,
    NC, after RW, where PN 1832; QLF 1933 from Mrs J S Welborn
    of High Point, NC, whose gdm was a Burton. R431
    Samuel, esf 1779 VA; PN ae 70 Amelia Co, VA, 1827. R431
    Thomas, esf 1779 Hanover Co, VA; b 1/26/1761; PN 1823 Albe-
    marle Co, VA, where dd 3/20/45; md there 3/16/1826 Dicey
    Reynolds; wid PN ae 66 there 1853 & dd there 1/19/64; s
    William res there 1823; s Andrew, only surv ch, res there
    1868. R431
    William, esf 1775 Orange Co, VA; PN ae 78 Chariton Co, MO,
    1833; dd 10/14/42; md Fall of 1783 Sarah Sandford, Albe-
    marle Co, VA; wid PN ae 81 Howard Co, MO, 1844, when wid
    sis Nancy & her h John Head made AFF there. R431
BURWELL, Lucy, former wid/o George BAYLOR. R431
    Nathaniel, esf 1775 VA; BLW issued 2/13/1798; dd 3/30/1802;
    md 3/5/1780 Martha Digges; wid PN ae 80 Botetourt Co, VA,
    1837, when her sis Elizabeth Nicolson & bro Dudley Digges
    made AFF there; QLF 1899 from desc Fanny Persinger, Wash-
    ington Court House, OH, states sol member/o Society of the
    Cincinnati. R431
BUSBY, James, esf 1776 Goochland Co, VA; b 5/2/1754-5; PN 1818
    Fayette Co, KY; res 1835 Bourbon Co, KY; dd 7/18 or 20/38;
    md 1790 Elizabeth Shackelford, Albemarle Co, VA, (MB dated
    3/4/90 & signed by Roger Shackelford); wid PN ae 68 Bour-
    bon Co, KY, & res there 1850; ch in 1820: Cynthia ae 25,
    Patsey ae 23, Gabriella ae 16, Sophia ae 14, George Ann ae
    12, James ae 8, Polly ae 6, & Sarah Jane ae 4; sol bro Ro-
    bert res Bourbon Co, KY, 1839; QLF 1917 from desc N McCra-
    ry, Park City, MT, states his m ae 91 gdd/o sol, further
    sol bro/o Robert, Mat, & John, all RW svc. R431
    Robert/Robart, esf 1776 Hanover Co or Goochland Co, VA; b
    Hanover Co 7/1759; PN 1833 Adair Co, KY; res 1839 Morgan
    Co, IL; bro/o James. R431
    William, esf 1780 Goochland Co, VA; b 4/5/1760 Henrico Co,
    VA; afp 1832 Goochland Co, VA, & PAR; s Jacob afp there

BUSBY (continued)
      1834, & PAR. R431
BUSH, Adam, esf 1781; dd 1814 Wheeling, VA; md 1779 Margaret
      Hagel, Buckhannon Fort, Monongalia Co, VA; wid blind when
      PN ae 79 Lewis Co, VA, 1842 when s Paulser res there; wid
      sis/o John Hagel. R432
   Charles, esf 1780 Orange Co, VA; b 1754 Culpeper Co, VA; PN
      1834 Henry Co,KY, where dd 4/17/34; md before RW Elizabeth
      d/o Henry & Mary Wood, Orange Co, VA; wid PN ae 87 Henry
      Co, KY, 1843, while res with s Levi ae 49; wid then had 4
      decd ch & 9 liv ch, including Henry, Levi, & Ambrose; QLF
      1925 from Kenyon Stevenson great great gds/o sol sis. R432
   Dennis, esf 1774 VA; PN aec 67 Newtown (Stephensburg), Fre-
      erick Co, VA, 1818; in 1820 family s David ae 30. R432
   Drury, esf 1770 Clinch River, now Russell Co, VA; PN ae 75
      Perry Co, KY, 1833; dd 4/4/44 Breathitt Co, KY; md before
      1794 Nancy Couch on Clinch River, VA; wid PN ae 87 Estill
      Co, KY, 1853; 4 ch mbnn. R432
   Enoch, esf c1779 Shenandoah Co, VA, where b 1747; PN ae 86
      Roane Co, TN, 1834. R432
   Jacob, esf 1778 Monongalia Co, VA; b 1756 Hampshire Co, VA;
      PN 1832 Lewis Co, VA, where dd 11/27-28/32 with Elias Fis-
      her adm/o his estate; md Fall/o 1779 Margaret Snar/Snarr/
      Snow, Augusta Co, VA (now Pendleton Co, WV); wid PN ae 87
      Lewis Co, VA, 1843, & dd 7/28/47 at home on Horn Creek,
      Gilmer Co, VA, leaving ch Peter, Susanah Simpson, Henry,
      Jacob, John, George, Elizabeth Stump, Margaret Stump, &
      Barbary Fisher; s Michael dd before m, leaving wid Mary &
      s Adam; QLF states sol md Margaret Swan. R432
   James, esf 1780 Orange Co, VA; b 9/26/1759 Culpeper Co, VA;
      PN 1833 Clark Co, KY; QLF states sol dd there 1849. R432
BUSHONG, Jacob, esf 1780 VA; PN ae 64 Columbiana Co, OH, 1818;
      res 1828 Stark Co, OH; QLF states sol res Shenandoah Vall-
      ey, VA, during RW. R434
BUSKILL, John, esf 1792 Fincastle, Botetourt Co, VA, for Gen
      Anthony Wayne's Campaign against indians; not RW sol; PN
      ae 78 Hopkins Co, KY, where BLW issued 1851; dd 2/23/55
      Pinckneyville, Perry Co, IL; md c10/18/1818 Hesther Hawk,
      Bracken Co, KY (MB dated 10/15/18, signed by Samuel Hawk);
      wid afp ae 54 Perry Co, IL, 1855, & PAR; sol surname some-
      times spelled BUCKELL & BUCKLE. R434
BUSKIRK, Aaron, esf VA; PN ae 80 Monroe Co, IN, 1834. R434
   John, esf 1775 Dunmore (now Shenandoah) Co, VA, surname also
      VAN BUSKIRK; b 9/26/1757 Frederick Co, MD; esf 1780 KY; PN
      1832 Greene Co,IN, when s Abram ae 49; dd 12/1/40. R434
BUSSELL, Matthew, esf VA; PN aec 75 Claiborne Co, TN, 1831; dd
      1/30/43-4; md c6/1/1791 Frances/Fanny Reynolds, Spotsylva-
      nia, Co, VA, her f's house where wid b; wid PN ae 71 Taze-
      well, TN, 1844, res there 1855 ae 98, & dd 10/29/57; ch
      births: John 10/1793, Robert 12/12/94, Wilson 2/9/96; ?
      2/1/1800, William 3/1/03, Nelley 12/12/04, Nancy 10/13/06,
      Sally 2/17/07, Bird 5/4/10, Shirley 1/15/11, Charles

BUSSELL (continued)
2/14/15, Matthew 6/14/19, & James 4/22/18--; other family
bible data: William Web Bussell md 8/24/1824 Juda/Juday b
10/1807; in 1844 Shirley & James Bussell res Claiborne Co,
TN; Charles Bussell res there 1855; QLF 1934 from great
gdd Mrs Harvey Sands, Lenoir City, TN. R435
William, esf 1780 Prince William Co, VA, where b 9/1759; PN
1833 Hawkins Co, TN, & dd there 10/13/40; md 1790 Sarah at
house/o her f James Wiatt, Prince William Co, VA (MB dated
1/21/90); wid PN ae 70 Hawkins Co, TN, 1841, when her sis
Rosamond Leavell made AFF ae 66 Gallatin Co, IL. R435
BUSSEY, Cornelius, esf 1781 Essex Co, VA; b 9/11/1765; afp Es-
sex Co, VA, 1835, while res Lincoln Co, TN; res later that
year Knox Co, TN; PAR. R435
BUSSLE, Vincent, see BUSTLE, Vincent. R435
BUSTER, Claudius, esf 1780 Albemarle Co,VA, where b 11/24/1763
s/o John; PN 1832 Augusta Co, VA, where had been Sheriff &
Justice of the Peace; dd 11/20/1843; md 11/28/1815 Eleanor
Paul there; wid PN ae 77 there 1854; QLF 1925 from desc
Mrs W B Allen, Amarillo, TX; QLF 1927 from desc Miss Wil-
lie Buster, Dallas, TX. R435
Michael, esf 1774 Fincastle Co, VA; b 8/6/1757 Caswell Co,
NC; to Fincastle Co (later Washington & Russell Co's) VA,
with parents 1772; to Pulaski Co, KY, 1812 where PN 1833;
QLF states w Rachel. R435
BUSTLE, Vincent, esf 1781 Stafford Co, VA, where PN 1820 aec
62 when family w Elizabeth aec 50, s George aec 15, & d
Polly aec 11; dd 12/26/39; md 12/1785 Elizabeth Jones,
Stafford Co, VA, both of Overwharton Parish; wid PN there
1840, & res there 1843 aec 80. R435
BUTCHER, Samuel, esf 1780 Loudoun Co, VA, where b 3/28/1756;
afp 1833 Wood Co, VA, & PAR, less than 6 months svc; ch in
1844: Thomas & Susan w/o Atwell Vaughan; QLF states sol dd
5/2/1847 Wood Co, VA, & was s/o Samuel Sr & Susanna Lewis.
R435
Sarah, former wid/o James WELLS. R435
BUTLER, Benjamin, esf 1781 sub for bro William, Culpeper Co,
VA, where b 1/7/1765; PN 1836 Henderson Co, TN. R436
Jacob, esf 1778 Loudoun Co, VA; b 10/1748 Germany; to PA
1773; PN 1832 near Leesburg, VA; dd 9/9/33; md 6/30/1791-2
Sarah who PN ae 77 Loudoun Co, VA, 1838; s William in Lou-
don Co militia 1813; QLF 1927 from gdd Mrs J Carter Bardin
of Dallas, TX. R436
James, esf c1777 Rutherford Co, NC; b 1749 Culpeper Co, VA;
PN 1832 Rhea Co, TN; dd 1/12/1836 leaving wid Agnes whom
he md 1785; wid dd 3/1/46; eldest ch Mrs Phoebe Ford ae 67
gtd PN due m, Meigs Co, TN, 1852. R436
James, esf 1778 Mecklenburg Co, VA; b 6/5/1758 St Paul's Parish, Hanover Co,VA; PN 1833 Elbert Co, GA; res 1837 Shelby Co, AL, to be with 10 ch res there. R436
John, esf 1779 King William Co, VA, where b 1/19/1764, & PN
there 1834. R437

BUTLER, John; esf 1780 Bedford Co, VA; PN ae 71 Morgan Co, KY, 1833. R437

John, esf VA; PN ae 56 Laurens District, SC, 1818. R437

John, esf 1776-7 King George Co,VA; BLW issued 4/28/1783; dd 8/28/1820;   2nd h/o Molly Arnold, whom he md 1/6/1793 King George Co, VA; Molly was wid/o Samuel Muse who also RW sol from King George Co; wid PN ae 80 Westmoreland Co, VA, 1849; wid had twins in 1793, then Charles b 2/16/95, Alexander, George, James, ? dd as infant, & Nancy who bc 1806; AFF 1841 Westmoreland Co, by William Berkley ae 62 that he md d/o of sol widow by her 1st h Samuel Muse. R437

John, esf Caroline Co, VA; dd 1826 Hanover Co, VA; will probated there 1/27/30 (dated 4/4/24) listed w Mary, ch Milley Hanes, David, Thomas, Samuel, William, & Peter, & gdd Polly B Thacker; md Mary Thacker there; wid PN there 1837 aec 98, when s John who b before RW made AFF; AFF then by 2nd ch David, Louisa Co,VA, that bro Peter eldest ch. R437

John Osborn, MA navy, esf 1778 MA where b 8/6/1763 Old Town; mvd to Norfolk, VA, 1786 where PN 1834. R437

Joseph, esf 1780 Mecklenburg Co, VA; b 1758 Caroline Co, VA; PN 1833 Mecklenburg Co, VA, where dd 8/3/43; md 6/16/1783 Frances at house of her f John Oliver there; wid PN ae 79 there 1846; QLF 1911 from great great gdd Mrs W R Taylor, Auburn, AL. R437

Lawrence, BLW issued 5/22/1789; QLF states sol also known as Lance Butler. R438

Patrick, esf 1780 Mecklenburg Co, VA; b 3/1/1760 Hanover Co, VA; to Elbert Co, GA, 2 years after RW where PN 1833; QLF 1930 from desc Mrs James L Stirling, Baton Rouge, LA, states sol & bro's James & Nathan s's of Zachariah. R438

Peter, esf 1779 Caroline Co, VA; b 8/24/1763 Hanover Co, VA; PN 1837 Louisa Co, VA; s Elijah; bro David AFF ae 72 Hanover Co, VA, that he 10 months younger than sol. R438

Reuben, esf 1777 King William Co, VA, where b 1/27/1750; dd there 1829; md 1/27/1780 Ann Lisle, Caroline Co, VA; wid PN 1837 Essex Co, VA, & dd there 1843; Lisle may have been wid's middle name; ch births: Samuel Warring 11/6/1780, Martha 3/6/82, Ann Smith 10/17/83, ? 17--, Thomas Perion Blunt 11/1/92, Henry Todd 10/19/94, Catharine 4/17/96, & William 3/26/98; d Lucy R Harris res Taylorsville, Hanover Co, VA, 1851. R438

Solomon, esf Bedford Co, VA; dd 9/5/1825; md 3/1801 Mary McFerson, Leaksville, NC; wid afp ae 63 Bedford Co, VA, 1844 & PAR, insufficient proof of svc. R438

Thomas, esf 1780 Bedford Co, VA; b 11/11/1763 Frederick Co, MD; to Bedford Co, VA, with parents as ch; PN 1834 Anderson Co, TN. R439

Thomas, esf 1780 Bedford Co, VA, where b 1758; to Madison Co KY c1792 where PN 1832; dd 5/13/39 leaving unnamed wid who recd unpaid portion of sol PN. R439

William, esf 1780 Bedford Co, VA; PN ae 96 Anderson Co, TN, 1834. R439

BUTLER, William, esf 1775 Culpeper Co, VA, where b 10/1754; to
    Lawrence Co, AL, 1818 where PN 1832; dd before 10/16/37,
    leaving no wid or ch. R439
  William, esf 1781 Culpeper Co, VA, as sub for Joseph Butler;
    b1762 Fauquier Co, VA; md after RW, mvd to Bourbon Co, KY,
    where res 40 years, thence Lincoln Co, MO, where PN 1833;
    record of 2nd VA Regiment states sol w Mary. R439
  William, esf 1776 Amelia Co, VA; b 11/11/1757 Prince George
    Co, VA, s/o John; family to Amelia Co when ch; to KY 1787
    where PN 1850 Trimble Co; QLF states sol md 1793 Nancy d/o
    Isaac Rawlings, further sol dd late 1835 Brunswick Co, VA,
    leaving wid Nancy who liv 1850 ae 80. R439
  Zachariah, esf 1781 Amelia Co, VA, where b 11/15/1764; mvd
    to Maury Co, TN, 1811 where dd 4/8/42; md 12/8/1787 Eliza-
    beth Noble, Amelia Co, VA (MB surety William Butler); wid
    PN ae 88 Maury Co, TN, 1850 & res there 1855; eld ch mbnn
    b 9/23/1788; QLF 1929 from gdd Mrs Lorena Butler Cox,
    Bristol, TN. R439
BUTT, Archibald, esf Prince Georges Co, MD, for svc in NC; POW
    SC 1780, escaped after 4 weeks, & esf MD; PN 1819 aec 55
    Greenbrier Co, VA; family in 1820 w ae 49 & ch: Betsy ae
    14, William ae 11, John ae 9, & Thomas aec 6. R440
  Barruck/Barrack, esf 1778 Prince Georges Co, MD; PN 1818 ae
    63 Berkeley Co, VA; family in 1820 w Diana ae 60 & d Mary
    ae 13. R440
  Edward, esf 1778 MD; KIA 3/15/1781; heir-at-law Thomas Butt
    of Greenbrier Co, VA, gtd BLW 1824; Barruck Butt, above,
    testified in support of claim then. R440
  Jacob, esf 1779 VA; PN ae 78 Botetourt Co, VA, 1832; dd
    8/8/38. R440
  Thomas, esf MD; BLW issued 2/1/1790; PN ae f70 Greenbrier Co
    VA, 1829, where dd 3/1/33; md 2/6/1809 Mary Taylor; wid PN
    ae 68 Red Oak Grove, Henry Co, IL, 1854, & res 1856 near
    Lancaster, MO; AFF by Thomas D Butt & Sarah Butt, Knox Co,
    IL, 1854; QLF 1934 from great great gdd Winifred Sweet of
    Geary Co, KS, states sol b Germany, dd Greenbrier Co, VA,
    md Mary & their ch George W (b 1817, dd 1863 Springfield,
    MO, md Jemmia Blake), Edward, Thomas Jr, & Lydia, further
    querier gdd/o sol s George W. R440
  Zachariah, esf 1778 MD; KIA 8/16/1780; older bro Edward KIA
    3/5/1781; Thomas Butt, heir-at-law of both Zachariah & Ed-
    ward gtd BLW 1824 Greenbrier Co, VA; Barruck Butt, above,
    testified in support of claim in Berkeley Co, VA. R440
BUTTEN, Luke, BLW issued 7/14/1792. R440
BUTTERTON, Samuel, see BATTERTON, Samuel. R441
BUTTS, Seth, esf Norfolk,VA, where b, s/o Josiah (not the Capt
    Josiah Butts in whose company he served); dd 10/7/1846 Au-
    taga Co, AL, ae 97, leaving 2nd w Mary Ann & her liv ch:
    Josiah aec 44, Sarah ae 38, Nancy Ann, Parthenia, & Joana
    Blackwell who dd before 1852; sol left ch James & Wilson
    by 1st w, they res near Nashville, TN; wid afp 1832 Autau-
    ga Co, AL, & PAR. R441

BUXTON, James; esf VA; PN 1810 for disability incurred in svc;
   res of Nansemond Co, VA; records lost in fire when War Office burned in 1814. R442
BUZAN, John, esf 1776 VA; PN ae 62 Bullitt Co, KY, 1819; family in 1821 w ae 64, d ae 22, s Philip ae 16 who crippled &
   of unsound mind. R442
   Philip, esf VA; PN 1831 Daviess Co, IN; dd 11/18/44, leaving
   ch James, Elgin, Jesse, & Allen; Elgin & James dd before
   1851 unmarried; only surv ch Jesse PN ae 62 Daviess Co, IN
   1851 when Andrew J Buzan adm/o sol estate; sol bro/o John.
   R442
BYAN, Samuel, see BYLAND, Samuel. R443
BYARLEY, Michael, see BYERLY, Michael. R443
BYARS, James, see BYERS, James. R443
BYBEE, Neilly/Neally, esf 1781 Fluvanna Co, VA; to KY 1785-6,
   then back to VA, thence KY 1792, where PN ae 69 Clark Co
   1832; to Monroe Co, MO, 1834 where dd 11/41; md 8/21/1837
   Mildred Wright there; wid PN aec 65 Audrain Co, MO, 1855 &
   gtd BLW, res there 1865; QLF 1926 from great great gdd Mrs
   Grace J Austin, Woodburn, OR, states sol d Frances md 1791
   in KY Thomas Jones, s/o Matthew (bc 1760 Southampton Co or
   Nansemond Co, VA, & md Mary Crumpler/Crumble) R443
   Pleasant, esf 1778 VA; PN ae 60 Fluvanna Co, VA, 1818; md
   9/3/1789 Mildred Preddy/Priddy; wid PN ae 81 there 1840; s
   Sherwood res there 1823. R443
BYERLY, Jacob, esf 1777 Westmoreland Co, PA, for svc in VA re-
   giment; PN ae 73 North Huntington Township, that Co, 1833;
   dd 7/7/58; QLF 1931 from great great gdd Mrs Grace Noble,
   Detroit, MI, states sol w Elizabeth; QLF states sol b 1760
   Westmoreland Co,VA, s/o Andrew, a butler for Gen Braddock.
   R443
   Michael, esf 1777 Berkeley Co, VA; PN ae 75 Washington Co,
   TN, 1832; to Jackson Co, IN, 1837 to be near ch; dd there
   8/20/44; md Rebecca, Berkeley Co, VA; wid dd Jackson Co,
   IN, 4/19/47, leaving ch: Hannah Morrison (aec 70 Palestine
   IL, 1853), Michael (b 12/23/1791, res 1847 Washington Co,
   TN), Rebecca Huffman, Mary Thacker, & Margaret, last 3 res
   Jackson Co, IN, 1847; QLF states another Michael Byerly,
   bro/o Jacob above, b 1746 Westmoreldnd Co, PA, dd 1829, md
   Mary who dd 1848, further an Andrew Byerly who RW sol md
   Phoebe Beatrice Goulden who RW nurse; QLF 1914 from desc C
   E Bireley, Los Angeles, CA; QLF from gdd Elizabeth Byarlay
   Turnbull, Roseville, IL, states sol b 7/1758 Shepherdstown
   WV, f/o her f Samuel who b 8/1797 there; QLF 1903 from gds
   L A Byarlay, St Joseph, MO. R443
BYERS, Hannah, former wid/o John Bunnell. R443
   James, esf VA; b 3/12/1761; res at one time Caroline Co, VA;
   dd 9/16-17/1817 Jefferson Co, KY; md 12/19/1782 Lovina
   Smith, Spotsylvania Co or Louisa Co, VA; wid dd 4/27/1842
   Oldham Co, KY; ch births: --tsey 4/13/1784, John S 2/1/88,
   --than 11/17/89, Nancey 10/24/91, Polly 10/23-25/93, James
   D 12/16/95, Patsey 1/5/98, Lucenda 7/22/1800, & Malindah

147

BYERS (continued)
  18--; in 1851 surv ch Polly Hinkle, Patsey Wellman & James
    D (res Jefferson Co, KY) recd PN due m Oldham Co, KY, when
    Samuel Hinkle (b 9/1792) made AFF there. R443
  Joseph, esf 1777 Chester Co,PA, where b 9/17/1761 on Brandy-
    wine Creek; served under bro Robert; apf 1834 Augusta Co,
    VA; PAR insufficient proof/o svc; s James & s Samuel C res
    there 1852; QLF states sol d Mary md Jacob Coiner. R443
BYLAND, Samuel, esf 1775 Loudoun Co, VA; PN ae 77 Campbell Co,
    KY, 1833, where dd 3/4/35; md 5/1809 Mary Bravard, Fleming
    Co, KY; wid PN ae 78 Covington, KY, 1853 when res with Eli
    J Rusk, her s-in-law. R444
BYRD, Andrew, esf 1776 Rockingham Co, VA, where b 11/40/1754
    Augusta Co, in that part now Rockingham Co, VA; PN there
    1832. R444
  Baylor, esf VA; dd 4/22/1830; md 10/4/1785 Nancy who afp ae
    82 Williamson Co,TN, 1839; ch births: Caty 7/9/1786, Tem-
    ple 10/24/87, Jenne 3/23/89, Richard 7/25/90, James 4/5/92
    John 2/9/94, Polly 9/25/96, & Tobey 2/9/99; wid PAR. R444
  Francis, esf VA; afp 1825 Marion Co, AL, & PAR; bro Thomas
    made AFF there then. R444
  Francis Otway, s/o William (dd 1777) of Westover, VA; sol
    midshipman in British Navy, who resigned 1775 to become
    aide de camp to Gen Lee of RW forces; md 46/1781 Ursula
    Anna "Nancy", 2nd d/o Col Robert Munford of St James Par-
    ish, Mecklenburg Co,VA; mvd after marriage to Charles City
    Co, VA, where High Sheriff, thence to Norfolk, VA, where
    dd 9/1800; wid PN ae 73 Lynchburg, VA, 1838, & dd there
    8/21/44, leaving ch Marta B Bradfate, Abby Davis, & Ann D
    Wright (who res Lynchburg 1845, adm/o m's estate); sol sis
    Maria H Page res Clarke Co, VA, 1838; QLF 1924 from desc
    Mary Byrd Deyerle, Richmond, VA. R444
  Henry, esf 1780 Montgomery Co, VA; b 1764 Prince Edward Co,
    VA; PN 1835 Hawkins Co, TN; res Morgan Co, KY, 1855; QLF
    1927 from great gds C T Byrd, Los Angeles, CA, states sol
    dd ae 105. R444
  Jesse, esf 1782 NC in section now Washington Co, TN; b 1764
    Franklin Co, VA; afp 1834 Roane Co, TN; PAR, less than 6
    monts svc; ch mbnn; QLF states sol dd Roane Co, TN, 1848.
    R444
  John, see BOARD, John. R444
  John, esf 1776 VA; PN aec 60 Bourbon Co, KY, 1819; to Fay-
    ette Co, IN, before 1823; dd c1830 leaving w Elinor ae 57
    & 1 ch at home; md 3/1780 who res IN 1870; d md IN; QLF
    states sol s Robert, b 5/22/1776 VA, who md 1/22/1799 Ra-
    chel Allen, Barren Co, KY, & dd OR 10/13/1855. R444
  Thomas, BLW issued 7/7/1792. R444
  William, esf 1781 Norfolk Co, VA; esf 1781 NC, where b Ber-
    tie Co; to Nansemond Co, VA, 1786 where PN 1833 ae 70; QLF
    states sol s Solomon md Nancy Bribb/Britt & their s Elijah
    md Annie E Hawkins, further Solomon & Nancy's d Cornelia
    md Rev Lewis Ledbetter. R444

BYRD, William, esf 1776 Prince Edward Co, VA; PN ae 65 Grayson
    Co, VA, 1818; in 1821 m/o w ae 99, & gdd Matilda ae 9; sol
    dd 5/31/29. R444
BYRNE, John, esf 1777 VA; PN ae 67 Alexandria, VA; res George-
    town, DC, 1820. R444
  John, esf 1778 VA; PN ae 78 Wayne Co, IN, 1818. R444
BYRNES, James, esf 1777 MD; esf 1782 Lancaster Co, PA; PN ae
    63 Brooke Co, VA, 1820 when w decd & ch supporting selves,
    & sol liv on bounty of gdd & her h, a shoemaker, res Ohio
    Co, VA; res 1821 Brooke Co, VA; QLF 1905 from great gdd
    Mrs Annie Forrest, Wapello Co, IA, states sol & w Margaret
    both b Ireland, further Margaret of royal blood & disinhe-
    rited by family when she md sol, further sol dd Wellsburg,
    WV. R444
  John, esf 1775 Hagerstown, MD, for svc in VA regiment; PN
    aec 68 Harrison Co, VA, 1818 where dd 11/7/36; md Esther
    Cavalier, Fayette Co, PA, 3/12/1792-3; wid PN aec 80 Har-
    rison Co, VA, 1850; ch births: d 1794 who dd infant, Samu-
    el c1803, Isaac c1811, & James c1813; Samuel md 1/6/1822
    Elizabeth Wadsworth, Harrison Co, VA; Samuel dd 7/8/22 &
    Elizabeth md (2) --- Matson, & she liv 1852. R444
BYRNS, John, see BYRNES, John, above. R444
BYRUM, Jacob, esf 1777 NC sub for f William; b 1761 VA, eldest
    s; to Granville Co, NC, as ch; PN Wake Co, NC, 1832. R444
  James, esf Norfolk, VA; b 1756 Essex Co, VA; to Warren Co,
    NC, thence Mecklenburg Co, NC, where PN 1832. R444
  Lawrence, esf 1776 Granville Co, NC; b 1759 Surry Co, VA; PN
    1832 Cumberland Co, NC. R444
BYRUN, Benjamin J, esf 1776 VA; dd 1793; md 5/20/1779 Mary c44
    miles from Pittsburg at Jacobs Creek, VA, where res; wid
    md (2) Michael Squire, Territory of IL & he dd 1/1820 near
    Edwardsville, IL; wid afp ae 89 Green Co, IL, & PAR. R444
CABBAGE, Adam, esf 1776 Shenandoah Co, VA; b 1755; PN Grainger
    Co, TN, 1836; w dd first; sol dd 3/17/44 leaving ch: Adam,
    John, Margaret "Peggy" (w/o William Idel & res IN 1856),
    Martha w/o John Nicely, Elizabeth (w/o Richard Kirby & res
    White Co, TN, 1856), Hannah w/o George Nicely (adm/o sol's
    estate), & Sarah; bro John res Campbell Co, TN, 1836. R445
  John, esf 1781 Shenandoah Co, VA; b 2/24/1758 Chester Co, PA
    & bro/o Adam above; PN 1834 Campbell Co, TN. R445
CABELL, Nicholas, esf VA; b 10/29/1750, 4th s/o William & Eli-
    za; dd 8/18/1803 leaving wid & 6 ch; md 4/16/1772 Hannah,
    d/o Col George Harrington; wid dd 8/7/1817 ae 67; gds Na-
    thaniel Francis Cabell afp Warminster, Nelson Co, VA, 1855
    for all heirs, stating Col Nicholas Cabell raised 2 compa-
    nies of Minutemen in 1775-6; sol bro/o Joseph; sole surv
    ch in 1855 Joseph C, uncle of Nathaniel Francis Cabell who
    PAR, gdc not authorized PN claim; gds William Cabell liv
    1853; in 1843 E A Cabell gave power of attorney to Joseph
    C Cabell. R445
  Samuel J, BLW issued 1/21/1796. R445
CAHOON, Charles, esf Kent Co, DE, where b 1747; to VA c1795;

CAHOON (continued)
　　afp ae 85 Botetourt Co, VA, 1832 res of Glade Creek & PAR;
　　dd 4/34;　power of attorney to J B Wilson 1851 by sol gds,
　　John B Cahoon, that Co.　R447
CAILES, John, esf aec 25 Staunton,VA; res Nicholas Co, VA, for
　　3 years before mvd to Washington Township,　Preble Co, OH,
　　where PN 1833, "unable to state present age."　R447
CAIN, John,　esf 1781 Winchester, VA;　esf later in PA sea svc
　　on brig BETSY;　b 1765-6 Manbridge, Ireland;　after RW res
　　25-30 years　Shenandoah Co, VA,　thence　Christian Co, KY,
　　were PN 1834 ae 67;　dd 12/25/40;　md 11/27/1786 Margaret;
　　wid afp ae 85 there 1842, & PAR, not wid at time of PN Act
　　of 1838.　R447
　　John, esf 1776 Harrison Co, VA;　b 12/27/1742 Buckingham Co,
　　VA; to Augusta Co, VA, 1775, thence Monongalia Co (section
　　now Harrison Co), VA; PN 1833 Harrison Co, VA.　R447
　　John, esf VA; PN 1833 Lewis Co,VA; PN apparently fraudulent-
　　ly obtained since he b 2/26/1769, per statement of his sis
　　Mrs Catherine Souther　(b 10/27/1766)　to Robert H Souther
　　1834 that sol "not old enough to serve"; sol name then re-
　　moved from PN rolls.　R447
　　William, esf 1775 Sussex Co, VA; b 11/1751;　PN 1818 Ruther-
　　ford Co, TN; QLF states sol dd 10/22/1828.　R447
CAINS, Richard, esf 1779 Augusta Co, VA; PN ae 64 Floyd Co, KY
　　1818.　R447
CAISY, John, see CASEY, John.　R448
CAKE, Lewis, see CLARK, Lewis.　R448
CALDERWOOD, James,　BLW issued 10/20/1796　to Adam Calderwood,
　　his heir-at-law, subject to dower/o sol wid Rachel Watson;
　　Records destroyed　1800 & 1814 by fire;　sol captain in VA
　　line;　QLF 1937 from Joseph C Calderwood,　Pittsburgh, PA,
　　states sol dd Battle of Brandywine　& probably b Scotland.
　　R448
CALDWELL, Alelxander, esf 1778 Washington Co,VA, res near head
　　of Holston River; b 11/13/1748 Hanover Co, VA; to Franklin
　　Co, GA, after RW,　thence Haywood Co, NC,　where afp 1835;
　　PAR, svc not in truly military unit.　R448
　　George, esf 1778　Bedford Co, VA;　b 2/15/1760 Prince Edward
　　Co, VA; PN 1833 Blount Co,TN, where res 47 years; QLF 1921
　　from desc Mrs Julia A Sherrett, Chattanooga, TN.　R448
　　James, esf 1779 Greenbrier Co, VA, as sub for f; also svc in
　　Indian War 1790;　b 7/4/1763;　PN 1833 St Francois Co, MO;
　　dd 9/6/36; md 11/30/1786 Meeke Perrin, Lincoln Co, KY; wid
　　b 2/27/1769, & PN 1844 St Francois Co, MO, res there 1858.
　　R448
　　John, esf 1776 Ohio Co, VA; b 1753 Ireland; to America ae 10
　　with f James to Baltimore, MD, thence 1773 to Ohio Co, VA;
　　PN 1832 there; bro judge there 1835.　R448
　　John, esf 1777 Prince Edward Co, VA;　b 1755;　to TN, thence
　　IN 1831 where PN 1833 Vigo Co.　R448
　　John, esf VA;　PN 1789 VA　for disability from wounds Battle
　　of Cowpens;　res 1823 Maryville,　Blount Co, TN;　res 1825

150

CALDWELL (continued)
　　Cloverhill, TN; QLF states a John Caldwell, b 1748 & dd
　　1829, md 1/7/1775 Dicey Mann, further his gdf John Cald-
　　well & w Margaret Phillips md Ireland, to America 1727 to
　　Newcastle, DE, thence Luneburg Co, VA, c1742; QLF states
　　sol PN 1789 Marshall Co, VA, mvd to TN where res with Eze-
　　kiel Caldwell. R448
　　Samuel, esf 1781 Ohio Co, VA; b 3/1765 Baltimore Co, MD; PN
　　1833 Morgan Co, IL; to Jefferson Co, Territory of IA, 1842
　　where 2 of ch res, one/o them just md; res 1850 Hancock Co
　　IL, recently moved from IA to be near d & s-in-law. R449
　　William, esf 1776-7 VA; PN ae 60 Nelson Co, KY, 1818; w ae
　　50 in 1820; sol dd 7/5/25; QLF 1914 from desc Lora R Riggs
　　of Morristown, TN. R449
　　William, esf 1780 Bedford Co, VA; b PA; PN ae 70 Jefferson
　　Co, TN, 1833; dd 11/24/40; md 9/1/1791 Eleanor Moor/Moore
　　(MB dated 8/30/91 signed by David Moor), Greene Co,TN; wid
　　PN ae 78 Jefferson Co, TN, 1843; QLF 1917 from great gdd
　　Margaret K Wilson, Dodd City, TX, states sol from Prince
　　Edward Co, VA. R449
CALHOON, Andrew, BLW issued 3/2/1799; trumpeter, Lee's Legion.
　　R450
　　George, esf 1776 Cumberland Co, PA; to VA (section now KY)
　　1781 where esf again; b 2/1/1754 Lancaster Co, PA; PN 1832
　　Daviess Co, KY; dd 10/20/35 at home of s Ralph C, leaving
　　8 ch; ch in 1850: John (circuit judge of KY), Sarah wid of
　　John Pyles, Ralph C, Rev Samuel (of Owensboro, KY), Mitch-
　　el, George, Henry, & Elizabeth w/o Gabriel Johnston; QLF
　　1936 from Margaret Calhoun (Mrs Clarence F) Bryan, Jeffer-
　　sontown, KY, states birth data from sol's old family bible
　　torn out; QLF 1902 from great gds C C Calhoun, Lexington,
　　KY; QLF 1905 from Birdy Calhoun (Mrs E H) Greer, Indiana-
　　polis, IN. R450
CALHOUN, William, esf 1777-8 Montgomery Co, VA; b 10/29/1762
　　Kent Co, PA; to Wayne Co, TN, for 20 years, thence Obion
　　Co, TN, 1833, were PN 1835; s S S appointed guardian of f
　　1837 when sol mentally deranged; dd there 2/15/39, leaving
　　no wid but ch Margaret Bedford, William, Mary Gore, & S S.
　　R450
CALL, Hugh, esf 1783 Augusta Co, VA; b 1/24/1764; afp 1835
　　Greenbrier Co, VA; PAR. R451
　Richard, BLW issued 8/19/1807; major in RW. R451
　Thomas M, see CAUL, Thomas M. R451
CALLAHAM, David, esf 1776 Luneburg Co, VA, sub for f Nicholas;
　　b there 2/1758; PN 1832 Russell Parish, Campbell Co, VA,
　　QLF 1917 from Bettie Callaham (Mrs William Lee) Cash, Bri-
　　stol, VA, states during RW following CALLAHAM's res VA:
　　David, Lightfoot, Nicholas, John, Dugger, Morris, Robert,
　　Leverett, & Matthew. R451
CALLAHAN, James, esf Spotsylvania Co, VA; b VA; afp 1833 Adams
　　Township, Guernsey Co, OH; PAR, insufficient proof of svc;
　　bro-in-law to Moses Kenney/Henney of Lexington, KY. R451

CALLAHAN, Joel, esf 1777 Watauga, East TN, for NC svc; bc 1754
Pittsylvania Co, VA; PN 1832 Greenville District, SC; w
Sarah dd there c1824; sol dd 1847 Spartanburg District,SC;
surv ch 1853 Catherine Compton ae 60 Marsh Creek, Greenville District,SC, & John of LA; QLF 1911 from great great
nephew Harry C Scott, Washington, DC. R451
CALLAWAY, Chesley, esf 17764 Bedford Co, VA, where b 1760; PN
1833 Ohio Co, KY, where res c40 years; QLF states sol buried 10-12 miles from Hartford, Ohio Co, KY, in old Calloway Burying Ground; QLF states sol dd 1846 leaving no w or
ch liv. R451
   Dudley, esf 1776 Bedford Co, VA; PN ae 66 Lynchburg, VA,
   1819; in 1821 w ae 65 & gds ae 8; house carpenter. R451
   James, esf 1777 Bedford Co, VA, where b 1756; PN 1832 Howard
   Co, MO; dd 7/13/35 MO; md 7/13/1784 Susan White, Bedford
   Co, VA; wid b 4/3/1767, PN 1840 Howard Co, MO, dd 9/30/44;
   ch births: Charles 9/3/1785, Stephen 8/12/87, Agatha/Aggy
   12/12/89 (md --- Hulse), John 10/28/91, Anna 2/15/93 (md
   --- Hutsell), Ambrose 3/15/95, Betsey 3/12/97 (md --- Elmore), Sally 4/12/1800, James 2/22/06, Flanders 9/22/08, &
   Seignea/Ceney 4/23/11 (md --- Swearingen); all ch but Sal-
   ly liv 1853; sol bro Micajah res IN 1834; QLF states a Col
   James Callaway, b 12/21/1736 & dd 11/1/1809 near New Lon-
   don, Campbell Co, VA, was s/o Col William Callaway who had
   French & Indian War svc & founded New London; QLF states
   sol mvd with family to KY 1787, & his s Charles, dd 1854,
   mvd with his family to Old Franklin, Howard Co, MO, & his
   f followed later; QLF 1930 from desc Mrs Pearl Callaway
   Codell, Winchester, KY. R451
   Micajah, see CALLOWAY, Micajah. R451
   Samuel, see CALLOWAY, Samuel. R451
CALLENDER, Samuel, esf 1776 VA; later esf PA; res after RW at
Wallkill, Orange Co, NY; PN ae 62 Greenfield, Luzerne Co,
PA; md c1778 an aunt/o David Slauson of Orange Co, NY, who
res there 1828; in 1820 sol & w ae 65 res Greenfield, PA,
with youngest s, sol then having 7 ch, he known as Samuel
the Elder; gtd BLW from state of VA; QLF states sol b VA
4/10/1756 & dd PA 3/12/1830; QLF 1924 from Alfred E Lister
of Scranton, PA, whose w desc/o sol; QLF 1923 from Nellie
Rose (Mrs Wilbur A) Jones, Klamath Falls, OR, states she
great gdd/o a Samuel Calendar who served in NY & VT militia; QLF 1929 from desc Mrs Bessie M Rightmire, Wenonah,
NJ; QLF states sol dd Scranton,PA, & w was Martha Slawson;
QLF 1937 from great great gds M Roy London states sol md
Martha Slossen. R452
CALLIS, George, esf 1777 Kingston Parish, Gloucester Co, VA,
where b; PN ae 72 Mathews Co, VA, 1832 where dd 2/21/43;
md 2/11/1834 Elizabeth Terrier, there; wid PN ae 60 there
1854; wid res there 1866 with s Samuel, & res there 1870
with s-in-law/stepson?; QLF 1933 from desc Anne V White,
Mobjack P. O., Mathews Co, VA; QLF 1915 from Ophelia Cooke
(Mrs Thomas S) Callis states sol md Nancy Genall & their

CALLIS (continued)
   ch were Daniel, George, John, Richard, Cye, & Samuel. R452
   William, esf 1780 Kingston Parish, Gloucester Co, VA, where
      b 1765; PN 1831 Mathews Co, VA. R452
   William Overton, esf 1777 VA; b 3/23/1757; dd 3/30/1814; md
      (1) 10/23/1782 Martha Winston who b 6/20/1765, dd 4/29/88;
      md (2) 5/4/1790 Anne Price, Hanover Co,VA; wid b 1/4/1774,
      PN 1838 Louisa Co, VA, where res since marriage; births by
      1st w: Eleanor Addison Callis 7/24/1784, Cleon M 1/14/86,
      & Martha Winston Callis 4/20/88; births by 2nd w: Lavinia
      2/11/1791, Otho W 10/13/92 (dd 6/6/1831), Jane Cosby Cal-
      lis 2/25/95, Arthur 12/23/96, Tobias Shandy 12/17/99 (res
      Louisa Co, VA, 1847), Caius Marcellus 4/26/1804, Mary Eli-
      zabeth 9/23/06 (dd 5/16/08), Mary Elizabeth 1811 & Barbara
      Ann 2/25/14; wid dd 12/8/46 leaving ch Tobias S, Caius W,
      Lavinia C Smith, Barbara E Jerdone, Jane C, Mary E Kean, &
      Arthur (not heard from since 1828); a William Overton Win-
      ston RW sol, & person of that name clerk of court of Hano-
      ver Co, VA, 1847; QLF 1934 from Mrs Margaret Monteiro Ber-
      ry, Washington, DC, who gdd/o sol d Martha Winston, stated
      DAR Chapter in Washington, DC, named for sol. R452
CALLOWAY, Chesley, see CALLAWAY, Chesley. R452
   James, see CALLAWAY, James. R452
   Micajah, esf 1777 Botetourt Co, VA; PN ae 74 Washington Co,
      IN, 1832, where dd 4/11/49; md 4/4/1805 Frances/Frank Haw-
      kins, Garrard Co, KY; wid PN aec 81 Washington Co, IN,
      1853, & res there 1859 with s John H. R452
   Samuel, esf 1779 Pittsburgh, PA, for svc in VA regiment; PN
      ae 66 Jefferson Co, KY, 1819; to Clark Co, IN, 1822 when w
      ae 52, & they had 4 s's & 4 d's, with 5 ch res MO, 2 res
      KY, & 1 res IN. R452
CALMES, George, esf 1776 near Winchester, Frederick Co, VA; PN
      ae 78 Alleghany Co, MD, 1834; bro/o RW Gen Marquis Calmes
      of Woodford Co, KY; sol dd 11/20/34, & wid dd soon after,
      leaving ch: Isabelle w/o John Rogers of Morgantown, VA, &
      Mary Hoge of Cumberland Co, MD; Mary Hoge afp 1849 as only
      surv heir of sol. R452
   Marquis, esf 1775 VA; PN ae 77, Woodford Co, KY, 1832; s M
      res Pettis Co, MO, 1855; QLF states sol Marcus Calmes dd
      2/27/1834, & his wid dd 1821, their res Versailles, Wood-
      ford Co, KY. R452
   William, esf 1777 Winchester, VA; b 5/15/1761 Frederick Co,
      VA; mvd 1782 to Ninety-Six District (now Newbury Co), SC,
      where PN 1832. R452
CALVERT, Jonathan, esf VA; surgeon's mate; s/o Max & Mary; dd
      12/17/1792; Norfolk Borough, leaving ch Newton & Rebecca;
      Newton dd c1804 underage & single; Rebecca md 11/21/1805
      Miles King, & dd leaving ch Newton Calvert & Charles, who
      gtd BLW for gdf svc, per AFF by Newton C King 1849 Norfolk
      VA; AFF 1832 Norfolk Co, VA, by Sarah Gilbert that her f
      Dr Ramsay served in VA state line troops with sol; Newton
      C King afp 1849, & PAR, insufficient proof of svc; John S

CALVERT (continued)
    Calvert adm/o sol estate 1792 Norfolk, VA; Miles King Sr &
    Jr adm/o sol estate 1805 there. R452
   Joseph R, svc in Illinois regiment of VA troops & left svc
    1782; Francis A Dickens, adm/o sol estate, applied for un-
    paid PN due sol & gtd; inquiry between 1844 & 1850 by Mrs
    Martha Clark; inquiry 1850 by I or J Calvert Clark; QLF
    states sol md Sidney Rundell (?), Iron Banks, settled near
    Natchez, MS, c1785, dd 1819 leaving wid Sidney, their ch:
    John, Thomas, & Martha who md Joshua G Clarke (later Chan-
    cellor of state of MS, his w Martha wid in 1830), further
    sol w possibly Elizabeth Sidney. R452
   Spencer, esf 1777 Prince William Co, VA; where b & raised;
    mvd to SC c10 years after RW for 20 years, thence Caldwell
    Co, KY, where PN 1833 ae 72; bro Raleigh also RW sol; QLF
    1908 from desc Mrs Charles Henson, Henderson, KY, states
    sol s/o Kirkland who res on James River & his home called
    "White House"; QLF 1939 from great great gdd/o sol bro Ra-
    leigh, Mary Gentry (Mrs B Hoff) Knight, Philadelphia, PA.
    R452
CALVITT, Joseph, see CALVERT, Joseph. R452
CAMEL, Thomas, colored, esf aec 16 c1777 Culpeper Co,VA, where
    b: mvd from Valley Forge 1778 to Salem, Washington Co, NY,
    thence Onandaga Co, thence Madison Co, NY, where afp 1832
    ae 72; sol illiterate; sol dd 5/6/49; s James CAMPBELL afp
    there 1854; both PAR, insufficient proof of svc. R453
CAMERON, Charles, esf 1776 Augusta Co, VA; dd 7/14/1829; md
    5/3/1792 Rachel Warwick; wid PN ae 67 Bath Co, VA, 1839, &
    BLW there 1833, PN increase 1854 & 1858; only ch Andrew;
    QLF 1927 from gdd Miss N C Lee, Pittsburgh, PA, states sol
    w Rachel Primrose mvd to Lexington, Rockbridge Co, VA from
    Bath Co; QLF 1900 from Miss Jean Cameron, Goshen Bridge,
    VA, states sol w dd 1858. R453
   James, see CAMRON, James. R453
CAMMACK, John, esf 1776-7 Caroline Co, VA; dd 3/10/1835; md ae
    17 there 12/25/1757 Nancy Miller; wid afp aec 90 Washing-
    ton Co, KY, 1839 when ch: James ae 70, Margaret aec 68,
    Martha aec 66, Mary aec 64, John aec 62, Thomas aec 60, &
    Delphy aec 58; s James AFF there then; d Margaret Montgom-
    ery AFF there then that sis Delphy Montgomery md but sis's
    Martha & Mary not md; Delphy Montgomery AFF there 1855
    that m Nancy then decd, & Delphy afp; both PAR, insuffi-
    cient proof of svc. R453
   William, esf 1780 VA; PN 1798 for disability from wounds at
    Battle of Guilford Court House; res Caroline Co,VA, thence
    Norfolk,VA; mvd c1819 to Elizabeth City,NC, where dd with-
    out issue 2/19/24; entered svc with bro George & bro John;
    bro George dd leaving ch but no claim for PN; bro John res
    Portsmouth, VA, 1837; QLF 1933 from desc L L (Mrs Charles
    J) Blake, Greensboro, NC. R453
CAMP, John, esf 1780 Brunswick Co, VA, where PN 1818 ae 57; in
    1822 w aec 60, d aec 21, s aec 19 mbnn; dd 11/25/32. R454

CAMP, John, esf 1781 Halifax Co, VA; b 5/1/1765; afp 1835 Ha-
fax Co, VA; PAR, less than 6 months svc. R454
John H, esf VA; LWT probated 5/1820 Giles Co, TN, listed w
Martha, s John H & s James W; James W Camp & Dorothy Camp,
guardians/o minor heirs of sol, power of attorney there to
obtain any compensation due sol 1832; heirs of sol in 1833
were James W Camp, Elizabeth W Camp, Sarah I Camp, Mary
Ann Camp, James T Camp, Martha w/o William C Flournoy, &
Maria w/o Albert Yerger; their PAR then; QLF states sol
res 1783 Greensville Co, VA. R454
Sharp, BLW issued 11/30/1795. R454
Thomas, esf 1777 Gloucester Co, VA; PN ae 61 Southampton Co,
VA, 1818, where dd 10/1825; md there 1789 Martha Westray/
Wester (MB dated 1/12/89); wid PN ae 73 Halifax Co, NC,
1825 where mvd after sol dd; s Humphrey ae 56 there 1848;
youngest s named for Lt Cavil/Cavel under whom sol served;
QLF 1913 states a Thomas Camp, b 1747, & a John Camp, b
b1742-3, both RW sol, further a Thomas Camp, b 1717 had 21
sons, further querier Miss N R Selman, Staunton, VA, desc
of RW sol Thomas Camp & w Susan Wagner, further Thomas
Camp, b 1747, md Miss Tarpley/Wester/Westray. R454
William, esf Gloucester Co, VA; adm/o sol estate 1852 Thomas
Ash afp & PAR. R454
CAMPBELL, Abraham, esf 1780 Newberry District, SC; b 1762 Cul-
peper Co, VA; PN 1833 Anderson District, SC. R455
Alexander, esf PA for PA svc, later transferred to VA regi-
ment; PN ae 72 Mercer Co, PA, 1828; dd 2/28/42 or 3/28/42
Indiana Co,PA; md 12/2/1778 Jane/Jeane who PN ae 87 Black-
lick Township, Indiana Co, PA, 1843, & res ae 88 Derry
Township, Westmoreland Co, PA; gds Samuel Palmer res 1844
near Blairsville, Indiana Co,PA; gds H D Campbell res 1848
New Alexandria, Westmoreland Co, PA. R455
Anthony, esf 1777 Amherst Co, VA; b 1761 Caroline Co, VA; to
Bedford Co, VA, 1790 where PN 1833. R455
Archibald, BLW issued 2/9/1796. R455
Archibald, esf 1778-9 Mecklenburg Co, VA, where b; to Granville Co, NC, 1782; dd c1802 Caswell Co, NC; md 1782 Elizabeth Pinson at her f's house Granville Co, NC, with her
bro John present; wid PN ae 90 Caswell Co, NC, 1842; wid
bro John AFF there 1843. R455
Archibald, esf 1781 Amherst Co, VA, where b 4/18/1763; mvd
c15 years after RW to Greenbrier Co, VA; PN 1834 there, a
minister; ae 100 there 3/11/57; dd at res there 7/20/57;
md 5/30/1844 Sarah Stuart Cook (license dated 5/27/44) Nicholas Co, VA; wid PN aec 67 Greenbrier Co, VA, 1859; her
last PN payment 6/3/81; bill for her coffin, burial clothing, & medical attendance paid 1882; sol gtd BLW; R455
Archibald, BLW issued 2/25/1799; dd Spring 1805; afb by John
Campbell 1805 Berkeley Co, VA, for svc of f & bro Archibald; John bro/o Jonathan. R455
Charles, esf 1777 Berkeley Co, VA; PN aec 86 ("8 years old
at time of Braddock's Defeat"), Butler Co, PA, 1833. R455

CAMPBELL, Charles, esf 1777 Augusta Co, VA, where b 1759; mvd
to NC, thence TN, thence Lauderdale Co, AL, where PN 1833;
dd 8/23/43 Hinds Co, MS, leaving wid & several ch, including George W of that Co; wid dd 9/1843; surv ch 1847 were
Hugh, William, John, Mary King; QLF 1928 from desc Miss
Irene Shipp, Rome, MS. R455
David, esf 1781 Rockbridge Co, VA; b 10/1/1761 Chester Co, &
mvd ae 6 with family to Augusta Co, VA; to East TN 1802,
thence McNairy Co, TN, where PN 1833. R456
Dennis, afb 1802 Jefferson Co, VA; BLW granted; surname also
spelled CAMPBLE. R456
Duncan, esf Orange Co, VA, where b 1760; to Gallatin Co, KY,
1812 where afp 1834; PAR, insufficient proof of svc. R456
Henry, esf 1781 Amherst Co, VA, where b 2/1764 in area now
Nelson Co, VA, where PN 1833; dd 1/3/35 at his res there;
md 5/19/1786 Sarah "Sally", Amherst Co, VA; wid PN ae 75
Nelson Co, VA, 1839, & gtd PN increase there 1843 ae 77;
eld ch William Jr ae 54 in 1841; AFF 1833 Nelson Co, VA,
by sol sis Matilda Cash ae 70. R456
James, esf 1780 Washington Co, NC; b 2/15/1759 Augusta Co,
VA; PN 1832 Knox Co, TN; dd 4/8/44; md 10/6/1779 Gennett/
Ganatt Allison, Washington Co, TN; wid PN ae 86 Knox Co,
1844; ch mbnn. R457
James, esf 1775 Leesburg, Loudoun Co, VA; PN aec 64 Montgo-
mery Co,MD, 1818; dd c9/1827; md 4/15/1819 Elizabeth Reed,
Leesburg, VA; wid PN ae 70 Springfield, Clarke Co, OH,
1855; d Etty 6 months old 1820; s Lenox liv 1855. R457
James, PN 1786 Berkeley Co, VA, for disability; records lost
in Washington, DC, fire 1800. R457
John, esf 1777 GA for svc in VA regiment; PN ae 56 Muskingum
Co, OH, 1818, when family w Eleanor ae 45 & d Polly ae 15;
QLF states sol res SC to 1809, thence Warren Co, OH, where
dd 3/18/24. R458
John, esf 1778-80 Rowan Co, NC; b 1759-60 Culpeper Co, VA;
PN 1833 Iredell Co, NC, where dd 3/23/34; md 1784-5 Cora/
Carah Collins, Wilkes Co, NC; wid PN aec 83 Iredell Co, NC
1843, & res there 1849; 2 small ch mbnn 1788; sol bro Per-
cival AFF 1834, Justice of the Peace Iredell Co, NC. R458
John, esf 1780 Rockbridge Co, VA; b 10/15/56 Augusta Co, VA;
PN 1834 Fulton Township,Hamilton Co,OH, where dd 11/26/39;
md 8/9/1802 or 8/9/05 a wid Sarah near Point Pleasant, Ma-
son Co, VA; wid b 9/11/1783, & md (1) John P Cruey/Crewey,
who dd 1798-9), their 4 ch: Polly Stevens (wid 1862 Hamil-
ton Co, OH), Martha (also wid there then), John (res near
Mayorsville, KY, then), & Abraham who dd young; wid PN ae
86 Warren Co, OH, 1862, ch by sol then: Betsey (dd young),
Daniel who dd 1834, Hiram who dd c1850, Sarah (w/o John
Wells/Walls of Terre Haute, IN), James ae 49, & youngest
Henry ae 44 with whom wid res at 20-Mile Stand, Warren Co,
OH. R458
John, esf 1780 Augusta Co, VA, where b 5/31/1765 s/o Andrew;
PN 1833 Cocke Co, TN. R458

CAMPBELL, John, esf 1777 Pittsylvania Co, VA, where b 1860;
PN 1832 Franklin Co, VA. R458
  John, esf 1778 Monongalia Co, VA; PN ae 64 Lewis Co, KY,
1818; in 1820 ae 68 there & w ae 75, they having raised 8
ch who all md. R458
  John, esf 1776 Augusta Co,VA; PN ae 63 Fayette Co, KY, 1820,
when ch: James, Archibald, Rachael, Sally, Jane, Mary, Anna, Rebecca, & Cynthia (ages 11-29); dd 12/18/35-38. R458
  John, esf 1778 Bedford Co, VA, where b 2/6/1761; after RW to
Knox Co, TN, thence Jackson Township, Preble Co, OH, c1818
where PN 1832; dd 5/14/46-7 there; md 12/1796 Sarah Vance,
MB dated 12/28/96 signed by her brother James, Jefferson
Co, TN; wid PN ae 75 Jackson Township, Preble Co, OH, 1849
& res there 1855; ch births: Samuel 11/13/1797, Jane
12/19/98, Elizabeth 10/28/1800, Archibald 1/9/03; Mary
1/11/05, James 8/11/07, Andrew 1/2/10, Robert 10/7/12,
William 1/1815, Alexander P 6/11/17, & Nancy 6/22/20; wid
bro James, b 1773, AFF 1850 that Sarah md sol at his house
& wid bro John b 9/1770 also AFF 1850, both res Jefferson
Co, TN; wid sis Elizabeth res there 1796; QLF 1935 from
Miss Edna Campbell, Richmond, IN, states sol b 2/5/61 & dd
5/14/1847, & w Sarah b 1/5/1772 & dd 12/12/1858. R458
  John, esf 1781 Amherst Co, VA; b 1750 Albemarle Co, VA; mvd
to Amherst Co as ch, where PN 1833; dd there 1/29/38, LWT
filed there 2/19/38; md 2/1779 Frances there; wid PN there
1841 ae 80, when eldest ch decd, 2nd or 3rd ch aec 55 res
there; ch Betsy, Nancy, & Wyatt, who made AFF, mentioned
1842. R458
  John, esf 1781 Lancaster Township, PA; PN ae 57 Frederick Co
VA, 1818, a shoemaker; res there 1820 with w ae 58 & s aec
16 a cripple; dd there 11/19/37; md there 1/13/1783 Ailce/
Elsey who PN there 1838; ch births: William 10/7/1785, Sarah 10/22/86, Dorchity 2/24/88, William 6/1/89, Samuel
5/7/91, Mary 10/18/93, Elizabeth 6/1/95, Caty 5/6/97, &
Fredis 1/8/99. R458
  Joseph, esf Albemarle Co, VA; b Culpeper Co, VA, s/o Joseph,
who mvd to Washington Co, VA, c1780 where sol esf 1780 as
sub for f; PN ae 73 Hamilton Co, TN, 1832; dd Bradley Co,
TN, leaving wid & ch mbnn; QLF 1908 from Ada McKinney Pet-
ty, Macon, MO, states sol s Samuel Givens had s Samuel
Rice who her gdf. R459
  Lawrence, esf 1781 Amherst Co, VA; b 11/1763; PN 1832 Green
Co, KY; QLF states sol f Lawrence dd Amherst Co, VA. R459
  Owen, esf 1777 Campbell Co, VA, where b & raised; PN ae 82
Culpeper Co, VA; dd 10/27/36; md there 11/30/1787 Jemima
Lear; wid PN ae 75 Rappahannock Co, VA, 1840, where res
1845. R459
  Richard, esf VA; KIA Battle of Eutaw Springs; LWT probated
3/28/1782 Shenandoah Co,VA; LWT dated 9/22/1778 Woodstock,
that Co, listed w Rebecca & ch mbnn; sol surv ch: Archi-
bald (also RW sol, who dd without issue), Joseph (US Army
lieutenant who dd Spring/o 1805 Fort Stoddard, leaving w &

CAMPBELL (continued)
    s), Richard (decd in 1805),   Jonathan liv 1800, & John res
    1805 Berkeley Co, VA. R459
    Robert, esf 1776 NC where mvd from VA; b 1/3/1759 Prince Ed-
    ward Co, VA; PN 1833 Carter's Valley, Hawkins Co, TN, when
    res there 40 years; QLF states a Robert Campbell, b Rock-
    bridge Co, VA, 1/3/1761, md 1/18/1785 Mary Young, Abingdon
    VA (she dd 4/1/1841), & settled Carter's Valley, TN, where
    dd 12/29/1841, further Mary Young b 17 miles from Rogers-
    ville, Rockbridge Co, VA, 2/12/1765, further sol appointed
    as one of 1st magistrates by VA government after RW; QLF
    states sol s Alexander of Sneedville, Hancock Co, TN, was
    War of 1812 sol. R459
    Robert, esf 1777 Botetourt Co, VA; PN ae 71 Jessamine Co, KY
    1832 as Robert Sr; dd there 7/4/40; md 11/1807-8 Katy Haw-
    kins; wid PN ae 87 P. O. Nicholasville, Jessamine Co, VA,
    1853; QLF states sol bro Patrick md Miss Ellison, whose f
    from Ireland; QLF 1932 from great grandniece Mrs Edna Mc-
    Guire, Nelson, MO, states sol md Catherine Hawkins, & his
    LWT filed Nicholasville, KY. R459
    Thomas, esf 1776 Baltimore, MD; PN 1818 Augusta Co, VA; res
    there 1820 aec 79, no family then. R460
    Thomas, esf 1776 Northumberland Co, VA; PN there 1818. R460
    Thomas, see CAMEL, Thomas. R460
    Thomas, esf Princess Anne Co, VA; b 1766 Northumberland Co,
    VA; afp 1849 Princess Anne Co, VA; PAR, insufficient proof
    of svc. R460
    Walter, esf Granville Co, NC; b 8/1752 Brunswick Co, VA; afp
    1833 Montgomery Co, AL; PAR, svc less than 6 months. R450
    William, esf 1775 Wilkes Co, NC; b 8/1/1756 Culpeper Co, VA;
    PN 1832 Crawford Co, IN; md 1790-1 Nancy Hendron, NC; in
    1822 family w Nancy ae 72, d Nancy ae 40, s William Hend-
    ron ae 33, s Enos ae 30, & 2 orphan gdc Nancy Campbell ae
    14 & Peggy Campbell ae 11; dd IL 1/19/40; wid dd 8/1/46
    there; Enos ae 60 Bureau Co, IL, 1852 only surv ch. R461
    William, esf 1776 Culpeper Co, VA; b 3/5/1753; PN 1829 Coop-
    er Co, MO, while res with gds Bradley Campbell aec 23 who
    had widowed m also liv with him. R461
    William, esf 1779 Amherst Co, VA; b 1754 Albemarle Co, VA;
    PN 1833 Nelson Co, VA, where dd 4/16/36; md 12/22/1785 Sa-
    rah; wid PN ae 70 there 1839; s James b 10/7/1786; d Nan-
    sy b 12/25/1788; sol bro/o Henry. R461
    William, esf 1775 VA; dd 10/23/1823; md 8/19/1783 Susan/Su-
    sanna Pierce, King & Queen Co, VA; wid PN ae 73 Orange Co,
    VA, 1838, & dd there 3/13/52, leaving ch: Catharine H Du-
    laney, Mildred, Arria Welch, America W, Eliza F, Mary B T,
    Susan Graves, John P, Joseph W, William, Virginia w/o Hill
    Maury, & Frederick W; sol sis Elizabeth res Madison Co, VA
    1851, wid of Churchill Gibbs; sol nephew of Judge Edmund
    Pendleton of VA; QLF 1908 from great great gdd Mrs A B Ad-
    ams, Memphis, TN; QLF states sol dd 1825 Orange Co, VA;
    QLF 1923 from desc Mrs N M Jordan Jr, Tennile,GA; QLF 1929

CAMPBELL (continued)
from great gds Alan W Graves, Haverford, PA, states sol b
12/12/1755 & dd 10/29/1823, & buried in family cemetery at
Campbellton, near Barboursville, VA; QLF states a William
Campbell & his s James (b Scotland 1754) came to America c
1768 & both esf VA, further s James d MD 1824 & was ae 68
when s Lenox b & also had d Mary Etta. R461
William, esf 1776 Albemarle Co, VA; b Scotland; PN ae 83
Franklin Co, GA, 1832, where dd 7/18/33; md 7/20/1783 Sa-
rah/Sally Gelie, Albemarle Co, VA; wid PN ae 81 Franklin
Co, GA, 1839. R461
William, esf VA; dd 3/15/1814 Cumberland Co, KY; md 3/9/1782
Jane d/o Adam Dean, Montgomery Co, VA; wid b 1/8/1760; wid
afp 1848 Jackson Co, AL, & PAR, insufficient proof of svc;
wid decd in 1857, when d Sarah w/o Wilson L Allen, Jackson
Co, AL; QLF mns a sol William Campbell, who had ch James,
Adam, Isaac, Betsy, John, Polly, William, Charles & Sally.
R461
CAMPER, John, esf 1781 Shenandoah Co, VA; bc 1749 Fauquier Co,
VA; PN 1832 Botetourt Co, VA; QLF states sol surname also
spelled KEMPER & KAMPER, sol bc 1747, d Newport, VA, 1857,
md (1) Sarah James & (2) Hannah Carney; QLF 1926 from desc
Mrs L Fay Ryan Thomas, Russellville, KY; QLF states sol dd
Fauquier Co, VA, md c1780 Elizabeth, sis/o Spencer & Ben-
jamin Morgan, further sol bro/o Moses, Tilman, & Charles,
who also RW svc, further sol bro-in-law Spencer & Benjamin
Morgan also RW svc, all serving under Daniel Morgan, who
1st cousin to Spencer & Benjamin; QLF 1906 from great gdd
Jennie Kemper Wysor, Muncie, IN; QLF states sol b 11/27/57
Fauquier Co, VA, & dd 1/22/1833 Garrard Co, KY. R462
Camper, Tilman, esf 1778 Fauquier Co, VA; b 4/11/1759; after
RW mvd to Fayette Co, KY, where PN 1832, where dd 12/3/36;
md 10/27/1779 Dinah Hitt, Fauquier Co, VA; wid b 4/15/1764
& PN 1838 Fayette Co, VA, when AFF there by 9th ch Nancy
Marsh ae 43; ch births: Thomas 9/9/1780, Anne 178-, Benja-
min 7/7/83, Sarah 1/5/86, Jonathan 1/13/88, Nimrod 11/3/89
Elizabeth 3/3/91, Polly 2/28/93, Nancy 3/2/95, Charles
Weaver 4/1/97; Joel Hitt 6/21/99, Peter 6/25/02, Miriam
3/7/04, Levi 3/10/06, & Reuben Hitt 3/19/08; AFF 1839 by s
Levi ae 33 Fayette Co, KY; name also spelled KAMPER. R462
CAMRON, James, esf 1779 Shenandoah Co, VA; PN ae 74 Floyd Co,
Co, 1832; dd 10/25/38; md 7/20/1784 Ann/Anna C Spangler of
Dutch extraction; wid PN ae 84 Tazewell Co, VA, 1846; ch
births: Elisabeth 10/17/1785, Daniel 12/13/1787, Jacob
2/5/92, Dungen/Duncan 9/5/94, James 2/7/9-, Mina 12/26/9-,
& Felix 10/17/98; s Duncan AFF 1846 Tazewell Co, VA. R462
William, esf 1776 Hanover Co, VA; b & raised Hanover Co, VA;
PN ae 73 Fluvanna Co, VA, 1853. R462
CANADAY, John, see CANNADAY, John. R462
Leroy, esf 1778 Essex Co, VA; mvd to Culpeper Co, VA, & esf
1781; PN ae 75 Madison Co, VA, 1833; surname also spelled
CANEDAY. R462

CANADAY, Merriday/Merideth, esf 1779 Culpeper Co, VA; b 1753
    on Rappahannock River, Essex Co, VA; to Lexington Co, KY,
    1795, thence Scioto Co, OH, c1818, where afp ae 80 Brush
    Township, 1834; PAR, less than 6 months svc; dd 8/27/38,
    leaving s Hezekiah & s Zanthus who afp there 1853 as heirs
    & PAR. R462
CANADY, John, see CANNDAY, John. R462
  John, esf 1776 at house/o nephew George's f George (d c1784)
    Westmoreland Co, VA; nephew George AFF 1834 Caroline Co,
    VA, that bro Andrew & other relatives entered svc with sol
    & Andrew KIA; sol bro/o George; sol who decd in 1834 never
    md; BLW issued to nephew George; surname at times spelled
    CANNADY & KENNEDY. R462
    William, esf 1781 Culpeper Co, VA; PN ae 67 Laurens District
    SC 1818; in 1821 family w ae 57 & d Nancy ae 22. R462
CANAFAX, William, esf Campbell Co, VA, where res; b7/9/1758
    Cumberland Co, VA; to KY 1800; PN 1834 Monroe Co, VA. R462
CANDLER, William, esf 1780 Bedford Co, VA, were b 1751; record
    of age in possession of Daniel Candler of Campbell Co, VA;
    PN there 1832. R463
CANFIELD, Daniel, esf NY 1775; b 2/10/1757; PN 1825 Randolph
    Co,VA; to Crawford Co,IN, 1830 to join 3 sons; dd 10/31/32
    Lewis Co, VA; md 10/1778 or 11/1778 Elizabeth, Dutchess Co
    NY, wid b 5/24/1759, & PN 1843 Jennings Co, IN; ch births:
    Nathan 6/20/1779 (dd 1813 near Chillicothe, OH), Mary
    11/12/81, Titus 8/28/84, Sarah 2/14/87, Zachariah 9/8/90,
    Daniel 8/17/91, Amos 6/14/94, Jedediah 9/20/96, Moses
    10/6/98, Henry 1/18/1801, & Margaret 6/10/04; Mary, Titus,
    & Zachariah decd in 1843; births in records of s Jedidiah:
    Priscilla 5/31/1809, Aaron 9/1828, Amos 1/25/3-, Daniel
    3/17/33, Anny 9/9/35, Philip 8/22/3- & Nancy 3/16/41. R463
CANK, Garret, BLW issued 1/19/1792. R463
CANN, William, esf 1776 Amherst Co, VA; b 3/19/1757; afp 1837
    (blind) Hart Co, KY, & PAR, insufficient proof of svc; s
    John afp 1854 there as heir/o sol, now decd, & PAR, since
    PN claim not established by sol before death. R463
CANNADAY, John, esf 1781 Bedford Co, VA; b 3/1/63 King George
    Co, VA; PN 1832 Casey Co, KY; res 1836 Montgomery Co, IL;
    dd 12/15/36; md 3/26/1787 Mary Shearer, Campbell Co, VA;
    wid afp ae 83 Montgomery Co, IL,1844, & PAR, for insuffi-
    cient proof of svc & marriage; ch births (all surnames KA-
    NADAY in family bible): James 1/27/1788, John 8/26/89 who
    decd in 1844, Robert 9/24/91, William 1/8/96, Sophiah
    5/3/98, Patsey 6/24/1800, & Elizabeth 5/9/06; AFF 1844 by
    s Robert Kanaday; surname variations: KENNADY, CANADAY, &
    KANADAY; QLF 1872 from great gdd Mrs J J Post, Chanute, KS
    states sol ch all b MD; another QLF states sol ch b Casey
    Co, KY, & w dd 1844 ae 83. R464
CANNADY, John, see CANADY, John. R464
  William, see CANADY, William. R464
CANNDAY, John, VA sea svc; esf 1781 near Mattox Bridge, West-
    moreland Co, VA, where b 8/21/1764; seafarer until 1804;

CANNDAY (continued)
  PN 1832 Stafford Co, VA; liv 1837. R464
CANNON, Ellis, esf 1781 VA; PN ae 81 Spartanburg District, SC,
  1829, when w ae 79 & d Phebe ae 57; dd 3/20/33; QLF states
  family tradition that sol taster of foods for Gen George
  Washington. R464
  Henry, esf 1775 Culpeper Co, VA; b 4/11/1751-2 Stafford Co,
  VA; to Spartanburg District, SC, 1784; PN 1832 Greenville
  District, SC, when Ellis CANNON, a clergyman of Spartan-
  burg District, SC, mentioned; bro/o Elam. R464
  Jesse, VA sea svc; esf 1781 VA; svc on DILIGENCE; dd 1792;
  heirs mbnn afp 1836, & PAR; Luke CANNON of VA sea svc then
  mentioned. R464
  Luke, esf Dumfries, VA, where PN 1828 & dd 2/29/29, & where
  heirs 1856: s Thomas T, d Mary B, d Edith A Norvell, Mary
  wid/o sol s Col Barnaby & her d Margaret Anne Goods. R464
  Luke, VA sea svc; no papers, but data in VA State Library,
  Richmond, VA. R464
  William, afp 1833 Green Co, TN, claiming svc in VA & NC; PAR
  R464
  William, esf 1776 VA; b & raised Caroline Co, VA; d 9/1824
  Roane Co, TN; md 12/17/1786 Elizabeth Brown, Caroline Co,
  VA; wid PN there 1842 ae 74; surname at times spelled KEN-
  NON. R464
  William, esf 1775 Richmond,VA; afp ae 71 Greenville District
  SC 1824 when w decd & 7 ch res with him: Polly, Peggy, Su-
  sanah, William aec 14, Uriah aec 12, Alfred aec 10, & Ca-
  tharine, other ch having already left home; PAR, svc not
  in regularly constituted unit. R464
CANTER, John, esf 1780 VA; PN ae 70 Jackson Co, OH, 1824 when
  w ae 60, d Mary ae 15, & s Hiram ae 27, all at home; other
  ch then: John ae 39, Henry ae 26, James ae 30 md, & Daniel
  not md; sol res Scioto Co, OH, 1826 & 1842; sol bro Thomas
  res 1826 Jackson Co, OH, when bro Truman res Rockcastle Co
  KY. R465
CANTERBURY, John, esf 1774 ae 14 when res settlement on Hol-
  stein River in area now Washington Co,VA; esf 1777 against
  indians; b 1759 Prince William Co, VA; to Monroe Co, VA,
  soon after RW, where afp 1834; afp again there 1839; both
  PAR, insufficient proof of svc. R465
  Sid, see FRANKLIN, James M. R465
CANTWELL, John, esf 1775 Orangeburg District, SC; mvd to Lou-
  doun Co, VA, where esf 1777, & where res till mvd 1790 to
  Spartanburg District, SC, thence Hawkins Co, TN, where PN
  1833; b 6/24/1745 Baltimore Co, MD; dd 9/20/1836; md Jane
  Barnett 12/10/1791; wid b 12/10/1770, afp 1843 Hawkins Co,
  TN, & PAR for further proof of marriage; ch births: Edward
  10/2/1792, Thomas 9/30/94, Susannah 9/11/96, John 9/29/98
  (res 1853 Hancock Co,TN), Patsy 11/17/1800, Nancy 10/23/02
  Jane 11/25/04, James 9/1/07, William Barnett 12/25/09, &
  David 1/23/11; AFF 1846 by s William Barnett, Hawkins Co,
  TN. R465

CAPE, John, esf 1776 Amelia Co, VA, where b 3/1745; to Bedford
    Co, VA, till 1796, thence Lincoln Co,KY, thence Cumberland
    Co, KY, till 1830, thence Russell Co, KY, where PN 1833.
    R465
CAPES, William, see COPIS, William. R465
CAPPS, William, esf 1780 Burke Co, NC; b Chatham Co, NC, later
    svc with VA militia; PN ae 81 Henderson Co, NC, 1845; md
    Nancy who afp 1847-8 & PAR; POA 1857 from sol d & heir Lu-
    cina Hammond, Fannin Co, GA, to Henry H Walker to claim PN
    PN due decd m, & PAR; queries 1856 by Hiram T Capps. R466
CAPSHAW, Catharine, former wid/o Johann Sensenbach. R466
CARDIN, Youen/Edwin, esf 1781 Cumberland Co, VA; PN ae 73 Flu-
    vanna Co, VA, 1845; dd 3/21/50 Greene Co, VA; only surv ch
    1853 William T, since sol d Judith & d Mary not heard from
    within past 20 years; AFF 1845 by s William T ae 53 Albe-
    marle Co, VA; sol 1st name at times spelled Edward or You-
    el, he "Dutchman who spoke very broken English". R467
CARDER, John, see CORDER, John. R467
    Sanford, esf 1780 Hampshire Co, VA; b 9/16/1760 Culpeper Co,
    VA; mvd 1794 to Bourbon Co, KY, thence 1800 to Union Town-
    ship, Fayette Co, OH, where PN 1832, & dd there 8/7/43; md
    12/19/1827 Sarah/Sally David there; wid b 3/1784 & PN Fay-
    ette Co, OH, 1856; QLF 1920 from great great gds Dr Brose
    Horne, Chicago, IL, states his own m gdd/o Francis Eviston
    (b Ireland, dd OH), who sol in either RW or War of 1812;
    QLF 1900 from desc Mrs Susan A Stoddard, Washington Court
    House, OH. R467
    William, esf 1780 Hampshire Co, VA, where b 1760; mvd to Mo-
    nongalia Co,VA, 1781 & esf there; PN 1833 Lewis Co, VA; in
    1834 sol stepd w/o John Mitchel; sol steps Isaac Washburn
    ae 58, Harrison Co, VA, AFF then that sol md his m when ae
    18 & Isaac ae 8 or 9; AFF 1834 by sol s Manly. R467
CARDONA, John, BLW issued 2/23/1792. R467
CARDWELL, James, esf 1780 Charlotte Co, VA; dd 10/26/1806 Mer-
    cer Co, KY, where md 5/4/1788 Sarah/Sally Crocket (MB da-
    ted 5/3/88 signed by Anthony Crocket); wid PN ae 76 there
    1841 & dd there 2/11/53, leaving ch John, Cuzza Forsythe,
    Anthony, James, & George; AFF there 1853 by s Col John;
    wid mvd to Mercer Co, KY, from Prince William Co, VA. R467
    Perrin, esf 1781 Powhatan Co, VA; b 7/12/1764 Cumberland Co,
    VA; PN 1832 Knox Co,TN, where dd 12/2/54; md 9/4/1785 Eli-
    zabeth Worsham/Worshom, Amelia Co, VA; wid PN ae 84 Knox
    Co, TN, 1855; ch mentioned: Daniel bc 1789 (decd in 1857),
    Thomas C b 1794, Perrin H b 4/17/1820 liv 1857; QLF 1911
    1925 from desc Rozina (Mrs N H) Rankin, Cleveland, TN; QLF
    1922 from Alvis Cardwell, Kansas City, KS, states sol Me-
    thodist minister & recd PN at Knoxville, TN; QLF 1916 from
    Mrs J W Cardwell, Johnson City, TN, states sol full name
    Perrin Henry Cardwell. R467
    Robert, esf 1776-7 Bedford Co, VA; esf 1781 Amherst Co, VA;
    PN ae 85 Campbell Co, VA; exec/o sol estate recd 1842 that
    PN due sol for 1838-1839. R467

162

CARDWELL, William, esf 1779 Spotsylvania Co, VA; PN Bullitt, Co, KY, 1819 aec 59; dd 3/1/28; md 3/1781 Famariah, Culpeper Co, VA; wid PN aec 81 Bullitt Co, KY, 1839 & dd 5/8/43 Jefferson Co, KY; ch mentioned 1839: Nancy wid/o Nicholas Brown, Elizabeth wid/o Robert Shirley & 1851 ae 76; Benjamin decd, Lewis b 12/25/1785 & dd 10/31/1832, William b 4/10/1787 & res Bullitt Co, Susan w/o Joel W Hundley; Jane decd who md William Kirk, George res Louisville, KY (1851 ae 51 & decd in 1852), John ae 65 in 1851, Mary w/o William Watson, & Edmund b 11/1/1801 & dd 10/26/1832; in 1852 William Cardwell, s/o sol s George, AFF Jefferson Co, KY, that John & Elizabeth Shirley only ch/o sol liv then; QLF from Harvey Cardwell, Louisville, KY, states sol w Famariah Hughes. R467

William, BLW issued 5/5/1790. R467

Wiltshire, esf 1781 Charlotte Co, VA; b 8/2/1764 Powhatan Co VA; PN 1832 Charlotte Co,VA, where dd 7/3/34; md Mary Russell there 12/18/1792; wid PN there 1838 ae 68. R467

CAREY, Michael, esf 1778 MD; PN 1818 Harrison Co, VA; in 1820 sol ae 64, w ae 61, d Nancy ae 19, & d Peggy ae 16; QLF states sol & f came to America before RW, further f also RW sol & KIA; surname sometimes spelled CARY. R468

CARGILE, Thomas, see CARGILL, Thomas. R468

CARGILL, Thomas, esf 1777 Wilkes Co, NC, where f mvd family before RW; b 3/30/1762 VA; after RW to GA, thence 1816 to AL where PN ae 72 Jackson Co 1832; dd 9/10/47; md Mourning Killingsworth, Marshall Co, AL, 9/14/1845; wid PN there ae 79 in 1855; wid declared non compos mentis 1853, & Barton S Clapp appointed her guardian; David Ricketts her guardian 1857. R468

CARGYLE, John, esf 1779 Pittsylvania Co, VA; mvd to Wilkes Co, NC, where esf 1780; b Halifax Co, VA, in area now Pittsylvania Co; afp ae 91 Haywood Co, NC, 1836, & PAR, less than 6 months svc; QLF 1939 from Miss Mary Lou Cargill, Winder, GA, states sol md Mary Allen, Brunswick Co, VA, his f John Sr md Rachel Lester there, further sol bro Cornelius & bro Daniel also RW svc, further querier gdm Elizabeth Garnett desc of Muscoe Garnett of "Elmwood, Essex Co, VA, who md Grace Fenton Mercer & member/o RW Committee/o Safety, further querier possibly desc/o sol John Cargyle. R468

CARLILE, James P, esf 1777 Augusta Co, VA, where b 2/8/1761; to KY 1780 where PN Green Co 1833. R470

CARLISLE, William, esf 1780 Surry Co, NC; esf 1781 Greenbrier Co, VA, where mvd 1780; b 11/18/1764 Guilford Co, NC; PN 1833 Jackson Co, TN; dd 4/5/43; md 4/19/1792 Nancy Kirkpatrick, Madison Co, KY; wid afp ae 70 Jackson Co, TN, 1844, & PAR per PN Act of 4/30/1844, total svc/o sol questioned; wid bro William AFF ae 67 there 1844 that he witnessed sis marriage; ch births: James 5/1/1793, Mary 8/7/95, Robert 12/8/98, Rachel 4/23/1801, & Mahalah 10/5/03. R470

CARLTON, Benoni, esf 1780 King & Queen Co, VA; PN ae 69 Saint Stephens Parish, that Co, 1832; ch mbnn liv 1839; w d/o

CARLTON (continued)
    Richard Rowe; QLF states s James h/o Miss McGuire mvd from
    King & Queen Co, VA, c1810-12. R471
  Christopher, esf 1781 King & Queen Co, VA; dd 6/1824; md
    9/1782 Jane Hart/Hurt there ; wid PN ae 75 Halifax Co, VA,
    1839; QLF states sol full name Christopher Charles Carlton
    & served with sol Anthony Hart, further s Christopher Jr
    War of 1812 sol. R471
  Humphrey, esf 1778 King & Queen Co, VA; PN ae 79 there 1833,
    when Molly Carlton ae 77 AFF there that sol several times
    served as sub for her h Richard. R471
  Kimball, b CT or MA; left MA before 1788 for KY, then part/o
    VA, in pursuit of man who owed him large sum/o money, lea-
    ving bro & sis in MA; md 6/17/1790 Elizabeth, d/o Henry
    Spillman, Mercer Co, KY, who mvd there from Fairfax Co, VA
    1779; sol dd 5/22/1830 Hardin Co, KY, ae 84; wid afp ae 82
    there 1851 claiming sol RW svc with MA, NH, & NY troops, &
    her PAR, insufficient proof of svc; wid res there 1855; ch
    births: James 4/9/1791, Rachel 7/21/93, Hiram 4/14/96,
    Henry -/14/98, John, & Eda 2/18/1804; s John res there ae
    52 in 1854; d Rachel to IL c1844; s Hiram sol War of 1812
    from KY; gds James Y, s/o sol s John, b 4/22/1830. R471
  Lewis, esf 1777 Albemarle Co, VA; esf 1781 Wilkes Co, NC; b
    9/12/1758, s/o John & Elizabeth; dd 3/13/1827 Wilkes Co,
    NC; md there 1/18/1781 Elizabeth, d/o Joseph & Mary Eve;
    wid b 2/26/1762 & dd 10/31/1839 leaving ch: Polly Laxton,
    Elizabeth Hagler, Nancy Pearson, William, Milly Tucker, &
    Thomas; other ch: Ambrose b 12/31/1781, John, Lewis, David
    & Howard; s Thomas ae 65 Burke Co, NC, 1853 afp due m for
    her surv ch, & PAR, no proof of her death, no proof wid at
    death, no proof of names of surv ch, & marriage occurred
    prior to sol last period of svc; sol bro Thomas was Tory &
    taken POW but released when showed discharge from previous
    svc against British; QLF states sol also bro/o John. R471
CARMACK, Cornelius, esf 1776 Montgomery Co (area now in Wash-
    ington Co), VA; b 1/8/1759 Frederick Co, MD; PN 1832 Over-
    ton Co, TN; dd 7/28/48; sis of sol md Henry Livingston who
    also RW sol & res there 1832; QLF states sol w Mary; QLF
    1927 from great great gds J R Carmack, Hilham,TN; QLF 1932
    from Mrs S C Carmack, Columbia, TN, states sol s/o Corne-
    lius, b 1732, res MD during RW, mvd to VA till all ch md,
    thence Overton Co, TN, to reside with s Cornelius & dd ae
    92 there 1824, further querier's h desc of sol bro Joseph
    who b 1768 & dd 1798, who had s Cornelius (1797-1851) who
    had s Francis M (1832-1861) who had s Sam Cornelius (1856-
    1925) & s Edward Ward (1858-1908). R471
  John, esf 1774 Washington Co, VA, where mvd with f 1773 from
    Frederick Co, VA, where b; afp 1832 Washington Co, VA, &
    PAR, svc less than 6 months. R471
  William, 1779 Washington Co, VA; b 1/5/1761; PN 1832 Lee Co,
    VA; dd 9/24/51; QLF 1913 from Luther Ambrose, Berea, KY,
    states a William Carmack bc 1735 England, esf Lee Co, VA,

CARMACK (continued)
     PN 1834 ae 73, f/o Levi who f/o Isaac who f/o Isabelle who
     m/o querier; QLF 1913 from Myrtle Wilson, Berea,KY, states
     above Isabelle Carmack Ambrose also m/o Ida Ambrose Wilson
     who m of this querier; QLF 1913 from Florence A Rowland
     Major, KY, states Isabelle Carmack Ambrose also m of Flo-
     rence Ambrose Rowland who m of Lester Rowland Major; QLF
     1913 from Dudley Roberts, gds/o Isabelle Carmack Ambrose &
     s/o Nellie Ambrose Roberts. R471
CARMAN, Nathaniel, esf Monmouth Co, NJ, early in RW; lost at
     sea 1807 en route from New Orleans, LA, to Philadelphia,
     PA; md 10/20/1782 Elizabeth Braten, Monmouth Co, NJ, where
     she b; wid afp ae 89 Brooke Co, VA, 1853 & PAR, md before
     sol 1st term/o svc & insufficient proof of svc; 9 ch with
     John 1st who b 1783-4 & dd ae 2; s David of Washington Co,
     PA, AFF ae 57 Brooke Co, VA, 1853 that family bible lost
     in fire when m res Jefferson Co, OH, 1811; AFF 1853 by sol
     bro Jehilah, Brooke Co, VA, he b Monmouth Co, NJ; surname
     at times spelled CARNAN. R472
CARMICHAL, John, see CARMICKELE, John. R472
CARMICHAEL, Thomas, see CARMICLE, Thomas. R472
CARMICKELE, John, esf 1777 Lancaster Co, PA; b 8/7/1757 Chest-
     er Co, PA; family to Lancaster Co, PA, when he ch; to Cum-
     berland Co, PA, for 10 years, thence Berkeley Co, VA for 5
     years, thence Montgomery Co, VA, for 15 years, thence New-
     port Cocke Co, TN, where PN 1832; res 1836 Carroll Co, GA,
     then known as John CARMICHAEL Sr to join ch; QLF 1938 from
     desc Beatrice (Mrs Burton W) Wands, Los Angeles, CA, who
     also desc of Benjamin Johnson Radford, RW sol who mvd to
     Christian Co, KY, c1817; QLF 1935 from desc Aurelia B Cate
     of Seaford, DE, states sol dd 1835. R472
CARMICLE, Thomas, esf 1778 Lancaster Co, PA; bc 1762; PN 1835
     Montgomery Co, VA; QLF 1939 from Mrs Burton Wands, above,
     states Benjamin Johnson Radford s/o John & w Jane of Buck-
     ingham Co, VA, who md 1767, R472
CARNALL, Patrick, esf 1778 Caroline Co, VA, where b; PN there
     1832 ae 73; PN Office letter states a James Carnal/Carneal
     had wid Mary M, who PN ae 78 Caroline Co, VA, 1871 & dd c
     9/2/1875; QLF mns a James Carnal who esf Essex Co, VA, for
     War of 1812, gtd BLW, res Caroline Co, VA, 1853 ae 73, dd
     there 3/11/1862, md 5/12/1812 Mary M Chapman. R473
CARNES, John, BLW issued 12/13/1791. R473
     Joshua, esf Drummonds, Stafford Co, VA; md there 1797 Catha-
     rine Randall (MB dated 12/7/97, signed by William Randall)
     & dd 5/11/1832 Charles Co, MD; wid dd there 8/1838 ae 65;
     s William R ae 41 afp there 1855 for himself & sis Frances
     E ae 51 who w/o John Crampsey also res there, & PAR. R473
     Patrick, esf VA; sol left wid, s Patrick (dd unmarried & in-
     testate c1808), & s Benjamin Smith (dd 9/1812 Charleston,
     SC; Benjamin LWT left estate to cousins Maria Lance, Eli-
     za Smith Frazer & Jane W Frazer, & mentioned Caroline Fra-
     zer & William Frazer, testator then res St Paul's Parish,

CARNES (continued)
Colleton District, SC; William Lance exec of sol LWT; BLW issued 1839 to Eliza Smith Frazer, Bordentown, NJ. R473
CARNEY, John, esf 1776 Botetourt Co, VA; b 4/15/1757 Frederick Co, VA; PN 1832 Jennings Co, IN. R473
Patrick, BLW issued 11/2/1792. R473
Thomas, afp ae 69 Lewis Co, VA; many court witnesses stated Thomas too young to be RW sol, labeling him "a man of bad character"; PAR, by evidence of age; this man one of several who apf in Lewis Co & afp found to be fraudulent. R473
William, esf 1781 Loudoun Co, VA; PN aec 60 there 1818 when crippled; PN increase ae 67 there 1820 when w Rosanna ae 60; dd 3/3/23; md 8/1784 Rosanna who PN 1839 ae 77 there; ch mbnn. R473
CARNINE, Andrew, see CONINE, Andrew. R473
Jeremiah, BLW issued 12/27/1794, see CONINE, Jeremiah; QLF from 1905 from gds J C Conine, Yelm, WA, states sol esf Berkeley Co, VA, & afp 1825 Richland Co, OH. R473
CARPENTER, Amos, esf 1776 Greenbrier Co, VA; PN ae 77 Scipio Township, Meigs Co, OH, 1832; dd 3/31/37 Columbia Township that Co; md (1) Caufel Bickle & (2) 2/18/1803 Margaret Mc-Glaughlin, West Fork Settlement, Harrison Co, VA; wid PN ae 76 Columbia Township, Meigs Co, OH, 1853, when s Jeremiah (1 of 3 ch) res there; also then Margaret Bickle ae 85 res Rutland,OH, AFF her h bro/o sol 1st w, further Margaret raised Randolph Co, VA; QLF 1927 from great gdd Mrs Ethel Curtis, Portland, IN; QLF states sol wid's d Nancy Carpenter Lotz. R474
Benjamin, esf 1777 Amherst Co, VA, where b 3/1/1755; to East TN 1790, thence West TN, thence IL where PN 1832 Schuyler Co; dd 6/12/40. R474
Christopher, BLW issued 4/21/1796. R474
David, svc in Indian Wars after 1785; afp Lewis Co, VA, 1834 age alleged to be 72; claimed he became res/o Harrison Co, VA, 1776, but witnesses AFF he b 1768-1771; PAR, by evidence of age as being too young to have RW svc. R474
Jesse, PN 1831 Lewis Co, VA; name dropped from PN rolls 1835 as being too young to have RW svc; sol claimed 1834 ae 83, & 1835 ae 74; witnesses AFF he aec 12 in 1787. R475
John, esf 1777 VA; PN ae 56 Green Co, KY, 1818; w aec 55 in 1821; mvd 1827 to Monroe Co, IN, to be near ch; QLF 1902 from S M Price, Newark Co, OH, states he great great gds/o a John Carpenter who RW sol, gtd BLW, & res near Mt Vernon VA till 1781-2, thence to Washington Co, PA, thence to OH, & had w Susan, further querier great gds of VA RW sol William Morrison. R475
John, esf 1780 Botetourt Co, VA, where b 1764; PN 1832 Hackers Creek Settlement, Lewis Co, VA; name dropped from PN rolls 1835 as having been too young to have RW svc. R475
Samuel, esf 1780 Culpeper Co, VA, where b in area now Madison Co, s/o John; sol sub for bro John & esf later for bro Mike; dd 8/1825 or 10/1825 Madison Co,VA, near birthplace;

CARPENTER (continued)
  md 3/26/1793 Margaret "Peggy" Blankenbeker, Culpeper Co,
  VA; wid b 10/13/-14/1772, & PN 1854 Madison Co, VA; sol f
  bro/o Andrew, William & Michael who owned & operated grist
  mill in Culpeper Co, VA; AFF 1845 by Joseph Carpenter ae
  85 that he md sis/o sol wid; AFF 1856 by Hannah res Madison Co, VA, that she d/o Andrew Carpenter & cousin to sol,
  further she b 12/25/1767 near birthplace of sol & md a s/o
  Michael Carpenter; QLF 1926 from desc Miss Oreina Clore
  states sol later a minister. R476
 William, esf 1780 Amherst Co, VA, where b on Rockfish River
  3/19/1761-2; res there till ae 45 when mvd to Knox Co, TN,
  for 18-19 years, thence to Wayne Co, KY, where PN 1832; dd
  9/14/35 Adair Co, KY; md 1/9/1786 Mary/Polly Strickling/
  Stricklen, Augusta Co,VA; wid afp ae 72 Adair Co, KY, 1840
  & PAR, no proof of marriage; wid dd 10/20/46, leaving ch
  Rebecca Pratt, Susan Ore, Nancy Money & Mary w/o McFarland
  Cantabury (she ae 39 in 1840, res/o Adair Co, KY); heirs
  afp 1855, & PAR; QLF 1924 from Mattie A (Mrs Owen) Carpen-
  ter, Covington, KY, states her gdd Roberta Adams Carpenter
  was desc/o sol, further sol & his f William Sr were Luthe-
  ran ministers, further sol f also RW sol who md Mary d/o
  Adam Wilhoite, further sol William Jr md Mary/Polly Aylor.
  R476
CARPER, John, esf 1780, b Frederick Co,VA; PN ae 73 Montgomery
  Co, VA; 1830 when w "aged"; dd 2/8/41; QLF 1929 from desc
  Florence Carper, La Grange, IL, who also desc/o RW sol Ba-
  sil Foster of MD or PA. R477
CARR, George, esf 1774 Wythe Co, VA; b 10/28/1746 NJ; mvd 1778
  to TN settling near Jonesboro where esf 1780; after RW res
  GA, TN, & MO; PN 1833 Cooper Co, MO, res of Morgan Co, MO.
  R477
 Gideon, esf 1778 Albemarle Co, VA, where b 11/5/1752; mvd 10
  years after RW to Dickson Co, TN, where PN 1833 when bro
  Meekins res Albemarle Co,VA; QLF states sol res ae 90 with
  John B Carr 1840, Dickson Co, TN; QLF states sol dd there
  1847. R477
 Hezekiah, esf 1780 Petersburg, VA, for svc as drummer in MD
  regiment; PN ae 54 Washington, DC, 1818; PN increase ae 58
  Chesterfield Co, VA, 1822, when family w Edith Parsons ae
  45 & ch: Joseph ae 11, Rachel ae 10, Caroline ae 8 & Deli-
  lah ae 3; dd c12/20/1823; md 1790 Edith Parsons Raglin (MB
  dated 9/22/90 signed by Joseph Raglin), Amelia Co, VA; wid
  PN ae 67 Chesterfield Co, VA, 1841; wid AFF 1851 Richmond,
  VA. R477
 James, BLW issued 7/7/1792. R477
 James, esf 1776 Berkeley Co, VA; b 1756 Ireland; to America
  with f, settled Newcastle,DE, for 5 years thence to Berke-
  ley Co, VA; after RW to PA for 2 years, to Berkeley Co, VA
  for c14 years, to Henry Co, KY, for c24 years, to Scott Co
  KY for c11 years, thence Johnson Co, IN, where PN Franklin
  Township 1833; QLF states sol there 1840 & dd there. R477

CARR, James, esf 1776 while res with f Washington Co, VA; b
Craven, SC (clerk error?, should be NC), 10/6/1764, & to
Washington Co, VA, 1775; res after RW there till 1784 when
mvd to Sumner Co, TN, thence to KY for 4 years; thence
Franklin Co, AL, 1820 where PN 1833, afp being made Sum-
ner Co, TN; res 1839 Franklin Co, AL, where mvd from Murry
Co, TN, to be near ch; dd 8/25/40; w mbnn; sol bro Richard
AFF 1833 Sumner Co, TN, who b 9/1766. R477
John, esf before 1776 Prince William Co, VA; afp ae 61 there
1818 while res Fairfax Co, VA; PN ae 72 Prince William Co,
VA, 1831 when no family liv with him. R478
John F, esf 1780 near Charlottesville, Albemarle Co, VA; esf
again 1781 as sub for Walter Carr; b 11/12/1764; PN 1832
Cedar Creek, Maury Co, TN; a Mr Carr sol lawful heir 1850;
QLF states sol md Elizabeth "Polly" Meekins, & their ch:
Nancy 1790 w/o Allan Jones, s Anderson later res Memphis,
TN, & other d's. R478
Meekins, esf 1780 Albemarle Co, VA, where b 8/30/1762; PN
there 1833. R478
Moses, esf 1780 Franklin Co,NC; b near Dumfries, Prince Wil-
liam Co, VA; PN aec 90 Franklin Co, NC, 1832; dd 3/6/41.
R478
Robert, esf 1780 Augusta Co, VA; b 1759 Ireland; mvd 1810 to
Franklin Co, IN; PN 1832 Marion Co,IN; dd 7/4/33; QLF 1909
from great gdd Marion Carr, Indianapolis, IN, states sol s
of David, who brought family to America 1762 & settled in
Chester Co, SC, where sol esf ae 17, further sol buried in
Marion Co, IN. R478
Solomon, esf 1776 Bute Co (now Franklin Co), NC; PN aec 60
Pitt Co, NC, 1818; dd 1/21/20; md 2/16?/1782 Sarah Owens,
Isle of Wight Co, VA; wid PN aec 76-77 Pitt Co, NC, 1843;
ch births: Polly 2/21/1783, Ferriby 3/27/85, John 8/3/04;
wid sis of Elisha who decd in 1843, when her bro Elias ae
85 there; AFF 1842 by wid sis Elizabeth there ae 68. R479
Thomas, esf 1781 Newtown, Berkeley Co, VA; esf 1791 Sinking
Creek, Washington Co, TN, for Northwest Indian War; dd Hanover Township, Butler Co, OH, c1837 & buried there at Ebenezer Church; md 4/11/1787 Ann/Anna Gates, Berkeley Co,
VA; wid gtd BLW ae 87 Butler Co, OH, 1855; wid afp there
1860 ae 94, & PAR, svc less than 6 months; AFF there then
by 7th s Samuel ae 53; sol bro/o James & John who both RW
svc from VA; QLF 1913 from gdd Ellen Carr Rogers, Toledo,
OH, states sol s/o Thomas, who also RW sol; QLF 1940 from
desc Z R Farmer, Washington, DC. R479
William, esf 1776 York District, SC; b 5/7/1744 Augusta Co,
VA; PN 1832 Hall Co, GA; dd 9/35 Benton Co, AL; md 10/1792
Elizabeth Denton, York District, SC; wid dd 9/16/1839 Benton Co, AL; ch included 1st ch Margaret b 5/2/1793, & Hugh
b 4/27/97 who adm/o m's estate, & he applied ae 48 for sis
Margaret & self for PN due m, & PAR; AFF 1845 by John, bro
of sol wid, Cherokee Co, GA; AFF by there then by Mrs Hannah Denton that she b 9/13/1781, & that her f James McCord

CARR (continued)
    dd 7/25/1793; sol surname at times spelled KERR. R479
  William, esf 1776 VA; PN ae 73 Knox Co, TN, 1823; twice md;
    in 1823 2nd w, d Elizabeth ae 22, & d Rebecca aec 10 res
    with him; other ch mbnn; dd 11/5/24. R479
CARRANCE, William, esf Taggarts Valley, VA, where res since
    1774; b PA; afp ae 70 Randolph Co,VA, 1834; PAR, less than
    6 months svc. R479
CARRICK, Patrick, esf 1776 Norfolk, VA; PN ae 68 Washington,
    DC; res there 1820 ae 70. R480
CARRINGTON, Clement, esf VA; PN 1828 Charles City Co, VA. R480
  Edward, esf 1776; dd 10/10/1810; md 12/8/1792, as her 2nd h,
    Mrs Eliza J Brent d/o Jacquelin Amber, Henrico Co, VA, (MB
    12/8/1792); wid PN ae 74 Richmond,VA, 1839; her eldest sis
    wid/o Chief Justice Marshall; wid sis Lucy N, w/o Daniel
    McCall, made AFF 1839 Richmond, VA, as did George Fisher h
    of another of wid sis's. R480
  George, BLW issued 1/21/1800. R480
  Mayo, BLW issued 2/22/1799. R480
CARROL, Bartholomew, esf 1780 New London,VA; PN ae 96 Dearborn
    IN, 1818 where res 1820 when w Catharine ae 76; QLF 1937
    from desc Grace Hart (Mrs D J) Scott, Hammond, IN, states
    her great gdf Adam Carol/Carroll s/o sol & adm/o f estate,
    Johnson Co, IN, further Adam md 8/20/1812 Sarah Surnford,
    Harrison Co, KY, (MB signed by Elisha Surnford), further
    Elisha dd 1813, further a gds/o Adam still liv & his m was
    cousin to Charles Carroll of Carrolton, a signer of Decla-
    ration of Independence. R481
  William, esf 1781 Granville Co, NC, where res; b Fairfax Co,
    VA; PN aec 80 Lincoln Co, NC, 1832; dd 12/26/1835; md Ke-
    ziah, Granville Co, NC, 9/1777; wid PN aec 83 White Co, TN
    1844, & dd TN 2/9/1845; ch births: Jesse 11/19/1777, John
    8/3/79, Betsy 9/13/80, Elijah 4/7/81, Henry 2/26/83, Nancy
    9/178-; d Betsy Dover afp 1846 Cleaveland Co, NC; sol sur-
    name at times spelled CARRALL. R481
CARROLL, Berry, esf 1777 King & Queen Co, VA; PN ae 72 Essex
    Co, VA, 1818; sol orig PN as Perry Carroll, & error later
    corrected. R481
  Daniel, esf 1781 Albemarle Co, VA, where b 6/10/1765; mvd to
    Goochland Co, VA, thence Warren Co,TN, where PN 1834. R481
  David, esf 1777 on south branch of Potomac River, Yogohania
    Co, VA; PN ae 77 Allegheny Co, PA, 1838 when w a cripple;
    name dropped from PN rolls 1848, when shown to have insuf-
    ficient proof/o svc; surname at times spelled CARREL. R481
  John, esf c1778 Annapolis, MD; dd 12/1789; md 4/9/1789 Isa-
    bella Bowman, Halifax Co, VA; wid md (2) 5/1795 Samuel
    Smith, who dd 1843; wid PN ae 76 Halifax Co, VA, 1844 as
    former wid of sol; wid dd 11/6/44 there, leaving ch Nancy
    Younger, Thomas Smith, & Martha Sneed; d Nancy afp there
    1844, & wid ch gtd remainder of PN due wid. R481
  John, esf VA early in RW; b Mecklenburg Co, VA, where md Ann
    Crowder; sol dd 10/15/1832 Warren Co, NC, leaving wid Ann,

CARROLL (continued)
who dd there 12/25/44, leaving 1 ch Nancy; Nancy, w/o John
Patterson, afp 1852 Chatham Co, NC; PAR for insufficient
proof of svc. R481
Malachi, esf 1777 Princess Anne Co, VA; PN there 1832 ae 78.
R481
CARSON, John, esf 1780 Henry Co, VA; b 5/3/1761; mvd after RW
to KY, thence Rush Co, IN, 1829 where PN 1833 Noble Town-
ship; QLF states sol dd c1843, & md Polly Lewis. R482
Robert, esf 1776 Washington Co, VA; b 11/20/1753 on Green-
brier River near English's Ferry; mvd 1782 to Greene Co,
VA, thence Jefferson Co, TN, for 14 years, thence Blount
Co, TN, for 12 years, thence Warren Co, TN, where PN 1834;
QLF states sol w Mary/Polly Thompson, & sol buried Cannon
Co (area formerly part/o Warren Co), TN. R482
Thomas, see PERKINS, John. R482
Thomas, esf 1776 Prince Edward Co, VA; PN ae 72 Butler Co,
KY; dd 1/18/40; QLF states sol b 2/18/1760, & md Anna Por-
ter. R482
William, esf Bedford Co (area later Campbell Co), VA; b 1748
Colerain, Ireland; to America 1764; PN 1834 Campbell Co,
VA; QLF 1937 from desc Mrs Valorie Guthridge McGuire, Wi-
chita, KS, states sol b 8/15/1748, & last PN payment 1838.
R482
CART, William, esf 1775 Northampton Co,VA; PN ae 69 Greenbrier
Co, VA, 1818 when w Catharine ae 68-9; res 1824 Gallia Co,
OH, with d Rachel w/o William Johnson & their ch Hannah ae
6 & Catharine ae 5; sol then had s George, s William & gdd
Nancy Cart; sol back to VA 1828 to be with ch; QLF 1926
from DAR re application of sol desc Mrs Mable Cart Hamil-
ton of Nebraska. R482
CARTER, Abraham, esf 1781 near Maysville, Buckingham Co, VA;
mvd 1820 to Yancey Co, NC, where afp Big Ivy 1850 ae 98;
PAR, insufficient proof of svc. R483
Arnold, esf 1778 Rockingham Co, VA; PN ae 74 Haray Township,
Holmes Co, OH, 1833. R483
Barnabas, esf c1777 VA; PN ae 71 Bardstown, Nelson Co, KY,
1827 when had w & 3 ch, & res KY 20 years; dd 8/24/41; md
10/15/1813 Rebecca Davis, Nelson Co, KY; wid PN ae 72 Ed-
ward Co, IL, 1841; wid res Wabash Co, IL, ae 74. R483
Charles, esf 1778 Granville Co, NC; b 4/19/1752 Goochland Co
VA; to GA after RW where PN 1832 Oglethorpe Co; res there
1840. R483
Charles, esf 1779-80 Powhatan Co, VA, where b 1762; PN 1833
McMinn Co, TN; QLF 1914 from desc Mrs W J Chambers, Tampa,
FL, who also desc/o RW sol William Moore, who res Roane Co
TN, 1840. R483
Charles, esf 1778 Dinwiddie Co, VA, where b 9/3/1762; after
RW to Mecklenburg Co, VA, for 40 years, thence Roane Co,
TN for 2 years, thence Smith Co, TN, where PN 1832. R483
Charles, esf 1777 Essex Co, VA, where reared; mvd to Cumber-
land Co, KY, 1810 where PN 1832 ae 74. R483

CARTER, David, esf 1774 Monongalia Co, VA; b 1758 eastern NJ;
    mvd to VA with parents as ch; esf 1777 Surry Co, NC, later
    taken POW; after RW res Pendleton District, SC, to 1825,
    thence Franklin Co, GA, where PN 1832; QLF 1934 from desc
    Edna Arnold (Mrs Z W) Copeland, Elberton GA. R483
  Henry, esf 1776 VA; b 6/25/1752 c18 miles from Fredericks-
    burg, VA; mvd to Barren Co, KY, c1801 where PN 1832; dd
    6/8/35. R484
  Henry, esf 1779 Albemarle Co, VA; PN ae 67 Stokes Co, NC,
    1829; dd 2/28/43; md 1785 Sarah White (MB dated 12/13/85,
    signed by Jesse White) Albemarle Co, VA; wid PN Stokes Co,
    NC, 1843 ae 72, when s John made AFF there sol ch births:
    John 10/8/1786, Elizabeth 12/28/88, Polly 11/9/90, Nancy
    3/21/94, Winston 2/15/98, Anderson 4/6/1801 & George Wash-
    ington 7/5/04; s George W appointed guardian of m there in
    1844; wid res there 1848 ae 78; AFF there 1829 by s Ander-
    son. R484
  Henry, esf 1777 Culpeper Co, VA; PN ae 67 Gallatin Co, KY;
    res 1820 Owen Co, KY, where dd 5/23/43; md 12/24/1783 Nan-
    cy Edwards, Culpeper Co, VA, where she b 1760; wid PN 1843
    Owen Co, KY, & dd there 11/15/44, leaving ch who gtd rest
    of PN due m: Henry, Andrew ae 44, Mary/Polly ae 58-9 w/o
    John Bibb, Elizabeth, Dicie w/o Moses Devore, Lucinda w/o
    John Bates, & Malinda/Milindy w/o Robert Sanders; in 1820
    sol mns gds Jefferson Carter ae 8 & gdd Kitty Carter ae 4,
    then res with him Owen Co, KY. R484
  Henry, esf c1780 Albemarle Co, VA, where b; mvd 1781 to Har-
    rold's Station (now Harrodsburg), KY, where svc in Indian
    Wars 1793-4, thence Bowman's Station, Mercer Co,KY, thence
    Smith's Station, KY, thence Fayette Co, KY, where more svc
    in Indian Wars 1795; afp ae 78 Washington Co, IN, 1843, &
    PAR, since RW svc less than 6 months. R484
  Hugh, esf 1777 Winchester, VA; b 1751 Chester Co, PA; mvd to
    Blount Co, TN, after RW for 8 years, thence Greene Co, TN,
    where afp 1834; PAR, svc not in truly military unit; QLF
    1836 from s Hugh Jr, Greeneville, TN. R484
  Hudsey, esf 1779 VA; afp 1830 when blind & PAR; afp again ae
    88 Buckingham Co, VA, 1833, & PN. R484
  James, esf 1781 Mecklenburg Co, VA, where b 11/13/1763; PN
    1832 Chatham Co, NC, when family w Mary aec 60 & ch: John
    ae 27 (deranged), William ae 18, Mary ae 23, Elizabeth ae
    20, & Amy ae 12; sol res there 1836. R484
  James, esf VA early in RW; PN ae 73 Northampton Co, VA, 1832
    & also gtd BLW. R484
  James, esf 1777 Leesburg, Loudoun Co,VA; b 11/12/1759 SC; to
    SC after RW where PN 1833 Pickens District. R484
  James, esf 1777 Winchester, Frederick Co, VA, where mvd aec
    9; b 2/1756 Chester Co, PA; mvd to Warren Co, OH, thence
    Clermont Co, OH, where PN 1833 Wayne Township; dd that Co
    6/6/41; md 9/1826 Eleanor, who b 11/13/1776; wid afp 1843,
    & PAR, md after PN law date; sol s Joshua AFF ae 28 there
    then. R484

CARTER, James M, see McCARTER, James. R484
   John, esf 1779 Edgefield District, SC, where mvd from VA aec
      10; colonel in War of 1812 & dd in svc c3/1815; md Eliza-
      beth when she ae 17 near Big Horse Creek, that District,
      where she b; wid PN ae 75 there 1838; wid decd in 1852, &
      surv ch Charles B, Rudolph, & others mbnn; QLF states sol
      md Elizabeth/Betsy Wise. R485
   John, esf 1776 Caroline Co, VA, where b; PN there 1832 ae 75
      where always res. R485
   John, esf 1779 Buckingham Co, VA; PN ae 72 Bedford Co, VA,
      1830 when family w ae 62, d ae 28, & s Lawson. R485
   John, esf VA; dd 1803-06 Albemarle Co, VA; md Mourning Bond
      11/13/1794 Fluvanna Co, VA; wid afp ae 87 Talladaga Co, AL
      1857, & PAR for proof of marriage; wid also afb then & gtd
      BLW; AFF then by youngest ch Charles ae 54 there. R485
   John B, esf Cumberland Co,VA; PN 1832 ae 82 Woodford Co, KY;
      dd 2/2/39; md 12/9/1775 Elizabeth d/o Edward & Martha Mos-
      by; wid b 7/12/1748, & PN 1840 Woodford Co, KY; ch births
      from ink-blotched & faded family bible: John 3/4/1777, Ed-
      ward 4/14/79, Patsey 3/3/80, Jeen 6/14/8-, Mary 1783, Su-
      sanah 12/18/87, Elizabeth 4/7/90, Benjamin Richard Mosby
      10/3/91, some unreadable, Povall? 10/12/95, Nancy 3/30/98.
      R485
   John Champ, BLW issued 8/26/1789; QLF gives following data:
      John Carter b 12/18/1761, dd 8/28/1820, md 2/14/1795 Anne
      Matilda Wray of Yorktown, VA, further John Carter b 1728,
      dd 1792, md Jane Michelle who b 1742 & dd 1791. R485
   Joseph, esf 1777 Northumberland Co, VA; PN ae 72 Washington
      Co, KY, 1832; QLF 1930 from desc Joseph N Wilson, Raywich,
      KY, an SAR member, states sol b 12/20/1760 & dd 8/20/1846
      Washington Co (area now Marion Co), KY; QLF states sol s/o
      Thomas; QLF states sol md (1) Jenny Shelton, & md (2) 1792
      Nancy Ann Winlock; QLF 1910 from desc Miss Margaret Beall
      Wilson, Lebanon, KY; QLF 1894 from gdd Miss Sara Carter,
      Lebanon, KY; QLF states sol from Lancaster Co or Stafford
      Co, VA. R486
   Joseph, esf 1776 Norfolk Co, VA; PN 1818 Portsmouth, VA, ae
      65; dd there 1825-6; md (2) 11/23/1821 Lucy Bullock who PN
      ae 47 Norfolk Co, VA, 1854, when AFF by sol s Edward ae 66
      & AFF by sol gds Joseph Carter ae 44. R486
   Landon, esf 1776 VA; PN ae 70 Stokes Co, NC, 1827, when liv
      him d Margaret aec 33, d Lucy aec 30 & her h; dd 9/5/38;
      ch gtd remainder of PN due him 1839. R486
   Martin, esf 1778 Goochland Co, VA, where b; PN ae 70 Mercer
      Co, KY, 1832. R486
   Nicholas, esf 1777 VA; PN ae 65 Nelson Co, VA, 1820; PN in-
      crease there 1830 when too infirm to come to court, & pe-
      tition presented by bro Barnabas Carter ae 79; sol then
      had aged w & one d. R486
   Obadiah, esf 1775 VA; PN ae 63 Lexington Co, KY, 1818; dd
      7/28/20; md 3/13/1781 Judith, who PN ae 84 Scott Co, KY,
      1838; d Judy b 1/22/1789; d Elizabeth b 10/7/1800; family

CARTER (continued)
    bible data presented in court 1838 by sol gds George Oba-
    diah Alsop: Spencer Alsop md Judith Carter 1/22/1809, John
    Hudson md Betsy Carter 11/28/1820, William H Smith md Emi-
    ly W Alsop 12/27/1831, George C Alsop md Catharine Green-
    up 2/26/1833, William B Shirley md Elizabeth D Alsop
    1/11/1835, James E Alsop md Sarah A Miller 8/20/1838, Sa-
    rah A Miller b 10/28/1820, Judith Carter Seigencourt
    b 11/18/1755, Spencer Alsop b 6/12/1785, Judith Alsop b
    1/22/1789, Eloisa Ann Alsop b 10/26/1809, Emily Watts Al-
    sop b 7/31/1811, George Obadiah Alsop b 4/21/1813, Sary
    Alsop b 2/21/1816, James Elliott Alsop b 2/19/1817, Eliza-
    beth D Alsop b 1/27/1819, Spencer Washington Alsop b
    7/3/1821, David H Hudson b 1/28/1821, Judith A Hudson b
    9/5/1822, John Obadiah Hudson b 4/27/1824, Elizabeth C
    Hudson b 11/30/1838, Elizabeth Carter b 10/7/1800, Eloisa
    Ann Alsop dd 2/15/1815, Mary Jane Alsop dd 3/6/1816, Spen-
    cer Alsop dd 9/13/1829, Elizabeth, w/o John Hudson, dd
    11/30/1834. R486
Philip, esf 1780 as sub for bro James, Halifax Co, NC, where
    b late 1760; mvd to Halifax Co, VA, 1806, where PN 1833;
    dd 7/16/35; md 6/12/1783 Sarah Gunn; wid PN ae 84 Halifax
    Co, VA, 1840; ch births: Polly Davis 3/11/1784, Thomas
    12/17/85, Sally 2/10/87, Bradley 3/17/89, Patsey 10/18/92,
    & Levi B 2/10/1800; other family bible data: Thomas Carter
    md 6/23/1804 Catey Carter who b 2/4/1787, Dudley Gunn b
    1/1792, James Carter b 11/1820, Benjamin Peary b 1820, ?
    Lowell Pery, his w Polley b 2/1803. R486
Philip, esf c1780 as sub for f John, Spotsylvania Co, VA,
    where b; PN 1832 Barren Co, KY; younger bro John. R486
Povall, esf 1779 Powhatan Co, VA; b 1762 Cumberland Co (now
    Powhatan Co), VA; PN 1832 Prince Edward Co, VA. 486
Robert, esf 1776 Hanover Co, VA; PN 1833 Clarke Co, GA, ae
    75; QLF 1938 from Mrs Ella Carter Eberhart, Cornelia, GA.
    R486
Samuel, esf 1777 Albemarle Co,VA; mvd 1778 to Fairfield Dis-
    trict, SC, where again esf; mvd 1795-6 to Rutherford Co,
    NC, thence Haywood Co,NC, 1810, thence Sevier Co, TN, 1813
    thence Blount Co, TN, thence Monroe Co, TN, where PN ae 78
    in 1832. R487
Thomas, esf 1777 VA; PN 1818 Lancaster Co, VA; QLF states a
    Thomas Carter b1734, md Winifred Hobson 7/10/1764, dd at
    "Greenrock", Pittsylvania Co, VA, further he sold land in
    Lancaster Co, VA, & mvd with bro Jesse to land inherited
    from f in Cumberland Co, VA, where he md & res till 1783
    when purchased "Greenrock"; QLF gives more data on latter
    Thomas who md eldest d of Adcock Hobson & Joanna Lawson,
    further ch/o Thomas & Winifred: Joanna, Elizabeth, Sarah,
    Edward, Thomas Jr, Jeduthan, Lawson Hobson, Christopher
    Lawson, Dale Miller, Raleigh Williamson, & Jesse; QLF mns
    a Joseph Rogers who dd Pittsylvania Co, VA, where res, md
    Elizabeth & they had ch: Polly Cosins, Elizabeth Nelson,

CARTER (continued)

Josiah, Frances (md 1782 James Soyars), William, Stephen, Reuben, & Rebecca. R487

Thomas, esf 177- Halifax Co, VA; b MD, & mvd to Fauquer Co, VA, as ch & left orphan; PN ae 86 Rockingham Co, VA, 1832. R487

Thomas, esf 1780 VA; PN ae 55 Knox Co, TN, 1818; dd 7/5/22; md 8/9/1784 Betsey, King & Queen Co, Va; wid b 8/4/1762, & PN 1846 Roane Co, TN; in 1789 ch Polly , Calep; ch later Legroy & another mbnn; in 1820 ch d ae 16 & s ae 14. R487

Thomas, esf 1779 as surgeon's mate; surgeon, Corps of State Cavalry, 1780; dd 1800, wid surv only a few months; ch liv 1832: James Brodnax, John Michell, Rebecca Brodnax Carter Stanard, Jane Maria, & Lucy Gray Edmunds, w/o William B Boyd, she res 1850 Medon, Madison Co, TN; 1/2 pay PN gtd to sol ch 1832; QLF 1908 from desc Miss Eliza Spence Norbury, Beardstown, IL, who also desc of RW sol David Spence of Surry Co, NC; QLF states sol from Williamsburg, VA; QLF states BLW issued to sol 8/6/1783. R487

Thomas, whose wid Judith afp for svc of her former h Thomas Palmer of VA Sea Svc. R487

William, esf 1778 Albemarle Co, VA, where b 4/21/1760; mvd to Burks Co, NC, 1780 & esf there; res there after RW for c10 yeare, thence Greenbrier Co, VA (area now Monroe Co), VA; PN 1833 Monroe Co, VA; sol & w liv 1838. R487

William, esf 1776 Pittsylvania Co (area now Patrick Co), VA; b 5/17/1761 on Staunton River, Campbell Co, VA; PN Patrick Co, VA, 1833, & dd there 12/17/45; md 1/31/1788 Susanna; wid b 5/12/1770, PN 1847 Patrick Co,VA, gtd BLW there 1855 & dd 2/4/57; ch: Archelaus H & Madison D res 1847 Hillsville, VA; s Madison D heir-at-law of m, Carroll Co, VA, 1857; sol younger brother Silas. R487

William, esf 1781 Chester Co, PA, where b 5/22/1748; mvd to Loudoun Co, VA, after RW where res 30-40 years, thence OH, thence Clinton Co, IN, where PN 1834; QLF states sol dd in Wayne Co, IN; QLF 1933 from Dr F R Nicholas Carter, South Bend, IN; QLF states sol res Butler Co, OH, before mvd to IN, further sol dd 9/21/1840 & buried near Frankfort, IN, further sol had several sons including Jesse who also buried near Frankfort, Clinton Co, IN. R487

William, esf Albemarle Co, VA; b 10/17/1758; PN 1832 Patrick Co, VA; dd 10/9/33; md 1/1782 Martha, Albemarle Co, VA, & she PN aec 77 Patrick Co, VA, 1842; ch births, all b Albemarle Co, VA: Alexander 1784, Elizabeth 1786, Nancy 1788, Milly 1790, & William 1792; AFF by sol bro Henry, Stokes Co, NC, 1840; AFF then by sol gds Alexander B Clark. R487

William, esf Amherst Co, VA, where b 8/2/1760; to Carter Co, TN, 1802, thence Washington Co, KY, thence OH Co, KY, 1805 where PN 1832; dd c10/14/42; md 1/7/1809 or 1/15/11 Sarah Williams, Breckenridge Co, KY; wid PN ae 74 Ohio Co, KY, 1853; QLF 1896 from gdd Armanda A (Mrs J M) Greenwood, Kansas City, MO, states sol dd 12/1841 & wid dd c1865, wid

CARTER (continued)
   b MD, also sol & w res P O Fordsville, Ohio Co, KY. R487
CARTMILL, Henry, esf 1779 Botetourt Co, VA; b Chester Co, PA,
   & family mvd to Augusta Co, VA, when he ch; family c1761
   to Botetourt Co, VA; PN there 1832 as Henry Sr. R488
CARTRIGHT, Robert, see CARTWRIGHT, Robert. R488
CARTWRIGHT, Jesse, see CARTWRIGHT, Justinian. R488
   Justinian, esf 1776 Amherst Co, VA; b 2/22/1752; PN Caldwell
      Co, KY, 1819 where mvd from Amherst Co, VA, c1782; md 1777
      Frances Gillespie who dd in late 1818; sol dd Caldwell Co,
      KY, 12/27/32; surv ch 1846: James A (Caldwell Co), Polly M
      w/o Elisha Thurman (Livingston Co,KY), Bennett G (res MS),
      Nancy S (Caldwell Co), Levin L (res MS), Justinian, Winne-
      fred (Caldwell Co), Sally w/o Leonard Brown (Caldwell Co),
      & Terresa w/o Tutt Brown; QLF 1917 from A J Cartwright,
      San Francisco, CA. R488
   Peter, esf 1777-8 Amherst Co, VA; mvd to KY 1791, where dd
      Caldwell Co 1809-10; md 1787 Christina Garven (MB 2/27/87
      signed by William Cartwright), Amherst Co, VA; wid dd at
      res of Sophia Wilcox 12/23/1838 Caldwell Co, KY, leaving s
      Rev Peter; d Rosanna Vineyard & d Polly Pentecost dd be-
      fore m; s Peter afp ae 64 Sangamon Co, IL, 1852, & PAR for
      insufficient proof of svc; 2 of sol bro's KIA in Battle of
      Brandywine; QLF states sol w Christine Garvin. R488
   Robert, esf c1779 Camden Co, NC, for svc in VA or NC troops,
      where b & reared; dd 4/1816 or 4/1818, Davidson Co, TN; md
      10/1784 Susannah Spence, Camden Co, NC, where she b; wid
      afp ae 74 Williamson Co, TN, 1839, & PAR for insufficient
      proof/o svc; wid dd there 10/15/50, leaving s David (2nd
      ch who ae 64 there 1853), & s John; in 1853 Mrs Elizabeth
      Cartwright referred to wid as her m-in-law; sol sis Eliza-
      beth Pritchard made AFF 72 Davidson Co, TN, 1839, & liv ae
      85 in 1853. R488
CARUTHERS, Elizabeth, former wid/o William Richardson. R489
   James, esf 1778 Augusta Co, VA; b 4/5/1760 Chester C, PA; to
      Augusta Co, VA, with parents when ae 10; PN 1833 Blount Co
      TN when res there c30 years; dd 1/13/46; md 1806 Margaret
      Jackson, Staunton, Augusta Co, VA; wid b 6/1/1769; wid PN
      1853 Blount Co, TN. R489
CARVER, James, esf 1780 Bedford Co, VA; b 11/1753 Louisa Co,
      VA; PN 1832 Madison Co, KY, where then res c40 years. R489
   Richard, esf 1st as sub for f James, Bedford Co,VA; esf 1781
      Washington Co, VA; b Albemarle Co, VA, & mvd to Bedford Co
      ae 12; mvd c1792 Spartanburg District, SC, for 20 years,
      thence Pendleton District (area now Pickens Co), SC; PN
      1833 Pickens Co, SC. R489
CARWILL, Zachariah, esf 1775 Prince William Co,VA; b 9/11/1750
      (old style date) Goochland Co, VA; to TN after RW, thence
      SC where res Spartanburg, Laurens, & Abbeville Districts;
      PN 1832 Abbeville District, SC; name at times spelled CAR-
      WILE; QLF 1936 from desc Mrs Lillian C Martin, Memphis, TN
      R489

CARY, Samuel, esf VA; afp 1850 by John N Carey, adm of sol estate 1850, seeking 1/2 pay PN due sol; PAR, already paid; sol surname at times spelled CAREY. R490

William, esf 1777 Chesterfield Co, VA, where b 4/14/1756; to Claiborne Co, TN, 1808, thence to Cumberland Co, KY, 1829 where PN 1832. R490

CASADAY, James, esf Halifax Co,VA, where b 1760; PN 1844 Charlotte Co, VA, having mvd there from Patrick Co, VA; QLF mns a James Cassidy, b Halifax Co, VA, who RW sol & w Mary whose s William KIA Battle of Brandywine. R491

CASBER, Jonathan, esf 1776 Sussex Co, NJ; mvd to Chambersburg where esf 1777; mvd to Yogohania Co, VA, where esf 1778; b near Philadelphia, PA; b 5/12/1752; PN 1838 Allegheny Co, PA. R491

CASE, John, see 2nd William Case below. R492

William, esf 1776 Winchester, VA; b 1753; POW, paroled & returned to f's res Redstone Settlement, PA, & svc against indians; PN 1820 Washington Co, IN, where dd 11/1/27; md 3/29/1798 Rebecca Glover, Shelby Co,KY; wid PN ae 69 Brown Township, Washington Co, IN; ch in 1821: James ae 21, Squire ae 18, Malinda ae 15, Hannah ae 13, Washington ae 11, Betsy ae 9, Ruth ae 7, Sally ae 5, Uriah ae 3 & Rebecca ae 1 1/2; s William mentioned; QLF 1921 from desc Katherine Duncan Rainbolt, Bedford, IN; QLF 1913 from great great gdd Miss Della Miller, McCune,KS, states sol b 1755, dd near Campbellsburg, IN, & wid dd there 11/16/1863; QLF states sol buried Trimble's Cemetery, Orange Co, IN. R492

William, esf VA; afb Accomac Co, VA, 1831 by Sabra A Case, heir-at-law to m Betty Case who only heir-at-law to RW sol William Case & RW sol John Case; BLW gtd. R492

CASEY, Archibald, esf Chesterfield Co, VA; PN there 1818 ae 62 R493

Charles, esf 1780 Chesterfield Co, VA, where b 1749; mvd to Clark Co, KY, 1795 for 1 year, thence Shelby Co, KY, where PN 1834; George W Casey his heir-at-law 1853; surname also spelled CAYCE. R493

Edward, esf 1776 Bedford Co, VA; PN ae 69 Amherst Co, VA, 1820 when family w ae 44 & ch: Edmund ae 7, Polly Caldwell ae 9 & Powhatan Bowling ae 2; res there 1822. R493

Jacob, esf 1776 for svc in MD & VA regiment; POW, paroled, & esf in PA regiment; PN ae 62 Franklin Co, OH, 1818; family in 1822 w aec 60, d aec 30, d aec 24, s aec 21, plus s res over 500 miles away. R493

James, esf 1777-8 Portsmouth, Norfolk Co, VA; PN aec 74 Isle of Wight Co, VA, 1832; dd before 1834-36; in 1861 s & heir John afp Nokomis, Montgomery Co, IL. R493

John, esf c1777 VA; raised in Culpeper Co, VA; esf Hillsborough, NC, 1779; PN ae 55 Casey Co, KY, 1818; res 1821 as widower Fayette Co, KY, with no family at home; res Franklin Co, KY, 1834; dd 7/10/38. R493

John, PN 1789 for disability & paid by VA agency; records lost in Washington, DC, fire 1800 & 1814. R493

CASEY, John, esf 1781 Prince William Co, VA; b 9/26/1763; PN
      1833 Davidson Co, TN; res there 1834. R493
   John, esf 1779 under ae 16 Amelia Co,VA; b Albemarle Co, VA;
      PN ae 69 Kanawaha Co, VA, 1833; dd ae 88 Mason Co, VA,
      1845; BLW issued 11/9/1784; md (1) Jean Bailey; md (2) Lu-
      cinda Miston; md (3) 5/26/1831 Mary Cox, Jackson, Jackson
      Co, OH; wid md (2) 1854-5 Jordan Luckadoo, a former slave,
      who gtd emancipation papers 1834 Albemarle Co, VA, when ae
      21; wid ch by 2nd h: Isaiah (ae 34 in 1887), Mathew & Ema-
      nuel; wid md Luckadoo in Jackson Co, OH; wid afp as former
      wid/o sol ae 68 Fayette Co, OH, 1878, & again ae 78 there
      1880; at this time only 1 RW sol wid living, & that lady
      ae over 100; much newspaper publicity when Mary Cox Casey
      attorney complained to government, & she PN 1887; that PN
      suspended when wid alleged to be living with former slave;
      however, Mary able to prove lawful marriage to Luckadoo, &
      PN resumed; both Mary & 1st h illiterate; many, many pages
      in this file & several old newpaper items; sol surname at
      times spelled CAISEY. R493
   Nicholas, esf 1781 Hampshire Co, VA, where b 11/17/1745; PN
      1832 Preston Co, VA; QLF 1914 from great gds John W Mason,
      Fairmont, WV. R493
   William, esf 1777 Southampton Co, VA, where b 1761; esf 1882
      Bute Co, NC; PN 1832 Warren Co, NC; dd 6/26/36; md 12/1786
      Mary/Polley Evans (MB 12/23/86), Mecklenburg Co, VA, who
      dd 9/14/1840, leaving ch: Thomas, Elizabeth, Peggy, Sally,
      Nancy, William, & Edmund; in 1845 s Edmund ae 42, adm of m
      estate, claimed for her ch PN due m, & PN gtd; QLF 1922
      from great gdd Mrs N B Prince, Odessa, MO; sol surname at
      times spelled KERSEY. R493
CASH, Bartlett, esf 1776 Amherst Co,VA, where b 12/18/1757; PN
      there 1832; dd 4/11/35; md 2/14/1781 Elizabeth b 1/15/1764
      & she PN there 1841; ch births: Joel 4/30/1783, Francess
      8/15/85, John 2/19/88, Willie 7/23/90, Mary 6/5/93, Nancy
      P 7/29/96, Henry W 3/5/1801, & William P 6/16/03 (md Eli-
      beth 12/3/1823); a Jefferson R Cash b 12/23/1825; ch of
      David & Nancy P Moore: William b 7/27/1822 & Bartlett b
      9/23/1823. R494
   James, esf 1780 Granville Co, NC; b 10/25/1764 Fairfax Co,
      VA; mvd after RW to Montgomery Co, NC, thence Franklin Co,
      GA, where PN 1832, Capt Vaughan's District; dd 7/3/1837;
      md 10/9/1783 Ann, Granville Co, NC; wid PN ae 75 Capt Tho-
      mas's District, Franklin Co, GA, 1839; sol sis mbnn res TN
      1832. R494
   John, esf Amherst Co, VA, where b 4/5/1757; to c1789 to Bed-
      ford Co, VA, thence 1802 to Elbert Co, GA, thence c1829 to
      Henry Co, GA, where PN 1832; dd 8/13/36; md 1/23/1782 Lucy
      Campbell, Amherst Co, VA, who b 3/3/1760; wid PN 1845 Pike
      Co,GA, & dd 1/23/48; ch: James b 11/6/1784 & dd 8/14/1848,
      Nancy ae 61 in 1853, Mary ae 52 in 1853, Stephen, Peter,
      William, & Innes. R494
   John, esf c1776 Amherst Co, VA, where b 2/1/1760; afp 1832

CASH (continued)
    Jackson Co, GA, where res 32 years; PAR, svc less than six
    months. R494
  Peter, esf 1780 Granville Co, NC; b 1756 Fairfax Co, VA; at
    ae 18 to Granville Co, NC, where PN 1832. R494
  Peter, esf Amherst Co, VA, with bro John & bro Howard, where
    b 5/21/1759; afp 1832 Henry Co, GA; PAR, svc less than six
    months. R494
  Warren, esf 1776 Albemarle Co,VA; b 4/4/1760; mvd to KY 1784
    where PN 1832 Hardin Co as Reverend; QLF states sol proba-
    bly b Culpeper Co, VA, drummer boy in svc ae 16, to Shelby
    Co, KY, after RW, dd 1849, md Susanna Baskit who b 1762 &
    dd 1842; QLF 1921 from Mrs R B Cash, El Dorado,AR, who re-
    quested data on sol for DAR membership; QLF states sol w
    Susanna Basket, further a William Cash, RW sol, dd c1837,
    Pulaski Co, KY, & md Dorothy Irwin. R494
  William, esf 1776 Spotsylvania Co, VA; b 1752 Westmoreland
    Co, VA; after RW to Wilkes Co, NC, thence c1811 to Pulaski
    Co,KY, where PN 1834 & where dd 6/14/37; md Dorothy/Dolly/
    Dorothea Irvin, Spotsylvania Co, VA; wid b 1759-60, & afp
    1840 & PAR for proof of marriage; ch: Larkin (res Clay Co,
    IN, 1843), Lewis (res Pulaski Co, KY, 1843), Waller (res
    MO 1843), Nancy w/o Perry Rush/Rash (res 1843 Pulaski Co,
    KY); James & William who both dd before m who dd 3/9/41-2;
    s James survived by ch: Jeremiah, Larkin, Rody w/o Willi-
    am Hare (?), Elizabeth, Christian, Pernina, & Richmond all
    res of Pulaski Co, KY, & Rachel w/o Hardy Long res TN; s
    William survived by ch John, Stephen, & Elizabeth w/o Le-
    muel Harris, all res Rockcastle Co, KY; births of ch of s
    Lewis & his w Mary: Wyley 7/3/1801, Eli 2/20/03, Nancy
    8/20/04, Elizabeth 8/2/06, Francis 3/6/08, Mary 11/2/09,
    Jesse 10/22/10, Dollah 8/16/12, William 4/16/14, & Lewis
    6/9/16; wid only surv heirs 1850 s Waller & s Lewis, who
    adm/o m estate Rockcastle Co, KY, then & afp; PAR since m
    not wid under current PN act & dd before 16 Aug 1842. R494
CASHIN, David, see CASHON, David. R494
CASHON, Burrel, esf 1777 Chesterfield Co, VA, where b 1758; to
    Mecklenburg Co, NC, 1800, where PN 1833 as Binwell CATHON;
    QLF 1933 from Blanche Cashon (Mrs J C) Caldwell, Charlotte
    NC. R494
  David, esf 1775 Chesterfield Co, VA, where b 5/13/1758; mvd
    after RW to Cabarras Co, NC, thence Iredell Co, NC, for 5
    years, thence Montgomery Co,TN, 1809, thence Sumner Co, TN
    1825, thence Weakley Co, TN, where PN 1832; dd 6/24/35; md
    Sally Harvell (MB 6/6/13 signed by David CASHION & Joel
    CASHION), Iredell Co, NC, per that Co Clerk certificate
    1853 (apparent error MB date, since PN record shows sol
    md 1788, & res TN 1813; wid dd 10/16/51 Weakley Co, TN
    leaving ch Eliza, Elizabeth, Pleasant, Martin, Sophia, Na-
    cy, Annis, Polly, Rebecca, David, Sintha, Emeline, & Pula-
    ska; s Pleasant afp as adm of m Sarah estate 1853, & PAR,
    claim submitted "subsequent to printed list 1852." R494

CASHON, Thomas, esf 1777 Chesterfield Co, VA, where b 1758; PN
1833 Mecklenburg Co, NC, where mvd 1800; 8 ch in 1802; dd
12/16/34 or 1/16/35; md 12/31/1780 Tabitha, Chesterfield
Co, VA; wid PN ae 81 Mecklenburg Co, NC, 1841, dd 6/12/44
leaving ch Jabez, Levi, Peter, & Thomas; afp by Jabez 1848
for any arrears due m. R494
CASHWELL, Henry, esf 1779 Amherst Co, VA, where b 10/1757; PN
there 1832. R494
  William, esf 1777 Amherst Co, VA, where b 2/1762; PN there
  1832; dd 6/9/47; md 11/1791 Betsey Penn, who PN there 1848
  ae 76. R494
CASNER, Adam, esf 1778 Cumberland Co, PA; b 8/10/1747 Germany;
to America with family of f 1764; res Franklin Co, PA, after RW; to Brooke Co, VA, 1814, where PN 1833, & res 1835.
R495
CASON, Edward, esf Hanover Co, VA, where res; b 1752 Spotsylvania, where PN 1832 & d there 3/13/34; md 1822 Ann F Allen, Louisa Co,VA; wid b 1/1785, & PN 1853 Hanover Co, VA;
wid res with d 1865 Henrico Co, VA, with P. O. address in
Richmond; sol sis-in-law Mrs Eliza M Hillman & her d Isabella P Hillman res 1854 Richmond, VA. R495
  James, esf 1777 Spotsylvania Co, VA; b 7/23/1758 Orange Co,
  VA; PN 1832 Jackson Co, TN; md 2/17/1785 Rebecca Smith, &
  she dd 9/8/36 Jackson Co,TN; ch births: Edward M 1/3/1805,
  Susan 1/1/90, Eliza S 10/17/1807; sol dd 7/12/42, leaving
  ch Edward M, Susannah, & Eliza S Cox; afp 1856 by Robert A
  Cox ae 23, adm/o sol estate, for any PN arrears. R495
  John, esf 1777 Spotsylvania Co, VA; PN ae 76 Anson Co, NC,
  1832. R495
  Thomas, esf 1780 Spotsylvania Co,VA; b 1762 Caroline Co, VA,
  where res till 1763 when family mvd to Spotsylvania Co,
  where sol res when PN 1832 Caroline Co; bro/o Edward; dd
  5/8/36; md 12/24/1784 Nancy, who PN ae 75 Harrison Co, KY,
  1839, when s John (b 10/15/1785) made AFF there; wid res
  there 1848 ae 84. R495
  William, esf 1776 Spotsylvania Co, VA; PN ae 72 there 1832;
  dd 11/14/1851; PN office letter 1850 indicates guardian of
  sol then Lewis A Boggs; QLF states sol mvd to MO & there
  PN, further a George Cason, War of 1812 sol, whose wid Maria E (Partlow) Cason PN in MO. R495
  William, esf VA; dd 3/1816; md 10/14/1782 Sally Beasley (MB
  10/11/1782), Buckingham Co, VA; wid dd there 10/30/1840 ae
  84, leaving ch: Fuqua, James, William, Hiram B, Mary Robertson, Mildred Woodall, Nancy Adcock, & Sarah Godrey; s
  Fuqua afp there 1/9/1841 for any PN due m, & PAR, insufficient proof of svc. R495
CASSADY, Michael, esf 1776 Berkeley Co, VA; mvd after RW to KY
where svc against indians; representative & senator, state
legislature, Mason Co, KY; dd 3/22/1829 Fleming Co, KY; an
"Irishman"; md 2/25/1795 Mary d/o Francis Evans, Mason Co,
KY; wid PN ae 79 Fleming Co, KY, 1851, & dd 2/1/56; large
family of ch mbnn; QLF 1933 from desc Mrs Emily Moore Da-

CASSADY (continued)
    vies, Humboldt, IL; QLF 1927 from desc J Cassidy Grimes,
    Cincinnati, OH. R496
CASSEL, Ralph, esf 1776 Newberry Co, SC; b VA; mvd to OH after
    RW thence IN 1839 where afp ae 79, Decatur Co; PAR for in-
    sufficient proof/o svc; surname also spelled CASSELL. R496
CASSETTY, Thomas, esf 1779 Botetourt Co, VA; b 9/9/1762 Augus-
    ta Co, VA, s/o Thomas who res Botetourt Co during RW; res
    after RW Franklin Co, VA, thence Jackson Co, TN, 1804; PN
    1832 Smith Co, TN; QLF 1935 from Mrs Marlin Cassetty Pull-
    ey, Oak Grove,LA, states Robert Casaty Jr heir/o sol. R496
CASSETY, Thomas, see CASSETTY, Thomas. R496
CASSIDY, Michael, see CASSADY, Michael. R496
CASSON, William, see CASON, William, dd 3/1816. R496
CASTLE, Bazle/Baswell, esf 1779 Fincastle Co (now Montgomery),
    VA; s/o Jacob who esf 1780; PN ae 73 Lawrence Co,KY, 1834;
    AFF by s John, Johnson Co, KY, 1851 that sol dd 10/8/1846,
    leaving no wid, & John only surv ch. R497
  Robert, enlisted in 1st or 5th VA Regiment as musician; POW
    Charleston, SC, for 2 years, escaped to Halifax, then re-
    turned to NY, where PN ae 76 New York, NY, 1832; dd there
    5/12/34; md there 1817 Charity Thompson, who PN ae 80 Or-
    ange Co, NY, 1853; wid gtd BLW 1855, Goshen, NY, where dd
    6/1855, willing BLW to bro, her only heir there; BLW taken
    back & voided, since wid dd before date/o issue; QLF 1905
    from Mrs Sadie C Gerow, Jersey City, NJ, gdd of sol wid.
    R497
  William, esf 1777 Winchester, VA; b 8/15/1750; mvd 1782 to
    NY & esf there; w & ch in Winchester, VA, when finished VA
    svc; PN 1818 Hurley, Ulster Co, NY, when family w & gdc, a
    boy ae 9; md VA during RW, w 3 months younger. R497
CASTLEBERRY, William M, esf near Augusta, GA, early in RW; b
    VA; res after RW Spartanburg District, SC, thence to Hop-
    kins Co, KY, where PN 1832 aec 77; QLF 1935 from Inez Cas-
    tleberry (Mrs Ernest) Mauldin, Gainesville, GA, a desc of
    Richard Castleberry who RW sol of Richmond Co, GA. R497
  Paul, see CASTLEBURY, Paul. R497
CASTLEBURY, Paul, esf 1777 Richmond Co, GA; b3/1/1761 on Tar
    River, VA, mvd as ch with parents to Orange Co, NC, thence
    to Newberry District, SC, thence Richmond Co, GA, where PN
    1832; dd 6/16/41 Spartanburg District, SC; md 2/15/1824
    Nancy Gillespie there; wid PN there 1855 ae 49, & dd there
    11/20/1865; ch (1) Sarah M b 11/14/1824 who md --- Pace &
    res 1857 Greenville District, SC, & res 1866 Pickens Co,
    SC, or Henderson Co,NC, (2) Tabitha b 4/5/1826, md William
    Stephens who drafted into Confederate army in Fall of 1862
    & dd 8/1863 Charleston, SC, wid res 1866 Spartanburg Dist-
    rict, SC, 4 ch under ae 8, (3) James A b 12/2/27, (4) Eli-
    zabeth J A b 10/7/29, (5) Winney b 4/13/32, md --- Marler,
    res 1865 Spartanburg District, SC, (6) Malinda b 2/17/34,
    md Charles Pearson who drafted into Confederate army 1864,
    & dd of disease in svc in VA 7/1864, wid & 6 ch under ae

CASTLEBURY (continued)
13 liv 1866, (7) Nancy Ann b 2/24/36, md --- King, she dd
12/1865 leaving 3 minor ch, (8) Rosey/Rosa b 12/28/37, md
Jackson Stephens who drafted into Confederate army 1863 &
dd of disease 7/1864 Richmond, VA, wid & 3 ch res Spartanburg District, SC, 1866, (9) Julia A, md --- Smith, res St
Clair Co,AL, some years before 1866, (10) Anderson, res St
Clair Co, AL, during Ciil War; in 1857 Richard Castleber-
ry, steps/o sol widow, res MS where mvd Fall of 1844; file
contains oaths/o allegiance of sol ch to US 1865; QLF 1913
from great gds Frank B Castleberry, Woodruff, SC. R497
CASEWELL, John, b on James River, Goochland Co, VA; mvd to
Charlotte Co, VA, where esf 1778; PN ae 68 (blind) Overton
Co, TN, 1832. R498
CATHON, Binwell, see CASHON, Burrel. R499
CATLETT, David, esf Frederick Co, VA; b near Dumfries, Prince
William Co, VA; mvd to Morgan Co, VA, c1810 where PN 1834
aec 78; dd 9/11/34; md 2/7/1783 Ann, who afp aec 73 Morgan
Co, VA, 1839, & PAR for proof of marriage; wid dd aec 74
10/21-26/1840; QLF 1918 from desc James E Catlett, Chicago
IL; QLF 1920 from desc Mrs Cecil R Gates, Morgantown, WV.
R499
   George, VA sea svc, esf VA 1776 in marines; dd 9/15/1814; md
   5/11/1798 Lucy Buckner, Caroline Co,VA; wid PN ae 75 there
   1848 & gtd BLW there 1855 ae 81; ch & heirs who afb, Port
   Royal, VA, 1832: William, George, Collin, Anna E, Harriett
   all claiming more bounty land since f an officer. R499
   Peter, svc in VA regiment; afp 1829 Covington, Campbell Co,
   KY, & gtd 5 years full pay in lieu of 1/2 pay PN for life;
   dd 5/18/31 there, LWT listing w Susan, no ch, & legatees
   Caleb Catlett & Elizabeth (Catlett) White, & LWT probated
   there 8/22/31; md 11/19/1789 Susannah, d/o RW officer Colonel Edward Meeks of NY, at 1st Baptist Church, New York,
   NY; wid afp ae 65 Boone Co, KY, 1839, & PAR, insufficient
   proof of svc; AFF 1839 by sol relative Thomas B Catlett,
   Scott Co, KY. R499
CATO, George, esf 1777 in VA regiment; discharged from svc at
Valley Forge for disability from disease; gtd PN as pauper
by MD 1810, when had w & 5 ch; afp ae 66 Durham Parish,
Charles Co, MD, 1818 when sol & w aec 56 res with d (m of
2 small ch), s aec 19, & s "a few years younger"; PAR 1822
since already receiving PN from MD. R500
   Henry, esf Elizabethtown, NJ, a "free born man of color"; b
   b 2/25/1756-7 near Newark, NJ, his f a Catawba indian, his
   m a Mustee; res 8 years in NJ after RW, thence 5 years in
   NY, back to NJ 1791, thence Knoxville, TN, for svc against
   indians, thence Rockbridge Co, VA, where res 38 years; afp
   1834, & PAR; heirs 1853 there William Cato & William Cato
   Jr. R500
CATRON, Peter, esf 1776 Montgomery Co, VA; b 1754 Germany s/o
Stuffle & came with parents to PA 1764; res with f Montgomery Co, VA, to 1786, thence Grayson Co, VA, 1804 when mvd

CATRON (continued)
      to Wayne Co, KY, where PN 1874; QLF 1926 from desc Miss
      Meda F Gross, Ogden, IL, states sol surname also spelled
      KETTERING, KETRON, & CATTRON; QLF states sol f/o Justice
      John Catron of Supreme Court of TN, & later of US Supreme
      Court 1837-65; QLF states sol w Elizabeth; QLF states sol
      bro of Frank & Catherine, & s/o Stuffle (Christopher) & w
      Susanna; QLF states sol had sis Julia Ann w/o William Hud-
      son who both dd 1840 Dade Co, MO. R500
CATT, Philip, b VA 1760 near Moorefield, & mvd with parents as
      ch to Brownsville, PA, where esf 1776-7; mvd to Northwest
      Territory 1785 where settled in what now Knox Co, IN, & PN
      there 1832; QLF states sol LWT gives w name Sarah & sol dd
      c1844, & had 5 d's. R500
CAUGHRAN, George, see COUGHRAN, George. R501
CAUGHRON, Joseph, see COUGHREN, Joseph. R501
CAUL, Thomas M, esf 1780 near Staunton, Augusta Co, VA, where
      b 10/1/1763; PN 1833 Lewis Co, VA; res there 1838. R501
CARUTHERS, Elizabeth, former wid/o William Richardson. R501
CAVANDER, Joseph, esf 1777 Amelia Co, VA; PN 1818 Franklin Co,
      VA; res ae 61 Christian Co, KY, 1820 with w & ch mbnn; dd
      8/13/26. R501
CAVE, Benjamin, esf Culpeper Co, VA, where b 6/15/1760; mvd to
      Guilford Co,NC, 1781; PN 1832 Perry Township, Fairfield Co
      OH, when Baptist minister; w mbnn; bro/o John & another
      mbnn; QLF 1926 from Joseph A Cave, Columbus, OH, who great
      gds of RW sol John Cave & gds of War of 1812 sol Benjamin
      Cave of Page Co, VA, further John's f from England; QLF
      QLF states a Benjamin Cave came to VA 1725 & a member of
      VA House of Burgesses from Orange Co; QLF states sol md to
      Keziah; QLF 1938 from Byron L Cave, Lancaster, OH, states
      sol dd Ross Co, OH, 1842 & wid Keziah res Harrison Town-
      ship, that Co. R501
    Reuben, esf 1776 Orange Co, VA; served apprenticeship Spot-
      sylvania Co, VA, near Fredericksburg & overseer there to
      1776; mvd after RW to Shenandoah Co, VA, where PN 1832 ae
      94 Page Co (formed from Shenandoah Co, 1831); referred to
      w & eldest s (who if liv would be ae 51) R501
    William, esf 177- Guilford Co, NC; b 1749 Culpeper Co, VA;
      mvd after RW to SC, thence KY where PN 1832 Montgomery Co;
      sol Uncle John Jenkins res 1832 Culpeper Co, VA; a Rachael
      Cave referred to 1844; QLF states sol wid Rachel. R501
CAVENAUGH, Garrett, BLW issued -- no date given. R501
CAVENDER, Joseph, see CAVANDER, Joseph. R501
CAVENDISH, Alice, former wid/o William McClintic. R501
CAW, Peter, esf 1776 Lancaster Co, PA, where b 5/1/1751; PN
      1834 Morgan Co, VA. R502
CAWOOD, Berry, esf Washington Co, VA; b Berkeley Co, VA; PN ae
      76 Harlan Co, KY, 1834, res on Clover Fork of Cumberland
      River; sol 1856 correspondence with attorney to make sure
      his wid gtd PN after his death. R502
CAWTHON, Richard, esf 1781 Amherst Co, VA; PN ae 69 Fluvanna

CAWTHON (continued)
    Co, VA, 1832; QLF states sol Richard Sr in 1840. R502
CAYCE, Ambrose, esf 1781 Chesterfield Co, VA, where b 4/1765;
    4/1765; afp 1833 & 1839, & PAR, insufficient proof of svc;
    dd 5/10/43 Davidson Co, TN, leaving no wid but ch: Levi
    (decd in 1852 without issue), Mathew, Betsey Porter, Lou-
    isiana Castleman, & Phebe w of James Smith (who ae 61 in
    1852 & res Davidson Co, TN); QLF 1931 from Jennie D Cayce
    (Mrs R M) Cavett, Chickasha, OK, states sol md cousin Han-
    nah. R502
CAZEY, Ambrose, see CAYCE, Ambrose, above. R502
CECIL, William, esf 1776 Montgomery Co (area now Tazewell Co),
    VA; b 5/28/1750; PN 1832 there; dd 12/11/36; md 3/29/1774
    Nancy, Fincastle, Augusta Co, VA, sis/o Thomas Witten who
    md sis/o sol; wid b 1/9/1775, afp 1843, & PAR since she dd
    9/6/43, several days after her PN claimed, leaving ch: Su-
    sannah Sayers b 2/19/1776, John b 3/17/78, Rebecca b
    10/21/80, Linny Price, Nancy Harman, Samuel, & Sally Cald-
    well; d Susannah & s John AFF 1843 Tazewell Co, VA, where
    m afp; QLF 1900 from desc Mrs Frances Harden Hess of New
    York, NY; QLF 1911 from gdd Mrs Lula Kennedy, Springfield,
    MO; QLF 1821 from great gds W H Cecil, Nevada, OH. R502
CHADDAIN, John, see CHAUDOUN, John. R503
CHADOIN, Andrew, esf 1781 Buckingham Co & Powhatan Co, VA; b
    11/1761; mvd c1796 to Green Co, KY, where PN 1832; AFF by
    bro Francis there then; sol dd 11/17/45; md a wid Sarah
    Mathews 12/20/21/1786 (MB 12/20/86), Buckingham Co,VA; wid
    PN ae 85 Green Co, KY, 1846, & res ae 87 there 1848. R503
John, see CHAUDOIN, John. R503
CHAFFIN, Christopher, esf 1776 Cumberland Co, VA; PN ae 76 Ta-
    zewell Co, VA, 1833, where dd 10/10/36; md 8/22/1778 Mary
    Ann Vawter, Powhatan Co, VA, a Nathan Chaffin present; wid
    PN ae 79 Clermont Co, OH, 1841, when d Tabitha Harvey, who
    b 11/22/1779, made AFF there that she & m res there since
    12/1836; wid afp increase there 1843 ae 82. R505
CHALFANT, Solomon, see CHALFFIN, Solomon. R506
CHALFFIN, Solomon, esf 1776 on Back Creek, Berkeley Co, VA; PN
    ae 80 Monongalia Co, VA, 1832; dd 2/26/1837; md Mrs Achsa
    Cotton, a wid who b 4/13/1759; wid md (1) Fall of 1780 RW
    sol James Cotton, Princeton, NJ; James b 12/25/1749 & esf
    as drummer 1775, & dd 2/20/1806; ch of Achsa by James Cot-
    ton: Elizabeth, William, Mary, James, Richard, Robert H,
    Anny/Nancy, & Jane; wid afp 1849 Monongalia Co, VA, for
    svc of 1st h; QLF 1892 by R H Cotton ae over 80 that sol
    mvd from Martinsburg, Berkeley Co, VA, to Dunkard Creek 15
    miles east of Morgantown,WV, where he died, further md (1)
    Miss Eaton, (2) Achsa, wid/o James Cotton; QLF states sol
    came to VA from Charles Co, PA (note: this Co in MD). R506
CHALMERS, Andrew, esf 1776 Westmoreland Co, PA; mvd to Hamil-
    ton Co, OH, c1795, thence near Batavia, Clermont Co, OH,
    where PN 1818 ae 64; dd 11/25/33 Brown Co,OH; md 6/20/1785
    Alice Beasley, near Pittsburgh, PA; wid b 11/14-15/1768 on

CHALMERS (continued)
   "Blue Ridge", Loudoun Co, VA, PN 1838 Brown Co, OH, & res
      there 1843, & res 1848 Perry Township, that Co; 13 ch in-
      cluding Rebecca (b 4/22/1786, liv 1839 as Rebecca Conn),
      Hannah (ae 50 in 1839, res IL as Hannah Crane), William,
      John, Ariance (ae 41 in 1839 w/o John Davison, Clermont Co
      OH), Isaac ae 20 in 1824, & youngest James (ae 16 in 1824,
      res Brown Co, OH, 1839); John Callahan stepf of sol; QLF
      states sol wid lived to be ae 100. R506
CHAMBERLAIN, George, see CHAMBERLAINE, George, below. R507
CHAMBERLAINE, George, VA sea svc; esf as 2nd lieutenant 1776 &
      served on brig MOSQUITO to close of RW 1783; dd 1/10/1792;
      sol gds Richard H Chamberlaine gtd 1/2 pay PN due sailor,
      Norfolk, VA, 1843 as only heir, & adm/o sailor estate 1850
      there; QLF states sailor b 1755 Warwick Co,VA, md Ann Har-
      low Lucas, & dd 7/10/1792. R507
CHAMBERLAYNE, Byrd, VA sea svc, also a lieutenant on MOSQUITO;
      afp 1856 by d Evelyn B wid/o Robert Pollard, King & Queen
      Co, VA, & PAR for proof of svc; afp earlier made by Robert
      Pollard & also PAR. R507
   Edward Pye, VA sea svc, esf 1776 res New Kent Co, VA; also a
      lieutenant on MOSQUITO; bc 1758 & dd 1806, when s William
      B adm/o his estate; ch William Byrd, Lewis W, Byrd, Eliza-
      beth B w/o Sterling Ruffin, & Lucy Parke w/o Robert C Wil-
      liamson; heirs who afp 1834 New Kent Co, VA: s William B,
      s Lewis W, Byrd, gds James Edward Ruffin (parents decd),
      gds Robert B Williamson & gdd Mary A Williamson, latter 2
      ch/o decd d Lucy P & her decd h; PAR; s William B afp 1850
      as adm/o f estate; PAR; sailor POW for time in the Jersey
      prison ship at New York. R507
CHAMBERLIN, John, esf 1775 Mecklenburg Co, VA; PN ae 63 Surry
      Co, NC, 1822 when family w Milly, s ae 13, d Kitty ae 22,
      d Patsy ae 20, d Lucenda ae 18, & gds John ae 2; md Amelia
      "Milly" Robinson, Mecklenburg Co, VA, 12/18/1779; wid PN
      ae 78 Surry Co, NC, 1839, when her bro John AFF that he ae
      12 when sol md sis; wid dd 6/9/1849 Yadkin Co, NC, leaving
      ch: John, William, Franklin, Catharine, Martha, & Cyndia;
      s William CHAMBERLAIN exec/o m's estate there 1852. R508
CHAMBERS, Alexander, esf 1777 Loudoun Co, VA; b Ireland & came
      with family to Philadelphia, PA, aec 15; esf 1780 near
      Jonesboro, Washington Co, NC (later area in TN); PN ae 80
      Knox Co,IN, 1833 where res 3 years; QLF 1909 from desc Mrs
      Bessie Chambers Haskins, Vincennes, IN, states sol name
      John Alexander Chambers, md a Miss Thomas; QLF from great
      great gdd Mrs F H Stonaker, Bedford, IN, states sol b Ire-
      land 1757, res Lewisburg, WV, shortly before RW, md 1782
      Miss Pheamstess & they had 4 ch, one her great gdf William
      & one named Thomas, further sol buried near Laporte, IN;
      QLF 1921 from W D Chambers, Muncie, IN, states he desc of
      another Alexander Chambers who md niece of President Mon-
      roe 1789, then mvd to his f's home in Rutherford Co, NC,
      further res after 1811 Jefferson Co, IN, where dd 1857 ae

CHAMBERS (continued)
101, further was RW sol in VA Continental Line. R509
David, esf 1777 Rockbridge Co,VA, where dd 4/1/1809; BLW issued 5/27/1783; md 10/23/1794 Isabel/Isabella Vachub, Augusta Co, VA, at her f house; wid PN ae 82 near Crawfordsville, Montgomery Co, IN, 1855 when AFF there by bro John
Vachub ae 68 that sol killed while working in mill; wid dd
leaving no surv members of her family; QLF 1912 from great
gdd Blanche McCray, Ouray Co,CO, states sol wid dd c1867 &
maiden name Isabella Walkup. R509
James, BLW issued 1/3/1794. R509
James, esf 1778 Westmoreland Co,VA, where b, & PN there 1818
ae 60; "raised & supported w & family; in 1820 w aec 70 &
3 ch who grown up & mvd away from home. R509
James, esf VA; dd 1/10/1833; md 3/30/1792 Anne Robertson,
(MB signed by Richard Robertson) Louisa Co, VA; wid dd on
2/28/36; afp there 1843 by surv ch: Harden ae 45, Willis,
& Louisa Ann w/o Solomon Gibson. R509
John, esf 1778 Halifax Co, VA, where b 5/1757; esf 1779 as
sub for Uncle Thomas Link; PN 1833 Carroll Co, TN. R509
John, esf 1778 in VA regiment; b Ireland, & came to America
1767, settling in Little York, PA; PN ae 80 Lincoln Co, MO
1819 & res there 1821 with Post Office at Monroe; mvd 1835
from MO to Butler Co,OH, to res with s; back to Lincoln Co
MO, 1839 to res with ch there; QLF states sol dd ae 110, &
on MO 1840 Census as RW pensioner; QLF states sol b Ireland 11/1739 & dd MO 1841; QLF 1925 from Mrs F H Stonaker,
Bedford, IN, states her great great gdf John Chambers who
b Ireland, esf VA in RW, md Margaret d/o William S Feem-
ster/Feimster & --- Black in 1786, Greenbrier Co, VA, further sol mvd to KY, & some/o his desc now res Harrodsburg,
IN, further sol had s Thomas & s William (her great gdf);
QLF states sol dd 12/30/1841 Warren Co, MO. R509
John, esf 1776 at Fork of Cheat River, Monongalia Co, VA; b
VA; mvd family to Knox Co, IN, 1809; PN ae 69 Gibson Co,
1818 when had s John; res 1823 Pike Co, IN; dd 6/22/24 IN;
ref to w mbnn 1823; d Mrs Rachael Welton mentioned in 1859
document; QLF 1935 from Mrs Charles R Emery, Bloomington,
IN, that she great great gdd/o a RW sol John Chambers, who
md Margaret Feamster, Greenbrier Co, VA, 1786, & 3 of sons
William, David, & Anthony mvd to Monroe Co, IN, 1817, further sol w liv 1814; QLF 1928 from Mrs F H Stonaker, Bedford Co, IN, that a RW sol John Chambers had w Margaret,
who d/o RW sol William Feamster of Greenbrier Co, VA. R509
Robert, esf 1777 Augusta Co, VA; b England 9/15/1753; to America 1774; mvd 1782 to Monroe Co, VA, where PN 1818; family in 1822 w Hannah ae 60, 2 md d's, 4 md s's, 1 single
s ae 20, another single s res Kanawaha Co, VA; in 1829 sol
s William had w & 4 ch; in 1835 sol res Monroe Co, VA; sol
dd 9/23/36. R509
William, esf Surry Co, NC, where res; b Lunenburg Co, VA; to
Madison Co, KY, after RW for 8-9 years, thence Jackson Co,

CHAMBERS (continued)
>IN, where PN ae 86 Salt Creek Township 1832, when bro Nathaniel, who served in RW with sol, res Washington Co, IN. R509

CHAMP, William, esf 1778 Paddytown, Hampshire Co, VA; PN ae 65 Pickaway Co,OH, 1818; in 1820 w ae 57 & d Elizabeth ae 17. R510

>John, see CHAMPE, John, below. R510

CHAMPE, John, esf 1776 Loudoun Co, VA, where b; mvd after RW to Hampshire Co,VA; dd c1798 when on tour of western country near Morgantown on Monongahela River; md 7/1782 Phebe, who res ae nearly 60 Franklin Co, OH, 1818, when ch: Eleanor w/o Jacob Hartman, Amelia w/o William Keys, Susannah w/o David Willfong (Ross Co,OH), William (Pickaway Co,OH), Mary (Pickaway Co, OH, later referred to as Mary Keys), John (Franklin Co, OH), & Nathaniel of Detroit (he b Hampshire Co, VA, & War of 1812 sol); wid PN 1838 Franklin Co, OH; surv ch 1847: William of Columbus,OH, Nathaniel of Detroit, MI, & John, + gds George W, s/o Susanna Willfong; QLF 1937 from great gdd Mrs Meady Champe Becker of Coatesville, PA; QLF 1925 from great gds Robert C Toy, Indianapolis, IN; QLF 1923 from Mrs Lewis M Pancake, Columbus, OH states her h desc/o sol & w Phebe Barnard; QLF states sol wid res ae 83 near Norwich, Franklin Co, OH, 1839-40 with s William; QLF 1917 from desc Floy S Champe, Logansport, IN. R510

CHANCE, James, esf 1780 VA; PN ae 64 Dinwiddie Co, VA, 1825 when family w ae 28, ch ae 4, & ch ae 1. R511

CHANCELLOR, David, esf 1779 VA; PN 1826 Spencer Co, IN, when w ae 69; both res there 1832, all ch md then; QLF 1928 from Franklin m Chancellor, Villa Park,IL, states sol buried in Chancellor Burying Ground, c3 miles north of Grandview in Spencer Co, IN. R511

>Julius, see CHANSLEY, Julius. R511

>Thomas, esf Hanover Co, VA, early in RW; b 1754 Goochland Co VA; PN 1833 Buckingham Co, VA. R511

CHANCLER, Julius, see CHANSLEY, Julius. R511

CHANDLER, Carter, esf 1780 Louisa Co, VA, sub for bro-in-law Barnett Mitchell; res Spotsylvania Co, VA, after RW for 4 years, thence Frederick Co, VA, where PN 1835 ae 72; illiterate; dd 8/16/1842 Clarke Co, VA; d Rebecca W, w/o Jacob Enders, afp there as sol sole heir 1851, & she had several ch by previous h. R512

>Claiborn/Claibourn, esf 1780 Spotsylvania Co, VA, where b 6/28/1761; PN 1832 Harrison Co, KY. R512

>David, esf c1780 VA; dd c7/10/1822 Mecklenburg Co, VA; md there c6/20/1801 Mildred Vaughan; wid afp ae 94 there 1855 & afp again ae 96 there 1856; PAR, insufficient proof of svc. R512

>James, esf 1776 Randolph Co, NC; b 8/10/1755 Pendleton Co, VA; mvd 1795 to Clark Co, KY, thence 1812 to Gallatin Co (later Owen Co), KY, where PN 1833; sis Sarah Dunaway, who

CHANDLER (continued)

b 1765, res Owen Co, KY, 1833. R512

John, esf 1776 Newberry District,SC; b 1755 Luneburg Co, VA; PN 1832 Gwinnett Co, GA; mvd 1839 to AL to be near part of family, including nephew Joel Chandler; QLF states sol dd AL; QLF states sol md Miss Nance; QLF 1904 from great gdd Mrs John M Duncan, Tyler, TX. R513

John, esf 1781 VA; b 2/1764 Halifax Co, VA; mvd to NC for 9 years, thence Russell Co, VA, for 9 years, thence Clay Co, KY, where PN 1833; dd 3/4/1842 leaving a ch mbnn. R513

Littleton, esf 1777 Accomac Co, VA, where b 3/10/1761 s/o John & Patience; dd 7/14/1832; md 9/7/1778 Susannah Drummond, Accomac Co, VA; wid b 5/1/1764, PN Accomac Co, VA, & dd there 4/22/1849; ch births: Nancy D 9/2/1789, William D 10/8/91 (md 5/23/1816 Peggy Wise), George P 10/24/93 (md 11/16/1820 Julian Riley), Susannah 3/27/96, John H 5/6/98, Peggy E 8/26/1800, Caty 9/11/02, & Eliza 3/14/06; ch of George & Julian Chandler: Susan E (b 9/18/1825, md 6/10/49 Richard W Ames), & her twin Sally A (b 9/18/25, md 3/25/44 William M Taylor); wid survived by ch Nancy, Margaret E, & Eliza, & they recd remaining PN due m Accomac Co,VA, 1851; other data in file: Mary E, d/o Daniel & Sally Drummond, b 2/19/1813 & md 8/28/33 Richard P Read. R513

Margaret, former wid/o George Purcell. R513

Meshack, esf 1775 Ninety-Six District, SC; b 11/7/1750 near the Great Falls on James River,VA; PN 1836 Ninety-Six District (now Union District), SC, & dd there 2/21/44; md there Sally when she ae 17; wid b 6/19/1762, & PN there in 1844; ch Elizabeth, Polly, ch dd as infant, Samuel, & others; sol sis Susan took family bible to KY. R513

Mordecai, esf 1777 Newberry District, SC; b 5/15/1762 Culpeper Co, VA; PN 1832 Union District, SC; dd c5/15/1846; bro of Meshack who AFF there 1833; sol wid Margaret dd 5/1852; surv ch who applied 1857 for unpaid PN due sol: Robert, Samson, Rosanah w/o Samuel Philips, Jane w/o Thomas Stevens, & Margaret w/o William James; PAR, since sol PN paid up to date of death; Samuel Philips adm/o sol estate 1857. R513

Robert, esf 1776 Orange Co, VA; dd 1806-7; md 2/25/1773-4 Susannah Edmunson at Court House, Orange Co, VA; wid PN ae 92 Marion Co, KY, 1839, when AFF there by s Richard who b 12/1776; other ch mbnn. R514

Shadrack, esf c1780 Newberry District, NC; b 8/1756-7 Luneburg Co, VA; res after RW Greeneville District, SC, thence Logan Co, KY, thence AL & TN; PN 1836 Dekalb Co, GA. R514

Thomas, esf c1778 NC; PN ae 65 Cabell Co, VA, 1827, when w aec 64. R514

Thomas, VA sea svc; afp 1846 by John B Ailworth, adm/o sailor's estate; 1/2 pay claim allowed. R514

William, esf 1776 Buckingham Co, VA; PN 1818 Garrard Co, KY; res 1822 Madison Co, KY, ae 70-80, w then ae over 50, & ch md & mvd away, except d aec 19 & s ae 17; res 1826 Posey

CHANDLER (continued)
   Township, Switzerland Co,IN; QLF states sol listed on 1835
   Census of Orange Co, IN, & dd there. R514
  William, esf VA in year of Gen Gates defeat; PN ae 70 Northampton Co, NC, 1822 while res with w in Co Poor House; sol
   then blacksmith & blind in one eye; dd there 7/16/1833; md
   there 12/24/1775 Sally Norwood; wid afp ae 87 Franklin Co,
   NC, 1845, & PAR. R514
CHANDLEY, William, esf 1780 Staunton, VA; PN ae 63 Greene Co,
   TN, 1818, where res 27 years; family in 1820: w Sarah & 6
   ch mbnn, all small except 1; dd 9/22/27 Sevier Co, TN; md
   c 12/20/1799 Sarah Prather (MB 12/19/99), Greene Co, TN;
   wid md (2) 4/8/1834 John Lovell who dd 11/30/45 Cincinnati
   OH, while visiting his ch; wid PN ae 73 Crawford Co, IN,
   1854, when John Lovell's s William B res there; wid gtd
   BLW there 1855 ae 74, & res there 1856; a James Chandley
   res there 1853; Jacob Sarver s-in-law/o John Lovell. R515
CHANDLY, William, see CHANDLEY, William, above. R515
CHANEY, Abraham, esf Pittsylania Co, VA, where PN 1832 ae 72 &
   dd there 12/25/48; md there 4/4/11 Nancy Donelson (license
   issued 12/17/1810); wid PN there 1853 ae 77, gtd BLW there
   1855, res P. O. Laurel Grove; sol bro Joseph res Pittsylvania Co, VA, 1832. R515
CHANSLEY, Julius, esf VA; dd 3/5/1799; md 2/14/1792 Ally Sneed
   (MB 2/9/92 signed by John Sneed & John Chandler) Albemarle
   Co, VA; ch birth: John 5/16/1793, Salley 1/4/95, & Julius
   6/6/99; wid md (2) John Utly who dd 2/15/38; wid PN 1844
   Jessamine Co, KY, & gtd BLW ae 81 there 1856, both for svc
   of 1st h. R515
CHAPIN, Benjamin, VA sea svc; esf VA navy 1777; William R Ashton, adm/o sailor's estate 1834, Baltimore Co, MD; sailor
   referred to as Dr Chapin who decd in 1838, when heirs apf
   & PAR. R516
CHAPLINE, Abraham, svc in VA Illinois Regiment; dd 1/19/1824,
   & 1/2 pay gtd to Isaac Chaplin, adm/o his estate; s A liv
   1856; QLF 1926 from Mrs George Chapline, St Louis,MO. R517
CHAPMAN, Benjamin, esf 1777 Baltimore Co,MD, where b 7/13/1760
   & mvd 1778 to Augusta Co, VA, where esf 1779; mvd 1797 to
   Washington Co, TN, thence Roane Co,TN, 1827 where PN 1832.
   R518
  Edmund, esf 1781 Caroline Co, VA, where b 1/8/1764 s/o Wil-
   liam; PN 1832 Sugar Creek Township, Randolph Co, MO, where
   mvd from KY. R519
  Erasmus, esf 1781 Spotsylvania Co,VA, where b 10/1759; after
   RW visited relatives in MS, & svc there in Creek & Semi-
   nole Wars; mvd to Lincoln Co, MO, thence St Francois Co,
   MO, thence Howard Co, MO, where afp (deaf) 1832; PAR, in-
   sufficient proof of svc. R519
  George, BLW issued for RW svc; War of 1812 sol. R520
  Isaac, esf 1776 Amelia Co, VA; PN ae 61 Ashe Co, NC, 1819, &
   mvd to Washington Co, VA, c1820 in area now Smyth Co; dd
   8/4/22; md 7/14/1787 Elizabeth who md (2) Richard Whitaker

CHAPMAN (continued)
who dd 10/18/38; wid PN ae 75 Smyth Co, VA, 1845, gtd BLW
ae 96 Washington Co,VA, 1855; ch births: Nathan 10/26/1788
William 3/3/90, Isaiah 8/27/91, James 2/7/93, Sara 9/27/95
Patey 6/3/97, Stephen /99, Rachel 1/26/1800, Peggy 12/2/02
John 6/18/04, Andrew 10/30/06, & Benjamin 11/23/08; other
family bible data: Rufus H Chapman b 5/30/1825, Aleyann b
1/6/20; AFF 1845 Smyth Co, VA, by s John & s James 1845 on
family bible data. R520
   Isaac, esf 1776 Montgomery Co (now Giles Co), VA, for indian
war; esf 1777 & 1778 for RW; afp ae 71 Giles Co, VA, 1835,
& PAR. R520
   Jacob, esf 1778 Greenbrier Co, VA; b Staunton, VA; PN ae 80
Nicholas Co, VA, 1833. R520
   James, esf 1775 Amelia Co, VA; b 11/10/1760-1; afp 1833 Scioto Co, OH, 1833; PAR, less than 6 months svc; QLF 1908
from Ira A Chapman, Indianapolis, IN, states a James Chapman esf 1777 Harpers Ferry, VA, mvd to OH c1790 where res
Portsmouth until dd c1834; QLF 1916 from DAR member, Fowler,IN, for data for application of Miss Ruby Chapman; QLF
states a Samuel Chapman & s John res Amelia Co, VA, further Samuel dd there 1775-80 while s John dd there 1816 leaving wid Oney & ch: John, James, Stephen, Benjamin, William, Jonathan, Ann, Jane, & Sarah, & further s James res
1833 Scioto Co, VA, when afp. R520
   John, esf 1780 Burke Co, NC; b 1750 Loudoun Co, VA; PN 1832
Wilkes Co, NC; dd 3/15-18/36; md 1/18/1779 Leanna Brown,
there; wid PN ae 82 there 1843. R520
   John, esf 1780 Halifax Co,VA, where b 10/16/1762; to Cumberland Co, KY, 1828 where PN 1832, blind; dd there 12/22/33;
md 2/1/1791 Lucy, Halifax Co,VA; wid b 12/14/1769, & PN
1838 Fentress Co,TN, when AFF there by s John (b 4/21/02),
1 of 4 ch, his eldest bro Rawley (b 6/30/1793) who md 1813
in VA, having 4 ch in 1838. R520
   John, esf for svc in VA regiment; KIA 9/2/1781 by indian am-
bush on Beargrass Creek near Louisville, KY; never md; nephew James Washington Chapman applied for all heirs of sol
1847, Logan Co, IL, for any PN due sol, & PAR; data on sol
siblings then as follows: (1) Joseph eldest, killed by his
negroes Adair Co, KY, leaving wid, liv 1837, s Joseph, s
Peyton res MO & d Dehoning who had s Dehoning res Adair Co
KY, (2) Thomas & w decd, leaving ch: John Strother (res
with 4 heirs Union Co, KY), William Cook (& w of Paducah,
McCracken Co, KY), Elisa (md cousin John Chapman, & res on
Wolfe Creek, Sangamon Co, IL), James Washington (res Logan
Co,IL, having 1 ch decd & 4 liv including d Sarah Jane who
md --- Burns & she survived by 4 heirs), Nancy (md William
McKinney & both dd Union Co, KY, leaving 4 ch), (3) Willi-
am md Fanny Rust of Frederick Co, VA, & they dd leaving ch
John (res on Wolfe Creek, IL), William (same res), Harri-
et (md --- Bryant, res near Springfield, Sangamon Co,IL)
& Polly (md --- Dowdall, same res), (4) Nutty md Adrian

CHAPMAN (continued)
    Davenport who dd Union Co, KY, & she dd Shawneetown, Gal-
    tin Co, KY, leaving 6 sons, (5) Rachel md Thornton Thorn-
    bury, & both dd Logan Co, KY, leaving ch: William decd in
    1847, Thomas, & Nancy who md, (6) ? md Thomas Ballard, &
    both dd Frederick Co, VA. R520
John, esf 1780 Frederick Co, VA; b 2/14/1766 Spotsylvania Co
    VA; esf 1781 Mercer Co, KY; res KY 1787; PN 1832 Anderson
    Co, TN, 1832, as John H; res there 1838. R520
Joseph, esf 1776 Guilford Co, NC; b 12/25/1745 Halifax Co,
    VA; PN 1833 Pickens District, SC; dd 1/18/36. R521
Nathan, esf Amelia Co, VA; POW; dd 1/29/1828-9; md 2/17/1791
    Elizabeth/Betsy Coleman (MB 2/12/91 signed by James Cole-
    man), Franklin Co, VA; wid PN ae 69 Bedford Co, VA, 1839 &
    res 1844 with s Henry Harison Chapman, Roane Co, VA, where
    she gtd BLW 1855; sol sis Mrs Elizabeth Bowls res Bedford
    Co, VA, 1839 aec 83; QLF 1939 from Guy H Wells, Milledge-
    ville, GA, desc of sol bro John, states sol b Watering
    Branch, VA. R521
Thomas, esf 1777 VA; mvd to SC shortly after RW; dd 11/1823;
    bro/o William; md 6/1785 Nancy Wise, Sumter District, SC;
    sol & w both b & raised VA; wid PN ae 94 Sumter District,
    SC, 1851 when AFF there by wid niece Jamime Richbourg ae
    64, also AFF there then by Thomas Richbourg & by Samuel
    Richbourg ae 75, s/o RW sol John Richbourg, & by Elizabeth
    Richbourg ae 76 who md 1796. R522
Thomas, esf 1778 VA; BLW issued 9/5/1828 to bro Nathaniel,
    his only heir, Bedford Co, VA; QLF states sol b England or
    VA & dd near Bowling Green, KY. R522
William, esf 1778 Montgomery Co, VA; b 1750 VA; PN 1835 San-
    gamon Co, IL; mvd from IL to Cannon Co, TN, 1837 to live
    among ch mbnn; dd 6/30/40; QLF states a William H Chapman,
    who RW sol, had 2 land grants in Montgomery Co, IL. R522
William, esf 1779 VA; PN 1819 Rowan Co,NC, & res there 1820;
    no ae given. R522
CHAPPEL, William, b 10/18/1760 Chesterfield Co, VA, where esf
    1776; PN 1833 Bullitt Co, KY; dd 12/12/33 Lexington, KY,
    at home of Laban Headington who bro/o w; md 7/29/1818 Ruth
    Quick, Bullitt Co,KY; wid PN there 1858, & res there ae 96
    P. O. Pitts Point; surname also spelled CHAPPELL. R523
CHAPPELL, Abner, esf 1780 Staunton, VA; b 4/10/1763 Amelia Co,
    VA; mvd 1807 to Bedford Co, TN, thence 1820 to Howard Co,
    MO, where PN 1833. R523
Benjamin, esf 1776 Williamsburg, VA; PN ae 62 New Kent Co,
    VA, 1818. R523
Hicks, b 3/5/1757 Brunswick Co, VA; mvd with f to Richland
    District, SC, c1764; PN there 1833, & dd there 4/22/36; md
    6/14/1780 Elizabeth Threewits/Thruwits who dd 7/4/1841; ch
    births: John Joel 1/9/1782 (member/o Congress from SC 1853
    when only surv ch of sol), William 6/12/83 (dd 9/1/83),
    Howell 2/3/85 (dd 9/19/85), James Henry 10/13/86, & Polly
    Ellen 12/17/88 (dd 10/26/90). R523

CHAPPELL, John, esf 1777 Fairfax Co, VA, where f res; PN there
    1832 ae 72; dd there 4/9/35; md there c1782 Mary Yayman;
    wid PN aec 77 there 1838, & res there 1848 ae 96; d Eliza-
    beth Marshall aec 56 there 1838, eldest of large family of
    ch; QLF 1937 from great great gdd Mrs Alice Chappell Sell-
    man, College Park, MD. R523
  William, esf 1781 Sussex Co, VA; PN there 1833 ae 71. R523
CHARITY, Charles, esf 1777 VA; PN 1827 Newberry District, SC;
    res there 1834 ae 78. R524
CHARLEVILLE, Francis; esf VA; res Kaskaskia, IL; dd c1793; ch
    1833: Joseph, John Baptist, Louise (decd), Charles, Popon,
    Andre, & Michael; afp 1833 St Genevieve Co, MO, by heirs
    Joseph, Charles, & Baptist Charleville; afp 1833 Randolph
    Co, IL, by heirs Mary, Henry, Genevieve, & Michael SHARLE-
    VILLE; all PAR. R524
CHARLEY, George, esf 1779-80 VA; PN 1832 ae 69 Harrison Co,IN,
    where dd 8/6/33; md 8/15/1790 Christena in PA by publica-
    ton of banns in church; wid PN ae 72 Harrison Co,IN, 1842;
    ch births: Peter 12/24/1791, Polly 3/24/94, Elizabeth
    3/24/96, Sarah 8/5/98, Anna 11/18/1801, Lydia 8/18/03,
    George Jr 1/14/05, Jacob 5/5/07, Christena 3/2/11, Susan-
    na 9/15/13, & Joseph 9/18/15; other family bible data: Pe-
    ter Charley md 3/10/1814, Polly Charley md 10/2/1813, Lyd-
    ia Charley md 9/1/1825 Philip Brandenburg who b 2/8/1803,
    George Brandenburg b 6/23/1826, Emanuel Brandenburg b
    8/5/18281, Joseph Brandenburg b 3/21/1830, Amos Branden-
    burg b 8/27/1833, Perry Brandenburg b 2/9/1836; Harden
    Fleshman b 10/18/1817; Christopher Fleshman b 11/9/1818;
    Harden Fleshman dd 2/27/1819. R524
CHARLTON, Francis, esf Montgomery Co, VA; b 2/3/1759; PN 1832
    Montgomery Co, VA, & dd there 11/23/1851; md there 2/1792
    Susanna Acres/Akers of that Co (MB 2/3/92 signed by James
    Carlton); wid PN aec 82 there 1852; s John W, b 7/8/1793,
    res there 1852; other ch mbnn; wid bro Jacob Akers res
    there 1852 aec 80; QLF states sol bro of John, who dd
    9/24/1833, & James; QLF states Francis & James served to-
    gether in RW & were sons of John & Elizabeth Charlton; QLF
    states John & Elizabeth Charlton md PA 1759, mvd to Mont-
    gomery Co, VA, c1763, their sons James, Francis & John svc
    together in RW; QLF 1906 from Mrs Wards Stephens, Martins-
    ville, Henry Co, VA, states her great gdf Samuel Caddall
    came to America from Ireland when quite young & settled
    in what is now McGavock's Farm near Dublin, Pulaski Co,VA,
    was RW sol, & dd there, & querier also desc of John & Eli-
    zabeth Carlton. R524
  Jacob, esf 1777 Powhatan Co, VA; b 4/25/1743 James City Co,
    VA; mvd after RW to Sullivan Co, TN, thence Hawkins Co, TN
    where PN 1834 after res for 14 years. R524
  John, esf 1781 Prince Edward Co, VA; b 4/12/1761 Cumberland
    VA; PN 1833 Davidson Co,TN; QLF from great great gdd Agnes
    Charlton, Canyon, TX, states sol & w buried near Nashville
    TN, his headstone reading: b 4/12/1761 Cumberland Co, VA &

CHARLTON (continued)
     dd 5/19/1839; QLF states sol md Anne Roberts/Robertson/Ro-
     binson; QLF 1893 from great gdd Mrs Evelyn B Leamon, Mem-
     phis, TN. R524
CHARNOCK, John, esf 1781 VA; b 8/2/1756; PN 1819 Accomac Co,
     VA; family in 1820 w Elizabeth ae 58, d Sally ae 28, d Ro-
     sy ae 16; also res with sol then Peggy Charnock ae 40, sis
     of w, & her ch Nanny ae 18, Molly ae 10, & William ae 7;
     sol dd 3/1/42; QLF 1934 from John N Charnock, Charleston,
     WV. R524
CHASE, Robert, esf 1777 VA; b 1/1/1761 Accomac Co,VA, where PN
     1832; dd 11/19/53; md c1787 Sally who PN there 1854 ae 87;
     4 or 5 ch mbnn. R527
CHASTEEN, James, esf 1777 Fluvanna Co, VA; PN ae 57 Madison Co
     KY, 1818; dd there 2/27-28/41; md 10/1783-4-5 Nancy Kenne-
     dy, Amherst Co, VA, who b Albemarle Co, VA; wid PN aec 83
     Rockcastle Co, KY, 1842; ch: eldest Elizabeth (md --- Dur-
     ham & AFF 1842 aec 60), John AFF 1842 aec 52, Polly, Jesse
     & Nancy + 1 mbnn; wid res ae 87 Rockcastle Co, OH, 1843.
     R528
CHAVERS, Anthony, esf Mecklenburg Co, VA, where res; dd 5/1831
     Granville Co, NC; afp by s Peter 1840, & PAR. R528
CHAVORS, Anthony, see CHAVERS, Anthony, above. R528
CHEATHAM, Benjamin, esf 1776 Charlotte Co,VA; b 9/8/1751 Ches-
     terfield Co, VA; mvd to Giles Co, TN, 1827 where PN 1832.
     R529
   Bernard, esf c1775 Chesterfield Co, VA; dd 1/23/1818 Char-
     lotte Co, VA; md there 12/10/1791 Judith Hampton; wid afp
     there 1839 ae 79, & PAR. R529
   Josiah, esf Amherst Co,VA; dd 2/13/1813 Albemarle Co, VA; md
     11/5/1786 Lucy, who afp ae 69 Nelson Co, VA, 1839, & PAR;
     wid PN ae 70 Albemarle Co, VA, 1840. R529
   Stephen, esf 1780 Chesterfield Court House, Chesterfield Co,
     VA; PN there 1818 ae 56 when had w mbnn. R529
   William, esf 1778 Chesterfield Co, VA, where b 8/28/1762; PN
     1832 Cumberland Co, KY; res 1837 Hempstead Co, AR, when 3
     ch mbnn res AR. R529
CHEATWOOD, William, esf 1779 VA; dd 2/28/1822; md c5/5/1777
     Susanna Nowlin, Bedford Co, VA; ch: Dicey, Joel, Squire,
     Frances, Matthias, & Sarah, all liv 1839, except Squire;
     sol LWT dated 2/10/1822 lists w Susannah & ch Squire, Mat-
     thias, Sally w/o Eli Perdue, Franky, Joel, & Dicey McMol-
     lin; will probated 5/6/22 Franklin Co, VA, in name of Wil-
     liam CHITWOOD; sol s/o John; wid afp ae 85 there 1839, &
     PAR, insufficient proof of svc & marriage; afp 1856 Sevier
     Co, TN, by s Matthias & s-in-law Eli Perdue stating they
     heard sol ch Joel & Frances already gtd PN for f svc; this
     PAR; different sources state wid dd 1840, 1842, or 1844.
     R529
CHEEK, James, esf 1781 Orange Co, NC; b 8/16/1762 Brunswick Co
     VA; PN 1832 Orange Co, NC; QLF 1930 from desc Alma Cheek
     (Mrs J A) Redden, Springfield, MA. R529

CHEEK, James, esf 1781 Frederick Co, VA, where PN 1834 ae 75.
     R529
CHEESEMAN, Thomas, VA sea svc, esf 1777 as surgeon aboard TAR-
     TAR; dd c1798-9 Hampton, VA, leaving wid mbnn, who md (2)
     Richard Garrett, & an only ch Lucy who md Robert Tabb. Ro-
     bert dd 1812, leaving ch William, Robert, & Mary (md Lewis
     Moreland, dd & left s Lewis who dd aec 9); William Tabb,
     adm/o Dr CHISMAN's estate, afb 1838, stating he & bro Ro-
     bert only liv heirs/o sailor, & they gtd BLW; Lewis More-
     land liv 1838. R529
CHEESMAN, Thomas, see CHEESEMAN, Thomas, above. R529
CHELTON, George, esf 1781 Lancaster Co, VA, where b; PN aec 85
     Woodford Co, KY, 1833. R529
   Stephen, esf 1779 Culpeper Co, VA, where b; POW 1780; PN aec
     73 Woodford Co, KY, 1833. R529
CHENAULT, James, esf 1776-7 VA; PN aec 61 Buckingham Co, VA,
     1819. R529
   John, esf 1776 VA; PN ae 65 Columbia Co, GA, 1820 when fami-
     ly w Nancy ae 45, s John ae 13, d Louisa ae 10, & d Mary
     Ann ae 7. R529
CHENOWETH, John, esf 1776 Hampshire Co, VA; b 11/15/1755 s/o
     William; dd 6/16/1831 Randolph Co, VA; md 1/7/1779 Mary
     Pugh; wid b 1/29/1762 & PN 1837 Randolph Co,VA; ch births:
     Ruth 7/8/1780, Robert 4/19/82, William P 2/2/84, Mary
     10/22/85, Ann 3/21/88, & John J 2/13/90; family bible mar-
     riage dates, all CHENOWETH: Robert 8/23/1802 & 4/10/11;
     Mary 3/25/03, William P 1/25/07, John J 8/5/10, Jehu
     11/19/13 to Nelly Skidmore, Gabriel 11/21/15 to Elizabeth
     Currants, & Nelly 9/23/19 to James Hart; John J & Lemuel
     Chenoweth res 1837 Randolph Co, VA; Michael Pugh 1837 Jus-
     tice of the Peace, Hampshire Co, VA; Samuel Pugh res 1837
     Wood Co, VA; QLF states sol wid dd 1849; QLF data on John
     Chenoweth III, b 1735 s/o John II, dd Hampshire Co, VA, md
     (1) Eleanor, & (2) Mary, & his ch births: William 1761,
     Absalom 1763, John 1765, James 1768, Elias 1770, Elizabeth
     1772, Eleanor 1774, Rachel 1777, & Mary 1779; QLF 1933
     from desc Mrs Marsalona Springston, Spencer, WV; QLF
     states sol lived & dd Frederick Co, MD, & his w Mary Pugh
     mvd from Randolph Co, VA, to KY & PN there as Mary Buskirk
     or Van Buskirk; QLF 1910 from Mrs Eva Chenoweth Robinson,
     Harrisville, WV; QLF 1902 from great great gdd Miss W V
     Chenoweth, Ellicott City,MD; QLF 1898 from desc W F Black-
     man, Hastings, NE. R531
CHENULT, John, see CHENAULT, John. R531
CHERRY, William, esf 177- VA; BLW gtd; res 1797 Berkeley Co,
     VA; dd 9/22/1804 Jefferson Co, VA; ch: eldest d Elizabeth
     w/o David Patten 1797, Richard res 1843 Highland Co, OH, s
     Mathias decd in 1833, Eleanor, Mary, John, & William Jr;
     William Jr md Mary G & they had Ellen (of Winchester, VA,
     who never md & dd 1843) & Mary E (unmarried & res with m
     1844 Winchester, VA) who w/o John B Gilkeson 1850 there;
     sol heirs who afp & afb 1844: William, Richard, John, &

CHERRY (continued)
     Harris Cherry & Eliza w/o Joseph Wysong; PN & BLW gtd; QLF
     1934 from desc Alison Struthers, Detroit,MI, who also desc
     of RW sol Jacob Wysong. R531
CHESHIER, James, esf Prince William Co, VA, where b 1749; afp
     1843 Fayette Co, IL; PAR, insufficient proof of svc. R532
CHESHIRE, John, VA sea svc, esf 1778; b Accomac Co, VA; survi-
     ved by one ch William H who md Sarah & had ch: William H
     C, Sarah T B Oliver, Margaret R, Thomas I or J, & George
     W; William H & Sarah decd when ch afp 1848 Norfolk, VA; no
     indication in record that PN approved; other spellings of
     surname CHESHER, CHESIRE & CHESSER. R532
CHESNEY, Benjamin, esf 1779 in Lee's Legion of VA troops; PN
     1818 Monongalia Co, VA; in 1820 ae 59, w Margaret aec 70,
     no ch res with them; QLF 19-- from desc Harriet B Chesney
     (Mrs Tusca) Morris states sol esf Rockingham Co, VA, & res
     after RW on Gustin River, branch of Scott's Run, Mononga-
     lia Co, VA, where dd; QLF states sol res Monongalia Co, VA
     1840 ae 80; surname at times spelled CHESNUT. R532
CHESSHER, James, esf Mecklenburg Co & Halifax Co, VA; afp aec
     87 Warren Co, TN; PAR, insufficient proof of svc. R532
CHESSHIR, John, esf 1778 VA; PN ae 76 Floyd Co, IN, 1829 when
     w Sarah ae 72 & 4 ch, all married; QLF states sol dd Floyd
     Co, IN. R532
CHESTERMAN, William, esf 177- Spotsylvania Co, VA; KIA Battle
     of the Santee; md Frances Payne, Spotsylvania Co, VA, when
     home on furlough 4/30/1779-80; wid md (2) 8/1785 William
     Thornton who dd 5/22/1819-20 & she PN on his RW svc aec 82
     Richmond, VA, 1844; wid sis/o John; sol s John Chesterman
     AFF ae 64 Hanover Co, VA, 1844 that he only s & heir/o sol
     & Frances Payne/Paine; QLF 1926 from Bernard Chesterman,
     Washington, DC; QLF states sol esf 1777. R532
CHEUVRONT, Joseph, esf VA; dd 1832; md 12/2/1802 Sarah in OH;
     wid afp ae 72 Harrison Co, VA, 1853, & PAR, insufficient
     proof of svc & marriage; AFF 1853 by s Aaron, Jackson Co,
     VA; AFF 1854 by Caleb Cheuvront, Harrison Co, VA, that he
     steps/o sol w Sarah; QLF 1934 from great great great great
     gdd Miss Margaret Rae Cheuvront, Lincoln, NE, states sol b
     2/2/1755 Strasburg, France, reared in city of Nantes, mvd
     to England 1771, to America 1774, & to Fredericksburg, VA
     1778, & was Methodist minister after RW, further querier
     sent copy of sol's dying statement which she copied from
     Walter G Cheuvront who copied from Lemuel G Cheuvront who
     copied from Andrew Cheuvront who copied from sol s Andrew.
     R533
CHEVALIER, Anthony, esf 1776 Winchester, VA; PN ae 63 Montgo-
     mery Co, OH, 1818; res there 1820 when w ae 63; QLF 1918
     from desc Mrs Scott Michener, Connersville, IN, states sol
     md Rachel Scott Wilson; QLF states sol came with LaFayette
     to America. R533
CHEW, John; PN 1789 for disability; papers lost in fire in DC;
     QLF states sol esf VA 1776 & wounded at Camden. R533

CHEW, Richard, VA res in 1834; PAR. R533
CHEWNING, Robert, esf 1780 Caroline Co,VA, where b 3/1752; afp
    ae 93 Greene Co,VA, 1845, & PAR, insufficient proof/o svc;
    dd Orange Co, VA; s Elisha afp as heir & adm/o sol estate
    ae 30 Greene Co, VA, 1851, & PAR; sol s-in-law Alexander
    Whitelaw AFF 1845 Greene Co, VA. R533
CHICK, James, esf 1776 King & Queen Co, VA; b 5/14/1760; PN
    1832 res on Greasy Creek, Knox Co, KY, when bro William
    res Buckingham Co, VA. R533
CHIEVES, Joel, esf 1778 VA; PN ae 74 Prince William Co, VA,
    1832. R533
CHILCOTT, Elihu, esf 1776; PN ae 63 Hardy Co, VA, 1820 when w
    Lydia ae 58 & ch: Ann ae 17, Rachel ae 20, Isaac ae 14,
    Joel ae 22, two older d's, + gdd Priscilla ae 5; sol dd
    5/25/31; md 1788 Lydia Payne; wid PN ae 78 Hardy Co, VA,
    1838. R533
CHILDERS, Abraham, esf 1776 Amherst Co, VA; b Buckingham Co,
    VA; raised Amherst Co, VA; bro Moseby KIA Battle of Bran-
    dywine; afp ae 82 Perry Co, KY, 1832, & PAR; w Elizabeth
    dd 2/17/1833; sol dd 5/6/49 Letcher Co, KY, leaving ch:
    William, Francis, Polly, Dicy, Abraham Jr, Seley, & Eliza-
    beth Goldsby; afp by s William 1854 Owsley Co, KY, & PAR;
    AFF there by gds John Childers 1855 ae 44. R535
  David, esf 1775 Charlotte Co, VA; POW, escaped & esf GA; PN
    ae 57 Sullivan Co,TN, 1818 where res 26 years; family 1820
    w, s ae 17, d ae 14, d ae 19 mbnn; surname also spelled
    CHILDRES. R535
  Goldsby, see CHILDERS, Goolsberry. R535
  Goolsberry, esf 1776-7 VA; b 1/1/1757; PN 1818 Garrard Co,
    KY; family in 1820 w ae 56 & 13 ch, of which 10 grew to
    adulthood, & but 2 res with sol then, a s b 4/1807 & d ae
    19; QLF states sol b SC & mvd to VA. R535
  Henry, esf Amherst Co, VA; b Albemarle Co,VA; PN ae 68 Grant
    Co, KY, 1833 where res 34-35 years. R535
  Jacob, esf York District, SC; b c1762-3 VA; mvd to NC as in-
    fant; afp aec 72 York District, SC, 1834, & PAR. R535
  Mosby, esf Charlottesville,VA; PN ae 55 Gallia Co, OH, 1818;
    in 1821 family res with him: w aec 55, s ae 18, s ae 14, 3
    d's ae 12-20, & 2 gc, eldest being ae 4; sol stated ae 66
    then; sol at one time res Hancock Co, IN; dd 8/3/43 leav-
    ing no wid but ch: John, Hannah, William, Mosby, Robert,
    Henry, Andrew, Martin, Nancy, Joseph, & Abraham, + 7 gdc
    mbnn; QLF states sol b 1747 & res Brown Co, IN, 1840 ae 93
    R535
  Patterson, see CHILDRESS, Patterson. R535
  Pleasant, esf Warren Co,NC; PN ae 57 Floyd Co, KY, 1818; res
    there 1823; dd 4/25/39 Pike Co,KY; md 4/16/1785 Sarah Jef-
    fries/Jeffriess, Buckingham Co, VA (MB 3/30/85 signed by
    John Jeffriess); wid afp ae 78 Pike Co, KY, 1839 & PAR, h
    living when Act of 7/7/1838 passed; wid dd 4/10/43 leaving
    ch (all liv 1851): Lucy, Elizabeth, Sally, Jesse/Jessie,
    Nathaniel, Pleasant, & Flemon. R535

CHILDRESS, Alexander, esf VA; PN ae 67 Henrico Co, VA, 1818;
family in 1820 w Temperance aec 40, d ae 14, d ae 12, s
aec 6 months; dd 12/22/39; md 9/1810 Temperance Bennett,
Henrico Co, VA; wid PN ae 75 there 1855 & dd 7/18/60; only
heirs s Joseph L & d-in-law Helen Childress afp 1866 Richmond, VA, for arrears due sol wid; PAR, since wid paid in
full to her death. R535
  Benjamin, esf 1780 ae 16 VA; afp 1850 Albemarle Co, VA; PAR;
AFF then by younger bro Samuel there. R535
  John, esf 1780 Surry Co, NC; b 5/5/1755 Cumberland Co, VA; f
KIA at Braddock's Defeat; esf 1781 Fayette Co, KY; after
RW mvd to Red River, TN, thence to near Nashville, thence
Laurens District, SC, for c18 years, thence Sevier Co, TN,
till 1826, thence to Rutherford Co, TN, where PN 1832; dd
1/9/44; md Martha, d/o Thomas Calhoon, Laurens Co, SC; QLF
1924 from desc Mrs W W Winders, Olive Branch, MS; QLF 1922
from desc Mrs P H Holland, New York, NY. R535
  John, esf 1778 Amherst Co, VA; b 12/2/1759 Albemarle Co, VA;
after RW mvd to Burke Co, NC, thence Wilkes Co, NC, for 7-
8 years, thence Knox Co, TN, where PN 1833; QLF states sol
bro Henry of Grant Co, KY; QLF 1922 from great great great
gdd Mrs F J Phippenney, Manhattan, KS. R535
  Mitchel, esf Wilkes Co, NC; b 10/23/1760 Henrico Co, VA; mvd
after RW to Greene Co, TN, for 1 year, thence Knox Co, TN,
where PN 1833 when res for 40 years; dd 8/5/44; md while
res Amherst Co, VA, wife unnamed; QLF 1937 from desc Mrs R
L Rose, Springfield, TN (on her m's side), Mrs Rose also a
desc of VA RW sol John Reed on her m's side, & she also a
desc of RA RW sol Zachariah Haden of Goochland Co, VA, who
md Elizabeth Poor, their ch births: Thomas Pore 6/16/1767,
Robert 8/10/65, Susaniah 9/29/68, Elizabeth 6/18/73, Jesse
9/6/76. R535
  Patterson, esf Buckingham Co, VA; dd 9/12/1831; md 5/12/1784
Nancy, who afp ae 76 Jefferson Co, TN, 1844; wid PAR, insufficient proof of svc; in 1853 d Nancy Hamilton address
P O Flint Gap, Jefferson Co, TN, & she one/o heirs/o m; in
1854 Nancy address P O Mecklenburg, Knox Co, TN; QLF 1939
from great gds W A Grant, Kansas City, MO; QLF states sol
had s Abraham. R535
  Robert, esf Amelia Co, VA; afp ae 78 Franklin Co, VA, 1834 &
PAR, insufficient proof of svc; QLF 1939 from Mrs Cora
Childress Ginnings, Macomb,IL, states she d/o Newton Chil-
dress who s/o John Milton Childress who s/o John Childress
who s/o Robert Childress who res 1782-1791 Prince Edward
Co, VA. R535
  Thomas, esf 1777 Charlotte Co, VA; b 1750 Chesterfield Co,
VA; res after RW Edgefield District, SC, for 30 years,
then mvd to Madison Co, AL; PN 1832 Lincoln Co, TN. R535
  William, esf Caswell Co, NC; later esf Ninety-Six District,
SC, where gdf William Vaughan res; b 12/25/1762 Buckingham
Co, VA; PN 1833 White Co,TN; dd 1/14/39; md 7/28/1784 Cha-
rity, Buckingham Co, VA; wid afp ae 83 DeKalb Co, TN, 1844

CHILDRESS (continued)
& PAR, proof of marriage; s Hiram liv 1834; QLF 1935 from
desc Mary Baker Simrall, ae 80, Cookeville, TN. R535
  William, see CHILDREY, William. R535
CHILDREY, William, esf 1776 Charlotte Co, VA, where b 1760; PN
1832 Halifax Co, VA; dd 2/29/40; md 12/27/1786 Anne Hanson
who PN ae 77 Charlotte Co, VA, res there 1848 ae 81. R535
CHILES, Henry, esf 1778 Caroline Co, VA, where b 12/18/1762;
PN 1832 Madison, Madison Co, VA; QLF 1932 from desc Mrs
Claude Rutherford, Parrott, GA. R536
  Hezekiah, b 1760 VA, mvd as ch to Granville Co,NC, where esf
1780; PN 1832 Lincoln Co, TN; QLF 1939 from Ira W Chiles,
Huntsville, AL. R536
  James, esf Orange Co, VA, where b; PN aec 70 there 1832; dd
1/7/52; d Susan R md Clayton Matthews who res 1854 Louisa
Co, VA; Susan one/o sol heirs. R536
  Thomas, esf VA; PN 1795 for disability from wounds; res 1820
Anson Co,NC; dd 9/15/20; records lost in DC fire; QLF 1915
from desc Mrs Jane Julian Chinn, Frankfort, KY, states sol
md Lucy, d/o RW sol Tarleton Woodson & w Ursula Fleming,
who res & dd Caroline Co, VA. R536
CHILTON, Andrew, esf 1778 VA; PN aec 58 Lancaster Co,VA, 1818;
dd 11/15/19; md 12/26/86 or 12/26/88 Elizabeth/Betsy Davis
who dd 5/15/1839 aec 74, leaving ch Richard D, Hiram & Mary; Hiram dd intestate leaving ch Richard & Margaret; wid
heirs afp Richmond, VA, 1856, & PAR, since wid dd before
her PN application approved. R537
  John, esf 1776 Fauquier Co,VA; KIA 9/11/1777 Battle of Brandywine; copy of sol LWT in file dated 8/24/1776 lists ch
but no w; LWT probated Fauquier Co, VA, 11/24/1777; s John
designed to receive sol's surveying instruments; s Thomas
afb 1810 for sol ch: Thomas, Joseph, George, Lucy & Nancy;
BLW gtd; s Joseph res Warrenton, VA, 1837; QLF 1925 from
desc Mrs Ben T Jordan, Houston, TX, states sol w probably
a Miss Blackwell, further sol s Thomas US congressman from
KY for several terms & later res AL. R537
CHINN, Perry, esf 1780 King George Co; b 1763 Stafford Co, VA;
PN 1833 Surry Co, NC; dd 3/7/47; md 12/30/1825 Elizabeth
Carr; wid PN ae 75 East Bend, Yadkin Co, NC, 1853; surname
also spelled CHIN. R537
CHISHAM, George, see CHISM, George. R537
  James, esf Orange Co, VA; b 1/25/1768; PN 1832 Scott Co, KY;
dd c9/15/38; md Fall of 1788 Catharine, Orange Co, VA, who
PN ae 76 Scott Co, KY, 1843, when nephew John Chisham res
there; ch mbnn; QLF 1934 from great great gdd Johnie K
(Mrs Vance O) Rankin, Atlanta, GA. R537
CHISHOLM, George, BLW issued 2/24/1794. R537
CHISHOLME, Walter, esf Hanover Co, VA, where b 4/19/1732, & PN
1832. R537
CHISM, George, esf 1776 Orange Co, VA; PN ae 62 Scott Co, KY,
1818; dd 12/13/30; md 3/15/1779 Mary, Orange Co,VA, who PN
ae 82 Scott Co,KY, 1837; ch births: George 8/24/1782, John

CHISM (continued)
8/5/84, Sarah 5/21/86, Betsey 3/1/88, Benjamin 5/1793, &
Rachel 1/18/96; d Polly ae 23 in 1820; QLF states wid res
ae 86 with s Benjamin, Georgetown, KY, 183-. R537
CHISMAN, Thomas, see CHEESEMAN, Thomas. R537
CHITWOOD, James, esf 1781 Rutherford Co, NC; b 6/21/1751 Cum-
berland Co (that area now Powhatan Co), VA; PN 1832 Camp-
bell Co, TN. R538
William, see CHEATWOOD, William. R538
CHIVVIS, William, esf 1777 Gloucester Co, VA; PN aec 69 New
York, NY, 1818; family in 1820 w ae 62 & ch: Mary ae 32,
Margaret ae 22, Eliza ae 17, & Peter ae 14; QLF from great
gdd Emma P Comes, New York, NY. R538
CHOAT, Christopher, b 1/1/1750 Bedford Co, VA; esf 1780 Ninety
Six District, SC; PN 1833 McNairy Co, TN. R539
Greenberry, b 1751 VA; esf on Holston River,NC, in that part
of Washington Co later TN; PN 1833 Johnson Co, IL. R539
CHOCKLEY, Thomas, esf VA/PA for VA regiment; PN Dunbar Town-
ship, Fayette Co, PA, 1819. R539
CHOICE, Tully, esf 1776 Pittsylvania Co (area now Henry Co),
VA; b 6/17/1753 Orange, Culpeper, or Pittsylvania Co, VA;
mvd 1784 to Ninety Six District,SC, thence 1792 to Hancock
Co, GA, where PN 1833; dd there 12/19/37; md 8/16/1791 Re-
becca Sims, Laurens District,SC; wid b 10/29/1775, PN 1843
Hancock Co,GA; ch births: John 1/8/1793 (dd 1/15/93), Fin-
ton 3/28/96 (dd 11/3/99), Anne 8/7/97, William 2/11/1800,
Tully 6/10/02 (dd 7/8/03), Ruth 4/15/04, Jesse 10/23/06,
Katharine 7/8/10, Martha 4/30/15, & Rebecca 10/29/18; sol
bro William res 1832 Greenville District, SC, also RW sol.
R539
William, esf 1778 Pittsylvania Co (area now Henry Co), VA,
with bro Tully; b 1/30/1756 Halifax Co (area now Pittsylvania Co), VA; PN 1842 Greenville District, SC, having mvd
there from VA 1784; dd there 9/30/43; md 5/10-11/1786 Mary
McDonald, Laurens District, SC; wid PN ae 81 Greenville
District, SC, 1848, & dd there 10/6/48; ch births: Tully
12/18/1787, Ann 7/30/90, Mary 7/7/92 (dd 8/12/92), John
10/11/93, William 10/24/96, Cyrus 10/18/99, Aralinta
7/20/02, Sophia 10/29/05, Joseah 3/28/08, & Jefferson
4/29/11; ch surv m: William, Joseah, Tully, Jefferson, Cyrus (Santa Fe, NM), Ann/Nancy w/o Samuel Cobb (res Cherokee Co, AL), & Aralinta w/o Joseph Dial (res Cherokee Co,
AL); s Cyrus decd in 1851; sol sis Sophia w/o Jesse Kerby
res 1848 Warren Co, KY (Sophia b 9/23/1760 & md 1778 Henry
Co, VA). R539
CHRISMAN, Joseph, esf 1782 Crab Orchard VA (now in KY) against
Shawnee Indians; afp ae 74 Wayne Co, KY, 1835; PAR, since
svc not considered RW svc; heir James S Chrisman afp Mont-
ville, Wayne Co, KY, 1853, & PAR. R539
CHRISP, John, b 12/23/1755 Prince George Co, VA; mvd as ch to
Chesterfield Co, VA, where esf 1779; after RW mvd to Cum-
berland Co, VA, thence 1817 Rutherford Co, TN, thence 1832

CHRISP (continued)
    to Gibson Co, TN, where PN 1833; QLF 1897 from Lt R O
    Crisp, Baltimore, MD. R539
CHRIST, Philip, esf 1776 Berks Co, PA, where b 1759; mvd 1785
    to Shepherdstown, VA, for 5 years, thence Greenbrier Co,
    VA, thence Botetourt Co, VA, where PN 1833 aec 74. R539
CHRISTIAN, Allen, esf 1780 Bedford Co, VA; b 5/22/1754 Cumber-
    land Co, VA; after RW res Bedford Co, VA 10-15 years, then
    res Guyandotte, VA, 10-12 years, thence Shelby Co, IN,
    where PN 1833 Liberty Township. R540
  Andrew, esf 1777 Hanover Co, VA, where b 3/17/1761; mvd aec
    25 to Amelia Co,VA, for 5-6 years, thence Prince Edward Co
    VA, for 20 years, thence Fayette Co, KY, where PN 1833, &
    where dd 12/30/37; md Mary/Polly Hatton, Amelia Co, VA, MB
    dated 11/23/1790, signed by Thomas Hatton; 12 ch who res
    1837 in KY, IL, IN, & MO; AFF 1843 by wid bro William (b
    12/1779) that he nephew of Townsen Wilkinson, & that sol's
    eldest ch then ae 52; wid PN ae 70, Bracken Co, KY, 1843,
    when stated she md sol in 1788. R540
  John, esf 1776 Washington Co, VA; b Ireland 1752; to America
    1760, & res on Church River in Fincastle, VA, before mvd
    to Washington Co, VA; mvd to East TN, thence KY, where PN
    1832 Fayette Co, having been blind for more than 23 years;
    w mbnn 1832. R540
  John, esf 1777 VA; b 10/16/1761 Kingston Parish, Gloucester
    Co, VA; PN 1832 Mathews Co, VA; dd 7/6/38. R540
  Rawleigh C, esf 1774 Northumberland Co, VA; PN there 1819 ae
    65; dd there 7/4/28; md 7/4/1782 a widow Elizabeth Pope,
    who ae 70 in 1821; wid PN ae 86 Lancaster Co, VA, 1839; 4
    ch; only s in US Army 1817 having already served at least
    10 years; in 1817 3 d's all md; wid dd 1/28/1840 leaving 3
    ch mbnn; QLF states sol middle name CHINN. R540
  Robert, b c7 miles from Staunton, VA; esf Augusta Co ae 17;
    PN ae 68 Kanawha Co, VA, 1832; bro/o Sarah Wilson. R540
  Thomas, esf Buckingham Co, VA, where b; PN there 1841 ae 81;
    dd at home there 10/3/53; md there 7/6/1814 Mary Adcock at
    her f's house; wid PN there 1854 ae 56 & BLW 1855. R540
  Walter, esf VA; b 9/23/1760 s/o Charles; gtd BLW for svc; dd
    8/1829; md 7/31/1783 Martha/Patsey, d/o Thomas & Phebe
    Walton, Cumberland Co, VA; wid b 12/12/1766 & PN 1840 Am-
    herst Co, VA, where res 1845 when gtd PN increase. R540
  William, 1775 Hanover Co,VA; PLN ae 60 Fayette Co, KY, 1818;
    AFF there by Judah Christian aec 69, wid of John Christian
    1819. R540
  William, esf 1776 Augusta Co, VA; PN ae 71 Montgomery Co, VA
    1821 where res over 25 years; mvd to Ross Co, OH, 1831, &
    dd there 1/14/33; md Fall of 1792 (MB dated 11/7/92) Mary,
    d/o Thomas Ally/Alley at her f's home, Montgomery Co, VA;
    wid PN ae 75 Ross Co, OH, 1848, & res there ae 88 when gtd
    PN increase & BLW 1857; ch births: Susanna 4/5/1795, Allen
    6/29/99, Margaret 4/25/1800, John 9/25/03, Mary 5/15/05,
    Gordan 11/10/08, & Thomas 1812. R540

CHRISTIE, James, esf 1777 Pittsylvania Co,VA; b 8/16/1758 Lancaster Co, PA; mvd after RW to NC, thence Franklin Co, VA,
thence Lincoln Co, KY, thence Shelby Co, KY, where PN 1832
& dd there 3/8/37; md 3/20/1781-2 Sarah, Orange Co,VA, who
b 4/19/1762; wid PN 1838 Shelby Co, KY, & dd 3/27/44 Ripley Co, IN; heirs of sol & w 1853 (all Christie): James &
Isaac (Ripley Co), William (Hendricks Co), John (Switzerland Co) & their 3 sis's; in 1838 sol 6th ch Israel ae 45,
Shelby Co, IN; QLF 1900 from great gdd M Katherine Wise,
Bloomfield, IA, states sol md Sarah/Sally Lemon, further
family res Christiansburgh, Shelby Co, IN; QLF 1939 from
desc Dora Lewis Sanders, Donna,TX, states sol md Sarah Lemon; QLF states sol s/o William who also RW sol, further
sol md Sarah Lemmon of Franklin Co, VA; QLF 1913 from Si-
meon Bush Christy, Murfreesboro, TN. R540
  Thomas, BLW issued 12/19/1793. R540
CHRISTLER, David, esf VA; dd 12/6/1824; md 10/12/1779 Eliza-
beth, Culpeper Co, VA; wid PN ae 78, Boone Co, KY, 1839;
ch births: Nancy 10/1/1780, Phebe 3/10/84, David 5/30/87,
Margaret 10/2/89, John 9/6/92, Fanny 5/19/95, Anna 3/31/98
Rhoda 6/20/1801, & Catharine 3/27/04; QLF states a Leonard
CHRISLER/CHRISTLER b 1743 Culpeper Co, VA, dd 12/6/1824,
Boone Co,KY, md (1) Margaret (b 1750) d/o John Khlor/Clore
& Dorothea Cafer/Caffer,VA, & md (2) 10/12/1799 Elizabeth,
Culpeper Co, VA, further names of ch of Leonard: Micheal,
Jeremiah, Lewis, Jemima, Anna, William Mason, Allen, Eli-
zabeth, Sally, John, Margaret, Silas, & Elishna, further a
Lewis Crisler b 6/1/1773 Madison Co (formerly part of Cul-
peper Co), VA, md (1) Catherine Chelb & had by her Elinor,
Jemima, Lucy, & Margaret, & md (2) 1806 Mary Zimmerman (b
4/4/1778 VA & dd 1/20/1857 Shelby Co, IN), Boone Co, KY, &
had by her Mildred, Cassandra, Nancy, Benjamin, Allen,
James, Sebria, Abraham, Lewis, & Mary Ann, further Lewis
Sr dd 5/19/1843. R541
CHRISTY, Daniel, esf 1780 Hickory Town, near Philadelphia, PA,
for svc in VA regiment; also US Army svc in War of 1812;
afp ae 72 Sullivan Co, NY, 1832, & PAR, insufficient proof
of svc; surname also spelled CHRISTIE; QLF states sol res
& dd Forestburg, Sullivan Co, NY. R541
  James, b 5/12/1746 London, England; mvd from eastern Augusta
Co, VA, to Greenbrier Co (area now in Monroe Co), VA, 1774
& esf there 1776; afp 1834 Monroe Co, VA, & PAR, svc not
in true military unit; apf again 1841 & PAR. R541
CHROUSHOUR, Nicholas, esf 1782 Morgantown, VA; b 1760 PA; afp
1833 Harrison Co, VA, & PAR. R541
CHUBB, John, BLW issued 7/14/1792. R541
CHUMBLY, John, esf 1778 VA; b 12/4/1760 Amelia Co, VA, & res
there for 10 years after RW, then mvd to Wilkes Co, GA,
thence Bourbon Co, KY, thence IN where PN 1833 Reeve Township, Daviess Co. R541
CHUMLEY, Daniel, esf Halifax Co, VA; PN aec 74 Wilson Co, TN,
1833; QLF 1937 from Virginia Chumley, Chattanooga,TN. R541

CHUN, Silvester, esf 1777 Halifax Co, VA; PN ae 60 Maury Co, TN, 1819; in 1826 ae 69-70, w aec 60 (his 2nd), ch all md, & had steps's Jack Harris & Moses Atkins; dd 4/12/41; surname also spelled CHUNN. R541

CHURCH, John, BLW issued 5/29/1792. R543

CITY, Jacob, esf near Sharpsburg, MD, 1775; mvd to Rockingham Co, VA, 1776 where esf 1781; b 6/28/1760 Lancaster Co, PA; mvd from Rockingham Co,VA, to Bedford Co, VA, c1800, where PN 1833, & dd there 5/6/36; md 3/1781 Elizabeth/Betsey d/o John Runion, Brock's Gap, VA; wid PN ae 80 Bedford Co, VA, 1841 & dd there 12/31/44; family bible entries in German & ch births (all surname ZETTI) were: Katarina 1/22/1782, Anna 9/11/83, Abraham 10/17/85, Johan 1/14/1790, Jacob 3/17/92, Magdalena 11/20/93, Sera 1/14/97, Christian 7/4/99, Sehm 3/17/1802, & Beddi 4/18/06; in 1841 William W Stevens AFF ae 64 that he md Nancy, 2nd d/o sol, & that sol eldest d Catharine md John Wood, & sol's other ch were Abraham, John, Jacob, Polly, Christopher, Elizabeth, Sally, Samuel, & Patsey; in 1841 John Wood AFF that he md sol d Catharine in 1803 when he ae 21; sol surname sometimes spelled CITTY. R546

CLACK, Moses, esf VA; BLW issued 11/26/1792; PN aec 64 Fleming Co, KY, 1828 & dd 9/25/42; md 10/19/1792 (MB 10/16/92) Ann d/o Samuel Deadman who signed MB, Albemarle Co, VA; wid PN ae 67 Fleming Co,KY, & res there 1848 ae 81; QLF 1933 from Kate Burke Moran, El Paso, TX, states sol w Ann/Nancy 10th ch/o parents, further sol s Philip Deadman md Mary Henderson, & their d res Paris, TX, 1933, very aged aunt of querier. R546

  Sterling, esf 1776 VA; b 11/17/1759; PN 1830 Sumner Co, TN; dd 11/6/37; md 8/17/1780 Mary/Polly, d/o Bennett Woods, Warren Co, NC; wid b 11/22/1766, & PN 1839 Sumner Co, TN; family bible damaged, & ch birth dates mostly unreadable: Nancy 11/5/17--, Eldridge, William, Bennett dd 10/22/1796, John Twitty, & James Caller; AFF 1839 by John Baynes, Sumner Co, TN, that his sis md bro/o sol w Mary. R546

CLAGETT, Samuel, see CLAGGETT, Samuel. R547

CLAGGETT, Samuel, esf 1777 Charles Co,MD, while student of mecine at Port Tobacco, MD, as surgeon's mate; settled in VA after RW; dd 4th Monday of March 1821; md 9/15/1785 Amie Jane Ramey of Cameron Parish at Leesburg, Loudoun Co, VA, per her AFF, but MB dated 8/22/1786 per Co clerk's certificate to court; wid PN ae 68 Fauquier Co, VA, 1838 & dd there 11/10/47 leaving ch: Ferdinand, Christopher, Thomas, Anne w/o Tomlin Bailey, Elizabeth w/o Thomas McCormick, Cecelia w/o John G Kirby, Sophia w/o Thomas Simpson, & Juliet w/o Robert Roach, all liv 1850; d Mary Cooper & s Samuel dd before m & had ch mbnn liv 1850; AFF 1838 by William Horner ae 69, res Warrenton, VA, high sheriff of Fauquier Co, that he halfbro/o sol, & also b & reared Charles Co, MD, further his m's s's Dr Samuel Clagett & Dr Gustavus Horner RW svc together, further his m Ann also md Sa-

CLAGGETT (continued)
muel Hanson Sr of Green Hills, Charles Co, MD, further Dr
William Brown, RW surgeon, near relative of sol; QLF 1929
from desc Mrs Samuel W Price, Searles, WV; QLF 1904 from
gds Charles W Cooper, res/o Ex-Confederate Soldiers' Home,
Richmond, VA, states sol wid dd c1848, further querier bro
of Mrs Price of Smyth Co, VA. R547
CLAIBORNE, Leonard, esf 1779 Chesterfield Co, VA, where b; PN
ae 73 Buckingham Co, VA, 1834; dd 12/9/39; md 11/27/1788
Frances/Fanny Tanner, Amelia Co, VA; wid PN ae 74 Bucking-
ham Co, VA, 1841; QLF states sol s John Tanner mvd from
Buckingham Co, VA, to TN. R547
  Richard, BLW issued 12/4/1794; papers lost in Washington, DC
  fire; QLF states sol b VA 1755 s/o William, & was aide to
  Gen Greene in RW; QLF states sol mvd to New Orleans, LA,
  & became judge. R547
CLAPPER, Valentine, esf c1776 MD; PN ae 72 Harrison Co, VA; in
1820 w ae 75. R548
CLARDY, Thomas, esf 1781 Halifax Co, VA, where b 10/23/1761;
PN 1832 there; dd 1/4/33. R548
CLARK, Birgess/Burgis, esf Chatham Co, NC; b 1763 Goochland Co
VA; family bible lost when Tories plundered f's house in
Chatham Co, NC; PN 1832 White Co, TN, where dd 10/22/50;
md 8/4/1799 Rhody Morris, Richmond Co, NC; wid PN 1850
White Co, TN; wid afb there 1855 ae 87, but dd before recd
BLW that was issued 7/31/56 & BLW cancelled; her ch Samuel
& Sally gtd BLW & mvd to Osceola Co, IA. R549
  David, BLW issued 4/21/1796. R551
  Dennis, esf 1775 Bedford Co, PA; esf 1781 Winchester, VA; b
  1756 Frederick Co, MD; PN 1832 Cincinnati, OH. R551
  Edmund, BLW issued 4/14/1800; papers lost in Washington, DC,
  fire; QLF states sol & bro Larkin b Orange Co, VA, s's of
  James who dd there 1789, further sol & Larkin dd GA. R552
  Edward, esf VA; b 12/27/1756; PN 1822 Elbert Co, GA, where
  res c30 years, when w ae 61 & d ae 19 mbnn; QLF 1934 from
  desc Mrs William W Stark, Commerce, GA. R552
  Elijah, esf 1779 Charlotte Co, VA; b 1759 Louisa Co, VA; PN
  1832 Charlotte Co, VA; QLF 1929 from desc Margaret McCor-
  mack, Columbus, IN. R552
  Field, esf 1775 Chesterfield Co, VA; b 4/30/1751 s/o Allison
  & Blanch; dd 1/29/1832; md 7/5/1774 Mary d/o Jacob Lester,
  Chesterfield Co, VA; wid afp ae 87 Lunenburg Co, VA, 1840,
  & PAR; another Field Clark b 3/2/1788 s/o Peter. R553
  James, esf 1779 Chester/Camden District, SC; b c1761 on Roa-
  noke River, VA; res SC to 1832 when mvd to Monroe Co, MS,
  where afp 1844 & PAR. R556
  James, esf 1780 Augusta Co, VA; PN ae 69-70 Blount Co, TN,
  1832. R556
  James, esf 1779 Chesterfield Co, VA, where b 1750; PN there
  1832; dd there 2/9/40 leaving 2 ch mbnn. R556
  James, esf 1781 Mecklenburg Co, VA, where b 2/18/1759; PN
  1833 Mercer Co, KY. R556

CLARK, James, esf Orange Co, VA; PN aec 50 Casey Co, KY, 1819;
in 1820 w Eleanor aec 60 & 5 ch all md. R556
James, esf Amherst Co, VA; dd 2/1832 Shelby Co, OH, aec 75;
md 9/1809 Nancy Clark in VA; wid dd 1835; surv ch 1832 Mc-
Lager, William, Albert, Rebecca, Nancy, & Horatio; afp by
only surv ch Horatio & Rebecca, Darke Co, OH, 1856, & PAR.
R556
John, esf 1775 Baltimore, MD; b 8/13/1747; PN 1818 Pickaway
Co, OH, 1818 where res c18 years; dd 7/26-27/1822; md
8/7/1794 Sarah Louden, Berkeley Co, VA, who bc 1774; wid
md (2) Simon/Simeon Andrews who dd 1845; ch births by sol:
Joseph 6/30//1795, Ann/Nancy Ann 2/19/97, John 3/7/99, Ca-
therine 6/19/1801, Sarah/Sally 8/9/04, Elizabeth 1/2/07,
Jane 8/20/11, & James 8/1/13; wid dd 10/5/53, leaving ch
Joseph, John, Nancy Ann Davis (res 1854 Franklin Co, OH),
Elizabeth Groves, & Jane Peltier who all gtd PN due m as
wid/o sol; other FB data: Nancy w/o John Clark dd 6/5/1839
& Joannah w/o John Clark dd 5/31/184-. R557
John, esf 1780 Middlesex Co, VA; b 2/18/1761 Essex Co, VA;
PN 1834 Middlesex Co, VA, where res since ch. R557
John, esf 1775-6 Essex Co, VA; PN ae 59 King & Queen Co, VA,
where dd 4/13/44; md (4) Miss Fogg; md (5) 3/32/1832 Mrs
Lucy Smither there; in 1828 family w mbnn & ch all surname
CLARKE: Benjamin F ae 13, Hannah B ae 11, Sam P ae 10, Mary E ae 8, Thomas I ae 7, & Martha E ae 6; wid b 4/22/1780
& PN 1851 Richmond, VA, & res there 1854 with Maria F Smither, d by her previous h; Rev Joseph H Davis, nephew of
wid res there then; wid s Gary res Richmond 1855, when wid
res Milton, Caswell Co,NC, with s-in-law Albert G Stevens;
wid dd 4/21/55; QLF 1928 from sol great gds Rev W T Hund-
ley, De Land, FL. R558
John, esf 1777 Charlottesville, Albemarle Co, VA; PN ae 75
Blount Co, TN, 1818; in 1821 aec 80 & w Letitia aec 65 in
that Co. R559
John, esf VA; dd 10/31/1845 Henderson Co,NC; md 3/9/1799 Catharine Ransom, Wilkes Co, GA; wid afp 1853 & 1855 Gilmer
Co, GA, & PAR, no proof of marriage; ch liv 1853: Lucy,
John, Sarah, George, William, Martha Ann, Robert, & Thomas
J; surname at times spelled CLARKE. R559
John, esf 1778-9 Ohio Co, VA; b 8/17/1765 PA; mvd from VA to
KY 1783; PN 1833 Greene Co, IL, where dd 9/13/44 leaving
wid Mary/Polly & ch: Absalom, Mary Atkins, Rebecca Wollingsford, & Miranda Bryan; wid dd 4/2/1846 Scott Co, IL;
ch who afp 1855: Absalom of Greene Co, IL, Nancy Atkins of
Paris, Lemar Co, TX, Rebecca Wollingsford of Muscatine Co,
IA, & Miranda Bryan of Warren Co, IA; ch PAR since m not
wid in 1838, dd bef 1851, & no proof of marriage. R559
Jonathan, b 1759 Bedford Co (later Campbell Co), VA; f mvd
family 1773 to Surry Co (later Stokes Co), NC, where sol
esf 1776; mvd 1784 to SC, thence 1803 to Christian Co, KY,
where PN 1832; youngest bro, Joseph too young to be RW sol
& res there 1832; QLF 1929 from Minnie Clark Keys states

CLARK (continued)

she great great gdd of RW sol Jonathan Clark, b Ireland, &
w Jane Rogers, b Scotland, who emigrated before RW & settled NC, later Christian Co, KY, where this sol dd 1850,
further sol s Nathaniel/Phanniel md Marsella Pennington
there having ch: Alonzo, Franklin, Jonathan, Phine, Polly
Ann (md Jacob Hainley), further both Alonzo & Franklin dd
Confederate sols Civil War, further Nathaniel mvd to Mississippi Co,MO, 1832 where dd 1839 & w dd 1866; querier gdd
of Alonzo who dd 12/16/1862 Pocahontas, AR, further Alonzo
md Mary Jane Ancell & they had d Nora & s James N who md
Miranda Elizabeth Alvord, & they parents/o querier. R560
Jonathan, BLW issued 12/11/1797. R560
Joseph, esf Orange Co,VA, where b 4/12/1752; PN there 1837;
dd there 2/5-6/1839; md (1) ?, (2) c1812 Catharine (no ch
by her); ch by 1st w: Larkin (res Morgan Co, GA), Martha
E w/o Reuben Clark (res Madison Co, VA), James (res Elbert
Co, GA), Mary w/o Col Herd (res Morgan Co, GA), Ann P w/o
Adjutant General John C Easter/Easton (res Elbert Co, GA),
Elizabeth w/o Col Thomas White (res Jones Co, GA), Sally T
w/o Lewis Shirler (res Louisa Co,VA), Tabitha w/o Cuthbert
Reese (res Jones Co, GA), Eunice w/o Solomon H McIntire
(res Madison Co, VA), William D (res Orange Co, VA), Bathsheba S (res Orange Co, VA); s William D afp 1851 for sol
surv ch: William D, Martha E Clark, Ann P Easter/Easton,
Elizabeth White, Sally T Shirler, Tabitha Reese, & Bathsheba S, & PN gtd; sol bro Robert/Robbin ae 90 Orange Co,
VA, 1850; QLF 1935 from Sally Graves (Mrs R M) Clark, Lexington, KY, states her h desc of sol; QLF 1933 from desc
Edna Arnold (Mrs Z W) Copeland, Elberton,GA; QLF 1913 from
great great gdd Mattie J White (Mrs John O) Ponder, For-
syth, GA, states sol md (1) Ann Haynes & their d Elizabeth
Haynes md querier's great gdf Thomas White who came to GA
1806-7; QLF 1906 from great gdd Mrs Jessie Reese Murphy
states sol b Culpeper Co, VA, md Anne Haines, & dd Willow
Grove, Orange Co, VA, 2/21/1839. R561
Lee, esf Brunswick Co,VA; parents mvd to NC, settling on Haw
River during RW; sol esf again 1780 NC; PN ae 76 Guilford
Co, NC, 1832. R562
Lewis, esf 1777 Gloucester Co, VA, where PN 1810 ae 64; sur-
name at times spelled CAKE. R562
Lewis, esf 1779 Dinwiddie Co, VA, where b 4/27/1763; mvd to
Franklin Co,TN, 1820, thence 1829 to Jackson Co, AL, where
PN 1833, & dd there 1/12/42; md 9/24/1800 Sally Rogers at
house of her f, Dinwiddie Co, VA, (MB 9/11/00); wid PN ae
73 Jackson Co, AL, 1853, when Joseph S Clarke AFF Lincoln
Co, TN, that he present at marriage of f to Sally Rogers;
AFF then by John R Clark, Benton Co, AL, that he also pre-
sent; QLF states a Lewis Clarke b1771, md 3/27/1799 Mary
Ligon Moseley, & dd 1854-6 leaving ch Asa, George R, James
P, & Martha A, further this Lewis s/o James; sol surname
also spelled CLARKE. R562

CLARK, Matthew, esf 1781 Goochland Co, VA, where b 2/7/1763; res Prince Edward Co, VA, after RW, thence to Pendleton District, SC; afp 1832 Anderson District, SC, & PAR insufficient proof of svc; dd 6/2/1841; QLF states sol one of 7 bro's to enlist; QLF 1912 from great gds Dr Clifton P Clark, Washington, DC. R563

Micajah, esf 1775 Surry Co, VA; b 1749 Albemarle Co, VA; PN 1833 Warren Co, KY; dd 12/22/38; 4 ch mbnn; QLF states a Micajah Clark bc 1749 Campbell Co, VA, md Mildred Martin, & they mvd to KY where they dd; QLF states a Micajah Clark an RW sol, s/o Christopher & h/o Judith Adams; QLF 1915 from desc Mary J Hendrick, Frankfort, KY. R563

Micajah, esf 1776 Powhatan Co, VA; esf 1781 Bedford Co, VA; dd 1/6/1821 Amherst Co,VA; md 9/23/1779 Keziah d/o Charles Harris, Powhatan Co,VA; wid PN ae 78 Amherst Co, VA, 1839; ch births: Elizabeth Dawson 7/8/1780, Charles Harris 3/16/82, William Madison 11/30/83, Sarah Dickerson 8/2/86, Nathaniel Harris 6/20/90, Ira Ellis 11/9/92, Joseph Garland 1/8/95, Keziah Snelson 11/2/97, Micajah Lynch 5/2/00 & Nancy Thomas 5/30/18--, Harriot Loving 7/7/18-- (family bible torn); QLF 1925 from desc Mary H Hume, Washington, DC, states she also desc/o RW sol John Hendrick. R563

Patrick, esf 1779 Orange Co, VA; b 1756 Caroline Co, VA; PN 1833 Mercer Co, KY. R564

Richard, esf 1779 Caroline Co, VA, where b 7/6/1760; gtd BLW for land near Louisville, Jefferson Co, KY, where res when dd 3/1784; bro-in-law of William Croghan; Col Attilla Cox, adm/o sol estate, recd sol PN arrears 1898. R564

Robert, esf 1777 Chesterfield Co, VA; b 7/20/1761 Middlesex Co, VA; PN 1833 Tipton Co, TN; dd 9/25/37. R564

Samuel, esf 1780 Augusta Co, VA, where b 4/18/1764; mvd 1786 to Greenbrier Co, VA, to area now Monroe Co where PN 1832; dd 1/12/1857. R565

Shadrack, esf 1775 Chesterfield Co, VA; mvd to Lunenburg Co, VA, where esf 1780; afp by s Field Clark Jr there 1841 for f ae 82 who had been insane for past 35 years; PAR, insufficient proof of svc & s not proved legal guardian of f; other ch mbnn. R566

Silas, PN 1789 paid by PA agency; dd 8/13/1800; records lost in Washington, DC, fire; QLF 1927 from Mrs Emma C Barry, gdd/o a Silas Clark b 9/7/1809, Harrisburg, states a Silas Clark of MD md Linnie & they had d Mary Anne b 5/13/1764 who md 1790 William Wood, Culpeper Co, VA. R566

Susannah Elizabeth, former wid/o John SCOTT. R566

Thomas, esf 1779 Charlotte Co, VA; b 1746 Louisa Co, VA; PN 1833 Charlotte Co, VA. R566

Thomas, esf 1777 VA; also War of 1812 svc from TN; family in 1820 w Sally ae 60 & d Jane ae 18; PN ae 65 Bledsoe Co, TN when occupation weaver. R566

Thomas, esf 1775 Gloucester Co, VA; b 8/28/1755 Fairfax Co, where f res during RW; PN 1786 for disability from wounds Battle of Brandywine; res 1824 Fayette Co, KY, res for c34

CLARK (continued)
years; dd there 2/7/42; md 1/28/1788 Jane, Fairfax Co, VA, who b 7/9/1767; wid PN 1843 Fayette Co, KY, & res there 1855; ch births: Charles 1/30/1789, Edward 5/2/91, Richard 7/14/93, Jefferson 6/9/97, James 12/12/03 (res Fayette Co, KY, 1843); other family bible data: Thomas Clarke s/o Edward & Hannah b 6/30/1815, Nancey Clarke b 4/16-17/1817, William Clarke b 7/31/1818, Charles Clarke b 4/20/1820, David Clarke b 3/8/1822, John Thomas Clarke b 4/12/1830, James William Clarke b 18--, Edward F & Hannah Clarke md 9/27/1814, Charles & Jane Clarke md 5/7/1822, James & Lydiann Clarke md 1/24/1828; QLF states sol wid dd 1857, her maiden name Jane Ford, further sol res Lexington, KY; QLF 1906 from W D Clark, National Soldiers Home, Los Angeles, CA, states he gds of RW sol Thomas M Clark who settled in what now Anderson Co, KY, & had eldest s Thomas M who War of 1812 sol; sol surname also spelled CLARKE. R566

Thomas, esf 1776 VA; PN ae 63 Essex Co, VA; res 1820 Middlesex Co,VA, when w ae 61; dd there 2/26/1822; md 12/24/1779 Lucy Tate (MB 12/21/1778), Essex Co, VA; wid b 1/26/1761 & PN 1838 Middlesex Co, VA; wid dd before 1st PN payment, & left s William & gdc Ware, Thomas Jones, & Lucy Jones who gtd PN due sol wid 1839; sol surname also spelled Clarke. R566

William, esf 1777 Washington Co, NC (later TN); b 4/7/1757 Shenandoah Co, VA; mvd 1784 to Pendleton Co, SC, where PN 1835 as res of Pickens District, SC; mvd 1837 to Hall Co, GA, where dd 6/4/43; md 2/14/1792 Ruth Goodwin, Franklin Co, GA; who b 2/14/1792, & PN 1844 Hall Co, GA; ch births: John 11/5/1793, Oliver 10/9/94, Sevier 11/11/97, & Sabra 3/3/99; sol bro George svc with sol; QLF states sol md (1) Ruth d/o Gen Sevier. R568

William, esf 1777 Hanover Co, VA; PN ae 60 Jackson Co, OH, 1819; dd there 3/29/27; md 9/1794 Nancy Ann Williams, Amherst Co, VA (MB 9/3/94); wid md (2) James Andrews, who dd 4/5/46; wid PN ae 70 Scioto Township, Jackson Co, OH, 1849 & res there 1855; in 1821 sol & w had ch mbnn including d ae 16; QLF 1936 from Esther Clark Naylor, Salt Lake City, states she desc/o an RW sol William Clark, b 8/3/1745 probably Ireland, dd 5/1/1819 VA, md 5/17/1785 Ann & they had 8 ch. R568

William, esf 1778 Hampshire Co, VA; b 1760 PA & mvd ae 10 to South Branch of Potomac River in VA; mvd after RW to Randolph Co, VA, thence Lewis Co, VA, where PN 1833, dd there 7/23/41; md 8/8/1798 Barbara/Barbary, d/o Jacob Helmick, Randolph Co, VA; wid PN ae 72 Upshur Co, VA, 1851, & dd 8/30/55. R568

CLARKE, Christopher, esf 1777 Fluvanna Co, VA; b 4/5/1763 Louisa Co, VA; PN 1844 Fluvanna Co, VA, & dd there 2/1/51; md 7/10/1810 Elizabeth Hope; wid PN ae 76 there 1854, & recd PN increase 1869 ae 92; QLF states an RW sol Christopher Clarke Jr md Rebecca Davis & settled Elbert Co, GA, with

CLARKE (continued)
f; QLF 1924 from Mrs J W Wright, Elberton, GA, states sol
of previous QLF s/o Christopher Sr who s/o Micajah, further that she desc of this sol & also desc/o George Eberhart
(s/o Jacob), of James Franklin Nunnelee of VA, & of George
Snellings of VA. R569
John esf 1776 Goochland Courthouse, Goochland Co, VA; PN ae
62 Garrard Co,KY, 1818; w mbnn ae 62 in 1821; last PN payment 1842 Butler Co, KY, where res for 7 years; res Logan
Co, KY, before then; QLF states sol res 1840 with Braxton
Clark; sol surname also spelled CLARK. R569
John, esf 1780 Amherst Co,VA, where raised; b 2/27/1764 Hen-
rico Co, VA; PN 1834 Washington Co, KY; dd 1/25/1839; md
5/19/1791 Ann, d/o Mrs Ann Whitten, Lincoln Co, KY; wid b
3/1772, & PN 1845 Washington Co, KY; QLF 1927 from desc
Mildred Marrs, Macomb, IL; QLF 1915 from desc Veta Frank-
lin, Glendale, CA; QLF 1911 from great great gdd Mabel
Franklin Ocker, Albuquerque, NM; sol surname also spelled
CLARK. R569
John, esf 1778 Washington Co, VA as sub for f George; afp ae
69 Macon Co, NC, 1832, & PAR. R569
John, esf 177- ; POW; dd intestate; BLW issued 1831 to Fran-
cis Jr, Sally w/o Marshall Munford, Patsey, & Eliza, ch &
heirs/o sol; heir Thomas B Clarke afb 1849 Cumberland Co,
VA; BLW issued 1849 to sol surv ch: Sally wid/o Marshall
Munford, Patsey, Eliza A Locke + ch/o sol decd s Francis I
(Mary, Eppa H, Jane w/o William Gordon, Nancy, William, &
Thomas B); QLF states an RW sol James Clark b 1737 Orange
Co, VA, dd 1789, LWT probated 9/21/1789 Culpeper Co, VA,
md Mary Marston, & their ch: Elizabeth, Lucy, Ann, John,
Thomas, Susanna, Frances, Mary, Reuben, Joanna, Joseph,
Rhoda, & Ambrose, further their s John also RW sol who b
5/30/1767 Culpeper Co, VA, & dd 11/7/1844 Hopkinsville,
KY, md (1) Mildred Gibs, (2) Mary Gaines, & had ch: Henry,
James, Mildred, Thomas, William, Mary Jane, Joseph, Eliza
Frances, & Sarah Ann, further d Mary Jane liv 1880 as Mrs
Mary Jane Glass; sol surname also spelled CLARK. R569
Joseph, esf 1776 Gloucester Co, VA, where b 12/15/1757; pa-
rents mvd to Fairfax Co, VA, where sol esf 1777; mvd 1792
to Fayette Co, KY, thence Montgomery Co,KY, where PN 1832;
QLF 1928 from desc Margaret McCormack, Columbus, IN. R569
Obadiah, esf 1776 Richmond, VA; b 1756 Henrico Co, VA; mvd
1795 to Shelby Co, KY, where PN 1834, & dd there 2/27/38;
md 6/1785 Nancy Miller, Henrico Co, VA; wid PN ae 72 Shelby Co, KY, 1838 when wid bro Edward AFF there ae 86 he also PN as RW sol & witnessed marriage of sis Nancy to Obadiah; sol surname also spelled CLARK. R570
Robert, esf Orange Co, VA; PN ae 98 there 1848; dd 5/26/1851
leaving d Josephine w/o William P Berry & gdd Martha w/o
Thomas J Adams (Martha d/o sol d Frances decd); BLW issued
sol 12/23/1784; heirs recd PN due sol. R570
Samuel, esf 1776 York Co, PA; PN ae 55 Bath Co, VA, 1818; in

CLARKE (continued)
    1820 d ae 30 res with sol; surname also spelled CLARK.
    R570
  Stephen, esf 1777 Goochland Co, VA, where b 1762; mvd 1805
    to Grayson Co, VA, where PN 1832; dd 1/12/37; surname also
    spelled CLARK. R570
  Spencer, esf 1780 VA; PN ae 57 Middlesex Co, VA, 1821; dd
    there 11/12/34; md there (1) Nancy Clondas (MB 4/23/1787),
    (2) 11/19/07 Elizabeth/Nancy Elizabeth Tool, wid of John
    Mercer (MB 11/2/07 bet sol & Mrs Eliza Mercer); wid afb
    1850 there ae 79 when AFF she md sol 4/23/1787, but later
    AFF she illiterate & was misquoted, stating sol md Nancy
    Cloud on that date, & that she md sol 11/19/07; wid PN ae
    81 there 1853 when AFF by sol s Lewis; surname sometimes
    spelled CLARK. R570
  Thomas, BLW issued 1/31/1794. R570
  Turner, esf 1778 Goochland Co, VA, where afp 1818 ae 61; PN
    there 1820 when had w ae 58 (a midwife), d Sally ae 18, &
    free negro girl Louisa Cousins ae 4 res with him; dd there
    5/8/28; md there 3/18/1789 Elizabeth Cragwell (MB 3/18/79
    between Turner Clarke Jr & Elizabeth Ann Cragwell, signed
    by Isham Clarke); wid b 8/26/1763, & PN there 1839, gtd PN
    increase there 1843, & res there 1848; sol surname also
    spelled CLARK. R570
  William, esf 1775 Washington Co, MD; b 12/18/1758 St Mary's
    Co, MD; mvd to Allegany Co, MD, after RW for 3-4 years, &
    thence Berkeley Co, VA, where PN 1832; ch mbnn 1854. R570
  William, esf 1779 Fluvanna Co,VA; b 2/19/1758 Louisa Co, VA;
    PN 1832 Jefferson Co, GA; dd 2/17/35; QLF 1914 from desc
    William Clarke Thompson, Cordele, GA. R570
  William, esf 1775-6 VA; PN ae 70 Culpeper Co, VA, 1818; fam-
    ily in 1820 w Hannah, 2 d's over ae 21, & gdd ae 3; dd
    12/8/27; md 3/19/1785 Hannah Peters, Stafford Co, VA; wid
    PN ae 80 Culpeper Co, VA. R570
CLARKSON, Constantine, b 12/17/1762 Goochland Co, VA; reared
    Goochland, Bedford, & Pittslvania Co's, VA; esf latter Co
    1779; mvd c1785 to TN & settled near Knoxville; mvd 1819
    to IL where PN Morgan Co 1832; QLF states sol dd Morgan Co
    IL; QLF 1922 from desc Mae W Avery, Jacksonville, IL,
    states sol buried Morgan Co; QLF states sol res Jackson-
    ville, IL. R571
  David, esf 1778 Louisa Co, VA; b 6/1761; PN 1833 Boone Co,
    KY, 1833; dd there 11/14-15/33; md 7/14-15 1790 Phebe/Phe-
    by Smith, Bourbon Co, KY; wid PN ae 65 Pendleton Co, KY,
    1839; wid mvd 1841 with s mbnn to Greene Co, MO, where s
    James I & s David S res with her 1845; wid gtd BLW Dade Co
    MO, 1855; QLF 1916 from desc Miss Frank Anna Eastin of
    Greenfield, MO. R571
CLARY, John, esf 1776 Sussex Co, VA; PN ae 70 Brunswick Co, VA
    1825 when had w Sarah ae 60 & ch: Polly aec 30, Betsey aec
    26, Rebecca ae 19-20, John ae 17-18, William ae 13-14, & 1
    ch mbnn; dd 3/19/25; md 2/1/1788 Sarah Mosely (MB 1/28/88

CLARY (continued)
     signed by William Mosely), Brunswick Co, VA; wid PN ae 76
     Warren Co, NC, 1841, & gtd PN increase there 1843. R571
CLASPY, John, esf Berkeley Co, VA; b 4/7/1760 MD; mvd to VA ae
     12; res after RW TN, thence KY where PN 1832 Warren Co;
     surname also spelled GILLASPEE & CLASBY. R571
CLATTERBUCK, James, esf 1776-7 Culpeper Co, VA; b Caroline Co,
     VA; res as ch Culpeper Co & Madison Co, VA, where PN 1832
     ae 72; illiterate. R571
   Reuben, esf 1776 Caroline Co,VA, where b 12/31/1755; f Dick;
     mvd 1810 to Shelby Co, KY, thence 1829 to Callaway Co, MO,
     where PN 1833 Round Prairie Township; dd 10/12/38; md 1782
     or 1783 Martha/Patsy/Patty, d/o Roy Griffin & w Elizabeth
     Gates, Caroline Co,VA; wid PN ae 79 Callaway Co, MO, 1846;
     10 ch, 7 liv 1846 & all res there: John, Leroy, James, Ca-
     gely/Catesby, Richard, William, & Nancey Darton/Dorton;
     wid res there 1848; QLF states a William S Clatterbuck of
     MO Confederate Army a POW 1864, his w Mary being res 1929
     of New Bloomfield, Calloway Co, MO. R571
CLAWSON, Garret, esf 1778 for svc in VA unit; b 12/25/1759; PN
     1822 Dunkard Township, Greene Co, PA; dd 4/14/30 Fayette
     Co, PA; md 7/29/1790 Kezia, Woodbridgetown, Springhill
     Township, Fayette Co, PA; wid b 4/27/1774 & PN there 1838;
     res 1848 Wood Co, VA, with one d mbnn; ch births: Lea
     4/3/1791, John 4/8/93, Mary 3/23/95, Phineas 8/10/97, Lo-
     tow 7/11/99, Thomas 8/22/1801, James 9/20/03, Isaac Stur-
     gis 11/20/05, Garret 7/18/08, Kezia 9/12/10 & dd 7/27/19,
     Abia 1/13/13 & dd 7/15/19, & Josiah 8/29/15 & dd --/16/19;
     wid sis Mary Fields res Fayette Co, PA, 1838; QLF 1930
     from desc Nellie M (Mrs U P) Ferguson, Vernon, MI. R571
   John, esf 1777 Sussex Co, NJ; b 1755 Middlesex Co, NJ; after
     RW res Berkeley Co, VA, for 30 years, thence to Meade Co,
     KY, where afp 1835 & PAR, service less than 6 months; lost
     hand when rifle blew up when fighting indians in RW & dis-
     charged disabled. R571
CLAY, Elijah, esf 1778 Cumberland Co (later Powhatan Co), VA,
     where b 8/27/1759; PN 1833 Edgar Co, IL; s mbnn & d Catha-
     rine referred to. R572
   John, esf 1777 Dinwiddie Co, VA, where b 1755; PN 1832 Ruth-
     erford Co, TN; dd 5/11-12/35; md 1779-82 Melison/Millerson
     Eppes, Dinwiddie Co, VA; wid afp ae 86-7 Rutherford Co, TN
     when s Joshua ae 55-6; wid PAR, no proof md before end of
     sol svc. R572
   Matthew, BLW issued 5/20/1797; records lost in Washington,
     DC, fire 1800. R572
   Thomas, esf 1779 Amelia Co, VA, where b 11/1760; PN 1833 Ha-
     lifax Co, VA. R572
   William, esf 1776 Chesterfield Co,VA, where b 1760; mvd 1781
     to Amelia Co, VA, for 3-4 years, thence to Halifax Co, VA,
     thence 1793 to Washington Co, VA, thence Jefferson Co, TN,
     for 1 year, thence Grainger Co,TN, where PN 1832; dd there
     8/4/41; md 12/30/1788 Rebecca, Halifax Co, VA, at home of

CLAY (continued)
her f Samuel Comer; wid PN ae 77 Grainger Co, TN, 1843; ch
births: Clement C 12/17/1789 (referred to in 1843 as the
Honorable Clement C Clay of AL), Margaret M 2/14/92, William 7/18/97, Cynthia 12/15/99, Maacah 6/18/1802, & Samuel
3/29/06; QLF states sol b 8/11/1760. R572
CLAYBORN, John, esf 1780 Bedford Co, VA; PN ae 72 Knox Co, TN,
1832. R572
CLAYCOMB, Frederick, b 1758 PA; mvd as ch to Berkeley Co, VA,
where esf 1781; res after RW KY, thence Knox Co, IN, where
PN 1832; QLF 1935 from H L Bruner, Indianapolis, IN, great
gds/o a Frederick Claycomb & w Mary All who had d Matilda,
who md Henry Bruner, & they grandparents of querier; QLF
1932 from William L Connor, Cleveland, OH, whose great gdm
Elizabeth Claycomb named her eldest s Frederick Connor for
her f who RW sol. R572
CLAYTON, Elisha, esf 1776 Monmouth Co, NJ, where b 12/11/1757;
mvd to Hancock, MD, 1792 for 2 years, thence PA, thence
Fifteen Mile Creek, MD, thence Fayette Co, PA, thence Monongalia Co, VA, where PN 1832, when res for c34 years; dd
3/31/45 Marion Co, VA; md 10/15/1793 Elizabeth Little, c15
miles from Cumberland, Allegany Co, MD; wid PN ae 70 Marion Co, VA, 1848; s John b 2/2/1796 was War of 1812 sol &
member of House of Delegates of VA; other ch mbnn; Elizabeth Dawson AFF 1846 ae 59 Marion Co, VA, that she d/o sol
by his 1st w who dd when Elizabeth ch; sol twin bro Elijah
also RW sol & PN, both taken POW together; bro Noah ae 71
in 1832 Greene Co, PA, also RW sol; another bro/o sol res
res 1832 Monmouth Co, NJ, as well as sol bro-in-law mbnn;
Sarah Cunningham, halfsis/o sol wid, ae 62 Marion Co, VA,
AFF she & sol w had same m but different f; QLF states an
Elisha Clayton, b 1757 DE or NJ, RW sol whose wid "Miss
King" dd 3/3/1845 ae 88; QLF 1909 from great gds U A Clay-
ton, Fairmont, WV; QLF 1907 from great gdd Mrs Rebecca J
Moore, Kearney, NE. R573
Joseph, esf VA; mvd to Nelson Co, KY, & dd there 1824; ch in
1848: William, John, Joseph, James, & Charles; d Polly (md
Mr Ford & then decd leaving ch: Robert, Shelton, Teresa, &
Nelly); d Catharine (md Mr Hayden & then decd leaving ch:
Robert, Ellen, Elizabeth, Jane, & Urban; d Sally & s Tho-
mas then decd without issue; s William afb for heirs 1848
Nelson Co, KY, & BLW gtd. R573
Phillip, BLW issued 4/16/1792; records lost in Washington,
DC fire 1800; QLF 1922 from desc Edna (Mrs Robert) Cromp-
ton, Flatbush, NY. R573
CLAYWELL, Shadrack/Shadrick, esf 1778 Bedford Co, VA; b 1760
Worcester Co, MD; PN 1833 Cumberland Co, KY. R573
CLEARWATER, Benjamin, see CLEARWATERS, Benjamin. R573
CLEARWATERS, Benjamin, esf 1776 VA; also War of 1812 sol; PN
ae 78 Madison Co, TN, 1827 when family w Elizabeth ae 23,
steps Jonathan Tucker ae 7, steps James Howard ae 5, & sol
d Betsey Ann ae 2; dd 3/7/1848; md 1778 Elenor Robbins, MB

CLEARWATERS (continued)
     12/21/88, Randolph Co, NC; sol became partially deranged &
     forgetful in later years & would leave & then return home
     from time to time; sol md 10/1822 bigamously Elizabeth who
     had 2 ch & res Madison Co, TN, with her; PN agent of legal
     w aware of sol alleged other w in TN & declared to PN Of-
     fice sol 2nd marriage not legal; wid Elenor/Elender PN ae
     90 Hall Co, GA, having been separated from h for c20 years
     before he dd, AFF she md sol 12/5/1776 & they res Pendle-
     ton District, SC, 1811; wid dd intestate 10/22/52; in 1854
     only ch/o sol & Elenor liv: Olive ae 60 w/o Thomas Steph-
     ens (adm/o sol wid's estate) of Hall Co,GA, Rachel Nichol-
     son ae 62 of Lumpkin Co, GA, & Deborah Raper ae 64-5 of
     Dade Co, GA. R573
CLEAVELAND, John, esf 1776-7 Shenandoah Co, VA, with younger
     bro William who KIA; mvd to KY c 1796 where PN ae 77 Har-
     rison Co 1832; dd there 8/5/32; md 2/1782 or 3/1782 Eliza-
     beth Robinson, Frederick Co, VA; wid PN ae 85 Harrison Co,
     KY, 1840; several ch including William, b 8/1785, who AFF
     1840 Harrison Co, KY, & with whom m res at Leesburg 1841;
     sol bro George AFF 1832 Harrison Co, KY, & res 1840 Jessa-
     mine Co, KY; wid bro James AFF 1834 Harrison Co, KY; sol
     sis Abigail Robinson AFF Scott Co, KY, that she md 1787;
     wid sis Jane A Hand res 1841 Pendleton Co, KY; QLF 1934
     from Nora L (Mrs C C) Collins, Roachdale, IN, states she
     great great gdd of sol bro George; QLF 1933 states sol b
     Frederick Co, VA, & dd Harrison Co, KY, further sol bro
     George b 1759, & dd 1850 Jessamine Co, KY; QLF 1891 from
     Howard Martin, Pittsburgh, PA, states his ch desc of sol.
     R574
   William, esf 1778 Albemarle Co, VA, where b 12/15/1757 s/o
     Alexander & Margaret; mvd after RW to Prince William Co,
     VA, for 6-7 years, thence Fauquier Co, VA, thence Loudoun
     Co, VA; thence Clark Co,KY, thence Pendleton Co, KY, where
     PN 1832; dd 7/18/42; md 4/14/1788 Margaret/Peggy who b
     11/12/1770; wid PN 1843 Pendleton Co, KY; ch births: Sally
     R 4/22/1790 (res 1843 Pendleton Co, KY), Henry W 1/13/93,
     Peggy 1/5/95, Nancy 8/13/97, Alexander Oliver 5/3/1800,
     William Franklin 6/10/03, Harriet Milton 3/27/06, Louisa
     Wilson 6/11/09, Jane Elliott 11/22/11, & Fenton Jackson
     9/11/17; QLF states sol md Margaret Wilson in VA; QLF
     states sol youngest of 6 bro's (one/o whom Alexander) who
     had RW svc. R574
CLEAVER, Benjamin, esf 1774 in Tigers VAlley of VA on Mononga-
     hela River against indians; b 1751 MD; esf 1779 in area
     now Nelson Co, KY; afp ae 81 Grayson Co, KY, 1832 when res
     16 years; AFF then by William Cleaver, who RW sol with him
     part of svc; PAR, less than 6 months svc in regularly con-
     stituted military unit; afp 1853 Grayson Co, KY, by Char-
     les C Cleaver, one/o sol's heirs & adm/o his estate, & PAR
     for same reason. R575
   William, esf 1776 same place as Benjamin above; b 1761 PA;

CLEAVER (continued)
PN 1832 Grayson Co, KY; AFF there by Benjamin Cleaver 1833
that he had RW svc with William. R575
CLEM, John, esf 1778 Shepherdstown, VA, as wagoneer; b 7/1753
PA c20 miles from Philadelphia; afp 1832 Jackson Co, TN, &
PAR, svc not in regularly constituted military unit. R575
CLEMANS, John, esf 1776 Augusta Co, VA, where b 1753; mvd 1806
Jackson Co, TN, where PN 1832; dd 8/20/34; name sometimes
spelled CLEMENS; QLF 1940 from Mrs Laura Thomas Clements,
Fallis, KY, states a John Clements came to America, settled Augusta Co, & was RW sol, md Elizabeth Thompson, had
s John KIA in Battle of Blue Licks & s Gustavus Adolphus
b 1769 who great gdf of querier; QLF 1915 from Miss Caroline Clements, Bowling Green,KY, states sol came from Rappahannock Co,VA, 1805 to TN & settled at what now Clement-
sville. R575
CLEMENT, Edmund, esf 1777 Amelia Co, VA, where b 9/18/1759; PN
1832 Spartanburg District, SC; dd 7/17/45; also known as
Edmond Clements; QLF states sol buried near Inman, SC;
QLF 1932 from desc Miss Gertrude Gilbert, Houston, TX, who
also desc of RW sol Aaron Wood. R576
Vachel, esf 1778 Pittsylvania Co, VA, where b 12/8/1762; mvd
1811 to Shelby Co, KY, for 2 years, thence to Hart Co, KY,
where afp 1833; PAR, insufficient proof of svc. R576
CLEMENTS, Benjamin, esf 1779 Charlotte Co, VA; b 12/1765; PN
1832 Stokes Co, NC, where dd 3/25/35; md 5/1831 or 9/13/31
Mildred Griffin, there; wid PN there 1853 ae 58; QLF 1932
from desc Mrs C S Patton, Scarsdale,NY; QLF 1920 from desc
Mrs Ola Freels, Laddonia, MO. R576
Bernard, see CLEMONS, Bernard. R576
Charles, esf 1778 Fluvanna Co, VA, where PN 1832 ae 74; QLF
1913 from great gds (on m's side) Bert C Thomas, Portland,
OR, states sol issued BLW by State of VA 1815. R576
Clement, b VA & mvd ae 7 with f to Darlington District, SC,
1780; PN ae 78-9 Lexington District, SC, 1844 & also gtd
PN by state of SC; mvd 1847 to Marion Co, GA, where res
1851; dd 11/11/51. R576
John, b Cumberland Co, VA; esf Goochland Co, VA, where PN ae
75 in 1832. R576
Mace, BLW issued 5/29/1792. R576
Roger, esf 1780 Rowan Co, NC; b 1/1/1762 Augusta Co, VA; mvd
1781 Fayette Co, KY, where esf 1781; PN 1832 Montgomery Co
KY, 1832, & dd 7/13/35; md 1/25/1787 Hannah Hathaway,
Clark Co, KY; wid dd 7/17/1846 Boone Co, IN, leaving ch:
John, Philip, Elizabeth, David, Keturah, James, Zachariah,
William, Gustavus, Hannah, Polly, Pamely/Parmelia, Nancy,
& Jonathan; s Lewis dd before m; ch afp 1851 Boone Co, IN,
for PN due m were: John, Philip ae 62, Elizabeth, David,
Keturah, Zachariah, William, Gustavus, Hannah, Polly, Pa-
mely, Nancy, & Jonathan; ch PAR; QLF 1919 from gdd Annie
Clements Ryle, Covington, KY; QLF 1913 from desc Miss Jen-
nie Clements, Kansas City, MO. R576

CLEMENTS, Thomas, esf 1776; PN ae 66 Fluvanna Co, VA, 1820 family then w aec 56, 5 d's ae 24,21,18,17,8, & 3 s's ae 15, 13,11; dd there 10/24/32; md there 1792 Mary Johnson (MB dated 11/10/92 bet sol & Molly Johnson, signed by Stephen Clements); wid dd there 6/28/40 leaving ch: Thomas, James, William, Frances, Martha, & Nancy, all res there 1845 when s James ae 39 afp for heirs, & PAR. R576

CLEMONS, Bernard, esf 1778 Charlotte Co, VA; PN ae 64 Franklin Co,KY, 1819; dd 7/21/38; md 3/1785 or 4/1785 Sally Goare, (MB dated 3/22/1785), Charlotte Co, VA; wid PN ae 80 Madison, Marion Co, IN, 1843; ch Allen (eldest), Catharine, Kitty, William, Jane, Sally, Oston, & Nancy; AFF 1843 Marion Co, IN, by youngest d Nancy Thornton aec 40 that bro William, now decd, would be aec 52 if living. R577

CLENCY, George, esf 1776 Staunton, Augusta Co, VA; PN Montgomery Co, OH, 1832 ae 85. R577

CLEVELAND, Absalom, esf 1778 Surry Co, NC; b 2/24/1759 Albemarle Co, VA; PN 1834 Greenville District, SC. R578

William, see CLEAVELAND, William. R578

CLEVENGER, Eden/Eben, esf 1775 VA; PN aec 62 Fayette Co, OH, 1818; sol res there 1820 with d Elizabeth ae 25; QLF 1934 from desc Mrs S M Sanders, Mentone, IN; QLF states sol b TN. R579

CLIBORNE, Leonard, see CLAIBORNE, Leonard. R579

William, esf 1780 Chesterfield Co,VA, where b 9/23/1766; mvd after RW to Halifax Co,VA, where PN 1832, dd there 3/12/45 & md there 8/24/1831 Sarah Hite (MB dated 8/4/31); wid PN 1857 Mecklenburg Co, VA, with res Halifax Co, VA, & ae 74 there 1866 P O Hyco, when md ch mbnn; wid signed Oath of Allegiance to US there 1868; her PN suspended during Civil War but later restored. R579

CLIFTON, Joshua, BLW issued 11/1/1791. R579

Joshua, esf Dageborough Co (now Blackford Co), DE, for svc in VA regiment; PN ae 77-8 Sussex Co, DE, 1822 when w aec 50. R579

William, b VA 1765 & mvd as ch to NC where esf 1781 Wake Co; PN there 1832 & dd there 3/16/38; md there 3/4/1787 Sarah Hunter (MB 2/19/87); wid PN there 1842 ae 75, & res there 1845 ae 80; AFF there 1842 by Edith Guffy ae 65 that she sis of sol wid; QLF 1936 from desc Frank O Goodlett, Tupelo, MS, states sol res near Raleigh,NC, when esf; QLF 1905 from gdd Mrs T D Duncan, Corinth, MS. R579

CLINCKENBEARD, John, esf 1775 NC; esf 1778 Berkeley Co, VA; b 7/9/1755 near Monolloway, PA, near MD line; parents mvd to Berkeley Co, VA, when he ch; sol mvd 1816 to Bourbon Co, KY, where res ever since; PN there 1834; bro William & bro Isaac served with sol in same company 1778; AFF 1834 by bro William ae 73 & bro Isaac 1834 Bourbon Co, KY, that they in svc with him. R580

CLINE, Andrew, esf 1776 York Co, PA; b PA; PN ae 85 Washington Co, VA, 1834; mvd to that Co c1794. R580

John, esf 1777 on North Branch of Potomac River in VA; PN

CLINE (continued)
aec 67 Harrison Co, IN, 1819; in 1822 w decd c3 years but
had ch Nancy ae 24, Peggy ae 21, Bennet ae 18, Jesse ae 13
& Polly ae 7 res with him there. R580
CLINKENBEARD, Isaac, esf 1776 Hancock, MD; esf 1777 Berkeley
Co, VA; b 11/20/1758; PN 1833 Bourbon Co,KY, when bro William AFF there that he sol in RW with Isaac & bro John;
QLF states a William Clinkenbeard f/o an RW sol Isaac who
b 1750. R580
CLINTON, William, b VA 1749; mvd as ch to Kershaw District, SC
& esf there 1777; mvd 1834 to Campbell Co, GA, where dd
2/16/47; md 1783-4 Violet Perry, Kershaw District, SC; wid
dd 2/12/1852 Campbell Co, GA, leaving ch: David ae 67 (res
LA), George P ae 42 (res Campbell Co, GA), Susan V Hollis
ae 45 (res Cobb Co, GA), & William P ae 48 (res Campbell
Co, GA); s William P afp then for all heirs of sol, & PAR,
insufficient proof of svc. R580
CLOPTON, Thomas, esf 1777 New Kent Co, VA, where b 2/10/1762;
mvd to Mathews Co, VA, after RW for 7 years, thence to res
with brother near Richmond in Henrico Co,VA, to 1812, when
returned to New Kent Co to res with sis Massie, a wid, until 1820, thence to Henrico Co, VA, where PN 1833; QLF
states sol res Henrico Co, VA, 1840. R581
Walter, esf 1775 Goochland Co, VA, where b 12/25/1756 near
Rockcastle; mvd 1803 to Sumner Co, TN, thence to Wilson Co
TN c16 miles from Lebanon where PN 1833 as Walter Sr. R581
CLOUD, Noah, esf 1775-6 SC; esf 1780 GA; b 1752 VA; PN 1832
Edgefield District,SC, where res c18 years; res there 1837
as Noah Sr; dd 8/15/38; md Unity several years before end
of RW; wid PN ae 83 Edgefield District, SC, 1838; many ch,
eldest b 1771-81; QLF 1932 from R E Cloud, Dallas,TX. R582
William, esf 1776 Henry Co, VA; b 9/17/1750 (old style), Ro-
wan Co, NC; PN 1833 Grayson Co, VA; dd 2/8/42 Carroll Co,
VA; md 9/1838 Nancy Vaughn, Carroll or Grayson Co, VA; wid
PN ae 42 Carroll Co, VA, 1853 where res with s-in-law, P O
St Paul; wid dd 2/20/98; only ch mentioned was Martin "son
of Nancy Cloud's late husband" who res 1866 Carroll Co,VA,
wid gtd BLW 8/9/1856; wid sis-in-law Martha Vaughan res
1866 Carroll Co, VA; QLF 1929 from desc M M Cloud, Los An-
geles, CA; QLF 1924 from desc Mrs E D Luhring, Evansville,
IN; QLF 1920 from Maude Madera, New Orleans,LA, states sol
md 3 times & 2nd wife Miss Morgan, further sol & wid Nancy
had d & a son Washington, further querier desc/o Wade Paschal, s/o Samuel Paschal of SC; QLF 1908 from desc Mrs N A
Greenwood, Mt Airy, NC, states she only surv d/o sol & wid
Nancy, & made claim for $500 due m. R582
CLOUSER, Mathias, BLW issued 1/19/1792. R583
CLOWER, George, esf 1776 VA; PN ae 63 Shenandoah Co, VA; family res with him 1820 w ae 57 & ch: Benjamin ae 18, George
ae over 21, Joseph ae over 21, & Henry nearly ae 21; dd
5/15/22; QLF 1937 from G W Glower Jr, Atlanta,GA; QLF 1935
from Rev J B Glower Jr, Virginia Beach, VA; QLF 1936 from

CLOWER (continued)
   desc Mrs Jennie T Grayson, Charlottesville, VA; surname at
   times spelled CLOUR. R583
 Henry, see CLOYER, Henry. R583
CLOYER, Henry, esf 1776 Warm Springs, Bath Co, VA; PN ae 75
   Jefferson Co, IN, 1819; family 1820 w only, sol then listed as ae 80 there. R583
CLUNG, Henry, see KLUNCK, Henry. R584
 William, BLW issued 7/14/1792. R584
CLUVERIUS, Gibson, esf early in RW, Gloucester Co,VA; dd there
   2/23/1789; md there 3/4/1786 Susan Whiting; wid md there
   (2) 9/29/1791 John Lowry/Loury, who dd 1821; wid PN ae 77
   as former wid of sol, Elizabeth City Co, VA, 1850 when res
   with eldest d Elizabeth S Lowry, b 1787, who md (1) 1802
   Anthony Armistead, & (2) 1818 Robert Lowry (decd in 1850);
   wid gtd BLW there 1855 ae 84. R584
COALDEN, James, esf 1774-5 Williamsburg,VA; PN aec 66 Stewart-
   burg, TN, 1818, a cripple; res c1821 Washington, DC. R585
COALTER, Samuel, esf 1776 Burks Co, PA; PN ae 71 Botetourt Co,
   VA, 1835, occupation millwright; only family in 1835 w ae
   60, who "aged & infirm"; surname also spelled COLTER. R585
COATES, John, esf 1780 Spotsylvania Co, VA; b 11/24/1762; PN
   1835 Halifax Co, VA; QLF 1918 from great gdd Mrs Gretchen
   F Gerhard, Kokomo, IN, states sol known as John Sr. R585
 William, esf 1778 Caroline Co, VA, where b; PN there 1832 ae
   77. R585
 William, esf 1775 VA; PN ae 59 Davidson Co, TN, 1820 when he
   & w cared for by s Austin who not md & about to depart TN;
   dd 10/6/44; md 3/4/1782 Susannah Dismukes of Berkeley Pa-
   rish, Spotsylvania Co, VA; wid PN ae 80 Davidson Co, TN,
   1845 when res Sumner Co, TN. R585
COATNEY, James, esf 1777 Fauquier Co, VA, where b 8/19/1749;
   PN 1832 Greene Co, TN; dd 3/12/36 leaving wid Sally, per
   AFF 1836 by Fielding & George COURTNEY, Greene Co,TN; sur-
   name also spelled COURTNEY. R585
 Michael, see COURTNEY, Michael. R585
COATS, William, see COATES, William, R585
COBB, Fleming, esf 1791 & 1793 Kanawha Co, VA, for Indian War
   svc; no RW svc; b 12/1767 Buckingham Co, VA; mvd 1787 to
   Albemarle Co, VA, thence 1789 to Kanawha Co,VA; gtd BLW ae
   66 there 1833; dd there 1/10/46; md there 1/10/1796 Sally
   Morris; wid gtd BLW there 1854 ae 79, & res there 1855 ae
   81. R586
 John, esf 1779 Halifax Co, VA, where b; esf 1780 Lincoln Co,
   NC; PN ae 74 Pickens District, SC, 1833 where dd 5/21/41;
   md 8/27/1786 Frances Smith, Spartansburg District, SC; wid
   b 5/1/1770, & PN 1845 Pickens District, SC. R587
 Samuel, bc 1761 Sussex Co, DE; mvd as ch to Augusta Co, VA,
   where esf 1776; res Randolph Co, VA, after RW for 4 years,
   thence Monongalia Co, VA, for 4 years, thence Fleming Co,
   KY for 22 years, thence Montgomery Co, MO, where PN 1833;
   QLF 1931 from Mrs Clayton F Daugherty, Champaign, IL, desc

COBB (continued)

of an RW sol Samuel Cobb of VA or NC who md Frances. R588

COBBS, John, esf 1779-80 Bedford Co (later Campbell Co), VA; b 10/8/1759 Buckingham Co,VA; PN 1833 Campbell Co, VA, where res since RW; QLF states sol res there 1840; QLF 1912 from gds Thomas E Cobbs, Martinsville, VA. R588

Robert, esf 1778 Bedford Co, VA; dd 8/2/1829; md 11/19/1783 Ann Gizaage Poindexter, Louisa Co, VA; MB 11/19/83 signed by John Poindexter; wid PN ae 79 Campbell Co, VA, 1841, & dd 2/1/42; surv ch 1848: Elizabeth Ann Mottley (Charlotte Co, VA), John P, Robert L, William, Charles L, & Sarah W Weaver; QLF states sol b 1754 & served under uncle Charles Lewis. R588

Samuel, esf VA; dd 1785-6, leaving only heir bro John C who dd 1799; BLW gtd 1807 Amelia Co, VA, to heirs of John C & w Rachel: Thomas M Cobbs, John C Cobbs, Edward S Cobbs, Edith Asselin, Sarah Booker, & Samuel Cobbs (s/o John C). R588

COBLER, Frederick, esf 1776 Guilford Co, NC; b 8/14/1758 Culpeper Co, VA; res Rockingham Co, NC, after RW, thence 1806 to Davidson Co, TN, where PN 1832; dd 9/21/40; bro res Rockingham Co, NC, 1832 mbnn; QLF states sol res 1840 ae 82 with John Corbitt. R588

COCHRAN, James, esf 1776 VA; PN ae 67 Harrison Co, VA, 1818; dd 11/13/30; md 7/20/1777 Temperance, Monroe Co, VA; wid PN ae 77 Harrison Co, VA, 1837, when s-in-law Eli Martin ae 63 made AFF there; QLF 1923 from desc Mrs E Denison, San Francisco, CA, states sol md Temperance Morgan, who b 1760 & dd 1849. R590

John, esf 1776 NC; b 1757 Hanover Co, VA; PN 1832 Robertson Co, TN; dd 1/24/33 leaving no wid but ch: Jeremiah, Lewis, Henry, James, William, Nancy, Elizabeth, Rebecca, Susan, & Sarah; w dd several years before sol; in 1837 d Susan decd leaving d Mary Ann Folk; in 1837 d Sarah decd leaving ch Benjamin & John Felts. R590

Joseph, see COUGHREN, Joseph. R590

Samuel, esf 1777 Henry Co, VA; esf 1781 Bedford Co, VA; b 4/24/1760, s/o William & Jemima; mvd to TN 1818 where PN 1832 Sumner Co; dd 1/7/42; md 8/10/1784 Sarah Northcutt/ Norcutt of Henry Co, VA, when res Bedford Co, VA; wid PN ae 78 Sumner Co, TN, 1844; ch births: Ann/Nancy 3/5/1785, Jemima 9/26/86, Sarah/Sally 11/4/88, William 4/24/91, Daniel 7/7/93, Mary/Polly 2/22/96, Milly 8/1798 dd infancy, Elizabeth/Betsy 3/10/1801 (md John B Buzendine/Bresendine) & Samuel 5/29/04; QLF 1927 from Mrs W H Bristow, Harrisburg, PA. R590

Sarah, former wid/o John Clark. R590

Thomas, esf 1778 Campbell Co, VA, were f res; esf 1779 Wilkes Co, NC, where res for c15 years after RW, thence Adair Co, KY, where PN 1832; b 4/8/c1760 Charlotte Co, VA. R590

William, esf VA 1777; PN ae 70 Clarke Co, AL, 1819. R590

William, esf VA; BLW issued 11/29/1783; dd 8/26/1825 Frede-

COCHRAN (continued)
rick Co, VA; LWT dated 8/20/25, & probated 11/1/25 Frederick Co, VA, listed w Mary & ch: Sarah, Mary, John, William, Edward, Thomas, Rebecca, Rachel, & Eliza Jane; md Mary
Bains 10/10/1816 Licking Co, OH; wid afp ae 72 Augusta Co,
VA, 1855, & PAR. R590
COCHRUN, Simon, esf 1777 Monongalia Co, VA; PN ae 62 Franklin
Co, OH; family 1820 w ae 50 & ch: Thomas ae 19, Christina
ae 18, Simon ae 15, Josiah, & William ae 6; dd 6/9/45 Allen Co,OH; 1st w dd before sol; md (2) 8/5/1831 Sarah Louden Clark, Franklin Co, OH; wid 1st h John Clark, who dd
1822, was RW sol from MD; Simon had no ch by 2nd w; wid PN
ae 79 Pleasant, Franklin Co, OH, 1853, & dd 10/5/53; sol
surname also spelled COCHRAN; QLF 1926 from desc Mrs Mead
Clark, Santa Rosa, CA, states her great gdm was Effie Cochran who md before 1812 William Boman & they res Allen Co
OH, further William Boman was War of 1812 sol who dd ae 76
Magnolia, IL, 1/3/57, further he s/o William Boman who had
VA RW svc & settled OH after RW; QLF 1920 from desc James
L Cochrun, Columbus, OH. R591
COCK, Charles, b 1762 Orange Co, VA; mvd aec 5 to Culpeper Co,
VA, where esf 1781; res Bedford Co, VA, after RW, thence
1802 to Caswell Co, NC, where PN 1832. R591
John, esf 1777 Montgomery Co (now Grayson Co), VA; single in
1781; b 2/12/1756 Bedford Co, VA; after RW res Cumberland
Co, KY, thence Overton Co, TN, thence 1811 Warren Co, TN,
where PN 1834 res on Barren Fork of Collins River where dd
7/20/34. R591
COCKE, Anderson, b Cumberland Co, VA; esf 1776 Prince Edward
Co, VA, where PN 1832 ae 74. R591
Charles, esf for Indian Wars 1774 & 1790 VA; esf for RW 1780
Washington Co, VA; b 11/12/1750; afp Lee Co, VA, 1838 when
res P.O. Greenville, Clarke Co, AR; PAR, svc against indians not in regularly constituted unit; AFF 1838 Lee Co, VA
by William George who b 1/4/1770, & by William Ewing who b
6/19/1764, both res of Lee Co. R591
John, BLW issued 6/19/1799. R591
John Catesby, VA sea svc; esf 1776 as captain of marines on
ship DRAGON; settled Culpeper Co, VA, after RW; dd intestate 1807-8 near Port Royal, Caroline Co, VA, leaving ch:
Thornton, Peter, Alice w/o Elias Edmonds, Mrs Joshua Tennison, & Mrs Fitzhugh; adm of sol estate Daniel Ward afp
for heirs 1839 & PAR; s Thornton mvd 1835-6 to MS where dd
leaving s Henry only heir; s Peter mvd 1837-8 from Loudoun
Co, VA, to OH or IN & dd leaving ch mbnn; d Alice dd c1807
Fauquier Co, VA, & her h also dd, leaving d Alice w/o Alexander Edmonds, d Helen w/o B R Bradford (Helen dd leaving
h, s B H, & d Margaret wid/o Sydnor Edmonds), & s John F
Edmonds res MO 1851; Joshua Tennison & w decd in 1851 survived by d Margaret A (res Fauquier & Loudoun Co, VA), d
w/o Mr Myers of Washington DC, & s who lieutenant US Navy;
Fitzhughs decd in 1851 survived by heirs in OH; adm of sol

217

COCKE (continued)
estate Alexander Edmonds & w Alice afp 1851, & PAR. R591
Nathaniel, esf 1776 VA; wid Rebecca afp 1830 Richmond Co,GA,
when family surv: d Eliza R Brown, d Mary Taylor, d Augusta, also heirs of decd s William (Nathaniel W), also heirs
of decd d Rebecca T Baldwin (Augustus C Baldwin, William H
Baldwin, & Alexander Cunningham h/o Louisa R T Baldwin);
wid PAR; in 1831 sol nephew Richard H Cocke ae 63 res Surry Co, VA. R591
William, esf 1779 Bedford Co, VA; b 1759 Hanover Co, VA; PN
1832 Rutherford Co, TN; QLF states sol s/o Abraham who s/o
Stephen who s/o Thomas who s/o Richard or Walter. R591
COCKEREL, Peter, see COCKRELL, Peter. R591
COCKERIL, Hanson, esf 1780 Loudoun Co, VA; dd Muskingum Co, OH
5/14/1814 or 4/1818; md c6/30/1784 Sarah/Sally Watson, Ca-
meron Parish, Loudoun Co, VA; wid PN ae 79 Muskingum Co,
OH, 1839; wid res Coshocton Co, OH, 1844 & 1855; wid dd on
farm/o of nephew John Watson, Perry Township, Coshocton Co
OH on 2/1855 or 2/1856, & was buried West Carlisle Cemete-
OH; ch: Thomas (eldest, dd as ch), Elias (2nd ch, dd be-
fore Civil War near Monroe, Greene Co,WI), Mary b 2/7/1803
VA, dd West Carlisle 4/20/1856, md 8/46/1827 John R Jurden
/Jordan b 4/1/1795 Greenwood, Mifflin Co, PA, dd 7/31/1859
West Carlisle, Coshocton Co, OH, where both buried), & Sa-
rah never md, dd 5/1885 ae 55-60 Dresden, OH, or West Car-
lisle; ch/o John & Mary Jurden: James C (b 11/8/29 Dresden
OH, or West Carlisle, OH, dd c1896 Newcomerstown, OH, md
11/20/51 Jane McCumber, Zanesville, OH, who md (2) c1900
David Starker who dd c1901), Hetty Ann b 3/14/32, Sarah C
(b 10/27/34, dd 1/9/45), Oscar M (b 7/22/37, dd 1/30/45),
Augusta "Gusty" Mitchell (b 6/1/40, md Jacob Steffe/Steffy
who had by former w s Thomas & d Sarah Ann Legg -- Gusty &
Jacob dd Calhoun, Richland Co, IL); ch of James C Jurden &
w Jane: Izett (b 3/1/52, md (1) Charles Google/Kugle, (2)
John E Wood, & res 1906 Newcomerstown, Tuscarawas Co, OH),
Augusta (b 10/26/55, md (1) Miles Jones b & reared Dresden
OH, & (2) Judson McPeak), Emma (b8/20/57, never md, & dd
5/25/73 Fraziersburg, Muskingum Co, OH), & Ella (b 6/3/60,
md Robert Vogenitz who dd before 1906 when she res Lorain,
OH); Charles Coogle & w Izett had s Denver who res Cleve-
land, OH, 1906; John E Wood & w Izett had ch Harry, Alta,
& Mark; Miles Jones & w Augusta had d Bessie who never md,
dd c1891 aec 23 at home of her uncle Mark Jones, Dresden,
OH; Augusta had no ch by 2nd h Judson McPeak; Robert Voge-
nitz & w Ella had s Justin P & s Chauncey who res 1906 Lo-
rain, OH, with m; sol bro Gabriel res near Zanesville, OH,
& md 3/5/1835 Lucinda Shiplet, both res Muskingum Co, OH.
R591
COCKRAN, John, esf 1781 VA; PN ae 76 Lynchburg, Campbell Co,
VA, 1828; dd 11/13/30; QLF 1927 from desc Miss Pauline E
Young, Chicago, IL. R592
COCKRAN, Mathew, esf Mecklenburg Co, VA; b Luneburg Co, VA; PN

COCKRAN (continued)
    aec 70 Morgan Co, GA 1833; dd c1847 leaving wid (2nd w, md
    c1830) mbnn who applied 1855 for PN unpaid to sol; surname
    also spelled COCKRAM. R592
  William, see COCHRAN, William. R592
COCKRELL, John, esf 1777 VA; PN aec 68 Montgomery Co, KY 1818;
    w decd when sol res Bath Co, KY 1822; surname also spelled
    COCKRILL. R592
  Peter, esf 1776 Northumberland Co, VA; PN ae 60 Bourbon Co,
    KY, 1818; family 1820 w ae 58, 5 d's, & 1 s mbnn; QLF 1938
    from Mrs B E Ragland, Lexington, MO, who desc/o RW sol Pe-
    ter Cockrill (1758-1834) Jefferson Co, VA; QLF 1934 from
    desc Laura B Kendall, Oklahoma City, OK. R592
COCKRIL, Hanson, see COCKERIL, Hanson. R592
COCKRUM, William, esf 1778 VA; PN aec 70 Hickman Co, KY, 1833;
    lost PN certificate & applied for new one there 1837; il-
    literate. R592
COCKS, Benjamin W, esf 1780 Surry Co, VA where PN 1819 aec 65;
    in 1820 sol stated ae 63 when had w Rebecca ae 54, d Susan
    ae 21, s William ae 18 & s Benjamin ae 16; dd 4/9/26; sur-
    name also spelled COX. R592
COFER, George, esf 1776 Culpeper Co, VA; mvd to KY 1789 thence
    1819 to St. Genevieve Co, MO, where PN 1832 ae 75. R594
  Joseph, see COFFER, Joseph. R594
  Reuben, see COFFER, Reuben. R594
COFF, William, "a free man of color", esf 1780 VA; illiterate;
    PN ae 60 Botetourt Co, VA, 1826 when family w ae 48-50, s
    ae 14, & s ae 11 mbnn. R594
COFFENBERRY, George, see COFFINBERRY, George. R594
COFFER, Joseph, esf Amherst Co, VA, when had w & 1 ch; afp ae
    86 Abbeville District, SC, 1832; PAR, insufficient proof/o
    svc. R594
  Reuben, esf 1778-9 VA; PN ae 55 Montgomery Co, KY, 1818; dd
    10/28/29-30 Bath Co, KY; md 2/4/1826 Jane "Gincey" McClan-
    nahan, Bath Co, KY; wid PN ae 72 there 1853; s Harrison/
    Hamin mentioned 1855; QLF 1926 from desc Mrs D H Bush,
    Sterling, KY, states she d/o Bettie Pendleton who d/o Sa-
    rah Nelson who d/o Cynthia Coffer who d/o sol; QLF states
    sol md twice. R594
COFFEY, Benjamin, esf 1776 Burke Co, NC; esf 1780 Wilkes Co,
    NC; b 1747 Spotsylvania Co, VA; PN 1833 Hawkins Co, TN.
    R594
  Eli, esf 1780 sub for uncle by marriage Thomas Field who had
    large family, Wilkes Co,NC; esf there 1781 sub for bro Am-
    brose; b 3/1/1764 Albemarle Co, VA; mvd to Wilkes Co, NC
    with f; mvd to KY 1784, thence Wayne Co, KY, thence McMinn
    Co, TN, where afp 1839; PAR, svc less than 6 months. R594
  Osbourn, esf 1776 Amherst Co, VA; b 7/29/1759; mvd 1797 to
    KY where PN 1830 when res on Green River, Casey Co; still
    res there 1834; dd 3/31/40; md 2/18/1783 Mary/Polly, d/o
    Mathew Nightingale, Amherst Co, VA; MB 2/15/83 signed by
    Mathew & Lucy Nightingale; wid PN ae 83 Casey Co, KY 1844;

COFFEY (continued)
in 1830 sol & w res with d Lucy; s Mathew dd before 1830;
eldest ch Jesse b 5/26/1784, & res 1833 P O Liberty, Casey
Co, KY, referred to in 1834 as Col Jesse Coffey, was State
Senator, & his res 1849 Middlebury, KY; sol also known as
Osburn COFFEE. R594

Reuben, esf 1780 Wilkes Co,NC; b 9/16/1759 Albemarle Co, VA;
family mvd to Amherst Co, VA, when sol aec 5, thence when
sol aec 15 to Wilkes Co, NC; after RW sol res Burke Co,NC,
thence Wayne Co, KY, where PN 1832 when res 13 years. R594

COFFINBERRY, George, esf 1780 near Martinsburg, Berkeley Co,
VA, where b 2/10/1760; PN 1832 Springfield Township, Richland Co, OH, where dd 7/13/51; md 12/5/1785-6 Elizabeth
Little, Martinsburg, VA; wid PN ae 82, Richland Co, OH,
1851; ch births: Mary 9/2/1787, Andrew 8/20/89, Sarah
6/26/91, twins George & Nancy 5/13/93, George 3/15/95, Jacob 5/25/97, John 9/22/99, Isaac 1/28/1802, Elizabeth
1/26/03, Wright Lewis 4/5/07, Salathiel Curtis 2/26/09, &
Abraham Pitcher 8/19/11; QLF 1928 from desc Madge McCaddon
of Peoria, IL, who also desc of RW sols Timothy Turner of
CT, Samuel Stewart of CT, William Pynchion of MA, & John
Pynchion of MA; QLF 1924 from desc Mrs F Berman, Covina,
CA, states sol middle name Lewis; QLF 1916 from G L Coffinberry, Columbus,OH; QLF 1914 from desc Mrs John B Campbell, South Bend, IN; QLF from A B Coffinberry, Grand Ra-
pids, MI, states sol dd Mansfield, OH. R595

COFFMAN, George, esf 1781 Woodstock, Shenandoah Co, VA; dd c
1/1/1833 Shenandoah Co, VA; md there 6/20/1786 Christena
Dellinger; wid afp there 1850 ae 83, & PAR, insufficient
proof of svc; surname also spelled KAUFFMAN. R595

Joseph, esf 1781 Essex Co, VA, ae 16; s/o Joseph who KIA at
Battle of Stony Point; bro Benjamin also KIA same battle;
afp ae 93 Marshall Co, VA, 1851, & PAR. R595

COGBURN, Henry, esf 1776 Caswell Co, NC; b 11/25/49 near home
of Gen George Washington, VA; mvd 1784 to Union District,
SC, where PN 1832. R595

COGER, Peter, esf 1777 Rockingham Co, VA; b 1753 PA, mvd to VA
when infant where reared Augusta Co & Rockingham Co; res
Franklin Co, VA, after RW; mvd 1824 to Elk River, Randolph
Co, VA, thence to Lewis Co,VA, where PN 1832; res 1837 Kanawha Co, VA; bro Joseph esf with sol 1778; QLF 1937 from
desc Mrs Emma Cogar, Hyattsville, MD. R595

COGHILL, James, esf 1776 Orange Co, VA; PN ae 61 Gallatin Co,
KY, 1819; s James ae 15 in 1823; QLF from great gdd Esther
King, Fort Scott, KS, states sol res 1840 Carroll Co, KY,
ae 80. R596

Ralph, see COWGILL, Ralph. R596

Thomas, esf 1780 Essex Co, VA, where b 5/9/1763; res there
except for 1 year after RW; PN there 1833, & dd 1/17/51
there. R596

COIEL, James, esf 1775 SC near Waxhaw Settlements; b 1750 Augusta Co, VA; res after RW Lancaster District, SC, to 1797

COIEL (continued)
      when mvd to Broad River, Franklin Co, GA; res 1824 Madison
      Co, GA, when w ae 64 & w sis Margaret Magrady aec 61; mvd
      1827 to Hall Co, GA, where PN 1832; dd 4/20/36; surname
      also spelled COILE. R597
COLBERT, John, esf 1781 near Winchester, VA; b Frederick Co,
      VA; PN ae 62 there 1827 when 2nd w aec 50; dd 10/20/38;
      sol sis Mrs Sarah Pernell AFF there after his death; sur-
      name at times spelled CALVERT. R597
COLDWELL, Robert; afp 1795 for disability for wounds at Siege
      of Ninety-Six in 1781; PAR for insufficient proof of svc
      because evidence lost. R600
COLE, Daniel, esf 1780 Prince William Co,VA, where b 2/20/1763
      near Dumfries; s/o Daniel; PN 1832 Culpeper Co, VA; md
      Whitehead of Prince William Co; s Richard res Culpeper Co,
      VA, 1850; sol dd 7/17/51; QLF 1929 from desc Mrs Basil G
      Culver, Leavenworth, KS. R602
   Daniel, esf 1780 Winchester, Frederick Co, VA; b 1755 Morris
      Co, NJ; PN 1833 Union Township, Fayette Co, PA; last PN
      payment 1841; QLF from great gdd Ferne Cole (Mrs J G) Ly-
      man, Shreveport, LA, states she d/o Ransome Taylor Cole,
      s/o Noah B Cole (b AL), s/o sol, further sol w Marye or
      Marie, further sol other s's Daniel, Thomas, & Mason. R602
   Francis, esf Chesterfield Co, VA, where b; PN ae 81 Dinwid-
      die Co, VA; mvd after RW to Prince Edward Co, VA, thence
      back to Dinwiddie Co, VA, 1819-20 where PN 1832 ae 81; dd
      8/17/34; md 12/25/1802 Martha Cliborn; wid PN 1853 Peters-
      burg, VA, ae 88 when res with niece Mrs Robertson Tucker;
      wid gtd BLW there 1856. R602
   Hamlin/Hamblin, esf 1777 VA; BLW issued 5/31/1783; PN aec 68
      (crippled) Chesterfield Co, VA, 1824 when w already decd.
      R603
   James, b 9/5/1755 Bedford Co, VA; family 1756 mvd to Anson
      Co (area now Richmond Co), NC, where sol esf 1776; PN 1832
      Carroll Co, TN; AFF 1833 Robertson Co, TN, by bro Stephen
      who b 5/16/1760 Anson Co, NC, also RW sol. R603
   John, esf Baltimore Co, MD; afp ae 78 Harrison Co, VA, 1834
      & PAR, less than 6 months svc. R604
   John, b 12/17/1752 & raised King George Co,VA; moved to Fre-
      derick Co, VA, 1773 where esf 1775 while res on Shenandoah
      River; PN 1833 Barren Co, KY. R604
   John, esf 1775 Dinwiddie Co, VA, where PN 1819 ae 74. R604
   Joseph, b 6/9/1746 Morris Co, NJ; mvd after marriage to Fre-
      derick Co, VA, where esf; later esf Montgomery Co, VA; mvd
      to Buncombe Co, NC, where PN 1833; PN increase there 1837.
      R604
   Joseph, esf 1776 VA; mvd 1779 to TN where f had mvd earlier
      & esf to fight indians; dd 11/28/1823 Wilson Co, TN; LWT
      11/24/1823, & probated there 12/1823, listing w Sarah, ch:
      Frances w/o William Bloodworth, Jemima w/o William Wood,
      David, James, William (eldest b12/21/1780) & gdc mbnn;
      md 11/30/1779 Sarah Barton, Sullivan Co, TN, b 8/29/1760;

COLE (continued)
wid PN 1851 Wilson Co, TN; d Jemima b 8/9/1788, her h William Wood b 1/28/1786; AFF 1851 by Jemima Wood that f came from MD to VA, & that family mvd to Wilson Co, TN, from Sullivan Co, TN, when Jemima aec 10, she being 4th ch of sol. R604

Richard, esf 1780 Warm Springs, Augusta Co, VA; b 3/8/1750 London, England; PN 1833 Bath Co, VA; QLF states sol w was Mary Richie/Ritchie. R605

Robert, esf Chesterfield Co, VA; dd 3/12/1816; md 1773 Dicey Bevill there; wid dd ae 91 Guilford Co, NC, 5/16/1844 before her PN application completed; wid PN paid to her only surv ch & heir James who afp ae 75 there 1845; AFF 1846 by John H Cole, Richmond, VA, (s/o Sally Bevill Cole, niece/o sol w), f/o Christopher & John H Cole Jr; AFF by Philip Bevill, Guilford Co, NC, 1846 ae 62, s/o Hezekiah (bro of sol w), that Hezekiah mvd family from VA to Guilford Co in 1791, & sol mvd his family there 1795; AFF 1846 by Lucy A Bevill ae 64 there. R605

Walter King, VA sea svc, esf 1776 as surgeon in VA Navy; s/o Walter King of Great Britain, who owned much land in Henry Co, VA; no reason given for sol adding surname COLE; sailor dd there 2/7/1794; wid Sally dd before 11/12/1850; only ch Samuel M dd 1817, leaving ch: Walter King, Edwin W (dd unmarried), Alonzo F, Nathaniel R, Sarah M w/o Patrick H Fontaine (who dd before 5/27/1851); Alonzo F dd, leaving wid Jane & d Mary Ann; Patrick & Sarah Fontaine had 6 ch mbnn; surv heirs of sailor 1851 were gdc Nathaniel R Cole, Walter King Cole, & Sarah M Fontaine + her ch; adm of gdf estate, Nathaniel R Cole, afp 1851 for all heirs, & PAR, since sailor svc in VA state organization & not provided for in the current RW PN laws. R606

William, esf 1777 VA; PN ae 63 Chesterfield Co, VA, 1822; dd 4/1824; md 1795 Martha/Patsy Miles, marriage license dated 12/29/1795; wid dd 1/1836 or 2/1836; d ae 13 mbnn 1820. R606

William, esf 1777 Charlotte Co, VA; b 12/12/1752 Prince Edward Co, VA; PN 1835 Halifax Co, VA; dd there 10/14/38; md there 6/1786 Mourning Hitson; wid PN ae 88 there 1844 when ch Nancy, Joel, Patsy, James, & Sally all over ae 50; AFF by Nancy Cole ae 73 there 1844 that she md sol bro Robert (MB 12/28/1789 between Nancy Carter & Robert Cole, signed by Richard Carter) when she ae 16, & that her 2nd ch now ae 53; QLF 1933 from Mrs Ella Cole Reid, Dallas, TX, desc of Robert & Nancy (Carter) Cole. R606

COLEGATE, Asaph, esf 1780 Baltimore, MD; BLW issued 1/16/1797; PN aec 55 Monongalia Co, VA, 1818; res there 1820 ae 57, when w Rosanna ae 61, s Thomas aec 24; res ae 92 Marion Co VA, 1855. R607

COLEMAN, Hawes, esf 1775 Spotsylvania Co,VA, where b 1/1/1757; mvd 1789 to Amherst Co, VA, to area now Nelson Co, where PN 1834. R607

COLEMAN, Jacob, esf 1776 VA; PN ae 63 Vigo Co, IN, 1818; res there 1826 ae 71; res 1828 Vermilion Co, IN. R607

James, BLW issued 9/26/1792. R607

Joel, esf 1780 Leesburg, Loudoun Co, VA; PN ae 71 Union Co, 1820 when w ae 66 mbnn. R608

John, b 10/20/1752; esf Prince Edward Co, VA, for GA regiment; PN 1818 Washington Co, TN, while res Sullivan Co, TN where res 1820 when w Esther ae 31 & s Nathan ae 2. R608

Joseph, esf Cumberland Co, VA, where b; mvd 1786 to SC where dd 1806 Union District; md 1/24/1782 Sithey/Scytha Glenn, Cumberland Co, VA, who b & raised there; wid md (2) 1820-3 John Bowles, Union District, SC, who dd there 2/1838, havno ch by him; wid dd there 7/16/44 at home/o s-in-law Benjamin Ellis; ch births: Lucy 1/27/1783 (md William Hollingsworth & they had Joseph Coleman & Barnet Glenn), Patience 3/9/84 (md Mr Triplett & they had Barnet, William, Mary, Nancy, Moses, & d who md George Cooper), Elizabeth 3/12/85 (md John Crosby), Nathan 12/21/86, Mason 3/3/88 (md Moses Crosby), Sarah/Salley 1/14/90 (md Benjamin Ellis), Mary/Polley 1/14/92 (dd no issue), Daniel 4/5/93 (dd no issue), Anna 5/5/96 (md Thomas Sartor), Sithey 5/25/97 (dd no issue), Susannah/Susan 11/22/1800 (md John Anderson), & Pamela/Permealey 11/22/02 (md Nathan Glenn); s Nathan afp due f 1846 Union District, SC, for himself & surv sis Elizabeth Crosby, Mason Crosby, Anna Sartor, Sarah Ellis, & Pamela Glenn, & PN gtd; wid bro William Glenn md Elizabeth Wright who bc 1788 Cumberland Co, VA, & res 1846 Union District, SC. R608

Naiad/Neniad, esf 1776-7 Leesburg, Loudoun Co, VA; PN aec 72 Hamilton Co, OH, 1818; res there 1820 ae 75 when w aec 75, 3 ch "capable of maintaining themselves", & s ae 42 an idiot. R608

Richard, BLW issued 1/17/1800 to heir Francis Coleman; QLF states sol bc 1761 Gloucester Co,VA, & md Ann Stubbs, also mns Auguston/Augustine Williams of Gloucester Co, VA, who dd 1849 & md (2) 1835 Elizabeth Coleman, also mns Stephen Goggin who b Bedford Co, VA, will probated 12/1831, who md 12/21/1773 Rachel Moorman, also mns Joseph Dickinson who b 4/11/1742, dd 9/16/1818 Bedford Co, VA, md 3/6/1769 Elizabeth Wooldrige. R608

Robert, esf 1780 VA sub for f Samuel; res after RW Buckingham Co, VA, where PN 1833 ae 67; stepm Elizabeth Coleman AFF there 1833. R608

Robert, esf 1776 Spotsylvania Co, VA, where b; PN ae 85 Mercer Co, KY, 1833, where dd 1/9/34; md 2/1774 Catharine Robinson, Botetourt Co,VA; wid PN ae 83 Mercer Co, KY, 1836; ch included James (eldest) & Sarah Alexander. R608

Samuel, esf 1782 Warren Co,NC; b 8/24/1762 Brunswick Co, VA; mvd to GA where res 43 years when afp 1835 Meriwether Co, & PAR; dd 5/11/38; md 1805 Sarah, who afp 1853 Meriwether Co, GA, & PAR; wid dd 11/1/53 leaving ch David, Samuel, Humphrey, Hybernia w/o W D Adair, Tempey w/o W Morgan, &

COLEMAN (continued)
Eden; s Eden afp 12/1853 there for all heirs, & PAR. R609
Samuel, esf VA; BLW issued 1/6/1795 to heirs;   KIA Battle of
Camden; papers lost Washington, DC, fire 1800;   QLF states
an RW sol Samuel Coleman md (1) Millie Coffie,   & (2) Ann;
QLF states sol KIA 8/16/1780. R609
Spencer, esf western VA;   b King & Queen Co, VA;   family mvd
to Stafford Co, VA, when he ae 2 & to Shenandoah Co, VA,
when he ae 15;   md there aec 23 & mvd to Seven Mile Ford,
(now Smyth Co), VA, where esf;   after RW mvd to "Big Pid-
geon", Cooke Co, TN, thence 1826 to Monroe Co, TN, where
PN 1832 ae 80 (ae 80 years & 10 months on 12/18/32). R609
Thomas, esf 1776 VA; PN ae 66 Woodford Co, KY, 1818. R609
Thomas, esf Culpeper Co, VA; PN 1832 Barren Co, KY; dd aec
70 there 8/17/32 where res c20 years; md 5/1785 Lucy Strother, Culpeper Co, VA; wid PN ae 72 Barren Co, KY, 1840;
ch mbnn. R609
Whitehead, BLW issued 8/8/1792; captain in VA troops; papers
lost in Washington, DC, fire 1800. R609
William, esf 1776 Mecklenburg Co, VA, for svc with GA regi-
ment; PN ae 58 Mecklenburg Co, VA, 1818; res there 1821 ae
59 (no explanation of ae discrepancy). R609
COLEY, Francis, esf 1776 Charles City Co,VA, where b 9/14/1757
& mvd 1779 to Halifax Co, NC, where esf that year;   later
esf 1781 Brunswick Co, VA; PN ae 77 Smith Co, TN, 1833.
R609
Isham/Isam, b 3/1762 Amelia Co, VA; esf Mecklenburg Co, VA,
where afp 1833, & PAR. R609
COLGAN, William, esf 1777 Berkeley Co, VA; PN ae 58 Madriver
Township, Champaign Co, OH, 1818; res there 1820 when w ae
58, d ae 18, & s ae 14; dd 11/14/37; bro Daniel res Berkeley Co, VA, during RW. R610
COLLETT, Isaac, esf 1781 Berkeley Co, VA; b 1760 Baltimore Co
MD; PN 1833 Henry Co, KY; s & 3 d's mbnn 1836. R611
John, esf 1777 VA; PN ae 60 Shelby Co, KY, 1818, when had
w Elizabeth, 3 s's (including John & Moses), & 7 d's;   dd
there 9/21/30; md 8/1790 Elizabeth McDaniel, Berkeley Co,
VA, who b 11/18/1769; wid PN 1838 Shelby Co, KY; QLF 1928
from desc John D Collett, Indianapolis, IN; QLF 1931 from
great gdd Iva N Harris, Uniontown, KY; QLF 1930 from great
great gdd Mrs Mary Collett Chapman, Malvern, AR, states
sol b Loudoun Co, VA, s/o John, further she also desc of
John Livesay whose s Charles res near Portsmouth, VA, in
Nansemond Co & Charles RW sol; QLF 1911 from great great
gdd Miss Bell Hubbell, Frankfort, KY. R611
COLLEY, Charles, see COLLIE, Charles. R611
Charles, esf 1776 VA; PN 1818 Madison Co, KY; res there 1820
ae 73 when house carpenter & no ch res with him. R611
Mainyard, esf 1777 VA; PN ae 68 Limestone Co, AL, 1829 when
w Elizabeth ae 68; dd 11/17/38 leaving wid. R611
COLLIE, Charles, b 1/25/1756 Stafford Co, VA; mvd aec 10 to
Pittsylvania Co, VA, where esf 1776; PN there 1832; bro

COLLIE (continued)
James res there then. R611
COLLIER, Aaron, esf 1780 Montgomery Co, VA; b 1/15/1750 Bed-
ford Co, VA; afp 1835 Lee Co,VA, & PAR, less than 6 months
svc; md 1770 Elizabeth, who dd 7/1830; sol & w res Grayson
Co, VA, for 40 years; sol dd 6/1842; s Shadrack ae 71 res
Carroll Co, VA, 1852; QLF 1931 from desc Mrs Dora Cochran
Smith, Humboldt, KS, who great gdd/o sol s Shadrack. R611
   William, b Franklin Co, VA, 1762; esf Northampton Co, NC, &
   res there c 14 years after RW, thence Giles Co, TN, where
   PN 1834. R611
   William, esf VA; PN ae 61 Mecklenburg Co, VA, 1820, for dis-
   ability from RW knee wound, when "rough carpenter without
   family." R611
COLLINGS, Jeremiah, see COLLINS, Jeremiah. R612
COLLINS, Elisha, esf 1778 Pittsylvania Co,VA; esf 1779 Lexing-
ton, KY; b 11/30/1759 Halifax Co, VA; res VA 1782 where md
1783; mvd to Lexington, KY, 1784, thence 1819 to Greene Co
AL where PN 1832; QLF 1926 from desc Mrs Catherine Collins
of Birmingham, AL, states she desc of William Collins, s/o
James Collins, s/o sol. Rec 612
   George, esf 1777 VA; PN 1833 Lewis Co, VA; after several ac-
   quaintances testified sol was too young to have had RW svc
   his name dropped from PN rolls; QLF 1904 from desc Mrs G W
   Felker, Jeffersonville, IN. R612
   Hezekiah, esf 1777 Albemarle Co,VA; afp 1832 Union Township,
   Madison Co, OH, & PAR, insufficient proof of svc. R612
   James, esf 1777 VA; esf 1778 Uniontown, PA, as sub for f; b
   1761 Lancaster Co, PA; mvd as infant to Loudoun Co, VA; PN
   ae 72 Monongalia Co, VA,1833; bro John mvd Fayette Co, PA,
   to Monongalia Co, VA, c1798, res 1833 Portsmouth, OH. R613
   Jeffrey, esf 1777 Settlement of Garney Manor (?), Shenandoah
   Co, VA, where bc 1756; PN 1832 Shenandoah Co, VA. R613
   Jeremiah, esf Albemarle Co, VA, where b & raised; md 1787 &
   w dd 1828; dd ae 94 Surry Co (area later Stokes Co), NC,
   9/27/1836; s George afp ae 55 Stokes Co, NC, 1843 as only
   surv heir, & PAR, no title to PN since sol dd before pas-
   sage of applicable PN act. R613
   John, esf 1776 VA; b 8/28/1758; PN 1818 Fleming Co, KY; dd
   1/21/1828 KY or Rush Co, IN; md 3/7/1786 Margaret, Westmoreland Co, VA; wid b 10/27/1768; wid PN 1839 Posey Township, Rush Co, IN; ch births: eldest mbnn dd before 1840,
   Elizabeth 11/9/1788 (md George Laurens, but known 1840 as
   Elizabeth Graham, Boone Co, KY), Elisha 2/8/91 (res Boone
   Co, KY, 1840), John 1799 6th ch, James 5/7/1801 (res Rush
   Co, IN, 1839), Sally 6/12/03, Levi 8/15/05, Margaret
   11/22/07, Polly (known as Polly Lawrence 1839); QLF 1933
   from desc Mrs C C Collins, Roachdale, IN. R613
   John, esf 1775 Spotsylvania Co, VA; b 2/10/1748 Orange Co,
   VA; PN 1832 Albemarle Co, VA. R613
   John, esf 1775 VA; PN ae 61 King & Queen Co, VA; dd 9/30/20.
   R613

COLLINS, John, esf 1777 King William Co, VA, where b & raised;
dd 1822; md 4/1780 Jane Richeson, Williamsburg, VA; wid PN
PN ae 88 King William Co, VA, 1836; AFF 1844 there by Jane
Hargrove that she md 1788 Baptist preacher Billy Hargrove
who res neighborhood of sol. R613
   John, b 9/10/1748 Amelia Co, VA; esf 1777 Halifax Co, VA, &
afp there 1835; PAR, svc less than 6 months; ch mbnn. R613
   Joseph, b 1745 Westmoreland Co, VA; family mvd when sol ch
to Prince William Co, thence Stafford Co, thence Bedford
Co, VA, where esf; PN 1838 Washington Co, TN. R614
   Joshuah, esf 1779 MD (area now Washington, DC); b 10/22/1747
on Rock Creek c5 miles from Georgetown, DC; PN 1833 Washington, DC; res VA for 9 months during RW. R614
   Josiah, esf 1778 VA enroute to KY; b 5/2/1757 Halifax Co,VA;
res Bath Co, KY, after RW where PN 1833; QLF states sol dd
1847. R614
   Lewis, esf 1776 SC; esf 1781 Montgomery Co, VA, where f res;
b 1754 VA; PN 1834 Hawkins Co,TN, when res Granger Co, TN;
afp 1853 by s Dowell & s Edmond, sol heirs 1853 Knox Co,
TN. R614
   Mason, esf 1777 VA; esf later 1777 PA; esf 1780 VA; PN aec
60 King & Queen Co,VA; res there 1820 ae 63 when w Minervy
ae 20, s Mason ae 17, d Mary ae 15, & d Eliza ae 11; illi-
terate mulatto. R614
   Ralph C, esf 1781 VA; afp & afb ae 72 Grant Co, KY, 1834, &
PAR, svc less than 6 months, & BLAR; dd Williamstown, that
Co; one heir liv 1838 mbnn. R614
   Solomon, esf PA 1777; PN aec 58 Lewis Co,VA, 1818; dd 2/8/38
R615
   William, esf 1780 as sub for f John, Orange Co, VA, where b
5/1767; mvd to KY after RW, thence 1816 to Ripley Co, IN,
where PN 1834. R615
   William, esf 1775 VA; b 12/20/1751; PN 1824 Charlotte Co, VA
R615
COLLINGSWORTH, John, esf 1776 as sub for bro Edmond, Culpeper
Co, VA, where b 1763; marine on ship LIBERTY 1776; esf
1777 near Norfolk, VA, in VA regiment; later esf Montgo-
mery Co, VA; res with f during RW; mvd from Culpeper Co to
Granger Co, TN, where PN 1832; mvd 1834 to St Clair Co, IL
with P.O at Lebanon; dd there 9/6/38. R616
COLLY, Asa, BLW issued 7/14/1792. R616
COLLYER, John, esf 1775 Pittsylvania Co, VA, where res; b 1757
Cumberland Co, VA; mvd 1775 to Wilkes Co, NC, & esf 1780;
after RW mvd to Pendleton Co, SC, for 4 years, thence to
Washington Co, VA, for 2 years, thence Russell Co, VA, for
13 years, thence Floyd Co, KY, for 4 years, thence Russell
Co, VA, for 3 years, thence Morgan Co, KY, for 8 years,
thence Franklin Co, IN, where PN 1833; res 1843 Grundy Co,
MO, to be near ch; res 1845 Mercer Co, MO, to be near ch;
surname also spelled COLYER. R616
COLONNA, Benjamin, esf 1779 Accomac Co, VA, where b 1763; mvd
to Northampton Co, VA, after RW, & later mvd back to Acco-

COLONNA (continued)
mac Co, where PN 1832. R616

COLQUITT, Ranson, esf 1777-8 Cumberland Co, VA; PN 1819 Rockingham Co, NC; dd 9/23/1818; md 11/25/1785 Susanna Baker,
Halifax Co, VA; wid PN ae 78 Greenbrier Co, VA, 1841; wid
dd 10/15/45 Rockingham Co, NC, leaving s James only survi-
vor; wid bro John present at her funeral; s James AFF 1854
Rockingham Co, NC, that m never got PN; surname at times
spelled COLQUETT. R616

COLSTON, Samuel, esf VA; dd 1778-9 Henrico Co, VA, intestate
without issue, leaving eldest bro William only heir; William dd 1780, his LWT listing ch William Traverse, Elizabeth L, & Susan; William Traverse dd Frederick Co, VA, &
left ch William, Armistead, Lucy L w/o Dr Joshua H Thomas,
& Susan P N w/o Jefferson Jennings all liv 1842, with William & Armistead res VA, Lucy & Susan res KY; Elizabeth L
md Dr Benjamin H Hall & dd KY, leaving ch William E, Caroline C w/o Alexander McGrew of Cincinnati, OH, & Nancy, of
which William E & Nancy dd intestate without issue; Susan,
d/o William Traverse, md Mr Turner, he since decd; heirs
1842 were William Colston, Armistead Colston, Lucy L Thomas, Susan P N Jennings, Caroline C McGrew, & Susan Turner
who gtd BLW. R616

COLTER, John, esf 1780 PA; gtd BLW when ae 74 Bedford Co, VA,
1829. R616

COLVILLE, James, esf 1777 Winchester,VA; b 10/7/1757 Frederick
Co, VA; res Shenandoah Co, VA, during RW; PN 1832 Newark
Township, Licking Co, OH; dd 12/30/38; QLF 1930 from Grace
F W Colville, Newark,OH, states sol buried Wilson Cemetery
near Newark, OH, further querier great gdd/o sol bro John,
who RW sol, & his w Mary Jamieson. R617

COLVIN, Benjamin, esf 1778 Culpeper Co, VA; PN ae 74 Boone Co,
MO, 1832. R617

Henry, esf 1779 Culpeper Co, VA; PN ae 70 Pendleton Co, KY,
1832; dd 1/31/39; QLF 1921 from great gds Leslie T Applegate, Covington, KY. R617

John, esf 1775 Culpeper Co, VA; b 3/16/1758; dd 5/29/1832;
md 10/7/1778 Sarah Dillard there, who b 1/11/1762; wid PN
1856 Culpeper Co, VA; ch births: Priscilla 7/16/1780, Robert 6/14/84, & John D 9/29/1800; sol bro of Mason & Harry
who both sub for him in RW svc 1781. R617

Mason, esf 1781 Culpeper Co, VA, where b; PN there 1832 ae
72; dd 1/23/53; QLF 1913 from great great great gdd Mrs
Will W Ward, Columbus, OH. R617

COLWELL, John, see CALDWELL, John. R618

COLYER, Charles, esf 1779-80 Henry Co, VA; b 12/1757 Fauquier
Co, VA; res after RW Washington Co, TN, thence Pulaski Co,
KY, thence Rockcastle Co, KY, where PN 1834. R618

John, see COLLYER, John. R618

John, esf VA; PN 1791 for disability from svc; res 1821 Lincoln Co, KY; dd 3/31/26 Rockcastle Co, KY; md 1772-3 Griz-
zey/Grizzy in VA; wid PN aec 90 Rockcastle Co, KY, 1843;

COLYER (continued)
AFF there 1843 by preacher Stephen M Collyer (b 4/10/1775)
that he mvd from VA to KY same time as sol & w; AFF there
then by preacher Richard Colyer ae over 64; no relationship stated between sol & preachers; QLF states sol w Griselda Taylor who b 1753 & dd 1844; QLF 1896 from desc Miss
Sue Williams, Carthage, IL. R618
COMBES, William, esf c1776 Stoverstown, VA; PN 1818 Bath Co,
KY, where res 1820 ae 63 when w aec 61 & no ch res with
them; sol dd 3/8/40; QLF states sol esf Shenandoah Co, VA,
& md Miss Cloud; QLF states a VA RW sol William Combs from
Chesterfield Co, VA, b 1745 & dd Fleming Co, KY. R618
COMBS, John, b 9/7/1764 Amelia Co,VA; esf Winter 1779-80 Fair-
field District, SC; mvd 1783 from SC to Wilkes Co, GA, &
PN there 1834. R618
  John, esf 1777 Frederick Co or Shenandoah Co,VA; b 2/7/1761;
PN 1825 Perry Co, KY, when w Margaret aec 55 & ch: John,
Sally ae 27 (wid with ch Samuel ae 9-10, Harvey ae 7, &
Thomas ae 1), & Margret ae 18 & her ch Hyskiah ae 1; QLF
states sol dd c1830; QLF states sol middle initial S. R618
  Mahlon, see COOMBS, Mahlon. R618
  Robert, esf 1775 Loudoun Co, VA; b near Berry Ferry on She-
nandoah River, Frederick Co, VA; PN ae 79 Fauquier Co, VA,
1832; QLF states sol dd 9/7/46. R618
  William, see COMBES, William. R618
  William, esf 1776 Stafford Co,VA; dd Fall 1780 in RW svc; md
12/7/1774 Sarah Ann Million, Prince William Co, VA; only
ch William Jr b 1/11/1777, res 1843 Russell Co, VA, when
m afp ae 90; wid res there 6 years, having res before in
Stafford Co, VA, SC, Russell Co, VA, & Montgomery Co, KY;
AFF 1843 by wid bro John Million (b 5/10/1760), res Madison Co, KY, that sol wid b Stafford Co, VA, that sol was
blacksmith, & John at sis wedding; wid PAR; sol surname at
times spelled COOMBS; wid PAR. R618
COMER, Augustine, esf 1776-7 Shenandoah Co,VA; PN ae 61 Monroe
Co,VA, 1818; dd there 1/22/24; md 4/23/1782 Catharine/Cor-
treen Rush, Shenandoah Co, VA; wid dd 4/11/1841 Mercer Co,
VA, survived by ch Jacob there, Sally (w/o John Peters of
Giles Co, VA), Elizabeth Miller (Logan Co, VA), Catharine
Ball (Logan Co, VA), Frederick (Monroe Co, VA), Barbara
(Monroe Co, VA), Michael (Cabell Co, VA), & Augustine (Ni-
cholas Co, VA); wid ch gtd PN due her 1849, except Frede-
rick who dd c1849. R619
  John, esf 1775 Amelia Co, VA; esf later as marine on ship
HERO; esf 1781 in VA militia; b 7/1753 Caroline Co,VA; mvd
to Grayson Co, VA, c1782 where PN 1832. R619
COMMANS, Robert, b 10/1750 Ireland; to America 1771; esf 1776
Carlisle, Cumberland Co,PA; PN 1832 Brooke Co, VA; surname
also spelled CUMMINS. R619
COMMINS, Harmon; esf 1776 Sharpsburg, Frederick Co,MD; PN 1819
Pendleton District,SC; res 1832 Anderson District, SC; fa-
mily mbnn 1819; QLF 1917 from desc Mrs S T Phillips, Co-

COMMINS (continued)
lumbus, GA. R619
COMPTON, Archibald, esf 1777 Amelia Co, VA; PN 1788 for disa-
bility from wound at Battle of Morristown, NJ; res 1822
Pittsylvania Co, VA; dd 4/1828; md 4/1783 Sally, d/o Hough
Carpenter of Charlotte Co, VA; wid PN ae 74 Halifax Co, VA
1838; QLF 1927 from great great gdd May Compton (Mrs F M)
Allen, Caney, KS. R620
 James, esf 1777 Annapolis, MD; PN ae 65 Guilford Co, NC; dd
3/10/1832 Russell Co, VA; md Frances, Caswell Co, NC; wid
PN ae 81 Russell Co, VA, leaving ch: David (ae 60 in 1847
who 2nd s), Polly, Clary, & Nancy. R620
 Jeremiah H, b 10/1754 Brunswick Co, NJ; esf 1780 Botetourt
Co, VA, where res till 1792 when mvd to Washington Co, NC,
(area later TN), for 8 years, thence Sevier Co, TN, where
PN 1832; dd 6/19/44; md 1784 Elizabeth Layman, Botetourt
Co, VA; wid PN aec 81 Sevier Co, TN, 1845, when AFF by her
bro Daniel Layman, a clergyman, that he attended her wed-
ding. R620
CONAWAY, John, esf 1776 Hampshire Co, VA, to fight indians;
mvd to Bedford Co, PA, 1780 where esf; b 10/6/1762; mvd to
Morgantown, VA, 1815, thence to res on line between Monon-
galia Co & Harrison Co, VA; while res there afp 1833 Lewis
Co, VA, & PAR; bro Thomas served with him in RW; surname
also spelled CONWAY. R623
 Richard, see CONWAY, Richard. R623
CONDREY, John, esf 1776 Chesterfield Co, VA, where b 2/7/1760;
PN there 1832. R623
CONDRY, William, esf Henry Co, VA; b 9/1753 Fauquier Co, VA;
later esf 1780 in what now Sullivan Co, TN, where bro res;
afp 1852 by s William H, Claiborne Co,TN, for all ch/o sol
& w who both then decd, & PAR. R623
CONGLETON, Moses, b 10/4/1763 s/o William & Mary, Allen Township, Northampton Co, PA, where esf 1776; PN 1833 Wells-
burg, Brooke Co, VA; dd 11/8/36; md 5/18/1788 Mary, Northampton Co, PA, who b there 9/20/1763 d/o Thomas & Margaret Grimes; wid PN 1848 Monroe Co, OH; ch births: Margaret
3/29/1789, Mary 4/30/91, John 5/31/93, Maria 12/1/95 (md
10/18/1820 Thomas Good), William 7/27/99, Juliana 7/180-
(md 11/14/1819 Cornelius F Randolph), & Thomas Grimes 1/05
R625
CONGROVE, William, esf Fauquier Courthouse, Fauquier Co, VA; b
Prince William Co, VA; mvd c1811 to Wood Co, VA, where PN
1833 ae 80 as William Sr; s William Jr AFF aec 58; other
ch res there mbnn. R625
CONINE, Andrew, b 10/22/1761 NJ; family mvd 1769 to Berkeley
Co, VA, where sol esf 1776; PN 1832 Henry Co, KY, where dd
6/11/36; md 9/1785 Lydia near York, PA, who b 4/19/1766;
wid PN 1841 Switzerland Co, IN; ch births: Richard
10/2/1786, Anna 2/3/88, Mary 2/10/90, Sarah 12/19/91, Ally
12/27/93, John 11/22/95 (dd 6/23/1835-6), Cornelius
10/22/97, Cornelius 6/29/1800 (dd 9/28/1839), Dennis 4/02,

CONINE (continued)
Andrew 5/8/04, David Demaree 4/2/09, & Mary 7/4/10. R625
Jeremiah, esf 1781 Martinsburg, VA; PN ae 63 Richland Co,
OH, 1825 when w decd & ch res with him: Jane ae 16, Deli-
lah ae 13, & Otho S ae 18, + orphan gdd Delilah Cissna ae
6; eldest s Richard afb 1859 Eddyville, Wapello Co, IA;
surname also spelled CARNINE; QLF 1908 from great gdd Ma-
ry L Terrell, Calliope, Sioux Co, IA, gdd/o sol s Richard
(War of 1812 sol) & wid/o Civil War sol. R625
CONKLIN, Daniel, esf 1776 Wallkill, NY; PN ae 61 Fayette Co,
PA, 1818; res there 1821 when w Ann ae 41; res Brooke Co,
VA, 1837 where mvd to res with d & s-in-law William Mc-
Connell; QLF 1938 from great great gds Vernon B Hampton,
Staten Island, NY, who also great great gds of RW sol
Charles Webb of NY, & great gds of Col Samuel Webb of War
of 1812 svc from Monroe Co, NY. R626
CONLEY, Charles, esf 1777 Goochland Courthouse, Goochland Co,
VA; b 7/22/1761 Chesterfield Co, VA; later esf Albemarle
Co, VA; mvd after RW ae 22 to Wilkes Co, GA, then back to
VA (Lee Co) for c12 years, thence Wayne Co,KY, 1816 where
PN 1835; surname also spelled CONLY. R627
CONLY, John, no RW svc, but esf 1792 Montgomery Co (now Giles
Co), VA, to fight indians; apf ae 64 Giles Co, VA, 1840 &
PAR, svc less than 6 months. R627
CONN, George, b 10/7/1758 VA; esf c1780 Craven Co, SC (later
Chester District), where PN 1832; surname also spelled
COLN. R627
Samuel, esf 1777 Loudoun Co, VA; b 1760 Fairfax Co, VA; PN
1834 Jefferson Co, KY, where res since 1796; QLF states
res there 1840 ae 78; QLF 1918 from great gdd Mrs E Craw-
ford, Atlantic, IA, states sol dd Jefferson Co, KY, & she
also great gdd of PA RW sol Christian Breneman who dd in
IN; QLF 1923 from desc Mrs H C Sears, Danville,IN, states
sol had s Hugh b 1788, further RW sol John M Conn, an in-
dian hunter, md Nancy & they later res Bourbon Co, KY;
QLF 1935 from Mary E Conn who desc of either sol or of RW
sol Timothy Conn, who PN Mercer Co, KY, & dd c1840 ae 84.
R627
William, esf 1777 Lincoln Co, NC; b 1760 Somerset Co, NJ;
res after RW Russell Co, VA; mvd 1810 to Henry Co, KY, &
PN there 1834; dd there 9/18/36 or 12/18/36; md 1779 or
10/1780 Elizabeth Alexander, Lincoln Co, NC; wid PN ae 78
Henry Co, KY, 1839, P O New Castle, when eldest of 8 ch
Elizanbeth Whitley, b 8/13/1781, res there; other ch mbnn
1840: 2nd ch ae 57, 3rd ch ae 55, 4th ch ae 51, & 5th ch
ae 49; AFF there then by Andrew Whitley that he neighbor
of sol & w c41 years; QLF 1934 from great great great gdd
Mrs D F Scott, Hammond, IN, states she desc/o sol d Charlotte who b 2/14/1789 Lincoln Co, NC, & md 10/12/1811
George Gilpin. R627
William Y, b & raised MD in area now Washington, DC, where
esf 1776; esf later Alexandria, VA, as pilot for ships

CONN (continued)
     evading British fleet; PN ae 78 Washington Co, VA, 1833.
     R627
CONNEL, Daniel, b 12/22/1749 Frederick Co,VA; esf Richmond Co,
     GA; res GA since RW where PN 1836 Jefferson Co; QLF states
     sol gtd ld Washington Co, GA, 1784. R628
CONNELL, Francis P, esf c1781 Lunenburg Co, VA, where res; afp
     ae 76 Lancaster District, SC, 1838, & PAR, insufficient
     proof/o svc; CONNELL births from bible: William 4/29/1759,
     Mary 2/21/61, Frank Pace 10/13/62, Elizabeth 11/1/64, Ro-
     bert 8/20/66, John 12/1/68, Walter 7/3/71, Lucresy 6/5/73,
     James 9/18/75, Stephen 12/1/77, Sarah 1/11/80, & Millah
     1/22/82; s Jefferson, heir-at-law, afp through power/o at-
     torney 1852 Lancaster District, SC, for f's claim, & PAR.
     R628
CONNELLY, John, esf 1777 Fairfax Co, VA; esf 1781 Loudoun Co,
     VA; b 8/22/1757 VA; PN 1839 Nelson Co, KY; QLF 1913 from
     desc Mrs Robert T Jenkins, Slater, MO. R628
   John, esf 1778 Brunswick Co, VA, where b 1/27/1760; mvd c2
     years after RW to Mecklenburg Co, NC, where res 44 years,
     thence 1831 to Bedford Co, TN, where PN 1832; dd there
     6/29/35; md 3/2/1790 Mary Stanford, Mecklenburg Co, NC;
     wd PN ae 79 Maury Co, TN, 1848; ch births: Jefferson
     11/3/1803, Charles L 8/10/07, Milton H 1/22/10, & James M
     12/21/11; in 1846 James M missionary in Africa; QLF 1937
     from Milton P Connelly, Fort Worth, TX, states he desc of
     a George Connally who came to VA from Ireland c1750 whose
     s Thomas (b 1742) RW sol who esf 1779 Brunswick Co, VA, &
     md 1770 Polly Price, further elder George had s George (b
     1763) RW sol who esf 1763 Lancaster Co, VA; QLF 1928 from
     great gdd A Albertha (Mrs W H) Curry, Sebro-Woodley, WA.
     R628
   William, BLW issued 9/25/1833 to only ch James, Nancy (w/o
     William G Clarke), & Albert, Lancaster Co, VA, at which
     time sol decd; surname also spelled CONNELY. R628
CONNELY, Arthur, esf VA; b 7/2/1756; dd 11/4/1813; md Marthew
     11/4/1784; wid b 6/19/1781, & PN 1839 Boone Co,KY, as Mar-
     tha; ch births: Peggy 11/19/1785, Jeane 12/18/87, & Poley/
     Coley 1/3/90; in 1839 Peggy Black AFF Boone Co, KY, that
     she eldest ch of sol & w Marthew. R628
CONNER, Arthur, esf 1777-8 Buckingham Co, VA, dd 9/22/1831; md
     10/1783 Ellena/Elenor; wid PN ae 85 there 1842; ch births:
     John 1/19/1784, Edmund Archdacon 11/19/85, Molley 1/11/86,
     Elenor 12/13/87, Charles 11/27/91, Salley 1/7/94, Luke
     2/19/96, & Arthur 8/22/98; gdc mbnn 1831; AFF then by Me-
     shach Boaz ae 66 that he nephew of sol wid. R629
   Daniel, esf 1776 Amherst Co, VA; PN aec 72 Nelson Co, VA,
     1820, where dd c1822; md 8/30/1815 Mrs Mary Hurt, Patrick
     Co, VA, who had ch mbnn by her former h; sol stated 1820
     that he had no ch; wid PN ae 80 Patrick Co, VA, 1853; her
     res 1855 Wythe Co, VA. R629
   James, esf 1814 Halifax Co, VA, for War of 1812; BLW issued

231

CONNER (continued)
11/6/1850 when sol ae 53 res Tuscumbia, Franklin Co, AL, where mvd Spring 1832; another BLW issued there 4/28/55; dd 4/7/57 or 4/8/57 there; md 7/11/1825 Martha T Scales, Courtland, Lawrence Co, AL, who mvd after h death to Iuka, MS, thence to Brownsville, Haywood Co,TN, where PN 1878 ae 70; ch mbnn; sol bro's Thomas & John also War of 1812 svc; file also mentions a John O'Connor who came from Ireland to VA c1740 who had sons John, William, Lewis, Charles, James, Philip, Thomas, & Timothy; QLF 1939 sol gds Ewell T Weakley, Dyersburg, TN, states sol b 3/9/1795; all of this data contained in file of RW soldier CONNER who not connected with VA. R629

James, esf c1778 Guilford Co, NC; b 10/3/1758 Culpeper Co, VA; PN 1832 Abbeville District, SC. R629

John, esf VA; dd intestate c1832 Norfolk Co, VA, leaving d Elizabeth Davis, only surv ch, who gtd BLW issued 8/8/34; in 1845 she decd & her heirs were: Elizabeth Conner, Edy Conner, William Conner Sr, Lydia Williams, William Conner Jr, James Conner, Mary Conner, & Thomas Conner. R629

John, see CONNOR, John. R629

Joseph, esf 1777 Berkeley Co, VA, while res Washington Co, MD; PN ae 67 Miami Co, OH, 1821 when w aec 60. R629

Lawrence, esf VA against Shawnee Indians; later esf VA for RW svc; PN 1789 Botetourt Co, VA, for disability from war wounds; PN increase ae 65 Cumberland Co, KY, 1818; ch in 1820: Ester ae 30, Cornelius ae 18, Jinny ae 16, Margaret ae 13; dd 3/7/26. R629

Maximilian, esf 1889 Ninety-Six District, SC; b VA; PN ae 69 Greene Co, TN, 1832; dd 11/27/34; md 11/14/1788 Phoebe Bishop at home of her m Elizabeth Bishop, Spartanburg District, SC; ch births: Benjamin 9/1789, Charlotta 3/14/91, James H 5/10/92, John 10/6/914, Elizabeth 10/18/98, Winney 8/19/98, Isaac 1800, Thomas 12/17/03, Maximilian 1/2/05, Mary 11/18/07, Brittanna 8/19/10, & Madison 12/13/12. R629

Philip, see CONNOR, Philip, R629

Philomen, esf 1779 Orange Co,VA, where b 6/29/1763 s/o John; mvd after RW with f & stepm Lucy to Washington Co, VA, for 1 year, thence Lincoln Co, KY, for c3 years, thence KY for c 10 years where res Mercer Co, Fayette Co, & Scott Co during which served against indians; settled 1795 Boone Co, KY, thence 1829 to Fayette Co, IN, where PN 1832 Harrison Township; dd 8/10/35; stepm Lucy ae 75 in 1832; bro John b 1774, res Fayette Co, IN, 1832; QLF 1940 from Mrs Ewell T Weakley, Dyersburg, TN, states she great great gdd of RW sol John Conner who md Elizabeth Kavanaugh 1734 & they res Orange Co, VA, & Culpeper Co,VA, further querier great gdd of RW sol John Conner who md Mary & dd Halifax, VA, 1798-1811, who had d Jane who md 1797 James Watson, Halifax, VA R629

Terrence, esf 1776 Prince William Co, VA; PN ae 64-67 Perry Co, IN, 1819; in 1821 w ae 65 & d Margaret ae 20; QLF 1928

CONNER (continued)
   from desc William S Vawter, New York, NY; QLF states sol b
   1757 Tipperary, Ireland, & dd 12/16/1841; QLF 1900 from
   gds F C Groves, Perry Co, IN; QLF states sol md Sarah Jane
   Speaks of VA; QLF undated from great great gdd Mrs E Marsh
   of Webster Grove, OH, who also great great gdd of RW sol
   Thomas Lewis who b 1742 Fairfax Co, VA, PN & dd KY c1822.
   R629
   William, esf 1779 Surry Co, NC; b Isle of Wight Co, VA; mvd
   as ch to King William Co, VA, where f dd; m then mvd fami-
   ly to neighborhood of her sis in Fauquier Co, VA, where m
   dd; sol bro then came from Surry Co,NC, & took sol home to
   live with him, sol then ae 10-12; sol mvd c1791 to Fayette
   Co, KY, thence to Montgomery Co, KY, 1829 where PN 1833 ae
   70. R629
   William, see CONNOR, William. R629
CONNERLY, William, esf 1776 Norfolk, VA; PN ae 63 Brunswick Co
   VA, 1818; d Elvira T ae 17 in 1820; surname also spelled
   CONNELLY; QLF states sol b Ireland. R630
CONNOLLY, George, esf 1779 Frederick Co,VA, while res Richmond
   Co, VA; b c5/20/1761 Lancaster Co, VA; res Richmond Co, VA
   for c18 years after RW, thence Harrison Co, VA, for c16
   years, thence Lewis Co,VA, for c2 years, thence Kanawha Co
   VA, where PN 1834; w dd shortly before sol PN, & sol later
   mvd to Lewis Co, VA, to live with d; sol last PN payment
   9/4/37. R630
CONNOR, John, esf 1778 VA; PN aec 65 Christian Co, KY, 1818;
   in 1820 had d Abigail aec 31 w/o Thomas C Withers & s Benjamin ae 24; Abigail & Thomas Withers res 1832 there, sol
   then decd; QLF states sol md twice & drowned at Dry Ford,
   Sinking Creek, Breckinridge Co, KY. R630
   Philip, esf 1775 Hampton, VA; w dd 1815, sol then res with s
   while other s res MO; PN ae 67 Hamilton Co, OH, 1819; PN
   increase ae 74 Jennings Co, IN, 1828; only 2 ch. R630
   Terrence, see CONNER, Terrence. R630
   William, esf 1776 VA; res after RW near Pittsburgh, PA; mvd
   to Beaver Co,PA, thence Scioto Co,OH, where PN 1820 ae 63;
   dd 3/14/27, 3/12/28, or 3/16/28; md 3/13/1782 Rosanna near
   Pittsburgh, PA, who b 3/1758; wid PN 1838 when res with d
   Sarah Stewart, Warren Co, IN; wid res 1841 & 1843 with another d, Coles Co,IL; wid dd 8/30/44; d Sarah b 2/17/1796
   youngest of 8 ch; sol s Cornelius res 1839 in "Mississippi
   County"; in 1846 d Sarah h George Stewart stated 3 heirs
   to sol wid: Sarah Stewart, Matilda Glaze, & Catharine Rankin; sol & w surv ch 1852: Margaret Eaton, Matilda Glaze,
   Catharine Wallace, & Sarah Stewart; QLF 1895 from gds Wil-
   liam Stewart Conner, Peirce City, MO, states sol & w res
   near Chillicothe, OH. R630
CONNOREY, John, BLW issued 11/20/1790. R630
CONRAD, Jacob, BLW issued 7/20/1792. R630
   Jacob, see CONROD, Jacob. R630
CONROD, Jacob, esf 1777 at Redstone Settlement on Monongahela

CONROD (continued)
River, PA or VA; b8/1754; PN 1820 Rockingham Co,VA; w mbnn
1821; sol dd 6/3/24; QLF 1939 from Mary M Conrad, Columbus
OH, states a Jacob Conrad Jr b 5/17/1744, s/o Jacob Sr, md
Hannah Rogers of Rockingham Co & Pendleton Co, VA, further
another Jacob Conrad md Eunice (b 1805 Cedarville, VA, &
dd there 1895). R631
CONSOLVER, John; esf VA; PN 1789; dd before 3/4/1810; papers
lost in Washington, DC, fire 1814. R631
CONWAY, Henry, esf 1777 VA; dd 9/10/1812; md 7/25/1769 Sarah,
Pittsylvania Co, VA; wid PN ae 86 Washington Co, TN, 1837;
during sol RW his ch Thomas aec 11, Nany aec 9, Elizabeth,
& Susana; BLW issued 1807. R632
James, esf 1776 New London, Bedford Co, VA; PN 1818 Greenville District,SC; res ae 77 with s Knox Co, TN, 1820; QLF
states sol dd 6/1/27 ae 91. R632
James, esf VA; dd in svc; heirs mbnn afp 1842; afp 1844 by
Christopher Conway, Pittsylvania Co, VA, & Mrs Lucy Harri-
son; both PAR; QLF states sol KIA or dd in svc 12/8/1776
near Trenton, NJ; QLF 1935 from desc Miss Ann F Conway,
Philadelphia, PA, states sol left wid & 4 small ch, one of
which named James. R632
Jesse, esf 1777 Reed Island,Montgomery Co, VA; esf 1779 Har-
rodsburg (now in KY) for svc in VA regiment; PN ae 71 Ma-
dison Co,IL, 1832; dd 10/9/40, Greene Co, IL; md 11/7/1825
Margaret Renfroe, Madison Co, IL; wid PN there 1854 ae 68;
QLF 1931 from George Pohlman, Macon, MO, whose w desc of
sol. R632
John, see CONAWAY, John. R632
John, esf 1776 Montgomery Co, VA; b 8/10/1758 Henrico Co,
VA; PN 1834 Nicholas Co, KY; dd 6/15/37; md 4/14-15/1790
Anna Sutton, Bourbon Co, KY, who b 6/24/1766; wid PN 1843
Nicholas Co, KY, & still res there 1848; ch births: Polly
3/30/1791, Anna 7/13/92, William 9/4/93, John 11/28/94,
Elizabeth 3/31/97, & Nathaniel Sutton 5/28/98; s Nathaniel
md 1/27/1825 Ann C Baker (b 7/7/1805) & their ch births:
John William 5/26/27, Elizabeth Ann 2/9/29, Washington
Franklin 8/27/32, & Mary Susan 8/7/35; in 1834 sol had bro
Jesse "if living res IL"; QLF sol s/o John, & sol wid dd
1850. R632
Joseph, BLW issued 2/17/1797; papers lost in Washington, DC,
fire 1814. R632
Richard, esf 1781 Hampshire Co, VA; b Queen Anne Co, MD; res
PA after RW for 5 years, thence to Mason Co, KY, for c30
years, thence Henry Co, IN, where PN 1832 aec 70; QLF 1937
from desc Mrs Ernest G Erler, Valparaiso,IN, states sol dd
1854, md Polly; QLF 1936 from desc Virginia H Buck, Madison,IN; QLF 1925 from J H Hayworth, Indianapolis,IN, whose
w desc of sol; QLF 1913 from desc Miss Damaris Metaker,
Plymouth, IN; QLF states sol dd ae 102, Henry Co, IN. R632
CONYERS, Benjamin, esf 1776 Fauquier Co, VA; b 7/12/1759; PN
1833 Shelby Co, KY; QLF states sol res there 1840. R632

COOK, Aaron, esf 1780 Philadelphia, PA, when res Surry Co, NC;
b 6/16/1760 Henry Co, VA, s/o William & w Elizabeth Clifton; family mvd 1761 to Surry Co, NC; afp ae 82 Hardin Co,
KY, & PAR; res ae 90 Elizabethtown, that Co; nephew of RW
sol William Clifton of NC whose s David also RW sol; William Clifton settled East TN where dd & s David settled NC
R633
  Benjamin, esf c1776 Charlotte Co, VA; b 4/8/1758 Hanover Co,
VA; dd 3/27/1806 Charlotte Co, VA; md there 12/25/1779 Catharine, d/o Sackville Brewer (MB 12/24/79 signed by William Cook); wid b 9/13/1759 & mvd to Green Co,KY, where PN
1839; eldest ch Martha b 1/25/1781. R633
  Benjamin, esf 1778 Yorktown, VA; b 6/9/1760 Princeton, NJ;
mvd 1782 to Middlesex Co, NJ, where PN 1832 New Brunswick;
dd 7/7/1832; md (2) 10/16/1799 Jemima, New Brunswick, NJ,
in presence of d Phebe Priestley by 1st marriage; wid b
11/11/1768, & PN 1848 Middlesex Co, NJ, when AFF by Phebe
Priestley ae 59 of New Brunswick, NJ, & by s Samuel C; ch
births: Benjamin G 9/13/1800, Samuel C 9/14/00, & Thomas
Hill 9/3/02. R633
  Charles, esf 1781 ae 16 Charlottesville,VA; PN 1818 Dearborn
Co, IN; family 1820 w Priscilla ae 60 & Thomas ae 16; sol
f res 1818 Albemarle Co, VA; surname also spelled COOKE.
R633
  Christopher, b 2/10/1756 Essex Co, VA; esf 1776 Northampton
Co, NC, where PN 1832. R633
  Dawson, see COOKE, Dawson. R634
  Henry, b 3/12/1753 on Thompson's Creek, VA; f mvd family to
Little Yorktown, PA, when sol ch, thence to Orange Co, NC,
near Balley's Fort where sol esf; sol mvd to Woodford Co,
KY, c1796 for c10 years, thence Bedford Co, TN, for 1 year
thence Franklin Co, TN, for 15 years, thence Carroll Co,
TN, where PN 1832. R635
  Henry, esf 1779 Lunenburg Co, VA, where b 5/16/1760 s/o John
& bro/o John; PN 1832 Williamson Co, TN. R635
  Jacob, b 7/2/1763 Rockingham Co, VA; mvd with f 1773 from
Washington Co,VA, to Cook's Fort, Indian Creek, Greenbrier
Co (area later Monroe Co), VA, & esf there 1779; afp Mon-
roe Co, VA, 1836, & PAR. R635
  James, b 1762 York Co, PA; mvd to VA as ch, where esf 1780
Bedford Co (area later Campbell Co), VA; res there for 40
thence Logan Co (area later Butler Co), KY where PN 1832.
R636
  John, esf 1776 Guilford Co, NC; b 12/9/1761 Hanover Co, VA;
mvd 1788 to Wilkes Co (later Elbert Co),GA, where PN 1832.
R636
  John, esf 1779 Winchester,VA; dd 6/3/1836; md 8/23/1786 Mary
at home of her f Robert Heshman, Culpeper Co, VA; wid b
6/5/1765; wid PN 1846 Greenbrier Co, VA; ch births: Nancy
7/12/1787, James 9/12/89, Thomas 5/31/91, Malinda 5/21/93,
John 10/3/95, Elizabeth 10/3/97, Sarah 3/9/99, Jesse
11/20/1800, Lewis 2/18/04, Andrew H 8/5/06, Eli 9/18/08, &

COOK (continued)
    Jennifer10/24/03; wid dd 1/14/53 Greenbrier Co,VA, leaving
      ch John, Nancy Church, Thomas, Malinda Thompson, Elizabeth
      Niece, Sarah Campbell, Lewis, Jesse, Andrew, & Eli; s John
      afp due m there 1853 for all surv ch & gtd; wid bro Moses
      Heshman, b 5/8/1760, made AFF 1846 Greenbrier Co, VA. R636
    Lewis, esf 1775 VA; PN 1818 Camden District, SC; PN increase
      ae 64 Kershaw Co, SC, when res with 2 d's & aged infirm w.
      R637
    Mathew, esf 1779 as cabin boy on ship FAIR AMERICA LIBERTY
      when res Northampton Co,VA, where b 4/11/1750; esf Lexing-
      ton Co, KY, for sea svc in War of 1812; afp 1835 Campbell
      Co, KY. R638
    Theodosius, esf 1780 Guilford Co,NC; b 5/31/1763 Mecklenburg
      Co, VA; afp 1833 3rd District of Henry Co, GA, & PAR, less
      than 6 months svc. R640
    Thomas, esf 1776 Guilford Co,NC; b 5/12/1752 Hanover Co, VA;
      PN 1832 Eleventh District of Henry Co,GA; dd that Co 1841;
      sons Fenton & Samuel & gdd Elizabeth Faulkner, w/o William
      Russell, mentioned in 1850; QLF states sol w Mary. R640
    Thomas, esf Rowan Co, NC; dd 8/31/1809; md 8/18/1763 Ann,
      Henrico Co, VA, who dd ae 100 Iredell Co, NC, 1/24/1844;
      ch: Ann, Robison, Thomas, Nancy, Sarah, Robert, Margaret,
      & John F (youngest); s John F ae 73 appointed adm of m's
      estate Iredell Co, NC, 1856 when he & sis Sarah (never md)
      only surv ch; John & Sarah afp & PAR. R640
    Thomas, esf 1777 Lunenburg Co,VA; dd 9/7/1819; md 12/27/1784
      Martha, d/o Robert Vaughan (liv then), Amelia Co, VA; wid
      PN ae 77 Charlotte Co, VA, 1839, & dd there 1840 leaving
      ch Elizabeth Franklin, Nancy Davis, Mary Adams, Martha
      Wilkinson, & Thomas; John A Adams adm of her estate. R640
    William, esf 1776 Amherst Co, VA; PN ae 78 Edgefield Dis-
      trict, SC, 1832 when ch & their families mbnn; AFF then by
      sol halfbro Bennet Henderson, Abbeville District, SC. R641
    William, b 10/15/1763 Pittsylvania Co, VA; mvd to NC during
      RW where esf 1779 Green Co; mvd after RW to SC for 18
      years, thence to KY where PN 1832 Graves Co. R641
    William, BLW issued 8/29/1791. R641
    William, esf 1780 Spotsylvania Co, VA, where b 10/11/1763;
      mvd after RW to Bath Co, KY, thence Morgan Co, KY, where
      PN 1834. R641
    William, esf 1780 Caroline Co, VA; b 4/1762; mvd after RW to
      Richmond, VA, thence King & Queen Co, VA, where PN 1832, a
      tailor; dd 3/12/37 when s mbnn present; md Clara/Clary who
      PN aec 77 King & Queen Co, VA, 1843; surname also spelled
      COOKE. R641
    Zachariah, esf 1781 Staunton,VA; bc 1/10/1751; PN 1830 Green-
      brier Co, VA, when w ae 52; mvd 1835 to Pike Co, OH, to be
      near ch, where dd 1/46 or 6/30/46, leaving ch: John, Eliza-
      beth, Mary Burgess, Nancy Gale, Margaret Zimmerman, Susan
      Zimmerman, & Sarah Butler; QLF states sol buried at Beaver,
      OH. R641

COOKE, Dawson, esf 1776 in VA Navy aboard brig LIBERTY & later
on ship GLOUCESTER, for which gtd ld by VA; dd 11/14/1829;
md 12/1775 Mildred, King & Queen Co, VA, when he assistant
Co clerk & was later Co sheriff; 7 ch: Mary (b 10/13/1776,
md -- Spencer, & dd 3/8/1802), Ann C (md John Didlake who
dd, then md James Brushwood who dd c1848, & their s George
W Brushwood ae 26 King & Queen Co, VA, 1851), Paschal (dd
2/25/1826), Mildred (md William Howlet & dd 10/16/1816),
Henry (dd 12/4/1837), Dawson (dd 3/8/1842 King & Queen Co,
VA & buried family burying ground there, md Ann L who ae
48 in 1851), & Giles (dd 1/28/1847 Elizabeth City Co, VA,
& his wid mbnn md there Reverend Cincinnatus Goodall who
ae 42 in 1851); sol wid dd 8/14/1836 King & Queen Co, VA;
Ann C Brushwood afp there 1850 ae 60, only surv ch of sol,
& recd PN; her PN application listed surv gdc of sol & w:
William Spencer, Alexander Howlet(t), Robert Didlake, & 3
unnamed d's of Paschal; John R Cooke sur for bond/o Robert
J Stubbs, adm of estate of sol wid; in 1851 Reverend John
Spencer (b 7/23/1775) pastor of Porporone Baptist Church,
King & Queen Co, VA; in 1851 Elizabeth R Newcomb ae 67 AFF
there that sol eldest ch Mary Spencer about same ae as her
bro John Newcomb; in 1851 William Collins ae 34 there, h/o
Johannah Matilda Newcomb, 3rd d/o John Newcomb by 2nd w
Johannah Robinson, brought NEWCOMB family record to court
with data as follows: John Newcomb & Clarrila Lockey Longest md 8/21/1802, their 1st ch Ann Longest b 6/21/03, 2nd
ch Clarrila b 6/16/05 & dd 8/19/08, above John Newcomb b
1/1/1777 (s/o William & Nancy) & dd 3/10/1829, above Clarrila Lockey b 12/20/1784 (d/o Robert Ross Longest & Nancy)
& dd 12/24/1806, John Newcomb md (2) 1/10/1809 Johannah
(1st d/o William & Uralia Robinson) who b 12/11/1788 & dd
3/5/1833, Rosey Ursula Robinson (1st d/o John & Johannah
Newcomb) b 6/4/1810 & dd 10/13/13, Evelina (2nd ch/o John
& Johannah) b 1/17/13 & dd 10/9/17, William Robinson (1st
s/o John & Johannah) b 8/28/15, Johannah Miltilda (3rd d/o
John & Johannah) b 11/17/17, John Garry (2nd s/o John &
Johannah) b 4/3/20, Mira Anna (4th d/o John & Johannah) b
10/19/22 & dd 11/12/33, Bradfute/Bradford Pettis (3rd s/o
John & Johannah) b 3/3/25; births records/o slaves belong-
ing to NEWCOMB's: India Keys (1st d/o Lydia) b 2/28/1821,
Bradick (1st s/o Lydia) b 4/26/23, Rachel Buckner (1st d/o
Dolly) b 7/10/28, Susannah Johnson (2nd d/o Dolly) b
4/25/31, Arrenah Curtis (d/o Fanny) b 2/15/1809, Harrott
Booth (d/o Fanny) b 1/27/15,Elizabeth Robinson (d/o Fanny)
b 9/27/16, Thomas Jackson (1st s/o Fanny) b 1/1/19, Joseph
Robson (2nd s/o Fanny) b 12/28/21, Julius (1st s/o Arrenah
above) b 1/7/28, Frances/Fanny Robinson (1st d/o Arrenah b 3/20/29, Mary Booker (1st d/o Salley) b 12/11/21,
George (1st ch/o Salley) b 11/12/19, John Robinson (2nd
s/o Arrenah) b 9/12/30, Warner Robinson (3rd s/o Arrenah)
b 5/5/32, John Joy Collins b 9/18/37, William Thomas b
5/18/18-- (record torn). R642

COOKE, John, esf 1780 Lunenburg Co, VA, where b 6/25/1763; mvd
1789 to Halifax Co, VA, thence 1822 to Williamson Co, TN,
where PN 1832; AFF then by bro Henry of same Co, also RW
sol. R642

John, esf 1777 Shenandoah Co, VA; PN ae 78 Logan Co, VA,
1832, where dd 11/21/32; md 6/28/13 Ann Hendrix, Monroe Co
VA; wid PN ae 78 Raleigh Co,VA, 1853; surname also spelled
COOK. R642

William, see COOK, William. R642

COOKERS, Michael, esf VA; dd 5/28/1829; md 5/12/1783 Elizabeth
Kiles, Frederick Co, MD, per her AFF; Co clerk report gave
marriage date as 5/10/1784; wid b 6/1761, & PN Berkeley Co
VA, 1838; wid res there 1844 when PN increased. R642

COOKINAN, William, esf ae less than 16 Northumberland Co, VA,
where b; res there until ae 40, thence to Frederick Co,VA,
for 6 years, thence Lewis Co, VA, where afp 1834 ae 75, &
PAR. R642

COOKSEY, Charles, esf 1781 Greensville Co, VA; b 1762 MD; PN
1834 Lunenburg Co, VA; QLF 1914 from gdd Mrs John L Yates,
Lunenburg, VA. R642

Zachariah, esf 1778 VA; PN aec 71 Franklin Co,IN, 1832. R642

COOLEY, James, esf 1778 Halifax Co, NC; b 4/16/1758 Charles
City Co, VA; mvd from Halifax Co, NC, to Montgomery Co, TN
for 12 years, thence Humphreys Co, TN, where PN 1832; surname also spelled COLEY; QLF 1913 from desc Mrs Lizzie
Cooley Hunt, Clarksville, TN. R643

James, esf 1776 Craven Co, SC; esf again 1776 Surry Co, NC,
where res; b 10/19/1760 VA; mvd from NC to Montgomery Co,
VA, for c7 years, thence Madison Co, KY, where PN 1832;
QLF 1930 from Mildred C (Mrs E C) Tallant, Santa Barbara,
CA, states sol her paternal great gdf. R643

COOMBS, John, esf 1781 Loudoun Co, VA, when had w & 3 ch; b
there c1754; PN there 1834, & dd there 1/16/1849; md (2)
1797 there wid Mrs Nancy Vinnander (MB 1/18/1797, signed
by Mahlon Combs & sol John Combs); wid PN 1849 there; wid
res ae 84 Morgan Co,OH, 1855; ch/o sol & 2nd w mbnn; surname at times spelled COMBS; QLF states Andrew Combs who
dd 3/1774 Loudoun Co, VA, survived by s Joseph (b 1740 &
dd 1804), Andrew Jr, Mahlon (b 1748), & this sol John (b
1745), all RW svc. R644

Mahlon, esf near Leesburg, Loudoun Co, VA; mvd to Licking
Co, OH, thence 1830 to IL, thence back to Licking Co, OH,
1832 where PN 1833 ae 64; w mbnn; s res IL 1830; sol bro
Joseph res Wayne Co, OH; QLF 1936 from great great gdd
Miss Leone D Harris, Aurora, IL, states sol 1st name also
spelled Malen, & res later Kendall Co, IL, during Black-
hawk War; QLF states sol dd 11/25/1834. R644

William, esf Wilkes Co,NC; dd 6/1809 Sullivan Co, TN, where
mvd earlier that year; md 6/22/1800 Michal Traylor, Charlotte Co, VA; wid b near beginning of RW Chesterfield Co,
VA, & raised there; wid md (2) c1816 Michael Staire, Sullivan Co, TN, who dd 12/30/1835, Jefferson Co, TN; wid PN

COOMBS (continued)
    aec 75 Washington Co, TN, 1853 for svc of 1st h, & res ae
    85 there 1855; s William Combs Jr dd 3/1853. R644
COON, Anthony, esf 1776 Monongalia Co, VA; PN 1818 Harrison Co
    VA; name dropped from PN rolls 1820 because of current law
    that his property worth in excess to warrant PN; PN ae 77
    Clarksburg, Harrison Co, VA, 1832; family res with sol in
    1826 w aec 65, d Nancy Petit, a wid, & her ch Richard aec
    7, Cylas aec 5, & Hezekiah aec 2; sol also had s Abraham &
    s Samuel liv then. R645
    Israel, BLW issued 9/9/1790. R645
    Michael, esf c1779 aec 14 with f Michael Sr, & bro's Daniel,
    Joseph, & Thomas in same company at Peter Sykes Mills near
    Lake of Salt-Spring, VA, while res Martinsburg, VA; esf
    again there c1781; family bible lost when f's farmhouse at
    Huntstown, NY, burned down, where f dd c1821; b 3/4/1766;
    bro Daniel dd c1822, bro's Thomas & Joseph dd c1829 near
    Huntstown, NY; 2 sis dd c1829; m dd soon after f; sol was
    youngest ch; afp 1854 Montgomery Co, PA, Township of Lower
    Marion, when res with d & her h John Hatchinson; PAR, in-
    sufficient proof of svc; bro's Joseph & Thomas & 2 sis all
    dd leaving ch. R645
COONS, Frederick, esf 1776 Culpeper Co, VA; PN ae 56 Fayette
    Co, KY, 1818; in 1820 w decd & all ch mvd away from home.
    R645
COOPER, Alexander, esf 1777 when res on Watauga River, Ruther-
    ford Co, NC (later East TN); b 1/28/1754 Lunenburg Co, VA;
    mvd from NC after RW to White Co, TN, where PN 1832; dd
    2/9/44; md c1774 Mary, Orange Co, NC; wid PN aec 89 White
    Co,TN, 1844; s Thomas AFF ae 59 there 1851 that sol wid dd
    3/12/49 leaving ch Thomas, Rheuben aec 70, Samuel aec 66,
    Nancy ae 64, Mary aec 63, Lucy aec 58, Elizabeth aec 54,
    Rebecca aec 52, & Drusilla aec 50. R646
    Apollos, esf VA; KIA 9/11/1777 Battle of Brandywine; wid Ma-
    ry md (2) William Stoker; sol & Mary ch: Robert, Jacob, &
    Sarah (md James Dobyns who dd 7/1834; wid & 2nd h dd seve-
    ral years before 1834; sol surv ch Jacob & Sarah res 1834
    Mason Co, KY; BLW issued to them 5/30/1839; QLF 1928 from
    great great gdd's Miss Ola V Cooper & Mrs Mayme Cooper,
    Emmett, ID, states sol res Loudoun Co, VA, before RW; QLF
    1906 from desc Mrs Alice Pauline Cooper Dobell, Greencas-
    tle, IN, states sol esf Loudoun Co, VA. R646
    Barnabas, esf 1779 Amherst Co, VA; b 1760 Black River Town-
    ship, NJ; PN 1832 Fayette Co, VA; dd 1/6/33 leaving s Abel
    res of Guyandotte, Cabell Co, VA. R646
    Benjamin A, esf 1776 Washington Co, VA; b 1/25/1756 Culpeper
    Co,VA; PN 1833 Saline Co,MO; QLF states sol dd there 1841;
    QLF 1935 from desc Burney Joseph Simpson, Chicago, IL,
    QLF states sol dd on Osage River,MO, 1842, md Anne Fuller-
    ton; QLF 1927 from great gds Jesse D Cooper, Kansas City,
    MO, states sol came to MO 1810 & settled Howard Co; QLF
    1920 from desc Mrs Richard W Haynie, Miami Co, OH. R646

COOPER, Caleb, esf 1776-7 Botetourt Co, VA, aec 15 to help in
driving cattle from there to Baltimore,MD, for troops; esf
again 1780 & 1781 there; b 1/6/17--; esf Sullivan Co, TN,
5 years after RW to fight indians; mvd to Lincoln Co, KY,
thence Pulaski Co, VA; esf Wayne Co, KY, for War of 1812,
mvd back to Pulaski Co, VA, where PN 1834 aec 72. R646
  Christopher, esf Botetourt Co, VA; dd ae 76 Greene Co, TN,
  5/29/1830; md 10/20/1786 Jane Brown, Botetourt Co, VA; wid
  afp ae 75 Greene Co, TN, 1844, & PAR, insufficient proof/o
  svc; ch births: Catharine 3/2/1789 (md 5/9/1805 Robert Maloney), Phebe 4/3/91, Elizabeth 7/8/93, & Christopher
  9/25/98 (mvd c1851 to MO); AFF 1852 by d Catharine Maloney
  res Greene Co, TN, that she b 3/2/1788 & her eldest ch b
  4/1/1807; AFF then by James Brown, Greene Co, TN, that he
  present at sol marriage; wid res 1855 Greene Co, TN, with
  s-in-law Ephraim Doty who ae 56 in 1852; sol gds William C
  Doty liv 1855. R646
  Christopher, b 5/12/1750 Culpeper Co, VA; mvd 1772 to Washington Co, VA, where esf 1777 against indians; f & bro KIA
  at Cowen's Fort 1777; sol later esf 1791-94 again to fight
  indians; afp Wilson Co,TN, 1833, & PAR; dd 9/21/33 leaving
  ch: Sarah ae 65, Frances ae 63, Mary ae 62, Francis ae 53,
  Abraham ae 60, Stephen ae 56, Elizabeth ae 51, Benjamin B
  ae 48, & Nancy ae 43; md 6/6/1784 or 5/6/1784 Permelia
  Hagg, Washington Co, VA; wid afp ae 84 Cannon Co, TN, 1850
  & PAR, when AFF by Francis Cooper ae 90 & Abraham Cooper
  ae 85; ch births: Sarah 3/13/1785, Frances 7/29/87, Mary
  5/20/88, Abraham 2/23/90, John 4/30/92, Stephen 11/14/94,
  Francis 3/27/99, Elizabeth 11/14/99, Benjamin B 2/23/1802,
  & Nancy 5/31/04; other Cooper births in bible: John s/o
  John C & Rebecca 9/13/1825, Alden 9/13/26, Sarah J 6/9/28,
  William B 10/30/29, Jeremiah M 12/18/31, Abner 8/12/34,
  Jackey H 9/23/40, Preston J 3/11/42, & Mary Elizabeth
  3/11/45. R646
 Dabney, esf 1776 Bedford Co, VA; b 11/22/1756 Albemarle Co,
 VA; after RW mvd to Franklin Co, VA, thence Botetourt Co,
 VA, thence 1810 to Smith Co, TN, where PN 1831; dd there
 5/4/42; md 6/16/1782 Henrietta Watts, Bedford Co (area now
 Franklin Co), VA, when both res of that Co; wid afp ae 81
 Mason Co, TN, 1843, & PAR, not qualified per current laws;
 wid dd there 12/7/48; AFF 1845 there by Jobe Meador ae 81
 & w Martha ae 74 that they present at marriage of sol; AFF
 1849 there by Daniel Claiborne Sr (b 5/1769) that he present at marriage of sol; sol & w had 11 ch of which 3 survived 1851 there to afp, Sally, Polly Candler, & William
 (b 1803 youngest), & PAR. R646
 Eiles, esf 1775-6 Bedford Co, VA; PN ae 84 Franklin Co, VA,
 1832; dd 12/4/43; md Sarah Monk in Fall 1784 Montgomery Co
 VA; wid PN aec 77 Franklin Co, VA, 1844 & gtd PN increase
 there 1851 ae 87; eldest ch Mildred; AFF there 1844 by Lewis Cooper ae 71 that he neighbor of sol when ch & had bro
 John b 1784. R647

COOPER, Ephraim, esf VA; afb 1810 Frederick Co, VA, by s Char-
les & d Mary w/o Samuel Filson, Fleming Co, KY; BLW issued
2/23/1826. R647
   James, esf Powhatan Co, VA; free man/o color; PN Augusta Co
   VA, 1818; PN increase ae 70 there 1820 when only member of
   family Lukey Orchard, free woman/o color, ae over 50. R647
   John, esf 1776 Chesterfield Co, VA; PN aec 70 Montgomery Co,
   VA, where res 17 years; res 1822 Dearborn Co, IN; dd Fall
   1825; md 2/1780-1 Anna Barbara Trout, Chester Co, PA; wid
   PN aec 90 Montgomery Co, VA, 1840; ch included Jacob who
   aec 58 there then. R648
   John, esf 1776 Washington Co, VA, where b 4/1759; PN 1834
   Morgan Co, KY, where res c12 years; dd there 3/3/37; md
   4/20/1789 Martha "Patsey" McDaniel/McDannel, Greenbrier Co
   VA; wid PN ae 64 Morgan Co,KY, 1839, res there 1855 aec 84
   when afb; BLW issued 5/22/56; s William ae 50 there 1840;
   QLF 1918 from gdd Mrs Elizabeth Bleam, Findlay, OH; QLF
   states sol w d/o RW sol Spencer McDaniel who dd KY. R648
   John, esf Henry Co, VA; mvd to GA Fall 1785 where afp ae 56
   Wilkes Co 1834 & PAR, insufficient proof of svc; dd there
   11/35; md 1778 ?, Henry Co, VA, who dd 8/1836; ch: John W,
   Joseph W, Elizabeth McMekin, Gideon, James, & Thomas; John
   (b 1/17/1783 3rd ch) dd 5/31/1850 Houston Co, GA, a minis-
   ter; sol surv ch Joseph W (Macon Co, GA), Gideon (Chambers
   Co, AL), Elizabeth McMekin (Wilkes Co, GA), & Thomas (Co-
   lumbus Co, GA) afp & PAR, insufficient proof of svc & mar-
   riage of parents; QLF 1906 from great gdd Sarah Cooper
   Holtzclaw, Chattanooga, TN, whose gdf b 1783 Bedford Co,
   VA. R648
 Leighton/Leaton, esf 1778 Albemarle Co, VA; PN ae 72 Adair
   Co, KY; ch mbnn; QLF 1903 from great gdd Mrs Ella Glenn
   Shields, Commerce, OK, states sol res 1830 Simpson Co, KY;
   QLF 1928 from desc Mrs G B Davis, Arkansas City,KS, states
   sol dd 1848 KY, she also desc of VA RW sol John Coombs b
   b 1754, dd 1849 of Loudoun Co, VA; QLF 1932 from desc Rose
   Schultheis, Vincennes,IN, states sol b 1757, dd 1848. R648
 Leonard, esf 1775 VA; b 5/1753-4; PN 1818 Shenandoah Co, VA;
   drowned in Shenandoah River,VA, 5/21/21; md 1796 Christina
   Troenberger, Shenandoah Co, VA, who b 12/25/1773-4; wid PN
   1851 Middletown, Frederick Co, VA; ch births: Aquilla
   3/25/1797 & dd 8/08, Mary M/Marian 12/2/1800 w/o William
   Stevens, Abraham who dd 1808, Presley 8/11/05, Margaret
   3/15/07 (md Mr Rhodes & res 1851 Middletown, VA), Letitia
   12/8/08, Catharine 3/20/10, Matilda 4/19/13, Manual (decd
   in 1821), John Henry 12/28/15, & Elizabeth 2/23/20; sol
   nephew Abraham Cooper b 9/9/1774, md 9/1804 wid sis Elizabeth & they res 1821 Hampshire Co, VA; in 1854 a David
   Rhodes res there; QLF 1936 from great gds Hugh E Naylor,
   Front Royal, VA, who gds/o sol d Catharine, states another
   RW sol Leonard Cooper came to Shenandoah Valley, VA, 1774
   & later settled Mason Co, VA, further states first Leonard
   Cooper s/o Leonard who sol in French & Indian War & whose

COOPER (continued)
    LWT recorded 1776 Frederick Co, VA, further LWT of Leonard
        Jr's w Christina dated 4/1859 & probated there 11/65 lists
        her gdc. R648
    Levin, esf 1776 VA; PN ae 65 Jefferson Co, KY, 1818; family
        1821 w ae 71, d Nelly ae 41, d Sally ae 39, & s Samuel ae
        26; sol dd 7/24/41. R648
    Richard, BLW issued 5/15/1795. R648
    Richard, esf 1776 Essex Co, VA; PN ae 64 Rhea Co, TN, where
        res since 1807. R649
    Spencer, esf VA; BLW issued 8/27/1800; papers lost in Wash-
        ington, DC, fire 1800; QLF 1917 from great gds Thomas C
        Shotwell, New York, NY. R649
    Sterling, esf 1777-8 Lunenburg Co, VA; b 6/20/1760 Amelia Co
        VA; PN 1832 Franklin Co, VA, where mvd soon after RW; dd
        there 1/9/36 leaving ch: Frances, William Langston, George
        W, Sterling Herbert, Benjamin F, Louisa M, Charity M, Sa-
        rah R, & James D (b 3/3/1835); w decd in 1855 when George
        Cooper AFF there that he guardian of sol son James D; QLF
        1925 from great gdd Mrs Martin Martin, Anaconda, MT. R649
    Thomas, esf 1776 Henry Courthouse,VA; PN 1819 Pendleton Dis-
        trict, SC; QLF states an RW sol Thomas Cooper esf 1777 VA,
        res Hampshire Co, VA, & md Rebecca Douthitt. R649
    Vincent, b 1756 Stafford Co, VA; res latter part of RW Fre-
        derick Co, VA, where esf 1780; mvd to Mason Co, KY; res
        1836 Hancock Co, IN, when afp ae 80; PAR, insufficient
        proof of svc. R649
    William, BLW issued 1/27/1793. R649
    William, esf 1780 VA; PN 1828 Fluvanna Co, VA. R649
COPELAND, James, b 8/1/1759 Ireland; came to Loudoun Co, VA,
        aec 4 with parents, where esf 1778; PN there 1832, & dd
        6/15/38; md 4/26/1787 Sarah Akers of Shelburne Parish; wid
        PN ae 70 Loudoun Co,VA, 1832, & res there 1843 ae 73. R650
COPENHAVER, Thomas, b 7/16/1763 Lancaster Co, PA; esf 1780
        Montgomery Co,VA; res there to 1831 when mvd to Lincoln Co
        MO, where afp 1834; PAR, less than 6 months svc. R651
COPES, Parker, esf 1781 Accomac Co, VA, where PN 1818 ae 56;
        PN increase there 1825 ae 63 when res on farm provided by
        s-in-law William Elliott; sol family then w Margaret, s
        Thomas aec 12, d-in-law Rachel Elliott, & Littleton T El-
        liott; sol md to wid of Teackle Elliott & she m/o William
        Elliott; sol also known as Peter P Copes. R651
    Southy, esf 1779 VA; b Accomac Co, VA; mvd to Lewis Co, KY,
        thence to near Portsmouth, Scioto Co, OH, where PN 1818 ae
        57; res there 1820 when 3rd w Ruth ae 60; dd 1/9/34 lea-
        ving w Ruth who mvd to IA where dd 1847; sol surv ch 1858:
        Easter Andrews, Annie Lancaster, Southey (of Adams Co, OH)
        & Parker (overseas for 7 years, res not known); QLF 1938
        from Lillie Copes Morgan, Hillsboro,OH, states sol s/o Sa-
        muel, further Wesley/William Copes adm/o sol estate. R651
COPIS, William, esf VA; PN ae 72 Stark Co, OH,1818; res there
        1820 when no family; surname also spelled COPES. R651

COPLIN, Benjamin, esf 1776 Nutter's Fort,VA; b 3/28/1752 Rock-
    ingham Co, VA; settled 1770 Harrison Co,VA, where PN 1833;
    dd 9/1834; had w during RW. R651
  William, esf 1777 Charlotte Co, VA, where b 1/26/1760; PN
    1832 DeKalb Co, GA; surname at times spelled COPELIN; QLF
    states sol res DeKalb Co, GA, 1840. R651
COPPAGE, John, esf 1777 Fauquier Co, VA; PN ae 67 Pendleton Co
    KY, 1818; AFF Lee Co, VA, 1825 ae 69; dd 2/7/34. R652
COPPEDGE, Thomas, esf 1776 Northumberland Co,VA, where b 1752;
    PN 1833 Amherst Co, VA, where res many years; dd 5/15/43;
    QLF 1932 from desc Miss Mary Eolian Coppedge, professor at
    State Teachers College, East Radford, VA; QLF 1921 from
    Irma Coppage (Mrs William T) Miller, Mattoon, IL, states
    she gdd/o John Coppage who b 1811 Culpeper Courthouse, VA.
    R652
COPPINGER, Higgins, esf 1780 Bedford Co, VA; PN ae 84 Washing-
    ton Co, TN, 1822 where dd 1/4/32, survived by wid who dd
    same year; heirs 1855 (all widows): Mary Coppinger Mitch-
    ell, Nancy Coppinger Harrell (both of Washington Co, TN) &
    Elizabeth Coppinger Mitchell of Sevier Co, TN; surname at
    times spelled COVVINGER; QLF from 1957 Cora Charles, Ber-
    keley, CA, who great gdd of sol s Higgins who md Margaret
    Skelton) Conklin. R652
COPSEY, John, esf 1778-9 Loudoun Co, VA; b 1760 St Marys Co,
    MD; afp 1836 Hampshire Co, VA, where res 50 years; Lucinda
    (Copsey) McIntire, Frederick Co, VA, gave power/o attorney
    to agent 1854 to afp; sol & agent both PAR. R652
COPUS, William, esf 1777 Berkeley Co, VA; PN ae 85 Sullivan Co
    TN, 1832; QLF 1936 from desc Mrs Lillian R Craig, Memphis,
    TN, who also desc of RW sol James Satterfield of Harpers
    Ferry, VA, whose w probably named Matheny. R652
CORAM, William, BLW issued 3/4/1794. R652
CORBETT, John, esf VA; PN 1789; papers lost in 1814 Washington
    DC, fire; QLF states PN transferred to TN. .R652
  John, esf 1777 Isle of Wight Co, VA, where b; esf 1779 Nor-
    thampton Co, NC; PN ae 76 Isle of Wight Co, VA, 1832; dd
    3/10/40 Onslow Co, NC; md 1827 or 8/1831 Elizabeth Blake,
    there or New Hanover Co, NC; wid PN ae 50 latter Co, 1844;
    s John res there 1849; QLF 1920 from great great gdd Mrs
    C L Sutherland, Canton, NC; QLF states another John Cor-
    bett VA RW sol dd several years before w Ann/Nancy Cooper,
    who dd 1835 & their eldest ch b 11/1774, further sol & w
    res on Snowden Creek, Tar River, NC, & mvd to upper part/o
    Orange Co, NC, between end/o RW & 1790 when had 7 ch. R652
  John, BLW issued 5/21/1799. R652
  Samuel, see CORBIT, Samuel. R652
CORBIN, Anderson, esf 1781 Hampshire Co,VA; b 2/13/1765 King &
    Queen Co, VA; PN 1832 Harrison Co, VA; dd 3/1/45; md there
    3/18/1789 Elizabeth Haines (Co clerk gave her surname as
    Harris from marriage records); wid PN there 1854 ae 81, &
    res Boone Co, KY, 1855 ae 82; ch births: May 10/30/1790,
    Sarah 3/11/93, Nancy 5/22/95, Frances 11/2/98, Henry B

CORBIN (continued)
3/20/1800, Elizabeth 10/18/02, Johanna 5/22/05, Benjamin
10/18/07, Edith 4/1/10, Anderson 3/15/13, O P 9/6/16 & A J
8/11/18; AFF 1854 there by David Coplin of Taylor Co, VA,
that he md d/o sol; QLF 1914 from desc Mrs Dwight Castlia,
by DAR Regent, MO. R653
George, esf 1789 Culpeper Co, VA, where b 11/28/1763; esf
1781 there as sub for David Corbin of Hampshire Co, VA; PN
1832 Culpeper Co, VA; dd 2/20-21/1840 Rappahannock Co, VA;
md 12/15/1814 Sarah/Sally Munroe, Culpeper Co, VA, who PN
ae 91 Rappahannock Co, VA, 1853. R653
John, esf 1775 Culpeper Co, VA; b 2/2/1750; PN 1832 Prairie
Township, Holmes Co, OH; md Sarah, Culpeper Co, VA, after
RW; mvd to OH c1824; family 1833 w Sarah ae 70, d Celey ae
48, & d Fanny ae 46 all res Holmes Co, OH. R653
Lewis, esf 1775 Culpeper Co, VA; b 4/4/1754 King George Co,
VA; res Culpeper Co, VA, to 1797, thence to KY where PN
1833 Bourbon Co, when Baptist preacher 45 years; s John R
res Henry Co, KY, 1854; QLF 1937 from Effie (Mrs C W) Sowers, Spokane, WA, states her gdm Joanna d/o John s/o sol;
QLF 1926 from desc Mrs Michael Buster, Bucklin, MO, states
a James Corbin b 8/28/1784 Bourbon Co, KY, f/o John C b
6/30/1808, f/o J M b 3/34/1839 near Bloomington, Marion Co
MO, f/o querier; QLF 1924 from gds James Wigginton, San
Diego, CA, states sol s/o William who also VA RW sol; QLF
from DAR Chapter Registrar, Paris,KY, for Mrs Effie S Hobson, desc/o sol, states sol dd 1840 Bourbon Co, KY, further Mrs Hobson desc of MD RW sol John Drebuler, b 1763, who
dd 1849 Bourbon Co, KY; QLF 1920 from desc Pauline E Young
of Chicago, IL. R653
Robert, esf 1778-9 Accomac Co, VA, where b 2/3/1764; dd
11/15/1843; afp 1851 there by s Robert for surv ch of sol:
Robert, Milcah Stant, & Edward, & PN gtd. R653
CORBIT, Samuel Sr, esf 1775 Isle of Wight Co, VA, where b
10/17/1759; PN 1832 Nottoway Parish, Southampton Co, VA;
QLF 1915 from desc Mrs Cecil A Casley, Rockfield, IN,
states sol md Miss Bird & they had d Edith & res 1840 with
Johnson Corbit, Southampton Co, VA, further querier has
family bible record. R653
CORDELL, John, esf 1777 Fauquier Co, VA, as unit chaplain; mvd
to Frederick Co, VA, thence to Louisville, KY, thence to
Vincennes, IN, thence c1798 to St Louis Co, MO, where dd
1800, a minister; md 6/19/1779 Judith Blackwell, Fauquier
Co, VA, who wid of Burnet/Bennett Price (md c1769 & he dd
c1774); wid b 1/6/1753; wid PN 1837 St Louis Co, MO, & dd
there 8/21/42; ch births: Stephen B 3/20/1780, Arthur
10/12/81, Harriet 5/22/83, & Hiram 3/27/85 (res St Louis
Co, MO, 1844); other ch mbnn; gdc mbnn; wid sis/o Captain
John Blackwell, also RW sol; AFF 1837 St Louis Co, MO, by
Mrs Catharine Cordell ae 86 that she wid of sol bro George
Edward (also RW sol), & she b & reared Northumberland Co,
& she m/o Presley (b 3/5/1779 & res Loudoun Co, VA, & res

CORDELL (continued)
in 1837 St Louis Co, MO); QLF states heirs/o sol recd 6000
acres of ld for sol svc; QLF 1931 from gds Joseph C Mason,
Washington, DC, states sol md twice, one w being Judith
Steptoe; QLF 1926 from desc Donna Cordell (Mrs J Carter)
Bardin, Dallas, TX; QLF 1923 from desc Clyde R Jeffords,
Jamaica, NY; QLF 1920 from desc Allan S Humphreys, Spring-
field, MO, states sol md Elizabeth Edwards. R654
CORDER, Benjamin D, b 4/4/1765 Fauquier Co, VA, where ran away
from f's res to enlist at Fredericksburg, VA; mvd to Fre-
derick Co, VA, where res c20 years, thence to Washington
Co, KY (area now Marion Co), thence to Hart Co, KY, where
PN 1834; AFF then by William Corder ae 102 & Nancy Corder,
Allen Co, KY, that sol esf from Fauquier Co, VA. R654
    John, esf 1777 Fauquier Co, VA; PN there ae 71 near Fiery
Run Meeting House 1832; s Vincent AFF Rappahannock Co, VA,
1836; QLF 1936 from desc Mrs Frank Gaines, Lubbock, TX,
who also desc of RW sol Morton Askey, native of MO (no record of Askey's svc at PN Office); QLF 1931 from Dorothy H
Corder, Waverly, MO, states sol blind when PN; QLF 1930
from desc Isa Y Wilson, Martinsville, IN; QLF 1924 from
Dixie Davis (Mrs J R) Gould, Lamar Co, Co, who great gdd/o
sol s Vincent; QLF 1912 from great great gdd Mrs Leslie
Wilson, Lexington, MO; QLF 1912 from great gdd Mrs Nannie
Corder Steele, Lexington, MO, sis/o Mrs Loula Corder Wilson of Amarillo, TX, provides following data: sol md Hannah Way & their s Nathan b 7/28/1788 Rappahannock Co, VA,
who md 1819 there Nancy Holloway who b 6/15/1798 there,
further Nathan dd 3/1/1858 Lafayette Co, MO, & his w Nancy
dd Corder, Lafayette Co, MO, 7/29/1882, further they had s
Nathan b 7/5/1834 Flint Hill, Rappahannock Co, VA, who md
12/14/1857 Octavia Hill, Liberty, Clay Co, MO, further Nathan the younger dd 11/5/1905 Waverly, MO, & his w Octavia
(b 12/20/1838 Liberty, Clay Co, MO) dd Lexington, MO, further querier their d b 11/20/1860 Lafayette Co, MO, & md
10/19/1881 William Boone Steele, Waverly, Lafayette Co,MO,
(b 3/12/1843 Owen Co, KY, & dd 6/28/1891 Ogden, UT); QLF
undated from sol gds Aldridge Corder, Waverly, Lafayette
Co, MO, states sol md Hannah Way. R654
CORDILL, James, esf Wilkes Co, NC; b Lunenburg Co, VA; PN ae
80 Perry Co, KY, 1833; surname also spelled CORDELL; QLF
1925 from desc L W Fields, Lexington, KY. R654
    Stephen, esf 1778 Wilkes Co, NC; b Lunenburg Co, VA; PN ae
70 Perry Co, KY, 1833 where mvd 1810; dd there 7/26/39; md
1792 Sarah Adams, Wilkes Co, NC; wid dd 10/1842 Letcher Co
KY; surv ch 1850: John A Caudill ae 52, Elizabeth Benson
ae 50, Nancy Adams ae 46, Easter Eldridge ae 45, Sarah Adams ae 41, Lydia Cornitt ae 38, Jesse Caudill ae 36,
& Watson Caudill ae 34; s John A afp due m 1850 for all
surv ch, & PAR; sol eldest ch Henrietta b 1792 & decd in
1850; surname also spelled CAUDILL. R654
CORE, Henry, b 2/23/1762-3 Hampshire Co, VA, & res there when

CORE (continued)
     esf 1781 Fayette Co, PA, where PN 1832; dd 1/17/35; md Sa-
     rah Barickman 2/17/1784 who b 9/22/1768; wid PN 1845 Fay-
     ette Co, PA, when s Isaac made AFF there; ch births: John
     11/24/1785, George 11/23/87, Rebecca 10/24/89, Isaac
     11/23/91, Elizabeth 5/17/95, Sarah 2/15/97, Jesse 5/15/99,
     Anne 8/8/1802, Catharine 3/19/05, & Henry B 180-. R654
CORLEY, Austin, esf 1776 Hanover Co, VA, where b 4/28/1757;
     mvd 1811 to Wilson Co, TN, where PN 1832 when AFF by Wil-
     liam Corley; dd there 7/28/41; QLF 1932 from desc Robert F
     Cole, Chicago, IL. R655
   William, esf 1779 Hanover Co, VA; b 3/2/1752; mvd to Louisa
     Co, VA, 1782, thence 1812 to Wilson Co, TN, where PN 1832;
     bro/o Austin who served in RW with him. R655
CORLY, Aquila, esf Culpeper Co, VA; dd 1785; md 1775 Mary Ann
     who md (2) 1791 Joshua Turner who dd 3/27/1825; wid afp ae
     94 Henry Co, KY, 1850 for 1st h svc when only surv ch Ri-
     chard (b 7/12/1778, now res Shelby Co, KY) & Nancy Wood ae
     69 (res Henry Co, KY), & Susan Coblin ae 71; wid PAR, in-
     sufficient proof of svc. R655
CORN, George, esf 1777 while res Redstone Fort, PA, on Monon-
     gahela River; esf 1780 KY for svc with VA unit; b 10/1758;
     res 1818 Boone Co, KY; res there 1820 with s-in-law when w
     ae 51, d Sally ae 14, s Tom Jefferson ae 11, & d Malinda
     ae 9; PN there 1832; QLF states sol dd Jackson Co,OH. R655
   Jesse, esf Albemarle Co, VA, early in RW; b 10/31/1753; dd
     3/5/1809 Patrick Co, VA; md 1780 Nancy, d/o John Hancock,
     (MB 2/21/1780 signed by Benjamin Hancock), Fluvanna Co,VA;
     wid b 2/17/1780; her f one time res Henry Co, VA; wid PN
     1841 Franklin Co, TN, & dd 6/17/48 at home of d Mrs Mary
     Sharp near Winchester, TN; ch births: Elizabeth 12/4/1780
     (md Richard Sharp), John Adam 1/26/83, William 1/11/8-,
     Jesse Jr 3/11/87, Mary 6/6/89 (md James Sharp, dd 8/12/47)
     Samuel 4/10/92, Suckey 12/16/94, Nancy 4/1/97 or 4/4/97
     (md George McCutchen), George 9/30/99, Dicea/Dicy 1803 (md
     Robert Sharp); ch who liv 1850: Elizabeth Sharp, John, Sa-
     muel, Mary Sharp, Nancy McCutchen, all res Franklin Co, TN
     & Jesse res Patrick Co, VA; m/o sol & his bro's George,
     Peter, Samuel res at one time Henry Co, VA, & those bro's
     all RW svc; bro/o wid R Major Hancock b 7/18/1770 Fluvanna
     Co, VA, & md Jane d/o Thomas Morrow & res 1849 Wayne Co,
     KY, & their ch mbnn res 1850 Clinton Co, KY; QLF 1933 from
     desc F F Lafon, Oklahoma City, OK. R655
   John Peter, esf 1776 with bro Jesse Albemarle Co, VA, where
     b 1752 s/o Molley; res VA c 12 years after RW, thence Sur-
     ry Co, NC for 5 years, thence Wilkes Co, NC, for 5 years,
     thence Buncombe Co, NC, where PN 1832; dd 10/14/43 Hender-
     son Co, NC, where res; md 5/1781-2 Elizabeth Parr, Henry
     Co, VA; wid b 6/14/1764, & PN 1844 Henderson Co, NC, & res
     there 1849 & dd 3/16/53; ch births: Adam 5/2/1783, William
     2/5/85, Samuel 2/6/87, John 12/2/89, Lot 2/24/92, & Sarah
     5/17/03; sol bro/o George & Samuel. R655

CORN, Timothy, mvd with f family from Redstone, PA, to area
of VA, later Mercer Co, KY, near McGary's Fort where esf
1781; PN ae 74 Mercer Co, KY, 1834, where dd 8/21/48; md
7/17/31 widow Mrs Elizabeth Yeast, (MB 6/23/31 signed by
George B Click), Harrodsburg, that Co; her eldest s by 1st
h md 4/1832 & had d b 18 months later, both mbnn; wid PN
1853 there; no mention of any ch of sol by Elizabeth; QLF
1940 from desc Mrs B B Sisco Jr, Bardstown, KY, also desc
of VA RW sol William Hicks who PN 1818 & dd 12/19/1822;
QLF 1937 from James F Corn, Cleveland, TN. R655
CORNELISON, Conrad, esf 1779 Rowan Co, NC; b 5/28/1763 Loudoun
Co, VA; PN 1832 Otter Creek, Madison Co, KY; dd 1/26/46;
md 2/15/1785 Susannah Strange (MB 2/9/1785), Rowan Co, NC,
who b 7/26/1760; wid PN 1846 Madison Co,KY; eldest ch John
b 11/14/1785 & dd 8/5/1843; s Richard liv 1853; QLF 1929
& 1935 from desc Sarah Cornelison (Mrs J C) Mason, Richmond, Madison Co, KY, also desc of VA RW sol James McWil-
liams of Albemarle Co, VA, near Charlottesville who had s
James H & mvd to KY after RW & dd 1808, who had bro RW sol
John who PN Madison Co, KY, after 1798 & dd there 3/12/24,
who md 12/10/1779 Elizabeth d/o Alexander Cleveland (1700-
1776) & w Margaret Doolittle who had 6 sons in RW: Lewis,
James, Eli, Oliver, Alexander, John (KIA 7/16/1779 Stony
Point), & William, further sol Conrad Cornelison md Mrs
Susanna Strange (nee Skinner); QLF 1929 from Mrs John D
Williams, Morenci, AZ; QLF states sol w Susanna Skinner.
R656
CORNELIUS, Charles, esf Culpeper Co, VA, where b; PN ae 70
Goochland Co, VA, 1832; res 1835 Madison Co, TN, where ch
res; res 1837 Pontotoc Co, MS, when "children living about
him"; wid Elizabeth liv 1846; QLF 1927 from great gds Re-
verend R E Cornelius, Hominy, OK, states sol md 1794 Eli-
zabeth Jenings, Culpeper Co,VA, & reared family at Hadens-
ville, Goochland Co, VA; QLF 1928 from desc Jeff Busby, US
Congressman from MS who also desc of VA RW sol Thomas Jennings. R656
CORNETT, Jesse, esf 1778-9 Henrico Co, VA, where b; PN aec 70
there 1832. R657
  William, esf 1779 Buckingham Co, VA; b Henrico Co, VA; PN ae
71 Perry Co, KY, 1833 where dd 12/26/36; md (2) 4/1796 Mary Everage, area later Washington Co, TN, now Sullivan Co,
TN; wid b 5/1770; wid PN 1850 Perry Co, KY, & dd 1/28/52;
sol s Archibald, by 1st w, b 1/12/1789 md & w mbnn; births
of sol ch by 2nd w: Robert Bustard 1/17/1798 (md 1/1822
Louisa/Louvisa Combs), Margaret 1798-9 dd infancy, Roger
(md Polly Lewis), Nancy (md Samuel Combs), Samuel (md Pol-
ly Adams), Nathaniel (md Lydia Caudle), Rachael (md John
Caudle), & Joseph E (md Sally Brown); QLF states sol res
Hazard, KY. R657
CORNEYLE, Jacob, esf 1776 Fluvanna Co, VA; b Goochland Co, VA;
PN ae 82 Campbell Co, VA, 1833. R657
CORNITT, William, see CORNETT, William. R657

CORNWELL, William, esf 1777 Pittsylvania Co, VA; b 1752 Amelia
    Co, VA; PN 1834 Jefferson Co, TN. R657
CORRY, Nicholas, esf 1775 Union District, SC; esf 1776 Meck-
    lenburg Co,NC; born 1752 County Down, Ireland; md c12/1776
    VA; mvd 1778 back to Union District,SC, where PN 1835; QLF
    1927 from Geraldine Corry Caddell, San Angelo, TX, states
    sol dd Union District, SC. R658
CORVIN, John, esf VA for Indian Wars & RW; dd c1823; wid dd
    4/10/1850; s Isaac afp 1853 Wythe Co, VA, & PAR, insuffi-
    cient proof of svc. R659
CORY, Elnathan, esf 1775 Essex Co, NJ, where b 1759; PN 1833
    Beaver Co, PA, where dd 2/14/1838; sol bro Samuel res 1842
    Brooke Co, VA, & AFF there that he served 1 month in 1778
    as sub for Elnathan. R659
   Samuel, esf 1777 Essex Co, NJ, where b 1/9/1763; esf 1778 as
    sub for bro Elnathan there; PN 1833 Brooke Co, VA; family
    bible in possession of Elnathan. R659
COSBEY, Sydnor, BLW issued 7/6/1793. R660
COSBY, Garland, esf 1776 Louisa Co, VA; b 1748-9 Hanover Co,
    mvd after RW to Fayette Co, KY for 6 years, thence Frank-
    lin Co, KY, for 6 years, thence Henderson Co, KY, where PN
    1834 when res 21 years; md near end of RW; w & ch mbnn.
    R660
   John, esf 1777 Louisa Co,VA; b 12/16/1737 Hanover Co, VA; PN
    1835 Barren Co, KY; QLF states sol dd there 1843; QLF 1925
    from desc Myrtie Merryweather, Greencastle Co, IN. R660
   Zacheus, esf 1776 Louisa Co, VA; b 1753 Hanover Co, VA, his
    family moving when he ch to Louisa Co, VA; PN 1833 Augusta
    Co, VA, where mvd 1811. R660
COTRELL, James, esf 1776 Amherst Co,VA; b 10/14/1748; afp 1840
    Pike Co, OH, & PAR, svc less than 6 months. R660
COTTEN, James, see COTTON, James. R660
COTTERAL, Thomas, esf when res on Hackers Creek, Monongalia Co
    (area later Lewis Co); b on George's Creek, PA; PN 1833
    Lewis Co, VA, where res since infancy; PN claim reexamined
    by US District Attorney 1834 when found sol b 1772 & thus
    too young to have svc in RW; name dropped from PN rolls in
    1835; QLF 1929 from gdd Anna B Smith, Oceanside, CA. R660
COTTERELL, Daniel, esf 1777-8 aec 15 VA for PA regiment; afp
    ae 76, Niles, Berrien Co, Territory of MI, 1835 formerly
    res of OH, & PAR. R660
COTTERILL, Thomas, see COTTRILL, Thomas. R660
COTTLE, Jedediah/Judiah, esf 1779 Greenbrier Co, VA; KIA Colo-
    nel Buford's Defeat at Waxsaw 5/29/1780; BLW issued 1810
    to heir-at-law bro William. R661
   Joseph, esf Fayette Co, KY, for svc in Indian Wars 1790-92;
    b 1772 Botetourt Co, VA, or Augusta Co, VA; res Greenbrier
    Co, VA, Floyd Co, KY, & Fayette Co, KY; afp 1832 Morgan Co
    KY, & PAR, svc not in RW. R661
COTTON, James, esf 1781 while visiting relatives in Henry Co,
    VA; b 10/1765 Guilford Co, NC; mvd 1789 to settlement near
    Nashville, TN, thence Smith Co, TN, thence Madison Co, AL,

COTTON (continued)
       where PN 1832; dd 2/18/38; md 12/20/1786 Nancy, d/o Gideon
       Johnson, at home/o sol uncle William Cotton, Rockingham Co
       NC; wid PN ae 78 Madison Co, AL, 1847, & res 1848 Jackson
       Co, AL; ch births: Peter Johnson 12/25/1787 (w & 2 ch mbnn
       1811), Mary 3/5/92, Martha 5/19/96, Tabitha A 2/3-23/1801
       md Mr Lewis), & Charles K 10/3/05; wid bro Abner ae 85 & w
       Nancy ae 82 res Maury Co, TN, 1848. R661
   William, esf Guilford Co, NC, 1780 where res; b 2/28/1750 on
       Smith River, VA; mvd after RW to Greenville Co, SC, for
       many years, thence Franklin Co, IN, where PN 1833; sis
       mbnn; QLF states sol dd Brookville, IN. R661
COTTRELL, Thomas, see COTTERAL, Thomas. R662
COTTRILL, John, esf 1777 Hampshire Co, VA; PN ae 62 Harrison
       Co,VA, 1825 when family at home w ae 52 & ch: Polly ae 18,
       John ae 17, Elisha ae 14, Barbara ae 12, William ae 10 +
       orphan gds Marshall ae 2; later stricken from PN rolls for
       proof/o svc but restored 1827; w mbnn liv 1840; dd 7/9/50
       Barbour Co,VA, where res c7 years, survived by ch: Watson,
       Elisha (res 1851 Barbour Co, VA), Elias (ae 32 in 1826),
       Polly, John, Barbara, & William; s Jackson decd in 1851;
       bro-in-law John McCullough neighbor 1826; QLF states sol
       from Clarksburg, Monongalia Co, VA. R662
   Thomas, esf 1774 VA; b 7/16/1750 Shenandoah Co, VA; mvd to
       Bourbon Co, KY, thence Nicholas Co, KY, thence Brown Co,
       OH, where PN 1833 & where dd 3/27/36; md 5/14/1775 Nancy
       Gerance, Redstone Settlement, PA, who b 1/6/57-8 Somerset
       Co, NJ; wid PN 1839 Brown Co, OH; 12 ch, eldest Elizabeth
       (b 11/1776 & md Hiram Harney), & youngest Millie/Mille (b
       3/1790, w/o John W Fight of Brown Co, OH); QLF 1928 from
       great great gdd Effie M (Mrs J F) Martin, Oceanside, CA,
       states sol b 1749. R662
COUCH, William, esf 1772 PA; dd 12/31/1807 or 1/1/08; surname
       also spelled COUTCH & CROUCH; md 9/19/1789 Guilford Co, NC
       Margaret, who mvd c1812 from Grayson Co, VA, to Hancock Co
       TN, thence to Lee Co, VA, c1850 where afp & afb & PAR &
       BLAR, insufficient proof/o svc & of marriage, & dd 9/30/56
       VA; afp 1857 Hancock Co, TN, by John CROUCH (b 6/1/08, 8th
       ch), youngest/o sol 6 surv ch, who AFF other surv ch were:
       Hanna, Peggy, Easter, Marriann, & Dempson; sol eldest ch
       William (b 9/30/1796, dd 8/30/1844) & 1 ch dd in infancy;
       ch res then Hancock Co, TN, Hawkins Co, TN, VA, & KY; ch
       PAR, insufficient proof/o svc & m marriage to sol. R662
COUGHRAN, George, esf 1781 Bedford Co, VA, ae 16-17; afp 1838
       Sevier Co, AR; afp ae 91 Scott Co, AR, 1853; both PAR, svc
       less than 6 months. R663
COUGHREN, Joseph, esf 1781 Hampshire Co, VA; b 1/16/1761 Bed-
       ford Co, PA; after RW res VA, PA, Scioto Co, OH, IL, & IN;
       PN 1834 Vermilion Co, IN, where dd 3/19/45; md 11/4/1794
       Prudence, d/o Alexander Mathews, Washington Co (now Beaver
       Co), PA; wid PN ae 74 Clark Co,IL, 1850, when res with her
       bro Alexander who b 1784; wid also sis/o Isaac; ch births:

COUGHREN (continued)
John M 6/20/1795, William 4/27/97, Rachel 4/11/99, Benjamin 4/11/1801, Joseph 4/24/04, Sarah 6/2/06, Isaac 7/17/09, James 7/5/11, Matilda 9/17/15, Jonathan 10/8/17, & Jesse 3/4/19; other family bible births (all CUNNINGHAM): Sally 12/19/1834, Mary Jane 11/10/37, Benton Jackson 2/17/41, Jefferson Franklin 3/6/43, John Marian 1/1/46, & Isaac Newton 18--; other family bible data: Johnson Cunningham & Matilda Cunningham md 3/30/1834 (dd 5/22/44), Johnson Cunningham & Eve Ritter md 2/27/1845. R663

COULSON, David, esf 1775 Charlotte Co, VA; b 2/16/1750 Amelia Co,VA; mvd after RW to Stokes Co,NC, for c20 years, thence to Bledsoe Co,TN, thence White Co, TN, where PN 1832. R663

COULTER, Nathaniel, esf 1777 Carlisle, PA, for svc with PA regiment, thence svc in VA regiment; esf 1780 Philadelphia, PA; esf 1813 PA in US Infantry regiment & discharged 1815 ae 53; res 1821 Lycoming Co, PA; PN ae 62 for RW svc 1822 Dauphin Co, PA; AFF 1823 that w decd & ch: Mary ae 37 (md Francis Lee & had 7 ch), Hughey ae 33 (had 5 ch), James ae 31 (had 2 ch), Nathaniel ae 29 (had 2 ch), & Betsey ae 19 (not md); sol res 1835 Springfield, Portage Co, OH, with ch, having mvd from White Deer Township, Northumberland Co PA; dd 1/27/39; md 6/5/1783 Isabella, d/o Hugh & Mary Coulter, Burt Township, Lancaster Co, PA; w b 5/2/1757, & liv 1839 (contrary to sol 1823 AFF), & PN then Tallmadge, Portage Co, OH, as sol's wid; she res 1843 Plymouth Township, Richland Co, OH; several QLFs point out discrepancy of sol 1823 AFF, but PN Office made no comment on subject; QLF 1896 from great great gdd Annie Shifer Walls, Lewisburg, PA. R663

William, esf 1778 MD; BLW issued 9/5/1828 to bro & only heir Samuel of Botetourt Co, VA; name also spelled COLTER. R663

COUNCE, Nicholas, b 1/12/1752 VA; mvd as ch to NC, where esf Orange Co; mvd after RW to Granger Co, TN, where PN 1833. R663

COUNCIL, Jesse, esf 1777 Southampton Co, VA; b 1/14/1760; PN 1832 Southampton Co, VA, & res there 1837. R663

COURSEY, James, esf 1774 Henry Co, VA, against indians; esf 1776 there for RW svc; b 1/16/1748-9 Granville Co, NC; f left m when sol ch, & m later md John Couch who mvd family to VA; sol mvd c1813 to Maury Co, TN, thence to Williamson Co, TN, thence Rutherford Co, TN, thence Bedford Co, TN, where afp 1833 when res there c9 years, & PAR, svc under 6 months; dd 5/8/1840; md 1777 Susannah Bennet, Henry Co, VA; wid afp ae 86-7 Bedford Co, TN, 1843, & PAR; AFF there then by d Nancy Haley (b 1/26/1778) & s Charles (b 6/4/1780). R663

COURTNER, Anthony, esf 1776 Hardy Co, VA; esf 1777 Rockingham Co, VA, where res; b 1740 Lancaster Co, PA; PN 1832 Greenbrier Co, VA; dd 4/30/33; md 12/6/1777 Catharine Wansturp, The Bullpasture, Augusta Co (area now Pendleton Co), VA, who b 8/10/1759; wid PN 1843 Greenbrier Co, VA; AFF then

COURTNER (continued)
there by d Phebe ae 42 & her h James Daugherty ae 52; AFF
1846 there by ch Phebe ae 46 (res Greenbrier Co, VA), Lew-
is ae 56 (res Fayette Co, VA) & David ae 54 (res outside
VA) that m dd 1/22/44; ch then afp for any PN due m. R664
COURTNEY, James, esf 1779 Washington Co, VA; b 10/17/1764 Cra-
ven Co, SC; res after RW SC, GA, AL, & MS; PN 1832 Simpson
Co, MS, & res there 1833. R664
Michael, esf Greenbrier Co,VA; PN ae 58 Jackson Co, IN, 1819
& res there 1820 when Sally w ae 56; res 1839 Jennings Co,
IN, to be near ch. R664
Samuel, BLW issued 7/7/1792. R664
Samuel, esf 1776 Caroline Co, VA; PN 1818 Fauquier Co, VA;
& res there 1820 ae 64-5 when "neither wife nor children
to help me"; bro mbnn liv then. R664
COUTCH, William, see COUCH, William. R664
COVERLY, Thomas, esf 1776 Accomac Co, VA; BLW issued 1808; PN
ae 71 Amelia Co, VA, 1818 where res 1820. R665
COVERT, Peter, esf NJ, later served in VA militia at Siege of
Yorktown; b 1/4/1761; PN 1818 Ridgeway, Genesee Co, NY; in
1825 no w & res with s-in-law George Houseman, Yates, Or-
leans Co, NY; s Benjamin AFF 1825 that he res with f for c
15 years; QLF 1939 from great gdd Mrs Edna Wilkin Bromley,
Pontiac, MI, d/o Alvira (Covert) Wilkin, d/o Nathaniel Co-
vert of NY who s/o sol, states Mary sis/o her m md Abraham
Covert of Farmersville or Trumansburg, NY, further family
data: RW sol Teunis Covert (b Somerset Co, NY, dd 1798 Co-
vert, NY), RW sol Peter Covert (b 1759 Seneca NY, dd 1849)
R666
COVEY, Samuel, esf ae 16 Dutchess Co, NY, where b 1761; mvd to
Washington Co, VA, where esf; PN ae 71 Jefferson Co, TN,
1832, & res there 1833. R666
COVINGTON, Robert, esf 1779 Culpeper Co, VA; b 1/1762; PN 1832
Madison Co, KY, where dd 8/10/47; md there 5/15/1843 Amy
Burk/Buirke; wid PN ae 70 there 1853 when AFF there by
John Buirke ae 64 that he present at marriage of sol & Amy
Buirke; QLF states sol b 1/3/1760 Culpeper Co, VA, & dd
3/8/47 Madison Co, KY; QLF 1912 from desc R C H Covington,
Richmond, KY, who also desc of RW sol Daniel Maupin of Al-
bemarle Co, VA, who later res Madison Co, KY. R667
COVVINGER, Higgins, see COPPINGER, Higgins. R667
COWGILL, Daniel, esf 1777 Culpeper Co,VA; b 10/9/1755 Burlington Co, NJ; PN 1832 Preble Co, OH, were res c3 years & res
OH 17 years; QLF states State Library in Columbus, OH, has
record that sol md 1785 Betsy Martin, Culpeper Co, VA, mvd
to Fayette Co, KY, thence to OH, where res Preble Co 1840.
R668
Ralph, esf VA; PN 1832 Anderson Co,KY, P O Lawrenceburg; res
later 1832 Spencer Co, KY; dd 11/9/1835 Anderson Co, KY;
md 1/30/1821 Mary/Polly Poindexter, Franklin Co, KY (his
name on marriage record Ralph COGHILL); wid PN ae 55 Cam-
denville, Anderson Co, KY, 1853; QLF 1934 from desc Dr

COWGILL (continued)
  Charles McNaull, Indianapolis, IN, states sol res Anderson
  Co, KY, 1840 ae 83. R668
COWHERD, Francis, esf 1779 VA; PN 1828 Orange Co, VA, where dd
  3/25/33; md 8/1787 Lucy Scott (MB 8/13/87 signed by John
  Scott), Orange Co, VA; wid b 3/1763, & PN 1838 Orange Co,
  VA; eldest ch Garritt H b 4/15/1786; wid dd 7/31/1847 lea-
  ving ch: Francis K, Mary S, Lucy, & John S (P O Gordons-
  ville, VA, 1843); QLF 1910 from great gdd Effie White Cox,
  Temple, TX. R668
  James, esf 1777 Culpeper Co, VA; b 1/1759; PN 1832 Green Co,
  KY, where res over 30 years; dd 4/12/41; QLF states sol s
  of Jonathan Cowherd & Miss Colby who also res Culpeper Co
  VA. R668
  Jonathan, esf 1775 Culpeper Co, VA, where b 10/1755; mvd to
  Green Co, KY, 1796 where PN 1833, & dd there 7/20/44; md
  4/1777 Elizabeth (MB 4/2/77 signed by her f Thomas Kirt-
  ley), Culpeper Co, VA; wid b 1/31/1760; wid PN 1845 Green
  Co, KY; 12 ch; in 1845 eldest decd, 2nd ch Willis ae 65,
  & youngest ch Simon Coleby aec 45; QLF 1939 from Miss Maud
  Cowherd, Campbellsville, KY, states sol bro/o RW sol James
  R668
COX, Andrew, esf 1776 Washington Co, VA; b 1761 Hampshire Co,
  VA, on the Potomac River; res Washington Co, VA, to 1790,
  thence mvd to KY, thence 1799 to Hamilton Co, OH, where PN
  1883 res Millerock Township. R670
  Bartlett, esf 1777-8 Powhatan Co, VA, where b; PN 1832 Cum-
  berland Co, VA, where dd 9/26/42; md 9/26/1799 Polly Hopper, Powhatan Co, VA, who PN ae 70 Cumberland Co, VA,
  1849, & dd 8/2/51. R670
  Benjamin, see COCKS, Benjamin. R670
  Curd, esf 1780, Halifax Co, VA; b 1762 on Little Roanoke River, Charlotte Co, VA; PN 1832 Knox Co, TN. R670
  George, esf 1776 VA in bro Capt Isaac Cox's company against
  indians; b 1749 Hampshire Co, VA; PN 1833 Brooke Co, VA;
  name dropped from PN rolls 1835 when reexamination by PN
  Office showed svc connected with protecting own property
  from indians & not in regularly constituted military unit;
  md 2/1775 w mbnn; settled on OH river 1772 or 1773. R670
  Isaac, esf Somerset Co, NJ, where b; PN 1832 Lewis Co, VA,
  when res on line between Lewis Co & Harrison Co, VA; name
  dropped from PN rolls 1835 after reexamination by PN Office showed proof of svc not adequate; f/o Philip who res
  1832 on line between Lewis Co & Harrison Co, VA; QLF 1928
  from desc Emma Cox Jewell, Ellenboro, WV, states an Isaac
  Cox, the Harrison Co, VA, pioneer, b 1731 NJ, s/o Philip
  & Hannah (Tremble) Cox, md Sarah Sutton of NJ, & after RW
  mvd to Harrison Co, VA, & dd 1838 ae 107, had 5 ch, & his
  f Philip dd NJ 1797 ae 112. R670
  James, esf 1780 Halifax Co,VA; b 1762-3 King & Queen Co, VA;
  mvd c1803 to Stokes Co, NC, where PN 1833; dd 9/10/46; QLF
  1926 from DAR Chapter Regent, Independence, MO, on behalf

COX (continued)

   of sol desc Mrs Oliver G Sheley; QLF 1915 from gds Thomas
   J Cox, Wapanucka, OK, states he small boy when his f recd
   word of sol's death. R670

James, esf 1778 Montgomery Co, VA; b 2/24/1763, Fort Chisel,
   Botetourt Co, VA, s/o John (area later Montgomery Co, VA);
   served in f's company; afp 1832 Grayson Co, VA, where res
   since RW; PAR, service under 6 months; dd there 4/17/41;
   md there 1/14/1815 Sarah/Sally Fielder; wid afp ae 75 Independence, Grayson Co, VA, 1835, & PAR; sol bro Joshua b
   3/3/1772, res 1852 Ashe Co, NC 1852; QLF states Capt John
   Cox, b 7/25/1739, of Grayson Co, VA, buried Ashe Co, NC;
   QLF 1938 from Richard P Eckels, Steelton, PA, desc/o James
   Cox (1735-1840) who b Buckingham Co, VA, whose w Elizabeth
   & he buried near ONA, Cabell Co, WV, where they mvd c1811;
   QLF 1932 from desc Mrs W H Welch, Lansing, MI, states sol
   md (1) 5/15/1783 Elizabeth Terrill, wid of Jesse Terrill
   who killed by indians, further births/o ch/o sol by 1st w:
   John 3/8/1784 (querier's ancestor), Susannah 12/1/85, Joshua 4/1/87, Mary 7/10/89, Catharine 6/1/91, Hardin
   4/8/94, Solomon 12/4/95, & James Robertson 6/2/98, further
   sol w Elizabeth, & sol md again; further sol dd 4/17/42,
   further sol s/o Capt John Cox whose ch: sol James who b
   2/17/1763, Joshua who b 3/13/72, Cynthia, Kate, Jennie, &
   Maggie. R670

John, esf 1779 Nash Co, NC; b 1753 Culpeper Co, VA; PN ae 79
   Anson Co, NC, 1832. R671

John, esf 1776 Orange Co, VA, where b; later visited bro in
   NC & esf there; res NC after RW, thence 1827 to Roane Co,
   TN, where PN 1833 ae 75; QLF states sol b 1758 & dd 1840,
   md 2/6/1782 Mary Bryson; QLF undated from desc Mrs Paul
   Maross, Chattanooga, T?N; QLF 1913 from great gds James M
   Cox, Carthage, TN; QLF 1913 states sol res with s Samuel,
   Roane Co, TN, 1840; QLF states sol md Mary Bryson, Orange,
   Co, VA. R671

John, esf 1774 Montgomery Co, VA, as sub for f; afp 1834 ae
   76 Scott Co, VA, & PAR, insufficient proof of svc. R671

John, esf 1781 Essex Co, VA, where b 1764; res there with w
   Nancy for 25 years, thence Pendleton District, SC, for 18
   years, thence Franklin Co, GA, thence MS Territory (area
   later Clarke Co, AL), where afp 1832 ae 68; dd 9/25/42; md
   11/6/1786 Nancy, Essex Co, VA; wid dd 10/9/1848; afp 1852
   by heir George Cox ae 56 Clarke Co, AL, & PAR. R671

John, VA sea svc, esf 1777 as Captain of ship HORNET, thence
   ship SALLY NORTON, thence ship MUSQUITO, thence ship GAME
   COCK; res 1833 Cosport; PN ae 82 Portsmouth, Norfolk Co,
   VA, 1834 where dd 12/17/1837; d Ann P Swift res there 1835
   & listed as sol only surv heir 1838. R671

Michael, esf 1779 Washington Co, PA; b 8/27/1759 Hampshire
   Co, VA; mvd after RW to Miami Co, OH, for c9 years, thence
   Logan Co, OH, where PN 1833; QLF states sol md Jeruthea
   Brooks, their ch being Isaac, Abraham, Betty, Samuel, Wil-

COX (continued)
    liam, Mahaley, & Ann, further a Benjamin Cox bc 1746 Hamp-
    shire Co,VA, RW sol with PA & VA troops, settled 1779 Nel-
    son Co, KY, dd OH, had ch Elizabeth, Sarah, Susannah, &
    others mbnn, further a Benjamin Cox dd 1840 Dayton, OH, md
    Rachael, had ch William, John, Benjamin, Charles, Rachael,
    & Lewis; QLF states sol had bro Benjamin who dd KY or OH.
    R671
Philip, esf Somerset Co, NJ, where b 1763; PN 1832 Lewis Co,
    VA, while res on line between Harrison Co & Lewis Co, VA;
    name dropped from PN rolls 1835 after reexamination of sol
    claim by District Attorney, who stated sol appeared to be
    10 years younger than earlier reported; sol refused to an-
    swer any more questions of District Attorney. R671
Philip, esf Surry Co, NC; b 9/25/1757 on Mago River, Halifax
    Co, VA; mvd after RW to SC for 3 years, thence Rutherford
    Co, NC for c4 years, thence WV on Horse Creek, thence back
    to Rutherford Co, NC, for 4 years, thence Crow Creek, Pen-
    dleton District (later Pickens District),SC; dd 3/22/1834;
    md 1772 Jemima Taylor who b 4/1757; wid PN 1840 Pickens
    District, SC, when AFF there by s Jacob R; ch births: Mil-
    ley 2/4/1773, Sarah/Salley 12/12/76, Nancy 12/26/78, Cath-
    arine/Catey 1/8/80, Elizabeth 1/17/82, Matthew 7/12/86,
    Jenny 11/15/87, Rebekah 2/5/89, William 12/5/91, Jacob
    1/29/93, & Richard 5/16/99; family bible mns a Thomas Man
    b 4/1/1769; wid sis/o Drury Taylor & had other bro's; AFF
    1841 Pickens District, SC, by Thomas Collings that he md
    sol d Catharine/Catey 4/12/1798; AFF there then by Martin
    tin Moss that he md Rebecca Cox 1/1/1833. R671
Phinehas/Phineas, esf 1779 Halifax Co,VA where b 10/10/1764;
    res Henry Co, VA, for time during RW; mvd after RW to Da-
    vidson Co, TN, thence Warren Co, KY, where PN 1833 & where
    dd 5/18/42; served in KY state legislature; md Barbara be-
    fore end of RW in what now Davidson Co, TN; wid PN ae 80
    Warren Co, KY, 1843; 12 ch, eldest William W ae 59 in 1843
    & Frederick ae 55 then; wid res ae 95 when gtd BLW 1855 at
    Warren Co, KY. R671
Samuel, esf 1776 Fauquier Co, VA; PN there 1818 ae 62; res
    1820 Frederick Co, VA, when w over ae 50, 2 d's "of age",
    & s aec 14 mbnn; dd 7/12/28; QLF states a Samuel Cox esf
    MD (probably Talbot Co), mvd to Loudoun Co, VA, where res
    res 1823, & md 1/9/23 Miss Sarah Chamblin. R672
Thomas, esf 1780 Washington Co, VA; b 1762 Halifax Co, VA;
    mvd after RW to Lincoln Co,NC, thence Greenville District,
    GA, thence 1818 to Gwinnett Co, GA, where PN 1832, & where
    dd 10/1/53; md 4/27/1807 Martha Smith, Franklin Co, GA;
    wid PN & gtd BLW ae 66 Whitfield Co, GA, 1856, res that Co
    near Dalton 1/1861 to 1866; ch included R D res Dalton, GA
    1869. R672
William, esf 1776 Halifax Co,NC; b 1762 VA; mvd to Edgefield
    District, SC, c1790, thence Pendleton District, SC, thence
    1822 to Habersham Co, GA, where PN 1845; dd 3/2/48 leaving

COX (continued)

no wid but ch: William, Jeremiah, Eli, Mordecai, Cary, Dianah Langston, & Frances Beard; s Mordecai ae 39 in 1852; sol f Cary also RW sol & wounded in battle. R672

William, BLW issued 4/12/1792. R672

William, b 1761 Halifax Co, VA; mvd as ch with family to Walkers Creek, branch of the New River, Montgomery Co, VA, where esf 1779; all svc as an indian spy; PN 1833 Lawrence Co, KY; PN suspended 1835 after reexamination of svc & requested to provide further proof of svc which sol did not provide; dd 1837. R672

COXE, Bartlett, esf 1779 Mecklenburg Co, VA, where b; lost leg at Battle of Guilford 1781 & PN for wounds 1788; res ae 73 Mecklenburg Co, VA, 1833; dd 12/23/45 leaving no wid but ch mbnn; surname at times spelled COX. R672

COYLE, Patrick, esf 1780 Washington Co, VA; b western part of VA; md Washington Co, VA, & had ch there mbnn; mvd aec 40 to Smith Co, TN, for 3 years, thence Wayne Co, KY, where PN 1833 ae 70 when res there 27 years; dd 2/21/45. R673

COZBY, Robert, esf 1775 SC; wounded at Battle of Ninety Six & taken to f John's home in Calhoun Settlement; mvd to VA where md 1782, thence back to f's home in SC for 1 year, thence to GA for 9 years, thence Blount Co,TN, thence 1818 to AL Territory (later Madison Co, AL) where PN 1818; AFF 1820 Rhea Co, TN, at court of Judge John Cozby by Dr James Cosby aec 69 & w Isabella of that Co that Dr Cosby bro of sol & they esf 1776 SC together, James not having seen sol since 1815-16, that Dr Cosby & Isabella md before Battle/o Ninety Six; AFF 1819 by sol s John, Madison Co, AL, that he res with f in Elbert Co,GA, when ch till 1809 when they mvd to Madison Co, AL R673

CRABB, John, esf 1779 Carters Valley, NC (area now Hawkins Co, TN) against indians; b 7/15/1763 Frederick Co,VA; res 1783 to 1808 Beans Station, TN, thence near Knoxville, Knox Co, TN, to 1828, thence Green Co, IL, where afp 1838, & PAR; ch mbnn. R674

CRABTREE, Abraham, esf 1776 Washington Co, VA; afp ae 74 Cumberland Co, KY, 1824 when w aec 70 & d aec 32, & PAR; sol dd 5/2/1838 Russell Co, VA; LWT dated 4/29/38, & probated that Co 7/5/38, left s Solomon 1 cent, d Ruth Spear 1 cent & balance/o estate to d Mary Crabtree who dd 8/22/40 Wayne Co, KY, her LWT dated 8/19/40 leaving her estate to cousin John Crabtree who s/o sol bro Isaac; AFF 1840 Clinton Co, KY, by this John Crabtree, who adm for sol heirs, that his f Isaac of Wayne Co, KY, was collecting RW PN; sol heirs 1840 ch Ruth Spear, Solomon, & Mary; sol wid dd before he dd; AFF 1844 by sol bro Isaac (member of KY state legislature) that other bro Parle also RW sol. R674

Isaac, esf 1775 Washington Co, VA; b 1757 Baltimore Co, MD; mvd after RW to Davidson Co,TN, thence Wayne Co,KY, thence to Overton Co,TN, where PN 1832; mvd 1840 to TN to be with s mbnn; QLF 1921 from desc Miss Edith Griffey, Unionville,

CRABTREE (continued)
MO; QLF 1929 from relative Mrs A E Simons, Princeton, MO,
states sol md Elizabeth Pike, Washington Co, VA, & sol dd
1847, further querier mns RW sol Benjamin Pike who md 1760
Abby Keith, Uxbury, MA, & had s Zebulon & d Elizabeth; QLF
1936 from DAR for sol desc Ruth M Crabtree (Mrs O C) Carmichael, whose h Vice Chancellor of Vanderbilt University,
Nashville, TN. R674

Jacob, esf 1776 Lee Co, VA, where PN 1833 ae 73, & dd there
3/19/46; md 8/4/1786 Mary Price, Russell Co, VA, who afp
there 1848 & 1849 (ae 87 then), & dd 7/27/49 before PN ac-
tion complete, leaving ch: Job, Richard, Hannah w/o Robert
Langham, Jane w/o Levi Brittain, Mary w/o John Langham,
Sarah w/o Wesley Bertram, & Rebecca w/o William Crabtree;
s Job afp 1850 Lee Co, VA, as adm/o m's estate for PN due
her, & PAR. R674

James, esf 1776 Washington Co, VA; b 2/20/1762 New London,
Bedford Co, VA; mvd 1785 to West TN near Nashville for c24
years, thence to IL where PN Washington Co 1833; QLF 1923
from desc Miss Lois Johnston, Chicago, IL. R674

Richard, esf 1776 Salisbury, Rowan Co, NC; b 1/29/1758 Loudoun Co, VA; res during RW mostly in Burk Co, NC; after RW
res NC, VA, TN; PN 1834 Morgan Co,KY; dd 6/29/49; md Sarah
Richerson, Russell Co, VA, 8/10/1792; wid PN ae 79 Scott
Co, TN, 1851, & gtd BLW ae 83 Clinton Co, KY, 1855 where
res since 1852; Russell Co, VA, Co clerk reported these
other marriages in verification of marriage of Sarah: William Kilgore & Jane Osborn 10/29/1791, Alden Williams &
Elizabeth Jackson 4/15/1792, William Whorton & Jemima Briers 12/5/1792, David Canady & Elizabeth Conway M/25/1792,
John Gilbert & Barbara Dowel 7/18/1792, James Kelly & Susanna Kezar 3/15/1792, & Thomas Ford & Sarah Compton
5/23/1792, all by Reverend Thomas Hansford. R674

CRACRAFT, Charles, see CRAYCRAFT, Charles. R674

CRADDOCK, Robert, esf VA; POW; BLW issued 7/15/1789; PN 1828
"The Hermitage", Warren Co, KY. R674

CRADLEBAUGH, William, came from NC 1776 to Boonesborough, KY
Territory, where esf in Capt Daniel Boone's Company; res
that area since 1776 when PN ae 88 Madison Co, KY. R674

CRAFTON, Anthony; b 1747 King William Co, VA; mvd 1771 to Lunenburg Co, VA, where esf 1778; mvd 1784 to SC, thence to
Charlotte Co, VA, 1785, thence 1796-7 Lincoln Co, KY, from
there to Nelson Co, KY, thence Shelby Co, KY, thence 1832
to Spencer Co, KY, where PN 1832. R675

James, esf VA; dd 5/6/1828; md (per AFF of wid) 4/25/1775
Frances Staples, Lunenburg Co, VA, by publication of banns
at Episcopal Church; per certificate of Lunenburg Co Clerk
1839, MB dated 12/10/1778 & signed by sol & John Crafton;
wid had 1 infant ch mbnn at time sol in RW; wid PN ae 85
Lunenburg Co, VA, 1839, when AFF by John Crafton who res
of that Co when sol md; wid res there 1850; AFF 1828 there
by Richard Crafton. R675

CRAFTON, Thomas, esf 1780 Lunenburg Co, VA; dd 1/28/1818; md
6/11/1785 Mary Sammons, Lunenburg Co, VA; wid PN 1840 ae
71 there & dd 11/17/1843; her unpaid PN amounts gtd to her
surv ch Elizabeth Powers & Thomas; AFF 1840 by John Crafton ae 79 there that he served in RW with sol Thomas. R675
CRAIG, James; afb 1828 Bedford Co, VA, by heir-at-law Charles
Craig to both James & Matthew Craig decd who esf 1779 PA;
Charles gds & one of heirs of James Craig, who was bro &
sole heir to Matthew Craig; BLW issued 9/5/1828. R676
James, BLW issued 12/5/1794; papers lost in Washington, DC,
fire 1800 when War Office destroyed; QLF states sol esf
1777 VA; QLF states sol b 7/23/1744 & res Augusta Co, VA.
R676
John, esf 1789 Washington Co, VA; b 5/24/1764 York Co, PA;
moved after RW to Greene Co (then NC now TN), thence c1810
to AL where PN 1832 Limestone Co. R676
John esf 1777 Bedford Co, VA, on day Thomas Brown's d Edy md
Ancel Goodman, & day Joel Davenport & bro Moses Davenport
enlisted; b 2/14/1755; signed MB 5/5/1808 between d Polly
& John Hatfield, Wayne Co, KY; dd 6/8/30; md 9/17/1780
Jane, d/o Thomas Brown, Bedford Co, VA; wid b 8/2/1760, &
wid PN ae 78 Wayne Co, KY, 1838 & gtd PN increase there in
1844 ae 83; AFF 1840 there by James Coyle that he md sol d
Rachel 1/14/1819, & further sol other ch: Polly (eldest)
w/o John Hatfield, Anna w/o David More, Rebecca w/o John
Savage, James, Robert (#5 ch) h/o Sooky Raines, Nancy twin
to Robert, John Henderson (dd 1/8/1815 shortly after Battle of New Orleans where sol), Betsy Smith, & Linn (aec
35); AFF 1839 there by James Pearcy, RW PN, that he knew
sol in Bedford Co, VA; also AFF then by Elizabeth Pearcy,
w/o James, that they md Bedford Co, VA, 1 year after her h
last RW svc, she niece of Thomas Dooley of Bedford Co, VA.
R676
John Hawkins, esf 1780 Spotsylvania Co, VA; b 3/1763; mvd
1781 with f & family to KY, where esf Bryants Station; PN
1833 Boone Co,KY, where dd 4/8/52; md 3/1802 Sally S Snelling, Woodford Co, KY; wid PN & gtd BLW there 1853 ae 86;
no mention of any ch; sol bro/o Lewis & they res in youth
Fredericksburg, VA; QLF 1912 from desc Frances E Emerson,
Plymouth, IN; QLF 1930 from great gds Henry H Craig states
sol d-in-law liv 1904 ae 89, further sol eldest s/o John
Hawkins Craig Sr, born probably 1732 Spottswood, VA, md in
VA Sally Page, came to KY 1781 with family, & dd Boone Co
1814, who also defender of Bryants Station during siege.
R676
Robert, esf 1776 Lancaster Co, PA; afp ae 89 Washington Co,
VA, & PAR, svc under 6 months; QLF 1939 states an RW sol
Robert Craig b 1746, esf Abingdon, VA, dd Washington Co,
VA, md Jean Denny. R677
Thomas, BLW issued 11/5/1789. R677
Thomas, esf 1776 Albemarle Co, VA, where b; PN ae 79 Frank-
lin Co, VA, 1832; dd 5/22/42; md c7/1/1797 Mary David (MB

CRAIG (continued)
6/26/97 signed by Williamson David), Henry Co, VA; wid PN
ae 76 Franklin Co, VA, 1849, & dd 6/20/52. R677
William, esf 1778 Albemarle Co, VA, where b 2/21/1757; PN
1833 Barren Co, KY; bro John liv 1833; QLF 1905 from desc
Mrs F H Eichorn, Boston, MA, states sol f William also RW
sol. R677
William, esf Washington Co, VA, just before Battle of Guilford Court House; b 12/8/1763 Cumberland Co, PA; PN 1832
Rockcastle Co, KY, where dd 3/25/35; md 4/8/1790 Mary, d/o
David Carson (MB 4/8/90 witnessed by William Carson), Washington Co, VA; wid & some of ch mvd shortly after h dd
to Macon Co, MO, where she dd 12/29/44; wid never afp; s
Joseph, adm/o her estate, afp 1852 for surv ch: Mary Tinsley, Elizabeth Guillis ae 60, Jane Elder ae 43, Margaret
Barnes ae 40, & Joseph ae 38; ch gtd PN due m. R677
William, esf 1777 VA; d Sally Karnes, one of his heirs, afb
Bedford Co, VA, & BLW gtd; QLF 1933 from Mrs W K Freudenberger, St Louis, MO, states her RW ancestor William Craig
bc 1747-8 Augusta Co, VA, res 1774 Botetourt Co (area later Greenbrier Co), VA, where he esf, & dd there 1799, res
there continuously after RW. R677
CRAIL, John, esf 1776 Pittsburgh, PA, in VA regiment; PN ae 84
Beaver Co, PA, 1829, where dd 4/3/39; md 1777 Allathea/Al-
lithia, d/o Peter Body; wid 2/16/1761; wid PN 1841 Raccoon
Township, Beaver Co, PA; ch births: Edward 4/24/1779, Jane
1/9/81, James 12/24/82, Mary Ann 2/19/85, Peter 7/24/87,
Allethea 3/2/89, Joseph 4/28/91, Benjamin 7/8/93, John Er-
vin 10/25/95, S Middleton 11/1/98, & Elizabeth 6/13/1801;
QLF 1904 from gds Abel M Crail, Janesville, Brenner Co,IA,
states sol res near VA border when esf; QLF 1912 great gdd
Mrs Bruce S Ratcliff, Fairfield, IA, d/o James D Crail who
s/o sol s Benjamin, further sol b 1745; QLF 1918 from desc
Mrs Mary Crail Smith, Los Angeles, CA; QLF 1918 from desc
Mary Helen Crail, Fairfield, IA; QLF 1924 from relative E
L Crail, West Fort Lee, NJ, gds of W W Crail who dd 1883
Louisville, KY. R678
CRAIN, Silas, esf 1780 Cherain District, SC; b 1762 Botetourt
Co, VA; res Montgomery Co, NC, after RW, thence Wilkes Co,
GA, to 1807, thence Robinson Co,TN, to 1811, thence Greene
Co, IL, where PN 1832, when cripple; f mvd c1781 to Mont-
gomery Co, NC. R678
Stephen, b VA at mouth of Commoco River; esf 1781 Halifax Co
NC, where res till 1806, thence to Chester District, SC,
where PN 1832 ae 72; dd 3/29/34; md 9/9/1784 Mary Brinkley
who dd 6/18/45; AFF 1846 Chester District, SC, by s-in-law
Hugh McLure, who exec of LWT of sol wid, afp for surv ch/o
sol: Sarah McCulla, Mary Heath, Margaret McLure, & James,
all res there; ch gtd PN due m; ch births: Sarah 6/26/1785
William 5/14/87, John 12/2/89, James 5/9/92, Stephen
7/24/95, Mary 4/16/98, & Isaac 2/1801. R678
Thomas, b King William Co, VA; mvd aec 15 to Goochland Co,

CRAIN (continued)
    where esf 1778 when bro already in svc; mvd after RW to
    Powhatan Co, VA, for c6 years, thence Cumberland Co, VA,
    thence TN, thence Buckingham Co, VA, thence Mercer Co, KY,
    where PN 1832 ae 77 when res for c20 years; sol dd 3/10/33
    & wid Polly recd his final PN payment Lexington, KY, 1833.
    R678
CRAINE, James, see CRANE, James. R678
CRANE, James, esf 1777 VA; dd c12/1788 Lancaster Co, VA; only
    ch Maria (b 2/1787 or 3/1787), w/o Edwin E Brown, afb 1808
    Northumberland Co, VA, & gtd BLW. R682
  William, esf 1781 Tryon Co, NC; b 1748 Culpeper Co, VA; PN
    1833 Rutherford Co, NC; dd 7/10/36; md 1789 Elizabeth; wid
    afp ae 80 Cleaveland Co, SC, 1846, & PAR; wid again afp ae
    81 there 1847, & PAR; several ch, including James & Polly,
    by 1792; surname also spelled CRAIN. R684
CRAWFORD, Charles, BLW issued 8/20/1791. R686
  David, esf 1777 Rockbridge Co, VA; dd 5/23/1815; md 7/8/1790
    Margaret Guthrie, Abbeville District,SC; wid PN ae 78 Cof-
    fee Co, TN, 1846; ch births: Ginne Meclon 5/22/1793, Ro-
    bert 2/28/95, Joseph 12/9/97, David 6/12/1800, & Margaret
    7/6/04 (dd 12/24/06). R686
  James, esf 1778-9 Augusta Co, VA, where b; PN ae 74 Fleming
    Co,KY, 1833; QLF 1926 from desc Miss Ida B Hoagland, South
    Bend,IN; QLF 1926 from desc Mrs Louisa M Gibbs, same city;
    QLF 1929 from great great gdd Miss Mildred Cadwalader, Wa-
    shington, DC, states sol b 1759 VA, md 10/20/1786 Sarah
    Vansandt, Botetourt Co, VA, who b 1767 VA, further they
    mvd to KY 1795 & settled near Hillsboro, Fleming Co, 1800,
    further w dd 11/23/27, sol dd 5/16/36, both buried on fa-
    mily farm near Hillsboro, further their s Alexander (great
    gdf/o querier) b 3/23/1789 Botetourt Co, VA, md 6/26/1810
    Rebecca Alexander (b 1/11/1793), Flemingsburg, KY, further
    Alexander War of 1812 sol from KY, mvd family 1827 to San-
    gamon Co (area later Menard Co), IL, & settled on farm at
    Indian Creek, further Alexander dd 11/30/1851 & Rebecca dd
    3/13/65, they having 10 ch; QLF 1916 from great gdd Jennie
    V (Mrs Richard) Johnson, Madison, IN; QLF 1906 from desc
    Minnie Vawter Harold, Indianapolis,MD, stating Jennie Vaw-
    ter Johnson, above, d/o her f's bro; QLF 1902 from desc
    Lucy (Mrs W A) Guthrie, Dupont, IN; QLF 1935 from Rebecca
    Crawford, Byron,GA, states an RW sol James Crawford of Bo-
    tetourt Co, VA (b c1754-5), PN 1832 Fleming Co, KY, md Re-
    becca Anderson. R687
  John, esf 1776 St Paul's Parish, Columbia Co,GA; b 7/16/1759
    Amherst Co, VA; PN 1834 Monroe Co, GA; dd 10/19/36 Monroe
    Co or Pike Co, GA; md 4/27/1781 Rebecca Snider/Snyder, Ri-
    mond Co (area later Columbia Co), GA; wid afp ae 84 Pike
    Co, GA, 1846, & PAR, proof of marriage; wid dd 5/25/46-7;
    ch births: David 1/24/1782, Rhoda 10/3/83, Elizabeth
    10/3/85, William 1/17/88, Susanna 1/8/90, Charles 5/30/93,
    Jean 7/3/95, John 10/2/97, Anderson 10/3/99, Ambrose

CRAWFORD (continued)
   5/19/1803, & Thomas (no birth date given but liv 1855 Lincoln Co, GA); s Thomas AFF 1855 Wilkes Co, GA, that heirs
   of sol then: David, Rhody, Elizabeth, Susan, John, Thomas,
   & Lee; QLF states sol parents mvd 1767 to Carolina, thence
   1775 to GA; QLF 1932 from desc Sara Stephens (Mrs H F)
   White, Thomson, GA, states sol s/o John (b VA) who md (1)
   Sara L Smith & (2) Elizabeth Moore; QLF states a John
   Crawford (b 1731-4 Amherst Co,VA, dd 1813 Columbus, GA) md
   (1) 3/3/1755 Sarah Smith & (2) 1/1767 Elizabeth Moore, had
   s Peter b 2/7/1765 who ran away from home, joined RW army,
   md 11/3/1791 his cousin Mary Crawford, & dd 10/1830; QLF
   states above Sarah Smith b 2/14/1731 Hanover Co, VA. R687
John, b 10/29/1762 seven miles below Staunton, VA; mvd with
   f from Augusta Co, VA, to Surry Co, NC, where esf 1778;
   after RW mvd to Washington Co, TN, thence several TN Co's,
   lastly to Rhea Co, TN, where PN 1833; dd 1/31/41 leaving
   ch mbnn; QLF 1910 from great gds H A Crawford, Dayton,
   Rhea Co, TN, states sol had s W A b SC, & had 2 bro's who
   RW sol's. R687
John, esf near Reading, PA; b 3/8/1748; after RW mvd to Stony Creek Glades, PA, for c5 years, thence Hampshire Co,
   VA, for c20 years, thence Pickaway Co, OH, for c12 years,
   thence Highland Co, OH, where PN 1832 Liberty Township; dd
   there 12/1/1848; md 2/5/1822 Catharina Mileisa, Pickaway
   Co, OH; wid PN aec 60 Liberty Township, OH, 1853; wid gtd
   PN increase 1857 Mahaska Co, IA, where res with s-in-law
   Joseph Phillips who mvd there from OH; witness then for
   wid afp increase Ruth Phillips & Henry M Phillips; sol &
   wid of Dutch descent. R687
John, esf 1777 VA; b Dinwiddie Co, VA; PN there 1828, dd Petersburg, VA, 3/3/33, leaving no wid or ch; John Rowlett
   exec/o sol LWT which listed no family; BLW gtd 8/27/1795.
   R687
John, esf VA; sol b Augusta Co, VA, & dd there 1/13/1832 ae
   91; md 2/24/1797 there "last wife" Sarah Newman; wid b
   3/1771, & afp 1849 Augusta Co, VA, when AFF made by ch:
   eldest d Mrs Nancy R Newman b 5/25/1800, eldest s James E
   Crawford b 10/25/02, & s William Crawford b 8/30/07; wid
   PAR, insufficient proof of svc. R687
Josiah, esf probably VA; dd 12/14/1827; md 1817 Sarah Hulse,
   Sullivan Co, TN (MB 7/1/1816); wid afp & afb ae 73 there
   1856, & PAR & BLAR. R688
Moses, esf 1775 Culpeper Co, VA; PN ae 60 Wilkes Co, NC,
   1820; family 1821 w Nancy ae 53, d Delilah ae 19, & d Betsy ae 15, both unmarried; dd 12/17/1826 Bledsoe Co, TN; md
   (2) 3/1790 Nancy Dorsey, Burke Co, GA; wid PN ae 81 Hamilton Co, TN, 1843, when s John ae 53 made AFF there that m
   other ch Elijah, Elisha, & James Y; AFF 1845 by William T
   P Crawford, DeKalb Co, GA, s/o sol by 1st w, that he witnessed marriage of f & Nancy Dorsey; QLF 1911 from desc
   Mrs A M Calvin, Atlanta, GA, that sol md (1) Miss Pickett,

CRAWFORD (continued)

further querier also desc/o RW sol Elisha Dyer h/o Melvina Wheeler & of RW sol William Pickett; QLF 1910 from great great gdd Mrs A G Weston, Chattanooga, TN, states sol middle initial B, that he probably b Scotland, further querier great gdd/o War of 1812 sol William Smith who b VA & md Mary Dyer. R688

Peter, esf Mecklenburg Co, VA, where b & raised; PN ae 68 Rockingham Co, NC, 1832; dd 2/19/42; md 12/27/1797 Hannah Christy, Rockingham Co, NC, who b 9/10/1771; wid PN & gtd BLW there 1851, & dd 7/2/58; QLF states sol md (2) Hannah Dill & they had s Johnson & s Elisha. R688

Thomas, esf 1776 PA in VA regiment; b 3/1759; PN 1819 Frederick Co, VA, 1819; family there 1820 w ae 68 (b 1/1753), & gdc ae 3; AFF 1837 Fayette Co, OH, that he recently mvd to OH to be near ch/o w. R688

William, indian trader 1767; esf VA as colonel 1776; fought indians who captured him 1782 & burned him at stake; sol survived by ch John (dd before 1820), Effey McCormick, & Sally (w/o Uriah Springer, RW sol who served under Colonel Crawford); AFF by s-in-law Uriah Springer 1819 Fayette Co, PA; BLW issued 6/1/1820 to sol surv ch Effey & Sally; QLF 1938 from desc Mrs Annie E Smith, New Washington, IN, states sol killed by indians at Sandusky, OH; QLF states states sol f/o RW sol John from Surry Co, NC, & had 2 older bros; QLF states an RW sol William Crawford b 1732 md Hannah Vance who PN; QLF 1932 from desc Dorothy Duvall (Mrs Sterling W) Obenaur, Roseville, OH, states sol dd 6/11/1782 near Carey, Wyandotte, OH, further Major William Harrison also burned at stake by indians 1782, he h/o Sarah Crawford d/o sol, further querier desc of Major Harrison & Sarah Crawford; QLF 1931 from Gilbert L Campbell, Evanston, IL, states he great gds of Mary Crawford whose f William Crawford LWT filed 1783 Rockbridge Co, VA, & who md 1797 Gilbert Campbell there, further Gilbert 2nd s/o RW sol George Campbell of that Co who mvd c1795 to Woodford Co, KY, & whose elder s Samuel h/o Phoebe Kirkham of Woodford Co, further George Campbell md probably Nancy as 2nd w; QLF states sol md (2) 1761 Hannah who recd PN from VA & dd 1817; QLF 1914 from Mrs P C Weston, Florence, SC, desc of an RW sol William Crawford, esf 1777 Goochland Co, who md Sarah & had 19 ch, 7 of which RW sol; QLF states a John Crawford & s William both RW sol from Botetourt Co, VA, further John h/o of Isabel Fulkerson, while William md (1) Mary McRoberts & (2) Margaret Kirkpatrick. R688

CRAWLEY, Samuel, esf VA; LWT dated 1/8/1793 Williamsburg, VA, & probated there 5/4/93 mns w Ann & ch; heirs 1849 Samuel C Ware, James S Mountcastle, & Elizabeth Wise, all of Williamsburg, afp & PAR; w decd in 1849. R689

Thomas, esf 1776 Pittsylvania Co, VA; b 4/25/1755; mvd after RW to Guilford Co, NC, thence Surry Co, NC, where res 1788, thence White Co, TN, where res 1818 & PN there 1832; dd

CRAWLEY (continued)
7/1 or 7/7/1843 Van Buren Co, TN; md 3/3/1786 Margaret, Stokes Co or Surry Co, NC; wid dd 12/5/1844 ae 83 Van Buren Co, TN, leaving ch (ae's in 1850); Nancy 60, Catharine Dunagan 57, John 54, Henry 41 (res 1854 Sparta, White Co, TN), & Thomas (no ae given); ch afp 1852 & PAR per current PN law. R689

William Robert, esf 1779 Williamsburg, VA; b 1/10/58-9; PN 1832 Burke Co, NC; dd 4/20/39; md 9/1/1812 Polly who PN ae 63 Yancey Co, NC, 1853; wid res 1866 Sevier Co, TN; sol s Richard liv 1832; ch surv sol: Elizabeth (md Mr Long), Alexander, George W, Israel, & Moses. R689

CRAYCRAFT, Charles, b Loudoun Co, VA, s/o Samuel; esf ae 14 Hampshire Co, VA, 1781; esf PA 1792 & 1793 Washington Co, PA, in PA militia; esf 1796 & 1804 in VA militia; in 1821 had 6 ch mbnn; md (2) 2/18/1828 Elizabeth Dillon, Greenup Co, KY; dd there 12/23-24/1832 leaving 7 ch including Henry Clay b 1/20/1830; wid md (2) John Price who dd 7/1/37; wid PN ae 70 Portsmouth, OH, 1857 for sol svc; sol bro Joseph res Scioto Co, OH, 1827 ae 59; bro Joseph AFF 1832 ae 64 that he also RW sol & sub for f Samuel; QLF states sol dd Washington Co, PA; QLF 1895 C C Parker, Trenton, MO, great gds of a Major Charles Cracraft, RW field surgeon; QLF 1905 from Dr W C Bane, Denver, CO, who desc of a Major Charles Cracraft, RW field surgeon (1748-1824); QLF states a Colonel Charles Cracraft, esf Monongalia Co, VA, d Washington Co, PA, md (1) Miss Atkinson & (2) Miss Ruple. R689

CREAMER, Daniel, b 3/1757 York Co,PA; mvd as ch with f to Frederick Co, MD, where esf 1776; esf VA later against Cherokee indians; PN 1833 Greene Co, TN, where dd 4/3/40; md there 12/9/1790 Sarah Wilson at res of Joseph Roberts by Rev Joseph Wilson; wid afp there 4/1840 ae almost 70 & PAR per current PN law that not wid in 1838; 6 ch of which 5 survived wid who dd 6/29/40; d Polly res there 1852 & afp for all sol ch but also PAR; in 1833 sol had bro mbnn who res OH. R689

CREASEY, John, esf 1781 Cumberland Co, VA, where b 1754; PN there 1834. R689

CRECK, Peter, BLW issued 5/29/1792. R689

CREED, Colby/Colbay, b 5/4/1758 Orange Co, VA; mvd aec 12 with parents to Surry Co, VA, where esf 1779; mvd c1815 to Henry Co, KY, for 1 year, thence Overton Co, TN, thence 1829 to Morgan Co, IL, where PN 1832; John A Creed adm of sol's estate there 1844; QLF 1927 from desc Willard Keen, Chattanooga, TN; QLF states sol dd Case Co, IL. R689

CREEL, John, esf Culpeper Co, VA, where b; PN there 1832 where always res; dd there 10/27-28/46; md 12/31/1811 Frances/Fanny Kilby; wid PN ae 80 there 1853, & dd there 7/21/54. R689

CREMER, Daniel, see CREAMER, Daniel. R690

CRENSHAW, Daniel, esf 1781 Lunenburg Co, VA; dd 9/15/1831 Williamson Co, TN; md 7/2/1789 Nancy Jennings, Lunenberg Co,

CRENSHAW (continued)
   VA; wid afp ae 75 Williamson Co, TN, 1848, & PAR, insufficient proof of svc; ch births: Cornelius 5/12/1790, -ze
   (bible record torn away) 7/6/92, Polly Jennings 10/25/94;
   wid liv 1856; a Nathaniel Crenshaw res Williamson Co, TN,
   1848 ae 44. R690
   John, esf 1781 Brunswick Co, VA; b & raised Amelia Co, VA;
   where res after RW; mvd to Guilford Co, NC, for 2 years,
   thence Brunswick Co, VA, for several years, thence Warren
   Co, NC, for 12-14 years, thence Edgefield Co, SC, thence
   Jackson Co, GA, thence Roane Co, TN, where PN 1832 ae 74;
   PN increase 1839 Morgan Co, TN. R690
   Nathaniel, esf 1777 VA; dd 11/7/1793 Lunenburg Co, VA; md
   there Unity Pamplin; wid PN ae 78 Charlotte Co, VA, 1838 &
   dd 9/2/41; no mention of ch. R690
   William, esf 1777 Nottoway Co, VA, where b 1/28/1760; PN
   there 1833; dd 11/27/34. R690
CRESS, George, PN 1809 for disability from wounds Rockbridge
   Co, VA; mvd 1822 ae over 83 to Gallia Co, OH; dd 2/23/23
   there; md before RW Christiana, who dd 7/30/1823 ae 85; s
   Henry res Gallia Co, OH, 1852 aec 85; d Christiana Williams liv then. R690
CRESWELL, Andrew; esf 1776 Washington Co, VA; PN ae 74 Sevier
   Co, TN, 1832; dd 7/1/38; QLF 1927 from E E Creswell, Sevi-
   erville, TN; QLF 1929 from desc Judge Sam O Houston, Knoxville, TN, states sol mvd 1787 from VA to TN; QLF states
   sol b 1/12/1753 PA, s/o William Henry Creswell who killed
   1776, further sol Andrew md 3/22/1780 Dorothy Evins/Evans
   of Washington Co, VA. R690
   Samuel, esf 1778 Bedford Co, PA, for svc in VA regiment; PN
   1818 Mason Co, KY; res ae 69 Lewis Co, KY, 1820 when w aec
   45 & 7 ch of which eldest d ae 18 & s aec 15; dd 4/15/39;
   QLF 1920 from desc Miss M B Adams, Orlando, FL, who also
   desc of RW sol Henry Robinson/Robeson of NY & RW sol John
   Brewster of NJ (later res PA). R690
CREWS, Gideon, esf 1776 Buckingham Co, VA; PN aec 66 Knox Co,
   TN, 1818; in 1820 w ae almost 60 & ch: 2 d's & w gdc mbnn;
   QLF states sol dd 1824. R690
   James, esf 1776 Buckingham Co, VA; PN aec 60 Knox Co, TN,
   1818; in 1829 w aec 60, sis aec 65; bro RW sol Gideon who
   res there 1818; dd 3/6/1841. R690
   Joseph, esf Amherst Co, VA; PN ae 75 Bedford Co, VA 1832, dd
   there 5/26/43; md there 1/4/1822 Nancy Eubank (MB 1/4/22);
   wid gtd BLW there 1855 ae 66; wid PN there blind ae 67; ch
   1832: d ae 7, d ae 3; wid liv there 1866 blind & deaf aec
   75 when PN restored, after cut off during Civil War, she
   first signing Oath of Allegiance to US government 5/3/66;
   also gtd another BLW then. R690
   Joseph, BLW issued 1/31/1794. R690
CRIHFIELD, William, esf 1778 Hampshire Co, VA, res on Patterson's Creek; b 1758 NJ; mvd 1781 to Somerset Co, PA, where
   PN 1837 Milford; AFF 1837 by brother Joshua CRITCHFIELD,

CRIHFIELD (continued)
Lancaster, Fairfield Co, OH; AFF then by cousin Nathaniel
CRITCHFIELD, Knox Co, OH, that he svd with sol in RW; QLF
1938 from great gdd Mrs J M Hellinger, Greencastle, IN,
states sol s/o Amos; surname at times spelled CRITCHFIELD.
R691
CRIM, Harmon, esf 1781 Fauquier Co, VA; b Culpeper Co, VA; mvd
c1808 to Harrison Co, VA, where PN 1832 ae 82; QLF 1928
from desc W Guy Tetrick, Clarksburg, WV, who also desc of
RW sol John Nay. R691
CRISP, John, see CHRISP, John. R691
CRISSWELL, Richard, esf Baltimore Co, MD, where b; PN 1832 ae
84 Brooke Co, VA; res occasionally with ch but more fre-
quently with one/o gdc; res there 1835 ae 87; AFF 1832 by
niece Susanna w/o Nicholas Gossage. R691
CRISWELL, Samuel, see CRESWELL, Samuel. R691
CRITCHFIELD, John, esf 1777 VA; PN aec 60 Wayne Co, OH, 1821
when w Rachel ae 60 & they res with sons Enoch & Asa; QLF
1902 from great gds A B Critchfield, Shreve, OH, states
sol dd 1850 Nashville, Holmes Co, OH; QLF states sol b DE
1758; QLF 1925 from desc Russell H Fluent, Seattle, WA;
QLF states sol dd 1851, md Rachel Shrimplin, & had s John;
QLF states sol a cooper res 1790 Washington Co, PA, & res
Knox Co, OH, c1807, dd 1851 Nashville, Holmes Co, OH, & md
Rachel Shrimplin. R692
Joshua, esf 1774 VA; esf 1777 Md; res 1778 Hampshire Co, VA;
b 5/27/1743 Sussex Co, NJ; PN 1832 Clear Creek Township,
Fairfield Co, OH. R692
Nathaniel, esf 1778 Bedford Co, PA for VA regiment; esf 1780
for PA regiment; b 11/1761 Shippestown, PA; PN 1832 Howard
Township, Knox Co,OH; bro John res 1832 Holmes Co, OH; QLF
1931 from great great gds Charles V Critchfield, Fairmont,
WV; QLF 1934 from great great gds Daniel E Dugan, formerly
member of TN state senate, Nashville,TN, states sol buried
Shrimplin Cemetery near Howard, Knox Co, TN. R692
William, see CRIHFIELD, William. R692
CRITTENDEN, John, esf VA for IL regiment; aide-de-camp to Gen
George Rogers Clark; elected 1783 to VA House of Delegates
from Fayette Co,KY; dd 1803 near res Woodford Co, KY, leaving wid Judith; s John member US Senate 1842; d md Randolph Hailey who adm/o sol estate & afp 1850 for heirs of
sol, & PAR. R692
Richard Hazlewood, esf 1778 Amherst Co, VA, as sub for f; b
3/6/1761 Charles City Co, VA; res after RW Fincastle Co &
Botetourt Co,VA, for 5 years, thence mvd to Salem, NC, for
1 year, thence KY for over 20 years, thence IN where PN
1832 Columbus Township, Bartholomew Co, when res 6 years;
dd IN 6/22/41; md 2/12/1789 Sally d/o Josiah & Martha Tanner at her f's house, Spartanburg District, SC; wid b
10/30/1773, & res afp 1843 Bartholomew Co, IN, & PAR, per
current PN law, md after end of svc/o sol; ch births: Josiah 10/24/1789, John 12/23/90, Charles Warde 1/11/93,

CRITTENDEN (continued)
Mary W 12/15/94, Matthew Tanner 1/14/97, Samuel 12/24/98,
Martha 6/22/1801, Nancy 8/16/03, & Richard Hazlewood
1/7/06; other bible data: James Harva Singer b 7/20/1819;
wid afp 1843 Bartholomew Co, IN, & PAR per current PN law,
md after end of sol svc; in 1845 s Richard H Jr & d Mary W
Singer res there, when wid m Martha Lemaster (wid/o Josiah
Tanner) res Johnson Co, IN; also then Patsey Tanner, sis/o
sol wid, AFF res Decatur Co, IN, she b 8/7/1777, md Lucius
Tanner 1/15/1793, & was present at sol wedding. R692
   William, esf 1780 as wagonmaster Albemarle Co, VA; PN ae 75
Orange Co,VA, 1834; PN increase there 1842 ae 82; dd there
3/27/1847 leaving no wid and only ch William who afp 1847
Culpeper Co, VA, stating f res for c18 years before death,
res Culpeper Co, VA; William gtd PN due sol 1848. R692
CRITTENDON, John, BLW issued 4/18/1792. R692
CRITTINGTON, William, esf 1776 King William Co, VA, where b
1761 s/o James who also RW sol from King William Co, VA,
who KIA at Battle of Brandywine; mvd c1793 to NC; PN 1833
Richmond, VA, res Wake Co,NC, when AFF by Joanna Blunt aec
63 of Hanover Co, VA, that sol md her eldest sis; sol nephew of James Mann, for whom sol once sub in RW; sol res
1836 Wake Co, NC. R692
CRITZ, Hamon, esf 1777 as Herman Critz Jr, Henry Co, VA; dd
8/5/1828 Patrick Co, VA; md 3/1786 Nancy Daulton; wid PN
ae 75 Patrick Co, VA, 1841 res near line of Stokes Co, NC;
ch births: Frederick 12/1786 (res 1845 Patrick Co, VA),
Sally 1/1788, William 7/1790, Hamon 3/1792, Jabe/Gabe
2/1794, Elizabeth 7/1795, Peter 6/9/97 (res 1841 Stokes Co
NC), Nancy 7/1799, Polly 11/1802, & Achilus 12/1804; James
Dalton witness to wid signature 1852 Patrick Co, VA; QLF
1921 from desc Miss Fannie Lee Shumate, Glen Lyn, VA,
states sol md Miss Dalton; QLF 1925 from Mrs C E Russ of
South Bend, IN, states her great gdm Catherine Critz b VA
12/1/1787 & md Jacob Treffel of Botetourt Co, VA. R692
CRITZER, Leonard; esf 1776 NJ; PN ae 73 Booth's Creek, Harri-
son Co, VA, 1832; 2 d's mbnn 1852, 1 res Harrison Co, VA,
& other res OH. R692
CROCKER, Jesse, esf c1776 Isle of Wight Co, VA; b 1760; PN
1832 Southampton Co, VA. R693
CROCKETT, Alexander, esf with VA troops; dd 9/15/1816; md Elizabeth 3/21/1793 "on the Waters of the French Broad River,
Grainger Co, TN"; wid afp ae 74 Stanford, Monroe Co, IN, &
PAR, insufficient proof/o svc; ch mbnn. R694
   Anthony, esf 1776 Botetourt Co, VA; b Prince Edward Co, VA;
PN ae 76 Franklin Co, KY, 1832; dd 12/6/38 leaving no wid;
names/o Dandridge S Crockett & William R Crockett mentioned; QLF 1914 from desc Lamar Washington, Summit, NJ, who
also desc/o VA RW sol Warner Washington; QLF states sol dd
1833-40 Franklin Co,KY, & b 1756 Prince Edward Co, VA; QLF
states sol md Sarah Blankenship. R694
   Joseph, esf VA; PN 1828 Nicholasville, Jessamine Co, KY; dd

CROCKETT (continued)
11/7/29; gds W Mead Woodson res KY 1829; Charles J Faulkner adm/o sol estate; QLF 1892 from great gdd Susan Crockett states sol dd ae 87; QLF states sol b 1742 Albemarle Co, VA. R694

Robert, esf Sullivan Co, NC, for VA troops; b 1755 Berkeley Co, VA; res after RW Greene Co,TN, to 1800, thence Cumberland Co, KY, where PN 1833; dd 2/26/36 survived by ch mbnn R694

CRODDY, John, esf 1776 Botetourt Co (area later Rockbridge Co) VA, where afp 1832 ae 77; PN 1834 Rockbridge Co, VA, after giving more RW svc proof; surname also spelled CRODY. R694

CROES, Joseph, esf 1778-9 Hanover Co, VA; PN ae 60 res on Ninety-Six Creek near Cambridge, Edgefield District, SC, 1818; in 1821 ae 72 when no w but 3 sons who had gone West R694

CROGHAN, William, BLW issued 3/4/1799. R695

CROMER, John, esf 1776 Lancaster Co, PA, where b 4/22/1758; after RW res PA, MD, VA, & KY, thence IN where PN Blue River Township, Harrison Co 1832; w mbnn 1838. R695

CROOK, Charles, esf Loudoun Co, VA; wounded Battle of Jamestown, for which gtd disability PN 1808-9 by VA; dd 1829; md c1/4/1791 Nancy Money, halfsis/o Nicholas Money at home Alexander Money, Fairfax Co, VA, per AFF Fairfax Co, VA, 1850 by Nicholas; wid afp 1850 & PAR, proof of marriage, & dd 1850; ch mbnn. R696

Henry, PN 1789 for disability & dd 3/18/1819 Washington Co, VA; papers destroyed by fire set by British in Washington, DC, 1814. R696

Jeremiah, esf Prince William Co, VA; b 1761 or 1764 Fairfax Co, VA, near Mt. Vernon; mvd to KY c1790 where res Bourbon Co & Pendleton Co; PN 1833 Grant Co, KY, where dd 6/14/34; md 10/7/1782 Jane Williams, Charles Co, MD; wid PN ae 82 Lewis Co, MO, 1846; large family of ch, including 4th ch Elizabeth who bc 1792, md 1810 Jesse Woodyard, who res Lewis Co, MO, 1848; wid already decd 2/1848. R696

CROOKE, John, esf 1781 Fauqier Co, VA; b St Mary's Co, MD; mvd 1789 to Madison Co, KY, where PN 1832 ae 66; Co surveyor there 1795; surname also spelled CROOK; QLF 1933 from desc Mrs Truman E Johnson, Paris, TX. R696

CROOKS, Michael, b 1760 near Philadelphia, PA; mvd as ch to Loudoun Co, VA, thence to Berkeley Co, VA, where esf 1781; res after RW VA, KY, & IN; afp Knox Co, IN, 1838, & PAR, less than 6 months svc. R696

CROOKSHANKS, John, esf 1776 Augusta Co,VA; PN ae 65 Greenbrier Co, VA, 1818; family 1820 w ae 53 & ch: Elizabeth ae 27, Catherine ae 17, Alexander ae 17, William ae 15, Hester ae 12, Nancy ae 6, & George ae 1. R696

CROPPER, James, esf 1778; b Acco Co, VA, per AFF 1820 there by Colonel John Cropper who knew sol since infancy; PN ae 61 York Co, VA, 1818; PN increase ae 63 there 1821 when had d Betsy aec 19 & s John ae 17. R696

266

CROPPER, John, esf 1776 Accomac Co, VA, where b 12/23/1755 at
    Bowman's Folly, s/o Sebastian & Sabra; member of General
    Assembly of VA 1784; dd 1/15/1821 Accomac Co, VA; md (1)
    there 8/15/1776 Margaret d/o William & Mary Pettit at res
    of George Abbott; 1st w b 7/12/1755 Occahannock, Northamp-
    ton Co,VA, & dd 6/1784; sol md (2) 9/18/1790 Catharine d/o
    Thomas & Ann Bayly at Hill's Farm, Accomac Co, VA; 2nd w b
    there 1/24/1772; ch births by 1st w (all b Bowman's Folly)
    were: Sarah C 3/21/1777 (md 4/18/1799 John s/o John & Mar-
    garet Wise at Bowman's Folly), Sabra 9/1/79 & dd infancy,
    days, Sabra 10/19/81 & dd 10/27/83, & Margaret Pettit
    5/13/84 (md Thomas M s/o Thomas & Ann Bayly at Bowman's
    Folly); ch by 2nd w: Catharine B (md 8/14/1826 Augustus
    s/o Charles & Ann Bagwell), Eliza W (md 10/23/1826 Joseph
    W s/o William & Frances Gibs), Ann C (md 9/28/1831 George
    W s/o Edward & Ann Arbuckle), John Washington (md 9/5/1832
    Mary Ann Savage), & Coventon Hanson (md 6/14/1837 Leah B
    d/o William & Isabella Seymour); wid PN 1838 Accomac Co,
    & dd 1/24/55; gds Henry A Wise member of US Congress 1839;
    QLF 1927 from desc Mrs R J Hancock, Sulphur, KY, states
    sol f also RW sol & she also desc/o RW sol Archibald John-
    ston & of RW sol William Skinner. R696
CROSBY, Jesse, BLW issued 5/16/1792. R697
   John, esf Fauquier Co, VA; b 5/10/1755; afp 1845 Shelby Co,
    1845, & PAR, insufficient proof/o svc; QLF states sol dd
    7/22/1853. R697
   Nelson, esf 1775 Hanover Co, VA; b VA; PN ae 61 Salem, Rock-
    ingham Co, NH, 1818, having left VA over 30 before; no ch
    or w res with him 1820; dd 11/18/1821; QLF 1925 from desc
    Mrs Grace F Linn, Indianapolis, IN. R697
   William, esf 1777 VA; PN 1820 Mansfield Township, Sussex Co,
    NJ. R698
CROSE, Philip, esf 1780 Hampshire Co, VA, where b 1757; after
    RW res Monongalia Co, VA, for c4 years, thence Fayette Co,
    KY, for c27 years, thence Ross Co,OH, for c4 years, thence
    Gallatin Co,IL, for c3 years, thence IN where PN 1834 Tip-
    pecanoe Co when res c13 years; Solomon Cross, clergyman, &
    Reuben Cross res there 1834; surname also spelled CROCE;
    QLF 1934 from desc Mrs O L Gilman, Webster City,IA, states
    sol had d Barbara. R698
CROSS, John, esf 1782 Point of Fork,VA; PN ae 50 Jefferson Co,
    VA, 1818; in 1820 w ae 51 & ch: Mary ae 30, Sarah ae 28,
    Elizabeth ae 16, Abraham ae 12, Samuel ae 10, & Eleanor ae
    7 & sol ae 59 there; mvd 1828 from res Berkeley Co, VA, to
    Fairfield, OH; dd 1847; s-in-law James Armstrong res Bant-
    ram, Clermont Co, OH; QLF 1930 from Frank C Cross, Moose-
    hart, IL, states sol dd Fairfield Co, OH; QLF states sol b
    3/2/1761, dd 4/22/1847, md Elizabeth Hardwick of VA; QLF
    from desc Miss Bess Ireton, Wilmington, OH, states sol dd
    at Royalton,OH; QLF 1921 from great gdd Miss Clara E Cross
    of Adrian, MN, states sol lived Martinsburg, VA, & his w
    buried beside him at Lancaster, OH; QLF 1917 from great

CROSS (continued)
  great gdd Bertha E Moore, Washington, DC, whose lineage:
  sol & Elizabeth Hardwick had James who md Frances McCaus-
  land, they parents of Elizabeth who md Major D A B Moore,
  they parents/o M Blackburn Moore who md Ida V Manley, they
  parents/o querier, who also niece of D.A.R member Mrs Ida
  Moore Tucker desc/o sol. R699
  John, BLW issued 10/26/1795. R699
  William, esf 1776 NC/VA (area now Sullivan Co, TN), for svc
  with NC troops; esf 1781 there for svc with VA troops; b
  3/5/1761-2 Baltimore Co, MD; res Sullivan Co, TN, to c1817
  when mvd to Knox Co, TN, for 1 year, thence Anderson Co,
  TN, were PN 1833. R700
  William, b 6/1/1759 near Hampton, Elizabeth City Co, VA; mvd
  with family as small ch to Sussex Co, VA, where esf 1778;
  mvd 1804 to Muhlenberg Co, KY, where afp 1832 & 1832; PAR,
  less than 6 months svc. R700
CROSSON, John, esf 1776 Vincent Township, PA; PN 1818 Lincoln
  Co,GA; dd 1/28/38 ae 82; md 7/3/88 Acksa/Achsa Lewis, Fauquier Co, VA; wid b 2/8/1769; wid PN 1842 Lincoln Co, GA,
  & dd 1/21/53 leaving ch: Lewis ae 64 (res AR), Mary Jackson ae 62 (res Stewart Co,GA), Elizabeth Rozier ae 60 (res
  Stewart Co, GA, wid/o Isham Rozier), Peninah Trammell ae
  58 (res Benton Co, AR, w/o Thomas W Trammell), James ae 57
  (res AR), & Felix ae 54 (res Stewart Co, GA). R701
  Robert, esf 1775 VA; esf 1776 & 1779 SC; PN ae 78 Burke Co,
  NC, 1818; res there ae 80 when w aec 64. R701
CROSTICK, Edward, b 8/25/1760 Chesterfield Co, VA, where esf
  1777; PN there 1832; liv 1835. R701
CROSTON, Gustavus, esf Newport, MD; later esf Alexandria, VA;
  PN ae over 60 Frederick Co, VA, 1813; res there 1818 aec
  aec 63; res 1824 ae 67 Hampshire Co, VA, & gtd PN increase
  there 1828; dd there before 1841, leaving no wid but seve-
  ral ch; sometimes called Travis Croston; surname at times
  spelled CROSSTON. R701
CROUCH, Jesse, esf 1778 VA; b 4/25/1760 Stafford Co, VA; f mvd
  to Halifax Co, VA, thence Henry Co, VA; mvd c1783 to what
  now TN; afp 1835 Washington Co, TN, & PAR, under 6 months
  svc. R702
  John, esf 1781 Prince William Co, VA, where b 1758; PN 1835
  Fairfax Co, VA; sol decd when PN due paid to s Reid, 1 of
  sol's 2 ch, 1843. R702
  John, b 5/1/1756 King George Co, VA; mvd as young man to
  Montgomery Co, VA, where esf 1777; mvd to Henry Co, VA,
  where esf 1779; PN 1834 Washington Co,TN, as John Sr. R702
  William, see COUCH, William. R702
  William, esf VA; PN 1822 Bedford Co, VA; dd there 12/29/23;
  md 1/1794 Elizabeth, who PN 1848 & gtd BLW 1855 Campbell
  Co, VA. R702
  William, esf 1780/1 VA; afp 1828 & 1829 Gooch Co, VA, & PAR.
  R702
CROUDUS, William, esf 1776 Charlotte Co, VA; dd 7/9/1825; md

CROUDUS (continued)
   6/1785 Doratha Arnold near Harrod's Station, Lincoln Co,
   KY (MB dated 6/7/85 between sol & Dolly Arnold, with con-
   sent of her m Gracey Arnold); wid PN ae 75 Marion Co, KY,
   1839 when AFF by s James ae 30; also had s George; PN increase there 1843 ae 78; res there 1849 ae 86; QLF 1904
   from great gdd Mrs John Mack Smith, Los Angeles,CA, states
   sol w Dorothy Crowdus; QLF 1906 from great gdd Janett Tow-
   ner (Crowdus) Menefee, states sol w from Appomattox Co, VA
   R702
CROUSE, Christian, esf York Co, PA; b near Lancaster, PA; PN
   ae nearly 80 Morgan Co, VA (area formerly part of Berkeley
   Co) where res c25 years; dd before 12/30/37; s Jesse. R702
CROW, Abraham, b 7/29/1763 Prince George Co, VA; mvd as youth
   to NC where esf 1780 Northampton Co; esf 1781 Brunswick Co
   VA; mvd from there 1784 to Rutherford Co, NC, thence 1822
   to Spartansburg District, SC, where PN 1832; mvd to Camp-
   bell Co,GA, where dd near Campbellton 10/4/48; md 2/1/1825
   Maria, Spartanburg District, SC, who PN ae 56 Fulton Co,
   GA, 1855 res city of Atlanta; wid gtd BLW 1856 there; wid
   res 1859 Red Oak, Fayette Co, GA, & still liv 1860. R702
   Benjamin, esf 1776 VA; afp 1824 St Louis, MO; afp 1829 Anto-
   ine Township, Clark Co, AR Territory; PAR, insufficient
   proof/o svc. R702
   Dennis, esf 1776 VA; PN ae 76 Madison Co,VA, 1832 when house
   carpenter with no family. R702
   John, esf 1776 Culpeper Co, VA; dd 3/2/1798; md 4/1779 Eli-
   zabeth Coleman, Culpeper Co, VA (MB dated 4/9/1779 between
   sol & Betty Coleman signed by Dennis Crow); wid PN aec 82,
   Madison Co, VA, 1839, when AFF there by her sis Mrs Ann
   Potts that wid 2nd ch of family of 8 ch, & Ann youngest.
   R702
   Robert, esf 1777 Fincastle Co (area later Wythe Co), VA; b
   1/1/1751; PN 1823 Roane Co, TN, when res c8 years; w ae 67
   in 1822; QLF states sol mvd 1837 to DeKalb Co, AL; QLF
   states sol buried near Webster, Roane Co, TN. R702
   William, esf 1779 Rockingham Co, VA, where b; res after RW
   Mason Co, VA, thence Gallia Co,OH, for c5 years; PN aec 75
   Clinton Township, Jackson Co, OH; mvd 1835 with s James to
   IL; res 1853 near Peoria, IL; dd 1/25/1854; QLF states sol
   buried Peoria, IL; QLF 1925 from desc Mrs Walter Roberts
   Jr states sol probably esf Christiansburg, VA; QLF undated
   from great gdd Mrs E A Cole, Peoria, IL; QLF states sol md
   Margaret d/o John Lewis of Augusta Co, VA, & had ch Tho-
   mas, John, & Andrew Lewis. R702
CROWDER, Philip, esf 1776 VA, sub for bro William; b 4/7/1760
   Amelia Co, VA; mvd 1785 to Rutherford Co, NC, thence 1791
   Green Co, KY, thence 1830 Sangamon Co, IL, where PN 1832;
   QLF 1911 from great gds Edward Crowder, Springfield, IL;
   QLF states sol esf Petersburg, VA; QLF 1927 & 1940 from
   great gdd Mrs Adria H Helmbrecht, Tonkawa, OK, states sol
   b near Petersburg,VA, sub RW for elder bro, dd Springfield

CROWDER (continued)
   IL 5/1844 whose eldest s Reuben f/o Martha (Crowder) Robison who gdm/o querier, further querier gdd/o Thomas Willi-
   ams, Union Civil War sol who esf 1862 Unionville, IL; QLF
   1934 from great gds Cary E Barnes, Springfield, IL. R703
   Sterling, esf 1777 Pittsylvania Co, VA;PN ae 59 Jessamine Co
   KY, 1818; in 1831 w & ch liv there including Currency Cro-
   der; QLF states Government Accounting Office records show
   sol dd 1/18/34 leaving wid Jemima. R703
   William, esf 1781 Mechlenburg Co,VA; mvd 1795-6 to Cleveland
   Co, NC; dd 11/9 or 11/10/40; md 1771-2 (1) ?, md 1825 (2)
   Miss Lucy Thompson (MB 9/15/25), Rutherford Co,NC; wid gtd
   BLW ae over 75 Cleveland Co, NC; s Jarral afp ae 69 Polk-
   that Co, 1854, & PAR, f less than 6 months svc; QLF states
   a William Crowder esf Mechlinburg Co, VA, & md Phoebe Elder; QLF 1919 from desc Charles R Conlee, Fort Morgan, CO,
   through sol & 2nd w; QLF 1938 from desc Mrs Lee Smith, Bi-
   ardstown, TX. R703
CROWDUS, William, see CROUDUS, William. R703
CROWEL, Thomas, esf 1776 Boston, MA, for service with VA regiment; esf later 1776 Winchester, ME; b 12/2/1760 Limerick,
   Ireland, & came to Brunswick, ME, shortly before RW; afp
   ae 73 there 1832, & PAR; dd 11/1844 md (1) ? & had ch by
   her; md after 1800 (2) Judith, who dd 1849 without issue;
   sol only surv ch Lucy, w/o Hiram Bowe, afp Topsham, ME,
   1851 & PAR; surname also spelled CROWELL. R703
CROWLEY, James, esf Henry Co, VA, while res with f about time
   of Battle of Guilford Court House; b 5/20/1764-5; PN 1836
   Fishing River Township, Clay Co, MO, when AFF made there
   by John Crowley who res Henry Co, VA, 1781 ae 13 (no relationship shown); QLF states sol mvd from VA to TN, thence
   Clay Co, MO, & buried as James Sr in Jack Crowley family
   cemetery 2 & 1/2 miles north of Excelsior Springs, MO, his
   w Sarah buried beside him, her headstone data b 10/10/1751
   & dd 4/4/1810 (possible stonemason's error), further sol
   had ch "Big Sam", John/Jack, & others, further Big Sam md
   (1) Celia Mayo, they parents of Mary/Polly (b 9/13/1812)
   who md Levi Casey Stephenson, they parents/o Jewell Mayes,
   further Big Sam md (2) Nancy Loe/Lowe, they having 13 ch
   of which eldest Francis Marion b 10/4/1828; QLF 1930 from
   desc Mrs H H King, Columbia, MO, states sol b 1765; QLF
   1933 from desc Alice Hamot, Portland,OR, states sol md (1)
   1778 Mary McLain & md (2) 1790 Sarah McLain, both VA. R704
CROWNOVER, Daniel; esf 1779 Union District, SC, as sub for bro
   Benjamin; esf 1781 VA; b 6/13/1763 NJ; PN 1833 Union District, SC; mvd 1840 to Pope Co, AR, where ch had mvd earlier; dd c1844 AR; surname also spelled CRONOVER or COWNOV-
   ER; QLF 1926 from Grace F (Mrs B B) Crownover, Benedict,
   NE, states sol surname variation of COVENHOVEN. R704
   Joseph, esf ae 17-18 Berkeley Co, VA; b 11/17/1759; PN 1833
   Franklin Co, TN, c100 miles from Nashville; son mbnn 1835;
   QLF 1909 from Arthur Crownover, Winchester, TN; QLF 1934

CROWNOVER (continued)
   from Arthur Crownover Jr, Nashville, TN. R704
CROXTON, Carter, esf 1776 Essex Co, VA; b 3/16/1761; PN 1833
   as Carter Sr, South Farnham Parish, Essex Co, VA; dd there
   4/29/45; md 11/26/1825 Frances Faulconer, who dd 11/26/49
   there; ch births: Fanny Ellen 7/3/37 who md Mr Broaddus,
   Louisa Carter 5/17/39, & Cornelia 6/1/40; QLF 1925 from
   Grace A Croxton states sol md more than once. R704
CRUIDSON, Benjamin, see CRUZAN, Benjamin. R704
CRUM, Adam, esf 1776 Burke Co, NC; esf 1781 Washington Co, VA;
   b 10/5/1756 of German parentage; PN 1834 Lawrence Co, KY;
   QLF 1908 from Dr E W Crum, Palmyra, IL, great gds of John
   Crum, who s/o Mathias (b Germany), both RW sol's. R705
CRUMLY, Thomas, esf 1781 Mecklenburg Co, NC; b 3/1762 Frede-
   rick Co, VA; res after RW Newberry District, SC, thence
   Buncombe Co, NC, thence Habersham Co, GA, where PN 1832;
   there 3/10/36; wid Ruth dd there 3/1837; d Hannah Berry ae
   64 res Lumpkin Co, GA, 1852 when an Elias Berry mentioned.
   surname also spelled CRUMLEY. R705
CRUMP, Abner, esf VA; member of Cincinnati Association; Clerk
   of Powhatan Co, VA, 1785 where dd 1/2 or 1/20/1802; bro of
   Goodrich & Richard, both decd in 1802; nephews George (s/o
   bro Goodrich) & Abner (s/o bro Richard); William Crump,
   Sheriff of Powhatan Co, VA, & adm/o sol estate, afp for PN
   PN due sol & claim allowed. R705
   Joshua, esf 1780 Bedford Co, VA; esf 1782 as sub for John P
   Crump; b 5/1765 New Kent Co, VA; mvd to KY 1795 where PN
   Hart Co 1832, & res there 1833; QLF 1922 from desc Mamie
   Hoyle (Mrs J D) Schnell, Columbus, GA, states sol md Mar-
   tha; QLF states sol known as Joshua Sr when PN; QLF states
   sol dd after 1840, md Mary/Polly Patterson. R705
   Thomas, esf 1776 VA; res KY 1832; dd 1/5/33 ae 75 Washington
   Co, KY, leaving s Daniel of that Co & d Polly Briscoe; sol
   w dd before him; QLF states sol b VA 1758. R705
   Thomas, esf 1777 VA; md (1) Fall/o 1784 King William Co, VA;
   mvd 1789 to Chesterfield Co, VA, when 2nd ch ae 2, & dd
   there 3/10/16; md Fall of 1784 Peggy, d/o George Gearton,
   ton, King William Co, VA; ch births: John 11/13/1785 &
   Elias 5/23/88; wid md (2) William Logwood (dd 11/7/1819);
   wid PN ae 76 Chesterfield Co, VA, 1843 when s Elias AFF
   bro John decd; wid sis Elizabeth md William Smith, uncle
   of Mrs Elizabeth Anderson, who AFF there 1843. R705
CRUTCHER, James, esf 1777 Philadelphia, PA; PN ae 55 Jefferson
   Co, VA, 1825 occupation blacksmith, when w ae 57 & 3 small
   male orphan ch ae 9,7, & 5 res with him. R706
   John, esf 1781 VA; PN ae 63 Franklin Co, KY, 1827; res 1845
   care of Thomas Crutcher, Elizabethtown, Hardin Co, KY; dd
   3/16/50 Barren Co, KY; md 7/10/1845 (1st & only w) Sarah/
   Sally Runner, Hardin Co, KY; wid PN ae 52 there 1853 & gtd
   BLW there 12/1855. R706
   William, esf Amherst Co, VA; mvd 1819 to TN, where dd Willi-
   amson Co 12/13/33; md 4/15/1782 Elizabeth, Amherst Co, VA;

CRUTCHER (continued)
wid afp ae 83 Williamson Co, TN, 1846, & PAR; ch births:
Polley 3/13/1783, Sarah 5/15/86, Robert 9/22/88, Elizabeth
5/21/90, William 12/30/92, Willis 4/25/95, Henry Lanson
1/25/98, & Parker 5/17/1800; wid dd 1/14/48; s William Jr
afp 1852 there for all surv ch: himself, Henry L, Elizabeth Bugg, Mary Padgett, & Robert T, & PAR; AFF 1846 there
by Henry G Padgett aec 50 that his f Beverly md (2) Mary/
Polley; sol d Sarah w/o John Hudson; sol d Elizabeth w/o
Allen Bugg. R706
CRUTCHFIELD, John, esf 1777 Charles City Co, VA, where PN 1818
ae 62; res there 1820 ae 64 & had w aec 64. R706
  Stapleton, esf 1777 Goochland Co, VA; b 9/20/1758; PN Gooch-
land Co, VA, 1832; dd 6/27/33; QLF 1927 from desc James
Stapleton Moore, Washington, DC; QLF 1927 from Dora E (Mrs
W E) Gunnett, Fullerton, CA, states her ancestor Benjamin
Burch md 1756 Jane Crutchfield in VA & after RW they set-
tled Lincoln Co, KY, where Benjamin's will recorded Stan-
ford, KY, further many of their descendants had given name
of Stapleton. R706
CRUTCHLEY, Benjamin, esf 1777 Baltimore, MD; PN ae 76 Wood Co,
VA, 1820 occupation carpenter, when w aged & infirm. R706
CRUTE, John, PN 1828, res P O Farmville, Prince Edward Co, VA,
for disability from wounds at Battle of Hanging Rock; dd
10/6/1840 Prince Edward Co, VA, leaving no wid but ch: Venable, Samuel, Clement, Maria M w/o Nathaniel Mottley, &
Mary w/o Thomas Ellington; d Maria M Mottley adm/o f's estate there 1854. R706
  Robert, esf 1775 Amelia Co, VA; b 1754 Northumberland Co, VA
(per family bible taken by m to GA); mvd 1804 to Halifax
Co, VA, where PN 1832. R706
CRUZAN, Benjamin, esf 1780 NC for svc with VA regiment; PN ae
67 Adams Co, IN, 1825; PN tranferred 1838 to Ripley Co, IN
where sol address P O Lawrenceburgh District; PN last paid
12/1846. R706
CRYDER, John, BLW issued 14/1792. R706
CRYSEL, Jeremiah, esf 1778 Culpeper Co, VA; PN ae 57 Wilkes Co
NC, 1819, & res there 1831 ae 70 when gtd PN increase; dd
8/26/36; md 5/5/1790 Mary Bruce, Culpeper Co, VA; wid PN
ae 67 Wilkes Co,NC, 1841; ch births: John B 4/6/1792, Nancy 12/13/95, Lucy 10/14/98, Mary 1/29/1801, Jeremiah B
7/7/03, Elenor C 11/18/05, William W 7/7/08, & Jane Mahala
9/29/10; wid dd 4/13/65 Wilkes Co, NC, leaving ch: Mary,
Nancy, John B, Lucy w/o John Walker, Elizabeth Saul (h decd), & Jane Haslin (h decd); d Mary, adm/o m's estate 1866
afp due m not recd during Civil War, & claim allowed after
all ch signed oath of allegiance to U S. R706
CUDDY, James, b 6/15/1754 Ireland where worked in iron foundry
before move to America 8/1774; settled York Co, PA, & esf
there 1777 to make cannon, bombs, & cannon balls for Army
at Pine Grove furnace near Carlisle, PA, at Hughes Furnace
in MD & at Hill's works in SC; afp 1835 Washington Co, VA,

CUDDY (continued)
 & PAR, svc not in military unit; dd there 1/9/39; md 1785
 Alcey Dunlap, Stokes Co, NC; wid afp ae 80-90 there 1853,
 & PAR; ch included Jane; QLF states bro James & bro John
 both had RW svc. R707
CUFFEY, Charles, esf 1780 VA; family then w Katy aec 30, 1 s,
 & 1 d aec 12; PN ae 75 Princess Anne Co, VA, 1830, where
 dd 10/1/44; md there (2) 12/1815 Catharine Fuller; wid PN
 there 1857 ae 60; her PN stopped during Civil War & after
 she took oath of allegiance to US, PN restored there 1867
 when she ae 65; surname also spelled CUFFEE. R707
CULLEN, Charles, see CULLIN, Charles. R707
 Daniel, esf 1780 Caroline Co, VA, where b 1761; PN Richmond,
 VA, 1832. R707
CULLENS, John, see CULLINS, John. R707
CULLEY, Armistead, esf 1776 Gloucester Co, VA, where b 1758
 Kingston Parish (area now Mathews Co); PN 1836 Baltimore,
 MD; dd 2/18/39; surname also spelled CULLY. R707
CULLIN, Charles, esf 1777 Caroline Co, VA; PN ae 82 Fayette Co
 KY, occupation cooper; res there 1820 when had w at home &
 all 15 ch grown up & left, youngest being ae 22. R707
CULLINS, John, esf 1778 Caroline Co, VA, where b & raised; PN
 ae 73 Powhatan Co, VA, where res 40 years. R707
 John, esf 1777 Hampshire Co, VA; res 1832 Muskingum Co, OH,
 with s mbnn; PN for disability 1835; dd 9/15/37; md 1783-4
 Jane d/o George Beatty of Hampshire Co, VA; wid afp ae 77
 Muskingum Co, OH, 1839 & PAR, svc less than 6 months; QLF
 1936 from great great great gdd Eula M (Mrs J G) Pittenger
 of Newell, WV. R707
CULTON, Joseph, esf 1780 Montgomery Co, VA, sub for f James; b
 1766 Augusta Co, VA; mvd after RW to SC for 10 years, then
 Garrard Co, KY, thence Knox Co, thence 1811 Floyd Co, KY,
 IN, thence 1821 Morgan Co, IN, where PN 1834; mvd 1842 to
 Jasper Co, MO, with s James; sol sis md Randolph Gibson,
 who res TN 1834; QLF 1940 from great gdd Mrs Hattie Henney
 of Martinsville, IN. R708
CUMMINGS, John, esf 1778 MD; PN ae 60 Ohio Co, VA, 1820 when w
 Araminta ae 59 & s Robert ae 21; QLF 1923 from great great
 gdd Mrs Edna Hill Moore Maholar, Zanesville, OH, d/o Mary
 Adelaid Gratigny Hill who great gdd of sol; QLF 1902 from
 great gdd Mrs A G Hill, Zanesville, OH, states sol dd ae
 96 years, 6 months, & 28 days on 4/28/1852, buried Bealls-
 ville, Monroe Co, OH, further sol former res Wheeling, WV.
 R709
 Joseph, esf 1781 Henry Co, VA; b 2/11/1762 Fauquier Co, VA;
 after RW mvd to Jackson Co, TN, thence 1807 White Co, TN,
 where PN Sparta 1833, res there 1836; QLF states sol dd
 White Co (area now Van Buren Co), TN; QLF 1908 from desc
 Bonnie Jean Cummings, Fresno, CA, states sol dd Van Buren
 Co, TN, 12/8/53; QLF 1935 from desc Elmer Cummings, Wash-
 ington, DC, states sol dd near Sparta, TN, 1853. R710
 Matthew, esf 1780 VA; PN 1818 Mercer Co, KY; PN increase ae

CUMMINGS (continued)
    73 Franklin Co, KY, 1823 when family w, widowed d, s, & an
    orphaned ch mbnn; dd 1839 KY; surname also spelled CUMMINS
    R710
CUMP, Henry, b 1757 Berks Co, PA; esf 1781 Hampshire Co, VA,
    where PN 1834; QLF 1912 states sol dd 1849 & w name possi-
    bly Catherine Swede. R711
CUNDIFF, Isaac, esf 1777 Bedford Co, VA; b 6/12/1759 Prince
    William Co, VA; PN 1833 Bedford Co, VA. R711
    John, b 1759 Lancaster Co, VA; esf 1775 that Co or Northum-
    berland Co, VA; mvd from latter Co after RW to Hampshire
    Co, VA, where PN 1833 when res c44 years; QLF 1939 from
    great gdd Miss Hannah M Cundiff, Ontario, Canada. R711
    John, esf Bedford Co,VA; b 1/14/1757; PN 1832 Hardin Co, KY;
    dd 9/18/37; md 5/15/1778 Sally; wid PN ae 80 Harding Co,
    KY, 1839; ch births: Gimmy 5/9/1779, Dick 12/7/81, John
    11/29/89, Pleasant A 9/18/94, Sally 4/7/97, Nancy 8/28/99,
    Polly 5/16/1803; Pleasant A & Polly res Harding Co, 1839;
    births/o ch/o sol parents Richard & Mary Cundiff: Benjamin
    8/23/1748, George 5/25/51, Nanne 3/30/54, John 1/14/57,
    Elijah 6/10/59, Winne 7/4/62, Charlotte 3/21/64, Joice
    9/18/66, Elisha 6/20/69, & Levice 3/21/72; Elisha Cummins
    AFF 1832 Harding Co,KY, that he res with sol family during
    RW. R711
CUNINGHAM, James, esf 1776 Cravens Co (area later Laurens Dis-
    trict), SC; b 1753 Bedford Co,VA; PN 1832 Laurens District
    SC, 1832; surname also spelled CUNNINGHAM; QLF 1925 from
    desc Mrs W P Blevins, Quitman, GA, states sol dd 12/11/35
    Laurens Co, SC. R711
    James, esf 1778 VA; afb ae 81 Nelson Co,VA, 1828; BLW issued
    11/25/28; surname also spelled CUNNINGHAM. R711
CUNNINGHAM, Ansel/Ansell, esf 1779 Mecklenburg Co, VA, where b
    7/27/1763; mvd after RW to Wilkes Co, GA, thence 1812 to
    Jackson Co, GA, where PN 1832; dd 8/24/40, & wid mbnn gtd
    arrears of his PN; QLF 1914 from W S Crosley, Commander in
    US Navy, states his w desc of sol & of John Cunningham of
    Wilkes Co, GA. R711
    Jacob, esf 1778 Cumberland Co, VA; PN ae 82 Prince Edward Co
    VA, 1832. R711
    James, esf 1776 Augusta Co, VA, where b 3/31/1760; mvd after
    RW to Washington Co, TN, thence McMinn Co, TN, where PN
    1833 when res c4 years; wid Perry L liv 1860. R711
    James, esf 1779 Mecklenburg Co, VA, where PN 1833 ae 69; QLF
    1936 from Mrs Henry Washburn, Rochelle, GA, desc of an RW
    sol John Cunningham, who md 1809 Polly Carleton, Mecklen-
    burg Co, VA, & they mvd to GA. R711
    James, esf 1775 VA; b 1/1756; PN 1833 St Francois Co, MO;
    QLF states sol gds Reece Cunningham res 1915 Farmington,
    MO, & sol buried near there. R711
    John, esf 1776 Lancaster Co, VA; PN ae 76 Rockbridge Co, VA,
    1832; QLF states sol w Anne Lurell dd before him, further
    sol dd c1856. R712

CUNNINGHAM, John, esf 1776 Lunenburg Co,VA, where b 2/10/1748;
     PN 1833 Warren Co, TN; gds John Cunningham Jr res there
     then; QLF 1927 from desc Carleton Brown Cunningham, Chica-
     go, IL. R712
   John, esf 1776 Prince Edward Co, VA; b 1758; PN 1832 St Pat-
     rick's Parish there; dd there 12/7/44; md there 2/8/1785
     Margaret Hill; wid PN ae 79 there 1845; QLF 1925 from Sem-
     ple Davidson (Mrs Andrew Lee) Roberts, Roanoke, VA, states
     she desc/o RW sol William Walker of Charlotte Co, VA, & of
     RW sol Benjamin Sublette of same Co. R712
   Matthew, esf 1778 VA; dd 5/14/1840 Bedford Co, TN; md 1791-2
     Elizabeth, Orange Co, NC; wid afp ae 84 Bedford Co, TN,
     1852, & PAR, proof of marriage; 1st ch b 1793. R712
   Murrell, esf 1777 Cumberland Co, VA, where b 11/15/1759; mvd
     to TN 1800, thence Hickman Co, KY, 1830 where PN 1832; res
     there 1834. R712
   Nathan, esf Mecklenburg Co, VA; dd 12/23/1823; md 1779-80
     Agness, Mecklenburg Co, VA; wid afp ae 89 Rockingham Co,
     NC, 1846, & PAR; eldest ch Sarah decd in 1846. R712
   Nathaniel, esf 1775 Prince Edward Co, VA; PN ae 64 Randolph
     Co, NC, 1818; dd 8/16/32 Putnam Co, IN; md 1790 Elizabeth
     Sneed (MB 9/24/1790 signed by Benjamin Snead), Caswell Co,
     NC; wid PN ae 66 Co, IN, 1838; in 1822 sol & w had s Ben-
     jamin ae 17 & d Lucy ae 12; d Amelia (b 10/1794) res 1843
     Greencastle Township, Putnam Co, IN. R712
   Peter, esf 1779 for svc in PA unit; dd 1808 VA; md 12/6/1786
     Louisa Fulgham, Isle of Wight Co, VA; wid dd 9/16/1846; in
     1849 surv ch Mary Denson, Caroline, & Louisa Wills (ae 55)
     afp Isle of Wight Co, VA, & gtd PN due m. R712
   Samuel, esf 1781 Halifax Co, VA; after RW mvd to Clark Co,
     GA, for 17-18 years, thence Maury Co, TN, where afp 1832
     aec 81, & PAR, svc less than 6 months. R713
   Thomas, b 3/2/1742; esf 1777 Pittsburgh, PA, for svc in VA
     unit; PN 1818 Huntington Township, Brown Co; OH. R713
   Thomas, esf VA; md 4/1776-7 Phebe, Precketts Fort, on Monon-
     galia River; in 1786 when res near bro Edward on Bingamon
     Creek, indians killed sol 4 ch & captured w Phebe who ran-
     somed & later had more ch; sol dd 6/2/1826; wid PN ae 79
     Lewis Co, VA, 1839 when AFF by her sis Mary Ann McKinney
     (b 10/1765) of Wood Co, VA; QLF states sol b Ireland 1761,
     md Phebe Tucker, & esf Culpeper Co, VA. R713
   Valentine, esf 1778 VA; PN ae over 65 Roane Co, TN, 1820 fa-
     mily then "present wife" Frances ae 36 + her ch by 1st h
     West Lahon (Hugh ae 16, William ae 12, & David ae 10) + s
     Martin aec 1 (sol s by Frances) + Rhoda his d by former w;
     sol dd 10/17/32; QLF states sol & w Mary La Prade were pa-
     rents of Alexander, who War of 1812 sol (enlisted ae 16) &
     who dd IN, md Nancy Archibald who PN IN. R713
   Walter, esf 1776 Shenandoah Co, VA, where b 12/1749; mvd af-
     ter RW to Harrison Co, VA, where PN 1832 Simpson Creek;
     bro Adam liv 1832. R713
   William, esf 1780 Shenandoah Co, VA, where b 7/23/1764 s/o

CUNNINGHAM (continued)
    John; mvd 1794 to Harrison Co, VA; PN 1832 Wood Co, VA;
    res 1855 Ritchie Co, VA. R713
    William, esf VA; md 1770 Susan Wood who dd 5/4/1828 Washing-
    ton Co, VA; sol dd there 11/13/1833, leaving ch John, Ann
    w/o John Hutton, Elizabeth w/o John Dickenson, Thomas,
    William, James, Samuel, Joseph, & Margaret Clark; s Thomas
    afp ae 76 there 1853 for PN due sol surv ch, & PAR, speci-
    fic period of svc not furnished. R713
    William, esf VA; BLW issued 3/22/1796; mvd after RW to NC,
    thence Smith Co, TN, where dd 1806-7; surv ch Betsey Ann
    w/o Philip Maury, Nancy w/o Richard Alexander, Polly, Su-
    sanna R (Cunningham) Hamilton, James, & Lucy B w/o Samuel
    P Howard afp 1832 Smith Co, TN, & PAR per current PN laws.
    R713
    William, VA sea svc; dd 1794; William E Cunningham, afp 1852
    as adm/o sailor's estate; afp later withdrawn before acted
    upon. R713
CUPP, Leonard, esf 1775 Northampton Co, VA, where b 1/17/1755;
    res there after RW, thence Berkeley Co, VA, thence Bedford
    Co, PA, thence Monongalia Co, VA,for 30 years, thence Pre-
    ston Co, VA, where PN 1833; dd there 8/17/34; md 6/21/1772
    Susannah, Northampton Co, VA; wid PN ae 83 Preston Co, VA,
    1838, & dd 4/3/41; AFF there 1853 by s John that he, Leon-
    ard, Christopher, Susannah Johnson, & William surv ch of
    sol & Susannah; s Leonard ae 78 there 1835, 3rd ch of sol;
    ages/o sol ch 1854: Leonard Jr 79, Susanna 74, Christopher
    76, John 70, & William 55; sol eldest ch dd infancy, & 2nd
    ch Conrad dd c1805. R714
CUPPY, John, b 3/11/1761 near Morristown, NJ; mvd with family
    as infant to near Romney, Hampshire Co, VA; esf there 1777
    or 1778 for RW svc; esf there 1790 for Indian War svc (for
    which BLW gtd); mvd aec 40 to Brooke Co, VA, thence Law-
    renceburg, IN, c1824, thence 1836 Wayne Township, Montgom-
    ery Co, OH, where apf 1844 & 1850, & PAR, RW svc less than
    6 months; dd there 1861; md (1) 1778-9 ?, & (2) 10/7/1824
    Lydia Russell; wid afp ae 85 there 1882 & PAR, ch then:
    Henry (res there), John (res Washington Co, NE), & Fletch-
    er P (res Washington,DC); sol d Ann Moore (aec 10 in 1790)
    AFF 1851 Tippecanoe Co, IN; QLF 1933 from desc Eugene A
    Riggs, Terre Haute,IN, who also desc/o RW sol Stephen Taft
    of Uxbridge, MA, of Stephen's s (RW sol of Albany Co, NY),
    & of Civil War sol William Taft of Sullivan Co, IN, also
    querier desc/o RW sol John Shelburne of Hanover Co, VA, of
    RW sol John Ingle of Kent Co,MD, & of War of 1812 sol Har-
    dy Hill of Nelson Co, KY. R714
CURD, John, esf 1778 Goochland Co,VA; b 9/16/1760; PN 1818 Lo-
    gan Co, KY; dd 9/10/38; md 7/10/1787 Nancy W Curd, Gooch-
    land Co, VA, who b 7/11/1762; wid PN 1839 Warren Co, KY, &
    res Bowling Green, that Co, with s Richard 1843; in 1826
    sol family included d Fanny ae 21, s William, & gds Rich-
    ard H Slaughter aec 4, both parents decd; QLF 1912 from

CURD (continued)
 desc Mrs H C Blackburn, Georgetown, KY, states sol d Polly
 md Spencer Curd, & they had d Elizabeth who md Nimrod Long
 & they had s Spencer Curd Long who md Cornelia Gano, they
 parents of querier Cornelia "Nellie" Long. R714
CURLE, Jacob, esf 1778 VA; bro/o Richard & John; sol & Richard
 dd intestate & unmarried before 1784; John dd leaving ch:
 Richardson/Richeson & Sally w/o John Hockaday; heir-at-law
 Richeson Curle afb Lynchburg, VA, 1834 on behalf of self &
 ch/o Sally Hockaday decd (William, Alexander, Judith, Elizabeth, & Robert, all minors), & BLW gtd; John Hockaday
 appointed guardian/o his ch for interest in BLW. R714
 Richard, esf 1778 VA; bro/o Jacob above; same afb as above,
 1834 & same heirs; BLW gtd. R714
CURRANCE, William, see CARRANCE, William. R714
CURRELL, James, VA sea svc; dd intestate Lancaster Co, VA,
 leaving s Isaac only heir-at-law; Isaac dd intestate there
 1810 leaving ch: James, Isaac, Alice, Polly, & Betsy, with
 all but James afp 1845 there & PAR. R714
CURRY, James, esf 1777 VA; PN 1818 Madison Co, OH, with res
 Franklin Co, OH; res 1828 ae 75 Union Co, OH; QLF states a
 Colonel James Curry, VA RW sol, b 1752, mvd 1800 to Highland Co, OH, thence Union Co, OH, where dd 1834. R716
 James, esf 1779-80 VA; dd 2/11/1828; md 2/25/1778 Ann Curry,
 Rockingham Co, VA; ch births: John 11/1782, James 2/26/84,
 Robert 1/7/86, Samuel 3/27/88 (other birth data torn, fa-
 ded, & unreadable); eldest ch b VA & dd aec 3; wid PN ae
 82 (blind) Mercer Co, KY, 1837; wid had 5 bro's in RW svc;
 her bro William KIA at Battle of the Point, & her bro Sa-
 muel KIA at Kings Mountain; d Nancy Brewer AFF Mercer Co,
 KY, that m dd 2/11/38, & afp arrears due m. R716
 Rachel, former wid/o RW sol James Halks. R716
 Thomas, esf 1779 Loudoun Co, VA; b 1762 Chesterfield Co, VA;
 after RW mvd to Amherst Co, VA, thence 1811 to Franklin Co
 IN, where PN 1833 res Posey Township; served in RW with a
 John Curry, no relationship given; QLF 1923 from Char-
 lotte Lafferty, Decatur, IL, desc of RW sol Thomas Currie
 b Ireland 1763, came to America 1777, esf VA, res Leesburg
 VA, thence IN where dd 1847 & buried Ebenezer, Franklin Co
 IN, md Miss Gordon. R716
 Torrence, esf VA; afp 1828 Sparta, Dearborn Co, IN, & PAR,
 insufficient proof/o svc. R716
CURTIS, Bowlin, esf VA; dd Fall 1808 near Yadkin River, Rowan
 Co, NC; bro Wyly KIA Battle of Brandywine; per wid AFF sol
 md Fall 1787-8 Mary Lee, Rockingham Co, VA; MB 11/10/1789
 per certificate of that Co Clerk; wid PN ae 73 Washington
 Co, TN, 1844; afb 1846 Carter Co, TN, by ch John, Nathan,
 William, & Mary (Curtis) Vest; John & Mary then res there;
 Nathan & William then res Washington Co, TN. R717
 James, esf 1775 King William Co, VA; b 3/4/1748; afp 1819
 Lincoln Co, TN; PN 1822 Lawrence Co, TN, when family d Ma-
 ry ae 20 & d Leticia ae 16; occupation shoemaker. R718

CURTIS, Jesse, afp Lewis Co, VA, 1832 & PAR, too young to have
    had RW svc. R718
  John, esf Dinwiddie Co,VA; b 1759-60 there or Sussex Co, VA;
    f dd when sol ch & m dd during RW; bro's & sis's mbnn; mvd
    after RW to Orange Co,NC, where res c20 years, thence Sum-
    ner Co, TN, for 2 years, thence Giles Co, TN, for 2 years,
    thence back to Sumner Co, TN, for 2 years, thence White Co
    TN, for c15 years, thence Bledsoe Co, TN, where PN 1833
    ae 74 when res over 8 years; dd 8/7/44; md 10/1793 Dolly
    Honeycutt, Chatham Co, NC; eldest ch b 1796; wid afp ae 78
    McMinn Co, TN, & PAR, no proof of marriage. R719
  Jonathan, b 1747 Frederick Co, VA; esf 1776 Burke Co, NC, &
    PN there 1832. R719
  Michael, esf 1780 MD; BLW issued 12/22/1798; PN ae 56 Fair-
    fax Co, VA, 1818, occupation carpenter, w decd & ch by her
    also decd. R719
  Richard, esf 1778 Beauford Co, NC, 1778; esf 1779 Craven Co,
    NC; esf 1780 Duplin Co, NC; b 3/1/1755 Snow Hill c14 miles
    from Richmond, VA; res after RW Orange Co,NC, thence Samp-
    son Co, NC, thence Guilford Co, NC, thence New Hanover Co,
    NC, where afp 1836 & 1837, illiterate; afp 1851 by s James
    there for himself & sol other surv ch: Charles H, Richard,
    Nancy Riley, & Sally Auboine; all PAR, insufficient proof
    of svc. R719
  Russel, Curtis, esf 1779 Montgomery Co, NC; b 1/6/1757 Fre-
    dericksburg, VA; PN 1832 Trigg Co, KY. R720
  William, esf 1777 Northumberland Co, VA; PN ae 63 New York
    City, NY, 1818, occupation tailor; family 1820 d Elizabeth
    ae 18. R720
CURTNER, Anthony, see Courtner, Anthony. R722
CUSHMAN, Isaac, b 1752 Essex Co,NJ; esf 1775 Wharton Township,
    Fayette Co, PA, for PA svc, where PN 1833; QLF 1939 from
    Alvah W Burt, Cincinnati,OH, states an RW sol Thomas Cush-
    man, b CT, mvd to NJ, thence Monongalia Co, VA, md Mary, d
    of Ephraim Frazee by 1st w, further Ephraim Frazee had d
    Deborah by 3rd w, that d md RW sol Isaac Cushman, further
    querier desc of Robert Cushman who possibly bro of Thomas
    since they md halfsisters; QLF 1936 from desc Dayse W (Mrs
    David Milton) Proctor, Kansas City,MO; QLF 1937 from great
    gdd Mrs J L Shroyer, Lake Park, IA, states sol prob son/o
    Thomas; QLF 1928 from desc Mrs Lenore C Jones, West Lafay-
    ette, IN. R723
CUSTAR, William, esf 1774 Greenbrier Co, VA; esf 1788 against
    indians; mvd to Mad River west/o Urbana, OH, thence Cham-
    paign Co, OH, thence 1825 Miami Co, OH; dd 2/28/1828; md
    1785 Anna Smith, Mason Co, KY; wid afp ae 82 Delaware Co,
    IN, 1851, & PAR, insufficient proof/o svc. R725
CUSTARD, Jacob, esf 1775 Rockingham Co, VA; later hired sub,
    since w seriously ill; b 2/1750; PN 1832 Jackson Township,
    Perry Co, OH; dd 8/17/33; QLF 1921 from great gdd Mary H
    Scarlett, Pocatello, ID, states sol dd 8/17/1838. R725
  Richard, b 6/1/1757 PA; mvd ae 5 with parents to Rockingham

CUSTARD (continued)
Co, VA, where sol esf 1781; PN there 1832; dd 2/14/37; per
wid AFF md 3/18/1790 Jane, d/o Conrad Humble, Rockingham
Co, VA; per that Co Clerk certificate MB 3/14/88 signed by
Conrad Humble; wid PN ae 70 there 1841; QLF 1937 from desc
Milo Custer, Bloomington, IL. R725
CUSTER, William, see CUSTAR, William. R725
CUTRIGHT, John, b 8/1754 near Moorefield, Hampshire Co,VA; esf
Buckhannon Settlement, Lewis Co, VA, where PN 1832; dd
3/8/50; md 1/2/1788 Rebecca Truby, Harrison Co, VA; wid PN
ae 87 Lewis Co, VA, 1851; wid gtd BLW 1855 res Upshur Co,
VA; QLF states sol res 1840 Lewis Co, VA, with Christopher
Cartwright; QLF states wid rec PN until 1860. R726
  Peter, esf 1780 Hampshire Co,VA, where b 1759; PN 1833 Macon
  Co, IL, having just recently mvd there from Sangamon Co,
  IL; QLF states sol res 1840 Dewitt Co, IL, with s Samuel.
  R726
CUTTING, John Browne; esf as apothecary before 1780; res Staf-
ford Co, VA, 1816 when transferred his BLW to Anna Angeli-
que, w/o bro Nathaniel of Washington, DC; PN 1828 Washing-
ton, DC. R727
CUTTS, William, esf 1779 Chesterfield Co, VA; b 3/15/1760 or
3/15/1763; PN 1833 Grainger Co, TN; mvd 1838 to Hamilton
Co, IN, to res with s; dd there 7/28/49; md m/o John Mul-
lins when returned home from RW; md (2) 4/6/1843 Elizabeth
Bentley/Bently, Hamilton Co, IN, who had 1 ch William by
sol; wid PN ae 39 there 1858 when s William aec 14; sol ch
by former marriage: Robert, Paschall & Mrs Elizabeth James
R727
CYPHERS, Andrew, BLW issued 3/4/1796. R727
CYPRESS, Andrew, see CYPRUS, Andrew, below. R727
CYPRUS, Andrew, esf 1775 Frederick Co, VA; PN ae 63 Madison Co
OH, 1818, where dd 10/16/47; md 8/20/1801 Hannah Marrl/
Marrle, Frederick Co, VA; wid PN ae 73 Franklin Co, OH,
1853; ch 2/21/1827: Rebecca ae 17, d Julian ae 11, George
ae 9, Jacob ae 8, Maria ae 6, Lawrence Washington ae 3, &
Michael ae 1 month; Jacob & Emily Sifritt res 1853 Frank-
lin Co, OH, their relationship to each other & to sol not
given; sol surname also spelled CYPHERS, CYPRESS, SYFRITT,
& SIFRITT; QLF 1937 from great gds L J Grafton, Philadel-
phia, PA. R727
CYRE, Nicholas, esf 1778-9 Chesterfield Co, VA, where b; PN ae
73-74 Campbell Co, VA; dd 11/17/1836; md 5/1/1819 Mrs Jane
(Cocke) Davidson, Campbell Co, VA; wid md (1) 2/1779 James
Davidson Jr (MB 2/6/1779 signed by James Davidson Sr),
Campbell Co, VA; James Davidson Jr RW sol from Bedford Co,
VA, who dd 1818 Campbell Co, VA; Polly Turner d/o wid AFF
Lynchburg, VA, 1847 that m dd 10/19/46. R727
CYRUS, Bartholomew, esf 1777 Chesterfield Co, VA; PN aec 60
Buckingham Co,VA, 1818; w Sally & Sally Tretwell aec 9 res
with him there 1820; md (2) 1/2/33 Mrs Phebe Gallaway (li-
cense same date), Campbell Co, VA; dd 7/11/55; wid PN ae

CYRUS (continued)
    61 Appomattox Co, VA, 1855; PN stopped during Civil War, &
    restored 1866; wid gtd BLW there 1879, dd there 2/28/1883
    ae 92. R727

::

End of Volume 1. Volume 2 will start with DABBS, John, Reel #
728

This index lists women with their married names and their maiden names, when known, and men who are not the subject of an entry. Children are also included.

ALBERT, Abiah 23 Abraham 6 Ca-
tharine 6 Eliza 65 Mary 62
ALDAY, Sarah 6
ALDER, Elizabeth 6 George 6
James 6 John 6 Lucy 6 Marcus
6 Mary 6 Nancy 6 Sary 6
ALDRIDGE, Barr 7 Darlington 7
Delilah 6 7 Eliza 6 7 Eliza-
beth 6 7 Erasmus 6 7 Henry 7
Jason 7 John 6 7 Joseph 6 7
Lucinda 7 Mary 6 77 Mehale 7
Nackly 7 Nathan 6 Philander
7 Polly 7 Rachel 6 Runzy 6
Ruhamar 7 Sarah 6 William 7
ALEXANDER, Abigail 7 Benjamin
7 Betsey 7 David 7 Easter 7
Ebenezer 8 Elias 8 Elizabeth
8 230 Esther 8 George 7 8
James 7 Jannett 7 John 7 Jo-
seph 8 Lydia 7 Luticia 7
Margaret 8 Martha 7 Mary 8
Nancy 276 Nelson 7 Polly 7
Rebecca 259 Richard 276 Sal-
ly 7 Sarah 7 Washington 7
William 71 8 127 Willis 7
ALFORD, Charles 8 Elizabeth 90
Jesse 8 John 8 Lucy 8 Mary 8
Nancy 8 Stephen 8 William 8
ALFRED, Elizabeth 8 Susan 8
ALGOOD, Sarah 8
ALISON, Martha 122
ALL, Mary 210
ALLAN, Archibald 8 Elizabeth 8
Eve 8 Mary 8
ALLBRITTON, John 9 Mary 9
ALLDER, Lucy 6
ALLEN, Achilles 10 Adaline 10
Allen 10 Anderson 11 Andrew
11 Ann 10,199 Apphia 9 Ar-
cher 10 Archie 11 Barbary 11
Bill 10 Catharine 9 Charles
10 11 101 David 11 Drucilla
11 Eliel 11 Elizabeth 9 10
11 Esther 11 F M 229 Fanny
11 Frances 9 11 12 George 10
11 Isham 10 James 10 11 Jane
10 Jeremiah 11 John 10 11
Julius 10 Kissey 11 Lewis 10
Lilly 10 Lucy 10 31 Margaret
11 Martha 10 Matthew 11 Mary
10 163 May 229 Molly 11 Nancy 10 Patsey 11 Phebe 9 Pol-

ALLEN (continued)
ly 10 11 Priscilla 11 Rachel
11 148 Robert 9 11 Sarah 10
11 159 Sims 10 Stanley 11
Susannah 9 Thomas 10 V Hale
11 Vincent 12 W B 144 William 10 12 35
ALLEY, Azby 12 Betsey 12 Catherine 12 Charity 12 Creecy
12 Cyrus 12 David 12 Dood-
ridge 12 Doshea 12 Elihu 12
Fanny 12 Hamlin 12 James 12
Jane 12 Jonathan 12 Joseph
12 Joyce 12 Joyday 12 Lanzel
12 Leah 12 Mary 12 199 Mas-
sey 12 Maud 12 Miles 12 Nan-
cy 12 Sally 12 Sampson 12
Samuel 12 Solomon 12 Thomas
100 Thursey 12 William 12
Wilson 159
ALLFRIEND, Casandra 25
ALLGOOD, Ishmael 122 Seleta 13
ALLHUE, Elizabeth 89
ALLIN, Ben 13 Charles 13 Grant
13 John 13 Mary 13 Nancy 13
Philip 13 Thomas 13
ALLISON, Archibald 13 Ganatt
156 Gennett 156 James 13
John 13 Nancy 13 Posey 13
Rebecca 13 Robert 13 William
13
ALLOWAYS, Anna 33
ALLPHIN, Ransom 13
ALLY, Mary 199 Thomas 199
ALMOND, Catharine 13 Clemen-
tine 13 Katy 14 Kelley 14
Lizza 13 Susanna 13 William
13
ALMY, Abigail 14 Gideon 14 Sa-
rah 14
ALSOP, Elizabeth 14 173 Eloisa
173 Emily 173 George 173
James 173 Judith 173 Mary
173 Sarah 14 Sary 173 Spen-
cer 173
ALTIZER, Mary 14
ALVERSON, Edward 14 Elender 14
Frances 14 John 14 Mary 14
Moses 14 Nancy 14 Nina 14
Polly 14 Sabitha 14 William
14 Wina 14 Winney 14 Zacha-
riah 14

ALVEY, Fanny 14 Frances 14 Susan 14
ALVIS, Betsy 14 David 15 Elizabeth 14 Jane 14 Nancy 14 Polly 14 Shadrach 14
ALVORD, Miranda 204
AMBROSE, Florence 165 Ida 165 Isabelle 165 Luther 164 Nellie 165
AMBER, Eliza 169 Elizabeth 169 Jaquelin 169 Lucy 169
AMBURN, Clifford 15 Jacob 15
AMES, Richard 187 Susan 187
AMMONETTE, John 15 Phoebe 15 Thomas 15
AMYX, Andrew 15
ANCELL, Mary 204
ANDERSON, Ailse 31 Alexander 18 Ann 17 Armistead 18 Audley 18 Bayles 17 Baly 31 Berimien 17 C M 56 Catherine 16,17,18 Cecelia 18 Charlotte 16 31 Christina 17 Clarissa 16 Daniel 18 Drucilla 31 Edward 18 Eliza 31 Elizabeth 17 18 19 276 Frances 16 Geny 18 George 16 17 Henry 17 18 Herbert 18 Isaac 17 18 James 16 19 Zane 18 74 Jeny 18 Jeruth 16 Joannah 19 Johannah 19 John 16 19 223 Joseph 18 Juliann 73 Kate 56 Lawrence 19 Lucy 16 Margaret 17 18 73 Mariana 18 Martha 3 19 Mary 16 17 18 19 Mathew 19 Merium 17 Milly 18 Molly 19 Nancy 17 19 31 120 Patsy 3 Peggy 17 Polly 17 31 Rachael 18 Rebecca 18 19 259 Richard 16 18 Robert 17 18 19 31 120 Rosanna 18 Sally 17 18 19 Samuel 19 Sarah 17 18 19 Sary 31 Susan 17 19 223 Susannah 223 Thomas 16 18 William 16 17 18 19 73
ANDRES Anna 105 106 E J 105
ANDREWS, Abraham 20 Ann 20 Andrew 19 Benjamin 19 Betsy 20 Catherine 20 Daniel 19 20 Easter 242 Elizabeth 19 20 Elkanah 19 20 Fanny 20 George 20 Hannah 20 James

ANDREWS (continued) 206 John 20 Joseph 20 Margaret 20 Margrit 20 Mark 20 Martha 20 Mary 20 Masey 19 Nancy 20 Nanny 19 Nely 20 Perley 20 Polly 20 Rachel 20 Rebecca 20 Richard 19 Robert 19 20 Salley 20 Samuel 19 Simeon 203 Simon 19 203 Tabitha 20 Thomas 20 William 20
ANGLEA, Drucilla 87 Scilly 82
ANGLING, Elizabeth 21
ANNIS, Peggy 21
ANSBAUGH, M 107
ANTILL Dorcas 21 John 21
APPERSON, Alcey 21 Alice 21 Alsey 21 Charles 21 Elbert 21 Francis 21 Homer 35 Jane 75 John 21 Polly 75 Reuben 21 Richard 21 Stephen 21 William 21
APPLEGATE, Elsie 21 Irwin 21 Leslie 227
APPLEWHAITE, Judith 21
ARBUCKLE, Ann 267 David 22 Edward 267 George 267 James 22 John 22 Mathew 21 William 22
ARCHER, Ann 22 Anna 22 Edward 22 Elizabeth 22 Frances 22 Jesse 22 John 22 Joseph 22 Martha 22 Mary 22 Mattie 22 William 22
ARCHIBALD, Nancy 275
ARGABRIGHT, Christina 23
ARGUBRIGHT, John 23 Abram 23
ARMAN, Charity 23 Elizabeth 23 Harry 23 Henry 23 Mary 23 Nancy 23 Thomas 23
ARMISTEAD, Abiah 23 Ann 23 Catherine 23 Elizabeth 23 132 Francis 132 Isaac 23 Jane 23 John 23 Juliann 23 Martha 23 Susan 23 Thaddeus 23
ARMONTROUT, Christiana 24 Christena 24
ARMSTEAD, Mary 33 Thaddeus 33
ARMSTRONG, A L 25 Amanda 24 Anaren 24 Andrew 24 Ann 25 Armistead 14 Byron 25 C C 25 Catharine 24 Elizabeth 24 Frances 121 Frank 24 George 24 H C 24 Hal 77 Hugh 24

ARMSTRONG (continued)
James 24 267 John 24 Joseph
25 Kitty 24 Langdon 24 25
Lucy 25 Mahala 24 Mary 24
Nancy 24 P H 24 Patsy 24
Purkins 25 Pyle 24 R G 24
Rebecca 24 Sarah 25 Susanna
24 Thomas 24 Will 25 William
24
ARNOLD, Andrew 26 Ann 26 An-
thony 26 Benjamin 25 Calberd
26 Dolly 269 Doratha 269 Dot
26 Edna 171 204 Elisha 25
Elizabeth 25 26 Harvey 26
Hayes 26 Hendrick 25 James
25 John 26 Lewis 26 Lucinda
26 Lucy 26 Martha 25 Mary 26
Molly 145 Nancy 26 Peter 25
Sally 25 26 Susan 26 Temper-
ance 26 Thomas 26 William 25
26
ARRINGTON, Susannah 27 William
27
ARTHUR, Ambrose 28 Betsy 94
Caleb 27 Cora 27 Dosia 27
Elizabeth 27 28 Emley 28
Henry 28 John 27 Larkin 27
Lilly 27 Lydia 27 Melindall
28 Melley 35 Mildred 35 Milley 35 Rachel 27 Sally 27 28
Sarah 28 Susan 28 Thomas 27
28 Willis 27 Winnifred 27
ARTIS, Chloe 28
ARUNDALL, Ann 28 Charles 28
Elizabeth 28 Jemima 28 Mary
28 Nancy 28 Peter 28 Polly
28
ASBERRY, Benjamin 28 Caleb 28
Elizabeth 28 Susan 28
ASBURY, Coleman 28 Mary 28
ASH, Anna 123 Betsy 28 Carol-
line 97 Curtis 97 Elizabeth
28 Lydia 97 Moses 97 Thomas
97
ASHBURN, Suckey 29, Susan 29
ASHBY, Absolom 29 Ann 29 Cindrella 29 Daniel 29 Elizabeth
29 Emily 29 Enos 29 Frances
29 Hannah 29 Henry 29 Hester
29 Huldah 29 James 29 Jesse
29 John 29 Lewis 29 Mary 29
Nancy 29 Peter 29 Presley 29

ASHBY (continued)
Rebecca 29 Rice 29 Rosy 29
Sarah 29 Stephen 29 Tabitha
29 Vincent 29 William 29
Wilson 29 Winnifred 29
ASHCRAFT, Uriah 30
ASHCROFT, Eleanor 30, Eliza-
beth 30 Emelia 30 Hannah 30
Isaac 30 Jadiah 30 James 30
Jediah 30 John 30 Lewiza 30
Luizean 30 Melia 30 Sally 30
Sarah 30
ASHER, Bartlett 30 Catharine
30 Daniel 30 Edmund 30 Jane
30 John 30 Levi 30 Levia 30
Linn 30 Margaret 30 Nancy 30
Thomas 30 William 30
ASHERST, Mary 30 Polly 30
ASHLEY, Andy 23 Callaway 23
Charles 23 Cinsy 23 Eliza-
beth 23 Mary 23 Milly 30 Mo-
ses 23 Peter 29 30 Susanna
23 Thomas 23
ASHLOCK, George 31 Josiah 31
Margaret 31 Philip 31 Sallie
31 Sarah 31 William 31
ASHWORTH, Elizabeth 31 Milly
31
ASKEY, Morton 245
ASRE, Joseph 31
ASSELIN, Edith 216
ATCHLEY, Benjamin 32 Easther
32 Elizabeth 32 George 32
Hannah 32 Isaac 32 James 32
Jean 32 John 32 Joshua 32
Liddy 32 Lydia 32 Mary 32
Nanna 32 Noah 32 Rhoda 32
Sarah 32 Thomas 32 William
32
ATHEY, Jonathan 32
ATHY, Martha 32
ATKINS, Joseph 32 Martha 25
Mary 203 Moses 201
ATKINSON, Anna 33 John 33 Mar-
garet 33 Mary 33 Nancy 33 83
Polley 37 Sally 33 Samuel 33
ATKISON, Littleton 33
ATWOOD, Mary 8
AUBOINE, Sally 278
AUSTIN, Anne 33 Daniel 34 Eli-
zabeth 34 Grace 147 John 34
Lucy 34 Nancy 34 Polly 34

AUSTIN (continued)
Stephen 33 William 33
AUXER, Andrew 34 Daniel 34
Enoch 34 Frances 34 John 34
Lyda 34 Mary 34 Nancy 34 Na-
thaniel 34 Samuel 34 Sarah
34
AVERY, May 208
AVIS, Martha 34
AWBRY, Craven 34 Margaret 34
AYERS, Mary 34
AYRES, Affey 35 Ann 35 Cassa-
mara 35 Daniel 35 Elizabeth
35 Elkanah 35 Jane 35 John
35 Kitty 35 Lemuel 35 Lucy
35 Lydia 35 Magdalene 35
Martha 35 Nancy 35 Nellie 35
Olive 35 Patsey 35 Susan 35
Susannah 35
AZBILL, W K 63
BABB, Err 35 Ezz 35 Hiram 35
Huldah 35 Mary 35 Nancy 35
Rachel 35 Rhody 35 Ruth 35
Seth 35
BABER, Anna 35 Barnabas 35
George 35 Hannah 35 Jane 35
John 35 Melley 35 Mildred 35
Milley 35 Rachel 35 Robert
35 Sally 35 William 35
BACK, John 34 Jacob 34
BACON, Edmund 10 Elizabeth 10
Washington 36 William 10
BAGBY, Charles 36 Elvira 36
James 36 Landon 36 Matilda
36 Nancy 36 R E 36 Richard
36 Roderick 36 Theodocia 36
William 36
BAGGS, Susannah 36
BAGWELL, Ann 267 Augustus 267
Charles 267
BAHR, Johannes 51
BAILEY, A A 37 Abigail 14 Anna
37 Anne 201 Anselm 37 Benja-
min 37 Betsey 37 38 39 Beth-
iah 64 Betty 38 Blane 37
Callum 38 Charles 38 Edmon
37 Eliza 39 Elizabeth 38
Francis 13 Hannah 37 Hetty
37 Hiram 37 Isaac 14 Isham
37 James 38 39 Jane 37 Jean
177 John 37 38 39 99 Jona-
than 38 Joseph 38 Juliana 37

BAILEY (continued)
Julina 37 Katy 38 Lehigh 37
Lewis 39 Lucinda 38 39 Mar-
garet 38 39 Marina 38 Martha
37 38 39 Mary 37 39 Nancy 38
39 89 Parmelia 76 Patsey 37
Peter 38 Phebe 64 Polley 37
Polly 37 Rebecca 37 106 Reu-
ben 38 Salley 38 Sally 38 39
Saluda 38 Samuel 38 39 Sarah
14 38 Susan 38 Susanna 37
Susannah 37 Terry 37 Thomas
37 Tomlin 201 Walter 38 Wil-
liam 37 38 39 Willis 38 Win-
ny 37 Winston 37 Wyuatt 38
BAILES, Sarah 36
BAILY, Ann 39 Elizabeth 39 Judy 39
BAIN, Margaret 52
BAINS, Mary 217
BAIRD, Amanda 39 Amelia 39 Anna 39 Ann 39 Archibald 39
Charles 39 Elizabeth 39 Jane
39 Joseph 39 Martha 39 Mary
39 Richard 39 Thomas 39
BAITH, Susanna 39
BAKER, Abraham 40 Ann 40 234
Anna 40 41 Armisted 41 Betsy
40 Catarina 41 Christina 41
Daniel 41 Dorothy 40 Eliza
41 Elizabeth 40 41 Frances
41 HC 41 Hanna 86 Henrich 41
Isaac 41 Jacob 41 James 40
Joseph 41 John 40 86 227 Ju-
liana 41 Mary 40 118 Michael
40 Ned 41 Philip 40 41 Paul-
ine 41 Rebecca 41 Robert 40
41 Rosa 41 Sarah 40 41 Susan
40 41 Susanna 40 227 Will-
helm 41 William 40 41
BAKES, Robert 105
BALDWIN, Agness 41 Augustus
218 Louisa 218 Rebecca 218
W H 41 William 218
BALL, Abraham 42 Catharine 228
Catrine 42 Elizabeth 42 Hen-
ry 42 Isaac 42 Jacob 42
James 42 John 42 Margaret 42
Mary 42 Samuel 42 Sarah 42
Susannah 42
BALLARD, A J 42 Belinda 43
Bland 42 Burnett 43 Catha-

BALLARD (continued)
rine 43 Elizabeth 42 Harris
43 James 43 John 43 Mary 43
Susanna 43 Thomas 43 190
William 43
BALLENGER, Nancy 103
BALLEW, Peter 44 Robert 44
BALLOW, America 44 Elizabeth
44
BALMAIN, Lucy 44
BALSEY, Anna 44 Christian 44
Elizabeth 44 George 44 Jo-
hannes 44 Jonathan 44
BALTHROP, Holly 44
BANDY, Cary 44 Elihu 44 Eliza-
beth 44 Horasha 44 James 44
Martha 44 Nancy 44 Polly 44
Richard 44 Robert 44 Thomas
44
BANE, Anne 45 Bythinia 45 Eli-
zabeth 45 Ellis 45 Henry 45
Jesse 45 Mordecai 45 R S 59
60 W C 262
BANES, Ellsworth 45 Sarah 45
Susannah 45
BANKS, Almirium 45 Daniel 45
Elizabeth 45 Emily 45 Fran-
ces 45 John 45 Joseph 45
Louisa 45 Mary 45 Nancy 45
Polly 45 Ruth 45 Salley 45
Thomas 45 Wesley 45 William
45
BANOW, Daniel 52
BARBEE, Ann 46 Daniel 46 Eze-
kiel 46 James 46 Joseph 46
Martha 46 Mary 46 Rose 46
Samuel 46 William 46
BARBER, Charles 132 Mary 46
BARBEY, Benjamin 46 Joseph 46
Nancy 46 Salley 46 William
46
BARBOUR, J S 46 Maria 46
BARDIN, Donna 245 J Carter 144
245
BARETH, Elizabeth 46
BARGER, Mary 17 Mary 17
BARKER, Anna 47 B L 47 Betsey
47 Edmund 42 Edward 47 Eli-
zabeth 47 138 Ellzey 47 El-
sey 47 Emily 138 Enoch 47
Frances 47 Ira 138 Irby 47
Jemima 47 Joel 47 John 47

BARKER (continued)
Leady 47 Letitia 47 Letty 47
Lucy 47 Mary 47 Medda 47
Penny 47 Polly 47 Sally 47
138 Susanna 47 Tazewell 138
Thomas 47 Vesta 47 William
47
BARKSDALE, Anna 47 Claiborne
47 Cynthia 47 Jemimia 48 Ju-
dith 47 Lucy 139 Molly 47
Patty 47 Richard 47 William
47 Unity 47
BARLOW, Barbara 48 Bluford 48
Catherine 48 Elizabeth 48
George 48 Jerusha 48 Judah
48 William 48
BARNARD, Abner 48 John 48 Phe-
be 186
BARNES, Ann 48 Armistead 49
Benjamin 68 Betsey 49 Cary
270 Charles 48 James 49 John
48 Margaret 258 Martha 48
Mary 48 49 Minna 68 Nancey
49 Nathaniel 48 Oren 48
Pleasant 48 Robert 48 Sally
49 Samuel 49 Stewart 48 Su-
sanna 49 William 48 49
BARNET, Ellender 124
BARNETT, Artax 50 Betsey 50
Daniel 50 Elizabeth 50 Esth-
er 50 George 50 Hannah 50
James 49 50 Jane 161 John 49
50 Jonathan 50 Judith 49
Louis 49 Louisa 50 Lucy 50
Marcey 49 Mary 130 Maryan 49
Massy 49 Robert 49 Sally 49
Sary 49 Spencer 50 Susannah
49 Thomas 50 William 49 Za-
dock 130
BARR, Alfred 29 Ann 51 Byram
50 Daniel 51 David 51 Eliza-
beth 51 George 50 51 Hugh 50
James 50 John 50 Joshua 51
Mary 51 Michael 50 Patsy 51
Polly 50 Rachel 51 Robert 51
Stapleton 51 W F 51 William
51
BARRET, John 51
BARRETT, Amy 51 Judith 51 Mary
51 52
BARRON, Ann 52 Mary 52 Susan-
nah 52

BARROTT, Jabez 52 John 52 Sa-
rah 52
BARROW, Aaron 53 Charles 52
David 52 Elizabeth 52 Hanna
52 Isaac 52 John 52 Martha
52 Mary 52 Moses 52 Nancy 52
Nathan 52 R W 52 Rebecca 52
Salley 52 Samuel 52 Susanna
52 Thomas 52
BARRY, Emma 105
BARTEE, John 53
BARTHOLD, Oscar 20
BARTLETT, Jefferson 53 John 53
Lavender 53 Morris 53
BARTLEY, Margaret 53
BARTON, Absalam 53 Charety 53
Eady 53 Elizabeth 53 Feby 53
Isaac 53 John 53 Rachel 53
Sarah 221
BASKERVILLE, Ann 54 James 54
Judith 54 Mildred 53 Millie
53 Richard 54 Samuel 54 Sta-
tina 54 William 54
BASKET, Susanna 178
BASKETT, Elizabeth 54 Frances
54 Henry 54 Jesse 54 John 54
Mary 54 Mildred 54 Nancy 54
Peggy 54 Sarah 54 Thomas 54
Walter 54
BASKIT, Susanna 178
BASS, Bird 54 Catherine 54
Dread 54 Elizabeth 54 Isaac
54 Jane 54 John 55 Jenney 54
Judith 54 Katy 54 Martha 54
Nancy 54 Patsy 54 Polly 54
Sarah 54 Tolbert 54
BASSETT, Elizabeth 55 Harriet
55 James 55 Melinda 55 Nan-
cy 55 Peggy 55 Polly 55 Re-
becca 55 Sally 55 Thomas 55
William 55
BASSHAM, Francis 55
BASYE, Nancy 55
BATCHELOR, Nancy 55
BATEMAN, Susan 28
BATES, Elizabeth 55 Isaac 55
James 55 John 171 Levina 55
Lucinda 171 Matthew 55 Micky
55 Mildred 55 Molly 55 Polly
55 Rebecca 55 Samuel 55 Su-
sanna 55 William 55 Winifred
55

BATHE, Susanna 39
BATSON, Rachel 56 Wesley 56
BATTERSHELL, Cynthia 56 Eliza-
beth 56 James 56 John 56 Ma-
ry 56 Nancy 56 Peggy 56 Ra-
chel 56 Sarah 56 Saryan 56
Susannah 56 William 56
BATTERTON, Lydia 56 Moses 56
BATTIN, F E 55
BATTLEY, Joseph
BAUGH, Adam 56 Alsey 56 Benja-
min 56 Judith 56 Kate 56 Lu-
cinda 56 Margaret 56 Mary 56
Nancy 56 Patsy 56 William 56
BAULDWIN, Drusilla 57 Henry 57
Herbert 57 Hiram 57 Mary 57
Nancy 57
BAWCUTT, Archibald 57 Letitia
57 Nancy 57 Sarah 57
BAYLES, Betsey 57 Haydon 57
Jane 57 Mason 57 Moses 57
BAYLEY, Betsy 58 Elijah 58
Elizabeth 58 John 58 Molly
58 Nancy 58 Ritter 58
BAYLIS, Eliza 58 Lucy 58 Maria
58 Mary 58 Nancy 58 Susan 58
BAYLISS, Anne 58 Elizabeth 58
BAYLOR, George 142 John 58 Lu-
cy 58 142
BAYLY, Ann 267 Catharine 267
John 58 Thomas 75 267
BAYNE, John 58 Molly 47 Rich-
ard 47
BAYNES, John 201
BAZWELL, John 58 Susan 58
BEADLES, Catherine 59 John 59
Martha 59
BEAL, Mary 59
BEALE, Betsy 59 Elizabeth 59
Grace 59 John 59 Mary 59 Ro-
bert 59 William 59
BEALL, George 66 Milly 59 Ruth
126 Samuel 66
BEALOR, Charles 60 Elizabeth
60 Frederick 60 George 60
Joseph 60 Mary 50 Nancy 60
Thomas 60
BEAM, Anne 94 John 94
BEARD, Betsy 60 Frances 255
Harvey 60 James 60 John 60
Mary 60 Nancy 60 Robert 60
Rosana 60 Rosena 60 Sarah 60

BEARDEN, Nancy 68 Richard 68
W H 60
BEARDON, John 60 Sarah 60
BEASLEY, Alice 183 Ammon 61
Edward 61 Elmer 61 Enoch 61
Fanny 61 John 60 Nancy 61
Rachel 60 Sally 11 179 Su-
sanna 61 Thomas 61
BEATTY, Andrew 60 Cyrene 60
Daniel 60 Elizabeth 60
George 60 273 James 60 Jane
273 John 60 73 Melly 60 Pri-
scilla 73 Roberta 60 Sarah
60 Thomas 60 William 122
BEATY, Alexander 60 James 60
John 60 May 60
BEAUFORD, Simeon 132
BEAUFORT, Simeon 132
BEAVERS, Ida 24 James 72 Jane
62
BEAZELEY, Durrett 62 Elizabeth
62 Ephraim 132 James 62 John
62 Lucy 62 Mary 62 Nancy 62
Polley 62 Robert 62 Sanford
62 Susan 132
BECHER, Benjamin 62 Betty 62
Jacob 62 John 62 Mary 62 Sa-
muel 62 William 62
BECK, Alexander 62 Ann 62 Cora
87 Elihu 62 Elizabeth 62 Eu-
genia 63 Fanney 62 Francis
62 63 George 63 James 63
Jesse 62 John 62 63 Mary 62
63 Matilda 63 Rachel 63 Re-
becca 62 87 Rebecka 62 63
Reuben 62 Samuel 63 Sarah 63
Susannah 62 63 William 62 63
187
BECKER, Meady 186
BECKETT, Florence 98 Jemima 63
Patsey 63 Susanna 63
BECKHAM, Maude 85 Salley 63
Susanne 63
BECKTEL, Susan 63
BEDFORD, Margaret 151 Matty 64
BEDINGER, Christopher 63 Dani-
el 64 Everett 64 Henrietta
63 64 Henry 63 64 Margaret
64 Mary 63 64 Matty 64 Nancy
64 Olivia 64 Phebe 63 Sarah
63 Susan 63 Virginia 64
BEDLE, Rhoda 64

BEECH, Elizabeth 64 Jane 64
Lodowick 64 Mary 64 Pheby 64
William 64
BEEKMAN, Aaron 64 Abraham 64
Christopher 64 Delilah 64
Elizabeth 64 Furman 64 Gab-
riel 64 John 64 Mary 64 Sa-
rah 64 William 64
BEELER, Joseph 65 Martha 65
BEEM, E C 60
BEETEM, Charles 65
BEGGS, James 60 Thomas 60
BEGLEY, William 65
BELCHER, Alice 65 Elizabeth 65
George 65 Jacob 65 James 95
John 65 Joseph 65 Lana 65
Sarah 65
BELEW, Elijah 65 Elinia 65
BELK, Darling 116 Sarah 116
BELKNAP, Emsey 65 John 65 Lu-
cerne 65 Mary 65 Nancy 65
Naomi 65 Polly 65
BELL, Andrew 66 Aza 66 Benja-
min 66 Brooks 66 Elizabeth
138 Grayce 16 Jake 66 John
66 Margaret 66 Mary 66 Nancy
73 Nathaniel 65 Rebecca 66
Rebekah 66 Samuel 66 Sarah
66
BELOTE, Byrd 67 Thuria 67
BENGE, Elizabeth 67 G C 67
Patsy 67 Robert 67 Sarah 67
W B 67
BENHAM, Elizabeth 135
BENIGER George 67 Mary 67 Sa-
muel 67 Sarah 67
BENJAMIN, D 67
BENNET, Susannah 250
BENNETT, Abram 68 Ann 68 Co-
vington 68 Daniel 68 Dorias
68 Elizabeth 68 Haywood 68
Henry 68 James 68 Jane 68
Margaret 68 Mary 67 68 Nancy
68 Peter 68 Polly 34 R M 68
Sally 68 Temperance 196
BENNING, Sally 26
BENSON, Alfred 68 Cynthia 68
Harry 68 Herod 68 Hiram 68
Jana 68 Job 68 Lina 68 Minna
68 Molly 69 Nancy 68 Parthe-
na 68 Pharaoh 68 Porter 69
Price 68 Sarah 69 Walter 125

BENSON (continued)
Zachariah 68
BENTLEY, Elizabeth 279 Jane 69
John 69
BERKLEY, John 69 Mary 69 Molly
69 Robert 69 Sally 69 Sarah
69 William 69
BERMAN, F 220
BERNARD, Elizabeth 70 F 70 F F
70 George 70 John 70 Mary 69
79 Nancy 70 Polly 70 Richard
70 Sarah 70 Susan 70 Susana
70 Thomas 70 Virginia 69
BERRY, Abraham 71 Andrew 71
Ankret 71 Ann 71 Benjamin 70
Catherine 71 Charles 271 Da-
niel 70 Elener 71 Eliza 71
Elizabeth 70 71 Ellender 71
Franklin 70 Hannah 71 271
Henry 70 Isaac 71 James 71
Jane 70 John 70 71 Joseph 70
Josephine 207 Lucy 71 Marga-
ret 70 71 153 Martin 70 Nan-
cy 57 70 71 Rebecca 70 Reu-
ben 70 Robert 71 Sarah 70 71
Seymour 71 Sue 70 Susan 70
Thornton 57 William 207
BERRYMAN, Susannah 103
BERTHEA, Louisa 23 Octavo 23
BERTRAM, Wesley 256
BERTRUG, Elizabeth 71
BEST, Elizabeth 72 Susan 72
BETHEA, Rachel 72
BETHEL, Margaret 72
BETSILL, Charity 72 John 72
Sarah 72
BETTERSWORTH, Ruth 72
BETTISWORTH, Betsy 72 Eliza-
beth 72 Evin 72 Sally 72
BEVILL, Dicey 222 Hezekiah 222
Lucy 222 Philip 222 Sally
222
BIBB, Agness 72 Benjamin 72
Fleming 72 Henry 73 John 129
Margaret 129 Peggy 129 R H
72 Richard 72 William 73
BIBLE, Magdalene 73 John 73
BICKEL, Mary 73
BICKERS, Benjamin 73 Janey 73
Joanna 73 Joel 73 Polly 73
BICKETT, Florence 98
BICKLE, Caufel 166 Margaret

BICKLE (continued)
166
BICKLEY, Sebastian 73
BIDDIE, Sarah 73
BIGGERSTAFF, M B 100
BIGGS, Alexander 74 Allen 73
Benjamin 73 74 Catey 74 Da-
niel 74 George 73 Ginny 74
Henrietta 73 Isabella 74
James 74 Jane 74 John 73 Ju-
liann 73 Lydia 73 74 Marga-
ret 73 74 Mary 73 74 Missis-
sippi 74 Nancy 73 74 Polly
74 Randal 74 Sampson 74 Sa-
rah 73 74 Thomas 74 Viney 76
William 74 Zaccheus 76
BILLS, Mary 75 Polly 75
BINGAR, Elizabeth 67 Jonathan
67
BINGHAM, Elizabeth 75 G M 75
Nancy 15
BINGLEY, Elizabeth 75 John 75
Mary 75 Nathaniel 75
BINNS, Nancy 33
BIRCH, George 75 Jane 75 Polly
75
BIRD, Joseph 128
BIRDSONG, J A 9
BIRELY, C E 147
BISCOE, Polly 75
BISH, Jacob 76
BISHOP, B L 105 Charlotte 76
Elizabeth 232 Fanny 76 Henry
138 James 76 Jeremiah 76
John 76 Mary 76 Parmelia 76
Phoebe 232 Sarah 76 Winifred
76 Winny 76
BLACK, Christopher 77 Eliza-
beth 77 Isabella 77 James 77
Mary 77 Milly 77 Peggy 231
Robert 76 Rudolph 77 Samuel
77 William 77
BLACKBURN, Edward 77 H C 277
Harrison 77 James 77 Rebecca
77
BLACKEY, William 81
BLACKMAN, W F 193
BLACKMORE, George 77 James 28
Sally 77 Sarah 77
BLACKNALL, O W 78
BLACKWELDER, Daniel 78 J S 78
John 78

BLACKWELL, Agatha 79 Alexander
78 Ann 78 79 Anne 78 Arthur
78 Betsey 79 Caty 78 Christopher 78 Elizabeth 78 79
Grant 79 Harriet 78 James 79
Jane 79 Joana 146 John 78 79
244 Joseph 79 Judith 249 Judy 79 Kitty 78 Lewis 78 Lucy
78 79 Mary 78 Octavia 79 Samuel 78 Sarah 78 Sophia 79
Susan 79 Thomas 79 Walter 78
William 78 79

BLAINE, James 79

BLAIR, Anne 79 Archibald 79
John 79 Mary 79 Violet 79

BLAKE, Benjamin 80 Charles 154
Dorothy 80 Elizabeth 243
Ethelred 80 Isham 80 Jemmia
146 John 80 L L 154 Lydia 80
Mary 80 Nancey 80 Polly 80
Richard 80 Samuel 80 Sarah
80 Thomas 80 William 80

BLAKELY, John 83 Margaret 83
Robert 83

BLAKEMORE, Buck 80 Caleb 80
Easther 80 Eliza 80 George
80 Hesther 80 Jessie 78 John
80 Joseph 80 Lucy 80 Thomas
80

BLAKEY, Ann 80 Churchill 80 81
Elizabeth 80 James 80 Lucy
81 Margaret 80 Nancy 80 Pamela 80 81 Reuben 80 81 Sally 80 Sarah 80 Susan 80 Thomas 80 William 80 81

BLALOCK, Elizabeth 81 Forest
81 Forrest 85 John 81 Lucy
81 Margaret 81 Mary 81 Polly
81 William 81

BLAND, Amy 81 Elizabeth 81

BLANE, Rachel 81

BLANKENBECKER, Margaret 167

BLANKENSHIP, Bland 82 Daniel
82 Fanny 82 Hudson 81 J C 82
James 82 Jesse 81 Mark 82
Melly 82 Polly 82 Sarah 17
265 Susan 82

BLANKINSHIP, Edmund 82 Frances
82 Henry 82 Mary 82 Reuben
82 Solomon 82

BLANTON, Aggy 82 Claiborn 82
Drucilla 82 Elizabeth 82

BLANTON (continued)
Hannah 82 Joel 82 John 82
Mary 82 Rutha 82 Scilly 82
Susanna 82 Vincent 82 Wil-
liam 82

BLEAKLEY, John 83 Margaret 83

BLEAM, Elizabeth 241

BLEDSOE, Betty 83 Iona 83 Jane
83 Joseph 83 Judith 83 Miller 83 Moses 83 Patience 83
Peachy 83 Polly 83 Sally 83
Sidney 83 Unice 83

BLEUFORD, Maria 85 William 85

BLEVENS, Daniel 83 John 83
Polly 83 Thomas 83 William
83

BLEVIN, Hannah 84

BLEVINS, Lydia 84 Sally 84 W P
274

BLIVINS, James 83

BLIZZARD, Sarah 84

BLODGETT, Benjamin 84 Hannah
84

BLOODWORTH, Sarah 221 William
221

BLOSS, E 84

BLOXON, Leah 84

BLUE, Jacob 84, John 84 Susannah 84

BLUFORD, Ann 84 Elizabeth 84
George 85 Hancock 85 Hariot
85 Heir 85 Henry 85 Jonathan
85 Maria 85 Mary 85 Priscilla 84 Rachel 84 Sarah 84
William 85

BLUNT, Joanna 265

BLY, Catharine 85 Elizabeth 85
Mary 85 Phebe 85 Rachel 85
Rebeka 85 Sarah 85

BOARD, Ann 85 Mary 85 Nancy 85
Polly 85 Thomas 85

BOAZ, Agnes 85 James 85 John
85 Mary 85 Meshach 231 Michael 85 Milly 85 Molly 85
Phebe 85 Robert 85 Shadrach
85 Tabitha 85

BOBBITT, John 85

BOCK, Abigail 86 Catharine 86
David 86 Hannah 86 John 86
Margaret 86 Michael 86 Nich-
olas 86 Sarah 86 Solomon 86

BODELL, R B 87

BODY, Allathea Allithia 258
BOGGS, Lewis 179
BOGGUS, Jeremiah 86
BOGLE, Agnes 86 Ann 86 Andrew
  86 Elizabeth 86 Hugh 86
  James 86 Jane 86 Jeane 86
  Joseph 86 Louise 86 Margaret
  86 Margret 86 O 86 Polly 86
  Rebecca 86 Samuel 86
BOHANNON, Helen 86
BOHON, John 87 Martha 87 Re-
  becca 87 Sallie 87 Sarah 87
  Walter 87
BOING, Reuben 94
BOISSEAU, O 87
BOLDER, John 87 Sargant 87
BOLDMAN, Anna 107 James 107
BOLEY, Anna 87 Harriet 87 John
  87 Martha 87 Polly 87 Pres-
  ley 87 William 87
BOLING, Joshua 87
BOLLES, Lemuel 16
BOLLING, Robert 87 Susan 87
  William 95
BOLT, Abram 88
BOLTINGHOUSE, John 93
BOMAN, Effie 217 William 217
BOMAR, Alexander 88 Armistead
  88 Bibby 88 Booker 88 Ed-
  ward 88 Fielding 88 John 88
  Peter 88 Reuben 88 Spencer
  88 Thomas 88 William 88
BOND, Allen 88 Anney 88 Eliza-
  beth 88 Frances 88 Jesse 88
  Joannah 88 John 88 Lindsey
  88 Lucy 88 Martha 88 Mary 51
  88 Maurice 88 Mehala 88
  Mourning 172 Nathan 88 Page
  88 Patsey 88 Peniser 88 Per-
  mele 88 Pleasant 88 Rhoda 88
  Richard 88 Sally 88 Sarah 88
  Sophia 88 Virginia 88 Willi-
  am 88
BONEWELL, Thomas 89
BONNELL, George 60
BONNER, Hannah 89 Peggy 89
  Ruth 89 Scipio 89 Susannah
  89 Thomas 89
BONNETT, Delilah 89 Eliza 89
  Elizabeth 89 Gracie 89 Jacob
  89 John 89 Lewis 89 Lucinda
  89 Martha 89 Peter 89 Samuel

BONNETT (continued)
  89 William 89
BONNEWELL, Arthur 89 Charles
  89 James 89 John 89 Smith 89
BOOKER, Ann 133 Frances 90
  George 90 Jacob 133 Mary 237
  Nancy 90 P R 90 Paul 90 Ri-
  chard 90 Sally 237 Sarah 216
  William 90
BOON, Anne 90 Elizabeth 90
  Frances 90 Henry 90 John 90
  91 Jonathan 90 Nancy 90 Re-
  becca 90 Sally 90
BOONE, Daniel 90 128 Israel 90
  James 90 Mary 128 Minnie 87
  Sarah 128 Squire 128
BOOTH, Caty 91 Fanny 239 Har-
  rott 237 Mary 91 Thomas 91
BOOTON, Amelia 91 Eleanor 91
  Elizabeth 91 Ellen 91 Emme-
  lia 91 Hiram 91 Mary 91 Rho-
  da 91 Rutha 91 William 91
BOOZ, Henry 92
BORDERS, Mary 92
BOSS, Harriet 92 Jacob 92
BOSTON, Elizabeth 92 Fanny 92
  Juliana 92 Juliet 92 Kitty
  92 Margaret 92 Mary 92 Nancy
  92 Phoebe 92 Sarah 92
BOSWELL, J V 112, Rice 7 Tho-
  mas 92
BOTHMAN, Catharine 92
BOTKIN, Margaret 92
BOTT, Elizabeth·91 Martha 92
BOUGHER, Abraham 90
BOULDIN, James 93 Joanna 93
  Louis 93 P 93 Robert 93 Tho-
  mas 93
BOULTENHOUSE, Abraham 93 Henry
  93
BOUNEY, Carlisle 93 Hiram 93
  Margaret 93 Martha 93 Nancy
  93 Rebecca 93 Sarah 93
BOURN, Catherine 93 Walker 93
BOURNE, Daniel 93 Mary 93
BOWDEN, Benjamin 93 Celia 93
  Dempsey 93 Francis 93 Jackey
  93 Margaret 93 Mary 93 Wil-
  liam 93
BOWE, Hiram 270 Lucy 270
BOWEN, Anne 94 Avis 94 Catha-
  rine 94 Charles 94 Elizabeth

BOWEN (continued)
94 Ephraim 94 Frances 94
James 94 John 94 Lydia 94
Martha 94 Mary 94 Micajah 94
Nancy 94 Polly 94 Reese 94
Sarah 94 Silas 94 Susan 94
Thomas 94 Thompson 94 Wil-
liam 94
BOWERS, Balaam 94 Betsey 94
H K 75
BOWLEN, Jarret 87
BOWLES, Betsy 94 John 223 Nan-
cy 95 Reuben 94 Zachariah 87
BOWLING, Charles 95 Letitia 95
Letty 95 Martha 95 Sally 95
Sarah 95
BOWLS, Elizabeth 190
BOWMAN, Abraham 95 96 Abram 95
Asa 96 Barbara 96 Catharine
95 96 97 Cornelius 96 Cosby
96 97 Daniel 96 Eadeth 96
Eli 96 97 Elizabeth 95 96
Emily 96 Ernest 96 George 95
96 Isaac 95 96 Isabella 169
John 95 96 Joseph 95 96 Lew-
is 96 Mary 95 96 Nancy 95 96
Patsy 96 97 Polly 95 96 Ro-
bert 95 Sally 96 Sarah 95
William 95 96 102
BOWSER, Betsy 97 Nathaniel 97
Thomas 97
BOWYER, Agatha 97 Henry 97
Nancy 97
BOXLEY, Joseph 134
BOXWELL, Deborah 97 Elizabeth
97 John 97 Joseph 97 Leona
97 Letty 97 Martha 97 Mary
97 Moses 97 Nancy 97 Robert
97 Sally 97 William 97
BOY, Andrew 97 Mary 97
BOYCE, Abraham 97 Anny 97 Da-
vid 97 Ezekiel 97 Hannah 97
Jacob 97 Jeremiah 97 John 97
Margaret 97 Mary 97 Nicholas
97 Robert 97 Sarah 97 Wil-
liam 97
BOYD, Abraham 98 Abram 99 Adin
98 Alonzo 98 Ann 98 Anna 98
Anne 98 Benjamin 98 Blancett
98 Blanchy 98 Charles 98 Em-
ma 98 Flora 98 Florence 98
George 98 Grace 98 Harriet

BOYD (continued)
98 Isabella 98 James 98 99
Jennie 98 John 98 Lucretia
98 Lucy 98 Margaret 98 Mary
98 Nancy 97 98 99 Nathan 98
Newton 98 Oscar 98 Patrick
98 Peggy 98 Robert 98 Sally
98 Samuel 99 Sarah 98 Spen-
cer 99 Thomas 98 99 William
174
BOYDSTUN, David 99
BOYERS, Anna 99 Elizabeth 99
Frederick 99 John 99 Marga-
ret 99 Mary 99
BOYLL, Enoch 99 Lydia 99
BOYLLS, America 100 Arabelle
100 Columbus 100 David 100
George 100 Melissa 100 Polly
100
BOYT, Sally 100
BOZORTH, Eli 100 Elizabeth 100
Jeremiah 100 John 100 Mary
100 Polly 100 Sally 100 Wil-
liam 100
BRABSON, Margaret 72 William
72
BRABSTON, Mary 100 Rachel 100
William 100
BRADBURY, Anna 99 William 99
BRADEN, Andrew 100 Brummett
100 Edward 101 Elizabeth 100
Elsey 100 Sarah 100 127 Wil-
liam 100
BRADFATE, Marta 148
BRADFORD, Catherine 101 Char-
les 101 Daniel 101 Fielden
101 Fielding 101 Harriet 101
Jane 101 John 101 Julia 101
Lucy 46 Mary 101 Nancy 101
Rose 46 S S 101 Sally 101
Samuel 101 William 46
BRADLEY, Elizabeth 102 Frankey
101 Mary 101 102 Susan 101
BRADSHAW, Barsheba 102 Betsy
102 Charles 102 Elizabeth
102 Fanny 102 Field 102 H C
102 John 102 Jonah 102 Lar-
kin 102 Larner 102 Mary 102
Matilda 103 Nancy 102 Orston
102 Patsy 102 Pierce 102
Polly 102 Pride 102 Robert
102 Selaw 102 Sinthia 127

BRADSHAW (continued)
Susannah 102 Unity 102 William 102

BRADY, Barbara 102 Elizabeth
103 George 103 James 103
John 103 Keziah 103 Nancy
103 Richard 103 Roseman 103
Susie 103 William 103

BRAGG, Cecelia 103 Cicely 103
George 103 Humphrey 103 Joseph 103 Nancy 103 Ruthy 103
Selah 103 Susannah 103 William 103

BRAITHWAITE, Catharine 103
Elizabeth 103 Emeline 103
Mary 103 Violett 103

BRAKE, Jacob 103 John 103

BRAMBLET(T), Ambrose 104 Hugh
3 Lewis 104 Lydia 104 Martin
3 Milly 104 Nancy 3 Sarah
104

BRAMLETTE, Thomas 104

BRANCH, Nancy 104

BRANDENBURG, Amos 191 Emanuel
191 George 191 Joseph 191
Lydia 191 Philip 191

BRANDOM, Agnes 104 Edward 104
Elizabeth 104 Margaret 104
Nancy 104 Peter 104 Suckey
104 Waldon 104

BRANDON, Agnes 104 Jennett 104
Mary 104 Robert 104 William
104

BRANHAM, Barthena 117 Eleanor
83 Elly 83 George 83 John
116 117 Mary 104 117

BRANN, Mathias 105 Nicholas
105 Rebecca 105 Sarah 104

BRANSFORD, Mary 105 John 105

BRASHEAR, Malcolm 105 Minnie
138 Walter 105

BRASHER, Mary 105 Susan 105

BRATEN, Elizabeth 165

BRAVARD, Mary 148

BRAXTON, Mary 105

BRAY, Amelia 105 Amy 105 Carolina 105 Daniel 105 David
105 Eleanor 105 Elizabeth
105 Ellen 105 Hanon 105 Jane
42 Lewis 105 Margaret 42
Martha 105 Nathan 105 Reuben
105 Samuel 105 William 105

BRAYHILL, James 106 Rebecca
106

BREATHITT, Susan 80

BRECHEEN, Margaret 106

BRECHEN, Josiah 106 Margaret
106

BRECKEN, Margaret 106

BREDEN, Mary 16

BREEDLOVE, Francis 106 Mary
106 Milly 106 Richard 106

BRENEMAN, Christian 230

BRENT, Elizabeth 106 Franky
106 Jane 106 Mary 78 Nancy
106 Polly 106 141 Samuel 106
Susannah 106

BRENTON, Davis 107 Henry 107
Horace 107 James 107 John
107 Mary 106

BRESENDINE, John 216

BRESSIE, Elizabeth 107 Francis
107 Joceming 107 Mary 107
Patsy 107 Thomas 107 William
107

BREWER, Anna 107 Catharine 235
Charles 107 Elijah 107 Elizabeth 107 John 107 Martha
107 Mary 107 Nancy 277 Peggy
107 Polly 107 Richard 107
Sackville 235 Sally 107 Sarah 107 Susan 107

BREWSTER, Eleanor 108 James
127 John 263

BRIBB, Nancy 148

BRICKEY, Elizabeth 108 Jared
108 Jarrett 108

BRIDGES, Benjamin 108 Betsy
109 Cornelia 108 Delly 108
Emma 108 Eving 108 Frances
108 George 108 Horace 108
Jenny 108 John 108 Joseph
108 Laura 108 Levina 108
Louisa 108 Margaret 25 Martha 108 Mary 1109 Nancy 109
Pauline 109 Polly 109 Preston 109 Sally 108 Seniorah
108 William 25 108

BRIDGEMAN, Mary 108

BRIDGEWATER, Mary 109

BRIDGWATER, Daniel 109 Elias
109 Elinor 109 Elijah 109
Elisha 109 Hanna 109 Isaac
109 Jack 109 Jonathan 109

BRIDGWATER (continued)
John 109 Joseph 109 Nathaniel 109 Patience 109 Polly
109 Rebecca 109 Solomon 109
William 109

BRIERS, Jemima 256

BRIGGS, Charles 109 Charloty
109 David 109 Elizabeth 109
George 109 110 Jeney 109
John 109 Judah 109 Hesakiah
109 Margaret 109 Marian 109
Thomas 109 William 109

BRIGHT, Barbara 110 Elizabeth
110 George 110 Margaret 110
Mary 110 Nancy 110 Samuel
110 Sarah 110 Susan 110 Susannah 110

BRIGHTWELL, Barnard 110 Charles 110 Nancy 110 Ronald 110

BRINKER, George 96

BRINKLEY, Henry 110 Mary 258
Sarah 110

BRISCOE, Caroline 126 Nettie
95 P W 126 Polly 271 William
126

BRISTER, Betsey 110 James 110
Lucy 110 Mina 110 Robert 110

BRISTOW, W H 216

BRITT, Nancy 148 Gertrude 111

BRITTAIN, Susan 111

BRITTEN, Emily 111 Hannah 111
John 111 Matilda 111 Richard
111

BRITTON, Mary 111

BRIZENDINE, Lucy 111, Mary 111
Milly 31 Nancey 111 Susan
111 Young 111

BROACH, Ann 111 Charles 111
Martha 111 Peggy 111 William
111

BROADDUS, Fanny 271

BROADUS, Catherine 112 Harriet
112 John 112 Juliet 112 Kitty 112 Lavinia 112 Maria 112
Martha 111 Patsey 112 Robert
112 Sarah 112 Thomas 112
Willilam 112

BROADWATER, Ann 112 Arthur 112
Charles 112 Guy 112 John 112
Sydney 112 Thomas 112

BROCK, Rose 112

BROCKMAN, John 112

BROCKUS, Betsey 112 David 112
John 112 Mary 112

BROIL, Jacob 125

BROMLEY, Edna 251

BRONSON, Bayless 29 Liner 29
Sarah 29

BROOD, Harriet 112 John 112

BROOKE, B E 113 H Y 113 Francis 113 Lucy 113 Mary 113
Michael 113 Robert 113 W T
113

BROOKES, Ann 113

BROOKOVER, Catharine 103

BROOKS, Ann 115 Barsheba 114
Catharine 115 Charles 115
Christina 113 Elizabeth 115
Everett 112 Fanny 112 Fielding 115 Frances 114 115 Giralda 114 Isham 115 Iverson
113 James 115 Jeruthea 253
John 114 115 Jonathan 114
Lucy 114 Malinda 113 Mary
114 Middleton 115 Nancy 114
115 Philip 115 Rhoda 114
Sallie 114 Sarah 114 Susannah 115 Thomas 114 115 William 114 115 Zachariah 114

BROOME, Chary 115 Ruth 115

BROSIUS, W G 115

BROSUS, Abraham 115

BROUGH, Eliza 115 Joseph 115

BROUGHTON, Mary 116 William
116 Winny 116

BROWDER, Addie 116 Elizabeth
116 Herbert 116 John 116 Mary 116 Polly 116 Rachel 116

BROWN, Abby 116 Abigail 121
122 Abraham 119 Agnes 117
Ailse 120 Alexander 123 Alfred 116 Alford 116 Alie 121
Alma 116 Alyce 120 Amanda
117 Ambrose 124 Anderson 121
Ann 34 Anna 123 Anne 121 Arabia 116 117 Barbara 120
Bessie 117 Betsey 116 119
123 Betsy 117 119 120 121
Betty 127 Brightberry 117
Caroline 119 Charles 118 123
Christiana 120 Clarissa 121
Clifton 117 Coleman 117 Corbin 121 Daniel 120 David 118
120 Deshy 117 Dicey 116

BROWN (continued)
Dosha 123 Doshy 116 Edgar
135 Edmund 117 Edward 118
Edwin 259 Edy 257 Eli 122
Elisha 123 Eliza 121 123 218
Elizabeth 45 116 118 122 123
124 135 161 Ellender 124 Esther 118 119 Franklin 122
Frances 118 121 122 George
116 117 119 121 Hannah 121
122 Harmon 118 Harvey 117
Henrietta 117 Henry 116 122
Hester 119 Horace 117 Hugh
122 124 Isaac 121 122 123 J
W 116 Jacob 121 James 89 116
119 120 123 240 Jane 116 118
120 122 240 257 Jennings 120
Jesse 120 Joanna 117 John 19
117 118 119 120 123 124 Joseph 116 121 124 Joshua 121
Katy 117 Labey 119 Leanna
189 Leonard 175 Levi 121 122
124 Lewcinda 116 Louvilia
117 Lucinda 121 124 Lucy 98
117 119 120 123 124 Luther
45 Lydia 123 Madison 122
Magdalen 122 Malinda 122
Margaret 116 120 121 124 Maria 259 Maredith 123 Martha
88 117 118 121 122 123 Mary
116 118 120 121 123 124 131
Matilda 123 Mattie 117 Maurice 121 Midy 123 Milley 122
Milly 117 Montgomery 123
Nancy 40 116 117 119 120 121
123 124 163 Nathaniel 34
Neal 121 Nicholas 163 Nimrod
117 Noah 118 Patience 117
Patsey 88 119 122 123 Peggy
116 120 Peter 122 123 Phebe
116 123 124 Pheby 124 Philadelphia 123 Pollard 122 Polly 100 117 118 119 121 123 R
D 193 Rachel 27 116 117 119
Rebecca 119 121 Richard 118
Robert 119 122 123 Sally 118
119 121 122 175 247 Samuel
122 123 124 Sarah 34 116 117
118 119 122 129 Sophia 117
Spicer 120 Stephen 116 117
Suca 117 Susan 118 Swingren
123 Sydney 121 Teresa 122

BROWN (continued)
Terresa 175 Thomas 116 117
119 120 123 257 Tutt 175 Van
Buren 123 William 117 118
119 120 121 122 123 123 202
Willis 119 Wilson 116 Zekiel
116
BROWNING, Betsey 125 Caleb 125
Charles 125 Edmund 125 Elizabeth 125 Frances 125 Fran-
cis 125 Henry 34 125 Jacob
125 James 125 Jane 125 Joel
125 John 125 William 125
BROWNLEE, Anna 125 Caroline
125 James 125 Jane 125 Mary
125 Polly 125 Sally 125 Wil-
liam 125
BROYLES, Jacob 125 James 125
BRUCE, Agnes 125 126 Austin
125 Austron 125 Barnett 126
Derret 125 Durritt 126 Eli-
zabeth 125 126 Ely 125 Han-
nah 126 Isaac 126 James 126
Kitty 126 Lucy 126 Mary 272
Mildred 126 Milly 125 Nancy
125 126 Oreon 120 Sallie 125
Sally 126 Sarah 125
BRUIN, Eliza 126 Mariah 126
Matilda 126 Sophia 126
BRUMBACK, Elizabeth 126 Ora
126
BRUMFIELD, William 126
BRUMMET, Anna 126 127 Banner
127 Belinda 126 Delila 126
Elijah 126 127 Hannah 126
James 126 127 Mary 126 Rhoda
126 Sarah 126 127 Sintha 126
Sinthia 126 Thomas 127 Wil-
liam 126 127
BRUNER, Henry 210 Matilda 210
BRUSHWOOD, Ann 237 George 237
James 237
BRUSTER, Polly 127
BRYAN, Abner 127 128 Andrew
127 Ann 127 Anthony 127 Ben-
net 128 Catharine 127 Cla-
rence 151 Daniel 127 David
95 Eleanor 128 Elizabeth 127
128 Foster 127 Hampton 127
Hannah 128 141 James 128
Jane 127 128 Jeremiah 128
John 64 127 128 Joseph 128

BRYAN (continued)
Luke 127 Margaret 127 128
151 Martha 127 128 Mary 64
127 128 Melinda 127 Miranda
203 Morgan 127 128 Phebe 127
128 Samuel 127 128 Sarah 64
85 96 127 128 Stella 141
Thomas 127 William 127 128
BRYANS, Augustine 128 Betsy
128 Else 128 Peggy 128
BRYANT, Elizabeth 128 129 130
George 128 Greenbury 129
Hartwick 130 Isaac 129 James
129 Jane 128 129 Jesse 130
John 128 129 130 Joseph 128
Margaret 129 Maria 128 Mary
129 130 Nancy 128 Peggy 129
Rodger 128 Roger 128 Ruth
128 130 Sarah 75 129 130 Si-
las 129 Stephen 129 Sylvanus
129 Thomas 129 130 Thompson
129 William 129
BRYSON, Mary 253
BUCH, Jacob 97
BUCHANAN, Andrew 1130 Frances
9 George 130 Hannnah 130
James 130 Jessie 130 Joshua
130 Thomas 130 William 130
BUCHANNAN, James 130
BUCHER, Ann 133 Emanuel 62 Ja-
cob 133 Mary 62
BUCK, Ann 130 Charlotte 130
Enoch 130 James 130 Jesse
130 John 130 Lucy 130 Mary
130 Miriam 130 Phebe 130
Thomas 130 Virginia 234
BUCKALEW, John 130
BUCKELL, John 143
BUCKHANNON, John 130
BUCKLE, John 143
BUCKLEY, Ann 130 Betty 131 Ca-
tharine 130 Colman 130 Eli-
zabeth 130 Emily 131 Ephra-
im 131 Hannah 130 J W 130
James 130 Louisa 130 Lucin-
da 131 Mary 130 Nancy 130
Susan 130 Susannah 130 W W
130
BUCKNER, Baldwin 132 Dolly 237
Dorothy 132 Elizabeth 132
Fanny 141 Mary 132 Rachel
237 Sally 122 Susan 132

BUFFINGTON, Catharine 132 John
132 Margaret 132 Mary 132
Peter 132 Rebekah 132 Rich-
ard 132 Susannah 132 William
132
BUFORD, Doldy 132 Elizabeth
132 Frances 132 John 132
Margaret 132 Martha 132 Mil-
ley 132 Rhoda 132 Samuel 132
Simon 132
BUGG, Allen 272 Elizabeth 272
BUHER, Ann 133
BUIRKE, Amy 272 John 272
BULL, Eliza 133 Rachel 133
BULLARD, B F 133 Juanita 133
BULLIN, Edward 133 Henry 133
Isaac 133 Jackson 133 Juston
Martin 133 Susanna 133 Wil-
liam 133
BULLOCK, Annie 133 Betty 134
Catharine 133 Charlotte 134
James 134 Jane 133 134 John
134 Lucy 172 Martha 134 Nan-
cy 134 Patsy 134 Polly 134
Rice 133 Sarah 133 Thomas
134 William 134
BUMGARNER, Catherine 134
BUMPASS, Betsey 134 Edmond 134
Elizabeth 134 Overton 134
Thomas 134 William 134
BUNNELL, Charles 134 Hannah
134 147 John 147 Margaret
134
BUNTIN, Elizabeth 134 Nancy
134
BUNTING, Leah 134 Peggy 134
Sally 134
BUNTON, William 134
BURBRIDGE, George 135 John 135
Lincefield 135 Robert 135
William 135
BURCH, Benjamin 272 Jane 272
BURCHER, Ann 135 Anne 135 Eli-
zabeth 135 Fanney 135 John
135 Landon 135 Margaret 135
Mary 135 Rebecca 135 Robert
135 William 135
BURDETT, Nancy 90 91 William
135
BURDICK, Chester 101
BURGESS, Daniel 136 Mary 236
Nancy 136

BURK, Alcy 136 Amy 251 Caty
136 David 136 Devarol 136
James 136 Jeer 136 Jerome
136 Joanah 136 John 136 Lew-
is 136 Lucy 136 Lydia 136
Mary 136 Polly 136 Priscilla
136 Robert 136 Sally 136 Su-
sanna 136 Susie 136 Thomas
136 William 137 Willies 136
Willis 136
BURKE, Hannah 137 John 137
Margaret 137
BURKS, Betsy 137 Charles 137
Elizabeth 137 Isham 137
James 137 John 137 Mahala
137 Nancy 137 Robert 137 Sa-
ly 137 Samuel 137 Sarah 137
Wesley 137 William 137
BURLEY, James 125
BURN, Harry 79
BURNETT, Absalom 138 Anna 138
Archibald 35 Clayton 36
George 138 James 138 John
138 Lucy 138 Lydia 35 Mabel
138 Margaret 138 Martha 3
Nancy 138 Priscilla 138 Ri-
chard 138 Sarah 36 138
BURNER, Abraham 139 Abram 138
Barbary 138 Catharine 134
Daniel 137 Elizabeth 138
Henry 137 Isaac 138 Jacob
137 John 138 Mary 137 Nancy
138 Polly 138 Sally 138 Su-
san 138
BURNLEY, Frances 138 Hannah
139 Harry 139 Israel 139 Ju-
dith 138 Lucy 138 139 Mary
139 Richmond 139 Sarah 138
Stephen 139
BURNS, Alexander 63 Allee 139
Ann 139 C E 140 Charles 139
Christopher 139 David 139
Elizabeth 63 139 Ezekeah 139
George 63 139 Jane 139 John
139 Lucretia 139 M S 139
Martha 99 Mary 139 Miles 139
Nancy 44 Rebekah 63 Robert
139 Riza 139 Samuel 139 Sa-
rah 139 189 Susannah 63
Uriah 139 William 139
BURNSIDE, Andrew 140 Charlotte
140 Ellen 140 John 140

BURRAGE, Catharine 140 Hal 77
Mary 140
BURRAS, Jean 140 William 140
BURRELL, Bartholomew 140 Han-
nah 140 Jane 140 Jesse 140
Mary 140 Polly 140 Rebecca
140
BURRIS, Elijah 127 Mary 126
BURROUGHS, Alex 104 Ann 140
Jean 140 Mary 104 140 Wil-
liam 140
BURROW, Barney 140 Holly 44
Lucy 140
BURROWS, Holly 44
BURRUS, Susanna 140
BURT, Alvah 278 Anne 141 Fran-
cis 141 Garland 141 Garrett
141 Harwood 141 John 141
Martha 141 Matthew 141 Mary
141 Moody 141 Nancy 141
Phillip 141 Robert 141 Sarah
141 Susan 141 William 141
BURTON, Andrew 142 Anne 141
Bazil 142 Benjamin 141 Beza-
bel 141 Bezaleel 141 Char-
lotte 142 Christian 142 Di-
cey 142 Elizabeth 141 Fanny
141 Frances 141 Hannah 141
Harriet 141 James 141 John
141 Judith 141 Kesiah 141
Kesine 141 Lucy 141 Margaret
141 Martha 141 Mary 141 Nancy 141 Patsey 141 Peggy 141
Polly 141 Sarah 141 Ursula
141 William 141 142
BURUS, George 140
BURWELL, Martha 142 Nathaniel
58
BUSBY, Cyntha 142 Elizabeth
142 Gabriella 142 George 142
Jacob 142 James 142 Jeff 247
John 142 Mat 142 Patsey 142
Polly 142 Robart 142 Robert
142 Sarah 142 Sophia 142
BUSH, Adam 142 Ambrose 143
Barbary 143 David 143 Elizabeth 143 George 143 Henry
143 Jacob 143 James 53 John
143 Levi 143 Lorena 53 Margaret 143 Mary 143 Michael
143 Nancy 143 Paulser 143
Rachel 36 Susannah 143

BUSKILL, Hesther 143
BUSKIRK, Abram 143 Mary 193
BUSSELL, Bird 143 Charles 143
   Fanny 143 Frances 143 James
   143 John 143 Juda 144 Juday
   144 Matthew 144 Nancy 143
   Nellie 143 Robert 143 Sally
   143 Sarah 144 Shirley 143
   William 143 144 Wilson 143
BUSTER, Eleanor 144 John 144
   Michael 244 Rachel 144 Willie 144
BUSTLE, Elizabeth 144 George
   144 Polly 144
BUTCHER, Jesse 89 Lucinda 89
   Samuel 144 Susan 144 Susannah 144 Thomas 144
BUTLER, Agnes 144 Alexander
   145 Ann 145 Catharine 145
   Charles 145 David 145 Elizabeth 146 Frances 145 George
   145 Henry 145 James 145 John
   146 Joseph 146 Lanc 145 Lorena 146 Lucy 145 Martha 145
   Mary 145 146 Milley 145 Molly 145 Nancy 145 146 Nathan
   145 Peter 145 Phoebe 144 Samuel 145 Sarah 144 236 Thomas 145 William 144 145 146
   Zachariah 145
BUTT, Betsey 146 Diana 146 Edward 146 George 146 Jemmia
   146 John 103 146 146 Lydia
   146 Mary 146 Roseman 103
   Thomas 146 William 146
BUTTER, Eleanor 83
BUTTS, James 146 Joana 146 Josiah 146 Mary 146 Nancy 146
   Parthenia 146 Sarah 146 Wilson 146
BUZAN, Allen 147 Andrew 147
   Elgin 147 James 147 Jesse
   147 John 147 Philip 147
BUZENDINE, John 216
BYARLAY, Elilzabeth 147 L A
   147
BYBEE, Frances 147 Mildred 147
   Sherwood 147
BYERLY, Andrew 147, Elizabeth
   147 Hannah 147 Margaret 147
   Mary 147 Michael 147 Phoebe
   147 Rebecca 147 Samuel 147

BYERS, Archibald 57 David 57
   Elizabeth 57 Hannah 134
   James 57 147 148 John 57 147
   Letitia 57 Lovina 147 Lucenda 147 Malindah 147 Mary 57
   148 Mattie 57 Nancy 147 Patsy 148 Polly 147 148 Rachel
   57 Robert 148 Samuel 57 148
BYLAND, Mary 148
BYRD, Abby 148 Ann 148 Anne
   148 C T 148 Caty 148 Cornelia 148 Elijah 148 Elinor
   148 James 148 Jenne 148 John
   148 Maria 148 Marta 148 Mary
   148 Nancy 148 Polly 148 Rachel 148 Richard 148 Robert
   148 Sarah 114 Solomon 148
   Temple 148 Thomas 148 Tobey
   148 Ursula 148
BYRNES, Elizabeth 149 Esther
   149 Isaac 149 Margaret 149
   Samuel 149
BYRUN, Mary 149
CABBAGE, Adam 149 Elizabeth
   149 Hannah 149 John 149 Mar-
   garet 149 Martha 149 Peggy
   149 Sarah 149
CABELL, E A 149 Eliza 149 Hannah 149 Joseph 149 Nathaniel
   149 William 149
CADDAL, Samuel 191
CADDLE, Geraldine 248
CADWALADER, Mildred 259
CAHOON, John 150
CAIN, Catherine 149 Margaret
   149
CAISEY, John 177
CAKE, Lewis 204
CALDERWOOD, Adam 150 Joseph
   150 Rachel 150
CALDWELL, Blanche 178 Dicey
   151 Eleanor 151 Ezekiel 151
   J C 178 James 150 John 151
   Margaret 151 Meeke 150 Mild-
   red 58 Susanna 183
CALENDAR, Samuel 152
CALHOON, Elizabeth 151 George
   151 Henry 151 John 151 Mar-
   tha 196 Mitchel 151 Ralph
   151 Samuel 151 Sarah 151
   Thomas 196
CALHOUN, Birdy 151 C C 151

CALHOUN (continued)
Margaret 151 Mary 151 S S
151 William 151
CALLAHAM, Bettie 151 David 151
Dugger 151 John 151 Leverett
151 Lightfoot 151 Matthew
151 Morris 151 Nicholas 151
Robert 151
CALLAHAN, Catharine 152 John
152 Sarah 152
CALLAWAY, Agatha 152 Aggy 152
Ambrose 152 Anna 152 Betsey
152 Ceney 152 Charles 152
Flanders 152 James 152 John
152 Micajah 152 Pearl 152
Sally 152 Seignea 152 Steph-
en 152 Susan 152 William 152
CALLENDER, Martha 152 William
132
CALLIHAM, Elizabeth 47 Ezekiel
47 Obadiah 47 Polly 47 Vesta
47 William 47
CALLIS, Anne 153 Arthur 153
Barbara 153 Caius 153 Cleon
153 Cye 153 Daniel 153 Ele-
anor 153 Elizabeth 152
George 153 Jane 153 John 153
Lavinia 153 Martha 153 Mary
153 Nancy 152 Ophelia 152
Otho 153 Richard 153 Samuel
152 153 Thomas 152 Tobias
153
CALLOWAY, Frances 153 Frank
153
CALMES, Isabelle 153 Marcus
153 Marquis 153 Mary 153
CALVERT, Elizabeth 22 154 John
153 154 221 Kirkland 154
Martha 154 Mary 22 153 Max
153 Newton 154 Raleigh 154
Rebecca 153 Sidney 154 Tho-
mas 154
CALVIN, A M 260
CAMERON, Andrew 154 Jean 154
Rachel 154
CAMMACK, Catharine 140 Delphy
154 Frances 140 George 154
James 140 154 John 154 Mar-
garet 154 Martha 154 Mary
154 Nancy 154 Thomas 154
CAMP, Dorothy 155 Elizabeth
155 Humphrey 155 James 155

CAMP (continued)
John 155 Maria 155 Martha
155 Mary 155 Sarah 155 Susan
155 Thomas 155
CAMPBELL, Adam 159 Ailse 157
Alexander 158 Andrew 156 Anna 157 Archibald 157 Betsey
156 Betsy 157 Bradley 158
Carah 156 Catherine 158 Caty
157 Charles 159 Cora 156 Co-
rah 156 Daniel 156 Dorchity
157 Edna 157 Eleanor 156
Eliza 159 Elizabeth 86 155
156 157 158 Elsey 159 Enos
158 Etty 156 Frances 157
Frederick 158 Fredis 157 Ganatt 156 Gennett 156 George
156 261 Gilbert 261 H D 155
Henry 156 158 Hiram 156 Hugh
86 156 Isaac 159 James 154
156 157 158 Jane 155 157 159
Jeane 155 Jemima 157 John
155 156 158 Jonathan 155 158
Joseph 157 Katy 158 Lenox
156 159 Lucy 124 177 Mary
120 157 158 159 Matilda 156
Mildred 158 Nancy 157 Perci-
val 156 Phoebe 261 Polly 156
159 Patrick 158 Peggy 158
Rachael 157 Rebecca 157 Richard 158 Robert 157 158
Sally 156 157 159 Sarah 155
156 157 158 159 236 Samuel
157 261 Susan·158 Susanna
158 Virginia 158 William 156
157 158 159 Wyatt 157
CAMPBLE, Dennis 156
CAMPER, Anne 159 Benjamin 159
Charles 159 Dinah 159 Elizabeth 159 Hannah 159 Joel 159
Jonathan 159 Levi 159 Miriam
159 Moses 159 Nancy 159 Nimrod 159 Peter 159 Polly 159
Reuben 159 Sarah 159 Thomas
159 Tilman 159
CAMRON, Ann 159 Anna 159 Daniel 159 Duncan 159 Dungen 159
Elizabeth 159 Felix 159 Jacob 159 James 159 Mina 159
CANADA, Sally 58
CANADAY, Hezekiah 160 Zanthus
160

CANADY, Andrew 160 David 256
George 160 Nancy 160
CANDLER, Daniel 160 Polly 240
CANEDAY, Leroy 159
CANFIELD, Aaron 160 Amos 160
Anny 160 Danny 160 Elizabeth
160 Henry 160 Jedediah 160
Margaret 160 Mary 160 Moses
160 Nancy 160 Nathan 160
Philip 160 Priscilla 160 Sa-
rah 160 Titus 160 Zachariah
160
CANN, John 160
CANNADAY, Elizabeth 160 James
160 John 160 Mary 160 Patsey
160 Robert 160 Sophiah 160
William 160
CANNON, Barnaby 161 Catharine
161 Edith 161 Elam 161 Eli-
zabeth 161 Ellis 161 Kathe-
rine 67 Luke 161 Margaret
161 Mary 161 Polly 161 Su-
sannah 161 Thomas 161 Uriah
161 William 161
CANTABURY, Mary 167 McFarland
167
CANTER, Daniel 161 Henry 161
Hiram 161 James 161 John 161
Mary 161 Thomas 161 Truman
161
CANTWELL, David 161 Edward 161
James 161 Jane 161 John 161
Nancy 161 Patsy 161 Thomas
William 161
CAPPS, Hiram 162 Lucina 162
Nancy 162
CARDER, Manly 162 R P 117 Sal-
ly 162 Sarah 162
CARDIN, Edward 162 Edwin 162
Judith 162 Mary 162 William
162 Youel 162
CARDWELL, Alvis 162 Anthony
162 Benjamin 163 Cuzza 162
Daniel 162 Edmund 163 Eliza-
beth 162 163 Famariah 163
George 162 163 Harvey 163
J W 162 James 162 Jane 163
John 162 163 Lewis 163 Mary
163 Nancy 163 Perrin 162
Sally 162 Sarah 162 Susan
163 Thomas 162 William 163
CAREY, John 175 Nancy 163 Peg-

CAREY (continued)
gy 163 Samuel 175
CARGILL, Mary 163 Mourning 163
CARGYLE, Cornelius 163 Daniel
163 Mary 163 Rachel 163
CARLETON, 274
CARLISLE, James 163 Mahalah
163 Mary 163 Nancy 163 Rach-
el 163 Robert 163
CARLTON, Ambrose 164 David 164
Eda 164 Elizabeth 164 Henry
164 Hiram 164 Howard 164
James 164 191 Jane 164 John
164 Lewis 164 Milly 164 Mol-
ly 164 Nancy 164 Polly 164
Rachel 164 Richard 164 Tho-
mas 164 William 164
CARIG, Mary 40
CARLILE, J H 70
CARLOCK, Mary 102
CARMACK, Cornelius 164 Edward
164 Francis 164 Isaac 45 165
Isabelle 165 J R 164 Joseph
164 Levi 165 Mary 164 S C
164 Sarah 45
CARMAN, David 165 Elizabeth
165 Jehilah 165 John 165
CARMICHAEL, John 165 Ruth 256
CARMICLE, John 165
CARNAL, James 165 Mary 165
CARNALL, Mary 165
CARNAN, Nathaniel 165
CARNEAL, Mary 165
CARNES, Benjamin 165 Catharine
165 Frances 165 Patrick 165
William 165
CARNEY, Daniel 74 Hannah 159
Julia 73 Lydia 74 Rosannah
166
CAROL, Adam 169 Bartholomew
169 Sarah 169
CAROTHERS, F A 91
CARPENTER, Andrew 167 Caufel
166 Edward 79 Hannah 167
Hough 229 Jeremiah 166 John
166 Joseph 167 Margaret 166
167 Mary 167 Mattie 167 Mi-
chael 167 Mike 166 Moncure
118 Nancy 166 167 Owen 167
Peggy 167 Polly 167 Rebecca
167 Roberta 167 Sally 229
Susan 166 167 Velner 79 Wil-

CARPENTER (continued)
liam 167
CARPER, Florence 167
CARR, Agnes 133 Anderson 168
Ann 168 Anna 168 Caroline
167 David 168 Delilah 167
Edith 133 Elizabeth 168 169
197 Ferriby 168 Hugh 168
James 168 John 133 168 Jo-
seph 167 Margaret 168 Marion
168 Meekins 133 Nancy 168
Polly 168 Rachel 167 Rebecca
169 Richard 167 Samuel 168
Sarah 168 Thomas 168 Walter
168
CARREL, David 169
CARRELL, Adam 169 Bartholomew
169 Sarah 169
CARRINGTON, Eliza 169 Eliza-
beth 169
CARROL, Betsy 169 Catherine
169 Elijah 169 Henry 169
Jesse 169 John 169 Keziah
169 Nancy 169
CARROLL, Ann 169 Charles 169
Isabella 169 Nancy 70 169
170 Perry 169 William 169
CARSON, Anna 170 David 258
Margaret 74 Mary 170 258
Polly 170 William 258
CART, Catharine 170 George 170
Mable 170 Nancy 170 Rachel
170 William 170
CARTER, Alexander 174 Amy 171
Anderson 171 Andrew 171 Anne
172 Archelaus 174 Barnabas
172 Benjamin 172 Betsy 172
173 Betsey 174 Calep 174 Catey 173 Charles 172 Christopher 173 Dale 173 Dicey 171
Edward 101 172 173 174 Eleanor 171 Elizabeth 171 172
173 Ella 173 F R 174 Frances
174 George 171 Henry 171 174
J 144 Jake 172 174 James 173
174 Jeduthan 173 Jeen 172
Jefferson 171 Jenny 171 Jesse 173 174 Joanna 173 John
171 172 173 Joseph 172 173
Joshua 171 Josiah 174 Judith
173 174 Judy 172 Kitty 171
Lawson 173 Legroy 174 Levi

CARTER (continued)
173 Lucinda 171 Lucy 172 174
Madison 174 Malinda 171 Margaret 172 Martha 174 Mary
171 172 Milindy 171 Milly
174 Mourning 172 Nancy 171
172 174 222 Patsey 172 173
Polly 171 173 174 Povall 172
Priscilla 138 Raleigh 174
Rebecca 170 174 Reuben 174
Richard 222 Rudolph 172 Sally 173 Sara 172 Sarah 171
173 174 Silas 174 Stephen
174 Susanah 172 Susanna 174
Thomas 172 173 William 171
174 Winifred 173 Winston 171
CARTWRIGHT, A J 175 Bennett
174 Christina 175 Christopher 279 David 175 Elizabeth
175 Frances 175 James 175
John 175 Justinian 175 Levin
175 Nancy 175 Peter 175 Polly 175 Rosanna 175 Susannah
175 Terresa 175 William 175
Winnefred 175
CARUTHERS, Margaret 175
CARVER, Elizabeth 21
CARWILE, Zachariah 175
CARY, Michael 163
CASASTY, Robert 180
CASE, Betsy 176 Betty 176 Han-
nah 176 James 176 John 176
Malinda 176 Rebecca 176 Ruth
176 Sabra 176 Sally 176
Squire 176 Uriah 176 Wash-
ington 176 William 176
CASEY, Edmund 176 177 Eliza-
beth 177 George 176 Jean 177
John 176 Lucinda 177 Mary
177 Nancy 177 Peggy 177 Pol-
ley 177 Polly 176 Powhatan
176 Sally 177 Thomas 177
William 177
CASH, Ann 177 Bettie 151
Christian 178 Dollah 178
Dolly 178 Dorothea 178 Doro-
thy 178 Eli 178 Francis 178
Henry 177 Howard 178 Innes
177 James 177 Jefferson 177
Jeremiah 178 Jesse 178 John
16 177 178 Larkin 178 Lewis
178 Lucy 177 Mary 177 178

CASH (continued)
Nancy 177 178 Pernina 178
Peter 177 R B 178 Rachel 178
Rody 178 Stephen 177 178 Su-
sanna 178 Waller 178 William
151 178 Willie 177 Wyley 178
CASHION, David 178 Joel 178
CASHON, Annis 178 Blanche 178
Burrel 181 David 178 Eliza
178 Elizabeth 178 Emeline
178 Jabez 179 Levi 179 Mar-
tin 178 Nancy 178 Peter 179
Pleasant 178 Polly 178 Pu-
laska 178 Rebecca 178 Sally
178 Sarah 178 Sintha 178 So-
phia 178 178 Tabitha 179
Thomas 179
CASHWELL, Betsy 179
CASLEY, Cecil 244
CASON, Ann 179 Edward 179 Eli-
za 179 Frances 107 Frederick
107 Fuqua 179 George 179 Hi-
ram 179 James 179 John 179
Lewis 107 Maria 107 179 Mary
179 Mildred 179 Nancy 179
Rebecca 179 Rheuben 107 Sal-
ly 179 Sarah 179 Susan 179
Susannah 179 William 179
CASSADY, Mary 179
CASSELL, Ralph 180
CASSETTY, Marlin 180 Thomas
180
CASSIDY, James 176 Mary 176
William 176
CASTLE, Baswell 180 Bazle 180
Charity 180 John 180
CASTLEBERRY, Frank 181 Inez
170 Richard 180 181
CASTLEBURY, Anderson 181 Eli-
zabeth 180 James 180 Julia
181 Malinda 180 Nancy 180
181 Rosa 181 Rosey 181 Sarah
180 Tabitha 180 Winney 180
CASTLEMAN, Louisiana 183
CASTLIA, Dwight 244
CASTON, Susannah 43
CASWELL, Rhoda 132
CATE, Aurelia 165
CATHON, Binwell 178
CATLETT, Ann 181 Anna 181 Ca-
leb 181 Collin 181 Elizabeth
181 George 181 Harriett 181

CATLETT (continued)
James 181 Lucy 181 Susan 181
Susannah 181 Thomas 181 Wil-
liam 181
CATO, William 181
CATRON, Catherine 182 Christo-
pher 182 Elizabeth 182 Frank
182 John 182 Julia 182 Stuf-
fle 182 Susanna 182
CATT, Sarah 182
CATTRON, Peter 182
CAUDILL, Easter 245 Henrietta
245 Jesse 245 John 245 Lydia
245 Nancy 245 Sarah 245 Ste-
phen 245 Watson 245
CAUDLE, John 247 Lydia 247
CAUTHORN, Sarah 98
CAVALIER, Esther 149
CAVE, Benjamin 182 Byron 182
John 182 Joseph 182 Keziah
182 Rachel 182
CAVENDER, Mary 2
CAVETT, Jennie 183 R M 183
CAWTHON, Richard 183
CAYCE, Betsey 183 Charles 176
Jennie 183 Levi 183 Louisia-
na 183 Mathew 183 Phebe 183
CECIL, John 183 Linny 183 Nan-
cy 183 Rebecca 183 Samuel
183 Sally 183 Susannah 183
W H 183
CHADOIN, Francis 183 Sarah 183
CHAFFIN, Achsa 183 Mary 183
Nathan 183 Rebecca 3 Tabitha
183
CHALMERS, Alice 183 Ariance
184 Hannah 184 Isaac 184
James 184 John 184 Rebecca
184 William 184
CHAMBERLAIN, William 184
CHAMBERLAINE, Ann 184 Richard
184
CHAMBERLAYNE, Byrd 184 Eliza-
beth 184 Evelyn 184 Lewis
184 Lucy 184 William 184
CHAMBERLIN, Amelia 184 Catharine 184 Cyndia 184 Franklin
184 Kitty 184 John 184 Lucinda 184 Martha 184 Milly
184 Patsy 184 William 184
CHAMBERS, Alexander 184 Anne
184 Anthony 185 Bessie 184

CHAMBERS (continued)
David 185 Harden 185 Isabel
185 Isabella 185 John 184
185 Louisa 185 Margaret 185
Nathaniel 186 Rachel 185
Thomas 184 185 W D 184 W J
170 William 184 185 Willis
185
CHAMBLIN, Sarah 254
CHAMP, Elizabeth 186
CHAMPE, Amelia 186 Eleanor 186
Floy 186 John 186 Mary 186
Meady 186 Nathaniel 186 Phe-
be 186 Susanna 186 William
CHANCELLOR, Franklin 186
CHANDLER, Caty 187 Eliza 187
Elizabeth 187 George 187
Jane 187 Joel 187 John 187
188 Julian 187 Margaret 187
Meshack 187 Mildred 186 Nan-
cy 187 Rebecca 186 Peggy 187
Phebe 85 Polly 187 Richard
187 Robert 187 Rosannah 187
Sally 187 188 Sampson 187
Samuel 187 Sarah 186 Susan
187 Susannah 187 William 187
CHANDLEY, James 188 Sarah 188
CHANEY, Joseph 188 Nancy 188
CHANSLEY, Ally 188 John 188
Julius 188 Salley 188
CHAPLIN, Isaac 188
CHAPLINE, George 188
CHAPMAN, Aleyann 189 Andrew
189 Ann 189 Benjamin 189
Betsey 190 Dehoning 189 Eli-
sa 189 Elizabeth 188 190
Fanny 189 Harriet 189 Henry
190 Ira 189 Isaiah 189 James
189 John 189 190 Jonathan
189 Joseph 189 Leanna 189
Lucy 189 Mary 165 224 Nancy
189 190 Nathan 189 Nathaniel
190 Nutty 189 Oney 189 Patey
189 Peggy 189 Polly 189 Rachel 189 190 Rawley 189 Ruby
189 Rufus 189 Samuel 189 Sara 189 Sarah 189 Stephen 189
Thomas 190 William 188 189
190
CHAPPEL, Ruth 190
CHAPPEL, Alice 191 Elizabeth
190 191 Howell 190 James 190

CHAPPELL (continued)
John 190 Mary 191 Polly 190
Ruth 190 William 190
CHARLES, Cora 243
CHARLEVILLE, Andre 191 Baptist
191 Charles 191 John 181 Jo-
seph 191 Louise 191 Michael
191 Popon 191
CHARLEY, Anna 191 Christena
191 Elizabeth 191 George 191
Jacob 191 Joseph 191 Lydia
191 Peter 191 Polly 191 Sa-
rah 191 Susanna 191
CHARLTON, Agnes 191 Anne 192
Elizabeth 191 Francis 191
James 191 John 191 Susanna
191
CHARNOCK, Elizabeth 192 John
192 Molly 192 Nanny 192 Nan-
ney 192 Rose 192 Sally 192
William 192
CHASE, E B 119 Sally 192
CHASTEEN, Elizabeth 192 Jesse
192 John 192 Nancy 192 Polly
192
CHAVERS, Peter 192
CHEATHAM, Judith 192 Lucy 192
CHEATOM, Mary 64
CHEATWOOD, Dicey 192 Frances
192 Franky 192 Joel 192 John
192 Matthias 192 Sally 192
Sarah 192 Squire 192 Susanna
192 Susannah 192
CHEDESTER, James 115 Nancy 115
CHEEK, Alma 192 Elizabeth 40
Menifee 40
CHEESEMAN, Lucy 193
CHENAULT, John 193 Louisa 193
Mary 193 Nancy 193
CHENOWETH, Absalom 193 Ann 193
Eleanor 193 Elias 193 Eliza-
beth 193 Eva 193 Gabriel 193
James 193 Jehu 193 John 193
Lemuel 193 Mary 193 Nelly
193 Rachel 193 Robert 193
Ruth 193 W V 193 William 193
CHERRY, Archie 52 Eleanor 193
Eliza 194 Elizabeth 193 El-
len 193 Harris 193 John 193
Mary 193 Mathias 193 Richard
193 William 193
CHESHIR, John 194

CHESHIRE, George 194 Sarah 194 William 194
CHESIRE, John 194
CHESNEY, Harriet 194 Margaret 194
CHESNUT, Benjamin 194
CHESSER, John 194
HESSHIR, Sarah 194
CHESTERMAN, Bernard 194 Frances 194 John 194
CHEUVRONT, Aaron 194 Andrew 194 Caleb 194 Lemuel 194 Margaret 194 Sarah 194 Walter 194
CHEVALIER, Rachel 194
CHEWNING, Elisha 195
CHICK, William 195
CHILCOTT, Ann 195 Isaac 195 Joel 195 Lydia 195 Priscilla 195 Rachel 195
CHILDERS, Abraham 195 Andrew 195 Dicey 195 Elizabeth 195 Flemon 195 Francis 195 Hannah 195 Henry 195 Jesse 195 Jessie 195 John 195 Joseph 195 Lucy 195 Martin 195 Mosby 195 Moseby 195 Nancy 114 195 Nathan 195 Pleasant 195 Polly 195 Robert 195 Sally 195 Sarah 195 Seley 195 William 195
CHILDRES, David 195
CHILDRESS, Abraham 196 Charity 196 Cora 196 Helen 196 Henry 196 Hiram 197 John 1196 Joseph 197 Martha 196 Nancy 196 Newton 196 Robert 196 Samuel 196 Temperance 196
CHILDREY, Anne 197
CHILES, Frances 47 Ira 197 Lucy 197 Susan 197
CHILTON, Betsy 197 Elizabeth 197 George 197 Hiram 197 John 197 Joseph 197 Lucy 197 Mary 197 Nancy 197 Octavia 79 Richard 197 Thomas 197
CHIN, Perry 197
CHINN, Elizabeth 197 Martha 8 Mary 101
CHISHAM, Catharine 197 John 197
CHISM, Benjamin 198 Betsey 198

CHISM (continued) George 197 James 104 John 197 Nancy 95 Rachel 198 Sarah 198
CHISMAN, Robert 193 Thomas 193
CHITWOOD, William 192
CHIVVIS, Eliza 198 Margaret 198 Mary 198 Peter 198
CHOICE, Ann 198 Anne 198 Aralinta 198 Cyrus 198 Finton 198 Jefferson 198 Jesse 198 John 109 Joseah 109 Katharine 198 Martha 198 Mary 198 Nancy 198 Rebecca 198 Ruth 198 Sophia 198 Tully 198 William 198
CHRISLER, Allen 200 Anna 200 Elishna 200 Elizabeth 200 Jeremiah 200 John 200 Leonard 200 Lewis 200 Margaret 200 Micheal 200 Sally 200 Silas 200 William 200
CHRISMAN, James 198 Lydia 104 Nathaniel 104
CHRISTIAN, Allen 199 Charles 199 Elizabeth 18 199 Gordon 199 John 199 Judah 199 Margaret 199 Martha 199 Mary 116 199 Nicholas 131 Patsey 199 Phebe 132 Polly 199 Sarah 199 Susanna 199 Thomas 199 William 18
CHRISTIE, Daniel 200 Isaac 200 Israel 200 James 200 John 200 Sarah 200 Simeon 200 William 200
CHRISTINE, George 51 Rowena 51
CHRISTLER, Allen 200 Anna 200 Catharine 200 David 200 Elishna 200 Elizabeth 200 Fanny 200 John 200 Jemima 200 Jeremiah 200 Leonard 200 Lewis 200 Margaret 200 Micheal 200 Nancy 200 Phebe 200 Rhoda 200 Sally 200 Silas 200 William 200
CHRISTY, Sarah 254
CHUMLEY, Virginia 200
CHUNING, R L 51
CHURCH, Nancy 236
CISSNA, Delilah 229
CITY, Abraham 201 Anna 201

CITY (continued)
Beddi 201 Betsey 201 Catharine 201 Christian 201 Christopher 201 Elizabeth 201 Jacob 201 Johan 201 John 201 Katarina 201 Magdalena 201 Nancy 201 Patsey 201 Polly 201 Sally 201 Samuel 201 Sehm 201 Sera 201

CLACK, Ann 201 Bennett 201 Eldridge 201 James 201 John 201 Mary 201 Nancy 201 Philip 201 Polly 201 William 201

CLAGGETT, Amie 201 Ann 201 Anne 201 Cecelia 201 Christopher 201 Elizabeth 201 Ferdinand 201 Juliet 201 Mary 201 Samuel 201 Sophia 201 Thomas 201

CLAIBORNE, Daniel 240 Fanny 202 Frances 202 John 202 William 202

CLAMINTZ, Elizabeth 102 Nancy 102

CLAPP, Barton 163

CLARK, Absalom 203 Albert 103 Alexander 174 Allison 202 Alonzo 204 Ambrose 207 Ann 17 Asa 204 Barbara 206 Barbary 206 Bathsheba 204 Benjamin 203 Blanch 202 Braxton 207 C C 101 Catharine 6 203 204 Charles 205 206 Christian 142 Christopher 205 Clifton 205 Edward 206 Eleanor 202 Eliza 207 Elizabeth 203 204 205 207 Eunice 204 Field 202 205 Frances 207 Franklin 204 George 203 204 206 Hannah 203 Harriot 205 Henry 207 Horatio 203 I 154 Ira 205 J 154 James 202 204 206 207 Jane 203 204 205 206 Jefferson 206 Joanna 207 Joannah 203 John 203 204 206 207 217 Jonathan 204 Joseph 203 204 205 207 Judith 1 205 Keziah 205 Larkin 102 204 Letitia 203 Lewis 204 Linnie 205 Lucy 203 206 207 Margaret 276 Marsella 204 Martha

CLARK (continued)
154 203 204 Mary 202 203 204 205 207 Mead 217 McClager 203 Micajah 205 Mildred 205 207 Miranda 203 204 Nancy 203 205 206 Nathaniel 204 205 Nora 204 Obadiah 207 Oliver 206 Peter 202 Phanniel 204 Phine 204 Polly 203 Rebecca 203 Reuben 204 207 Robert 203 204 Rhoda 207 Rhody 202 Richard 206 Robbin 204 Ruth 206 Sabra 206 Sally 202 203 204 205 Sam 203 Samuel 202 208 Sarah 203 205 207 217 Sevier 206 Silas 205 Spencer 208 Stephen 208 Susannah 205 207 Tabitha 204 Thomas 203 206 207 Turner 208 W D 206 Ware 206 William 203 204 205 206

CLARKE, Ann 207 Asa 204 Benjamin 203 Charles 206 David 206 Edward 206 Eliza 207 Elizabeth 14 206 208 Eppa 207 F B 67 Francis 207 George 204 207 Hannah 203 206 208 Isham 208 James 204 206 Jane 206 207 John 206 207 Joseph 204 Josephine 207 Joshua 154 Lewis 204 Lydiann 206 Martha 154 203 204 Mary 203 207 Micajah 206 Nancy 206 207 208 231 Patsey 207 Rebecca 206 Sally 207 208 Sam 203 Thomas 203 206 207 William 206 207 231

CLARKSON, David 208 James 208 Phebe 208 Pheby 208

CLARY, Betsey 208 John 208 Polly 208 Rebecca 208 Sarah 208 William 208

CLASBY, John 209

CLATTERBUCK, Cagely 209 Catesby 209 James 209 John 209 Leroy 209 Martha 200 Mary 209 Nancey 209 Patsy 209 Patty 209 Richard 209 William 209

CLAWSON, Abia 209 Garret 209 Isaac 209 James 209 John 209 Josiah 209 Keziah 209 Lea

CLAWSON (continued)
209 Lotow 209 Mary 209 Phineas 209 Thomas 209
CLAY, Catharine 209 Clement 210 Henrietta 64 Joshua 209 Maacah 210 Margaret 210 Matty 64 Melison 209 Millerson 209 Rebecca 209 William 210
CLAYCOMB, Elizabeth 210 Matilda 210 Mary 210
CLAYPOLE, Elizabeth 70 71
CLAYTON, Catharine 210 Charles 210 Elijah 210 Elizabeth 210 James 210 John 210 Joseph 210 Noah 210 Polly 210 Sally 210 Thomas 210 U A 210 William 210
CLEARWATERS, Betsey 210 Deborah 211 Elender 211 Elenor 210 211 Elizabeth 210 211 Olive 211 Rachel 211
CLEAVELAND, Abigail 211 Alexander 211 Elizabeth 211 Fenton 211 Frances 132 George 211 Harriet 211 Henry 211 Jane 211 Louisa 211 Margaret 211 Nancy 211 Sally 211 William 211
CLEAVER, Benjamin 212 Charles 211 William 211
CLEMENS, Allen 213 Catharine 213 Jane 213 John 213 Kitty 213 Nancy 213 Oston 213 Sally 213 William 213
CLEMENTS, Caroline 212 David 212 Edmond 212 Elener 71 Elizabeth 212 Ellender 71 Frances 213 Gustavus 212 Hannah 212 James 212 213 Jennie 212 John 212 Jonathan 212 Keturah 212 Laura 212 Lewis 212 Martha 213 Mary 213 Mildred 212 Nancy 104 212 213 Pamely 212 Parmelia 212 Philip 212 Polly 212 Salathiel 71 Stephen 213 Thomas 213 William 104 213 Zachariah 212
CLEVELAND, Alexander 247 Eli 247 Elizabeth 247 James 247 John 247 Lewis 247 Margaret 247 Oliver 247 William 247

CLEVENGER, Elizabeth 213 George 102
CLIBORN, Martha 221
CLIBORNE, Sarah 213
CLICK, George 247
CLIFTON, David 235 Edith 213 Elizabeth 235 Josiah 80 Lydia 80 Sarah 80 213 William 235
CLINCKENBEARD, Isaac 213 William 213
CLINE, Bennet 214 Jesse 214 Nancy 214 Peggy 214 Polly 214
CLINKENBEARD, Isaac 214 John 214 William 214.
CLINTON, David 214 George 214 Susan 214 Violet 214 William 214
CLOCK, Nancy 121
CLONDAS, Nancy 208
CLOPTON, Massie 214
CLORE, Oreina 167
CLOUD, M M 214 Martin 214 Nancy 208 214 Unity 214 Washington 214
CLOUGH, Elizabeth 18
CLOUR, George 215
CLOWER, Benjamin 214 G W 214 George 214 Henry 214 J B 214 Joseph 214
CLUVERIUS, Susan 215
COATNEY, Sally 215
COATES, Austin 215 Susannah 215
COBB,Ann 198 Frances 215 216 Nancy 198 Sally 215 Samuel 198 216
COBBS, Ann 216 Charles 216 Edith 216 Elizabeth 216 Edward 216 John 216 Rachel 216 Robert 216 Sarah 216 Thomas 216 William 216
COBLIN, Susan 246
COCHRAN, Ann 216 Betsy 216 Daniel 216 Dora 217 Edward 217 Effie 217 Eliza 217 Elizabeth 216 Henry 216 James 216 Jemima 216 Jeremiah 216 John 217 Lewis 216 Mary 216 217 Milly 216 Nancy 216 Polly 216 Rachel 217 Rebecca 216

COCHRAN (continued)
217 Sally 216 Samuel 216 Sarah 216 217 Simon 217 Susan 216 Temperance 216 Thomas 217 William 216 217
COCHRUN, Christina 217 James 217 Josiah 217 Sarah 217 Simon 217 Thomas 217 William 217
COCKE, Abraham 218 Alice 217 Augusta 218 Eliza 218 Henry 217 Jane 279 Mary 218 Peter 217 Rebecca 218 Richard 218 Stephen 218 Thomas 218 Thornton 217 Walter 218 William 218
COCKERIL, Elias 218 Gabriel 218 Lucinda 218 Mary 218 Sally 218 Sarah 218 Thomas 218
COCKRILL, John 219 Peter 219
COCKS, Benjamin 219 Rebecca 219 Susan 219 William 219
CODELL, Pearl 152
COFFEE, Osburn 220
COFFER, Cynthia 219 Gincey 219 Hamin 219 Harrison 219 Jane 219
COFFEY, Ambrose 219 Jesse 220 Lucy 220 Mary 219 Mathew 220 Polly 220
COFFIE, Millie 224
COFFINBERRY, A B 220 Abraham 220 Andrew 220 Elizabeth 220 G L 220 George 220 Isaac 220 Jacob 220 John 220 Mary 220 Nancy 220 Salathiel 220 Sarah 220 Wright 220
COFFMAN, Benjamin 220 Christena 220 Martha 29 William 29
COGAR, Emma 220
COGER, Joseph 220
COGHILL, James 220 Ralph 251
COILE, James 221
COINER, Jacob 148 Mary 148
COLBERT, Sarah 221
COLBURN, Margaret 89
COLE, Alonzo 222 Christopher 222 Daniel 221 David 19 221 Dicey 222 Edwin 222 Ella 222 F H 269 Ferne 221 Francis 221 James 221 222 Jane 222

COLE (continued)
Jemima 221 222 Joannah 19 Joel 222 John 222 Marie 221 Martha 19 221 222 Mary 19 222 Marye 221 Mason 221 Mourning 222 Nancy 222 Nathaniel 222 Noah 221 Patsy 222 Ransone 221 Rebecca 10 Richard 19 Robert 19 222 246 Sally 222 Samuel 222 Sarah 221 222 Stephen 221 222 Thomas 221 Walter 22 William 221
COLEBURT, Mary 105
COLEGATE, Rosanna 222 Thomas 222
COLEMAN, Ann 223 224 Anna 223 Betsy 190 Betty 269 Catharine 223 Daniel 223 David 223 Eden 224 Elizabeth 190 269 Esther 223 Humphrey 223 Hybernia 223 James 190 223 Lucy 223 Mary 223 Mason 223 Millie 224 Nathan 223 Pamela 223 Patience 223 Permealey 223 Salley 223 Samuel 223 Sarah 223 Scytha 223 Sithey 223 Susan 223 Susannah 223 Tempey 223
COLEY, James 238
COLGAN, Daniel 224
COLLETT, Elizabeth 224 John 224 Mary 224 Moses 224
COLLEY, Elizabeth 224
COLLIE, James 225
COLLIER, Elizabeth 225 Shadrack 225
COLLINGS, Catey 254 Catharine 254 Thomas 254
COLLINGSWORTH, Edmond 226
COLLINS, C C 225 Carah 156 Catharine 225 Cora 156 Dowell 256 Edmond 226 Elisha 225 Eliza 226 Elizabeth 225 George 225 Hannah 83 James 225 Jane 226 Johannah 237 John 225 237 Levi 225 Lucy 141 Margaret 71 225 Mary 226 Mason 226 Minervy 226 Nora 211 Polly 226 Sally 235 William 225 237
COLLYER, Stephen 228

COLN, George 230
COLQUETT, Ranson 227
COLQUITT, James 227 Susanna 227
COLSTON, Armstead 227 Elizabeth 227 Lucy 227 Susan 227 William 227
COLTER, Samuel 215 William 250
COLTON, Carrie 119
COLVILLE, Grace 227 John 227 Mary 227
COLVIN, Harry 227 John 227 Mason 2227 Priscilla 227 Robert 227 Sarah 227
COLYER, Griselda 229 Grizzey 227 Grizzy 227 John 226 Richard 228
COMBS, Andrew 238 John 228 238 Joseph 238 Mahlon 238 Margaret 228 Sally 228 Sarah 228 William 228 239
COMER, Barbara 228 Catharine 228 Cortreen 228 Elizabeth 228 Frederick 228 Jacob 228 Michael 228 Rebecca 209 210 Sally 228 Samuel 210
COMES, Emma 198
COMPTON, Catharine 153 Clary 229 David 229 Edward 21 Elizabeth 229 Frances 229 May 229 Nancy 229 Polly 229 Sally 229 Sarah 256
CONAWAY, Thomas 229
CONDRY, William 229
CONGLETON, John 229 Juliana 229 Margaret 229 Maria 229 Mary 229 Thomas 229 William 229
CONINE, Ally 229 Andrew 229 Anna 229 Cornelius 229 David 229 Delilah 229 Dennis 229 J C 166 Jane 229 John 229 Lydia 229 Mary 229 Otho 229 Richard 229 Sarah 229
CONKLIN, Ann 230 Margaret 243
CONLEE, Charles 270
CONLY, Charles 270
CONN, Charlotte 230 Elizabeth 230 Hugh 230 John 230 Mary 230 Nancy 230 Rebecca 184 Timothy 230
CONNALLY, George 231 Thomas

CONNALLY (continued)
231 Polly 231
CONNELL, Elizabeth 231 Frank 231 James 231 Jefferson 232 John 231 Lucresy 231 Mary 231 Millah 231 Robert 231 Sarah 231 Stephen 231 Walter 231 William 231
CONNELLY, Daniel 54 Jefferson 231 William 233
CONNELY, Coley 231 Jeane 231 Martha 231 Marthew 231 Peggy 231 Poley 231 William 231
CONNER, Arthur 231 Benjamin 231 Britanna 231 Charles 231 Charlotte 231 Cornelius 231 Edmond 231 Edy 231 Elizabeth 72 231 Ellena 231 Elenor 231 Ester 231 Isaac 231 James 231 Jane 231 Jinny 231 John 231 Lucy 231 Luke 231 Madison 231 Margaret 231 Martha 231 Mary 231 Matthew 72 Maximilian 231 Molly 231 Phoebe 231 Sally 231 Sarah 231 Thomas 231 William 231 234 Winney 231
CONNERLY, Elvira 233
CONNOR, Abigail 233 Benjamin 233 Catharine 233 Cornelius 233 Frederick 210 Margaret 233 Matilda 233 Rosanna 233 Truman 44 William 220
CONRAD, Eunice 234 Hannah 234 Jacob 234 Mary 234
CONWAY, Ann 234 Anna 234 Christopher 234 Elizabeth 234 256 Harriet 79 James 234 Jesse 234 John 234 Margaret 234 Mary 234 Nathaniel 234 Polly 234 Washington 234 William 234
COOK, Andrew 235 236 Ann 236 Benjamin 235 Catharine 235 Charles 231 Clara 236 Clary 236 Eli 235 236 Elizabeth 235 236 Fenton 236 James 231 235 Jemima 235 Jennifer 235 Jesse 235 236 John 235 236 Lewis 235 236 Lydia 62 Malinda 235 236 Margaret 236 Martha 235 236 Mary 235 236

COOK (continued)
Milton 231 Nancy 235 236
Phebe 235 Priscilla 235 Robert 236 Robison 236 Samuel
235 236 Sarah 155 235 236
Susan 236 Thomas 235 236
William 235
COOKE, Ann 237 238 Charles 235
Dawson 237 Elizabeth 132
Giles 237 Henry 237 238 John
237 Mary 237 Mildred 237
Ophelia 152 Paschal 237 Thomas 152
COOKERS, Elizabeth 238
COOLEY, Lizzie 238
COOMBS, John 241 Joseph 238
Malen 238 Michal 238 Nancy
238
COON, Abraham 239 Daniel 239
Joseph 239 Michael 239 Nancy
239 Samuel 239 Thomas 239
COONIES, Betsey 105 Elizabeth
105
COONS, Polly 138
COOPER, Abel 239 Abner 240 Abraham 240 241 Albert 231 Alden 240 Alice 239 Anna 241
Anne 239 Benjamin 240 244
Catherine 240 241 Charles
202 241 Christopher 240 Drusilla 239 Elizabeth 239 240
241 Francis 240 George 223
Henrietta 240 Jackey 240 Jacob 239 Jane 240 Jeremiah
240 Jesse 239 John 240 241
Lewis 240 Lucy 239 Mary 69
201 239 240 241 Mayme 239
Mildred 240 Nancy 231 240
243 Ola 239 Permelia 240
Phebe 240 Polly 240 Preston
240 Rebecca 242 Rheuben 234
bert 239 Sally 240 241 Samuel 239 241 Sarah 239 240
241 242 Stephen 240 Thomas
239 241 Victor 63 William
240 241 242
COPES, Annie 242 Easter 242
Margaret 242 Parker 242 Peter 242 Ruth 242 Samuel 242
Southey 242 Thomas 242 Wesley 242 William 242
COPELAND, Edna 171 204 Sarah

COPELAND (continued)
242 Z W 171 204
COPELIN, William 243
COPLIN, David 244
COPPAGE, Irma 243 John 243
COPPEDGE, Mary 243
COPPINGER, Elizabeth 243 Higgins 243 Margaret 243 Mary
243 Nancy 243
COPSEY, Lucinda 243
CORBETT, Ann 243 Elizabeth 243
John 243 Nancy 243
CORBIN, Anderson 244 Benjamin
244 Celey 244 David 244 Edith 244 Edward 244 Elizabeth
243 244 Fanny 244 Frances
243 Henry 243 J M 244 James
244 Joanna 244 Johanna 244
John 244 Lewis 101 May 243
Milcah 244 Nancy 243 O P 244
Robert 244 Sally 244 Sarah
243 244 William 244
CORBIT, Edith 244 Johnson 244
CORBITT, John 216
CORDELL, Arthur 244 Catharine
244 Donna 244 Elizabeth 244
George 244 Harriett 244 Hiram 244 James 245 Judith 244
Presley 244 Stephen 244
CORDER, Aldridge 245 Dorothy
245 Hannah 245 Loula 245
Nancy 245 Nannie 245 Nathan
245 Octavia 245 Vincent 245
William 245
CORDILL, Easter 245 Elizabeth
245 Henrietta 245 Jesse 245
John 245 Lydia 245 Nancy 245
Sarah 245 Watson 245
CORE, Anne 246 Catharine 246
Elizabeth 246 George 246
Henry 246 Isaac 246 Jesse
246 John 246 Rebecca 246 Sarah 246
CORLEY, Austin 246 William 246
CORLY, Mary 246 Nancy 246 Richard 246 Susan 246
CORN, Adam 246 Dicea 246 Dicy
246 Elizabeth 246 247 George
246 James 247 Jesse 246 John
246 Lot 246 Malinda 246 Mary
246 Nancy 246 Peter 246 Sally 246 Samuel 246 Sarah 246

CORN (continued)
Suckey 246 Tom 246 William 246
CORNELISON, John 247 Richard 247 Sarah 247 Susannah 247
CORNELIUS, Elizabeth 247 R E 247
CORNETT, Archibald 247 Joseph 247 Louisa 247 Louvisa 247 Lydia 247 Margaret 247 Mary 247 Nancy 247 Nathaniel 247 Polly 247 Rachael 247 Robert 247 Roger 247 Sally 247 Samuel 247
CORNISH, James 93
CORNWALL, Mary 91 N E 63 Susan 63
CORY, Elnathan 248 Samuel 248
COSBY, Isabella 255 James 255 Mary 96
COSINS, Polly 173
COTTLE, William 248
COTTON, Abner 249 Achsa 183 Anny 183 Charles 249 Elizabeth 183 James 183 Jane 183 Martha 249 Mary 183 249 Nancy 183 249 Peter 249 R H 183 Richard 183 Robert 183 Tabitha 249 William 183
COTTRILL, Barbara 249 Elias 249 Elisha 249 Elizabeth 249 Jackson 249 John 249 Marshall 249 Mille 249 Millie 249 Nancy 249 Polly 249 Watson 249 William 249
COUCH, Dempson 249 Easter 249 Hanna 249 John 250 Margaret 249 Mariann 249 Nancy 143 Peggy 249 William 249
COUGHREN, Benjamin 250 Isaac 250 James 250 Jesse 250 John 250 Jonathan 250 Joseph 250 Matilda 250 Prudence 249 Rachel 250 Sarah 250 William 249 250
COULTER, Betsey 250 Hugh 250 Hughey 250 Isabella 250 James 250 Mary 250 Nathaniel 250
COURSEY, Charles 250 Nancy 250 Susannah 250
COURTNER, Catharine 250 David

COURTNER (continued)
251 Lewis 251 Phebe 251
COURTNEY, Fielding 215 George 215 James 215 Sally 251
COUSINS, Louisa 208
COUTCH, William 249
COVERT, Abraham 251 Alvira 251 Benjamin 251 Mary 251 Nathaniel 251 Peter 251 Teunis 251
COVINGTON, Amy 251 Francis 118 John 118 Lucy 118 Margaret 118 R C 251 William 118
COWEN, Benjamin 219 Elizabeth 77
COWGILL, Betsy 251 Mary 251 Polly 251
COWHERD, Elizabeth 252 Francis 252 Garritt 252 James 252 John 252 Jonathan 252 Lucy 252 Mary 252 Maud 252 Simon 252 Willis 252
COWNOVER, Daniel 270
COX, Abraham 253 Ann 253 254 Attilla 295 Barbara 254 Bartlett 255 Benjamin 254 Betty 253 Cary 255 Catey 254 Catharine 253 254 Charles 254 Cynthia 253 Dianah 255 Eli 255 Eliza 179 Elizabeth 253 254 Frances 255 Frederick 254 George 253 Hannah 252 Hardin 253 Henrietta 74 Isaac 252 Jacob 254 James 253 Jemima 254 Jenny 253 Jeremiah 255 Jeruthea 253 John 253 254 Joshua 253 Kate 253 Lewis 254 Lorena 146 Maggie 253 Mahaley 254 Martha 254 Mary 177 253 Matthew 74 254 Milley 254 Mordecai 255 Nancy 253 254 Philip 252 Polly 252 R D 254 Rachel 254 Rebecca 254 Rebekah 254 Richard 254 Robert 179 Sally 253 254 Samuel 253 Sarah 252 253 254 Solomon 253 Susannah 253 254 Thomas 253 William 253 254 255
COYLE, James 120 257 Rachel 257
COZBY, John 255

CRABTREE, Elenor 29 Elizabeth 256 Hannah 256 Isaac 255 Jane 256 Job 256 John 29 255 Lucinda 29 Mary 255 256 Parle 255 Richard 256 Rebecca 256 Rosy 30 Ruth 255 256 Sarah 256 Solomon 255 William 30 256

CRACRAFT, Charles 262

CRAFTON, Elizabeth 257 Frances 256 John 256 257 Mary 257 Richard 256 Thomas 257

CRAGWELL, Elizabeth 208

CRAIG, Anna 257 Betsy 257 Charles 257 Elizabeth 258 Henry 257 James 257 Jane 120 257 258 Jean 257 John 120 257 Joseph 258 Lewis 257 Lillian 243 Linn 257 Margaret 258 Martha 141 Matthew 257 Nancy 257 Polly 257 Rachel 257 Rebecca 257 Robert 257 Sally 257 258 Sooky 257 William 258

CRAIL, Abel 258 Allathea 258 Allithea 258 Benjamin 258 E L 258 Edward 258 Elizabeth 258 James 258 Jane 258 John 258 Joseph 258 Mary 258 Peter 258 S Middleton 258 W W 258

CRAIN, Isaac 258 James 258 John 258 Margaret 258 Mary 258 Polly 259 Sarah 258 Stephen 258 William 258 259

CRAMB, L E 31

CRAMP, Sarah 73

CRAMSEY, Edward 269 Frances 163 John 163

CRANE, Elizabeth 259 Hannah 184 James 259 Maria 259 Polly 259

CRANSON, Sally 88 Sarah 88

CRAVEN, Idela 50 Margaret 34 Theodore 50

CRAWFORD, Alexander 259 Ambrose 259 Anderson 259 Betsy 260 Catharina 260 Charles 259 David 256 260 Delilah 260 E 230 Effey 261 Elijah 260 Elisha 260 261 Elizabeth 259 260 Ginne 259 H A 260

CRAWFORD (continued) Hannah 261 Isabel 261 James 259 260 Jean 259 John 260 261 Johnson 261 Joseph 259 Lee 260 Margaret 259 262 Mary 260 261 Nancy 260 Peter 260 Rebecca 259 Rhoda 259 Rhody 260 Robert 259 Sally 261 Sara 260 Sarah 259 260 Susannah 259 Thomas 260 W A 260 William 259 260 261

CRAWLEY, Alexander 262 Anne 261 Catharine 262 Elizabeth 262 George 262 Henry 262 Israel 262 John 262 Margaret 109 262 Moses 262 Nancy 262 Polly 262 Richard 262 Thomas 262

CRAWLY, Margaret 109

CRAYCRAFT, Elizabeth 262 Henry 262 Joseph 262 Samuel 262

CRAYMOR, Amelia 89

CREAMER, Polly 262 Sarah 262

CRECY, Patsy 119

CREED, John 262

CREEL, Fanny 262 Frances 262

CRENSHAW, Cornelius 263 Nancy 262 Nathaniel 263 Polly 263 Unity 263

CRESS, Christiana 263 Henry 263

CRESWELL, Dorothy 263 E E 263 William 263

CREWEY, John 156 Sarah 156

CREWS, Gideon 263 Nancy 263

CRIDER, John 88 Sally 88 Sarah 88

CRIHFIELD, Amos 264

CRISLER, Abraham 200 Allen 200 Benjamin 200 Cassandra 200 Catharine 200 Elinor 200 James 200 Jemima 200 Leonard 200 Lewis 200 Lucy 200 Margaret 200 Mary 200 Mildred 200 Nancy 200 Sebria 200

CRISP, R O 199

CRITCHFIELD, A B 264 Amos 264 Asa 264 Charles 264 Enoch 264 John 264 Joshua 263 Nathaniel 264 Rachel 264 William 263

CRITTENDEN, Charles 264 John

CRITTENDEN (continued)
264 Josiah 264 Judith 264
Martha 265 Mary 265 Matthew
265 Nancy 265 Richard 265
Sally 264 Samuel 265 William
265
CRITTINGTON, James 265
CRITZ, Achilus 265 Catherine
265 Elizabeth 265 Frederick
265 Gabe 265 Hamon 265 Her-
man 265 Jabe 265 Nancy 265
Peter 265 Polly 265 Sally
265
CROCKET, Anthony 162 Sally 162
Sarah 162
CROCKETT, Andrew 17 Asher 17
Charlotte 17 Dandridge 265
Elizabeth 17 265 Gertrude 17
Sarah 17 265 Susan 266 Wil-
liam 265
CROCKSIN, Joanna 117
CROGHAN, William 205
CROMPTON, Edna 210 Robert 210
CRONOVER, Daniel 270
CROOK, Elizabeth 266 Jane 266
John 266 Nancy 266
CROOKSHANKS, Alexander 266 Ca-
therine 266 Elizabeth 266
George 266 Hester 266 Nancy
266 William 266
CROPPER, Ann 267 Betsy 266 Co-
venton 267 Catharine 267
Eliza 267 John 266 267 Mar-
garet 267 Sabra 267 Sarah
267 Sebastian 267
CROSBY, Elizabeth 223 John 223
Mason 223 Moses 223
CROSE, Barbara 267
CROSLEY, W S 274
CROSS, Clara 267 Eleanor 267
Elizabeth 24 267 268 Frank
267 James 268 Maclin 24 Mary
267 Sarah 267 Solomon 267
William 24
CROSSON, Achsa 268 Acksa 268
Elizabeth 268 Felix 268
James 268 Lewis 268 Mary 268
Peninah 268
CROSSTON, Gustavus 268
CROSTON1, Travis 268
CROUCH, Cynthia 47 Dempson 249
Easter 249 Hannah 249 John

CROUCH (continued)
249 Mariann 249 Peggy 249
William 249
CROUDUS, Dolly 269 Doratha 269
Dorothy 269 George 269 James
269
CROUSE, Jesse 269 Washington
16
CROW, Andrew 269 Betty 269
Dennis 269 Elizabeth 269 El-
la 116 James 269 John 269
Margaret 269 Maria 269 Tho-
mas 269
CROWDER, Ann 169 Currency 270
Edward 269 Jarral 270 Jemima
279 Lucy 270 Martha 270
Phoebe 270 Reuben 270 Wil-
liam 269
CROWEL, Judith 270 Lucy 270
CROWELL, Thomas 270
CROWLEY, Celia 270 Francis 270
Jack 270 John 270 Mary 270
Nancy 270 Polly 270 Sam 270
Sarah 270
CROWDUS, Dorothy 269 Janett
269
CROWNOVER, Arthur 270 B B 270
Benjamin 270 Grace 270
CROXTON, Cornelia 271 Fanny
271 Frances 271 Grace 271
Louisa 271
CRUEY, John 156 Sarah 156
CRUM, E W 271 John 271 Mary 5
Mathias 271
CRUMBLE, Mary 147
CRUMLEY, Thomas 271
CRUMLY, Hannah 271
CRUMP, Abner 271 Arthur 127
Daniel 271 Elias 271 Eliza-
beth 78 George 271 Goodrich
271 John 271 Martha 271 Mary
271 Peggy 271 Polly 271 Ri-
chard 271 William 271
CRUMPLER, Mary 147
CRUTCHER, Elizabeth 271 272
Henry 272 Parker 272 Polley
272 Robert 272 Sally 271 Sa-
rah 271 272 Thomas 271 Wil-
liam 46 272 Willis 272
CRUTCHFIELD, Jane 272 Staple-
ton 14
CRUTE, Clement 272 Maria 272

CRUTE (continued)
Mary 272 Samuel 272 Venable
272 Samuel 272
CRYSEL, Elenor 272 Jane 272
Jeremiah 272 John 272 Lucy
272 Mary 272 Nancy 272
CUDDY, Alcey 273 James 273
Jane 273 John 273
CUFFEE, Charles 273
CUFFEY, Catharine 273 Katy 273
CULLINS, Jane 273
CULLY, Charles 273
CULTON, James 273
CULVER, Basil 221
CUMMINS, Elisha 274 Matthew
274 Richard 126 Robert 228
Susannah 2
CUMMINGS, Araminta 273 Bonnie
273 Elmer 273 Robert 273
CUMP, Catharine 274
CUNDIFF, Benjamin 274 Char-
lotte 274 Dick 274 Elijah
274 George 274 Gimmy 274
Hannah 274 John 274 Joice
274 Mary 274 Nancy 274 Nanne
274 Polly 274 Richard 274
Sally 274 Winne 274
CUNNINGHAM, Agness 275 Alexan-
der 218 Amelia 275 Ann 276
Anne 274 Benjamin 275 Benton
250 Betsy 276 Carleton 275
Edward 275 Elizabeth 275 276
Eve 250 Frances 275 Isaac
250 James 274 276 Jane 3
Jefferson 250 John 250 274
275 276 Johnson 250 Joseph
276 Louisa 218 275 Lucy 276
Margaret 275 276 Martin 275
Mary 250 275 Matilda 250
Nancy 275 276 Perry 274 Phebe 275 Polly 274 276 Reece
274 Rhoda 275 Sally 250 Samuel 276 Sarah 210 275 Su-
sannah 276 Thomas 276 Wil-
liam 276
CUPP, Christopher 276 Conrad
276 John 276 Leonard 276 Su-
sannah 276 William 276
CUPPY, Ann 276 Fletcher 276
Henry 276 John 276 Lydia 276
CURD, Elizabeth 276 Fanny 276
Nancy 276 Polly 276 Richard

CURD (continued)
276 Spencer 277 William 277
CURLE, John 277 Richard 277
Richardson 277 Richeson 277
Sally 277
CURRANTS, Elizabeth 193
CURRELL, Alice 277 Betsy 277
Isaac 277 James 277 Polly
277
CURRIE, Thomas 277
CURRY, A Albertha 231 Ann 277
James 277 John 277 Margaret
30 Mary 140 Nancy 277 Robert
277 Samuel 277 W H 231 Wil-
liam 30 277
CURTIS, Arrenah 237 Charles
278 Dolly 278 Elizabeth 278
Ethel 166 Fanny 237 James
278 John 277 Julius 237 Le-
tecia 277 Mary 277 Nathan
277 Nancy 278 Richard 278
Sally 278 William 277 Wyly
277
CUSHMAN, Deborah 278 Mary 278
Robert 278 Thomas 278
CUSTAR, Anna 278
CUSTARD, Jane 279
CUSTER, Milo 279
CUTRIGHT, Rebecca 279 Samuel
279
CUTTING, Anna 279 Nathaniel
279
CUTTS, Elizabeth 279 Paschall
279 Robert 279 William 279
CYPRUS, George 279 Hannah 279
Jacob 279 Julian 279 Law-
rence 279 Michael 279 Rebec-
ca 279
CYRE, Jane 279
CYRUS, Phebe 279 Sally 279
DABNEY, A L 63 Catharine 95
Richard 95 Sarah 98
DAILY, Mary 74
DALTON, Nancy 265
DANIEL, Esther 50
DARE, Naomi 65
DARK, Martha 34
DARTON, Nancey 209
DAUGHERTY, Clayton 215 James
251 Phebe 251
DAUGHMER, Sarah 69
DAULTON, Nancy 265

DAVENPORT, Adrian 189 190
Braxton 64 Elizabeth 64 Jane
129 Joel 129 Lucy 139 Moses
257 Nutty 189
DAVID, Mary 257 Sally 162 Sarah 162 Williamson 258
DAVIDSON, J E 34 James 279
Jane 279 N B 34 Polly 279
Semple 275
DAVIES, Emily 179 180
DAVIS, Abby 148 Betsy 197 Dixie 145 Elizabeth 26 197 232
Frances 108 G B 241 James
119 Jonathan 26 Joseph 203
Josiah 121 Matilda 36 Mattie
71 Nancy 203 216 Polly 107
Rebecca 170 206 Richard 65
Sarah 97 William 97 Winny
116
DAVISON, Ariance 184 Cora 39
John 184
DAWKINS, Dorcas 21 John 21
DAWSON, Elizabeth 210
DEAN, Henry 35 Hiram 35 Kitty
35 Nancy 35
DEADMAN, Ann 201 Nancy 201 Samuel 201
DEFREES, Alice 82 Joseph 82
DeHOUSE, Edward 3 Margaret 3
Mary 3 Polly 3
DELLINGER, Christena 220
DeLOACH, A G 80
DEMASTERS, Rachel 81
DENISON, E 216
DENNISTON, Polly 102
DENNY, Jean 257
DENSON, Mary 275
DENTON, Alice 82 Elizabeth 168
Hannah 168 John 168
DEVERICKS, Margaret 92
DEVORE, Dicie 171 Moses 171
DeWITT, Jane 42 Peter 42
DEYERLE, Mary 148
DEYO, J N 67
DIAL,Aralinta 198 Joseph 198
DICKEN, Emma 139
DICKENS, Francis 154
DICKENSON, Elizabeth 276 John
276
DICKINSON, Elizabeth 223 Helen
90 Joseph 223
DIDLAKE, Ann 237 John 237 Ro-

DIDLAKE (continued)
bert 237
DIERS, W C 107
DIETRICK, Elizabeth 122
DIGGES, Dudley 142 Elizabeth
142 Martha 142
DIGGS, Bailey 114 Barsheba 114
DILL, Hannah 261
DILLARD, Sarah 227
DILLIARD, Irving 108
DILLON, Elizabeth 262
DISMUKES, Susannah 215
DIX, Mariah 126
DIXON, Robert 36 Sally 28 Sara
123 Sarah 28 57 Susan 111
DOBELL, Alice 239
DOBYNS, James 239 Sarah 239
DODD, Elizabeth 19
DOGGETT, Lucy 120
DONELSON, Nancy 188
DONNEGAN, Ruth 130
DOOLEY, Betsy 116 Elizabeth
116 Thomas 257
DOOLITTLE, Margaret 247
DORMAN, John 81 Polly 81
DORMANT, John 81 Polly 81
DORSEY, Nancy 260
DORTON, Nancy 209
DOTY, Ephraim 240 William 240
DOUDLE, Peggy 54
DOUGHERTY, Margaret 124 Mary
124 Robert 124
DOUGHTY, Ann 85 Nancy 85
DOUGLASS, Margaret 141
DOUTHITT, Rebecca 242
DOVER, Betsy 169
DOWDALL, Polly 189
DOWEL, Barbara 256
DOWLING, Helen 94
DOWNING, Millie 128
DOZIER, Susnnah 3
DRAKE, Mark 105 Mary 105
DRAPER, Caty 91
DRAPIER, Elsie 21
DREBULER, John 244
DREW, Socrates 45
DRUM, O L 17
DRUMMOND, Daniel 187 Mary 97
187 Sally 187 Susan 187
DUFF, J Boyd 90 Jane 21
DUGAN, Daniel 264
DULANEY, Catharine 158

314

DUMA, Magdalen 122
DUNAGAN, Catharine 262 Ruth
   130
DUNAWAY, Sarah 186
DUNCAN, Ann 140 John 187 Julia
   112 T D 213
DUNIGAN, Ruth 130
DUNKLIN, Ann 26 Hance 26
DUNLAP, Alcey 273 Eleanor 108
DUNN, Elizabeth 108 Nathaniel
   127 Polly 127
DURHAM, Elizabeth 192
DUVALL, Dorothy 261
DYE, Sally 30 Sarah 30
DYER, Blanche 16 Charles 16
   Elisha 261 Mary 261 Melvina
   261 Ruth 128
DYSON, Mary 46
EASTER, Ann 204 John 204 Nancy
   13
EASTIN, Frank 208
EASTON, Ann 204 John 204
EATON, Christina 23
EBERHART, Ella 173 George 207
   Jacob 207
ECKELS, Richard 253
EDDINS, Mary 141
EDLEE, Henry 110
EDMONDS, Alexander 217 218
   Alice 217 218 Betsey 79 He-
   len 217 John 217 Margaret
   217 Sydnor 217
EDMUNSON, Susannah 187
EDWARDS, Elizabeth 245 Mary 66
   68 Nancy 171
EICHELZER, Nola 112
EICHORN, F E 258
ELDER, Jane 258 Phoebe 279
ELDRIDGE, Easter 245
ELGIN, Ann 112 Fannie 112
   James 40
ELLINGTON, Mary 272 Thomas 272
ELLIOTT, Eliza 80 Littleton
   242 Margaret 242 Mary 85 Ra-
   chel 242 Sarah 104 Teackle
   242 William 242
ELLIS, Benjamin 223 Elizabeth
   64 G B 26 Martha 112 Nancy
   64 Susanna 20 William 20 64
ELLISTON, Mary 136
ELLZEY, Letitia 47 Letty 47
ELMON, Thomas 142

ELMORE, Betsey 152 O W 49
ELSEY, Letitia 47 Letty 47
ELSTON, Allen 79
EMBY, Joel 91 Mary 91
EMERSON, Frances 257
EMERY, Charles 185
ENDERS, Jacob 186 Rebecca 186
ENOMONGER, Margaret 86
EPPERSON, Hyrum 21 Jane 75
   John 21 Polly 75 William 21
EPPES, Melison 209 Millerson
   209
ERLER, Ernest 234
ESTILL, James 91 Rutha 91
EUBANK, Elizabeth 114 Nancy
   114 263 Royal 114 Sally 114
EUSTACE, Agatha 79 Ann 79
EVANS, Catharine 127 Daniel
   127 Dorothy 263 Francis 179
   Jane 127 Mary 177 179 Polley
   177 Reese 127 Thomas 122
EVE, Elizabeth 164 Joseph 164
   Mary 164
EVERAGE, Mary 247
EVERMAN, Rhoda 91
EVINS, Dorothy 263
EVISTON, Francis 162
EWING, Lucy 128 William 217
FARLEY, Kesine 141
FARMER, Z R 168
FARNSWORTH, F J 19
FARR, Elizabeth 112 Guy 112
   Samuel 112 William 112
FAULCONER, Frances 271
FAULKNER, Charles 266 Eliza-
   beth 236
FAVOR, Alcey 21 Alice 21 Ann
   21 William 21
FAVOUR, Alcey 21 Alice 21 Ann
   21 William 21
FEAMSTER, Margaret 185 William
   185
FEEMSTER, Margaret 185 William
   185
FEIMSTER, Margaret 185 William
   185
FELKER, G W 225
FELTON, Estella 52 Thomas 52
FELTS, Benjamin 216 John 216
   Sarah 216
FENNER, Lilly 10
FERGUSON, Dougald 22 Frances

FERGUSON (continued)
22 Nellie 209 U P 209
FERRALL, Mary 40
FIELD, Thomas 219
FIELDER, Sally 253 Sarah 253
FIELDS, Elizabeth 132 Mary 209
FIGHT, John 249 Mille 249 Millie 249
FILSON, Mary 240 Samuel 240
FINCH, Barnet 114 Lucy 119 Mina 114
FINLEY, Henry 101 John 101 Julia 101
FISHER, Barbary 143 Elias 143
Elizabeth 107 Emsey 65
George 169 Israel 107 James
107 Mary 91 Sarah 107
FITZHUGH, George 2
FLEMING, Hampton 130 J T 50
Ursula 197
FLESHMAN, Christopher 191 Harden 191
FLETCHER, Isham 137 Martha 4
Sally 137 William 137
FLOURNOY, Martha 155 William
155
FLOYD, Sally 47
FLUENT, Russell 264
FOGG, Miss 203
FOLK, Mary 216 Susan 216
FONTAINE, Patrick 222 Sarah
222
FOOSE, Sarah 141
FORD, Elisha 54 Elizabeth 31
Jane 206 Nelly 210 Phoebe
144 Polly 210 Robert 210
Shelton 210 Teresa 210 Thomas 256 Walter 5
FORNEY, Christiana 1
FORREST, Annie 149
FORSEE, Jane 129 Judith 87
William 83
FORSYTHE, Cuzza 162
FORWOOD, May 23
FOSTER, A B 116 Ann 51 Basil
167 Margaret 64 116 Sarah 41
W T 129 William 41
FOUCHE, Dudley 76 Ruth 76
FOUTZ, Doldy 132 Milley 132
FOWLER, Lanzel 12 William 12
FOX, C P 73 Frank 73
FRANCIS, Nancy 136

FRANKLIN, Elizabeth 236 Veta
207 Virginia 37 Wirt 37
FRAZEE, Deborah 278 Ephraim
278 Mary 278
FRAZER, Caroline 165 Elizabeth
165 Ella 165 Jane 165 William 165
FRAZIER, Caroline 73
FREELS, Ola 212
FREEMAN, Polly 18
FREUDENBERGER, W K 258
FRIEND, C C 90 Mary 65 Polly
65
FRIZZLE, John 132 Rebeckah 132
FROST, Mahala 137 Rowland 137
FUGOTA, Lewis 29 Nancy 29
FULKERSON, Isabel 261
FULLERTON, Anne 239
FURMAN, Sarah 64
FUTTER, Catharine 273 Caty 273
GAINES, Frank 245 Kitty 126
Mary 207
GALBRAITH, Andrew 18 Sarah 18
GALBREATH, Jemima 74 William
74
GALE, John 121 Nancy 236 Sally
121
GALLAWAY, Phebe 279
GAMEWELL, Mahaly 24
GANN, Martha 49 Nathaniel 49
W 49
GANO, Cornelia 277
GANSON, Emma 22
GANT, Joyday 12
GARDNER, John 21 Sarah 84
GARNER, Amanda 75 Anna 87 Fannie 75 R F 87 Sarah 75
GARNETT, Elizabeth 42 163
Grace 163 Muscoe 163
GARRETT, Elizabeth 42 Richard
193
GARVEN, Christena 175
GARVIN, Christine 175 Margaret
96
GASKINS, Ann 79 John 79 Margaret 2
GATES, Albert 39 Ann 168 Anna
168 Cecil 181 Cora 39 Elizabeth 39 209 Pickens 21
GAUS, Albert 125 Anna 125
GAY, Hannah 37 Peggy 37 Thomas
37

317

GRIFFIN, Elizabeth 209 Henry
110 Martha 209 Mildred 212
Patsy 209 Patty 209 Roy 209
Sarah 110
GRIFFITH, Asa 97 Hannah 97
Jesse 97
GRIMES, J Cassidy 180 Margaret
229 Mary 229 Thomas 229
GROOM, Betty 32 Solomon 32
GROSJEAN, Jane 10
GROVES, Elizabeth 203 F C 233
W J 129
GRUBBS, Sarah 70
GUERRANT, Jane 129
GUILLIS, Elizabeth 258
GUNN, Dudley 173 Sarah 173
GUNNER, James 136 Ruth 136
GUNNETT, Dora 272 W E 272
GUTHRIDGE, America 100 Ara-
belle 100
GUTHRIE, Lucy 259 Mae 50 Mar-
garet 259 W A 259
GWIN, John 55 Mildred 55 Tho-
mas 55 Winifred 55
GWINNER, Gertrude 133
HACKER, Newton 65
HADEN, Elizabeth 102 196 Jesse
196 Nancy 81 Pamela 81 Ro-
bert 196 Sally 81 Susannah
196 Thomas 196 Zachariah 196
HADDEN, Rosanna 18
HAGEL, John 143 Margaret 143
HAGG, Permelia 240
HAGGARD, Elizabeth 125 126 Na-
thaniel 126
HAGLER, Elizabeth 164
HAILEY, Randolph 264
HAINES, Ann 204 Elizabeth 243
HAINLEY, Jacob 204 Polly 204
HALEY, Nancy 250
HALKS, James 277
HALL, Benjamin 227 Caroline
227 Catherine 23 Elizabeth
106 227 Everard 23 H E 9 Ly-
dia 27 Nancy 141 227 Phoebe
15 Sarah 119 Susannah 106
Thomas 106 William 227 Wil-
lis 119
HAMIL, Margaret 92
HAMILTON, John 55 Nancy 196
Susanna 276
HAMMOND, Lucina 162 Martha 141

HAMOT, Alice 270
HAMPTON, Jane 74 Judith 192
Vernon 230
HANCOCK, Ann 127 Benjamin 246
Jane 246 John 246 247 Nancy
246 R J 267 R Major 246
HAND, Jane 211
HANES, Milley 145
HANNA, Elouise 65 Scott 65
HANKS, Lucy 25
HANSBERRY, Peggy 107
HANSBROUGH, Eliza 121
HANSFORD, Thomas 256
HANSON, Anne 197 Samuel 202
HARDEN, Frances 183
HARDESTY, C E 72 Cecelia 72
HARDWICK, Elizabeth 267
HARDY, Stella 72
HARE, Rody 178 William 178
HARGIS, Mary 190
HARGROVE, Billy 226 Jane 226
HARLOW, Louisa 50 Susannah 5
HARMAN, Frances 29 Isaac 29
HARMON, Nancy 138 Sarah 118
HARNEY, Elizabeth 249 Hiram
249
HAROLD, Minnie 259
HARPER, Lillie 132 Sarah 52
HARRALSON, Anderson 38 Eliza-
beth 38
HARRELL, Nancy 243
HARRINGTON, George 149 Hannah
149
HARRIS, Betsy 134 Charles 205
Elizabeth 134 139 178 243
Iva 224 Jack 201 John 94 Ke-
ziah 205 Lemuel 178 Leone
238 Lucy 145 Nancy 94 Sally
26
HARRISON, Lucy 234 Major 261
Sarah 261 Susan 79
HART, Anthony 165 Elizabeth 3
Grace 169 James 193 Jane 164
Lentite 3 Nelly 193 William
3
HARTMAN, Eleanor 186 Jacob 186
HARTWELL, J L 27
HARVELL, Sally 178
HARVEY, Tabitha 183
HARWOOD, W F 78
HASKINS, Bessie 184
HASLIN, Jane 272

HATCHER, Benjamin 28 Mary 28
    Thomas 139
HATCHINSON, John 239
HATFIELD, Elizabeth 12 Jeremi-
    ah 12 John 257 Polly 257 Sa-
    rah 60
HATHAWAY, Hannah 212
HATTON, Mary 199 Polly 199
    Thomas 199 William 199
HAWK, Hesther 143 Samuel 143
HAWKINS, America 44 Ann 135
    Annie 148 Catherine 158
    Elizabeth 50 Frances 153
    Frank 153 Katy 158 Marcey 49
    Massy 49 Nathan 49 Nicholas
    49 Polly 73
HAYDEN, Catharine 210 Eliza-
    beth 210 Ellen 210 Jane 210
    Robert 210 Urban 210
HAYES, Hazel 41 Louise 86 Reu-
    ben 86
HAYNES, Ann 204
HAYNIE, Richard 239
HAYS, D T 98 Jane 98 John 98
    Rebecca 66
HAYSE, Nancy 30 Peter 30
HAYWORTH, J H 234
HEAD, Benjamin 141 James 141
    John 142 Lucy 141 Nancy 142
    Sarah 141
HEADINGTON, Laban 190 Ruth 190
HEARNE, Warren 7
HEATH, Mary 258
HEISEL, Dicey 116
HELLINGER, J M 264
HELM, H D 133
HELMBRECHT, Adria 269
HELMICK, Barbara 206 Barbary
    206 Jacob 206
HELVESTINE, Maria 50 William
    51
HENDERSON, Bennet 236 James 63
    John 63 Mary 201 N R 78
HENDRICK, John 205 Mary 205
HENDRICKS, Sophia 88
HENDRON, Nancy 158
HENIGER, JZane 18 John 18
HENNEY, Hattie 273 Moses 151
HENSON, Charles 154 Dyce 5
HERD, Mary 204
HERRING, John 69 Molly 69
HESHMAN, Mary 235 Moses 236

HESHMAN (continued)
    Robert 235
HESS, Abraham 89 Delilah 89
    Frances 183
HETCHUCK, Lucy 9
HICKS, Ann 70 John 70 Mary 69
    Maude 105 Meshack 69 70 Nan-
    cy 70 Sally 70 Sarah 94 Vir-
    ginia 69 William 247
HIGGINBOTHAM, Lenora 49
HIGGINS, Isabella 98 99
HIGHLEYMAN, Cora 87
HILL, A G 273 Adelaid 273 Eli-
    zabeth 118 Hardy 276 Lucy 3
    Margaret 275 Octavia 244
HILLMAN, Eliza 179 Isabella
    179
HINKLE, Polly 148 Samuel 148
HINSCH, V B 96
HINSON, Susannah 131 William
    131
HITCH, Mary 46
HITE, Mary 96 Sarah 213
HITSON, Mourning 222
HITT, Dinah 159
HOAGLAND, Ida 259
HOBBS, Azby 12
HOBSON, Adcock 173 Effie 244
    Joanna 173 Winifred 173
HOCKADAY, Alexander 277 Eliza-
    beth 277 John 277 Judith 277
    Robert 277 Sally 277 William
    277
HODGES, Betsey 94
HOGE, Mary 153
HOLCH, A E 104
HOLDERNESS, Robert 113
HOLING, Mattie 117
HOLLAND, P H 196
HOLLIDAY, Joannah 88
HOLLINGSWORTH, Barnet 223 Jo-
    seph 223 Lucy 223 William
    223
HOLLIS, Susan 214
HOLLOWAY, Nancy 245
HOLTZCLAW, J A 25 Sarah 241
HONEYCUTT, Dolly 278
HONEYWELL, A M 70
HOOPER, Barbara 96 W P 126
HOPE, Elizabeth 206
HOPKINS, Arthur 112 Martha 112
HOPPER, Polly 252

HORN, Maud 32 Walter 60
HORNE, Brose 162 Martha 89 Samuel 89
HORNER, Ann 201 Gustavus 201 William 201
HORSELEY, Lucinda 38
HORSLEY, Lucy 161
HOUCHINS, Henry 102 Nancy 102
HOUGHTON, Mary 75
HOUGLAND, Catherine 71
HOUSEMAN, George 251
HOUSTON, L H 30 Margaret 86 Martha 31 Sam 263
HOW, Julianna 92 Juliet 92
HOWARD, Anne 131 Elizabeth 210 Jackey 93 James 210 Lucy 276 R C 66 Samuel 276
HOWEL, Lewis 50
HOWELL, Hannah 29 James 29 Lewis 50 Nancy 29 Vincent 29
HOWLET, Alexander 237 Mildred 237 William 237
HOWLETT, Alexander 237
HOYLE, Mamie 271
HUBBARD, Ann 52
HUBBELL, Bell 224
HUCKELBRIDGE, Mary 8
HUDGINS, Mary 114 Robert 132
HUDSON, Betsy 173 David 173 Elizabeth 173 John 173 272 Judith 173 Sarah 272 William 182
HUFF, Elsey 100
HUFFMAN, Rebecca 147
HUGUENIN, Ann 63
HUGHES, Ann 62, 138 David 138 Delia 1 Famariah 163 Fannie 75 Janie 78 John 138 Margaret 138 W O 46
HULL, Ann 79 Edwin 79 Mary 137
HULSE, Agatha 152 Aggy 152 Sarah 260
HULSEY, Helen 94
HUMBLE, Catharine 85 Conrad 279 Jane 279 Michael 85
HUME, Lizza 13 Mary 205
HUMPHREYS, Allen 245 Sally 90
HUNDLEY, Joel 163 Susan 163 W T 203
HUNLY, Elizabeth 126
HUNT, Allen 10, Isabella 127 Jonathan 127 Lizzie 238 Mary

HUNT (continued)
127 Nathaniel 10 Rebecca 1
HUNTER, Charles 106 Edith 213 Harriet 101 Jacob 4 Nancy 8 Sarah 213
HUNTON, Charles 101 Harriet 101
HURLEY, Mary 136 Thomas 136
HURT, Franky 101 Jane 164 Mary 231
HUSTIN, Peggy 121
HUTSELL, Anna 152
HUTTON, Ann 276 John 276
IDEL, Margaret 149 Peggy 149 William 149
INGLE, John 276
INMAN, Martha 7
IRBY, Lucy 47
IRETON, Bess 267
IRION, George 1 Polly 1 Rebecca 1 Robert 1 William 1
IRVIN, Dolly 178 Dorothea 178 Dorothy 178 Henrietta 73 William 73
IRWIN, Dorothy 178
ISON, Nancy 83
IVERSON, Sarah 113
JACKSON, Elizabeth 256 Fanny 237 Margaret 175 Susanna 133 Thomas 237
JAMES, Elizabeth 279 Margaret 124 187 Sarah 159 William 187
JAMIESON, Elizabeth 107 Mary 227 Sarah 107
JARVIS, Elizabeth 23
JEFFORDS, Clyde 245
JEFFRIES, Agatha 79 Enoch 79 Sarah 195
JEFFRIESS, John 195 Sarah 195
JENINGS, Elizabeth 247
JENKINS, John 182
JENNINGS, Baylor 117 Jefferson 227 Nancy 262 Susan 227 Thomas 247
JERDONE, Barbara 153
JEWELL, Amanda 75 Ema 252
JOHNSON, Agnes 10 Albert 52 Alley 30 Archer 11 Armilda 56 Blancett 98 Blanchy 98 C S 96 Cynthia 56 Dolly 237 Elizabeth 56 64 Jacob 56

JOHNSON (continued)
  James 50 Jennie 259 John 30
  L C 69 Lenore 278 Louisa 108
  Margret 56 Mary 213 Matilda
  56 Molly 213 Nancy 56 Polly
  106 Richard 259 Robert 65
  Sally 87 Sarah 138 Squire 56
  Susannah 237 276 T M 108
  Thomas 64 Truman 266
JOHNSTON, Aggy 82 Archibald
  267 Elizabeth 151 Gabriel
  151 Lois 256
JONES, Allan 168 Augusta 218
  Bessie 218 Betsy 120 Eliza-
  beth 118 144 Esther 2 Fran-
  cis 147 Hannah 137 Jekyl 18
  John 53 Judson 127 Mark 218
  Martha 87 Mary 147 Matthew
  147 Merriwether 18 Miles 218
  Nancy 168 Nellie 152 Rachel
  53 Raymond 39 Rhoda 114 Rose
  112 Sally 18 100 138 Skelton
  18 Thomas 147 W W 40 Wilbur
  152
JOPLING, Hanna 109 Josiah 109
JORDAN, Ben 197 Elizabeth 79
  John 218 N M 158
JURDEN, Augusta 218 Gusty 218
  Hetty 218 Izett 218 James
  218 Jane 218 John 218 Mary
  218 Oscar 218 Sarah 218
JUSTICE, Sally 108
KAMPER, John 159
KANADAY, Elizabeth 160 James
  160 John 160 Patsey 160 Ro-
  bert 160 Sophia 160 William
  160
KARNES, Sally 258
KAUFFMAN, George 220
KAVANAUGH, Elizabeth 232 Rutha
  91 William 91
KAYS, Rebecca 135
KEAN, Mary 153
KEEN, John 95 Mary 95 Nancy 95
  Polly 95 Willard 262
KEENE, Elizabeth 28
KEEZER, Mary 85
KEISTER, Sarah 84
KELLY, Elizabeth 17 James 256
  Jesse 34 Joseph 17 Sarah 34
KELTCH, Susanna 84
KEMPER, G W H 129 John 159

KENADAY, Susan 8
KENDALL, Laura 219 Polly 75
KENNEDY, Hannah 121 Lula 183
  Nancy 192 Susan 8
KENNEN, Martha 117
KENNEY, Moses 151
KENNON, William 161
KEPPEL, Frederick 8
KERBY, Jesse 198 Sophia 198
KERR, William 169
KERSEY, William 177
KETRON, Peter 182
KETTERING, Peter 182
KEYES, Daniel 135
KEYS, Amelia 186 Bradick 237
  India 237 Lydia 237 Mary 186
  Minnie 203 William 186
KEZER, Susanna 256
KICER, Polly 85
KILBY, Fanny 262 Frances 262
KILES, Elizabeth 238
KILGORE, William 256
KILLEBREW, Louisa 131 Thomas
  131
KILLIAN, T D 28
KILLINGSWORTH, Mourning 163
KILLMAN, Sallie 31 Sarah 31
  Wesley 31
KIMBLE, Martha 70
KIMBOROUGH, Frances 125
KINBOROUGH, Frances 125
KINCHELOE, Daniel 105 Eleanor
  105 Ellen 105
KING, A J 9 Charles 154 Dean
  9 Elizabeth 54 Esther 220
  H H 270 Mary 124 156 Miles
  153 154 Nancy 181 Newton 154
  Rebecca 154 Sarah 9 William
  54 124
KINGKADE, Margaret 83
KINGORE, Hannah 131
KINNETT, Melly 82 Peter 82
KINSBOROUGH, Frances 125
KIRBY, Cecelia 201 Elizabeth
  149 John 201 Margaret 133
  Richard 149
KIRK, A D 11 Bernice 11 Jane
  163 William 163
KIRKHAM, Phoebe 261
KIRKPATRICK, Margaret 261 Nan-
  cy 163
KIRTLEY, Elizabeth 252 Marga-

KIRTLEY (continued)
ret 132 Thomas 252
KISNER, Barbara 110
KITCHEN, Susan 14
KLUNCK, Henry 215
KNIGHT, B Hoff 154 Mary 154
KREMER, Margaret 137 Peter 137
KRIEGER, C H 109 Glennora 109
KUGLE, Charles 218 Izett 218
KYLE, Sallie 98
LACY, Abner 107 Martha 107
LAFEVER, Elizabeth 129
LAFFERTY, Charlotte 277
LAFON, F F 246
LAHON, David 275 Frances 275
Hugh 275 West 275 William
275
LAMB, William 93
LANCASTER, Annie 242
LANCE, Maria 165 William 166
LANDRUM, Whitfield
LANE, Joseph 96 Martha 20
LANGHAM, Hannah 256 Robert 256
LANGSTON, Dianah 255
LANHAM, Joseph 39 Martha 39
LANIER, Nancy 24
LANKFORD, Mary 59 Seleta 13
LANNERT, Janet 8
LANTEN, Frances 88
LaPRADE, Mary 275
LATEMAN, Thomas 45
LAUCK, Mary 63 Simion 63
LAURENS, Elizabeth 225 George
225
LAW, J E 53
LAWRENCE, Celia 93 Polly 225
LAWSON, Joanna 173 Mary 51 Sa-
rah 130
LAXTON, Polly 164
LAYMAN, Daniel 228 Elizabeth
229 Elsie 52
LAYTON, Delilah 6 Ninette 75
LEAMON, Evelyn 192
LEAR, Jemima 157
LEATHERWOOD, Edward 139 John
139 Mary 139 Samuel 139 Sa-
rah 139
LEAVELL, Rosamond 144
LEDBETTER, Cornelia 148 Lewis
148
LEE, E I 63 Hazel 20 Henrietta
63 John 20 Mary 277 N C 154

LEE (continued)
Sarah 4 Tabitha 20
LEGG, Sarah 218
LEMASTER, Martha 265
LEMMON, Sarah 200
LEMON, Sally 200 Sarah 200
LENNON, John 123
LESLEY, Betsy 57
LESTER, Nancy 37 Rachel 163
LEWIS, A K 64 Ann 78 Apphia 9
Charles 216 Hazel 100 John
113 269 Margaret 269 Mary 78
Polly 247 Susanna 144 Thomas
232 William 118 Zachariah 78
LIGHTFOOT, Sallie 11 Sarah 11
Thomas 11
LIGON, Jane 69
LINDSAY, Elizabeth 34 Olivia
64 Richard 64
LINEAR, Nancy 24
LINK, Thomas 185
LINN, Grace 267
LIPSCOMB, A B 106 Granville
106 William 106
LISLE, Ann 145
LISTER, Alfred 152
LITTELL, Hardin 21
LITTLE, Elizabeth 210 220
LIVESAY, Charles 224 John 224
LIVINGSTON, Barbary 138 Henry
164
LLOYD, Fanny 14 Frances 14
LOCKE, Eliza 207
LOE, Nancy 270
LOGWOOD, Peggy 271 William 271
LONDON, M Roy 152
LONG, Cornelia 277 Elizabeth
262 277 Hardy 178 Nellie 277
Nimrod 277 Rachel 178 Sarah
64 William 64
LONGEROT, J B 52
LONGEST, Clarrila 237 Nancy
237 Robert 237
LOTT, Hannah 111
LOTZ, Nancy 166
LOUDEN, Sarah 203 217
LOURY, John 215 Susan 215
LOVE, Jane 83
LOVELL, John 188 Sarah 188
William 188
LOWE, Nancy 270
LOWRY, Elizabeth 215 John 215

322

McCLINTIC, Alice 182 William 182
McCONCHIE, Catharine 9
McCORD, Hannah 168 James 168
McCORMACK, Margaret 207
McCORMICK, Effy 261 Elizabeth 201 Isaac 50 Mary 50 Micajah 47 Sally 47 Thomas 201
McCRACKEN, Julia 58
McCRARY, N 142
McCRAY, Blanche 185
McCRELLIS, James 68
McCULLA, Sarah 258
McCULLOUGH, Fanny 121 John 249
McCUMBER, Jane 218
McCUTCHEN, George 246 Nancy 246
McDANIEL, Elizabeth 224 Fanny 5 Martha 241 Patsey 241 Spencer 241
McDANNEL, Martha 241 Patsey 241
McDONALD, Mary 198
McDOWELL, Ann 98 Anna 98 James 98 Jennie 98
McELROY, Frances 90
McFERSON, Mary 145
McGAHEE, Andrew 40 Mary 40
McGAHEY, Andrew 40 Mary 40
McGARITY, J L 58
McGEE, Dale 125 Jane 4
McGLAUGHLIN, Margaret 166
McGREW, Alexander 227 Caroline 227
McGROARTY, A S 46 Rose 46
McGUIRE, Edna 158
McINTIRE, Eunice 204 Lucinda 243 Solomon 204
McINTOSH, Cecile 70
McKAN, Edy 96 Polly 96
McKEAN, Harriet 133 James 133
McKEE, Frank 40
McKINNEY, Mary 275 Nancy 189 Robert 72 Robertson 72 William 189
McKINZEY, Nancy 117
McKIZECK, Ann 139 Daniel 139
McKONKEY, Catharine 9
McLAIN, Mary 270 Sarah 270
McLURE, Hugh 258 Margaret 258
McMEKIN, Elizabeth 241
McMILLION, Edward 37

McMOLLIN, Dicey 192
McMULLIN, Nelson 22
McMURTREY, Parthena 68 W H 68
McNAULL, Charles 252
McNEIL, Elizabeth 75
McNIER, Elizabeth 18
McPEAK, Augusta 218 Judson 218
McREA, Rebecca 13
McROBERTS, Mary 261
McWILLIAMS, Dorothy 132 Elizabeth 247 James 247 John 247 William 132
MEAD, John 22
MEADOR, Jobe 240 Martha 19 240
MEADOWS, Martha 19
MEANS, Mary 48 Robert 6
MEDLEY, Hannah 141 L B 50
MEEKINS, Elizabeth 168 Polly 168
MEEKS, Edward 181 Susannah 181
MEGLASSON, Mary 85 Molly 85
MELTON, Clara 35 Fanny 102
MENEFEE, Janett 269
MERCER, Elizabeth 67 208 Grace 163 Nancy 208
MERRILL, Betsey 102 Timothy 102
MERRILLS, Virginia 34
MERRYWEATHER, Myrtle 248
METAKER, Damaris 234
METCALF, Allen 73 Priscilla 73
METCALFE, T 101
METZGER, Harry 41 Hazel 41
MICHELL, Gideon 54 Joab 54 Mildred 54 Thomas 54
MICHELLE, Jane 172
MICHENER, Scott 194
MICHLER, Carlos 46
MILEISA, Catharina 260
MILES, Martha 222 Patsy 222
MILLER, Barbara 103 Brison 140 Charlotte 17 Della 176 Dixie 32 E B 57 Edward 17 207 Elizabeth 228 Irma 243 Margaret 124 Mary 140 May 61 Molly 69 Nancy 207 Nathaniel 62 Polly 176 Robert 61 Sarah 173 William 243
MILLESPAUGH, F H 137 F W 136
MILLION, John 228 Sarah 228
MILLS, Rhoda 64
MISKELL, Susanna 52

MISTON, Lucinda 177
MITCHEL, John 162
MITCHELL, Ann 23 Barnett 186
  Elizabeth 243 Mary 60 243
MOBLEY, J C 15
MOHOLAR, Edna 273
MONEY, Alexander 266 Nancy 167
  Nicholas 266
MONTEIRO, Margaret 153
MONTGOMERY, Anne 90 Delphy 154
  Margaret 154
MOON, W G 119
MOOR, David 151 Eleanor 151
MOORE, Adelaid 273 Ann 276
  Bertha 268 D A B 268 David
  177 Edna 273 Eleanor 151
  Elizabeth 96 260 268 Emily
  179 H C 8 Ida 268 James 272
  John 17 54 M Blackburn 268
  Nancy 177 Nell 74 Peter 46
  R B 77 Rebecca 210 Susan 110
  William 170
MOORMAN, Rachel 223
MORAN, Kate 201
MORE, Anna 257 David 257
MORELAND, Lewis 193 Mary 193
MORGAN, Benjamin 159 Catherine
  101 Daniel 159 Elizabeth 159
  Esther 118 Hannah 126 Lillie
  242 Nancy 10 Spenser 159
  Temperance 216 W 223
MORRIS, Elizabeth 75 Harriet
  194 Morris 25 Sally 215 Sa-
  rah 25 70 Tusca 194 William
  70
MORRISON, Hannah 147 James 64
  Margaret 64 William 166
MORROW, John 246 Thomas 246
MORTIMER, Arthur 25
MOSBY, Edward 172 Elizabeth
  172 Martha 172
MOSELY, Sarah 208 William 209
MOSER, Ethel 47 Walter 47
MOSS, Edwin 88 Martin 254 Re-
  becca 254
MOTTLEY, Elizabeth 216 Maria
  272 Nathaniel 272
MOUNTCASTLE, James 261
MULLINS, John 279 Martha 54
  Patsy 54
MULLNER, Margaret 62
MUNDAY, Henrietta 73

MUNDY, Hazel 100
MUNFORD, Marshall 207 Nancy
  148 Robert 148 Sally 207 Ur-
  sula 148
MUNROE, Sally 244 Sarah 244
MURPHEY, Charles 29 Jessie 204
  Leleticia 29
MURPHY, Ann 68 Anne 121 Nancy
  68
MUSE, Samuel 145
MYRES, Frances 90
NANCE, Levina 55
NANTZ, Nancy 90 Thomas 90
NASH, Mary 30 Polly 30
NAY, John 264
NAYLOR, Esther 206 Hugh 241
NELCOMP, Charles 5
NELSON, Charity 12 Cynthia 219
  Elizabeth 123 J C 47 Medda
  47 Sarah 219
NEVILLE, Judith 49
NEWBY, Nancy 38
NEWCOMB, Ann 237 Bradford 237
  Bradfute 237 Clarrila 239
  Elizabeth 237 Evelina 237
  Johanna 237 John 237 Mira
  237 Nancy 237 Rosey 237 Su-
  sannah 131 William 237
NEWMAN, Ann 78 Eleanor 96 El-
  len 91 Nancy 260 Sarah 260
  Waller 91
NEWSOM, John 68 Lina 268
NICELY, George 149 Hannah 149
  John 149 Martha 149
NICHOLS, O E 15
NICHOLSON, Rachel 62
NICOLSON, Elizabeth 142
NIGHTINGALE, Lucy 219 Mary 219
  Mathew 219 Polly 219
NOBLE, Elizabeth 146 Grace 147
NOELL, Avie 20
NOLAND, Jerre 77
NORBURY, Eliza 174
NORCROSS, Ruth 72
NORCUTT, Sarah 216
NORFLEET, Ann 40
NORMAN, Eli 1 Mary 132 Sary 1
  Thomas 132
NORRIS, Fanny 11
NORTHCUTT, Sarah 216
NORTON, Charles 120 James 77
  John 77 Milly 77

NORVELL, Edith 161
NORWOOD, Sally 188
NOWLIN, Susanna 192
NUNNELEE, James 207
NUNNS, Mary 74
NYSWENDER, Barbara 62
OBENAUR, Dorothy 261 Sterling 261
OCKER, Lukey 240
O'CONNOR, Charles 232 James 232 John 232 Lewis 232 Philip 232 Thomas 232 Timothy 232 William 232
OGLESBY, J W 133 Juanita 133
OHR, Mary 78
OLDACRES, Hannah 71
OLIVE, Mary 93
OLIVER, Frances 145 George 20 John 145 Sarah 194
OLSON, E M 99
ORCHARD, Lukey 240
ORE, Susan 167
OREAR, Luticia 7 Martin 7
OSBORN, Jane 256
OSBORNE, Mary 12
OSBURN, Mary 12
OURLEY, Mary 26
OUSTOTT, Gertrude 111
OVERSTREET, R B 24
OWENS, Sarah 168
OWSLEY, Mary 129 Patience 83
PACE, Sarah 180
PACK, George 124
PADGETT, Henry 272 Mary 272
PAFFORD, William 133
PAGE, Lucy 58 Maria 148 Mann 58 Sally 257
PAINE, Frances 194
PALMER, Samuel 155 Thomas 174
PAMPLIN, Unity 263
PANCAKE, Lewis 186
PARISH, Martha 37 Uriah 37
PARKER, C C 262 Drucilla 11 Elizabeth 25 Faye 47 Joseph 63 Mary 1 Priscilla 11
PARKMAN, N P 79
PARR, Elizabeth 246
PARTLOW, Maria 179
PASCHAL, Samuel 214 Wade 214
PASCHALL, Addie 116
PATTEN, David 193 Elizabeth 193

PATTERSON, Margaret 66 Mary 271 Polly 271 Uriah 107
PATTON, C S 212
PAUL, Eleanor 144
PAVEY, Dot 26 G M 26
PAXON, Catharine 62
PAYNE, Frances 194 John 194 Lydia 195 Nancy 74 S E 91 Sarah 141
PEARCE, John 30
PEARCY, Elizabeth 257 James 257
PEARL, Martha 117
PEARSON, Charles 180 Malinda 180 Nancy 164
PEARY, Benjamin 175
PEDCOCK, A B 29 Martha 29
PEDIGO, Agnes 85 Daniel 85
PEEL, W L 69
PELTIER, Jane 203
PENDLETON, Bettie 219 Edmund 158 Mildred 53 Millie 53
PENNEBAKER, L A 44
PENNINGTON, Elizabeth 53 Margaret 31 Marsella 204 Micajah 53 Milton 31 Rachel 53
PENTECOST, Polly 175
PENTICOST, Thomas 116
PEPPER, Frances 12
PERDUE, Eli 192 Sally 192
PERKINS, P H 88
PERKINSON, J E 18 Mary 20
PERNEL, Sarah 221
PERRIN, Meeke 150
PERRY, Violet 214
PERRYMAN, Albert 4 Anthony 4 Eliza 4 Elizabeth 4
PERSINGER, Fanny 142
PERY, Lowell 173 Polly 173
PETERS, Hannah 208 John 228 Sally 228
PETERSON, Winona 80
PETIT, Cylas 239 Hezekiah 239 Nancy 239 Richard 239
PETTIJOHN, Celia 126
PETTIT, Margaret 267 Mary 267 William 267
PETTY, Ada 157 P W 58
PEW, Rachel 20
PEYTON, Elizabeth 41
PFANDER, Winona 122
PHILIPS, Matthew 38 Nancy 38

PHILIPPI, Margaret 56
PHILLIPS, Henry 260 John 34
   Joseph 260 Margaret 151 Nan-
   cy 40 Rosanah 187 Ruth 260
   S T 228 Samuel 187 Sarah 34
   40
PHILPOTT, Bert 60 Grace 60
PHILPUTT, Alan 127
PHIPPENNEY, F J 196
PHIPPS, Minta 100
PICKETT, William 261
PIERCE, C A 135 Catharine 23
   Elizabeth 135 Nancy 82 Susan
   158 Susanna 158 William 23
PIERCEFUL, Sally 17 Sarah 17
PIKE, Benjamin 256 Zebulon 256
   Elizabeth 256
PILLARS, Mary 64 Josiah 64
PING, Nancy 19 Robert 19
PINSON, Elizabeth 155 John 155
PITMAN, Susan 105
PITT, Ann 71 Douloss 71 Rich-
   ard 71
PITTENGER, Eula 273 J G 273
PLEASANTS, Lucile 72
PLOT, Margaret 70
PLUMER, Mrs. 28
POHLMAN, George 234
POINDEXTER, Ann 216 Elizabeth
   24 John 216 Mary 251 Polly
   251
POLLARD, Evelyn 184 Judith 47
   Robert 184
POMFRET, Elizabeth 68
PONDER, John 204 Mattie 204
POPE, Elizabeth 199 Sarah 141
POPHAM, Elizabeth 124
PORTER, Betsy 183 David 38
   John 103 Margaret 39 Samuel
   12
POST, J J 160
POTTERF, Casper 27 Nancy 27
POTTS, Ann 269
POWERS, Elizabeth 257 Grace 16
POYTHRESS, Mary 27 William 27
PRATHER, Ann 29 James 29 30
   Philip 29 Polly 29 Priscilla
   29 Rachel 60 Sarah 188 Ste-
   phen 30 Thomas 29 Washington
   30
PRATT, Rebecca 167
PRAY, A L 24

PREDDY, Mildred 147
PRESSON, Mary 91
PRESTON, Milley 122
PREWITT, L D 76 Lela 76
PRICE, Bennett 244 Burnet 244
   Harrison 89 Judith 244 Linny
   183 Mary 256 Polly 231 S M
   166 Samuel 202
PRIDDY, Mildred 147
PRIESTLY, Phebe 235
PRINCE, N B 177
PRITCHARD, Elizabeth 175
PRITCHETT, Jamima 29 Robert 29
PROCTOR, David 278 Dayse 278
PROVOST, Charles 96 Emily 96
PUGH, Mary 193 Michael 193 Sa-
   muel 193
PULLEY, Marlin 180
PURCELL, George 187 Margaret
   187
PURKHISER, H H 51
PURVINES, Sarah 116
PYLES, John 151 Sarah 151
PYNCHION, John 220 William 220
QUERY, Margaret 98
QUICK, Ruth 190
QUINN, James 126
QUIRK, Jane 132 Thomas 132
RADFORD, Jane 165 John 165
   Benjamin 165
RAGLAND, B E 219
RAGLIN, Edith 167 Joseph 167
RAGSDALE, Iona 83 V 83
RAINBOLT, Katherine 176
RAINES, Sooky 257
RAINEY, Patsey 11
RALSTON, Mae 50
RAMEY, Amie 201
RAMSAY, Mary 120 Sarah 153
RAMSEY, Francis 11 Joyce 12
   Joyday 12 Martha 11 Patsey
   11
RANDALL, Catharine 265 Gordon
   36 John 101 Rachel 36 Wil-
   liam 165
RANDOLPH, Abigail 7 Ann 20 Ca-
   therine 20 Cornelius 229 Ju-
   liana 229 Robert 20 William
   20
RANKIN, Johnie 197 Rozina 162
   Vance 197
RANKLEY, Mary 21

RANNE, Sarah 69
RANSDELL, Harriet 92
RANSOM, Catharine 203 Frances 54
RAPER, Deborah 211
RASH, Nancy 178 Perry 178
RATCLIFF, Bruce 258
RAWLINGS, Isaac 146 Nancy 146
READ, Mary 19 187 Richard 187 William 19
READE, Mary 19 William 19
READER, W H 90
RECORD, Elizabeth 50
REDDEN, Alma 192 J A 192
REECE, Anna 120
REED, Elizabeth 156 John 196 Mary 4
REEDER, Sarah 104
REEL, Mary 75
REESE, Cuthbert 204 Harriet 70 Jessie 204 John 70 Mary 70 Samuel 70 Susan 70 Susanna 70 Tabitha 204 Thomas 70 William 70
REEVES, Susannah 9
REGAN, W S 26
REID, Ella 222
RENFROE, Margaret 234
REPILOW, Eliza 115 116 Helen 115 116 Robert 115 116
REXFORD, J C 115
REYNOLDS, Fanny 143 Frances 143 Dicey 142
RHEA, Isaac 18
RHODES, David 241 Henrietta 117 Lucy 71 Margaret 241
RICE, John 22 Lucy 114 Martha 22 Mattie 22 Polly 55
RICH, J R 18
RICHARDS, Lydia 32
RICHARDSON, Ann 131 Catherine 97 Elizabeth 74 182 Francis 122 John 18 Martha 35 111 Mary 18 131 Miriam 131 Patsy 97 Samuel 35 William 182
RICHBOURG, Elizabeth 190 Jamine 190 Samuel 190 Thomas 190
RICHERSON, John 18 Mary 18 Sarah 256
RICHESON, Jane 226
RICHEY, Malinda 113

RICHIE, Mary 222
RICHMOND, William 72
RICKETTS, David 163
RIDGEWAY, James 131 Mary 131
RIGGS, Eugene 276 Lora 151
RIGGSBY, Lucy 3
RIGHTMIRE, Bessie 152
RILEY, Agnes 108 Conny 108 Elizabeth 42 Fielding 108 Henry 108 Isom 108 Jesse 108 Julian 187 Lavina 108 Nancy 70 278 Seton 108 Thomas 70
RINGO, Burtis 28 Hannah 28
RISNER, Stella 67
RITCHIE, Mary 222
ROACH, Juliet 201 Robert 201
ROBBINS, Elender 211 Elenor 210 211
ROBERTS, Andrew 275 Anne 192 Catharine 115 Dudley 165 Johnnie 32 Joseph 262 Nellie 165 Semple 275 Suckey 29 Susan 29 Walter 269
ROBERTSON, Ann 29 Anne 185 192 John 20 Lewis 29 Mary 179 Richard 185 Sterling 79 Violet 79
ROBESON, Henry 263 Scisely 50 William 50
ROBINSON, Abigail 211 Alcey 136 Amelia 184 Anne 192 Arrenah 237 Catharine 223 Clarissa 16 Daniel 16 Elizabeth 211 237 Eva 193 Fanny 237 Henry 263 James 211 Jane 211 Johannah 237 John 184 237 Margaret 81 Milly 184 Susannah 37 Uralia 237 Warner 237 William 237
ROBISON, Martha 270 Wayne 22
ROBSON, Fanny 237 Joseph 237
ROE, Anthony 74 Sarah 74
ROGERS, Elizabeth 173 Ellen 168 Frances 174 Hannah 234 Isabelle 153 James 39 Jane 204 John 91 153 Joseph 174 Josiah 174 Mary 91 Polly 173 Rebecca 174 Reuben 174 Sally 204 Stephen 174 W C 45 William 174
ROLAND, Mary 73
ROLLINS, Anne 27

ROOKER, Jabez 113 Mary 113
ROOME, Elmina 6
ROONEY, Elizabeth 46
ROSE, John 40 Nellie 152 R L
196 Sarah 40
ROSS, Harriet 70 John 70 Mary
59 70 Peter 26 Samuel 70 Sarah 25 Susan 70 Susana 70
Temperance 26 Thomas 70 William 70
ROWLETT, John 10 260 Lucy 10
Mary 10 William 10
ROY, Catharine 133 Thomas 30
92 Walker 133
ROYDON, David 126 Mary 126
RUDD, Rebecca 1
RUFFIN, Elizabeth 184 James
184 Sterling 184
RUNDELL, Sidney 154
RUNION, Betsy 201 Elizabeth
201 John 201
RUNNELS, J R 85
RUNNER, Sally 271 Sarah 271
RUNNION, Adren 100 Mary 100
RUSH, Catharine 228 Cortreen
228 Nancy 178 Perry 178
RUSK, Eli 148
RUSS, C E 265
RUSSELL, Elizabeth 236 Lydia
276 Mary 163 William 236
RUSSEY, James 35
RUST, Fanny 189
RUTHERFORD, Claude 197 Sarah
63
SADLER, Rebecca 53 Samuel 53
SAGNER, Betty 62
SALLE, Jane 35
SALLEE, Jane 35
SALLY, Jane 35 William 35
SAMMONS, Mary 257
SAMUEL, Amy 81 Henry 81 John
81
SANDERS, Dora 200 John 127 128
Malinda 171 Mary 63 127 Milindy 171 Phebe 63 Robert
171 S M 213 Sarah 127
SANDFORD, Nancy 141 Sarah 141
SANDS, Harvey 144
SANFORD, Mary 62
SANGER, Eve 17
SAPPINGTON, Polly 100
SARTOR, Anna 223 Thomas 223

SARTORE, Catherine 54 John 54
SARVER, Jacob 188
SATTERFIELD, James 243 Matheny
243
SAUL, Elizabeth 272
SAUNDERS, George 28 Massey 12
SAVAGE, John 257 Mary 267 Rebecca 257
SAWYER, Joseph 90
SAYERS, Susannah 183
SCALES, Martha 232
SCARCE, Elizabeth 116
SCARLETT, Mary 278
SCATES, Jean 140 William 140
SCEARCE, Elizabeth 116
SCHERIEBLE, Faye 48
SCHNELL, J D 271 Mamie 271
SCHOOLS, John 2 Lucy 2 Sally 2
SCHRIVER, Sarah 41
SCHULTHEIS, Rose 241
SCHUMAKER, Juliana 41
SCHWARTZWALDER, Daniel 78
Isaac 78 John 78
SCOTT, Affey 35 Anne 31 D F
230 Grace 169 Harry 152 John
35 252 Lucy 252 Mississippi
74 Nancy 74 Sallie 31 Samuel
74 Sarah 31 William 74
SEALE, John 69 Sarah 69
SEARS, H C 230
SEATCH, Susan 41
SEBASTIAN, Alcy 136 Julia 112
SECREST, A T 6
SEELY, Elizabeth 3
SEIGENCOURT, Judith 173
SELF, Elizabeth 50
SELLMAN, Alice 191
SELMAN, N R 155
SENSENBACH, Catharine 162 Johann 162
SEVIER, General 206 Ruth 206
SEXTON, George 137 Nancy 137
SEYMOUR, Isabella 267 Leah 267
William 267
SHACKELFORD, Elizabeth 142
George 12 Roger 142
SHACKLEFORD, Nancy 54 Sarah 54
SHARLEVILLE, Genevieve 191
Henry 191 Mary 191 Michael
191
SHARP, Dicea 246 Dicy 246 Elizabeth 246 James 246 Mary

SHARP (continued)
246 Richard 246 Robert 246
SHAVER, Abigail 86 Catharine
86 Margaret 86 Michael 86
Sarah 86
SHAW, Sally 100
SHEARER, Mary 160
SHEEHAN, J V 142
SHELBURNE, John 276
SHELEY, Oliver 253
SHELOR, Daniel 45 George 45
Ruth 45
SHELTON, Jenny 172
SHEPHERD, Frances 54 John 54
Nancy 17 Sophia 116 Susan 38
SHEPPARD, Sarah 119
SHERRET, Julia 150
SHERROW, Philadelphia 123 Reu-
ben 123
SHIELDS, Ella 241 Harriet 133
James 18 Rachel 18
SHIPLETT, Lucinda 218
SHIPP, Irene 156
SHIRLER, Lewis 204 Sally 204
SHIRLEY, Elizabeth 163 Mildred
35 Robert 163 William 173
SHOEMAKER, George 73 Magdalene
73
SHOTWELL, Thomas 242
SHREVE, Betsy 121 Isaac 121
SHREWSBURY, Milly 104 Natha-
niel 132 Rhoda 132
SHRIMPLIN, Rachel 264
SHROPSHIRE, Reuben 55
SHROYER, J L 278
SHUFFLEBARGER, Mary 17
SHUMATE, Fannie 265
SIFRITT, Andrew 279 Emily 279
Jacob 279
SIGN, Margaret 22 Martha 22
William 22
SIMES, Mary 107 Taylor 107
SIMMONS, J D 77
SIMPKINS, Daniel 76 Fanny 76
SIMPSON, Burney 239 C P 62 E W
126 Elizabeth 126 137 John
137 Margaret 128 Martha 19
Mary 62 Sarah 137 Sophia 201
Susanah 143 Thomas 201
SIMRALL, Mary 197
SINGER, James 265 Mary 265
SINGLETON, Ann 46

SINNOTT, Mary 86
SIMS, Ann 10 Rebecca 198 W S
35
SISCO, B B 247
SISK, Elizabeth 29 Stephen 29
SKELLEM, John 18 Mary 18
SKELTON, Margaret 243
SKIDMORE, Nelly 193
SKINNER, Susannah 247 William
267
SLAUGHTER, Richard 276
SLAUSON, David 152
SLAWSON, Martha 152
SLAYTON, Rachel 116
SLOSSEN, Martha 152
SMITH, Anna 7 248 278 Annie
261 Austin 29 Betsy 257 Ca-
tharine 29 Clarissa 121 Dora
225 Elizabeth 271 Ellen 140
Emily 173 Frances 106 215
Georgiana 64 Gregory 23 Han-
nah 134 Harriet 4 Howard 50
Isabella 169 James 183 Jar-
rett 13 John 64 269 Julia
181 Lavinia 153 Lee 270 Lo-
vina 147 Lucy 79 Mahala 7
Martha 169 254 Mary 45 258
Massa 27 Phebe 131 183 208
Pheby 208 Rebecca 179 Sallie
114 Samuel 169 Sara 260 Sa-
rah 260 Thomas 169 Viola 125
William 79 106 127 173 261
Zola 50
SMITHER, Ethel 213 Gary 203
Lucy 203 Maria 203
SMITHSON, Elizabeth 70 Francis
69 70
SMOOT, Nancy 134 Samuel 134
SNAR, Margaret 143
SNARR, Margaret 143
SNEAD, Benjamin 275
SNEED, Ally 188 Elizabeth 275
John 188
SNELLING, Sally 257
SNELLINGS, George 207
SNIDER, Rebecca 259
SNIVELY, Harriet 78
SNODDY, Mary 5
SNYDER, Rebecca 259
SOLOMONS, Priscilla 136
SOMERFIELD, Gladys 89
SONGER, Eve 17

SOUTH, David 34 Sally 24
SOUTHER, Catherine 150 Robert
150
SOWARD, Sarah 34
SOWERS, C W 244 Effie 244
SOYARS, Frances 174 James 174
SPANGLER, Ann 159 Anna 159
SPARKES, Alfred 102
SPARKS, Nola 112
SPEAKS, Sarah 233
SPEAR, Ruth 255
SPEER, Anna 41
SPEERS, Margaret 142
SPENCE, David 174 Philip 80
141 Susannah 175
SPENCER, John 237 Mary 237
Unity 47 Williamm 237
SPILLMAN, Elizabeth 164 Henry
164 Mary 121 Polly 121
SPINDLE, William 14
SPRATT, John 117 Thomas 117
SPRINGER, Sally 261 Uriah 261
SPRINGSTON, J D 119 Marsalona
193
SPROUSE, Eliza 89 Fleming 89
Sally 38 Sarah 38
SQUIRE, Mary 149 Michael 149
STAGGERWALT, Frederick 30 Jane
30
STAIRE, Michal 238 Michael 238
STALLARD, Nancy 55 Walter 55
STANARD, Rebecca 174
STANFORD, Mary 231
STANHOPE, Nancy 95 William 95
STANSFIELD, Kenneth 72
STANT, Milcah 244
STAPLES, Frances 256 Mary 79
Phebe 116
STARKER, David 218 Jane 218
STAUNTON, Benjamin 9
STEEL, Henry 49
STEELE, Adam 59 Betsy 59 Ja-
nett 7 Nannie 245 William
245
STEFFE, Augusta 218 Gusty 218
Jacob 218 Sarah 218 Thomas
218
STEFFY, Jacob 218
STEPHENS, Catherine 71 Eliza
41 Jackson 181 John 71 Olive
211 Rosa 181 Rosey 181 Sara
260 Tabitha 180 Thomas 211

STEPHENS (continued)
Ward 191 William 180
STEPHENSON, Easter 7 Elizabeth
59 Jewell 270 Levi 270
STEPTOE, Judith 245
STETTON, Absalom 138 Mabel 138
STEVENS, Albert 203 Emma 22
James 136 Jane 187 Marian
241 Mary 136 241 Nancy 201
Polly 136 156 Sally 84 Tho-
mas 127 William 22 201 241
STEVENSON, Edith 71 Elwood 71
F H 75 Kenyon 143
STEWART, Clara 233 Foster 92
George 233 Samuel 220 Sarah
233
STIERS, Alfonso 7 Cyrus 7 Eli-
zabeth 6 7 John 7 Rafe 7
STILWELL, Patience 109
STINSON, Joel 84 John 67 Mary
67 Sally 84
STIRLING, James 145
STODDARD, Susan 162
STODGHILL, Elizabeth 29 John
29
STOKELY, Henrietta 89
STOKER, Mary 239 William 239
STOKES, John 123 Matilda 123
STONAKER, F H 184 185
STONE, Enoch 95 Sally 95
STOREY, Margaret 114
STOVALL, Bartholomew 38 Jona-
than 38
STRAIGHT, Betsey 57
STRANGE, Susanna 247
STRICKLEN, Mary 167 Polly 167
STRICKLING, Mary 157 Polly 167
STRINGER, Edmond 38
STRODE, Martha 127
STROTHER, Margaret 118 John
118 Lucy 118 224
STRUTHERS, Alison 194
STUBBS, Ann 223 Robert 237
STUMP, Elizabeth 143 Margaret
143
SUBLET, Nancy 54
SUBLETTE, Benjamin 275
SULLIVAN, Sarah 31
SUMMERS, Sarah 98
SURNFORD, Elisha 169 Sarah 169
SUTHERLAND, C L 243
SUTTON, Ailse 120 Anna 234

SUTTON (continued)
  Elizabeth 31 James 120 Sarah
  252
SWAMPSTEAD, Leroy 7 Sarah 7
SWAN, Elizabeth 64 Margaret
  143 W R 64
SWEARINGEN, Ceney 152 Nancy 64
  Seignea 152
SWEDE, Catharine 274
SWEENY, Lenora 49 William 49
SWEET, Winifred 146
SWENEY, Susanna 136
SWIFT, Ann 253
SYFRITT, Andrew 279
TABB, Mary 193 Robert 193 Wil-
  liam 193
TAFT, Stephen 276 William 276
TALIAFERRO, Elizabeth 132 John
  113 Philip 58
TALLANT, Mildred 238
TALLEY, Francis 138 James 138
  Louisa 138 Margaret 138 Mar-
  tha 138 Mary 138
TANDY, Jane 10 Sally 83 Sarah
  83 William 10 11
TANNER, Josiah 264 Lucius 265
  Martha 264 Patsey 265 Sally
  264
TARPLEY, Martha 155
TATE, Agness 72 Lucy 206 Uriah
  72
TAYLOR, Barbara 81 Catherine
  20 Drury 254 Edmund 138 Eli-
  za 133 Frances 138 Garland
  138 Griselda 228 Hardenia
  138 James 81 Jane 138 Jemima
  254 Lucy 44 Mary 146 218 Ro-
  bert 44 Sally 114 187 Sarah
  138 Tabitha 85 W R 145 Wil-
  liam 138 187
TEBBETTS, Louisa 126
TEIM, Jane 125
TENNISON, Joshua 217 Margaret
  217
TERNER, Elizabeth 152
TERRELL, Mary 229
TERRILL, Elizabeth 253 Jesse
  253
TERRY, Jane 133
TETRICK, W Guy 264
THACKER, Mary 145 147 Polly
  145

THOMAS, Bert 212 Joshua 227 L
  Fay 159 Laura 212 Lucy 80
  227 Mary 77 Richard 33 Sarah
  42 William 237
THOMPSON, Catharine 112 Chari-
  ty 180 Elizabeth 212 George
  30 Kitty 112 Levia 30 Lucy
  270 Martha 112 Mary 112 Mer-
  riwether 112 Patsey 112 Ri-
  chard 112 W S 112 William
  112 208
THORNBURY, Rachel 190 Thornton
  190
THORNHILL, Grace 98
THORNTON, Dozier 3 Frances 194
  Mark 3 Nancy 194 Susannah 3
  William 194
THREEWITS, Elizabeth 190
THRELKELD, George 87 Sarah 87
THRELKELL, John 29 Martha 29
THROCKMORTON, Elizabeth 132
THRUWITS, Elizabeth 190
THURMAN, Elisha 175 Polly 175
TIMMONS, George 29 Hannah 29
  James 29 Margaret 29 Mason
  29 Rosy 29 Winifred 29
TINSLEY, Martha 117
TODD, Mary 9
TOLIBEE, Betsey 110
TOOL, Elizabeth 208 Nancy 208
TOPY, Alice 67
TORBET, Geny 18 Jeny 18 Samuel
  18
TORBORNE, Andrew 27 Elizabeth
  27
TOWLER, John 23 Martha 23
TOXELL, Catharine 43
TOY, Robert 186
TRAVERSE, Mary 124
TRAVIS, Julia 110 Mary 124
TRAYLOR, Michal 238
TREFFEL, Jacob 265
TREMBLE, Hannah 252
TRENT, Frances 114 Mina 114
TRETWELL, Sally 279
TRIBBEL, Hyram 4
TRIGG, Drusilla 57 Joshua 57
  Mary 57
TRIMBLE, Mary 73
TRIPLETT, Barnet 223 Mary 223
  Moses 223 Nancy 223 Patience
  223 William 223

TROENBERGER, Christena 241
TROUT, Anna 240
TRUBY, Rebecca 279
TUCKER, Cyntha 56 Elizabeth
210 G G 36 Ida 268 Jonathan
210 Kelly 56 Milly 164 Os-
burn 56 Phebe 275 Robertson
22 Susanna 56
TUMBERLIN, Elizabeth 23
TUMBLIN, Elizabeth 23
TURLEY, Daniel 29 Sarah 29
TURNER, Catharine 131 Polly
279 Susan 227 Timothy 220
TURVEY, Margaret 68
TUTT, Maria 58 Mary 58
TYLER, David 55 Joanna 93 John
75 Susanna 55
TYSON, Isaac 4
UNDERWOOD, John 70 Mary 70
Polly 70
URBAN, Abbie 90
UTLY, Ally 188 John 188
VACHUB, Isabel 185 Isabella
185 John 185
VanARSDELL, J C 88
VanBUSKIRK, Aaron 143 Mary 193
VanCULIN, Lillie 132 William
132
VanWINKLE, Mary 127
VANCE, Elizabeth 55 157 Hannah
261 James 157 John 157 Jo-
seph 101 Mary 101 Sarah 157
Zachariah 75
VANOVER, Juicey 44 Nancy 44
VANSANDT, Sarah 258
VAUGHAN, Atwell 144 Elizabeth
55 107 John 27 Martha 59 214
236 Mary 27 Mildred 186 Ro-
bert 236 Sarah 107 Susan 144
Susannah 27 William 196
VAUGHN, Nancy 214
VAWTER, Jennie 259 Mary 183
Minnie 259 William 233
VENABLE, Martha 119 Patty 119
VERMONET, John 101
VERMONNET, John 101
VESEY, D M 99
VEST, Mary 277
VINASDOL, Lucretia 139
VINEYARD, Rosanna 175
VINNANDER, Nancy 238
VOGENITZ, Chauncey 218 Ella

VOGENITZ (continued)
218 Justin 218 Robert 218
VOLKNER, Dorothy 41
WADE, Frank 61
WADSWORTH, Elizabeth 149
WAGNER, Susan 155
WALKER, Elijah 85 Elizabeth 63
Henry 162 John 61 272 Lucy
272 Mary 70 Minerva 126 Sa-
luda 38 Samuel 126 William
275
WALKUP, Isabella 185
WALL, Martha 92
WALLACE, Elizabwth 107
WALLER, Agnes 133 Annie 133
John 133
WALLS, Annie 250 John 156 Sa-
rah 156
WALTER, Mary 17
WALTERS, Catharine 30 William
30
WALTON, Martha 199 Patsey 100
Phebe 199 Thomas 199
WAMSHER, Jonathan 97 Mary 97
WANDS, Beatrice 33 165 Burton
33 165
WANSLEY, Sara 63
WANSLOW, Sara 63
WANSTURP, Catharine 250
WARD, F M 119 Henry 112 Juliet
112 L T 135 Martha 5 Patsey
4 Philip 112 Una 135 Will
227 William 112
WARE, Samuel 261
WARREN, H E 141 Helen 141
WARWICK, Rachel 154
WASHBURN, Henry 271 Isaac 162
WASHINGTON, Benjamin 63 Daniel
63 Elizabeth 63 George 64
Georgiana 64 John 64 Lamar
265 Lawrence 63 Mary 64 Mil-
dred 64 Sally 63 Susan 64
Warner 265
WATKINS, Elizabeth 71 J C 58
O L 94
WATLINGTON, John 10 Susanna 10
WATSON, James 232 Jane 232 Ma-
ry 163 O P 126 Polly 119 Ra-
chel 150 Sophia 126 William
163
WATTS, David 106 Henrietta 240
Mary 106 Milly 106

WAUGH, George 121
WAY, Hannah 245
WAYLAND, Ann 83
WEAKLEY, Ewell 232
WEAVER, Elizabeth 42 Lucy 21
  Sarah 216
WEBB, Alice 119 Charles 230
  J L 74 Judith 141 Mary 81
  Samuel 230 Susan 131
WEBBER, Nancy 54 William 54
WELBORN, J S 142 John 53 Kat
  53
WELCH, Arria 158 W H 253
WELLMAN, Patsey 148
WELLS, Guy 190 Hannah 97 James
  144 John 156 Sarah 156 Tho-
  mas 97
WELTON, Rachel 185
WENDEL, Rosana 60 Rosena 60
WESSELS, Betsy 58 Elizabeth 58
WEST, Gracie 89 Ursula 107
WESTER, Martha 155
WESTON, A G 261 P G 261
WESTRAY, Martha 155
WEYSER, Christiana 17
WHEELER, John 69 Melvina 261
  Sally 72 Sarah 69
WHETZEL, Ann 133
WHITAKER, Elizabeth 188 Rich-
  ard 188
WHITE, Anna 127 Anne 152 Coro-
  la 20 Elizabeth 181 204 H F
  260 Jesse 13 171 Kissey 11
  Mattie 204 Rachel 11 Samuel
  68 Sara 260 Sarah 133 Susan
  152 Thomas 204
WHITELAW, Alexander 195
WHITFIELD, Sarah 118 Thomas
  118
WHITING, Susan 215
WHITLEY, Andrew 230 Elizabeth
  230
WHITMIRE, Mary 52 Polly 68
WHITNEY, Eli 33
WHITSITT, Ann 80
WHITTEN, Ann 207
WHITTINGTON, Asa 122 Azariah
  122 Winona 122
WHORTON, William 256
WIATT, James 144 Rosamond 144
  Sarah 144 Susan 82
WICKHAM, May 45

WIGGINTON, James 244 William
  101
WILEY, Rebecca 55
WILHOITE, Adam 167 Mary 167
WILKERSON, Sarah 38
WILKES, Archibald 138 Lucy 138
WILKIN, Alvira 251 Edna 251
WILKINSON, Catherine 20 J B 20
  Townsend 199
WILLFONG, David 186 George 186
  Susanna 186
WILLIAMS, Alden 256 Augustine
  223 Auguston 223 Byron 132
  Christiana 263 David 119
  Elizabeth 223 Emelia 30 Est-
  her 119 Hester 119 Jane 266
  John 247 Lydia 232 Martha 95
  Nancy 206 Nettie 95 Sally
  107 Sarah 174 Sue 228 Thomas
  30 270 Winifred 76 Winny 76
WILLIAMSON, J T 119 Lucy 184
  Mary 184 Robert 184 Uriah 76
WILLIS, John 45 Mary 45
WILLS, Agnes 125 Grace 27
  Isaac 126 Louisa 275 Nancy
  125 Thornton 126
WILLSON, Susanna 39
WILSON, Abigail 121 Betsy 19
  Cicely 103 Ednah 62 Eliza-
  beth 109 Ida 165 Isa 245 J B
  150 Jane 10 Janie 78 John
  134 Joseph 172 262 Leslie
  245 Loula 245 Margaret 151
  172 211 Myrtle 165 Polly 52
  Rachel 194 Sarah 199 262 Ta-
  mey 19 Thomas 52 William 19
WIMERCAST, Elizabeth 125 John
  125
WINDERS, W W 196
WINGFIELD, Jemima 48
WINLOCK, Nancy 172
WINSTON, Martha 153 William
  153
WIRT, Marjorie 66
WISE, Betsy 172 Elizabeth 171
  261 Henry 267 John 267 M Ka-
  therine 200 Margaret 267
  Nancy 190 Peggy 187 Sarah
  267
WISEMAN, Dorothy 40
WISER, Christina 17
WITHERS, Abigail 233 Thomas 233